Beginning New Testament Greek Made Easier

Fifth Edition

by
Robert K. McIver

Barnard Publishing Company
Cooranbong NSW 2265
2019

Copyright © 2019 by Robert K. McIver

Barnard Publishing Company
PO Box 275
Cooranbong NSW 2265
Australia

Cover design: Miriam Kingston

National Library of Australia Cataloguing-in-Publication entry:
Creator: McIver, Robert K. (Robert Kerry), 1953- author.
Title: Beginning New Testament Greek made easier / Robert K. McIver.
Edition: Fifth edition.
ISBN: 978-0-6485114-2-7 (Paperback)
978-0-6485114-3-4 (Kindle ebook)
Subjects: Bible. New Testament. Greek.
Bible. New Testament--Language, style.
Bible. New Testament--Study and teaching.
Greek language, Biblical--Grammar.
Dewey Number: 487.4

In memoriam
Dora Lorelie McIver
1916-1990

4

Contents

Preface 13
   About this Book (for Students and Teachers) 13
   About this Book (for Teachers) 16
   My Thanks to 17

Recommended Resources 19
   Needed 19
   Recommended 20

Methods of Study 22
   Study Habits 23
   Oral Learning 24
   Tactile Learning 24
   Vocabulary Cards 25
   The Danger of Getting Behind 25

PART 1 27
   How to read simple sentences in the present tense 27

Chapter 1: The Alphabet 29
   Why Study New Testament Greek? 29
   1.1 The Alphabet 30
   1.2 Pronunciation 32
   1.3 Breathing Marks 33
   1.4 Transliteration 33
   1.5 Accents 34
   Vocabulary 1 34
   1.6 Writing Greek Text by Hand 35
   Exercise 1.1 35
   1.7 Typing Greek Text using the Greek Polytonic Keyboard 37
   Exercise 1.2 40

Chapter 2: The Present Tense of λύω 41
   2.1 What is a Verb, and How Are Greek Verbs Recognized? 41
   2.3 Present Indicative Active of λύω 42
   2.2 Paradigms 42
   2.4 Greek as an Inflected Language 43
   2.5 Tense, Mood, Voice 44
   2.6 Learning the Verb Paradigm 44

2.7 Pronouncing Greek Words 45
Vocabulary 2 45
Exercise 2.1 45
2.8 Accents on Verbs 46
Exercise 2.2 47

Chapter 3: Masculine Second Declension Nouns 48

3.1.1 What is a Noun? 48
3.1.2 What Is a Declension? 49
3.1.3 Gender 49
3.1.4 The Subject and Direct Object in English 49
3.1.5 Nominative and Accusative Cases 50
3.1.6 The Article 51
3.1.7 How to Recognize which Paradigm or Declension to Apply to a Vocabulary Item 52
Vocabulary 3.1 53
Exercise 3.1 53
3.2 Vocative, Genitive and Dative Cases 54
3.3.1 The Complete Second Declension Masculine Noun 56
3.3.2 The Masculine Article 56
Vocabulary 3.2 57
Exercise 3.2 58
3.4 Accents on Nouns 58
Exercise 3.3 60

Chapter 4: Neuter Second Declension Nouns; The Present Tense of the Verb "To Be" 61

4.1 Neuter Second Declension Nouns 61
4.2 The Neuter Article 62
4.3 The Verb "To Be" 62
4.4 Indeclinable Nouns and Irregular Names 63
4.5 Punctuation Marks 64
Vocabulary 4 65
Exercise 4 65

Chapter 5: -εω Verbs 67

Vocabulary 5 68
Exercise 5.1 69
Accents on -εω verbs 70
Exercise 5.2 70

Chapter 6: Feminine First Declension Nouns 71

6.1 Feminine First Declension Nouns 71
6.2 The Full Declension of the Article 72
Vocabulary 6 72
Exercise 6 73

Chapter 7: Adjectives of the First and Second Declensions 75
Vocabulary 7 76
Exercise 7 77

Chapter 8: -αω Verbs 79
Vocabulary 8 80
Exercise 8.1 81
Accents on -αω verbs 82
Exercise 8.2 83

Chapter 9: The Present Indicative of Middle [and Passive] Verbs 84
Vocabulary 9 86
Exercise 9 87

Chapter 10: Third Person Pronoun 89
Vocabulary 10 90
Exercise 10 91

Chapter 11: Review of Part 1 92
Greek is an inflected language. 92
Remember the following 93
Checklist for revision 94
Exercise 11 (Review) 94

PART 2 99
The aorist tense, third declension nouns, the infinitive and subjunctive moods, and beginning to translate sentences from the Greek NT 99

Chapter 12: The Aorist Indicative Active 101
Overview of Greek Tenses in the Indicative Mood 101
12.1 The Strong Aorist Indicative Active[1] 102
Vocabulary 12.1 104
Exercise 12.1 105
12.2 The Weak Aorist Indicative Active 108
Vocabulary 12.2 111
Exercise 12.2 112
12.3.1 The Aorist Indicative Active of -μι Verbs 114
12.3.2 The Aorist Indicative Active of Some Other Verbs 115
Vocabulary 12.3 116
Exercise 12.3 118

Chapter 13: The Demonstrative Adjective οὗτος 120
Exercise 13 121

Chapter 14: Third Declension Nouns 122
14.1.1 Masculine and Feminine Third Declension Nouns 122
14.1.2 Dictionaries 126
Vocabulary 14.1 127

Notes on Vocabulary 14.1 128
Exercise 14.1 128
  14.2.1 Neuter Third Declension Nouns 130
Vocabulary 14.2 131
Exercise 14.2 132
  14.3.1 πᾶς, πᾶσα, πᾶν 134
  14.3.2 τις, τι, and τίς, τί 134
  14.3.3 First and Second Person Pronouns: ἐγώ and σύ 136
Vocabulary 14.3 136
Exercise 14.3 137

Chapter 15: The Infinitive Mood 138
Overview of Greek Moods 138
15.1 The Infinitive Active 139
15.2 δύναμαι 142
15.3 Parsing 142
Vocabulary 15 143
Exercise 15 144

Chapter 16: The Subjunctive Mood 147
16.1 Forms of the Subjunctive 147
16.2 Common Uses of the Subjunctive 152
Vocabulary 16 153
Exercise 16 155

Chapter 17: Review of Parts 1 & 2 158
Progress thus far 158
Grammar covered to date includes: 158
Translation strategies: 160
Using Logos to Search for Examples of Grammatical Features 162
Checklist for revision 163
Translation Passage 17: John 1:1-11 163
Exercise 17 (Review) 164

PART 3 167
Participles, the perfect and imperfect tenses, and beginning to translate whole chapters from the Gospel of John 167

Chapter 18: The Relative Pronoun 169
18.2 Using the Dictionary Functions of *Logos* 171
18.3 Using Burer & Miller's or Kubo's *Reader's Greek-English Lexicon* 173
18.4 Gentle exhortation and encouragement 174
Vocabulary 18 174
Exercise 18 175

Chapter 19: Translation of 1 John 2:1-11 177
Vocabulary 19 177
Translation Passage 19: 1 John 2:1-11 178

Chapter 20: Participles 179
20.1.1 The Present Participle Active 179
20.1.2 The Weak Aorist Participle Active 180
20.1.3 The Strong Aorist Participle Active 181
20.1.4 The Present Participle Active of the Verb εἰμί 183
20.1.5 The English Participle 183
20.1.6 Uses of the Participle 1: "The One Who ..." 184
Exercise 20.1 185
Vocabulary 20.1 (John 5:19-32) 186
Translation Passage 20.1: John 5:19-32 187
20.2.1 Present & Aorist Participles of -μι Verbs 189
20.2.2 The Present Participle Middle & Passive 191
20.2.3 Uses of the Participle 2: "When/while/as/After ..." 191
20.2.4 Uses of the Participle 3: "-ing" 192
20.2.5 Translation Strategies for Participles 192
Vocabulary 20.2.1 (for Ex 20.2) 192
Exercise 20.2 193
Vocabulary 20.2.2 (John 9:1-41) 194
Translation Passage 20.2: John 9:1-41 194

Chapter 21: The Perfect Tense 198
21.1 The Perfect Tense in English 198
21.2 The Perfect Indicative Active 198
21.3 The Perfect Participle Active 200
21.4 The Perfect Indicative of Middle and Passive Verbs 201
21.5 The Perfect Participle Middle and Passive 201
21.6 The Perfect Infinitive 201
21.7 Examples of Translating the Perfect Tense 202
Vocabulary 21.1 (for Ex 21) 202
Exercise 21 203
Vocabulary 21.2 (for John 8:12-59) 204
Translation Passage 21: John 8:12-59 204

Chapter 22:
The Imperfect Indicative Active 207
22.1 The Paradigm of the Imperfect Indicative Active 207
22.2 The Imperfect Indicative of -εω and -αω Verbs 208
22.3 The Translation of the Imperfect Tense 209
Exercise 22.1 209
22.6 The Difference Between the Imperfect and the Aorist Tenses 210
22.4 The Imperfect Indicative of Middle and Passive Verbs 210
22.5 The Imperfect Indicative of εἰμί 210
Vocabulary 22 212
Exercise 22.2 212

Chapter 23: Review of Parts 1-3 .... **215**
   The Major Things Learnt Thus Far 215
   Principal Parts of Regular and Irregular Verbs 218
   Exercise 23 (Review) 221

PART 4 225

   The passive voice, the future tense, the imperative mood, and the translation of John 1-11 225

Chapter 24: The Passive Voice 227
   24.1.1 The English Passive Voice 227
   24.1.2 The Indicative Passive of λύω 228
   24.1.3 Translating the Tenses of the Indicative Passive 229
   24.1.4 Agent and Instrument 230
   24.1.5 Middle and Passive Voices and their Translation 230
   24.1.6 Irregular Passives 232
   24.1.7 Principal Parts 233
   Vocabulary 24.1 234
   Exercise 24.1 235
   24.2.1 The Subjunctive Passive of λυω 236
   24.2.2 The Infinitive Passive of λύω 237
   24.2.3 The Passive Participles of λύω 237
   Vocabulary 24.2 239
   Exercise 24.2 239
   Translation Passage 24.2: John 3:1-36 240

Chapter 25: The Future Tense 242
   25.1 The Future Indicative 242
   25.2 The Future Participle 245
   Vocabulary 25 245
   Exercise 25 247

Chapter 26: The Imperative Mood 250
   26.1 Imperative Mood 250
   26.2 The Present Imperative Mood of εἰμί 252
   26.3 The Aorist Imperative of βαίνω & γινώσκω 252
   26.4 The Imperative Active of -μι Verbs 252
   Vocabulary 26 253
   Exercise 26 253

Chapter 27: Present & Imperfect Indicative Active of -μι Verbs .. 256
   Vocabulary 27 258
   Exercise 27 258

Chapter 28: Potpourri 261
   28.1 -οω Verbs 261
   28.2 The Unthematic Aorists of βαίνω, γινώσκω and δύνω 262

- 28.3 The Aorist Indicative Middle ... 263
- 28.5 Third Declension Nouns that Have a Stem which Ends in a Vowel ... 264
- 28.4 The Other Moods of the Middle Voice ... 264
- 28.6 Other Translations of the Present Tense ... 265
- 28.7 μέγας and πολύς ... 265
- Vocabulary 28 ... 265
- Exercise 28 ... 266

Chapter 29: Translation of John 1-11 ... 269
- Vocabulary 29.1 (For John 1-2) ... 269
- Notes on Translation Passage 29.1: John 1-2 ... 270
- Vocabulary 29.2 (For John 3-6) ... 273
- Notes on Translation Passage 29.2: John 3-6 ... 273
- Vocabulary 29.3 (For John 7-11) ... 277
- Notes on Translation Passage 29.3: John 7-11 ... 277

Chapter 30: Comprehensive Review of Parts 1-4 ... 283
- 30.1 Verbs ... 283
- 30.2 Nouns ... 287
- 30.3 Adjectives ... 287
- 30.5 Pronouns ... 288
- 30.4 Conjunctions ... 288
- 30.6 Prepositions ... 289
- 30.7 Adverbs ... 290
- 30.8 Vocabulary ... 290
- A Checklist for revision: ... 290
- Exercise 30: Review of Parts 1-4 ... 291

Chapter 31: Where to Go From Here ... 295

APPENDICES ... 297

Appendix A: Answers to Exercises ... 299
- Part 1 ... 299
- Part 2 ... 305
- Part 3 ... 314
- Part 4 ... 322

APPENDIX B: Paradigm of the Regular Verb ... 332

APPENDIX C: Selected Principal Parts of Regular & Irregular Verbs ... 335

APPENDIX D Appendix D: -μι Verbs ... 338

APPENDIX E: The Declension of Nouns & Adjectives ... 341

APPENDIX F: Words Which Differ Only in Accent, Breathing Mark, or in Only One Letter ... 349

APPENDIX G: Modifications of Vowels and Consonants in Inflection 353
APPENDIX H: Cumulative Vocabularies 354
Cumulative Vocabulary for Part 1 (chaps. 1-11) 354
Cumulative Vocabulary for Part 2 (chaps. 12-17) 356
Cumulative Vocabulary for Part 3 (chaps 18-23) 359
Cumulative Vocabulary for Part 4 (chaps 24-30) 361
APPENDIX I: Pronunciation of Modern Greek 364
APPENDIX J: Abbreviations 366

Preface

About this Book (for Students and Teachers)

Beginning New Testament Greek Made Easier is based on the following principles:
1. Start translating from the New Testament at the earliest opportunity.
2. Don't confuse beginners with unnecessary information at the start, yet by the end of the book, provide comprehensive coverage of beginning New Testament Greek grammar. Thus, only a minimal amount of new material is introduced in the early chapters. More complex matters are saved for later chapters where possible. At the same time, by the end of the book students have enough grammar and syntax to competently translate from the Gospel of John (incomplete grammar in not easier!).
3. Practice what is learnt in a variety of ways. Use repetition in the exercises to build familiarity with and confidence in the material. Give answers to odd-numbered questions.
4. Provide frequent revision.
5. Give full explanations for each new point of grammar. In the first parts of the book, begin by explaining the equivalent English grammar before moving on to the Greek grammar. A shorter textbook does not necessarily equate to an easier learning experience!
6. Study the New Testament's most frequently encountered tenses and moods of the verb first, and those less frequently encountered after translation has begun.
7. Learn all the words occurring over 50 times in the New Testament first.
8. Move from the familiar to the unfamiliar.
9. Design a study program that will enable an average college-level student to learn to translate from John at the end of one year (*Beginning New Testament Greek Made Easier*), and any part of the Greek New Testament within two year's classwork (*Intermediate New Testament Greek Made Easier*) by the investment of approximately one hour's study per day, six days a week.

While I do not pretend to have written the perfect textbook for learning NT Greek, this is the book I wished I could have had as a student. It offers a fresh approach to NT Greek, one that has grown out of my own experiences, first as a student learning the language, then as a lecturer teaching it. What follows is a brief explanation of how the different principles of the course have been developed.

Even the easiest textbooks on NT Greek tend to overwhelm students with non-essential details at a beginning stage. It is a sound teaching principle to keep things simple to start with. Yet textbooks that keep things as simple as possible too often leave students far short of where they need to be before they are proficient at translating the New Testament. To address these two issues, *Beginning New Testament Greek Made Easier* first introduces the bare minimum needed to begin translating from the NT, and then systematically builds up knowledge of basic grammar and syntax in parallel to providing translation experience. The companion volume, *Intermediate New Testament Greek Made Easier*, is then devoted to giving a systematic overview of intermediate grammar and syntax to leave the student with enough grounding in the language to be able to translate anything in the New Testament with confidence.

There are several other innovations in the approach offered in this book. For some reason it is usual to omit answers to exercises in Greek textbooks. Two things have caused me to break with this tradition. The first derives from my experience teaching high school mathematics, where it is normal for textbooks to provide answers to odd-numbered questions. Providing answers enables students to get instant feedback on how well they are understanding the exercise, and the teacher has the opportunity to set the even-numbered questions for assignments that can be marked. Secondly, I taught myself New Testament Greek without the benefit of either a teacher or fellow students. It would have often been most helpful to have access to a set of answers during that process.

My experience teaching myself Greek laid the basis for several other convictions which reveal themselves in this book. I was working systematically through the recommended textbook [Eric G. Jay, *New Testament Greek: An Introductory Grammar* (London: SPCK, 1958)] and was about halfway through it when I realized my examinations would overtake me before I had finished. The London University BD preliminary examinations had two papers dealing with New Testament Greek—one on grammar and one on the Greek text of the Gospel of Mark. From that point I began translating Mark—without having finished the grammar—and used the textbook as a reference for forms that I had not met. This was of tremendous value. It is more interesting using grammar to solve a translational problem than tackling it as a barren exercise in rote learning. It became obvious too that some tenses and moods of the verb which are normally left to the later chapters of textbooks were essential to the translation of just about any passage. In particular, this is true of infinitives, subjunctives, participles, and strong aorists. In most textbooks subjunctives and participles are left till towards the end, and as a consequence, students cannot start their translation of the Greek NT until very late.

By way of contrast, strong aorists, infinitives, subjunctives and participles are dealt with very early in *Beginning New Testament Greek Made Easier,* using carefully chosen material so as not to overwhelm the learner, but providing enough grammar so that practice with materials drawn directly from the NT can begin. The positive benefits of being able to begin actual translation of the Greek New Testament at an early stage are self-evident—most students learn NT Greek as part of their wider theological training, and can immediately gain the benefit of their new knowledge in their exegetical classes. Since they wish to use Greek to understand their NT better, they gain real motivation from applying their newly forming language skills to the actual NT texts, rather than artificially-sounding constructed sentences. Extended reading from the Greek NT also quickly raises both the students' level of proficiency, and their desire to learn enough grammar to help understand the particular translation difficulties of a text.

Finally, *Beginning (and Intermediate) New Testament Greek Made Easier* has been shaped by the exigencies of teaching New Testament Greek to tertiary-level students as part of their fairly intensive theological training. At Avondale College (NSW, Australia), where the textbook was developed, NT Greek is one of several subjects of a student's study load. The time allocated to the subject is three hours classroom contact per week, plus up to an hour a day, six days a week, outside of class. The challenge has been to design a course which will enable average college students to translate from the Gospel of John after one year, and be proficient at translating from anywhere in the Greek NT after two years, while keeping within this time limitation. Again, this has caused me to concentrate on the bare essentials in the beginning chapters of the book, and to concentrate on those parts of intermediate grammar that have greatest impact in helping the students translate from the New Testament. I suspect that much New Testament Greek is taught under similar time constraints, with similar kinds of students. Those teachers/classes with more time, or with better students, will still find that this book ideal for their needs, as much enrichment material is made available in the latter parts of some of the longer exercises. Furthermore, more translation passages have been provided than might usually be covered in class. Those with less time could cut down on the number of exercises, and perhaps omit some of the systematic presentation of grammar towards the end of the book. In any event, I hope you find this book helpful to you in your learning/teaching, and in your endeavors to better understand the New Testament.

About this Book (for Teachers)

The accompanying teacher's manual further explains the aims and teaching methodologies adopted in *Beginning ...* and *Intermediate New Testament Greek Made Easier*. It also contains answers to all exercises (only answers to odd-numbered questions are provided in this book); a comprehensive set of tests and exams with answers; masters for making overhead transparencies; and a listing of early vocabulary items by exercise and chapter together with a cumulative vocabulary for the whole text. PowerPoint presentations and a distance education implementation delivered through Moodle are also available. Prices and terms of use may be requested by emailing rob.mciver@avondale.edu.au.

New Testament Greek Made Easier is divided into two volumes:

Beginning New Testament Greek Made Easier:
Part 1 gently introduces the different ways of representing the present indicative tense in New Testament Greek, as well as nouns and adjectives of the first and second declension. A small number of carefully selected vocabulary items are introduced, and mastered by continuous repetition in the exercises.
Part 2 introduces the aorist tense, the infinitive and subjunctive moods, and third declension nouns. Sentences from the Greek New Testament are presented for the first time.
Part 3 begins translation from extended passages of the NT, and introduces participles and the perfect tense. By the end of Part 3, the student will have encountered several continuous chapters from the Greek NT.
Part 4 introduces the passive voice and the imperative mood. By the end of Part 4, John 1-11 will have been translated, and elementary grammar will have been completed. The vocabulary lists in Parts 1 through 4 include all words that occur more than 50 times in the NT, as well as many forms of irregular verbs.

Intermediate New Testament Greek Made Easier [Int]:
This volume systematically covers intermediate grammar and syntax. By the end of it, the student will be equipped to translate with relative expertise any passage from the Greek New Testament. There are exercises that accompany the text, as well as questions, answers and notes on 41 chapters from the New Testament which illustrate the various grammatical and syntactical points made in each chapter.

Preface

The aim of the early part of the *Beginning New Testament Greek Made Easier* is to get the student reading the Greek New Testament as quickly as possible. To facilitate this, third declension nouns, as well as the subjunctive and participial voices, are covered much earlier than is customary. One cannot translate without subjunctives and participles! The aorist indicative, subjunctive and participial forms of -μι verbs are also covered early, although the more difficult and less frequently used present indicative forms are left until later. Some of the forms of the strong verbs are learned as vocabulary items – an innovation which has produced very pleasing results.

Once the student has done some reading of the Greek New Testament, the intermediate grammar begins to make a lot more sense. Actual translation shows the need for a more detailed grammar of the kind covered in *Intermediate New Testament Greek Made Easier*. I have long felt that most textbooks of the Greek either make too many demands of the student at the beginning of the course by launching into intermediate grammar right from the beginning, or leave them without an adequate grounding in grammar and syntax. Perhaps the approach adopted here might strike the happy balance.

While it is advisable to keep closely to the sequencing of vocabulary, grammar, and translation passages for *Beginning New Testament Greek Made Easier*, for *Intermediate New Testament Greek Made Easier* the sequencing need not be observed, as each chapter of the intermediate grammar has been written to stand in its own right, independent of the others. Furthermore, more translation passages are provided in *Intermediate ... Greek ...* than can be covered each time, providing an opportunity to vary the set passages used each year.

Feedback from my own students and from other teachers has greatly enriched this book. I welcome your advice. Should you find on these pages any infelicities, or if you can advise of material that could usefully be added or better ways of going about things, don't hesitate to write to me at rob.mciver@avondale.edu.au. I would greatly value your input and will give it careful attention.

My Thanks to ...

Looking back, it almost seems an act of hubris to try to write a new Greek textbook. I had expected it to make considerable demands on my time, but was not quite prepared for the reality. Along the way there have been many who have encouraged and helped me, and I would like to take this opportunity to express my deep gratitude.

First, a big "thank you" to all my students, particularly the Avondale College Greek class of 1989-90. When we started together, I had little more than the first couple of chapters ready, and while I had a reasonably clear idea of where I was heading, it required some courage on the class's part to blindly follow my lead. The textbook evolved tremendously during those two years, and the input of the class had a great deal to do with it. While just about everybody was able to help me with corrections and suggestions, four students stand out as having gone beyond what was required for the class: Steven Hebbard, Susan Mankelow, Mark Falconer and Andrew Skeggs. Steven probably deserves the prize for finding most mistakes, Sue for her attention to correct English expression, and all four for acting in the capacity of unofficial proof readers of both the teacher's answers and also of the beta version of the textbook. Subsequent classes have also been helpful, and among many others, I should thank such students as David Reilly, Victor Acuna, Khamsay Phetcharuen, Paul Hopson, Carol Livingston, Chrissie Cooper, Marius Jigau and Tim Turner for their continuing contributions.

Second, I would like to thank other teachers who have used my textbook for their very helpful feedback, including: Herb Brasher, Jeff Crocombe, David Thiele, and Norman (Norm) Young. Of these, I would particularly like to thank my colleague, Norm Young, who before he retired, had been prepared to try the text with several of his New Testament Greek classes. Norm began with a version that only included parts 1-3, and took it on faith that parts 4-5 would eventuate. His feedback was extraordinarily valuable, and he saved me from some embarrassing errors, as have a number of other teachers who have been using the book in more recent times.

Third, a large number of others have read through this manuscript and given valuable input. Anne Reilly, David Sutcliffe, Doug Robertson, Mike Brownhill, and Bert Cozens read it with a view to improving the English. Darryl Palmer, who for many years taught in classics department of the University of Newcastle (NSW) was kind enough to go through the intermediate grammar and circumvent some infelicities.

To all of the above, and many others not mentioned by name, my sincerest thanks.

RKM July 2019

Recommended Resources

Students quickly learn to wait to see if they really need a recommended textbook before they purchase it. Rightly so, because some recommended books are only opened once or twice at best. The situation is different with language study, however. Textbooks are referred to repeatedly, and often end up completely worn out by frequent handling. Language reference works are also books that will be consulted again and again, so a language reference book is a good investment, and several will need to be purchased during the course of working through this book.

Needed

The following resources are required to complement *Beginning New Testament Greek Made Easier*:
* From Chapter 18 onwards: access to a Greek-English Dictionary;
* From Chapter 21 onwards: access to a Greek New Testament.
This access may be achieved by the purchase of an electronic resource, or by published books as follows:

Either: 1. An Electronic Dictionary, Greek New Testament, and Parsing Guide

There are several computer resources that will provide the Greek-English dictionary, access to the text of the Greek New Testament, and a parsing guide that you will need from Chapters 18 and 21 onwards. One such resource is Logos (www.logos.com). If you are using Logos, it is important that you either obtain a copy of the Biblical Language package (a package designed for theological colleges and seminaries), or a version of the software that contains all the dictionaries and other language tools that are in the Biblical Languages package. Included are several versions of the Greek New Testament, the Septuagint, the Hebrew Bible, and several dictionaries of various sophistication (including the 11-volume reference work *Theological Dictionary of the New Testament [TDNT]*).

Or: 2. A Dictionary and a Greek New Testament

The following options are available if you prefer to use physical books rather than an electronic resource:

From Chapter 18 onwards either Burer and Miller's Lexicon or any other good dictionary is required. The great advantage of Michael H. Burer and Jeffrey E. Miller, *A New Reader's Lexicon of the Greek New Testament*

(Grand Rapids, MI: Kregel, 2008), is that, rather than listing all the words in the NT alphabetically, most words you will not know are listed under the verse in which they occur. This saves a lot of time which is otherwise spent looking for entries in a dictionary. Sakae Kubo's, *A Reader's Greek-English Lexicon of the New Testament* (Grand Rapids / Berrien Springs, MI: Zondervan / Andrews University Press, 1975), does the same thing, and a number of copies of Kubo are available on the second hand market. How to use Burer & Miller or Kubo effectively is explained in Chapter 18.

From Chapter 21 onwards a Greek New Testament is required. Either the United Bible Societies' (UBS) *The Greek New Testament*, ed. Barbara Aland, et. al, 5th rev. (or subsequent) ed. (Stuttgart: Deutsche Bibelgesellschaft / American Bible Society / United Bible Societies, 2014), or the *Novum Testamentum Graece: Nestle-Aland*, 28th (or later) ed. (Stuttgart: Deutsche Bibelgesellschaft, 2012), ed. Barbara Aland, et. al., may be used.

There is little to choose between these two. The UBS Greek Testament has a slightly larger type face, and has maps. The most important consideration, though, is that this edition can be bought with a small dictionary as an Appendix. This is a great convenience.

The Nestle version lists more variants, although these are not as fully attested nor given an indication of probability as they are in the UBS. One very valuable thing that the Nestle Greek Testament has, however, is the Eusebian canon which is reprinted at the beginning. This gives passages which have parallels in all four Gospels, in three of them, in two, etc.

3. *Intermediate New Testament Greek Made Easier*

A companion volume, *Intermediate New Testament Greek Made Easier,* also written by Robert K. McIver, provides a systematic presentation of the grammar and syntax of New Testament Greek. It will be useful to have it available even in the early chapters, and the book is frequently referred to when longer translation passages are met from Chapter 20 onwards [where the abbreviation *Int* is used to refer to it].

Recommended

Vocabulary Aids

Several aids will assist with your vocabulary. Some will find the electronic vocabulary cards in Quizlet very helpful (quizlet.com – search for "Avondale Greek"). This Ap works on most types of computers and smart phones, and provides very convenient access to vocabulary lists that are portable.

Many will prefer to use cards (see later comments on Methods of Study on the advantage of being able to select words that need extra practice, and review less frequently already known words). The set of vocabulary cards put out by Vis-Ed, "Biblical Greek Vocabulary Cards," by Robert Gromacki (Visual Education Association, 581 West Leffel Lane, PO Box 1666, Springfield, Ohio 45501, USA) includes all the words that occur over 15 times in the New Testament. While it is possible to make your own set of cards, it is somewhat time consuming. So, even though there are one or two extra cards that you will need to make, this box of cards will most likely repay the investment in time saved overall.

Trenchard

Warren C. Trenchard's *Complete Vocabulary Guide to the Greek New Testament,* rev. ed. (Grand Rapids, MI: Zondervan, 1998) does in a more complete way what Bruce M. Metzger's, *Lexical Aids for Students of New Testament Greek* (Princeton, N.J.: published by author, 1978) did for several earlier generations of students. They both list the words of the New Testament according to their frequency—down to those words that occur more than ten times in Metzger, and down to those words which occur only once in Trenchard. They both have all kinds of other useful information. It is worth owning Trenchard or a second-hand copy of Metzger by the end of Part 4 of *Beginning New Testament Greek Made Easier.*

Print or e-Book Version of *Beginning NT Greek Made Easier*

This textbook is available in both print and e-book versions. They are available through amazon.com and other book stores. The advantage of the e-book version is that it is portable. For example, the Kindle book reader, free from amazon.com, can be installed on both PC and Mac computers and laptops, on iPad, iPhone, and android devices - phones and tablets. In this way, your textbook can conveniently travel with you wherever you go. On the other hand, there are certain advantages to using a print-based version for your study. You can then more efficiently use your computer for its dictionary functions, etc.

Parsing Guide

It is always going to be faster using a computer based resource as a parsing guide than using a print version (after all, it is just a matter of placing the curser over the relevant Greek word to have the parsing of the word pop up), but if a print-based guide is desired, two very good ones are available: Either Max Zerwick and Mary Grosvenor, *A Grammatical Analysis of the Greek New Testament*, rev. ed. (Rome: Gregorian & Biblical Press, 2010); or Clean L. Rogers Jr., and Cleon L. Rogers III, *The New Linguistic and Exegetical Key to the Greek New Testament* (Grand Rapids: Zondervan, 1998).

RESIST USING INTERLINEARS!
    Students are frequently tempted to use an interlinear Greek—English New Testament. An interlinear gives the Greek text with the equivalent English word listed underneath. May I urge you strongly, *do not use interlinears*. Your eye automatically reads the English, which means you may never learn to read the Greek if you use an interlinear. It is a crutch you will find extremely difficult to give up. A similar danger exists with computer-based resources. The temptation is to skimp on learning vocabulary and declensions, but without a certain minimum level of vocabulary and understanding of grammar, you will be confined to reading the parsing and dictionary help, rather than reading the Greek text itself.

Methods of Study

    Learning another language requires two things—commitment and nerve. Commitment, because there are few effective short cuts, and learning the necessary vocabulary and grammatical forms takes time and some pain. Nerve, because even the best student will feel overwhelmed by the task once in a while. Occasionally every student will feel underprepared for a test or a reading assignment. The ability to make the best of whatever knowledge you do have, and the nerve not to be overwhelmed by the task set is something that all students must draw upon sometime in their study career. They will certainly be called upon to use it in their language study. There is a fairly large body of material that must be mastered and memorized before any real translation is possible in Greek. The teacher's task is to break up this body of material into digestible lumps, and to judge when the student is in a position to move to the next step. There is rarely time to completely master each level, and the teacher must use judgment in knowing when the student can move forwards.

    Learning Greek is like moving upward through different plateaus of complexity. At first students feel as though they are drowning in an overload of data. Then they begin to make sense of the material, whereupon the teacher again overloads the system with a whole new set of things to be learnt. Eventually these are mastered, and then the process is repeated. Having the nerve to face this process will get even the most mediocre student through the subject. Lack of nerve will cause even the brightest student to fail.

    This textbook has been designed in four parts. Each part represents a major step along the road to developing the skills to translate the Greek New Testament. Each part introduces a significant new level of difficulty, and then gives students time to absorb the new information needed to perform at that level of complexity. This is reinforced by a review process at the end of each part, after which it is time to move onward. Each separate part lays the foundation for all work that follows it and, if mastered, will ensure the comprehensibility of what follows.

Study Habits

A famous academic often told his students that they waited for the ideal time and environment for study, then no study would ever be done, and this is generally true. There always seems to be something to prevent optimum study—the chatter in the library, the children at home, or colds and 'flu. Study must always be done in the face of obstacles, although there are several strategies for at least making such obstacles manageable.

Habit Patterns

One thing that can be helpful is the establishment of regular study habits. It does not take long before you will discover your peak times for study—some study best in the mornings, others at night. It then makes sense to arrange your study times so that they take place during those most effective times.

With your study of Greek, it is important that you quickly establish the pattern of study you plan to follow, and that you consistently follow it. It is remarkable how habit patterns can take over. We have experienced work feeling a bit below par on waking, only to find that once at work habit patterns carry us through. If your body always experiences study at a certain time of the day, then it will carry you through those many times that for some reason you feel a bit off.

Peak Performance

Study is a demanding activity. It is best done with the body at peak performance. Frequently missing out on adequate sleep is guaranteed to lead to poor study, as does habitually skipping meals or continuously eating the wrong types of food. Another factor is the fitness of the body. Regular exercise and rest are two of the factors that can prevent burnout.

Priorities

I would rather do most other things than learn languages—even doing the dishes and dusting become attractive when compared to the pain involved in memorizing vocabulary or grammatical forms. But, to learn Greek, a high priority must be attached to the process. It is a good idea to set aside a regular part of your daily study program for Greek. It takes good time management to achieve this, as without planning, it is so easy for a major essay due the next day to become a crisis that comes before the Greek.

Repetition

One of the principles of memorization is repetition. Languages need to be rehearsed every day or else they are lost. This is the danger if a day's study is skipped. Doing two hours study the following day does not always make up for the loss of missing one hour's study one day. More is usually lost in missing one day than can be made up in the next.

Repetitious exposure to the material is vital. It is one of the means by which short- and medium-term memory becomes long term memory. Greek needs to be looked at almost every day. Do take one day a week off, though, on the biblical principle of one day of rest a week.

Attention Spans

Depending on the activity, most people's attention span ranges from 5 to 40 minutes. For intensive memorization work, attention spans are generally very short. This means that to sit in one place for one hour is not as productive as breaking up the study time. Intensive bursts of 10 to 15 minutes, separated by breaks of 3 to 5 minutes where you get up from your chair and move around, are probably the most effective way to study.

Environment

Contrary to popular myth, the TV or radio does not enhance study. Absolute quiet may also not be the ideal—as the smallest noise can then disrupt concentration. Remember, there is nowhere absolutely suitable for study—there is always background chatter in the library, there are always distracting things going on at home. However, it is desirable to remove as many of these distractions as possible, and then refuse to be distracted by what cannot be changed.

Oral Learning

Speaking out loud has long been recognized as a way to enhance the process of memorization. It devotes more attention to the item being learned. Aural memory complements the visual memory.

Tactile Learning

Different people learn things via different processes. Some learn best visually, some aurally, and some by touch. It can be helpful to write out your verb charts, for example. Examine how you best learn, and use your characteristics to their best advantage.

Vocabulary Cards

A constant review of vocabulary is an esesntial part of learning languages, and NT Greek is no exception. The electronic resource quizlet.com (search for "Avondale Greek") works with laptops, and smart devices such as iPad, iPhone and Android devices and phones, and most students find it a very helpful aid in learning vocabulary. In addition to this electronic resource, there are several advantages in also using vocabulary cards. For some reason, some words are always easier to memorize than others. After a couple of days' review, these easily memorized words can be put aside for reviewing every second day, then every third day, and finally only once a week. Words that refuse to stick for one reason or another can be put in a special pile and reviewed several times each day. Of course, individual words will move between the different categories. Also, shuffling the cards means that words can be reviewed in any sequence.

The Danger of Getting Behind

It scarcely needs pointing out that if you are slightly ahead of or on top of the work, you will then generally feel much better than if you are desperately trying to keep up. A little each day is much more effective than a lot at once. Most failures in Greek come from those who fall behind and are unable to catch up. If you are behind, you are doing things that depend on material that you have not mastered, and so it will look confusing and hard. If you keep up, it looks and feels easy.

Part 1

How to read simple sentences in the present tense

Chapter 1: The Alphabet

As Greek is written with an alphabet that is different to that used for English, learning the Greek alphabet is the first step towards learning the language. This chapter explains the letters of the Greek alphabet and how they are pronounced. Many of these letters will be already familiar, and as with the English alphabet, the first part of the sound of the name of a Greek letter reveals the sound the letter represents. By the end of the Chapter, you will have learned your first Greek words (Vocab. 1), and gained familiarity with the alphabet by means of the practice provided in the exercise.

Why Study New Testament Greek?

Why does almost all serious theological education insist on the sometimes-painful experience of learning New Testament Greek? There are at least four reasons:

1. Perhaps most important is that it gives students access to information they could not obtain in any other way. Culture and meaning are embedded within a language, and there is no better way to be fully sensitive to this than to be able to read the original language in which writers expresses themselves.

2. All translations of the Bible have merit, but they also all have weaknesses. Translation has to be interpretation to some extent, and without access to the original language the student has no real means of ascertaining the interpretive options available, and their relative merits. Choosing the English translation that happens to fit best what one would like the text to mean is not always the best way to understand what is being said by the New Testament writer!

3. Many of the better commentaries are based upon the Greek text, as are most of the best journal articles on the New Testament documents. All this is opened up to the student who acquires even a rudimentary knowledge of Greek.

4. Finally, while dependence upon experts of various kinds is unavoidable, a degree of exposure to the original language at least gives some basis by which to evaluate their comments. Greek is one of the tools of trade that professionals need in dealing with the New Testament, whether the profession is academic or pastoral.

1.1 The Alphabet

The alphabet was only invented once. All modern alphabets derive from the one brilliant invention of a Semite living in Palestine in the second millennium BCE. Thus the order of letters between the Latin alphabet used in written English and the Greek alphabet is quite similar.

The Greek lower-case letters are used much more frequently than the upper-case letters. Their form is different from the Latin alphabet, but many of them will be familiar as they are often used in high school mathematics classrooms. This reflects the classical education enjoyed by many of the pioneers of mathematics.

Here is the complete lower-case alphabet:

The Greek alphabet: lower-case letters

Letter	Name	Letter	Name
α	alpha	ν	nu
β	beta	ξ	xi
γ	gamma	ο	omicron
δ	delta	π	pi
ε	epsilon	ρ	rho
ζ	zeta	σ, ς	sigma
η	eta	τ	tau
θ	theta	υ	upsilon
ι	iota	φ	phi
κ	kappa	χ	chi
λ	lambda	ψ	psi
μ	mu	ω	omega

The first task is to memorize the lower-case letters and their names. Notice the following points:
1. There are two forms of the Greek letter sigma. One form, σ, occurs at the beginning and middle of the word, but never as the last letter, while ς occurs only as the last letter of a word (e.g. σοφος, στασιαστης).
2. There are two letters for the "o" sound, and two for the "e" sound: ο is used for the short "o" sound, while ω is used for the longer "o" sound. Likewise, ε is short, while η is long.
3. The Greek vowels are α, ε, η, ι, ο, υ, ω. When two vowels occur together they are called diphthongs. Information on how diphthongs should be pronounced may be found below (at 1.2).

Part 1

4. A small iota is sometimes written under a vowel. It is called an iota subscript (e.g. ῳ, ῃ).

The upper-case letters can be learnt next. New Testament Greek does not always start each sentence with a capital letter, so they occur less often in Greek than in English. Upper-case letters are used for proper names (persons, places), at the beginning of a new paragraph, and at the beginning of direct speech. Many upper case Greek letters are the same as in the Roman alphabet (the exceptions being Γ, Δ, Θ, Λ, Ξ, Π, Σ, Φ, Ψ, Ω). Note also that the Greek upper-case ρ is not R but P.

Here is a complete list of the lower-case (lc) and upper-case (UC) Greek letters, including some further information on the sound and transliteration of each letter (which will be explained in due course):

The alphabet: lower- and upper-case, sound and transliteration

lc	UC	Sound	Transliteration (lc/uc)	
α	Α	a	a	A
β	Β	b	b	B
γ	Γ	g [get]	g	G
δ	Δ	d	d	D
ε	Ε	e [met]	e	E
ζ	Ζ	z or dz	z	Z
η	Η	e [fête]	ē	Ē
θ	Θ	th [thin]	th	TH
ι	Ι	i	i	I
κ	Κ	k	k	K
λ	Λ	l	l	L
μ	Μ	m	m	M
ν	Ν	n	n	N
ξ	Ξ	x	x	X
ο	Ο	o	o	O
π	Π	p	p	P
ρ	Ρ	r	r	R
σ, ς	Σ	s	s	S
τ	Τ	t	t	T
υ	Υ	u	u	U
φ	Φ	f	ph	PH
χ	Χ	ch [loch]	ch	CH
ψ	Ψ	ps [lips]	ps	PS
ω	Ω	o [tone]	ō	Ō

1.2 Pronunciation

A glance at the guide to modern Greek pronunciation listed in Appendix I will show why students of New Testament and classical Greek tend to use a different system of pronunciation. Several of the vowels and vowel combinations in modern Greek sound the same, and this makes learning more difficult if the goal is only to read the Greek New Testament. It is no longer known what Plato, Aristotle, and Paul sounded like when they spoke Greek, but the sounds suggested in the column labeled "Sound" in the table above are those generally used by students of classical and New Testament Greek. As they distinguish between the different vowels, it is easier to learn vocabulary items using this system.

While this "classical" system of pronunciation makes it easier to learn the written language, it does mean that, without some effort to re-learn the sounds of the various words, modern Greek speech remains inaccessible to a student who has learned using a "classical" system. For this reason, some teachers and students prefer to use modern Greek pronunciation. There are benefits and losses whichever system of pronunciation is chosen.

Many Greek letters are pronounced in the same way as their English equivalent in the classical system of pronunciation. This is true of α, β, γ, δ, ζ, ι, κ, λ, μ, ν, ξ, ο, π, ρ, σ, τ, υ, φ. English also has equivalent sounds to ε, η, θ, ψ, ω. The consonant χ, is a guttural, and sounds rather like the "ch" as a Scot would pronounce the word "loch."

The Greek vowels are α, ε, η, ι, ο, υ, ω. Where some combinations of two vowels occur together, they are called diphthongs. They are pronounced thus:

αι	as ai in **ai**sle
αυ	as au in F**au**st
ει	as ei in v**ei**l [some prefer ei as in h**eig**ht]
ευ, ηυ	as eu in f**eu**d
οι	as oi in b**oi**l
ου	as ou in gr**ou**p
υι	as ui in q**ui**t

Note that γγ is pronounced "ng." Thus ἄγγελος (angel), is pronounced "angelos," and ἐγγύς (near), is pronounced "engus." By the way, ἄγγελος occurs 175 times in the Greek New Testament, and ἐγγύς 31 times.

1.3 Breathing Marks

All NT Greek words which start with a vowel have a breathing mark over the initial vowel. A diphthong is considered as one vowel sound—the breathing mark is placed on the second character.

Although the "h" sound exists, there is no Greek letter corresponding to the English letter "h." The sound (a rough breathing in Greek) is indicated by placing an ʽ over the first vowel of the word (e.g. ὁδός, "way, path"). A smooth breathing denotes the absence of a rough breathing, and is indicated by an ʼ over an initial vowel. It has no effect on the sound of the vowel. Note that in all cases in which a word begins with the letter ρ, the letter ρ has a rough breathing.

Where the vowel at the beginning of the word is capitalized, the breathing mark is placed before it, unless it is a diphthong.

Some examples of smooth and rough breathings might make them easier to understand:

Greek	Sound	Greek	Sound
ἐν	en	αὐτός	autos
ἕν	hen	οὗτος	houtos
ὄν	on	εὑρίσκω	heuriskō
ὅν	hon	Ἀδάμ	Adam

1.4 Transliteration

Transliteration is the term used to describe the process of using the English alphabetic script to represent the Greek alphabet. The commonly used conventions are listed in the column labeled "Transliteration" in the table on p. 31.

Note: when transcribing into English, long "e" sounds (η), and long "o" sounds (ω), are indicated with a bar across the top of the letter. Thus η is transliterated by "ē" and ω by "ō." You can type these characters on a Mac by pressing the e or o key, and holding it down. A set of options should appear, including the two characters ē and ō. On a PC, if you press and hold the <alt> key while typing 275 on the number pad, when you release the key, the ē character should appear. Here is a list of five of the special characters that are available on the PC in this manner:

<alt> 275 = ē
<alt> 274 = Ē
<alt> 139 = ï
<alt> 333 = ō
<alt> 332 = Ō

1.5 Accents

There are three accents in the Greek NT: the acute accent (´) indicates that the voice should rise and that vowel should be stressed, while the grave (`) accent indicates that the voice should fall on the accented vowel. The circumflex accent (˜ or ˆ), originally a mark to indicate the fusion of two vowels, is usually thought to be a rise in the voice followed by a fall, but in practice it is the virtual equivalent of the acute accent [so Chrys C. Caragounis, *The Development of Greek and the New Testament* (Tübingen: Mohr Siebeck, 2006), p. 386]. Most students probably will note accents by stressing the accented vowel or diphthong when the word is said. Places where accents have grammatical importance will be discussed as they arise, and a list of words which differ only by their accents is given in Appendix F. This appendix will be useful from time to time when translating from the Greek NT, but for now there is no need to worry further about it.

Accents are provided throughout this book to assist in pronunciation, and some help with the rules of accents is provided in the early chapters. Learning accents might seem a distraction at the very beginning, but if they are not learned then, they become very difficult to master later. Better students will probably wish to familiarize themselves with accents, and from time to time will no doubt supplement what is said about accents in the various chapters in the book by referring to parts of Chapter 7 in *Intermediate New Testament Greek Made Easier* – the chapter on accents. As a general rule of thumb, most students will find accents on verbs easy to master, but there is more challenge with accents on nouns and adjectives.

Vocabulary 1

Ἀβραάμ (73)	Abraham
Δαυίδ (59)	David
θεός (1314)	God, god
Ἱεροσόλυμα (62), Ἱερουσαλήμ (71)	Jerusalem
Ἰησοῦς (919)	Jesus
Ἰωάννης (135)	John
Πέτρος (156)	Peter
Χριστός (531)	Christ, christ

Notes on Vocabulary 1

1. See comments in the introductory material on the usefulness of vocabulary cards.
2. Most of these words should be recognizable just by sounding them out.

The one that might appear new is θεός, but remembering that "theology" is literally the study of God should help.

3. Sometimes an "I" becomes a "J" when a name passes from Greek into English (note how Ἰησοῦς becomes Jesus, and Ἰωάννης becomes John). Note also that the vowel combinations ιε and ιη are not listed amongst the diphthongs [in 1.2], and so form two separate sounds. Thus the breathing marks for Ἱεροσόλυμα, Ἱερουσαλήμ, Ἰησοῦς and Ἰωάννης belong to the initial iota.

4. The number 1314 after θεός indicates that the word is used 1314 times in the New Testament. The vocabulary lists in the various chapters have been carefully chosen so that the most frequently occurring words are learned first. The first goal is to learn all words that occur more than 50 times in the Greek New Testament, and this should have been achieved by the end of Part 4. [For the curious: The statistics are generally taken from Sakae Kubo, *A Reader's Greek-English Lexicon of the New Testament* (Berrien Springs, MI: Andrews University Press, 1975), or (less often) from H. Bachmann & W. A. Slaby, *Computer-Konkordanz zum Novum Testamentum Graece* (Berlin: de Gruyter, 1980), or Gramcord. Kubo says he derived his statistics from Robert Morgenthaler, *Statistik des neutestamentlichen Wortschatzes* (Zürich: Gotthelf, 1958). The meanings given in the vocabularies usually follow Kubo, but on occasion are drawn from other sources.]

1.6 Writing Greek Text by Hand

The following, taken from J. W. Wenham, *Elements of New Testament Greek* (London: Cambridge University Press, 1965), p. 20, is a useful guide to how the characters of the Greek alphabet should be written by hand. The asterisk (*) indicates where the pen should begin the letter.

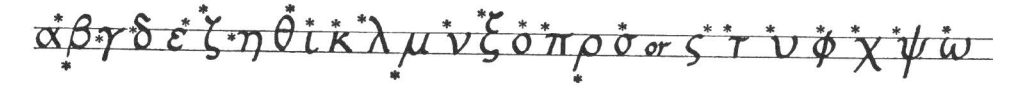

α β γ δ ε ζ η θ ι κ λ μ ν ξ ο π ρ σ or ς τ υ φ χ ψ ω

Exercise 1.1

1. Write out or type Luke 3:23-37 in English characters, using the normal conventions for transliteration. This passage is the genealogy of Jesus found in Luke. Many of the words may be recognized from an English Bible, especially towards the end. The Greek idiom used in this genealogy has no equivalent in English, which must add the words "the son of" where Greek only has "of the" (του).

Luke 3:23-38:

[23] Και αὐτὸς ἦν Ἰησους ἀρχομενος ὡσει ἐτων τριακοντα, ὢν υἱος, ὡς ἐνομιζετο, Ἰωσηφ του Ἡλι [24] του Μαθθατ του Λευι του Μελχι του Ἰανναι του Ἰωσηφ [25] του Ματταθιου του Ἀμως του Ναουμ του Ἐσλι του Ναγγαι [26] του Μααθ του Ματταθιου του Σεμεϊν* του Ἰωσηχ του Ἰωδα [27]

του Ἰωαναν του Ῥησα του Ζοροβαβελ του Σαλαθιηλ του Νηρι [28] του Μελχι του Ἀδδι του Κωσαμ του Ἐλμαδαμ του Ἢρ [29] του Ἰησου του Ἐλιεζερ του Ἰωριμ του Μαθθατ του Λευι [30] του Συμεων του Ἰουδα του Ἰωσηφ του Ἰωναμ του Ἐλιακιμ [31] του Μελεα του Μεννα του Ματταθα του Ναθαμ του Δαυιδ [32] του Ἰεσσαι του Ἰωβηδ του Βοος του Σαλα του Ναασσων [33] του Ἀμιναδαβ του Ἀδμιν του Ἀρνι του Ἑσρωμ του Φαρες του Ἰουδα [34] του Ἰακωβ του Ἰσαακ του Ἀβρααμ του Θαρα του Ναχωρ [35] του Σερουχ του Ῥαγαυ του Φαλεκ του Ἐβερ του Σαλα [36] του Καϊναμ του Ἀρφαξαδ του Σημ του Νωε του Λαμεχ [37] του Μαθουσαλα του Ἐνωχ του Ἰαρετ του Μαλελεηλ του Καϊναμ [38] του Ἐνως του Σηθ του Ἀδαμ του Θεου.

*The double dot over the iota of Σεμεϊν in v. 26 is called a "dieresis." It means that the two vowels ε and ι, which usually are pronounced together as a diphthong, should be pronounced separately in this instance. English uses the same punctuation mark to indicate the same thing, e.g. naïve. Cf. also Καϊναμ in v. 36.

2. Write by hand the following in Greek letters. It is given in the normal conventions for transliteration (as a matter of interest, the word ἐγεννησεν is a form of the verb γεννάω, "to be a father of; bear, give birth to," and will be met officially in Vocabulary 8):

Matt 1:6-11:
[6] Iessai de egennēsen ton Dauid ton basilea. Dauid de egennēsen ton Solomōna ek tēs tou Ouriou, [7] Solomōn de egennēsen ton Hroboam, Hroboam de egennēsen ton Abia, Abia de egennēsen ton Asaph, [8] Asaph de egennēsen ton Iōsaphat, Iōsaphat de egennēsen ton Iōram, Iōram de egennēsen ton Ozian, [9] Ozias de egennēsen ton Iōatham, Iōatham de egennēsen ton Achaz, Achaz de egennēsen ton Hezekian, [10] Hezekias de egennēsen ton Manassē, Manassēs de egennēsen ton Amōs, Amōs de egennēsen ton Iōsian, [11] Iōsias de egennēsen ton Iechonian kai tous adelphous autou epi tēs metoikesias Babulōnos.

Note: Complete answers to this exercise and the exercises in the review chapters are given in Appendix A, which also lists answers to odd numbered questions for all other exercises. These answers are an important way to check whether or not you have understood the exercise.

1.7 Typing Greek Text using the Greek Polytonic Keyboard

Some years ago, as computers were being adapted for countries which did not use the alphabet used to write English, a standard set of characters were added to most fonts so that Greek, Arabic, Cyrillic, Hebrew, and a number of other languages could be typed. These formed the so-called unicode character set. Most fonts on PCs and Macs today are unicode, so all the Greek characters are available in most fonts.

In Microsoft word these characters can be accessed by the insert symbol command. This is fine for just a few characters, but for fluent typing, a keyboard needs to be installed. There is more than one keyboard that produces Greek characters, but the one you wish to have installed is the Greek Polytonic keyboard, which has all the correct accent marks.

Install a Greek Polytonic Keyboard on your computer
- It must be Greek Polytonic – modern Greek lacks some of the accents and other marks you need
- On a PC: Press the Windows key, and from the start menu click on the gear symbol for settings. Then choose Time & Language/ Region & language/+ Add a language/Ελληνικά Greek. Then click on Ελληνικά/options/+ Add a keyboard/ Greek Polytonic [Note: for Windows 7 and 8: use Control Panel / Region and Language / Keyboards and Languages / change keyboards / Add / Greek / Greek Polytonic]
- On a MAC: System Preferences / Languages and Regions / Add a language / Greek / Greek Polytonic

Once you have the Greek Polytonic keyboard installed, you will see an option appear on your screen that will enable you to choose which keyboard you wish to use. On the PC it is possible to use hot-keys to move from one keyboard to another. The hotkey is usually either <shift><alt>, or <shift><ctrl> [press them both together at the same time].

Once you have chosen the Greek Polytonic keyboard, the following Greek letters are associated with the standard English Letters [English alternating with Greek Polytonic equivalents underneath]

Q	W	E	R	T	Y	U	I	O	P
;	ς	Ε	Ρ	Τ	Υ	Θ	Ι	Ο	Π

q	w	e	r	t	y	u	I	o	p
;	ς	ε	ρ	τ	υ	θ	ι	ο	π

A	S	D	F	G	H	J	K	L
Α	Σ	Δ	Φ	Γ	Η	Ξ	Κ	Λ

a	s	d	f	g	h	j	k	l
α	σ	δ	φ	γ	η	ξ	κ	λ

Z	X	C	V	B	N	M
Z	X	Ψ	Ω	B	N	M

Z	x	c	v	b	n	m
Z	χ	ψ	ω	β	ν	μ

Most of these choices make sense: a for α, b for β, d for δ for example, but note that:
- u produces θ
- y produces υ
- j produces ξ
- w produces ς
- c produces ψ
- v produces ω

Some will find it helpful to turn on the **on-screen keyboard**, which provides a map of what the Greek letters the various keys produce. On a PC running Windows 10 (or 7 or 8 for that matter), the on-screen keyboard may be activated in the following manner: Press the windows key (i.e. go to start menu), and type in "on" over the list of apps (on Windowns 7 or 8, type "on" in the search box); several options will appear, one of them being the "on-screen keyboard." That will show the various Greek or English characters available on the keyboard that you are using at the time, and will change as you move between an English keyboard and a Greek keyboard. Alas, on a PC, only the Greek letters show via this method - accents have to be added using a technique described below.

To obtain a **floating keyboard** on a Mac, go into System Preferences, then select keyboard. Check the box labelled: Show Keyboard & Character Viewers in menu bar. Then click on the Input Sources button. Press the + button to add a new one. Scroll down to Greek in the list of languages on the left and click on it. Then select Greek Polytonic from the box on the right. Click on 'Add'. Now you will be able to easily change between Australian and Greek Polytonic from the menu bar as well as bring up the floating keyboard which will show you how to type all of the characters. Just select the tiny Australian flag in the menu bar. As you type in accents, notice how the keyboard changes to show how that accent will appear with the next letter you input. You can press multiple accents and then enter a letter. Hold shift to get alternate accents and capital letters.

Adding accents adds an extra layer of complexity, so I suggest that you do Exercise 1.2, no. 1, and then come back and read how to type breathing marks and accents once you have completed that.

Breathing marks are added by making two consecutive keystrokes in the Greek Polytonic keyboard.
- Smooth breathing: if you type 'a, the Greek Polytonic keyboard would produce ἀ. Typing 'y produces ὐ, etc.
- Rough breathing: "a produces ἁ; and "i produces ἱ, etc.
- [note: only the Greek Polytonic keyboard does this, the normal Greek keyboard does not; if you are having trouble check which keyboard you are using]

Accents are (also) produced by two key strokes.
- Acute accent: typing qa produces ά; qe produces έ, etc.
- Grave accent: typing]a produces ὰ;]v produces ὼ, etc.
- Circumflex accent: typing [a produces ᾶ; [y produces ῦ, etc.

On a PC, **combined breathing marks and accents** are produced by only two keystrokes (Mac users may find they are permitted more than two key strokes).

Smooth breathing with:
- Acute e.g. /a produces ἄ; /y produces ὔ
- Grave e.g. \a produces ἂ; \i produces ἲ
- Circumflex e.g. =a produces ἆ; =y produces ὖ

Rough breathing with:
- Acute e.g. ?a produces ἅ; ?y produces ὕ
- Grave e.g. |a produces ἃ; |i produces ἳ
- Circumflex e.g. +a produces ἇ; +u produces ὗ

Iota subscripts can be found with vowels, combinations of vowels and accents, and combinations of vowels, accents and breathing marks. Iota subscripts combined with accents and breathing marks are produced by typing the right <alt> key with the first of the two strokes that produce the rest of the character needed.
- Iota subscript with a vowel: e.g. {a produces ᾳ; {v produces ῳ
- With combinations: <[right] alt>=h produces ᾖ; <[right] alt>qv produces ῴ; <[right] alt>[h produces ῇ

To add a **dieresis** with the Greek Polytonic keyboard, type : then character (e.g. :i produces ï); while the Greek semi-colon or colon (·) is produced by typing together <shift> <right alt>]. Commas and full stops are the same on both the English and Greek keyboards, while the Greek question mark (; – see 4.5) is found on the Greek Polytonic keyboard by typing q and then hitting the space bar.

Exercise 1.2

1. Type Luke 3:23-29 [without breathing marks or accents] using the Greek Polytonic keyboard. You will recognize this passage from Exercise 1.1 where you transliterated it.

Luke 3:23-28:
    [23] Και αυτος ην Ιησους αρχομενος ωσει ετων τριακοντα, ων υιος, ως ενομιζετο, Ιωσηφ του Ηλι [24] του Μαθθατ του Λευι του Μελχι του Ιανναι του Ιωσηφ [25] του Ματταθιου του Αμως του Ναουμ του Εσλι του Ναγγαι [26] του Μααθ του Ματταθιου του Σεμεϊν του Ιωσηχ του Ιωδα [27] του Ιωαναν του Ρησα του Ζοροβαβελ του Σαλαθιηλ του Νηρι [28] του Μελχι του Αδδι του Κωσαμ του Ελμαδαμ του Ηρ

2. Type John 1:1-10 [including breathing marks, accents, iota subscripts, etc] using the Greek Polytonic keyboard.

John 1:1-10:
    [1] Ἐν ἀρχῇ ἦν ὁ λόγος, καὶ ὁ λόγος ἦν πρὸς τὸν θεόν, καὶ θεὸς ἦν ὁ λόγος. [2] οὗτος ἦν ἐν ἀρχῇ πρὸς τὸν θεόν. [3] πάντα δι' αὐτοῦ ἐγένετο, καὶ χωρὶς αὐτοῦ ἐγένετο οὐδὲ ἕν. ὃ γέγονεν [4] ἐν αὐτῷ ζωὴ ἦν, καὶ ἡ ζωὴ ἦν τὸ φῶς τῶν ἀνθρώπων• 5 καὶ τὸ φῶς ἐν τῇ σκοτίᾳ φαίνει, καὶ ἡ σκοτία αὐτὸ οὐ κατέλαβεν.
    [6] Ἐγένετο ἄνθρωπος, ἀπεσταλμένος παρὰ θεοῦ, ὄνομα αὐτῷ Ἰωάννης• [7] οὗτος ἦλθεν εἰς μαρτυρίαν ἵνα μαρτυρήσῃ περὶ τοῦ φωτός, ἵνα πάντες πιστεύσωσιν δι' αὐτοῦ. [8] οὐκ ἦν ἐκεῖνος τὸ φῶς, ἀλλ' ἵνα μαρτυρήσῃ περὶ τοῦ φωτός. [9] Ἦν τὸ φῶς τὸ ἀληθινόν, ὃ φωτίζει πάντα ἄνθρωπον, ἐρχόμενον εἰς τὸν κόσμον. [10] ἐν τῷ κόσμῳ ἦν, καὶ ὁ κόσμος δι' αὐτοῦ ἐγένετο, καὶ ὁ κόσμος αὐτὸν οὐκ ἔγνω.

Part 1 41

Chapter 2: The Present Tense of λύω

A verb is at the heart of nearly every sentence, and thus it makes sense to begin with Greek verbs. This chapter will first define what is meant by the term "verb," and describe how they are recognized in Greek. It will then introduce the various terms needed to recognize and understand the Greek present tense. By the end of the chapter, you will have learned the forms of the present indicative active, the meaning of several commonly used verbs, and how to place accents on verbs. The exercises will allow you to become comfortable and familiar with the present tense of the indicative active verb.

2.1 What is a Verb, and How Are Greek Verbs Recognized?

Not everybody using this book will feel a master of English grammar. So a feature of Greek Grammar will usually be introduced by a brief description of the English grammar to which it corresponds most closely. This chapter introducing the Greek verb will be no exception.

What, then, is a verb? Generations of school children have learnt that a verb is "an action word." Vocabulary 2 lists nine separate verbs which are given the English equivalents: "hear, write, eat, find, have, want, take, say, loose." Several of these describe an action – e.g. "write, eat, take, say" – and thus fit the definition "action word." On the other hand, the verb "want" expresses an intention, not an action, and later vocabularies will introduce verbs such as "be" (Vocab. 4) and "love" (Vocab. 8), verbs which describe a state of being or state of mind. Thus a better definition of a verb might be such as that found in Webster's dictionary: a verb is "a word expressing action, existence, or occurrence." Amongst other things, verbs may make statements, express intentions, and give commands.

The form of the word in Greek actually indicates whether or not it is a verb. Words in the vocabulary lists that end in -ω, -μι or -ομαι ***must*** be verbs. So here is another way to understand what a verb is – observe what happens to words with these endings and you will gain a very good understanding of what a verb is and what it can do in a sentence. Indeed, one of the consequences of learning a second language is usually a better understanding of the grammar and structure one's own language.

2.2 Paradigms

Every native English speaker automatically knows whether something is correct or incorrect English. All would realize that the sentence "the boys sat down, he ate a sandwich," has a mistake in it; and that "I want eat" is bad grammar, whereas "I want to eat" is correct. It is surprising to realize, but each English speaker knows the correct patterns to use for spoken or written language. For verbs these patterns are called paradigms.

For example, here is the verb pattern (paradigm) for the English present-sent tense [active voice]:

Examples of English Verb Patterns [Present Tense, Active Voice]			
I say	I hear	I eat	I have
you say	you hear	you eat	you have
he says	he hears	he eats	he has
we say	we hear	we eat	we have
you say	you hear	you eat	you have
they say	they hear	they eat	they have

The pattern unconsciously followed by all English-speakers always puts an "s" on the verb for "he .....s" or "she .....s" in the present tense. One of the keys to learning another language is to consciously study the patterns of that language. Once these patterns are learned, then the language is accessible. These patterns (paradigms) for the verb in New Testament Greek are listed in Appendix B. The most commonly used parts of the paradigm will be explained first.

2.3 Present Indicative Active of λύω

The simplest form of the verb is the present indicative active (what these terms mean is explained below in 2.5). The present indicative active of λύω, "I loose" is as follows:

Person	Form of λύω	English Meaning
1st pers sing	λύω	I loose
2nd pers sing	λύεις	you loose
3rd per sing	λύει	he/she/it looses
1st pers pl	λύομεν	we loose
2nd pers pl	λύετε	you loose
3rd pers pl	λύουσι / λύουσιν	they loose

Part 1 43

Notes:
1. λύω, "I loose," is used by itself 42 times in the New Testament, and a further 99 times in compound verbs such as ἀπολύω [ἀπό + λύω] (66), "I release, dismiss, divorce." It has the basic meaning of loose, but can also be used in other ways (e.g. breaking [loosing] the Sabbath). It is the verb normally used to show the paradigm because it is completely regular. This means it follows the general pattern of how a verb should be formed without any exceptions [irregularities].
2. The term "first person" is shorthand for the form of the verb that fits "I" or "we," second person "you" (singular and plural), while third person fits "he, she, it, they."
3. One part of the word stays the same, while the last few letters are different. The part that stays the same is called the [present] verb stem. The form of the verb given in the dictionary generally is the first person present indicative active. For this kind of verb, the ending added to the verb stem is ω. If this ω is taken from the dictionary form of the verb, what is left is the verb stem for the present tense, and its present indicative is then formed by adding to the verb stem the ending from the pattern of λύω. This sounds harder than it is. For example, the Greek word for "I say" is λέγω. Removing the ω gives the verb stem λεγ-, to which endings should be added that follow the pattern of the endings on the present indicative active of λυω:

λύ-ω	λέγ-ω
λύ-εις	λέγ-εις
λύ-ει	λέγ-ει
λύ-ομεν	λέγ-ομεν
λύ-ετε	λέγ-ετε
λύ-ουσι / λύουσιν	λέγ-ουσι / λέγουσιν

4. Generally speaking, if the verb is the last word in the sentence, or if the next word in the sentence starts with a vowel, the third person plural has a final ν. This extra ν [called a moveable ν] was used to make pronunciation easier, in much the same way that an "n" is used with the word "an" in English. So, in English one says, "a banana," "a car" or "an orange," "an elephant."
5. The personal pronouns need not be written in Greek [see 2.4 below].

2.4 Greek as an Inflected Language

English distinguishes between "I say" and "you say" by the addition of the personal pronouns "I" or "you." Greek does this by varying the endings of the words (i.e. by inflection), and one of the major differences between Greek and English is that Greek is an inflected language. English still has remnants of inflection, for example, "I say ... he say**s**," or "he, him, his, she, her, hers, it, its, etc.," or "thou say**est**" in King-James-Version English. But English mostly indicates grammatical form by means other than inflection. So, person is indicated in English by the addition of the personal pronouns "I, you, he/she/it, we, you, they." In Greek, on the other hand, the personal pronouns need not be used with the verb, although they can be used when the writer wishes to stress the "I," or "you," or "we," etc.

All the words of Vocabulary 2 are like λύω: i.e. they are verbs which end with the vowel ω. They follow the same pattern of inflection as λύω. So once the way λύω declines (i.e. how it changes as it inflects) is learnt, the way all the verbs in Vocabulary 2 decline for their present indicative active may be worked out.

2.5 Tense, Mood, Voice

The part of the paradigm dealt with in this chapter is the present indicative active. The word "present" refers to the tense, the word "indicative" refers to the mood, the word "active" refers to the voice.

In English, the tense of a verb is primarily a reference to time. Most verbs deal with actions. Actions can be considered to be happening in the present (the present tense of the verb), in the past, or in the future (the future tense of the verb). The Greek tense system is not quite the same as the English tense system, but it will make it easier if we leave discussion of the differences to a later place in the book, and learn the closest equivalent English tense at first. As might be expected, the English present tense is the closest in meaning to the Greek present tense.

It will be best to postpone a discussion of mood and voice until other moods and voices have been met [most students are content to follow the step by step approach to learning the language, but some, who are "big picture" thinkers prefer to see everything at once. They may find an overall summary of mood in the review chapter for Part 4, Chapter 30, and more on voice in Chapter 24. Those wanting access to the really big picture on tense, mood and voice should consult Chapters 3, 1 and 4 in *Intermediate New Testament Greek Made Easier*]. For now it is probably enough to know that the indicative mood is used for making statements about real events, and that the active voice is used where the subject of the verb does the action.

2.6 Learning the Verb Paradigm

It is one of the less pleasant facts of life that the memorization of vocabulary and language patterns that was natural while learning to speak a language as a child becomes something that an adult must deliberately do. For example, verb paradigms just have to be learnt. Each student will develop

Part 1 45

their own strategies for learning. Some find it helpful to chant paradigms aloud and to write them out on paper. However it is done, though, there is no way of avoiding this task, just as there is no way to avoid spending the time necessary to learn vocabulary.

2.7 Pronouncing Greek Words

The pronunciation of Greek letters has been explained in some detail in 1.2, and the importance of saying vocabulary out loud has been stressed in the section of methods of study. It is important to begin reading out loud as soon as possible, and you actually know almost everything you need to be able to do just that. The exercise on transliteration in the previous chapter will have given most readers a grasp of how the words may be pronounced. It will soon become second nature to read from words written using the Greek alphabet, although at the very beginig some may find it a helpful aid to pronunciation to transliterate the word. Thus, ἀκούω is transliterated and pronounced, as "a-k*ou*-ō"; γράφω is transliterated and pronounced "gr*a*ph-ō"; ἐσθίω is transliterated and pronounced as "es-th*i*-ō"; etc.

Vocabulary 2

ἀκούω (427)	I hear, listen
γράφω (190)	I write
ἐσθίω (165)	I eat
εὑρίσκω (176)	I find
ἔχω (705)	I have
θέλω (207)	I will, wish, want
λαμβάνω (258)	I take, receive
λέγω (1318)	I say, speak
λύω (42)	I loose

Exercise 2.1

A. Paradigms: Write out or type in full the present indicative active of:
i. ἀκούω   ii. θέλω   iii. γράφω   iv. ἔχω
[Note: When an exercise, test or exam asks you to write out in full one part of the paradigm of a verb, it is expected that you write out the forms of the 1st, 2nd and 3rd persons for both singular and plural for the indicative tense, mood and voice of that verb.]

B. Translate into English
1. λέγει 2. ἀκούεις 3. γράφουσιν 4. θέλομεν 5. ἔχω 6. εὑρίσκετε 7. ἐσθίουσιν
8. λαμβάνει 9. ἔχει 10. εὑρίσκεις 11. ἐσθίω 12. ἀκούουσιν

13. γράφομεν 14. θέλετε 15. λέγω 16. γράφεις 17. λαμβάνετε 18. θέλεις
19. ἀκούομεν 20. ἔχουσι 21. λέγομεν 22. λαμβάνεις 23. εὑρίσκουσιν
24. θέλει

C. Translate into Greek
[note: accents on Greek verbs are covered in 2.8. You need not put accents on the verbs in this part of the exercise]
25. I wish 26. I receive 27. They say 28. You (sing) eat 29. I hear 30. We take 31. You (pl) say 32. He finds 33. I write 34. I find 35. You (sing) have 36. She hears

37. They take 38. You (sing) say 39. We have 40. You (pl.) hear 41. They want 42. We eat 43. You (pl.) eat 44. He writes 45. You (pl) have 46. We find 47. It eats 48. You (pl.) write

2.8 Accents on Verbs

For most verbs, the question of where to place an accent is relatively straight forward, and can be determined by knowing: (a.) about short and long syllables, (b.) the general rules for accents, and (c.) a few rules specific to verbs.

a. Long and Short Syllables: A syllable is part of a word that contains a vowel (the Greek vowels are α, ε, η, ι, ο, ω, υ, plus diphthongs), and can sometimes consist of only that vowel. The following are examples of the various syllables that make up selected English words: con-tain, vo-wel, fol-low-ing, ob-ser-va-tion, de-ter-min-ed, etc. In a Greek word, a syllable is long if its vowel is long; and short if its vowel is short. The following vowels [and diphthongs] are:
  always short: ε, ο
  always long: η, ω, αυ, ει, ου, ευ
  usually short: αι, οι
Whether α or ι is long or short must be determined by observation, although at the end of nouns and verbs, α or ι is often short.

b. The General Rules for Accents might be summarized as follows:
i. The grave accent (`) may only be found on the last syllable of a word (e.g. θεὸς in John 1:1).

Part 1

ii. Generally speaking, the circumflex accents (˜ or ˆ) may only be found on the last two syllables of a word (e.g.ἐκεῖνος, ἀρχῇ in John 1:1, 8). However, when the last syllable is long, the circumflex accent must be on the last syllable (E.g. αὐτοῦ in John 1:3).

iii. Generally speaking, the acute accent (´) may be found on any of the last three syllables of a word (e.g. ἐγένετο, σκοτία, θεόν in John 1:1-4). However, if the last syllable is long, it can ***only*** appear on the last two syllables of a word (e.g. φωτίζει in John 1:9). Note: the acute accent on the last syllable usually changes to a grave accent if another word follows.

Note: if an acute accent is found on the last syllable of a word (the *ultima*), it is called *oxytone*; if it is found on the second to last syllable of a word (the *penult*) it is called *paroxytone*; if it is found on the third to last syllable of a word (the *antepenult*) it is called *proparoxytone*. If a circumflex accent is found on the last syllable of a word, it is called *perispomenon*; if it is found on the second to last syllable of a word, it is called *properispomenon*.

c. Rules specific to verbs

i. The accent, which is usually acute, must be placed as far from the end of the verb as is consistent with the main accents for verbs. For λαμ-βαν-ω, as the last syllable (ω) is long this means that the accent must be found on the last two syllables, and the furthest from the end of the word that is possible is λαμβάνω. On the other hand, the last syllable (εν) of λαμ-βαν-ομ-εν is short, and thus the accent may fall on any of the last three syllables, and the furthest possible from the end of the word is λαμβάνομεν.

ii. If the accent stands on the second to last syllable, which is long, it must be circumflex if the last syllable is short. This rule will become important in Chapter 12 where we will meet εἶπον "I said," and ἦλθον "I came/went."

Exercise 2.2

Write out or type each example and provide appropriate accents:
1. λεγει 2. ἀκουεις 3. γραφουσιν 4. θελομεν 5. ἐχω 6. εὑρισκετε 7. ἐσθιουσιν 8. λαμβανει 9. ἐχει 10. εὑρισκεις

Chapter 3: Masculine Second Declension Nouns

In addition to one or more verbs, a sentence almost always contains nouns. This chapter introduces nouns and explains the way their grammatical function in a Greek sentence is indicated by the various endings that they take. These endings designate the case of a noun, and by the time the chapter is finished, you will have met all five cases that are used in the Greek New Testament: the nominative, vocative, accusative, genitive and dative cases, together with some of their most common uses. All this will be illustrated by using one of the significant types of Greek noun: second declension nouns that end in –ος.

The chapter is divided into three sections, each one followed by an exercise, and the first two accompanied by vocabularies listing, among other things, some commonly used nouns. The first section shows how the nominative and accusative cases are used to indicate the subject and direct object of a verb, and the accompanying exercise will introduce you to some simple sentences in Greek. The second section deals with the genitive, dative, and vocative cases, while the last one shows how accents should be placed on nouns.

3.1.1 What is a Noun?

A noun is a word that is the name of something. It might name a thing, a collection, a quality, or a person. English grammar distinguishes four types of noun: common nouns (e.g. rock, lake, sheep), collective nouns (e.g. flock, people), abstract nouns (e.g. love, righteousness), and proper nouns (a name of a person or place, e.g. Jesus, Capernaum), and each of these types of noun may be found in Greek. For example, of the twenty nouns in Vocabularies 1, 3.1 and 3.2, six are proper nouns (Abraham, David, Jerusalem, Jesus, John, Peter), twelve are common nouns (god, Christ, brother, man, bread, slave, word, son, angel, world, law, house), and two are collective nouns (people, crowd). Examples of abstract nouns such as "love" and "sin" will be met in Vocabulary 6.

3.1.2 What Is a Declension?

Just as the verb changes its endings (inflects) to show its number, tense and mood, so also the Greek noun inflects by changing its endings. It is the ending of the noun that indicates what part of the sentence it is (subject, direct object, etc). The pattern that the verb follows is called a paradigm. The pattern a noun follows is called a **declension**. There are three declensions of the Greek nouns. This merely means that there are three broad categories of Greek nouns, and that nouns follow patterns which are similar to each other within these categories. There are a large number of masculine second declension nouns that end in -ος used in the NT, and this is the first kind of noun that will be dealt with in this book. First and third declension nouns will be met in subsequent chapters (see Chapters 6, 14, and Appendix E).

3.1.3 Gender

Greek has three genders (masculine, feminine, and neuter), and every Greek noun has gender. While it is sometimes possible to see why a particular noun is masculine or feminine (e.g. ἄνθρωπος "man" is masculine; γυνή "woman" is feminine), the gender of a noun is often arbitrary. On occasion gender can be helpful in making the meaning of a sentence clear.

3.1.4 The Subject and Direct Object in English

A simple English sentence is usually in the order: subject – verb – direct object. For example, in the sentence, "The boy hits the ball," the subject is first ("The boy"), the verb is next ("hits"), and the direct object is after the verb ("the ball").

Word order is very important in determining the subject and object of an English sentence. For example, the meaning of the sentence, "The man bites the dog" is quite different from "The dog bites the man." This is because the subject of an English sentence is usually indicated by the fact that it comes before the verb, and "man" is the subject of the verb "bites" in the first sentence, while "dog" is the subject of the verb "bites" in the second sentence. Furthermore, "dog" is the direct object of the verb "bite" in the first sentence, while "man" is its direct object in the second sentence. Hence, although the two sentences use exactly the same words, the different order in which the words are found gives them different meanings in English. In Greek, on the other hand, it is the form of the ending of the word (i.e. case, etc.) that shows its grammatical meaning, and thus word order is much less important. Nouns in New Testament Greek may have five different cases. Two of them – the nominative and accusative cases – are used to indicate the subject and direct object of a verb.

3.1.5 Nominative and Accusative Cases

In almost every sentence there is at least one verb, and each verb has a subject (and usually a direct object). One of the key skills needed to translate accurately is the ability to pick out these three elements in the sentence. Once they are recognized, the rest of the elements of the sentence normally make sense. The subject and direct object of a Greek verb is revealed by the case endings of the nouns. **The nominative case of the Greek noun is used for the subject of a verb, while the accusative case is used for the direct object of a verb.**

Masculine nouns of the second declension follow the pattern of λόγος, "word." The nominative and accusative cases of λόγος are:

Nominative masculine singular:	**λόγος**
Accusative masculine singular:	**λόγον**
Nominative masculine plural:	**λόγοι**
Accusative masculine plural:	**λόγους**

A subject, a verb, and direct object can be used to make a complete sentence. In Greek, the process of recognizing the various grammatical forms in a sentence is called parsing, a highly important skill in translation. For example, parsing the sentence, ἄνθρωπος λέγει λόγον gives: ἄνθρωπος (nominative masculine singular; i.e. the subject of the sentence); λέγει (third person singular, present indicative active—the main verb); λόγον (accusative masculine singular; i.e. the direct object of the verb). The sentence could be translated: "A man says a word." Note that because word order does not determine grammatical function in Greek, this sentence could equally well have been written, λέγει λόγον ἄνθρωπος.

Where there is a clearly expressed subject of the verb (aside from the personal pronouns "I," "we" or "you"), the verb is in the third person. It is singular or plural depending on whether the subject is singular or plural. Thus if the sentence was "men say a word" (ἄνθρωποι λέγουσι λόγον), then the verb would be in the third person plural, to agree with the plural subject "men." The number of the direct object does not affect the number of the verb. Thus:

λέγει λόγον ἄνθρωπος	A man says a word
λέγει λόγους ἄνθρωπος	A man says words
λέγουσι λόγον ἄνθρωποι	Men say a word
λέγουσι λόγους ἄνθρωποι	Men say words

What you need to know about the nominative and accusative cases at this stage might be summed up as follows:

3.1.5.1 The Nominative Case

The nominative case is indicated by the -ος (sing.) or -οι (pl.) ending on masculine second declension nouns such as λόγος. The most common use of the nominative case is to indicate:

i. The **subject** of a verb. For example, Πέτρος λέγει ... ("Peter says ...") or δοῦλος λαμβάνει ... ("a servant takes ...").

3.1.5.2 The Accusative Case

The accusative case is indicated by an -ον (sing.) or -ους (pl.) ending on masculine second declension nouns such as λόγος. There are two common uses of the accusative case:

i. The accusative case is used to identify the **direct object of a verb**. For example, Δαυίδ εὑρίσκει ἄρτον ("David finds bread"), or Ἰησοῦς λέγει λόγους ("Jesus says words").

ii. The accusative case is found with **certain prepositions**. As this is the first time the term preposition has been met, perhaps it should be defined. A preposition is used to show the relation between a noun and something else. Prepositions comprise many of the little words of a language—words like "of," "to," "for," etc. There is a list of common prepositions found at 30.6, and if you look at the list, you will see a number of them are found with the accusative case. In Part 1, you will meet prepositions that uses the accusative case in Vocabulary 5 (κατά + acc. "according to"), Vocabulary 9 (εἰς + acc. "into"; πρός + acc. "towards"), and Vocabulary 10 (ἐπί + acc. "across"). See also 3.2.1, 3.2.2, and 30.6 for prepositions that are used with the genitive and dative cases.

3.1.6 The Article

English has two kinds of article: the definite article "the"; and the indefinite article "a." Greek has only one article. At this beginning stage of learning Greek it is probably best to consider the Greek article as the equivalent of the definite article in English, although, as will gradually emerge throughout the rest of the book, there are some differences in how the two languages use the article.

The Greek article has case, gender, and number. Three of the four endings have already been met:

Nominative Masculine Singular   ὁ
Accusative Masculine Singular   τόν
Nominative Masculine Plural   οἱ
Accusative Masculine Plural   τούς

The use of the article can be illustrated by the following sentences:

λέγει λόγον ἄνθρωπος	A man says a word
λέγει λόγον ὁ ἄνθρωπος	The man says a word
λέγει τὸν λόγον ἄνθρωπος	A man says the word
λέγει τὸν λόγον ὁ ἄνθρωπος	The man says the word
λέγει τοὺς λόγους ἄνθρωπος	A man says the words
λέγουσι λόγον οἱ ἄνθρωποι	The men say a word
λέγουσι τοὺς λόγους οἱ ἄνθρωποι	The men say the words, etc.

Notes:

1. The definite article is used 19,734 times in the Greek New Testament in its different forms. It is helpful to be able to instantly identify whether the article is singular/plural, nominative/accusative, etc. Thus the different forms of the definite article have been listed as separate items in the vocabulary lists in this chapter.

2. Because Greek has only the definite article, a decision has to be made whether to include the indefinite article or not when translating into English: e.g. ἄνθρωπος could be either "a man" or "man," depending on the context and a judgment of what is the best way to express the intent of the Greek original in English.

3. Greek often uses an article before a personal name. In particular, the name Ἰησοῦς is almost always found with an article. Thus, rather than Ἰησοῦς λέγει λόγους, the examples given in 3.1.5.2 would have better expressed, ὁ Ἰησοῦς λέγει λόγους ("Jesus says words").

3.1.7 How to Recognize which Paradigm or Declension to Apply to a Vocabulary Item

Beginning Greek students regularly report that they find difficulty in working out which paradigm or declension to apply to a word in their vocabulary lists. Thus far one paradigm has been learnt: the present tense of the verb. Verbs in vocabulary lists can be recognized because, with only the rare exception, they will end with an -ω, an -ομαι or a -μι. Thus, because none of the words in it end with an -ω, an -ομαι or a -μι, there are no further verbs in Vocabulary 3.1, although there is one in Vocabulary 3.2 (πιστεύω which ends in -ω). The one declension met thus far is for second declension nouns that end in -ος. Many of the words in Vocabulary 3.1 finish with -ος (eg. ἀδελφός, ἄνθρωπος, etc.). These words are nouns, and follow the pattern learned for λόγος. Some words do not decline (e.g. καί, which is a conjunction usually translated "and," and used to join two nouns or two larger parts of a sentence together), and others are already shown in their declined form (e.g. οἱ, τόν, etc.).

Vocabulary 3.1

Second Declension Nouns
ἀδελφός (343)   brother
ἄνθρωπος (548) human being, man
ἄρτος (97)   bread
δοῦλος (124)   slave, servant
λαός (141)   people [cf. the English word, "laity"]
λόγος (331)   word, matter, reason
υἱός (375)   son

Other Words
καί (8947) **and**, also, even [for now, translate this as "and"]
ὁ (2300+) the [nom. masc. sing. definite article]
τόν (1330+) the [acc. masc. sing. definite article]
οἱ (950+) the [nom. masc. pl. definite article]
τούς (630+) the [acc. masc. pl. definite article]

Exercise 3.1

A: Translate into English

1. οἱ ἄνθρωποι εὑρίσκουσι τοὺς δούλους.   2. ἄνθρωποι εὑρίσκουσι τοὺς δούλους.   3. οἱ ἄνθρωποι εὑρίσκουσι δούλους.   4. τοὺς ἀνθρώπους εὑρίσκουσι δοῦλοι (think carefully about this one).   5. εὑρίσκει τὸν δοῦλον ὁ ἄνθρωπος.   6. ἄνθρωπος εὑρίσκει δοῦλον.   7. εὑρίσκει δοῦλον ὁ Χριστός.   8. ὁ Χριστὸς ἀκούει τὸν λόγον.   9. ὁ υἱὸς λαμβάνει τὸν λαόν.   10. τὸν ἄρτον ὁ Πέτρος ἐσθίει.

11. ὁ Ἀβραὰμ θέλει υἱοὺς καὶ δούλους. [Unlike English, Greek often puts the definite article in front of a person's name. This is not always done, although the name Jesus generally has a definite article. Beginning students should probably always include an article with a name when translating from English into Greek.] 12. θεοὺς ὁ λαὸς ἔχει (think carefully about this one also). 13. ὁ θεὸς λαὸν ἔχει. [Unlike English, Greek usually puts the definite article in front of θεός. Beginning students should probably always include such an article when translating from English into Greek.] 14. ὁ Δαυὶδ ἐσθίει τὸν ἄρτον. 15. ἔχει ἀδελφὸν ὁ Ἰωάννης. 16. ἐσθίει τὸν ἄρτον ὁ Ἰησοῦς. 17. ὁ Ἀβραὰμ ἔχει υἱὸν καὶ ὁ Δαυὶδ ἔχει υἱόν. 18. οἱ ἀδελφοὶ λαμβάνουσιν τὸν ἄρτον. 19. λέγει λόγους ὁ Ἰησοῦς. 20. οἱ ἀδελφοὶ καὶ οἱ δοῦλοι ἐσθίουσιν ἄρτον.

B. Translate into Greek
[Note: accents on nouns are not introduced until 3.4. You may either write this part of the exercises without putting accents on the nouns, or pre-read 3.4 before starting it.]

21. The slave has a brother. 22. The brother has a slave. 23. The brothers have slaves. 24. The brothers have a slave. 25. The slave has brothers. 26. David

writes a word. 27. The people eat bread. 28. The people take gods. 29. The Christ has a people. 30. The men take the slaves. 31. Jesus finds the slaves and he says words. 32. Abraham takes bread and the slaves eat the bread.

3.2 Vocative, Genitive and Dative Cases

The Greek noun has five cases: nominative, vocative, accusative, genitive and dative. Nominative and accusative were dealt with in 3.1.5. Section 3.2 will cover the genitive, dative, and vocative cases.

3.2.1 The Genitive Case

The genitive case is indicated by an -ου (sing.) or -ων (pl.) ending on masculine second declension nouns such as λόγος. There are two common uses of the genitive case:

i. With **certain prepositions**. [Note: prepositions have already been defined at 3.1.5.2.ii; see also 30.8.] Many prepositions are followed by the genitive case. When the prepositions ἀπό ("from") and ἐκ ("out of, from") are used, for example, they are followed by a noun in the genitive case. Examples:
ὁ Δαυὶδ λαμβάνει ἄρτον ἐκ τοῦ οἴκου   David takes bread out of the house
ἀπὸ τοῦ νόμου   from the law (Matt 5:18)

ii. To show **possession**. English indicates that a house belongs to a man by using the words "the man's house," or "the house of the man." In Greek the word "man" would be in the genitive case, which indicates that he possesses the house: ὁ οἶκος τοῦ ἀνθρώπου (οἶκος is the Greek word for "house" [Vocab. 3.2], while ἀνθρώπου is the masculine singular genitive of ἄνθρωπος). When a genitive noun is used in the possessive sense it is usually found immediately following the word denoting what or who is possessed.
Examples:
ὁ οἶκος τοῦ Πέτρου   The house of Peter (i.e. Peter's house)
ὁ ἄνθρωπος τοῦ θεοῦ   The man of God (or God's man)
οἱ υἱοὶ τοῦ Ἀβραάμ   The sons of Abraham (or Abraham's sons)

3.2.2 The Dative Case

The dative case is indicated by an -ῳ (sing.) or -οις (pl.) endings on masculine second declension nouns such as λόγος. There are three common uses of the dative:

i. With **certain prepositions**, particularly ἐν + **dat**. The frequently occurring preposition, ἐν, "in," is invariably followed by a noun or adjective in the dative case. E.g.: οἱ δοῦλοι εὑρίσκουσιν ἄρτον ἐν τῷ οἴκῳ "The slaves find bread in the house."

ii. **Some verbs are followed by a dative case**. For example, the verb πιστεύω

("I believe [in]"; Vocab. 3.2) is usually followed by the dative case, as are the verbs ἀκολουθέω ("I follow"; Vocab. 5) and προσκυνέω ("I worship"; Vocab. 5). A list of these verbs followed by the dative case may be found in Chapter 5 of *Intermediate New Testament Greek Made Easier*, but for now it will be sufficient to learn them as they occur in vocabulary lists.

iii. The **dative case** is used for the **indirect object**. In English the indirect object is normally indicated with the words "to" or "for." For example, in the sentence, "God speaks words to the people," the main verb is "speaks," the subject of the verb is "God," the direct object is "words," and the indirect object is "people." In Greek this would be, ὁ θεὸς λέγει λόγους τῷ λαῷ (λαῷ is the dative of λαός). Another example of an indirect object might be found in the sentence, "I give bread to the slave." The different parts of this sentence are: "I" (subject of verb) "give" (verb) "bread" (direct object of verb) "to the slave" (indirect object). The verb δίδωμι means "I give," so this sentence could be written in Greek as follows: δίδωμι ἄρτον τῷ δούλῳ.

If you find the concept of an indirect object difficult to grasp you are not alone. Many students find that it can take a little while for the concept of an indirect object to make sense. It will do so in the end, but in the meantime, it is probably useful to note that almost all occurrences of the dative case used as an indirect object involve verbs of saying (e.g. λέγω, "I say" in Vocab. 2; or λαλέω, "I speak"in Vocab. 5), or giving (e.g. the verb δίδωμι, "I give" in Vocab. 12.3). Look particularly for indirect objects associated with these verbs.

3.2.3 The Vocative Case:

The vocative case is used when talking directly to somebody. For example, in the sentence, "O Lord, hear our prayer" the words "O Lord" would be expressed in the vocative case. Unlike the second declension masculine nouns ending in -ος, most nouns do not have a different form for the vocative case.

3.2.4 Shortcuts re. Case

If it is ...	It must be ...
The subject	Nominative
The direct object	Accusative
Possession	Genitive
The indirect object	Dative

3.3.1 The Complete Second Declension Masculine Noun

The complete declension of λόγος	
Case	Form of λόγος
nom masc sing	λόγος
voc masc sing	λόγε
acc masc sing	λόγον
gen masc sing	λόγου
dat masc sing	λόγῳ
nom masc pl	λόγοι
voc masc pl	λόγοι
acc masc pl	λόγους
gen masc pl	λόγων
dat masc pl	λόγοις

3.3.2 The Masculine Article

The masculine article is as follows [note how closely the article corresponds to the case endings found on λόγος.]

Case	Article	Meaning
nom masc sing	ὁ	the
acc masc sing	τόν	the
gen masc sing	τοῦ	of the
dat masc sing	τῷ	to/for the
nom masc pl	οἱ	the
acc masc pl	τούς	the
gen masc pl	τῶν	of the
dat masc pl	τοῖς	to/for the

Note: the feminine and neuter forms of the article may be found at 6.2.

Vocabulary 3.2

ἄγγελος (175) — angel, messenger
ἀπό + genitive (645) — from, away from[1]
γινώσκω (221) — I know, learn
εἰς (1753) + acc. — into, towards
ἐκ, ἐξ + genitive (915) — **out of,** from, away from[1, 2]
ἐν + dative (2713) — **in,** by [instrument[3]]
κόσμος (185) — world, adornment
νόμος (191) — law
οἶκος (112) — house, household
ὄχλος (174) — crowd
πιστεύω +dat.[4] or εἰς (241) — I believe (in), entrust

τοῦ (1940+) the [gen. masc./neut.[5] sing. definite article]
τῷ (1050+) the [dat. masc./neut. sing. definite article]
τῶν (1034+) the [gen. masc./neut./ fem. pl. definite article]
τοῖς (540+) the [dat. masc./neut. pl. definite article]

Notes on Vocabulary 3.2

1. The difference between ἀπό and ἐκ is that ἀπό has the meaning "away from," while ἐκ also has the meaning "out of."
2. ἐκ, ἐξ: ἐκ is used before a word starting with a consonant, and ἐξ before a word starting with a vowel (both smooth and rough breathing).
3. The terms agent and instrument will be discussed in more detail in Chapter 25, and you do not really need to know the difference yet. But if you are curious, agent refers to a person, while instrument does not. For example, if we say, "the man was killed by the stranger," the "stranger" is the agent. If we say, "the man was killed by a sword," then the "sword" is the instrument. The preposition ἐν ("in") plus the dative may be used in New Testament and Hellenistic Greek for the instrument, although in classical Greek, instrument was expressed by the dative case only. The dative case (without ἐν) is also used in the New Testament to express instrument.
4. Certain verbs are usually followed by the dative case; πιστεύω is one of them.
5. Even though neuter and feminine nouns and articles are covered in later chapters [Chapters 4 and 6], neut. & fem. are indicated in this vocabulary list because it makes sense to get all the information needed on the vocabulary card the first time, rather than have to find it again to add things to it later.

Exercise 3.2

A. Declensions: Write out in full the declension of
i. δοῦλος ii. νόμος iii. λαός iv. ὄχλος

[Note: if you are asked to "write out in full the declension of" in a test or exam, you are being asked to write out the forms of the nominative, vocative, accusative, genitive and dative for both singular and plural. Where the vocative is the same as the nominative there is no need to list it separately, although you may wish to note N./V. in the margin to show that you did this intentionally.]

B. Translate into English
1. ὁ οἶκος τοῦ δούλου. 2. ὁ οἶκος τῶν δούλων. 3. ὁ οἶκος τοῦ ἀγγέλου. 4. ὁ οἶκος τῶν ἀγγέλων. 5. ἄνθρωπος λαμβάνει τὸν οἶκον τοῦ δούλου. 6. οἱ ἄνθρωποι λαμβάνουσι τὸν οἶκον τοῦ δούλου. 7. ὁ ἄνθρωπος λαμβάνει τοὺς οἴκους τοῦ δούλου. 8. ὁ ἄνθρωπος λαμβάνει τὸν οἶκον τῶν δούλων. 9. ὁ Ἰωάννης λέγει λόγον τῷ ὄχλῳ. 10. γινώσκεις τὸν νόμον τοῦ θεοῦ. 11. γινώσκεις τὸν νόμον τοῦ θεοῦ; [The ";" at the end of this sentence is the Greek punctuation mark for a question. Thus, this sentence should be translated as a question. To do so, start with the words, "Do you …?" This is true for many such questions. Often the appropriate form of the word "do" has to be added by the translator to make a question in English: "Do I …?", "Does he …?", "Do we …?", etc.] 12. γινώσκει τὸν ἄνθρωπον τοῦ θεοῦ; 13. ἐσθίει ἄρτον ἐν τῷ οἴκῳ ὁ υἱός. 14. οἱ ἀδελφοὶ ἀκούουσι λόγους ἐκ τοῦ οἴκου. 15. πιστεύω τῷ θεῷ. 16. λέγει τοὺς λόγους τοῦ θεοῦ ὁ Ἰησοῦς. 17. λέγει τοὺς λόγους τοῦ θεοῦ ὁ Ἰησοῦς; 18. οἱ υἱοὶ λαμβάνουσι τὸν ἄρτον ἐκ τοῦ οἴκου. 19. ὁ ὄχλος πιστεύει; 20. πιστεύεις εἰς τὸν υἱὸν τοῦ θεοῦ; 21. οἱ υἱοὶ λαμβάνουσι τὸν δοῦλον ἀπὸ τοῦ οἴκου. 22. γινώσκω τὸν κόσμον.

C. Translate into Greek
23. I believe in angels. 24. I know from the law. 25. The Christ has the people of God. 26. The angel has the law of God. 27. Abraham eats bread from the house. 28. David eats bread in the house. 29. Jesus speaks to the world. 30. John wants [wishes] a slave in the house.

3.4 Accents on Nouns

As genitives and datives are difficult for many students, it would be good to be able to postpone a discussion of the extra complexity of accents on nouns, but alas, that cannot be. If accents on nouns are to be mastered, they need to be learned when a noun is first met, so we must look at accents on nouns here. [Your teacher will inform you as to whether or not you should learn accents or just confine yourself to noting those places in the book where a difference in accent makes a difference to the meaning of the words.]

The main rules of accents and the explanation of terms such as proparoxitone are given in 2.8.b and Chapter 7 [7.1 and 7.4, in fact] of *Intermediate New Testament Greek Made Easier*. The basic rule for first and second declension nouns is that as far as is consistent with the main rules of accents [see 2.8-b or *Int*.7.1], the accents remain on the syllable on which it is found in the nominative singular. What this means in practice can be discerned in the following examples [note that this list will be useful as a reference as the lists of words under each example include all of the relevant nouns found in Part 1 – the number in square brackets gives the chapter in which the noun is found]:

Nominative with acute accent on third syllable from end (Proparoxytone)

ἄνθρωπος
ἄνθρωπε
ἄνθρωπον
ἀνθρώπου
ἀνθρώπῳ
ἄνθρωποι
ἀνθρώπους
ἀνθρώπων
ἀνθρώποις

Explanation: ἄνθρωπος keeps its proparoxytone accent for ἄνθρωπος, ἄνθρωπε, ἄνθρωπον, ἄνθρωποι because -ος, -ε, -ον, -οι are syllables with short vowels; on the other hand, because -ου, -ῳ, -ους, -ων, -οις are long, the accents of ἀνθρώπου, ἀνθρώπῳ, ἀνθρώπους, ἀνθρώπων, ἀνθρώποις must become paroxytone.

The same pattern of accents [as ἄνθρωπος] is used by: [3] ἄγγελος [4] δαιμόνιον, πρόσωπον [10] θάνατος, κύριος

Nominative with acute accent on second syllable from the end (Paroxytone)

[βιβλίον, "book," is a word that will be met in the next chapter]

βιβλίον
βιβλίον
βιβλίον
βιβλίου
βιβλίῳ
βιβλία
βιβλία
βιβλίων
βιβλίοις

The same pattern of accents [as βιβλίον] is used by: [1] Πέτρος [3] ἄρτος, κόσμος, λόγος, νόμος, ὄχλος [4] ἔργον, παιδίον, τέκνον [5] Note: all first declension feminine nouns accent the genitive plural perispomenon: -ῶν: ἀγάπη, ἁμαρτία, δόξα, ἐκκλησία, ἐξουσία, ἐπαγγελία, ἡμέρα, σοφία [7] δικαιοσύνη

Nominative with acute accent on last syllable (Oxytone)
θεός
θεέ
θεόν
θεοῦ
θεῷ
θεοί
θεούς
θεῶν
θεοῖς

The same pattern of accents [as θεός] is used by: [1] Χριστός [3] ἀδελφός, λαός, υἱός [4] ἱερόν [5] Note: all first declension feminine nouns accent the genitive plural perispomenon: -ῶν: ἀρχή, ἐντολή, ζωή, φωνή, χαρά [8] συναγωγή

Note also that on words followed by another word, most oxytone accents become grave. E.g.
λέγει θεός, ...
θεὸς λέγει, ...

Nominative with circumflex accent on second to last syllable (Properispomenon)
δοῦλος
δοῦλε
δοῦλον
δούλου
δούλῳ
δοῦλοι
δούλους
δούλων
δούλοις

Explanation: because the final syllables -ος, -ες, -ον, -οι contain short vowels or diphthongs, δοῦλος, δοῦλε, δοῦλον, δοῦλοι may keep their properispomenon accent; on the other hand, because the endings -ου, -ῳ, -ους, -ων, -οις all contain long vowels or diphthongs, and a properispomenon accent requires a short vowel in the last syllable, the circumflex accent is changed to acute in δούλου, δούλῳ, δούλους, δούλων, δούλοις.

The same pattern of accents [as δοῦλος] is used by: [3] οἶκος [10] πλοῖον

Exercise 3.3

Write out or type each example and provide appropriate accents:
1. γινωσκεις τον νομον του θεου; 2. γινωσκει τον ἀνθρωπον του θεου; 3. ἐσθιει ἀρτον ἐν τῳ οἰκῳ ὁ υἱος. 4. οἱ ἀδελφοι ἀκουουσι λογους ἐκ του οἰκου. 5. πιστευω ἐν τῳ θεῳ. 6. λεγει τους λογους του θεου ὁ Ἰησους. 7. λεγει τους λογους του θεου ὁ Ἰησους; 8. οἱ υἱοι λαμβανουσι τον ἀρτον ἐκ του οἰκου. 9. ὁ ὀχλος πιστευει; 10. πιστευεις ἐν τῳ υἱῳ του θεου;

Chapter 4: Neuter Second Declension Nouns; The Present Tense of the Verb "To Be"

The Greek noun has three genders: masculine, feminine and neuter. The previous chapter introduced one type of masculine noun, and this chapter will deal with one type of neuter noun, as well as the present tense of the verb εἰμί ("I am") and indeclinable nouns. It then provides more information on punctuation marks.

You may be pleased to know that the steepest part of the learning curve for Part 1 is now behind you. What you have learned about cases in the previous chapter is still true of the cases of the neuter nouns, and this chapter will help you further consolidate what you have previously learned. Later chapters in Part 1 will introduce new information, but the new content will largely be extensions of what you have already learned about verbs and nouns. By the review chapter (Chap. 11) you should be quite comfortable with how simple present-tense sentences are formed in NT Greek.

4.1 Neuter Second Declension Nouns

Neuter second declension nouns follow the pattern of ἔργον, "deed, work." The declension of ἔργον is as follows:

Case	Form of ἔργον
Nom/Voc neut s	ἔργον
Acc neut sing	ἔργον
Gen neut sing	ἔργου
Dat neut sing	ἔργῳ
Nom/Voc neut pl	ἔργα
Acc neut pl	ἔργα
Gen neut pl	ἔργων
Dat neut pl	ἔργοις

Notes:
1. Neuter nouns like ἔργον may be distinguished from masculine nouns like λόγος by their different nominative endings (-ον instead of -ος). Vocabu-

lary items are listed in the nominative case.
2. The vocative is the same as the nominative, as it is for most nouns.
3. Neuter nouns have the same endings for both the nominative and accusative. In practice, this is rarely a problem for translation.
4. The endings for the genitive and dative cases are the same as for λόγος.
5. One peculiar feature of neuter nouns is that their plurals take a singular verb. While there are exceptions to this rule in the Greek New Testament, when translating into Greek in tests and exams it should be observed. This rule may be illustrated using the second declension neuter word δαιμόνιον, "demon":

A demon speaks: δαιμόνιον λέγει [as would be expected]
Demons speak: δαιμόνια λέγει [**not** δαιμόνια λέγ<u>ουσιν</u> as might be expected]

4.2 The Neuter Article

The neuter article is as follows [notice how close it is to the pattern of endings found on ἔργον]:

Case	Form	Meaning
Nom/Voc neut s	τό	the
Acc neut sing	τό	the
Gen neut sing	τοῦ	of the
Dat neut sing	τῷ	to/for the
Nom/Voc neut pl	τά	the
Acc neut pl	τά	the
Gen neut pl	τῶν	of the
Dat neut pl	τοῖς	to/for the

The article takes the gender of the noun it qualifies. Thus "the man" would be ὁ ἄνθρωπος – the article is masculine because the noun ἄνθρωπος is masculine. On the other hand, "the work" would be τὸ ἔργον – the article is neuter because the noun is neuter.

4.3 The Verb "To Be"

The present tense of the English verb "to be" is as follows:
I am
you are
he/she/it is
we are
you are
they are

It is quite irregular (there is no pattern to am/are/is), and this is typical of the verb "to be" in all languages, including Greek. Here, then, is the present indicative of the Greek verb "to be":

Present Indicative of εἰμί		
1st pers s	εἰμί	I am
2nd pers s	εἶ	you are
3rd pers s	ἐστίν	he/she/it is
1st pers pl	ἐσμέν	we are
2nd pers pl	ἐστέ	you are
3rd pers pl	εἰσίν	they are

Notes on εἰμί:
1. The verb εἰμί takes the nominative for both the subject and complement (a complement corresponds to the direct object in other verbs; this verb does not have a direct object). Thus, the Greek for "David is a man" would be ὁ Δαυίδ ἐστιν ἄνθρωπος (**not** ὁ Δαυίδ ἐστιν ἄνθρωπον).
2. Since the different forms of εἰμί are used so frequently and the verb is so irregular, it is worth making a separate vocabulary card for each of its forms.
3. It is important to learn the accent of εἶ as this is one of the words that differs from another only in accent. The word without the accent, εἰ, means "if."
4. Textbooks often list the third person singular of εἰμί as having an optional ν [i.e. ἐστί(ν)]. In fact, the form ἐστί is only found once in the New Testament (at Acts 19:10). The other 814 verses which have the third personal singular have the form ἐστίν.
5. In the Greek New Testament, the accents of εἰμί are usually found on the previous word. The term "enclitic" is used to describe this phenomenon [see 7.16.3 in *Intermediate New Testament Greek Made Easier* for a full explanation if one is desired]. The exception is εἶ, which needs to retain its accent to be distinguished from the word εἰ, "if." There is usually no need to worry about the enclitic nature of this verb in translating from the Greek.

4.4 Indeclinable Nouns and Irregular Names

Names in the New Testament often have their origins in Hebrew and Aramaic names. Many of them have endings which are normally not found on Greek words. Normal Greek words end only with a vowel or ν, ρ, or ς. Words ending in ξ or ψ are considered to end in ς. The only exceptions to this are ἐκ (Vocab. 3.2), and οὐκ, οὐχ (forms of οὐ "not," Vocab. 5). Names which finish with letters other than a vowel or ν, ρ, or ς do not decline in the different cases, hence they are called "indeclinable nouns." Examples include: ὁ Ἀβραάμ (73), ὁ Δαυίδ (59), ἡ Μαριάμ (27; "Mary"), ἡ Ἰερευσαλήμ (77), ὁ Ἰσραήλ (68; "Israel"), ἡ Καφαρναούμ (16; Capernaum).

Many other names show irregular declensions. For example, the frequently occurring name Μωϋσῆς [80] "Moses," is declined Μωϋσῆς, Μωϋσῆν, Μωϋσέως, Μωϋσεῖ; and Μωϋσέα is also found for accusative in one place [Luke 16:29]. This name is usually found without an article, so can cause momentary problems to the translator. Besides Moses, the other irregularly declined name frequently found in the Greek New Testament is that of "Jesus," but his name is more frequently found with the definite article, which is a great help. Here is the way the names Jesus and Moses are declined:

Case	Ἰησοῦς	Μωϋσῆς
Nominative	Ἰησοῦς	Μωϋσῆς
Vocative	Ἰησοῦ	Μωϋσῆς
Accusative	Ἰησοῦν	Μωϋσῆν
Genitive	Ἰησοῦ	Μωϋσέως
Dative	Ἰησοῦ	Μωϋσεῖ

4.5 Punctuation Marks

New Testament Greek uses a comma and a full stop much as they are used in English. The ";" is used instead of a "?" to indicate a question mark, and the punctuation that corresponds to the English semi-colon or colon is a "·" (a dot above the line). As in the English word "don't" in which the ' is used to indicate a missing vowel from the expression "do not," an ' is placed where a vowel is missing in a Greek word. This is called "elision." For example, κἀγώ is used instead of καὶ ἐγώ.

A dieresis (two dots placed over a vowel) is used to indicate that two vowels which would otherwise make a diphthong, are to be pronounced separately. An example of dieresis is found in the name Ἰάϊρος in Mark 5:22, which should, therefore, be pronounced "Ia-iros." The RSV writes this name as Jãirus; the KJV as Ja-i-rus.

Reminder: To add a dieresis using the Greek Polytonic keyboard, type : then character (e.g. :i produces ï); while the Greek semi-colon or colon (·) is produced by typing together <shift> <right alt>]. Commas and full stops are the same on both the English and Greek keyboards, while the Greek question mark (; – see 4.5) is found on the Greek Polynotic keyboard by typing q and then hitting the space bar.

Vocabulary 4

Second Declension Neuter Nouns
βιβλίον (34)   book [cf. the English word, "Bible"]
δαιμόνιον (63)   demon
ἔργον (169)   work, deed
ἱερόν (70)   temple
παιδίον (52)   child, infant
πρόσωπον (74)   face
τέκνον (99)   child

Other Words
εἰ (513)   if
εἶ (89)   you are (sing.)
εἰμί (131; in its different forms, 2450)   I am
εἰσίν (142)   they are
ἐστίν (815)   is, he/she/it is, there is
Μωϋσῆς (80) Moses
τά (710+) the [nom./acc. neut. pl. definite article]
τό (1370+) the [nom./acc. neut. sing. definite article]

Exercise 4

A. Declensions
Write in full or type the declension of:
i. τέκνον   ii. βιβλίον   iii. κόσμος   iv. παιδίον

B. Translate into idiomatic (i.e. natural) English
[Hint: for longer sentences, first find the verb(s) and parse them. Parsing a verb means to work out its grammatical form. All the verbs in the current exercise are present indicative, but the person (is it "I ..." or "you ...," etc.) still has to be determined. Next find the subject and direct object if there is one. The rest of the sentence will fit around these three elements: the main verb, the subject and the direct object.]
1. ὁ Ἀβραάμ ἐστιν ἄνθρωπος τοῦ θεοῦ. 2. εἶ ὁ Χριστός. 3. εἶ ὁ Χριστός; 4. εἶ ὁ ἄγγελος ἀπὸ τοῦ θεοῦ; 5. εἶ ὁ ἄγγελος ἀπὸ τοῦ θεοῦ. 6. παιδίον γράφει λόγους ἐν τῷ βιβλίῳ. 7. εἰμὶ ὁ Δαυὶδ ὁ ἀπὸ Ἰερουσαλήμ. 8. τὰ τέκνα ἐσθίει ἄρτον ἐν τῷ ἱερῷ. 9. ἐστὶν δαιμόνια ἐν τῷ κόσμῳ. 10. ἐστὶν δαιμόνια ἐν τῷ κόσμῳ;

11. εἰ εἶ ὁ Ἰησοῦς, εἶ ὁ Χριστὸς τοῦ θεοῦ. 12. εἰ ἐστὶν ὁ Ἰησοῦς, ἐστὶν ὁ Χριστὸς τοῦ θεοῦ. 13. οἱ ἀδελφοὶ λαμβάνουσι τὰ βιβλία τοῦ τέκνου. 14. τὸ ἱερόν ἐστιν ὁ οἶκος τοῦ θεοῦ. 15. ὁ Ἰησοῦς θέλει ἔργα τοῦ νόμου; 16. τὰ

δαιμόνια γράφει ἐν τῷ βιβλίῳ. [Notice again that the neuter plural subject takes a singular form of the verb.] 17. ἐσμὲν οἱ δοῦλοι τοῦ λαοῦ. 18. ἐστὲ τὰ δαιμόνια τοῦ κόσμου. 19. ὁ Ἰησοῦς καὶ ὁ ἀδελφὸς τοῦ Δαυὶδ εὑρίσκουσι τὰ παιδία ἐν τῷ ἱερῷ. 20. ὁ ὄχλος πιστεύει δαιμονίοις.

21. ὁ δοῦλος γινώσκει τὰ πρόσωπα τῶν τέκνων. 22. εἰ ἔχεις τὸν Ἰησοῦν, ἔχεις τὸν θεόν. 23. δαιμόνια γινώσκει τὸν υἱὸν τοῦ θεοῦ. 24. ἐστὶν τὸ ἔργον τοῦ δαιμονίου. 25. ἐσμὲν ὁ λαὸς τοῦ νόμου. 26. ὁ Ἰωάννης εὑρίσκει τὰ βιβλία τοῦ δαιμονίου ἐν τῷ ἱερῷ. 27. ὁ Ἰησοῦς ἐστιν ἐκ θεοῦ. 28. τὰ παιδία γράφει λόγους ἐν τῷ βιβλίῳ. 29. ὁ νόμος ἐστιν ἐκ τοῦ θεοῦ. 30. ὁ Δαυὶδ εὑρίσκει τὸν νόμον τοῦ θεοῦ ἐν τῷ ἱερῷ.

C. Translate into Greek
31. Demons are in the world. 32. Children take bread out of the house. 33. Jesus is the Son of God. 34. The temple slaves find a book in the house. [hint for 34: temple slaves = slaves of the temple] 35. We are the people of the Christ. 36. It is the work of the children. 37. Abraham knows God. 38. I believe in demons. 39. Do you (sing.) believe in demons? 40. You (pl.) are the children of God.

Chapter 5: -εω Verbs

Not all verbs follow the exact pattern of λύω for their present indicative active. One type of difference occurs when the [present] verb stem of a verb finishes with an ε. The changes that occur in the present tense of -εω verbs most likely flows from the fact that when two vowels are spoken together, the resultant sound is slightly different. The most common verb of this kind, λαλέω, "I speak," has the verb stem λαλε-. If the pattern of λύω was used to write out the present indicative active of λαλεω in full, it would look like this: λαλέ-ω λαλέ-εις λαλέ-ει λαλέ-ομεν λαλέ-ετε λαλέ-ουσιν.

In every instance, the ε is immediately followed by a vowel. In these cases, the vowels are modified when the words are said. Fortunately, they follow a consistent pattern as they change (by contracting). For -εω verbs the rules of contraction are these:

Vowel combination	Result
ε + ε[ι]	ει
ε + ο	ου
ε + long vowel or diphthong	long vowel or diphthong (i.e. no change; the ε disappears)

The long vowels are ω and η, while the diphthongs are αι, ει, οι, αυ, ου, ευ, ηυ, and υι. In the endings for λύω are found the long vowel ω, the diphthongs ει and ου, and the short vowels ο and ε. Applying the rules of contraction gives two differences from λυω in the present indicative of λαλέω (in the first and second person plural). Thus the present indicative active of λαλέω is:

λαλε-ω → λαλῶ
λαλε-εις → λαλεῖς
λαλε-ει → λαλεῖ
λαλε-ουμεν → λαλοῦμεν
λαλε-ετε → λαλεῖτε
λαλε-ουσιν → λαλοῦσι(ν)

By the way, these rules of contraction also work for other parts of the verb paradigm of -εω verbs, so that most of the time, learning the paradigm for λύω and remembering the rules of contraction will make it possible to work out how these verbs should decline.

How may the verbs that follow these rules of contraction be recognized? They are listed in vocabularies and dictionaries in their uncontracted form (i.e., with the ending -εω), even though the uncontracted form is not found in the New Testament. So if a word in a vocabulary list ends in -εω, then these rules of contraction should be applied. The following vocabulary list has several such words (e.g. αἰτέω, ἀκολουθέω, δοκέω).

Vocabulary 5

-εω verbs

αἰτέω (70)	I ask, demand
ἀκολουθέω (90)+dat.[1]	I follow
δοκέω (62)	I think, believe; I seem
ζητέω (117)	I seek
θεωρέω (58)	I behold, see
καλέω (148)	I call
λαλέω (298)	I speak, utter
μαρτυρέω (76)	I testify, bear witness
παρακαλέω (109)	I summon, request, entreat
περιπατέω (95)	I walk
ποιέω (565)	I do, make
προσκυνέω (59) + dat.	I worship, prostrate myself before
τηρέω (70)	I keep, watch

Other Words

κατά (471)	+ acc. (347+): according to
κατά (471)	+ gen. (39+):[2] down, against
ὅτι (1285)	because, that, "[speech marks]"[3]
οὐ, οὐκ, οὐχ[4] (1619)	not

Notes on Vocabulary 5

1. Notice that the Greek idiom for the verb ἀκολουθέω, "I follow," is different from that of English. English places a direct object after the verb "to follow." Greek uses the dative case. This is just an instance of different languages expressing things differently.

2. From the perspective of the student learning New Testament Greek, it can be problematic that the same preposition has different meanings depending on the case with which it is found. Yet, because these prepositions are used very frequently, it is impossible to avoid learning the different meanings with the different cases. Perhaps one way to do so would be to make separate vocabulary cards for the different cases, and put the other case on the back of the card to remind yourself of it. These prepositions will be introduced one

at a time to try to lessen the strain of learning them. Prepositions are used very idiomatically, and there is seldom one English preposition that exactly corresponds to a Greek preposition in meaning. Only practice in translating will give any real confidence in handling prepositions. This practice will be provided in the remainder of the book!

3. Where written English would use speech marks, New Testament Greek often uses ὅτι to introduce direct speech. In these cases ὅτι is not translated. The word ὅτι is also often translated 'that' in indirect speech – e.g. Ἰησοῦς λέγει ὅτι … could be translated as either "Jesus says that …" or "Jesus says, '…'"

4. Generally speaking, οὐ is used if the next word begins with a consonant, οὐκ if the next word begins with a vowel with a smooth breathing, and οὐχ if it begins with a vowel with a rough breathing. This is just to make the word easier to say in a sentence.

5. Vocabulary 5 includes all the -εω verbs that occur more than 50 times in the NT.

Exercise 5.1

A. Paradigms
Write out in full the present indicative active of:
i. τηρέω   ii. ποιέω   iii. λαμβάνω   iv. καλέω

B. Translate into idiomatic English

1. ὁ ἀδελφὸς περιπατεῖ κατὰ τὸν νόμον τοῦ θεοῦ. 2. οἱ ἀδελφοὶ περιπατοῦσι κατὰ τὸν νόμον τοῦ θεοῦ. 3. τὰ τέκνα περιπατεῖ κατὰ τοὺς νόμους τοῦ θεοῦ. 4. οἱ υἱοὶ περιπατοῦσι κατὰ νόμους τῶν ἀνθρώπων. 5. ὁ υἱὸς περιπατεῖ κατὰ τὸν νόμον τοῦ θεοῦ. 6. ὁ λαὸς περιπατεῖ κατὰ τὸν νόμον τοῦ κόσμου. 7. ζητοῦμεν τὸν Ἰησοῦν. 8. προσκυνοῦμεν τῷ θεῷ. 9. προσκυνοῦμεν τῷ Ἰησοῦ καὶ τηροῦμεν τὸν νόμον τοῦ θεοῦ. 10. ὁ Ἰησοῦς καλεῖ τῷ ὄχλῳ.

11. μαρτυρῶ κατὰ τοῦ Ἰερουσαλήμ. 12. ὁ Δαυὶδ λαλεῖ λόγους τῷ λαῷ. 13. ὁ ὄχλος οὐ περιπατεῖ κατὰ τὸν νόμον τοῦ κόσμου. [Hint: translate the οὐ with the words "does not."] 14. αἰτοῦσιν ἄρτον ἀπὸ τοῦ ἱεροῦ οἱ ἄνθρωποι. 15. προσκυνοῦμεν οὐκ ἀνθρώπῳ. 16. ἄγγελοι μαρτυροῦσι τῷ κόσμῳ. 17. τηρεῖτε οὐ τὸν νόμον τοῦ θεοῦ. 18. αἰτοῦσι τὸν Ἰησοῦν οἱ δοῦλοι. 19. δοκῶ ὅτι δαιμόνιά ἐστιν ἐν τῷ κόσμῳ. 20. ζητῶ τὸ ἱερὸν τοῦ θεοῦ.

21. ὁ Ἰησοῦς καλεῖ ἀνθρώπους ἐκ τοῦ κόσμου. 22. περιπατοῦσιν ἀπὸ Ἰερουσαλήμ. 23. ζητεῖ τὸν Ἰησοῦν ὁ ὄχλος. 24. τὰ δαιμόνια δοκεῖ ὅτι ὁ Ἰησοῦς ἐστιν ὁ Χριστός. 25. δοκῶ ὅτι εἶ ὁ Χριστὸς τοῦ θεοῦ. 26. δοκῶ ὅτι ὁ Ἰησοῦς ἐστιν ὁ Χριστὸς τοῦ θεοῦ. 27. ὁ Ἰησοῦς μαρτυρεῖ κατὰ Ἰερουσαλήμ. 28. ὁ Ἰωάννης μαρτυρεῖ κατὰ τοῦ λαοῦ. 29. ὁ Ἰησοῦς λαλεῖ κατὰ τὸν νόμον

τοῦ θεοῦ. 30. προσκυνῶ τῷ θεῷ κατὰ τὸν νόμον. 31. ποιεῖ τὰ ἔργα τοῦ θεοῦ ὁ Ἰησοῦς. 32. θεωροῦμεν τὸν θεόν. 33. ἀκολουθοῦμεν τῷ Ἰησοῦ.

C. Translate into Greek

34. The slaves walk according to the law of God. 35. The sons do not walk according to the laws of man. 36. He does not keep the law of God. 37. You [plural] speak words to the crowd. 38. Do you [plural] seek Jesus?

Accents on -εω verbs

Accents on -εω verbs are discovered by placing the accent on the uncontracted form of the verb (e.g. λαλέ-εις, λαλέ-ομεν), and adding a grave accent to all other non-accented vowels (e.g. λὰλέ-εὶς, λὰλέ-ὸμὲν). Where two accents follow acute-grave (e.g. έ-εὶ, έ-ὸ), contract the vowels using the usual rules, and use a circumflex accent (e.g. λαλεῖς, λαλοῦμεν). This, in fact, was the original use of circumflex accent in the earliest Greek inscriptions. Where two accents follow grave-acute, contract the vowels according to the usual rules, and use an acute accent (this does not occur in the present tense, but in a later chapter the following form of λαλέω will be met: ἐλὰλέ-όμὴν which gives ἐλαλούμην).

Exercise 5.2

Add accents to the following:

1. μαρτυρω κατα του Ἰερουσαλημ. 2. ὁ Δαυιδ λαλει λογους τω λαω. 3. ὁ ὀχλος οὐ περιπατει κατα τον νομον του κοσμου. 4. αἰτουσιν ἀρτον ἀπο του ἱερου οἱ ἀνθρωποι. 5. προσκυνουμεν οὐκ ἀνθρωπῳ. 6. ἀγγελοι μαρτυρουσι τῳ κοσμῳ. 7. τηρειτε οὐ τον νομον του θεου. 8. αἰτουσι τον Ἰησουν οἱ δουλοι. 9. δοκω ὀτι δαιμονια ἐστιν ἐν τῳ κοσμῳ. 10. ζητω το ἱερον του θεου.

Chapter 6: Feminine First Declension Nouns

6.1 Feminine First Declension Nouns

There are three basic variations of first declension feminine nouns. These nouns either finish with an η or α, and those that finish with an α vary according to whether or not the α follows either ε, ι or ρ or not. If the three are put side by side it is easier to see the similarities and differences between them:

Feminine First Declension Nouns			
Case	γῆ (earth)	ἡμέρα (day)	δόξα (glory)
N/V	γῆ	ἡμέρα	δόξα
Acc	γῆν	ἡμέραν	δόξαν
Gen	γῆς	ἡμέρας	δόξης
Dat	γῇ	ἡμέρᾳ	δόξῃ
N/V	γαῖ	ἡμέραι	δόξαι
Acc	γᾶς	ἡμέρας	δόξας
Gen	γῶν	ἡμερῶν	δοξῶν
Dat	γαῖς	ἡμέραις	δόξαις

Notes:
1. Feminine first declension nouns with nominative singulars which end in:
   - -η decline like ἀρχή (beginning, ruler). E.g. ἀρχή, γῆ, ἐντολή, ζωή, and φωνή in Vocab. 6.
   - -α preceded by ε, ι, or ρ decline like ἡμέρα (day). These are sometimes known as alpha-pure nouns. The alpha-pure nouns in Vocab. 6 are ἁμαρτία, ἐκκλησία, ἐξουσία, ἐπαγγελία, ἡμέρα, σοφία, χαρά.
   - -α preceded by a consonant other than ρ decline like δόξα

   One of these forms should be memorized well. Once this is done, it should be possible to reproduce others on request.
2. All the plural endings are the same for all feminine nouns of the first declension.
3. Note that all the singular datives met so far have an iota subscript.
4. Note also that all the plural genitives met so far have had the -ων ending. Indeed all plural genitive nouns in all declensions end with -ων. However,

unlike the accent on the genitive plurals of the second declension nouns λόγος and ἔργον (which are λόγων and ἔργων, resp.), first declension feminine nouns accent the genitive plural with a circumflex accent on the last syllable (-ῶν).

5. With the exception of the genitive plural which is accented -ῶν, like other nouns and as far as is consistent with the main rules of accents [see 2.8-b; *Int.* 7.1], the accent on first declension feminine nouns tends to stay on the same syllable on which it is found in the nominative singular.

6.2 The Full Declension of the Article

Nouns from the three Greek genders have been met: masculine, feminine and neuter, so the full article can now be given. It is worth learning the complete range of forms of the article thoroughly. There are other nouns that decline somewhat differently from those met thus far, but if they are found with a known article, they may then be parsed even if they are unfamiliar.

The Article				
	Masc	Fem	Neut	Meaning
Nom s	ὁ	ἡ	τό	the
Acc s	τόν	τήν	τό	the
Gen s	τοῦ	τῆς	τοῦ	of the
Dat s	τῷ	τῇ	τῷ	to/for the
Nom pl	οἱ	αἱ	τά	the
Acc pl	τούς	τάς	τά	the
Gen pl	τῶν	τῶν	τῶν	of the
Dat pl	τοῖς	ταῖς	τοῖς	to/for the

The article takes the gender of the noun it qualifies. Thus "the man" would be ὁ ἄνθρωπος—the article is masculine because the noun ἄνθρωπος is masculine. "The work" would be τὸ ἐργόν—the article is neuter because the noun ἐργόν is neuter. "The day" would be ἡ ἡμέρα—the article is feminine because the noun ἡμέρα is feminine.

Vocabulary 6

ἀγάπη (116)   love
ἁμαρτία (173) sin
ἀρχή (55)   beginning, ruler, authority
γῆ (248)   earth, ground, land
δόξα (165)   glory, splendor, fame

Part 1

δοξάζω (61)   I glorify, praise
ἐκκλησία (114)   church
ἐντολή (68)   commandment
ἐξουσία (102)   authority, ability, right
ἐπαγγελία (52)   promise, pledge
ζωή (135)   life
ἡμέρα (388)   day
σοφία (51)   wisdom
φωνή (137)   voice, sound
χαίρω (74)   I rejoice
χαρά (59)   joy

αἱ   (132) the [nom. fem. pl. definite article]
ἡ   (793) the [nom. fem. sing. definite article]
ταῖς (181) to/for the [dat. fem. pl. definite article]
τάς   (313) the [acc. fem. pl. definite article]
τῇ   (750) to/for the [dat. fem. sing. definite article]
τήν   (1273) the [acc. fem. sing. definite article]
τῆς   (1070) of the [gen. fem. sing. definite article]

Exercise 6

A. Declensions: Write out in full the declension of
i. φωνή ii. σοφία iii. χαρά iv. ἄρτος v. πρόσωπον vi. ζωή

B. Translate into idiomatic English
1. ἡ ἐκκλησία τοῦ θεοῦ τηρεῖ τὸν νόμον τοῦ θεοῦ. 2. χαίρω ἐν τῇ φωνῇ τοῦ θεοῦ. 3. ἡ ἀγάπη τοῦ θεοῦ ἐστιν ἡ ἀρχὴ τῆς σοφίας. 4. ἐστιν χαρὰ ἐν τῇ ἀγάπῃ ἁμαρτίας; 5. ἡ ἐντολή τοῦ Ἰησοῦ ἔχει ἐξουσίαν. 6. ζητῶ τὴν ἐπαγγελίαν τῆς ζωῆς. 7. ἡ δόξα τῆς ἐκκλησίας ἐστὶν ἐν τῇ ἀγάπῃ τῶν ἀδελφῶν. 8. δοξάζουσι τὸν θεόν. 9. χαίρω ἐν τῷ νόμῳ τοῦ θεοῦ. 10. ἡ ἀγάπη τοῦ Ἰησοῦ ἐστιν ζωή.

11. χαίρω οὐκ ἐν ταῖς ἐντολαῖς τῶν ἀνθρώπων. 12. ὁ θεὸς ἔχει ἡμέραν τῆς δόξης. 13. αἱ ἐντολαὶ τῶν ἀνθρώπων ἔχουσιν οὐκ ἐξουσίαν. 14. ἡ ἀρχὴ ἔχει οὐκ ἀδελφόν. 15. ζητῶ τὴν σοφίαν τοῦ θεοῦ. 16. ἔχω οὐ χαρὰν ἐν τῇ σοφίᾳ τοῦ κόσμου. 17. ὁ Ἰωάννης λαλεῖ κατὰ τῆς ἁμαρτίας τῶν ἀνθρώπων. 18. πιστεύω τῇ ἐντολῇ τοῦ Ἰησοῦ. 19. ὁ Ἰησοῦς μαρτυρεῖ ὅτι ὁ θεός ἐστιν ἀγάπη. 20. ἡ ἐκκλησία τοῦ θεοῦ ποιεῖ τὰ ἔργα τοῦ θεοῦ.

21. οἱ υἱοὶ τοῦ θεοῦ περιπατοῦσι κατὰ τὴν ἐντολὴν τοῦ θεοῦ. 22. τὸ πρόσωπον τῆς γῆς. 23. ἀκούω τὴν φωνὴν τῆς χαρᾶς ἐν Ἰερουσαλήμ. 24. δοξάζω τὸν θεὸν ἐν τῇ ἐκκλησίᾳ. 25. ἔχει οὐχ ἡ ἁμαρτία τὴν ἐπαγγελίαν τῆς ζωῆς. 26.

ἡ γῆ ἐπαγγελίας. 27. οἱ υἱοὶ τοῦ θεοῦ ποιοῦσι τὰς ἐντολὰς τοῦ θεοῦ. 28. ἡ ἡμέρα τοῦ θεοῦ. 29. ἡ ἀρχὴ τῆς ἁμαρτίας. 30. χαίρω ἐν τῷ Ἰησοῦ.

31. χαίρετε ἐν τῷ Ἰησοῦ; 32. τὰ τέκνα αἰτεῖ τὸν δοῦλον τῆς ἀρχῆς. 33. τηρεῖτε τὰς ἐντολὰς τοῦ Ἰησοῦ; 34. δαιμόνια οὐ χαίρει ἐν τῇ δόξῃ τοῦ θεοῦ. 35. ὁ Ἰησοῦς καλεῖ ἀνθρώπους ἀπὸ ἁμαρτίας.

C. Translate into Greek
36. Abraham and David keep the commandments of God. 37. The land of David. 38. The day of sin and the day of promise. 39. It has the authority of a pledge. 40. They praise the wisdom of life.

D. Add Accents
41. οι υιοι του θεου περιπατουσι κατα την εντολην του θεου. 42. το προσωπον της γης. 43. ακουω την φωνην της χαρας ἐν Ἰερουσαλημ. 44. δοξαζω τον θεον ἐν τη ἐκκλησια. 45. ἐχει οὐχ ἡ ἁμαρτια την ἐπαγγελιαν της ζωης. 46. ἡ γη ἐπαγγελιας. 47. οι υιοι του θεου ποιουσι τας ἐντολας του θεου. 48. ἡ ἡμερα του θεου. 49. ἡ ἀρχη της ἁμαρτιας. 50. χαιρω ἐν τω Ἰησου. 51. χαιρετε ἐν τω Ἰησου; 52. τα τεκνα αιτει τον δουλον της ἀρχης. 53. τηρειτε τας ἐντολας του Ἰησου; 54. δαιμονια οὐ χαιρει ἐν τη δοξῃ του θεου. 55. ὁ Ἰησους καλει ἀνθρωπους ἀπο ἁμαρτιας.

Chapter 7: Adjectives of the First and Second Declensions

Adjectives qualify nouns, and have the end result of giving greater precision of expression. For example, the noun "men" names all male humans above a certain age. Adding the adjective "good" to "men" ("good men") names only those male humans who are of a certain age and who are also good: a more precise naming. In a similar fashion, "evil men," "dead men," "faithful men" and "righteous men" are all more specific than just the noun "men."

Greek adjectives do not usually provide a difficulty in translation. Indeed, they are often used rather like they are in English. For example, in Greek "the good man" would be ὁ ἀγαθὸς ἄνθρωπος. "The good men" (plural) would be οἱ ἀγαθοὶ ἄνθρωποι. "The good work" would be τὸ ἀγαθὸν ἔργον, while "the good works would be τὰ ἀγαθὰ ἔργα. "The good day" would be ἡ ἀγαθὴ ἡμέρα, while "the good days" would be αἱ ἀγαθαὶ ἡμέραι. From these examples it can be seen that the adjective takes the same case, number and gender as the noun that it qualifies. The most common adjectives follow the pattern of ἀγαθός:

Adjectives of the 1st & 2nd Declension			
	Masc	Fem	Neut
Nom sing	ἀγαθός	ἀγαθή	ἀγαθόν
Voc sing	ἀγαθέ	ἀγαθή	ἀγαθόν
Acc sing	ἀγαθόν	ἀγαθήν	ἀγαθόν
Gen sing	ἀγαθοῦ	ἀγαθῆς	ἀγαθοῦ
Dat sing	ἀγαθῷ	ἀγαθῇ	ἀγαθῷ
N,V pl	ἀγαθοί	ἀγαθαί	ἀγαθά
Acc pl	ἀγαθούς	ἀγαθάς	ἀγαθά
Gen pl	ἀγαθῶν	ἀγαθῶν	ἀγαθῶν
Dat pl	ἀγαθοῖς	ἀγαθαῖς	ἀγαθοῖς

Notes:
1. Greek has two ways of using the adjective. The one discussed so far resembles English usage. The other way is slightly different. Thus while "the good man" is often written ὁ ἀγαθὸς ἄνθρωπος, it can also be written ὁ ἄνθρωπος ὁ ἀγαθός. In practice this does not make translation from Greek to English difficult. Furthermore, when translating from English

to Greek, the English word order can be used as this is correct Greek.
2. As far as is consistent with the main rules of accents [see 2.8-b; *Int.* 7.1], the accent on first and second declension adjectives tends to stay on the same syllable on which it is found in the nominative singular.
3. Some adjectives do not follow the pattern of γῆ for their feminine forms, but rather follow the pattern of ἡμέρα. It will not be surprising to find that these have word stems that finish in ε, ι or ρ. You can recognize these because they are listed in the dictionary thus: ἅγιος, -α, -ον [ἀγαθός would be listed as ἀγαθός, -ή, -όν]. When the full pattern of ἅγιος is written out, the differences from the way ἀγαθός is declined are apparent:

Alpha-pure Adjectives of the 1st & 2nd Declension			
	Masc	Fem	Neut
Nom sing	ἅγιος	ἁγία	ἅγιον
Voc sing	ἅγιε	ἁγία	ἅγιον
Acc sing	ἅγιον	ἁγίαν	ἅγιον
Gen sing	ἁγίου	ἁγίας	ἁγίου
Dat sing	ἁγίῳ	ἁγίᾳ	ἁγίῳ
N,V pl	ἅγιοι	ἅγιαι	ἅγια
Acc pl	ἁγίους	ἁγίας	ἅγια
Gen pl	ἁγίων	ἁγίων	ἁγίων
Dat pl	ἁγίοις	ἁγίαις	ἁγίοις

In Vocabulary 7, which includes all adjectives that occur over 50 times in the Greek New Testament, ἅγιος, δίκαιος, νεκρός and πονηρός follow the pattern of ἅγιος, -α, -ον in forming their declension. The other adjectives in the vocabulary follow the pattern of ἀγαθός, -ή, -όν in forming their declension.

Vocabulary 7

ἀγαθός, -ή, -όν (104)	good
ἀγαπητός, -ή, -όν (61)	beloved
ἅγιος, -α, -ον (233)	holy, sacred, dedicated
αἰώνιος, -ον[1] (70)	eternal
δίκαιος, -α, -ον (79)	just, righteous
δικαιοσύνη (91)	righteousness, justice
κακός, -ή, -όν (50)	bad
καλός, -ή, -όν (99)	beautiful, good
μόνος, -η, -ον (66)	only, alone

Part 1

μού (460), or ἐμοῦ (108)	my (a genitive)
νεκρός, -ά, -όν (128)	dead
πιστός, -ή, -όν (67)	faithful, believing
πονηρός, -ά, -όν (78)	evil, wicked
τυφλός, -ή, -όν (50)	blind

Notes on Vocabulary 7

1. As is indicated, αἰώνιος, -ον has no separate feminine forms. It is one of those adjectives which use the masculine forms for both masculine and feminine, and the neuter forms for neuter. This is the only such adjective that occurs more than 50 times in the Greek New Testament.
2. In dictionaries (and from here on in this book), adjectives are listed with an indication of the endings they take for the three genders. For example, τυφλός, -ή, -όν shows the way the adjective declines: its nom. masc. sing. ends with -ος, its nom. fem. sing. ends with -η, and its nom. neut. sing. ends with -ον.
3. It is helpful to learn the three endings while learning vocabulary. If it is your practice to say the word out loud as you review it – and it is a good practice – for τυφλός, -ή, -όν you would say out loud, τυφλός, τυφλή, τυφλόν. In this way an aural memory of how the adjective is declined will be formed.
4. μού is enclitic – where possible it throws its accent onto the previous word (see notes on εἰμί number 5, on p. 63).

Exercise 7

A. Declensions: Write out in full the declension of
i. κακός   ii. νεκρός

B. Translate into idiomatic English
1. ὁ ἀγαθὸς ἄνθρωπος 2. οἱ ἀγαθοὶ ἄνθρωποι 3. ὁ ἄνθρωπος ὁ ἀγαθός 4. οἱ ἄνθρωποι οἱ ἀγαθοί 5. ἡ ἀγαθὴ ἡμέρα 6. αἱ ἀγαθαὶ ἡμέραι 7. ἡ ἡμέρα ἡ ἀγαθή 8. αἱ ἡμέραι αἱ ἀγαθαί 9. τὸ ἀγαθὸν ἔργον 10. τὰ ἀγαθὰ ἔργα

11. τὸ ἔργον τὸ ἀγαθόν 12. τὰ ἔργα τὰ ἀγαθά 13. ὁ νεκρὸς ἄνθρωπος 14. οἱ νεκροὶ ἄνθρωποι 15. ὁ ἄνθρωπος ὁ νεκρός 16. οἱ ἄνθρωποι οἱ νεκροί 17. ἡ νεκρὰ ἐκκλησία 18. αἱ νεκραὶ ἐκκλησίαι 19. ἡ ἐκκλησία ἡ νεκρά 20. αἱ ἐκκλησίαι αἱ νεκραί

21. τὸ νεκρὸν ἔργον 22. τὰ νεκρὰ ἔργα 23. τὸ ἔργον τὸ νεκρόν 24. τὰ ἔργα τὰ νεκρά 25. τὸ ἅγιον βιβλίον 26. οἱ ἅγιοι ἄγγελοι 27. ὁ δοῦλος ὁ ἀγαπητός 28. τὰ πονηρὰ δαιμόνια 29. τὸ τυφλὸν παιδίον 30. ἡ ἐκκλησία ἡ πιστή

31. προσκυνοῦμεν τῷ μόνῳ θεῷ. 32. κακοὶ ἄνθρωποι ποιοῦσι πονηρὰ ἔργα. 33. τὸ τέκνον ἔχει καλὸν πρόσωπον. 34. ἡ ἐκκλησία ἔχει οὐ δικαιοσύνην, Χριστὸς μόνος ἔχει δικαιοσύνην. 35. εἰ ἔχεις τὸν Χριστόν, ἔχεις αἰώνιον ζωήν. 36. δικαιοσύνή ἐστιν ἐπαγγελία τοῦ θεοῦ. 37. ὁ θεὸς μού ἐστιν δίκαιος. 38. ὁ Ἰησοῦς λέγει λόγους τῆς ζωῆς. 39. ὁ πιστὸς λαὸς ἔχει αἰώνιον ζωήν. 40. ἀγαθοὶ ἄνθρωποι λέγουσιν οὐ πονηροὺς λόγους.

41. εἶ καλὸν παιδίον. 42. εἶ καλὸν παιδίον; 43. ὁ Ἀβραάμ ἐστιν δίκαιος ἄνθρωπος. 44. ὁ Δαυὶδ ἐσθίει ἄρτον ἐκ τοῦ ἁγίου ἱεροῦ. 45. οἱ νεκροὶ γινώσκουσιν οὐ τὸν θεόν. 46. ἅγιοι ἄγγελοι λέγουσι τοῖς δικαίοις ἄνθρωποις. 47. δοκῶ ὅτι θεός ἐστιν δίκαιος. 48. ἡ σοφία μού ἐστιν κακή, ἡ σοφία τοῦ θεοῦ ἐστιν ἀγαθή. 49. ἡ ἐντολὴ τοῦ Ἰησοῦ ἐστιν ἀγαθή.

C. Translate into Greek
50. The good slave. 51. The evil slave. 52. The bad slaves. 53. The holy man. 54. The holy day 55. The holy days

D. Add Accents
56. το νεκρον ἐργον 57. τα νεκρα ἐργα 58. το ἐργον το νεκρον 59. τα ἐργα τα νεκρα 60. το ἁγιον βιβλιον 61. οἱ ἁγιοι ἀγγελοι 62. ὁ δουλος ὁ ἀγαπητος 63. τα πονηρα δαιμονια 64. το τυφλον παιδιον 65. ἡ ἐκκλησια ἡ πιστη 66. προσκυνουμεν τῳ μονῳ θεῳ. 67. κακοι ἀνθρωποι ποιουσι πονηρα ἐργα. 68. το τεκνον ἐχει καλον προσωπον. 69. ἡ ἐκκλησια ἐχει οὐ δικαιοσυνην, Χριστος μονος ἐχει δικαιοσυνην. 70. εἰ ἐχεις τον Χριστον, ἐχεις αἰωνιον ζωην.

Chapter 8: -αω Verbs

Like -εω verbs (Chap. 5), verbs with stems that end in an α (-αω verbs) have minor differences in their present indicative active when compared to the pattern of λύω. The most probable explanation for such differences is that in speech the α on the verb stem interacts with the vowels of the endings of the regular verb. The most frequently occurring -αω verb is ἀγαπάω. If ἀγαπάω was written out following the pattern of λύω, the result would look like this:

ἀγαπά-ω
ἀγαπά-εις
ἀγαπά-ει
ἀγαπά-ομεν
ἀγαπά-ετε
ἀγαπά-ουσι(ν)

In every instance the α is immediately followed by a vowel. In these cases the vowels are modified when the words are said. Fortunately, they follow a reasonably consistent pattern as they change. For -αω verbs the rules of contraction are these:

Vowel combination	Result
α + ε	α
α + η	α
α + ο	ω
α + ω	ω

Notes: .
1. An iota in the second syllable becomes an iota subscript (e.g. αει becomes ᾳ)
2. An υ in the second syllable disappears, and does not effect the way the other vowels contract (e.g. αου becomes what αο would become, i.e ω)
3. The contractions, α + ε and α + η, changes a short α into a long α, which can effect the type of accent

It is possible to simplify these contractions and notes by observing:

Vowel combination	Result
α + "e" sound	α
α + "o" sound	ω
α + ?υ	Upsilon disappears
α + ?ι	An iota becomes an iota subscript

Applying these rules of contraction shows that the present indicative active of ἀγαπαω would be:

ἀγαπῶ [α + ω]
ἀγαπᾷς [α + εις]
ἀγαπᾷ [α + ει]
ἀγαπῶμεν [α + ομεν]
ἀγαπᾶτε [α + ετε]
ἀγαπῶσι(ν) [α + ουσι(ν)]

There are more changes from the basic pattern of λυω with -αω verbs than there are with the -εω verbs. However, as with the -εω verbs, a separate paradigm for the -αω verbs need not be learned. All that is necessary to memorize is the present indicative active of λύω, and the rules of contraction. The various forms of the verb can then be derived.

Vocabulary 8

-αω Verbs

ἀγαπάω (141)   I love
γεννάω (97)   I beget; bear, produce
ἐπερωτάω (56)   I ask
ἐρωτάω (62)   I ask
ζάω (140)   I live[4]
ὁράω (114)   I see

Other words

ἀλλά (635)   **but**, yet, nevertheless
ἀπολύω [1] (65)   I release; dismiss, send away
ἀποστέλλω (131)   I send away, send
ἀπόστολος (79)   apostle, messenger
ἐγώ (1713)   I[2]
σύν + dative (127)   with[3]
συνάγω (59)   I gather
συναγωγή (56)   synagogue, place of assembly

Part 1

Notes on Vocabulary 8

1. Notice that ἀπολύω is made up of ἀπό + λύω. The next vocabulary item, ἀποστέλλω, is made up of ἀπό + στέλλω. Many Greek verbs are made up from prepositions plus existing verbs
2. The first person personal pronoun (ἐγώ) is not strictly needed by the verb, and is generally only used when the writer wishes to stress the pronoun "I."
3. σύν means "with," in the sense of accompanying someone or something– "together with."
4. The verb ζάω is irregular. Its present indicative active is as follows: ζῶ, ζῇς, ζῇ, ζῶμεν, ζῆτε, ζῶσιν. While ζάω is usually listed in dictionaries and grammars as an -αω verb, as Chrys Caragounis points out, "This form is incorrect, anyway, since the correct uncontracted form [in classical Greek] was ζήω (or ζώω)" [*The Development of Greek and the New Testament* (Tübingen: Mohr Siebeck, 2006), p. 118, fn. 105].
5. This vocabulary includes all the -αω verbs that occur more than 50 times in the Greek New Testament.

Exercise 8.1

A. Paradigms: Write or type in full the present ind. act. of
i. γεννάω   ii. ἐρωτάω   iii. ζητέω   iv. συνάγω

B. Translate into English
1. ὁρῶμεν 2. ζῶσιν 3. ἀγαπᾷ 4. ἐρωτᾷς 5. ἀποστελλέτε 6. ἀγαπᾶτε 7. ἐπερωτᾶτε 8. ποιοῦμεν 9. γεννᾷ 10. ἀκολουθεῖτε

C. Translate into Greek
11. They beget 12. She sees 13. You (sing.) live 14. We love 15. We ask

D. Translate into idiomatic English
[Remember: When translating, first look for the verb, then the nominative, then the accusative. These can then be placed in the English sentence order, which is generally Subject (usually identified by the presence of a the nominative case of a noun in the Greek sentence), Verb, Direct Object (identified by the presence of the accusative case on a noun in the sentence). Greek does not keep to the word order used in English, and some of the sentences towards the end of this exercise will act as a reminder of that fact. The subject and direct object will need to be recognized from the case endings on the nouns in such sentences.]

16. ὁ ἀπόστολος ἐρωτᾷ τὸν Ἰησοῦν. 17. ἡ δικαιοσύνη γεννᾷ τὴν ἀγάπην. [Abstract nouns such as ἀγάπη are generally found with the article in Greek.] 18. ὁ Ἰησοῦς ζῇ σὺν τῷ Πέτρῳ. 19. ὁρᾷς ἁμαρτίαν ἐν τῇ ἐκκλησίᾳ; 20. ἀπολύει τὸν ὄχλον ὁ Ἰησοῦς. 21. ὁ θεὸς ἀγαπᾷ τὸν κόσμον, ἀλλὰ ὁ κόσμος οὐκ ἀγαπᾷ τὸν θεόν. 22. οἱ ἀδελφοὶ καὶ οἱ δοῦλοι ἐπερωτῶσι τὸν Ἰησοῦν. 23. ἡ σοφία τοῦ θεοῦ οὐχ ἁμαρτίαν γεννᾷ. 24. ὁ θεὸς ἀποστέλλει τὸν ἀπόστολον ἐκ τοῦ ἁγίου ἱεροῦ.

25. ὁρῶμεν τὴν ἀγάπην τοῦ θεοῦ ἐν τῷ προσώπῳ τοῦ Ἰησοῦ. 26. ὁ Δαυὶδ ἀποστέλλει τὸν λαόν. 27. γράφεις τὸν νόμον ἀνθρώπου, ἀλλὰ ἐγὼ λέγω ἐντολὰς τῆς ἐξουσίας. 28. ὁ λαὸς συνάγει ἐν τῷ οἴκῳ. 29. τὸν ἀδελφόν μου ἀγαπῶ. 30. ὁρᾷς ἁμαρτίαν ἐν τῇ συναγωγῇ; 31. ὁ ἄνθρωπος ἀπολύει τοὺς δούλους ἀπὸ τοῦ οἴκου. 32. ὁ ἀπόστολος μαρτυρεῖ ὅτι ὁ θεός ἐστιν ἀγάπη. 33. ἐγὼ ὁρῶ τὸν Ἰησοῦν σὺν τῷ Πέτρῳ. 34. ἀγάπη γεννᾷ χαράν.

35. ὁ Ἰησοῦς μαρτυρεῖ κατὰ τῶν ἐντολῶν τῆς συναγωγῆς. 36. ἄγγελοι συνάγουσιν ἐν τῷ ἁγίῳ ἱερῷ. 37. τὰς ἁμαρτίας τοῦ κόσμου ὁ Ἰησοῦς οὐκ ἀγαπᾷ. 38. οἱ ἄνθρωποι οἱ νεκροὶ ἐπερωτῶσιν οὔ. 39. πονηροὶ ἄνθρωποι λαλοῦσι κατὰ τοῦ νόμου τοῦ θεοῦ. 40. δικαιοσύνη γεννᾷ αἰώνιον ζωῆν. 41. τοὺς πονηροὺς λόγους λαλεῖς, ἀλλὰ ἐγὼ τοὺς λόγους τῆς ζωῆς λαλῶ. 42. ὁ Δαυὶδ ἐν τῇ Ἰερουσολὴμ ζῇ. 43. τὸν ὄχλον ὁ Ἰησοῦς ἀποστέλλει ἀπὸ τοῦ οἴκου. 44. ὁ ὄχλος συνάγει ἐν τῇ συναγωγῇ.

E. Translate into Greek
45. The angels dismiss the apostles. 46. Jesus sees the crowd. 47. The people do not see God. 48. God does not love sin.

Accents on -αω verbs

As with -εω verbs, accents on -αω verbs are discovered by placing the accent on the uncontracted form of the verb (e.g. ἀγαπά-εις, ἀγαπά-ομεν), and adding a grave accent to all other non-accented vowels (e.g. ἀγὰπά-εὶς, ἀγὰπά-ὸμὲν). Where two accents follow acute-grave (e.g. ά-εὶ, ά-ὸ), contract the vowels using the usual rules, and use a circumflex accent (e.g. ἀγαπᾷς, ἀγαπῶμεν). Where two accents follow grave-acute, contract the vowels according to the usual rules, and use an acute accent (this particular combination of accents does not occur in the present tense, but in a later chapter the following form of ἀγαπάω will be met: ἀγὰπὰ-όμὴν which gives ἀγαπώμην).

Part 1 83

Exercise 8.2

Add accents

1. ὁ ἀποστολος ἐρωτᾳ τον Ἰησουν. 2. ἡ δικαιοσυνη γεννᾳ την ἀγαπην. 3. ὁ Ἰησους ζῃ συν τῳ Πετρῳ. 4. ὁρᾳς ἁμαρτιαν ἐν τῃ ἐκκλησιᾳ; 5. ἀπολυει τον ὀχλον ὁ Ἰησους. 6. ὁ θεος ἀγαπᾳ τον κοσμον, ἀλλα ὁ κοσμος οὐκ ἀγαπᾳ θεον. 7. οἱ ἀδελφοι και οἱ δουλοι ἐπερωτωσι τον Ἰησουν. 8. ἡ σοφια του θεου οὐχ ἁμαρτιαν γεννᾳ. 9. ὁ θεος ἀποστελλει τον ἀποστολον ἐκ του ἁγιου ἱερου. 10. ὁρωμεν την ἀγαπην του θεου ἐν τῳ προσωπῳ του Ἰησου.

Chapter 9: The Present Indicative of Middle [and Passive] Verbs

All the verbs met so far either follow the pattern of λύω for their present indicative active, or something close to it. There are two other types of pattern that are translated by an English verb with a present indicative active meaning – the pattern followed by a group of verbs which have a Greek middle voice but no active voice, and the pattern followed by -μι verbs. The -μι verbs will be met later (starting in 12.3.1), but because they are so frequently encountered, an acquaintance with verbs using the Greek middle voice that are translated by the English active voice cannot be delayed.

The Greek verb has three voices: active middle and passive. The difference in meaning between the three revolves around the relationship between the subject of the verb and the action of the verb. In the active voice, the subject initiates the action of the verb; in the middle voice, the subject of the verb participates in the action; while in the passive voice, the subject of the verb receives the action of the verb.

The English verb only has two voices: active and passive. Because English speakers do not have a middle voice in their language, they usually find it a challenge to understand the meaning of the Greek middle voice. There is good news, though. The middle voice is almost always translated by the English active voice. And that is pretty much all you need to know about the middle voice at this stage of your learning. One of the principles used in this textbook is not to confuse beginners with unnecessary information at the start, but ensure that by the end of book provide a comprehensive coverage of grammar. This chapter is in Part 1 of the textbook, and at this stage, all you need to know is to translate middle voice verbs by an active voice in English. There will come a time when you need to understand the Greek passive voice and come to terms with the Greek middle voice, but that can be postponed until chapter 24 (24.1.5; see also Int. 4).

If you consult the paradigms in Appendix B, you will find that Greek uses the same form for the middle and passive voice. The context will indicate which meaning to use. The majority of the times you meet a verb using -ομαι forms, it will be on a verb in the middle voice, and translated by the English active voice.

You will notice from the vocabulary that there are three verbs that have passive forms that are usually translated by the English active voice: ἀποκρίνομαι (231) I answer; φοβέομαι (95) I fear; πορεύομαι (150) I go.

Verbs such as those found in vocabulary 9 (i.e. verbs have only middle and passive forms and which are usually translated with the English active voice) are sometimes called Deponent verbs. As we have seen, they are really middle and passive verbs that are best translated by the English active voice [your teacher may still prefer to use the term Deponent verb as a kind of shorthand for this class of verb].

The following table summarizes the manner in which the Greek active, middle and passive voices are usually translated

Greek Voice	Equivalent English Voice	Voice Usually Used in English Translation
Active	Active	Active
Middle	-	Active
Passive	Passive	Passive [although some verbs, such as those found in this chapter, are translated with the English active voice]

Translating into the English passive voice will not take place until Chapter 24. So in the meantime, any verb that you meet in exercises using middle or passive forms should be translated by the English active voice, and you can postpone needing to know more about the meaning of the middle and passive voices until Chapter 24.

The pattern we will use for learning the present tense of the middle and passive voice will be the verb δέχομαι (I receive, take), as it is one of the verbs that when found in the middle voice are almost always translated by an English active voice.

Present indicative middle [& passive] of δέχομαι		
Person	Form	Meaning
1st pers sing	δέχομαι	I receive
2nd pers sing	δέχῃ	you receive
3rd pers sing	δέχεται	he/.. receives
1st pers pl	δεχόμεθα	we receive
2nd pers pl	δέχεσθε	you receive
3rd pers pl	δέχονται	they receive

Notes:
1. Verbs that use middle or passive verbal forms that are usually translated by the English active voice may be recognized in vocabularies and dictionaries because they are listed with an -ομαι ending (almost all of them are not found with the active voice endings in the Greek NT). Such verbs should be translated with the English active voice, at least until Chapter 24 where it will be discovered that the endings may also indicate the middle and passive voice. [Most readers will be content to wait until Chapter 24 for further explanations. Those who desire to know more may consult the paradigm of the regular verb in Appendix A and the explanations in Chapter 24 if they wish.]
2. This verb pattern has to be memorized, and there is no short cut to avoid the task. In future tests, you can be sure that you will be asked to reproduce this pattern (or paradigm). Not only this, in translating the Greek New Testament, you must be able to recognize these endings.
3. The rules for accenting verbs also apply to middle and passive verbs [see 2.8; Ex 5.2; Ex 8.1].
4. The same rules of contraction already learnt for the -εω and -αω verbs also work for middle and passive verbs which have verb stems that end with an ε or α. For example, the verbs φοβέομαι – which has a present verb stem which ends in an ε – would look like φοβε-ομαι, φοβε-η, φοβε-εται, φοβε-ομεθα, φοβε-εσθε, φοβε-ονται if written in full. But because ε + ε becomes ει, and ε + ο becomes ου, and ε + long becomes long, these turn out to be φοβοῦμαι, φοβῇ, φοβεῖται, φοβούμεθα, φοβεῖσθε, φοβοῦνται. [See Chapter 5 for how to work out accents on -εω verbs; the method is the same for φοβέομαι.]

Vocabulary 9

Verbs with middle and passive forms in the NT, whose middle forms are usually translated by the English active voice:

ἀπέρχομαι (116)	I go away, depart (ἀπό + ἔρχομαι)
ἀσπάζομαι (59)	I greet
γίνομαι[1] (667)	I become, come to be, happen
δέχομαι (56)	I receive, take
εἰσέρχομαι (192)	I come in, go in (εἰς + ἔρχομαι)
ἐξέρχομαι (216)	I go out, come out (ἐκ + ἔρχομαι)
ἔρχομαι[2] (631)	I go, come
προσέρχομαι (87)	I come or go to, approach
προσεύχομαι (86)	I pray

Verb with only passive forms in the NT, whose passive forms are usually translated by the English active voice:

ἀποκρίνομαι (231)	I answer
φοβέομαι (95)	I fear

Part 1 87

A verb which as both middle and passive forms in the NT, which are often translated by the English active voice:
πορεύομαι (150)   I go

Other words:
εἰς (1753) + acc.   **into**, towards   [from Vocabulary 3.2]
πρός (696) + acc.³   **toward**, to,⁵ with, against

Notes on Vocabulary 9

1. Like the verb εἰμί, the verb γίνομαι takes a nominative for its complement.
2. While English has two separate verbs, "go" and "come," New Testament Greek does not. Ἔρχομαι can mean either "go" or "come." If direction is important, Greek makes this clear by the use of a preposition such as πρός "towards," or ἀπό "from."
3. The most common use of πρός is with the accusative to mean "to, towards." It is used 8 times with the dative to mean "near, at, by" [e.g. Mark 5:11; John 20:12]. It is found once with the genitive [Acts 27:4], where it means "to the advantage of."
4. The verb εἰσέρχομαι is almost always followed by εἰς in the New Testament. The verb ἐξέρχομαι is often (but not always) followed by ἐκ. This appears redundant in English, but was correct Greek usage.
5. The difference between εἰς and πρός + acc. is somewhat like the difference between ἀπό and ἐκ. Εἰς has the sense of "into," while πρός + acc. has the sense of "towards," though there is a large overlap in their meanings.
6. Vocabulary 9 contains all the verbs with middle or passive voices that are translated by the English active voice that occur more than 50 times in the Greek New Testament.
7. If you consult Appendix B, you will discover that the present tense of the middle and passive voices are the same. It is only when we get to the aorist and future tenses (chapters 12 and 25) that it will become important to know which verbs are middle and which are passive. The vocabulary lists which verbs use middle voice and which use passive voice in preparation for Chapters 12 and 25.

Exercise 9

A. Paradigms: Write or type in full the present indicative of
i. προσεύχομαι ii. παρακαλέω iii. φοβέομαι

B. Translate into English
1. δέχονται 2. δέχῃ 3. δεχόμεθα 4. πορεύεται 5. ἀποκρίνῃ 6. ἀποκρίνεται 7. ἀπέρχομαι 8. προσέρχονται 9. προσεύχεσθε 10. φοβούμεθα 11. γίνεσθε 12. ἀσπαζόμεθα

C. Translate into Greek
13. We pray 14. You (sing) come in 15. They fear 16. You (pl) fear 17. She fears 18. You (plural) receive [Hint for qus. 15-17: the verb stem of φοβέομαι ends in ε, so apply the same rules of contraction which you learnt for –εω verbs.]

D. Translate into Idiomatic English
19. ὁ Ἰωάννης ἀσπάζεται τὸν Ἰησοῦν. 20. ὁ υἱὸς τοῦ ἀνθρώπου ἔρχεται εἰς τὸν κόσμον. 21. ὁ υἱὸς τοῦ ἀνθρώπου εἰσέρχεται εἰς τὸν κόσμον. [See notes on Vocab. 9 no. 4] 22. ὁ υἱὸς τοῦ ἀνθρώπου ἔρχεται ἐκ τοῦ κόσμου. 23. ὁ υἱὸς τοῦ ἀνθρώπου ἐξέρχεται ἐκ τοῦ κόσμου. 24. ὁ Ἰησοῦς πορεύεται πρὸς τὴν Ἰερουσαλήμ. 25. ὁ Ἰησοῦς πορεύεται εἰς Ναζαρέθ. 26. ὁ Ἰωάννης ἔρχεται ἀπὸ τῆς Ἰερουσαλήμ. 27. ὁ Ἰωάννης ἐξέρχεται ἐκ τῆς Ἰερουσαλήμ. 28. φοβούμεθα οὐκ ἄνθρωπον. 29. προσέρχομαι πρὸς τὴν αἰώνιον ζωήν.

30. οἱ ἅγιοι ἄνθρωποι πορεύονται εἰς τὸ ἱερόν. 31. ὁ δοῦλος δέχεται τὸ ἅγιον βιβλίον ἀπὸ τοῦ δικαίου ἀνθρώπου. 32. ὁ Ἰησοῦς ἀποκρίνεται τὸν Ἰωάννην. 33. λόγοι μου γίνονται οὐ νόμος, ἀλλὰ οἱ λόγοι τοῦ Ἰησοῦ γίνονται νόμος. 34. δαιμόνια ἀπέρχεται ἀπὸ τῆς πιστῆς δούλης. 35. τὰ τέκνα ἔρχεται εἰς τὸν οἶκον. 36. οἱ δίκαιοι ἄνθρωποι εἰσέρχονται εἰς τὴν αἰώνιον ζωήν. 37. τὸν ἄρτον δέχεται ἀπὸ τῆς καλῆς δουλῆς ὁ Δαυίδ. 38. δικαιοσύνη πορεύεται ἐκ τοῦ ἁγίου ἱεροῦ. 39. τὸν Χριστὸν ὁ κόσμος οὐ δέχεται.

40. ἐγὼ φοβοῦμαι τὸν θεόν, ἀλλὰ οὐ φοβοῦμαι ἄνθρωπον. 41. κακοὶ ἄνθρωποι γίνονται δίκαιοι εἰ πιστεύουσιν εἰς τὸν Ἰησοῦν. 42. ὁ Ἰωάννης ἀσπάζεται τὸν Χριστόν.

E. Translate into Greek
43. We receive life from God. 44. Peter and John go into Jerusalem. 45. The people greet Jesus. 46. Do you pray? 47. Do you fear God?

F. Add Accents
48. ὁ υἱος του ἀνθρωπου εἰσερχεται εἰς τον κοσμον. 49. ὁ υἱος του ἀνθρωπου ἐρχεται ἐκ του κοσμου. 50 ὁ υἱος του ἀνθρωπου ἐξερχεται ἐκ του κοσμου. 51. ὁ Ἰησους πορευεται προς την Ἰερουσαλημ. 52. ὁ Ἰησους πορευεται προς την Ἰερουσαλημ. 53. ὁ Ἰωαννης ἐρχεται ἀπο της Ἰερουσαλημ. 54. ὁ Ἰωαννης ἐξερχεται ἐκ της Ἰερουσαλημ. 55. φοβουμεθα οὐκ ἀνθρωπον.

Chapter 10: Third Person Pronoun

The usefulness of pronouns might be illustrated by the following two sentences which are written without their help: "John went to school today. When John arrived, John was told by John's teacher that John was late." With pronouns the sentences could have been written this way: "John went to school today. When he arrived, he was told by his teacher that he was late." The words, "he, she, it, they" are the third person pronouns in English. Interestingly enough, though the words used in English do not usually decline, its pronouns do:

	The English Third Person Pronoun		
	Masc	Fem	Neut
Nom sing	he	she	it
Acc sing	him	her	it
Gen sing	his, of him	hers, of ..	its, of it
Dat sing	(to/for) him	(to/for) ..	(to/for) it
Nom pl	they	they	they
Acc pl	them	them	them
Gen pl	their	their	their
Dat pl	(to/for) them	(to/for) them	(to/for) them

Each of these meanings can be matched with the declension of αὐτός, the Greek third person pronoun:

	The Third Person Pronoun (αὐτός, αὐτή, αὐτό)		
	Masc	Fem	Neut
Nom sing	αὐτός	αὐτή	αὐτό
Acc sing	αὐτόν	αὐτήν	αὐτό
Gen sing	αὐτοῦ	αὐτῆς	αὐτοῦ
Dat sing	αὐτῷ	αὐτῇ	αὐτῷ
Nom pl	αὐτοί	αὐταί	αὐτά
Acc pl	αὐτούς	αὐτάς	αὐτά
Gen pl	αὐτῶν	αὐτῶν	αὐτῶν
Dat pl	αὐτοῖς	αὐταῖς	αὐτοῖς

Notes:
1. Apart from αὐτό (the nominative and accusative neuter singular), the endings are exactly the same as for an adjective. Thus the task of learning how αὐτός declines should be relatively straight-forward.
2. αὐτός can also be used as an adjective, in which case it means "himself/ herself/ itself/ themselves." For example, αὐτὸς Δαυίδ David himself (Mark 12:36); αὐτὸς Ἰησοῦς Jesus himself (Luke 24:15).
3. Notice particularly that the nominative and accusative neuter singular is αὐτό (*not* αὐτόν).
4. The third person personal pronoun is used in a way that is similar to English. It takes the same gender and number as the noun it replaces. Its case is determined by its function in the sentence. For example:

αὐτὸς λέγει	he says	(nom used for subject)
ὁ θεὸς ἀγαπᾷ αὐτόν	God loves him	(acc used for dir object)
τὸ βιβλίον αὐτοῦ	his book [lit.: the book of him]	(gen of possession)
ὁ Ἰησοῦς λέγει αὐτῷ	Jesus says to him	(dat used for indirect object)
αὐτοὶ λέγουσιν	they say	(nom used for subject)
ὁ θεὸς ἀγαπᾷ αὐτούς	God loves them	(acc used for dir object)
τὸ βιβλίον αὐτῶν	their book [lit.: the book of them]	(gen of possession)
ὁ Ἰησοῦς λέγει αὐτοῖς	Jesus says to them	(dat used for indirect object)
αὐτὴ λέγει	she says	(nom used for subject)
ὁ θεὸς ἀγαπᾷ αὐτήν	God loves her	(acc used for dir object)
τὸ βιβλίον αὐτῆς	her book [literally: the book of her]	(gen of possession)
ὁ Ἰησοῦς λέγει αὐτῇ etc.	Jesus says to her	(dat used for indirect object)

Vocabulary 10

ἄγω (66)	I lead, bring, take along, arrest
ἀποθνῄσκω (113)	I die
αὐτός, -ή, -ό (5534)	he/she/it [third person personal pronoun]; [him/her/it]self; same
αὐτοῦ (1200+)	his [gen. masc. sing. of αὐτός]
βάλλω (122)	**I throw**; put, place, bring
ἐκβάλλω (81)	I cast out, send out, remove
ἐπί (878)	+ acc. (317+): across, to, against
ἐπί (878)	+ gen. (188+): **upon**, near, before, over, on the basis of, in the time of

ἐπί (878)   + dat. (137+): at, by, on
θάνατος (120)   death
κύριος (718)   lord, master
πίπτω (90)   I fall
πλοῖον (66)   boat
φέρω (68)   I bear, bring, carry

Exercise 10

Translate into idiomatic English
1. ὁ Ἰησοῦς ἔρχεται εἰς τὸν λαὸν αὐτοῦ, ἀλλὰ ὁ λαὸς αὐτοῦ οὐ δέχεται αὐτόν.
2. ὁ Ἰησοῦς εἰσέρχεται εἰς τὸν κόσμον, ἀλλὰ ὁ κόσμος οὐ δέχεται αὐτόν. 3. ὁ Ἰησοῦς φέρει τὰς ἁμαρτίας τοῦ κόσμου, ἀλλὰ ὁ κόσμος οὐ γινώσκει αὐτόν. 4. ὁ Ἀβραὰμ πίπτει ἐπὶ τοῦ προσώπου αὐτοῦ καὶ αὐτὸς προσκυνεῖ τῷ θεῷ αὐτοῦ. 5. ὁ Δαυὶδ βάλλει τὸ βιβλίον αὐτοῦ ἐν τῷ οἴκῳ αὐτοῦ.

6. ὁ Ἰησοῦς ἐκβάλλει τὸν ὄχλον ἐκ τοῦ ἁγίου ἱεροῦ. 7. ὁ Πέτρος προσέρχεται πρὸς τὸ πλοῖον αὐτοῦ. 8. ὁ Ἰησοῦς ἄγει τὸν λαὸν αὐτοῦ εἰς ζωήν. 9. αὐτοὶ εὑρίσκουσι τὸν Πέτρον ἐπὶ τῷ πλοίῳ. 10. αὐτοὶ εὑρίσκουσι τὸν Πέτρον ἐπὶ τοῦ πλοίου. 11. αὐτὸς Πέτρος εὑρίσκει αὐτοὺς ἐπὶ τοῦ πλοίου. 12. ὁ Πέτρος εὑρίσκει αὐτοὺς ἐπὶ τῷ πλοίῳ. 13. ὁ Ἰησοῦς ἀποθνῄσκει.

14. οἱ νόμοι αὐτοῦ εἰσιν ἀγαθοὶ καὶ αἱ ἐντολαὶ αὐτοῦ εἰσιν δίκαιαι. 15. προσκυνοῦμεν τῷ θεῷ καὶ τηροῦμεν τοὺς νόμους αὐτοῦ. 16. ἐγὼ γινώσκω ὅτι ὁ Ἰησοῦς μου ζῇ. 17. ὁ κύριος ἔρχεται εἰς τὸν λαὸν αὐτοῦ. 18. τὸ παιδίον αὐτοῦ πίπτει. 19. ὁ κύριος προσέρχεται πρὸς τὸ ἅγιον ἱερὸν αὐτοῦ. 20. θάνατος ἔρχεται εἰς τὸν Ἰησοῦν. 21. ὁ Ἰωάννης λαλεῖ ἐπὶ τὸν ὄχλον πρὸς Πέτρον.

22. αὐτὴ ἀποθνῄσκει ἐν οἴκῳ αὐτῆς. 23. ὁ Ἰησοῦς ὁ Χριστός ἐστιν ὁ κύριος. 24. αὐτὸς ἀποθνῄσκει ἐν οἴκῳ αὐτοῦ. 25. αὐταὶ οὐκ ἀποθνῄσκουσιν ἐν οἴκοις αὐτῶν. 26. αὐτοὶ οὐκ ἀποθνῄσκουσιν ἐν οἴκοις αὐτῶν. 27. ὁ Ἰησοῦς ἐκβάλλει δαιμόνια ἐκ τοῦ τέκνου. 28. ὁ κύριος εὑρίσκει τὸν τυφλὸν ἄνθρωπον ἐπὶ τῷ οἴκῳ. 29. ὁ κύριος εὑρίσκει τὸν τυφλὸν ἄνθρωπον ἐπὶ τοῦ οἴκου. 30. ἁμαρτία γεννᾷ θάνατον.

31. ὁ δοῦλος φέρει τὸ παιδίον αὐτοῦ. 32. ὁ Ἰωάννης ἄγει τὴν τυφλὴν δούλην πρὸς τὸν Ἰησοῦν. 33. ἄγγελοι ἄγουσι τὴν ἐκκλησίαν τοῦ θεοῦ. 34. Πέτρος βάλλει ἄρτον ἐν τῷ πλοίῳ αὐτοῦ. 35. οἱ δοῦλοι πίπτουσιν ἐπὶ τῶν προσώπων αὐτῶν. 36. ἡ δούλη φέρει τὸ τέκνον αὐτῆς. 37. ὁ θεὸς οὐκ ἀποθνῄσκει. 38. τὰ ἔργα τῆς ἁμαρτίας ἄγει εἰς θάνατον.

Translate into Greek
39. The brother leads his child. 40. They cast out demons. 41. We worship the Lord. 42. They eat their bread. 43. Jesus speaks words to them.

Chapter 11: Review of Part 1

By now you will be well over the initial shock of starting to learn Greek. The new alphabet will have become familiar, and the basic way the language is put together will be beginning to make sense. Your confidence should now be building up. It is probably a good time to do a quick review of the things covered so far, to put everything in perspective, and ensure that Part 1 has been mastered before moving on to Part 2.

Greek is an inflected language.

That it inflects is perhaps the biggest difference between Greek and English. In English we show the different parts of the sentence by their position in the sentence. The English sentence typically is made up of:

Subject + Verb + [Direct Object] + [Prepositional Phrase(s)]

Real life English sentences are often more complicated than this scheme, but it does show the normal way of expressing things. In English the verb need not have a direct object, but it always has a subject.

In contrast to English, Greek does not use position to show the different parts of the sentence. Instead, it changes the endings on the words – it inflects. Word order is not as important. Thus, the basic skill in translating from Greek to English is to recognize these different parts of the sentence, and then reassemble them into their English word order. This gives us the following **translation strategy:**

1st find the verb
2nd find the nominative [the subject]
3rd find the accusative [the direct object]
Fit the rest of the sentence around these

Because being able to recognize the different parts of the sentence by their form is so important in translation, it is vital that the different paradigms and declensions are learnt thoroughly. Furthermore, it is important that you feel confident with the material covered to date before beginning the next part of the course. The following section will begin to introduce the next level of complexity in the language, and if you do not know what has been done so far, Part 2 will seem hard. However, if you have faithfully memorized the different forms, and can recognize and use them, you will find the next sec-

Part 1 93

tion relatively easy. You can test your performance by trying to do Exercise 11 from memory. There is no new grammar or vocabulary in it.

Remember the following

Quirks of grammar:
1. The verbs εἰμί and γίνομαι take nominative for both subject and complement
2. Plural neuter subjects are found with third person singular verbs.
3. There is one item of grammar which could not be introduced when you met the verb ἀκούω. This verb is usually followed by the accusative of the thing heard, and /or the genitive of person heard. E.g. ὁ Ἰησοῦς ἀκούει τὴν φωνὴν τοῦ Πέτρου [τὴν φωνὴν is the thing heard, therefore is in the accusative; τοῦ Πέτρου is the person heard, so is in the genitive]. This rule is sometimes broken in the New Testament.
4. The definite article (ὁ, ἡ, τό) is mostly used in Greek rather as it is in English – i.e. to make nouns "definite" (e.g. ὁ ἄνθρωπος is *"the* man," rather than *"a* man," which would be ἄνθρωπος). There are two usages in Greek which are different to that of English, and you may already have noted these: the Greek definite article is usually used with personal names (e.g. ὁ Ἰησοῦς) and with abstract nouns (e.g. ἡ ἀγαπή).

Tricky bits:
1. The difference between εἰ and εἶ [you may consult Vocab. 4 if you have forgotten]
2. The verb ζάω declines in its own unique way [see notes on Vocab. 8].

Paradigms and Declensions
If asked to write in full the **paradigm** of the present indicative active of any verb (the only part of the verb paradigm met so far), or any other part of the verb paradigm, this means that you are being asked to write out the:

                First person singular   First person plural
                Second person singular Second person plural
                Third person singular   Third person plural

of the verb. If asked to write in full the **declension** of a particular noun, you should give the:

                Nominative singular   Nominative plural
                Vocative singular   Vocative plural
                Accusative singular   Accusative plural
                Genitive singular   Genitive plural
                Dative singular   Dative plural

for that noun. Remember, if you have not learnt a separate vocative for a particular noun (and so far only second declension masculine nouns such as λόγος have had a separate form for the vocative), then the vocative is the same as the nominative.

Checklist for revision

◊ Revise the paradigm for the present indicative of λύω and δέχομαι, and how to write out the paradigm of other verbs which follow the pattern of these two verbs.
◊ Revise the second declension masculine (λόγος) and neuter (ἔργον) nouns, and the first declension feminine nouns (γῆ, ἡμέρα, δόξα). Also review all cases and genders of the article.
◊ Look over the rules of contraction for -εω and -αω verbs, and how to write out the present indicative active of these verbs. You should also be able to write out the paradigm for middle or passive verbs that have a present stem that ends in an ε (e.g. φοβέομαι).
◊ Ensure that you know all the vocabulary to date, especially the different meanings of the prepositions with the different cases. Appendix H gives a listing of the cumulative vocabulary for each part of the book, including a separate listing of all the words in the vocabulary lists in Part 1.
◊ Revise the different uses of the cases (nominative, accusative, genitive, dative).
◊ Ensure you know the different (present indicative) forms of the verb εἰμί.
◊ Revise the declension of adjectives of the first and second declension.
◊ Do Exercise 11, checking your answers against those in Appendix A.

Exercise 11 (Review)

The following exercise will use every vocabulary item met so far at least once. There is a complete set of answers in Appendix A.

Translate into English

1. ἐσθίομεν 2. ἐπερωτᾷς 3. ζητεῖτε 4. προσεύχομαι 5. φέρεις 6. ὁρῶσιν
7. ἀποστέλλει 8. δοξάζετε 9. δέχεται 10. δοκεῖτε 11. γίνονται 12. ζῶ
13. φοβούμεθα 14. λαμβάνει 15. γινώσκεις 16. περιπατοῦμεν 17. γεννᾷς
18. θέλω 19. χαίρουσιν 20. ἀποθνῄσκεις

21. ἔρχομαι 22. συνάγει 23. μαρτυροῦμεν   24. εὑρίσκετε 25. πιστεύω
26. καλοῦμεν 27. ἀγαπᾷ 28. ἀπέρχονται 29. πίπτω 30. ἀκούετε 31. ποιῶ
32. ἐρωτῶσιν 33. ἀποκρίνεσθε 34. βάλλει 35. λέγεις 36. αἰτεῖ 37. ἀπολύεις
38. πορεύομαι 39. γράφεις 40. ἀσπάζονται

Part 1

41. εἰσέρχεσθε 42. ἔχω 43. ἐκβάλλετε 44. ἐξέρχομεθα 45. ἄγετε 46. προσέρχῃ 47. προσκυνεῖτε 48. τηρεῖς 49. ἐσμέν 50. λαλεῖτε

Translate into Greek
51. We wish 52. You (sing.) fear 53. You (pl.) fear 54. They gather 55. We think 56. He begets 57. They pray 58. I glorify 59. You (sing.) greet

Translate into English
60. ἡ ἁγία ἡμέρα 61. ἡ ἐπαγγελία τῆς αἰωνίου ζωῆς 62. ἀγαπητὴ ἐκκλησία 63. ἡ ἀρχὴ σοφίας 64. θάνατος αὐτοῦ 65. νεκρὰ ἔργα 66. αἱ ἐντολαὶ τοῦ κυρίου 67. τὸ τέκνον τὸ μόνον 68. ὁ υἱὸς τοῦ ἀνθρώπου 69. ἡ ἀγαθὴ γῆ 70. εἰ εἶ ὁ Χριστός

71. οἱ δίκαιοι ἀπόστολοι 72. τὸ ἱερὸν τοῦ θεοῦ 73. βιβλίον μου 74. οἱ δοῦλοι οἱ πονηροί 75. ἡ φωνὴ τῆς ἐξουσίας 76. οἱ ἀδελφοὶ ἀπὸ τῆς Ἰερουσαλήμ 77. ὁ κόσμος τῶν δαιμονίων 78. ὁ ἄγγελος ὁ πιστός 79. τὰ τυφλὰ παιδία

80. ὁ νόμος ὁ κακός 81. αἱ χαραὶ τῆς δικαιοσύνης 82. οἱ καλοὶ λόγοι 83. ὁ λαὸς τοῦ Ἀβραάμ 84. ὁ Πέτρος καὶ ὁ Ἰωάννης 85. ἐν τῷ συναγωγῇ 86. ἡ ἀγάπη τῆς ἁμαρτίας 87. αἱ δόξαι τῆς ἐκκλησίας 88. ὁ ἄρτος αὐτῶν 89. οἱ ὄχλοι ἐκ τοῦ οἴκου 90. τὸ πρόσωπον τοῦ Ἰησοῦ

Translate into Greek
91. The holy man 92. The holy men 93. The holy day 94. The holy days 95. The only God 96. The dead child 97. His words 98. Their words 99. Child of the synagogue 100. The work of demons

Fill in the gaps
Contraction of vowels
101. α + ε becomes ____
102. α + ω becomes ____
103. ε + ε becomes ____
104. α + ει becomes ____
105. α + ου becomes ____
106. ε + ω becomes ____
107. α + ο becomes ____
108. ε + ει becomes ____
109. α + η becomes ____

Prepositions
110. ἐπί + ____ = upon, near, before, over, on the basis of, in the time of
111. ____ + genitive = from, out of, away from
112. σύν + dative = ____
113. πρός + genitive = to the advantage of [see note 3 concerning πρός + gen. in notes on Vocabulary 9]
114. κατά + ____ = according to

115. ἐπί + _____ = at, by, on
116. ἀπό + _____ = from
117. πρός + _____ = toward, with, against
118. ἐπι + _____ = across, to, against
119. κατα + _____ = down, against
120. πρός + dative = near, at, by [see note 3 concerning πρός + dat. in notes on Vocabulary 9]
121. ἐν + _____ = in
122. εἰς + _____ = into, towards

Write the full declension of:
123. λόγος 124. κύριος 125. ἔργον 126. βιβλίον 127. ἀρχή 128. φωνή 129. χαρά 130. τυφλός, -η, -ον 131. ὁ, ἡ, το 132. αὐτός, -ή, -ό

Write out the paradigm for the present indicative active of:
133. ἀπολύω 134. καλέω 135. ἀγαπάω 136. δέχομαι

Correct the following sentences
The following sentences and phrases have *at least one error. Correct them, and give the English translation of the corrected sentence.*
137. ἡ ἀγαθὸς ἡμέρα. 138. οἱ ἀπόστολοι ἔρχεται πρὸς τὸν Ἰησοῦν. 139. Πέτρος εὑρίσκει αὐτοὺς ἐν τὸν οἶκον. 140. ἐγὼ ἀκούω τὸν Πέτρον. 141. θεός ἐστιν ἀγάπην. 142. Δαυὶδ λαμβάνεις ἄρτον ἐκ τὸν ἱερόν. 143. δαιμόνια οὐκ ἐσθίουσιν τὸν ἄρτον. 144. ἐγὼ προσκυνεῖ θεόν. 145. φοβόμεθα οὐκ ἄνθρωπος.

Translate into Idiomatic English
146. καλοῦμεν ἐπὶ τοῦ κυρίου. 147. γινώσκω ὅτι ὁ θεός ἐστιν ἀγαθὸς ἀλλὰ ἄνθρωπός ἐστιν πονηρός. 148. πονηροί ἄνθρωποι ἐκβάλλουσιν τὸν Πέτρον καὶ τὸν Ἰωάννην ἐκ τῆς συναγωγῆς ὅτι αὐτοὶ πιστεύουσιν ὅτι ὁ Ἰησοῦς ἐστιν ὁ Χριστός. 149. ὁ Ἰησοῦς λέγει, Εἰμὶ ὁ υἱὸς τοῦ ἀνθρώπου. εἰ πιστεύεις εἰς τὸν υἱὸν τοῦ ἀνθρώπου ἔχεις ζωῆν εἰς τὸν αἰώνιον. 150. ἁμαρτία γεννᾷ θάνατον, ἀλλὰ δικαιοσύνη γεννᾷ ζωήν.

Translate into Greek
151. Angels lead righteous men. 152. Jesus calls the dead to life. 153. Do only good men keep the law of God?

[In the exercises leading up to this chapter, there have been many sentences for you to translate. It would be good revision to go over these again before you move on. You may well be pleased to find how easy they are now.]

* * * * *

Part 1

Were you wondering when you might be able to read some of the Greek New Testament? You will begin to be able to read some sentences immediately after learning one more thing (aorists in Chap. 12), and by Chapter 20 you will have learnt the absolute minimum you will need to get started with longer passages. After that it will be a matter of filling in gaps in your grammar and vocabulary.

Well then, let's think about aorists …

Part 2

The aorist tense, third declension nouns, the infinitive and subjunctive moods, and beginning to translate sentences from the Greek NT

[1]Note to teachers on Chapter 12: Reasons for covering the strong aorist before the imperfect are given in the teacher's manual. If you wish, you may still teach imperfects before aorists. The first part of Chapter 22 (Imperfects) has been designed so that it does not use any vocabulary that a student has not met before chapter 11. Thus, if you so desire, you may go straight to Chapter 22, do Exercise 22.1, then returning to this chapter and do Exercise 12.1 & 12.2, and finally do Exercise 22.2, numbers 1 to 27.

Reasons for doing the strong aorist before the weak aorist are also given in the teacher's manual. It is still possible to do the weak aorist first by doing 12.2 before 12.1. If this is done, class assignments from Exercise 12.2 should be set from numbers 1-22, 34-48, 57-70, 74-81, 83-91.

Chapter 12: The Aorist Indicative Active

Overview of Greek Tenses in the Indicative Mood

Two metaphors can be used to describe the approach to learning New Testament Greek adopted by this book. The first is: "Divide and conquer." Applying this principle to learning New Testament Greek, one might say although the overall task is great, if it is divided up into smaller parts, each part can easily be mastered. As a consequence of this insight, you have yet to be given the bigger picture, on the quite reasonable grounds that the bigger picture is a bit overwhelming at first. The second metaphor is this: "A long journey is completed a step at a time." Once again, one achieves the overall objective by concentrating only on the task immediately in the foreground. But sometimes it is good to look up to see where the total journey is taking us. So here is a brief overview of the tense system of the verb in NT Greek, at least as they are used in the indicative mood.

The following table gives a summary overview of the six tenses as they are used in New Testament Greek. It provides the name of the tense, the form it takes in the first person singular of λύω, the closest English tense, and the usual translation of the tense.

\multicolumn{4}{c	}{**Uses of Tenses in the Indicative Verb Active Voice**}
Tense	Form of λύω	Closest English Tense(s)	Normal Translation
Present	λύω	Simple pres act Pres continuous act Pres emphatic act	I loose I am loosing I do loose
Imperfect	ἔλυον	Past continuous act Past inceptive	I was loosing I began loosing
Future	λύσω	Future active	I shall loose
Aorist	ἔλυσα	Simple past active	I loosed
Perfect	λέλυκα	Perfect active	I have loosed
Pluperfect	ἐλελύκειν	Pluperfect active	I had loosed

Uses of Tenses in the Indicative Verb Passive Voice			
Tense	Form of λύω	Closest English Tense(s)	Normal Translation
Present	λύομαι	Simple pres pass Continuous pres pass	I am loosed I am being loosed
Imperfect	ἐλυόμην	Past continuous pass Past inceptive passive	I was being loosed I began to be loosed
Future	λυθήσομαι	Future passive	I shall be loosed
Aorist	ἐλύθην	Simple past passive	I was loosed
Perfect	λέλυμαι	Perfect passive	I have been loosed
Pluperfect	(ἐ)λέλυμαι	Pluperfect passive	I had been loosed

Attempting to learn all of these tenses at once would be challenging to say the least. So while it has been helpful to take a brief look at the bigger picture, our attention will be now directed to just one of these tenses, the aorist tense.

12.1 The Strong Aorist Indicative Active[1].

New Testament Greek has four past tenses: the aorist, the imperfect, the perfect and the pluperfect. The aorist is used much more often than the imperfect, perfect or pluperfect, and so will be studied first. The differences between the four past tenses will be explained in due course (in Chapters 21, 22 and *Int*.3.2.1, *Int*.3.2.2, *Int*.3.5). For now it is enough to know that the aorist tense corresponds best to the simple past tense in English.

In English an important part of the meaning of tense relates to time: past tenses refer to actions which have taken place in the past, and the simple past tense is no exception. Examples of the English simple past tense may be observed in the vocabularies of this chapter. For example, the English simple past tense of die, throw, see, say, find, eat, take, fall, have, lead and come are: died, threw, saw, said, found, ate, took, fell, had, led, came (Vocab. 12.1). After only a small amount of practice, most English speakers have little difficulty in working out the correct simple past English translation of aorist verbs.

There are two types of aorists. The names for these vary. Some call them first and second aorists, others weak and strong aorists, and yet others more bluntly describe them as regular and irregular aorists. In strong (or second) aorists, the verbs not only get a different kind of ending, they have a different stem from the one they use for the present tense.

Part 2

Most of Vocabulary 12.1 consists of aorists of strong verbs that have already been met. It is worthwhile learning these strong aorists as separate vocabulary items. As with most languages, the irregular verbs tend to be those that are used most, and these aorists are used with great frequency. [At a rough count, of the 45 verbs that have appeared in the vocabulary lists of Part 1 – which include the greater part of the most frequently used verbs in the New Testament – 20 are strong aorists, 7 are middle or passive, and several of the other 18 verbs show irregularities of one kind or other in their aorist tenses.] Because of this, it is perhaps best to start with the strong aorists, which has the added advantage that several complications of weak aorists can be left until Section 12.2, until you have had the opportunity to become familiar with translating the aorist tense.

The paradigm of the strong aorist is as follows:

Strong Aorist Indicative Active of λαμβάνω		
Person	Form of λαμβάνω	English Meaning
1st pers sing	ἔλαβον	I took
2nd pers sing	ἔλαβες	you took
3rd pers sing	ἔλαβεν	he/she/it took
1st pers pl	ἐλάβομεν	we took
2nd pers pl	ἐλάβετε	you took
3rd pers pl	ἔλαβον	they took

[Note: Many textbooks suggest that the third person singular of strong aorists should have a movable ν; this is incorrect for almost all instances of strong aorists in the NT (e.g. ἦλθεν πρὸς τὸν Ἰησοῦν in Mark 10:50); although one can find the rare example of a movable ν, such as ἦλθε τὸ in Acts 19:6.]

For the most part, aorists are not a translation difficulty. They are translated by a simple past tense in English. The meanings given in the vocabulary can generally just be plugged straight into the translation of the Greek sentence. For example:

ὁρῶ τὸ τέκνον	I see the child [present indicative active]
εἶδον τὸ τέκνον	I saw the child [aorist indicative active]
ἔρχομαι εἰς τὸ ἱερόν	I go into the temple [present indicative active]
ἦλθον εἰς τὸ ἱερόν	I went into the temple [aorist indicative active]
ὁ ἄνθρωπος ἀποθνήσκει	The man dies [present indicative active]
ὁ ἄνθρωπος ἀπέθανεν	The man died [aorist indicative active]
αὐτὸς ἐσθίει τὸν ἄρτον	He eats the bread [present indicative active]
αὐτὸς ἔφαγεν τὸν ἄρτον	He ate the bread [aorist indicative active]

Perhaps it is worth noting that not only are the verbs ὁράω, ἔρχομαι, ἀποθνῄσκω and ἐσθίω irregular in Greek, most their English equivalents are also irregular [go/went, see/saw, eat/ate, etc.].

While the first person singular has the same form as the third person plural, it is not normally a problem as the context usually makes the subject of the verb clear. For example, in the sentence ἐγὼ ἔφαγον, "I ate," the verb ἔφαγον is in the first person singular because it has a first person subject. In the sentence δοῦλοι ἔφαγον, "slaves ate," the verb ἔφαγον is in the third person plural because it has a plural subject, and therefore needs to be in the third person.

Vocabulary 12.1

Strong Aorists[1]

ἀπέθανον (45)	I died [aor. of ἀποθνῄσκω]
ἔβαλον (40+18)	I threw, put [aor. of βάλλω]
εἶδον (146)	I saw [aor. of ὁράω]
εἶπον (647+52)	I said [aor. of λέγω]
εὗρον (52+3)	I found [aor. ind. act. of εὑρίσκω]
ἔφαγον (25+3)	I ate [aor. of ἐσθίω]
ἔλαβον (66+29)	I took [aor. of λαμβάνω]
ἔσχον (12+9)	I had [aor. of ἔχω]
ἤγαγον (32+23)	I led [aor. of ἄγω]
ἦλθον[2] (168+288)	I came, went [aor. of ἔρχομαι]

Other words

δύο[3] (136)	two
ἑπτά (87)	seven
ἦν (289)	he/she/it was,[4] there was
Φαρισαῖος (98)	Pharisee

Notes on Vocabulary 12.1

1. **It is hard to overemphasize the importance of thoroughly learning the strong aorists in Vocabulary 12.1.** These need to be learnt in two ways. First, if you were given the present of a verb (e.g. ἐσθίω), you must be able to write down its aorist (ἔφαγον). Second, if given the aorist (e.g. ἔφαγον), you must be able to write down the present (ἐσθίω). This is particularly important because dictionaries do not usually give a separate entry for the aorist of strong verbs. Their present indicative form must be known before they can be found in a dictionary. Furthermore, **if this**

vocabulary is not mastered, many of the things that will be dealt with in later chapters will not make sense. Time spent learning this vocabulary properly is time well invested.

2. Learning the aorist of ἔρχομαι means that the aorist of all of the verbs that are formed by adding a preposition onto it have also been learnt:

   Verb: *Aorist*
   ἀπέρχομαι   (= ἀπό + ἔρχομαι):   ἀπῆλθον
   εἰσέρχομαι   (= εἰς + ἔρχομαι):   εἰσῆλθον
   ἐξέρχομαι   (= ἐκ + ἔρχομαι):   ἐξῆλθον
   προσέρχομαι (= πρός + ἔρχομαι):   προσῆλθον

   This is true of the compounds of other verbs, as well. E.g.: ἐκβάλλω (= ἐκ + βάλλω), aor.: ἐξέβαλον

   This means that the effort of learning the irregular aorists is doubly worthwhile because there are many compounds of these verbs.

3. The form δύο is used for nom., acc., and gen. For dative the form δυσί(ν) is used. There is no difference in form between masc., fem, or neut.

4. ἦν is actually the third person singular imperfect indicative active of εἰμί. This verb does not have aorist forms. In most cases ἦν can be translated by the English word "was." The third person singular of the word is included here because it is so commonly used in the New Testament. Its full paradigm will be given in Chapter 22 [22.5].

5. Reminder: accents on verbs go as far away from the end of the word as is permitted by the general rules of accents. Thus many aorist indicative active forms are proparoxytone (e.g. ἔφαγον, ἔλαβον, ἔσχον, ἤγαγον, etc.). However, in those cases where the aorist form has only two syllables, the rule is that if the second to last syllable is long and the last syllable is short, then the word must be properispomenon (e.g. εἶδον, εἶπον, εὗρον, ἦλθον).

6. Vocabulary 12.1 includes all the verbs occurring in the Greek New Testament over 50 times which have strong aorists formed after the manner of ἔβαλον. Note that the frequencies given are the number of times these verbs are found in the aorist indicative active in the NT. These verbs are also found in compounds (e.g. see note 2), which increases the count for many of the verbs. Thus the frequencies are given with a + to indicate the frequency of compounds of this form in the NT (e.g. ἦλθον (168+288) indicates the aorist indicative active of ἔρχομαι is found 168 times in the NT; and a further 288 times is compounds of ἔρχομαι). The aorist indicative form is also used as the basis for the aorist of other moods.

Exercise 12.1

A. Paradigms
Write out the aorist indicative active of: i. λέγω   ii. ὁράω   iii. ἔρχομαι

B. Translate into English
1. βάλλει 2. ἔβαλεν 3. ἐβάλομεν 4. βάλλομεν 5. ἐβάλετε 6. βάλλετε
7. βάλλεις 8. ἔβαλες 9. εἶδον 10. ὁρῶσιν 11. εἴδετε 12. ὁρᾶτε 13. ἦλθεν
14. ἔρχεται 15. ἔρχομαι 16. ἦλθον 17. ἐφάγετε 18. ἐσθίετε 19. ἐφάγομεν
20. ἐσθίομεν 21. λαμβάνω 22. ἔλαβον 23. ἔλαβες 24. λαμβάνεις
25. ἀπέθανεν 26. ἀποθνῄσκει 27. ἀπέθανον 28. ἀποθνῄσκουσιν

29. ἤγαγεν 30. ἄγει 31. ἠγάγετε 32. ἄγετε 33. ἔσχες 34. ἔχεις 35. ἔσχομεν
36. ἔχομεν 37. εἶπεν 38. λέγει 39. εἴπετε 40. λέγετε 41. ἐκβάλλετε
42. ἐξεβάλετε 43. εἶδες 44. ὁρᾷς 45. προσῆλθεν 46. εἰσῆλθες 47. προσέρχεται
48. ἀπήλθομεν 49. οἱ Φαρισαῖοι ἔσχον τοὺς νόμους αὐτῶν. 50. οἱ Φαρισαῖοι ἔχουσι τοὺς νόμους αὐτῶν. 51. ὁ Ἀβραὰμ εἶδεν τὸν θεόν.

52. ὁ Ἀβραὰμ ὁρᾷ τὸν θεόν. 53. ἐγὼ εἶδον τὸν κύριον. 54. ἐγὼ ὁρῶ τὸν κύριον. 55. τὰ δύο τέκνα λαμβάνει ἄρτον. 56. τὰ δύο τέκνα ἔλαβεν ἄρτον. 57. τὰ ἑπτὰ τέκνα ἔφαγεν ἄρτον. 58. τὰ δύο τέκνα ἐσθίει ἄρτον.

C. Translate into Greek
59. We eat 60. We ate 61. We saw 62. We see 63. They died 64. He said
65. He says 66. You (pl.) fell

D. Sentences and Phrases from the Greek New Testament
Note: This is the first time that there have been actual sentences from the Greek New Testament to read. Answers to odd-numbered exercise are provided, as are the text references, so you can also check your translation against an English Version of the Bible. You may wish to choose a fairly literal translation of the Bible to do this, such as the RSV. Translators for published English versions of the Bible exercise more freedom in their translation than most beginning students are comfortable with. *Intermediate New Testament Greek Made Easier* will give the reasons for many of the differences from what you might expect at this stage of your learning. Still, there are a good number of texts in the New Testament which show that translation is an art, not a science.

To read the New Testament is to move beyond the carefully managed vocabulary which has so far been used. At this stage the goal is to learn all words that occur more than 50 times in the Greek New Testament, so such words that occur in the set passages will be included in the vocabulary lists. Words that occur fewer than 50 times will be listed at the end of the exercise, their meanings given, together with their frequency of occurrence. You may judge for yourself which of these you would like to remember. Of course, many students will not learn words that are not specifically listed in the vocabularies, and this book has been designed on that assumption. From

Part 2 107

time to time, a grammatical form or a point of syntax will be met that has not yet been covered in the textbook. These will either be explained in an accompanying note or after the text in the exercise.

Now let us use all that grammar we have been learning, and begin translating from the Greek New Testament ...
67. εἶπεν αὐτοῖς ὁ Ἰησοῦς, Ἐγώ εἰμι ὁ ἄρτος τῆς ζωῆς. **68.** εἶδεν ἄνθρωπον τυφλὸν ἐκ γενετῆς.[1] **69.** Ἐν ἀρχῇ ἦν ὁ λόγος, καὶ ὁ λόγος ἦν πρὸς τὸν θεόν, καὶ θεὸς ἦν ὁ λόγος. οὗτος[2] ἦν ἐν ἀρχῇ πρὸς τὸν θεόν... ἐν αὐτῷ ζωὴ ἦν, καὶ ἡ ζωὴ ἦν τὸ φως[3] τῶν ἀνθρώπων. **70.** Ἄγουσιν αὐτὸν πρὸς τοὺς Φαρισαίους τόν[4] ποτε[5] τυφλόν. **71.** Ἰωάννης ταῖς ἑπτὰ ἐκκλησίαις ταῖς ἐν τῇ Ἀσίᾳ[6] ...
72. Ἐγώ εἰμι τὸ Ἄλφα[7] καὶ τὸ Ὦ, λέγει κύριος ὁ θεός. **73.** These things εἶπεν ἐν συναγωγῇ ... ἐν Καφαρναούμ.[8]

Vocabulary helps for questions 71-77 (above)

1. (qu. 68) γενετή, ῆς (1) birth. Words like this, which are only used once in the Greek New Testament, are called *hapax legomena*. At this stage, no effort to learn this kind of word need be made. In this case, though, its meaning might have been able to be deduced from the context, and from the verb γεννάω [from Vocab. 8].
2. (qu. 69) οὗτος, αὕτη, τοῦτο (1338) this. The word οὗτος is used a great deal, and will be met officially in the next chapter. Here it has the same function as αὐτός, "he," though it is a bit stronger than αὐτός would have been. In this context it literally means "this man," but should be translated as "he."
3. (qu. 69) φῶς, φωτός, το (73) light. This is a neuter third declension noun. From the article το it may be seen that it is in the nominative (or accusative) case. Third declension nouns will be met in Chapter 14.
4. (qu. 70) In this sentence and the next a Greek idiom that is quite different from English will be met for the first time. In Greek the article carries the gender and number of the noun with which it is associated, and so sometimes it is used instead of a pronoun, as here. Translate the τόν as "the one who ..."
5. (qu. 70) ποτέ (29) once, formerly [the word is enclitic; i.e. it throws it accent back on the previous word if possible; see *Int*.7.3]
6. (qu. 71) Ἀσία (18) Asia
7. (qu. 72) You probably recognized Ἄλφα (3) as "Alpha," the name of the letter α.
8. (qu. 73) Καφαρναούμ (16) Capernaum

12.2 The Weak Aorist Indicative Active

12.2.1 The Aorist Indicative Active of λύω
The weak aorist is also called the first aorist. The pattern for the weak aorist is as follows:

Weak Aorist Indicative Active of λύω		
Person	Form of λύω	English Meaning
1st pers sing	ἔλυσα	I loosed
2nd pers sing	ἔλυσας	you loosed
3rd pers sing	ἔλυσεν	he/she/it loosed
1st pers pl	ἐλύσαμεν	we loosed
2nd pers pl	ἐλύσατε	you loosed
3rd pers pl	ἔλυσαν	they loosed

[Note: Many textbooks suggest that the third person singular of weak aorists should have a movable ν; this is incorrect for almost all instances of weak aorists in the NT (e.g. ὁ Χριστὸς ἠγάπησεν τὴν ἐκκλησίαν in Eph 5:25); although one can find the rare example of a movable ν, such as ἔδοξε κἀμοὶ in Luke 1:3.]

The weak aorist [indicative active] uses the same verb stem as the present [indicative active]. There is one important difference from the way the present tense is formed. Not only do the endings change, the verb gets an ε in front of it. This is called the augment. Thus there are two parts to the formation of the weak aorist: the augment and the endings:

ἐ-λυ-σα
ἐ-λυ-σας
ἐ-λυ-σεν
ἐ-λυ-σαμεν
ἐ-λυ-σατε
ἐ-λυ-σαν

12.2.2 Verbs with Stems that End in a Consonant
Because all the endings begin with a σ, some of the changes that occur in the endings with certain verbs are generally predictable. Saying a consonant followed by an "s"-sound causes natural changes. Try saying -κσ- or -χσ- quickly, and you will see what is meant. The consonants have been subdivided into several subgroups, depending on which part of the mouth forms them. When the gutturals (γ, κ, χ), the labials (β, π, φ), and the dentals (δ, τ, θ) combine with an "s"-sound, these consonants show a consistent set of changes, as follows:

Consonant combination	Result
guttural (γ, κ, χ) + σ	ξ
labial (β, π, φ) + σ	ψ
dental (δ, τ, θ) + σ	σ

Many of the stems of verbs that have already been met end with one of these consonants. The above rules work consistently, so a separate vocabulary item is not needed for weak aorists. They may be worked out. Of course, in actual translation, the process is reversed – you have to be able to look at the word and see what it might have been in the present tense before an s-sound was added to the verb stem.

The following table gives some examples of the aorists of verbs with consonant endings:

	Present		Aorist	
I see	βλέπω	I saw	ἔβλεψα	π+σ=ψ
I write	γράφω	I wrote	ἔγραψα	φ+σ=ψ
I send	πέμπω	I sent	ἔπεμψα	π+σ=ψ
I glorify	δοξάζω	I glorified	ἐδόξασα	dz+σ=σ
I save	σῴζω	I saved	ἔσωσα	dz+σ=σ
I persuade	πείθω	I persuaded	ἔπεισα	θ+σ=σ

[Note: While it is necessary to memorize strong aorist forms, two different approaches to learning weak aorist forms are possible. Many will find that knowing the rules which determine how gutturals, labials and dentals interact with sigma is sufficient. For them, just knowing the aorist of λύω and the rules of contraction enable the verbal forms to be recognized and remembered. Others though, may prefer to make separate vocabulary cards for each of these forms.]

12.2.3 Verbs with Stems that End in the Vowels α or ε

The σ of the endings also affects **contracted verbs** (i.e. -εω and -αω verbs). Verbs with stems that end in either ε or α tend to replace these with an η. In other words, both -εω and -αω become -ησα. For example:

	Present		Aorist
I ask	αἰτέω	I asked	ᾔτησα
I love	ἀγαπάω	I loved	ἠγάπησα
I beget	γεννάω	I begat	ἐγέννησα
I ask	ἐρωτάω	I asked	ἠρώτησα
I speak	λαλέω	I spoke	ἐλάλησα
I do	ποιέω	I did	ἐποίησα
I bear witness	μαρτυρέω	I bore witness	ἐμαρτύρησα

There are only a few exceptions to this (e.g. the aorist of καλέω is ἐκάλεσα, that of δοκέω is ἔδοξα), and those that occur do not usually cause a problem when translating from Greek into English.

[Note there are 7 instances of the aorist indicative active of δοκέω in the NT, and they all follow the pattern of ἔδοξα – as though the verb was δόκω rather than δοκέω, and despite the fact that the verb shows the normal contractions of an -εω verb in the pres. ind. act. On the other hand, the compound verb εὐδοκέω (I am well pleased, take delight), which is found 21 times in the NT, 16 of which are aor. ind. act., follows the pattern εὐδόκησα in the aor. ind. act., as might be expected of an -εω verb.]

12.2.4 Verbs with Stems that Begin with a Vowel

Another thing that may be noticed from the examples given above, is that further changes occur when the verb starts with a vowel (see αἰτέω, ἀγαπάω, ἐρωτάω in 12.2.3). This makes sense, because in the weak aorist, the verb stem not only takes different endings, it receives an ε at the front. When the verb begins with a vowel already, some change has to take place to indicate the aorist tense. Notice that this is not a contraction caused by the combining of two vowels. It is actually a lengthening of the initial vowel: α and ε become an η, while an ο becomes an ω. An ι can become a subscript, though there is no regular pattern in this.

12.2.5 Compound Verbs

Some of the verbs that have already been met in vocabulary lists are actually compounds of a preposition plus another verb (e.g. ἀπολύω = ἀπό + λύω). The aorists of these verbs are formed as though the aorist of the verb was formed first, and the preposition was tacked on afterwards. Thus the aorist of ἀπολύω is ἀπέλυσα: the aorist of the verb is formed first (ἔλυσα), and the preposition is then tacked on. The ο of ἀπο disappears, although that should not be a surprise, as the same phenomenon has been met already with verbs such as ἀπέρχομαι (= ἀπό + ἔρχομαι).

12.2.6 Translating the Weak Aorist

The translation of the weak aorist is no different from that of the strong aorist. It corresponds best with the English past tense, and your knowledge of English should provide the appropriate English past tense without any real problems:

ἀγαπῶ τὸν ἀδελφόν μου	I love my brother
ἠγάπησα τὸν ἀδελφόν μου	I loved my brother
ὁ Ἰησοῦς λαλεῖ	Jesus speaks
ὁ Ἰησοῦς ἐλάλησεν	Jesus spoke
ὁ Ἰωάννης ἀπολύει τὸν ὄχλον	John dismisses the crowd
ὁ Ἰωάννης ἀπέλυσεν τὸν ὄχλον	John dismissed the crowd

Part 2

A word of encouragement
There seem to be a lot of new things happening with the weak aorists. Take heart, while they can be confusing for a start, they begin to make sense after some practice. Exercise 12.2 is a long one because it is designed to build up more confidence with weak aorists.

Vocabulary 12.2

ἀμήν (126)	so let it be, truly, amen
βασιλεία (162)	kingdom[1]
βλέπω (132)	I see
γάρ[2] (1036)	for; certainly, so, then
δέ (2271)	but, and[3]
ἔτι (92)	still, yet [οὐκ ἔτι = no longer]
ἠθέλησα (18)	I wished, wanted [aor. ind. act. of θέλω; note irregular augment]
θάλασσα (91)	sea
ἴδιος (113)	his/her/its own, private
ὁδός, ἡ[4] (101)	way, road, path
οὐρανός (272)	heaven [note: this word is normally found in the plural in the NT]
πείθω (52)	I convince, persuade; depend on, trust in
πέμπω (79)	I send
πρῶτον (60)	adv. first[5]
πρῶτος, -η, -ον (92)	first [cf. the English word "prototype"]
σάββατον (68)	Sabbath[6]
σύ (1057)	you (sing. nom)
σῴζω (106)	I save, heal (aor. ἔσωσα)
ὑμεῖς (1830)	you (nom. pl. of σύ; acc. pl. ὑμᾶς; dat. pl. ὑμῖν)
ὑμῶν (489+)	your (gen. pl. of σύ)

Notes on Vocabulary 12.2

1. The third declension masculine noun βασιλεύς, which will be met in Vocabulary 28, means "king."
2. One of the features of γάρ is that it is never found first in a sentence. It is always the second word. This is true also of δέ in this vocabulary. γάρ should usually be translated "for" and placed as the first word in the sentence of an English translation.
3. δέ is frequently used in the Greek New Testament. Its meaning is about half way between ἀλλά and καί. In other words, usually it can be translated as "but," but often it would be best translated as "and." In practice this is not

as confusing as it sounds. Like γάρ, δέ never occurs as the first word of a sentence, always the second. Conjunctions like γάρ and δέ which do not occur as the first word in a sentence are called "postpositive conjunctions."
4. ὁδός declines in the pattern of λόγος (the second declension), even though it is feminine. In his book, *Complete Vocabulary Guide to the Greek New Testament* rev. ed. (Grand Rapids, MI: Zondervan, 1998), 295-96, Warren Trenchard lists 33 second declension feminine words that occur in the NT which decline like λόγος [cf. Metzger, *Lexical Aids*, pp. 91-93], and 15 more that follow this pattern but are sometimes masculine and sometimes feminine. Of the second declension feminine words, ὁδός is the only one that occurs more than 50 times in the Greek NT. With the exceptions of βίβλος (10; book, sacred book, record), ἔρημος (34; desert, wilderness), νόσος (11; disease, illness) and ῥάβδος (12; staff, rod), all the rest occur less than ten times each (most only in one or two occurrences). There are some words that follow this pattern which are sometimes feminine and sometimes masculine. The common ones [διάκονος (29; servant, deacon); θεός (1314); παρθένος (15; virgin)] present no problem, and the rest occur only rarely. So, while there are exceptions [including some you will meet in 14.2.1], nouns which end in -ος are usually second declension masculine nouns.
5. πρῶτον is an adverb, while πρῶτος is an adjective. Adverbs qualify verbs, while adjectives qualify nouns. This will make sense as you come to translate these, so don't worry too much about this distinction at the moment. By the way, adverbs do not decline.
6. σάββατον is generally found in the plural, and sometimes needs to be translated with a singular "Sabbath" in English.

Exercise 12.2

A. Paradigms: Write in full the aorist indicative active of
i. βλέπω   ii. λαλέω   iii. πείθω   iv. γεννάω

B. Translate into English
1. πέμπει 2. ἔπεμψα 3. ἐπέμψαμεν 4. ἀπολύουσιν 5. ἀπελύσατε 6. γεννᾷς 7. ἐγέννησας 8. ἐγεννήσατε 9. ἐγράψατε 10. ἐγράψαμεν 11. γράφετε 12. λαλοῦμεν 13. ἐλάλησαν 14. ἐλάλησεν 15. ἔσωσα 16. σῴζεις 17. ἔσωσαν 18. ποιεῖτε 19. ἐποιήσαμεν 20. ἔβλεψα 21. ἐδόξασεν 22. ἐμαρτύρησας 23. ἤγαγεν 24. ἠγάπησα 25. ἠρώτησας 26. πείθομεν 27. εἴδομεν 28. ἔπεισα 29. ἐπείσατε 30. βάλλεις 31. ᾔτησεν 32. ἀπεθάνετε 33. ἐβάλομεν 34. ἐπείσαμεν 35. λέγετε 36. ᾔτησαν 37. ᾐτήσαμεν 38. ἔπεισας 39. ἐλαλήσαμεν 40. περιπατοῦμεν 41. ἐσώσατε 42. ἐποίησα 43. ἐκάλεσεν

Part 2 113

44. ἐγέννησα 45. ἐδοξάσατε 46. πείθεις 47. ἔβλεψαν 48. ἠρώτησεν
49. ἔσχετε 50. σῴζει 51. ἐμαρτύρησας 52. ἐγράψατε 53. ἠγάγετε
54. ἠγάπησας 55. ἐλαλήσαμεν 56. ἐκαλέσατε

C. Translate into Greek
57. We love 58. We loved 59. I write 60. I wrote 61. We threw 62. We throw 63. They wrote 64. She bore witness

D. Translate into English
65. ὁ Ἰησοῦς ἔσωσεν ὑμᾶς. 66. ὁ Ἰησοῦς σῴζει ὑμᾶς. 67. ὁ Ἰησοῦς ἔσωσεν αὐτούς. 68. οἱ οὐρανοὶ λέγουσι τῆς δόξης τοῦ θεοῦ. 69. οἱ οὐρανοὶ λέγουσι ἔτι τῆς δόξης τοῦ θεοῦ. 70. ὁ κύριος ἔπεμψεν τοὺς ἀποστόλους αὐτοῦ εἰς τὸν κόσμον. 71. ἡ βασιλεία ἦλθεν ἐν τῷ Ἰησοῦ; 72. Δαυὶδ ἔγραψεν ὅτι τὸ σάββατόν ἐστιν ἁγία ἡμέρα. 73. ὁ Ἰησοῦς εἰς τὸν ἴδιον ἦλθεν.

74. ἐγὼ βλέπω τὸ πλοῖον ἐπὶ τῆς θαλάσσης. 75. ἐγὼ ἔβλεψα τὸ πλοῖον ἐπὶ τῆς θαλάσσης. 76. αὐτὴ βλέπει τὸ πλοῖον ἐπὶ τῆς θαλάσσης. 77. αὐτὴ ἔβλεψε τὸ πλοῖον ἐπὶ τῆς θαλάσσης. 78. ὑμεῖς βλέπετε τὸ πλοῖον ἐπὶ τῆς θαλάσσης. 79. ὑμεῖς ἐβλέψατε τὸ πλοῖον ἐπὶ τῆς θαλάσσης. 80. ὑμεῖς ὁρᾶτε τὸ πλοῖον ὑμῶν ἐπὶ τῆς θαλάσσης. 81. ἀμὴν ἀμὴν λέγω ὑμῖν ὅτι ἐγώ εἰμι ὁ Χριστός.

82. ὁ υἱὸς τοῦ ἀνθρώπου ἦλθεν ἐκ τῶν οὐρανῶν. 83. ὁ Ἀβραὰμ περιεπάτησεν ἐπὶ τῆς ὁδοῦ τῆς δικαιοσύνης. 84. τηροῦμεν τὸν νόμον τοῦ κυρίου καὶ περιπατοῦμεν ἐπὶ ὁδῶν τῆς χαρᾶς. 85. ὁ Δαυὶδ ἔγραψεν νόμους καὶ ἐντολάς. 86. σὺ ἔσωσας; 87. ὑμεῖς ἐσώσατε; 88. ὁ Ἀβραὰμ ἤκουσεν τὴν φωνὴν τοῦ θεοῦ. 89. οἱ Φαρισαῖοι ᾔτησαν τὸν Ἰησοῦν. 90. ὁ Ἰησοῦς ἠγάπησεν πρῶτον ὑμᾶς. 91. ὁ Πέτρος ἦν ὁ πρῶτος τῶν ἀποστόλων;

E. Translate into Greek
92. Do you see Jesus? 93. Did you see Jesus? 94. The slave loved his brother.
95. The Christ came from heaven.

F. Sentences and Phrases from the Greek New Testament
96. λέγει αὐτοῖς ὁ Ἰησοῦς, Ἀμὴν λέγω ὑμῖν ὅτι οἱ τελῶναι[1] καὶ αἱ πόρναι[2] προάγουσιν[3] ὑμᾶς εἰς τὴν βασιλείαν τοῦ θεοῦ. ἦλθεν γὰρ Ἰωάννης πρὸς ὑμᾶς ἐν ὁδῷ δικαιοσύνης, καὶ οὐκ ἐπιστεύσατε αὐτῷ, οἱ δὲ τελῶναι καὶ αἱ πόρναι ἐπίστευσαν αὐτῷ ... 97. εἰς τὰ ἴδια ἦλθεν, καὶ οἱ ἴδιοι αὐτὸν οὐ παρέλαβον.[4]

98. Καὶ εἶδον οὐρανὸν καινὸν[5] καὶ γῆν καινήν. ὁ γὰρ πρῶτος οὐρανὸς καὶ ἡ πρώτη γῆ ἀπῆλθαν[6] καὶ ἡ θάλασσα οὐκ ἔστιν ἔτι. 99. ἦν δὲ σάββατον ἐν τῇ[7] ἡμέρᾳ τὸν πηλὸν[8] ἐποίησεν ὁ Ἰησοῦς 100. εὑρίσκει οὗτος[9] πρῶτον τὸν ἀδελφὸν τὸν ἴδιον Σίμωνα[10] καί λέγει αὐτῷ "We have found the Messiah (which is interpreted the Christ). ἤγαγεν αὐτὸν πρὸς τὸν Ἰησοῦν. ἐμβλέψας[11] αὐτῷ ὁ Ἰησοῦς εἶπεν, Σὺ εἶ Σίμων ὁ υἱὸς Ἰωάννου, σὺ will be called Cephas (which is interpreted Peter).

Vocabulary help for questions 96-100 (above)

1. (qu. 96)τελώνης, ὁ (21) tax-collector, revenue officer. Note: even though this is a first declension masculine noun of a type that will not be met until Vocabulary 20.2.2 and Appendix E, its case can be recognized by looking at the article. As the article is nominative masculine plural, the noun must be nominative masculine plural. 2. (qu. 96)πόρνη (12) prostitute 3. (qu. 96)προάγω (20) I lead forward, lead or bring out; go before, lead the way 4. (qu. 97)παραλαμβάνω (49) receive, accept 5. (qu. 98)καινός, -ή, -όν (42) new 6. (qu. 98)ἀπῆλθαν is a mixed up form (from the compound verb, ἀπέρχομαι = ἀπο + ἔρχομαι). The verb should use the strong aorist, and in fact uses the strong aorist stem. The ending, however, is that of the third person weak aorist. This is done occasionally in the New Testament, and causes no translation problems. 7. (qu. 99)This is a slight change from the New Testament, which has a relative pronoun here. Relative pronouns will be met in Chapter 18. 8. (qu. 99)πηλός (6) clay 9. (qu. 100)οὗτος, literally, "this man." Translate with the word "he." 10. (qu. 100)Σίμωνα is the accusative singular of the third declension Σίμων, Simon. 11. (qu. 100)ἐμβλέπω (11) look at, fix one's gaze upon; ἐμβλέψας is an aorist participle. It may be translated "when [Jesus] saw." Participles will be met in Chapter 20.

A Gentle Exhortation and a Suggestion

The number of different verb paradigms is increasing. The temptation is to concentrate only on the paradigm or declension for the current exercise, and forget previous patterns. This is likely to be a mistake. One of the greatest challenges in translating from Greek into English is to recognize the tense, mood, voice, etc. of verbs. Learning the verb paradigm is perhaps the most important part of learning Greek, and real effort needs to be put into mastering it.

One suggestion that may be helpful is that the paradigm is easier to remember if recited aloud from memory. If this is done several times each day, it quickly becomes second nature and need not take much time. Another good idea is to regularly practice writing out all the paradigms and declensions on a piece of scrap paper. Tests and exams in New Testament Greek classes almost always ask for paradigms or declensions, because most teachers are convinced of the importance of this knowledge and wish to make sure that students know these patterns.

12.3.1 The Aorist Indicative Active of -μι Verbs

So far the -μι verbs have been avoided. This is because they show considerable irregularities in their present tenses. In their aorist tenses, though, they are reasonably regular. These verbs are frequently used, and so it is a good idea to meet their easier tenses as early as possible.

The aorists of -μι verbs can be divided into those that use the same endings as weak aorist indicatives [-σα, -σας, -σεν, -σαμεν, -σατε, -σαν], and those that almost use the endings of weak aorist indicatives, but without the initial sigma [i.e. -α, -ας, -εν, -αμεν, -ατε, -αν]. The -μι verbs which use the endings of the weak aorist indicatives are:

ἀπώλεσα	I destroyed	(aorist of ἀπόλλυμι	I ruin, destroy)
ἔδειξα	I showed	(aorist of δείκνυμι	I show)
ἔστησα	I placed	(weak aorist of ἵστημι	I stand, place)

[The verb ἵστημι also has a strong aorist; cf. *Int*.6.14 and appendix D.]

The -μι verbs which use the endings of the weak aorist indicatives without the sigma are:

ἀφῆκα	I forgave	(aorist of ἀφίημι	I forgive)

[The aorist of the verb ἀφίημι has irregular plural forms in classical Greek. The aorist plural of this verb is not found in the Greek New Testament.]

ἔδωκα	I gave	(aorist of δίδωμι	I give)
ἔθηκα	I placed	(aorist of τίθημι	I place)

These "relatively regular" aorists are lacking a σ in their endings, but otherwise use the regular endings of the weak aorist. For example, the aorist of δίδωμι is as follows:

Aorist of δίδωμι	
1st pers sing	ἔδωκα
2nd pers sing	ἔδωκας
3rd pers sing	ἔδωκεν
1st pers pl	ἐδώκαμεν
2nd pers pl	ἐδώκατε
3rd pers pl	ἔδωκαν

12.3.2 The Aorist Indicative Active of Some Other Verbs

There are several common verbs whose aorists show irregularities of one sort or another, and some of these are gathered together here. For example, the two verbs ἀποστέλλω and φέρω use the endings for the weak (regular) aorist, even though the verb stem they use for the aorist shows a large difference from the verb stem they use for the present. These are two examples of so-called "liquid verbs" (verbs which have a stem that ends in λ or ρ). Liquid verbs have many irregularities (cf. *Int*.6.15).

ἀπέστειλα   I sent   (aorist of ἀποστέλλω)
ἤνεγκα   I bore, carried (aorist of φέρω, I bear, carry)

Like ἔδωκα, their aorists do not finish with a σ, but they do use the rest of the endings from the regular aorist tense. Thus, the aorist indicative active of these verbs are:

	Aor of ἀποστέλλω	Aor of φέρω
1st pers sing	ἀπέστειλα	ἤνεγκα
2nd pers sing	ἀπέστειλας	ἤνεγκας
3rd pers sing	ἀπέστειλεν	ἤνεγκεν
1st pers pl	ἀπεστείλαμεν	ἠνέγκαμεν
2nd pers pl	ἀπεστείλατε	ἠνέγκατε
3rd pers pl	ἀπέστειλαν	ἤνεγκαν

The aorists of middle and passive verbs will be met at 28.3, although the aorist of ἀποκρίνομαι is so common it should be met now: ἀπεκρίθη (he/she/it answered) is its third person singular. Likewise, the form ἐγένετο, "he/she/it became," is found 195 times in the New Testament, and as it is also used so often it needs to be learnt now: ἐγένετο is the 3rd pers. sing. strong. aor. ind. middle passive of γίνομαι. This word is used highly idiomatically in the Greek New Testament. It has the basic meaning of "become," but at times is best translated as "happen," "appear," or "be." Καὶ ἐγένετο is often best translated "And it came to pass." Initially γίνομαι is hard for beginners to translate, but after a while it ceases to be a problem.

Not an aorist, but also worth meeting now, ἔλεγε(ν) is used 71 times, and is the imperfect indicative active of λέγω. ἔλεγε(ν) may be translated as "he/she/it said"; in other words, it may be treated as a synonym of εἶπε(ν) [cf. *Int*.3.5.1.7].

Vocabulary 12.3

–μι verbs

ἀπόλλυμι (90)   I ruin, destroy. In middle voice: perish, die
ἀφίημι (142[+36])   I forgive, cancel, remit (of sin or debts), leave, allow, divorce
δείκνυμι (32+34)   I show, point out
δίδωμι (415+534)   I give
τίθημι (101+258)   I place
ἵστημι (152+325)   I place, set, put; stand; stop

Part 2

Aorist indicative active of –μι verbs

ἀπώλεσα (6)   I destroyed [aor. of ἀπόλλυμι]
ἀφῆκα (28[+9])   I forgave, etc. [aor. of ἀφίημι]
ἔδειξα (106)   I showed [aor. of δείκνυμι]
ἔδωκα (84+41)   I gave [aor. of δίδωμι]
ἔθηκα (23+26)   I placed [aor. of τίθημι]
ἔστησα (25+65)   I placed [wk. aor. of ἵστημι]

Other verbs

ἀπέστειλα (61)   I sent [aor. of ἀποστέλλω]
ἀπεκρίθη (82)   He/she/it answered [3rd pers. sing. aor. ind. pass. of ἀποκρίνομαι, I answer]
ἐγένετο (195)   He/she/it became, appeared, happened; often used impersonally: it happened, it came to pass that [3rd pers. sing. str. aor. ind. mid. of γίνομαι, I become]
ἔλεγεν (71)   He/she/it said [3rd pers. sing. imperfect ind. act. of λέγω, I say] [Note: the form ἔλεγε is not found in NT]
ἔπεσα[1] (42+31)   I fell [aor. of πίπτω]
ἤνεγκα (23+11)   I carried, bore [aor. of φέρω]
παραδίδωμι[2] (120)   I deliver, entrust, commit, pass on [παρά + δίδωμι]
εἶπαν[3] (94)   They said: 3rd pers sing aor ind act of λέγω.

Other words

ἄλλος, -η, -ο (155)   other, another
Γαλιλαία (61)   Galilee
δώδεκα (75)   twelve
καρπός (66)   fruit
μέσος, -η, -ον (56)   middle, in the middle
ὅτε[4] (102)   **when**, while, as long as
οὕτως (208)   adv.: thus, so, in this way
πάλιν (139)   adv. again, once more
παραβολή (50)   parable
τότε (159)   then

Notes on Vocabulary 12.3

1. πίπτω uses weak aorist endings for the indicative mood, but strong aorist endings for other moods.
2. παραδίδωμι = παρά + δίδωμι
3. εἶπαν is a varient of εἶπον that uses a weak aorist ending (which can happen in Koine Greek). εἶπον can be either 1st pers sing or 3rd pers pl. It is used at least 25 times as a 3rd pers plural in the Greek NT.
4. Note the difference between ὅτε, "when," and ὅτι, "because" [from Vocab. 5].

5. The double numbers in the vocabulary [e.g. δίδωμι (415+534)], indicate that δίδωμι is found 415 times in the NT, and that there are a further 534 compounds of that verb in the NT [e.g. παραδίδωμι (120)]. The verb, ἀφίημι (142[+36]), is actually a compound verb (ἀπό + ἵημι); 142 examples of ἀφίημι are found in the NT, and a further 36 other compounds of -ιημι [συνίημι (26) I understand].

Exercise 12.3

A. Paradigm: Write out in full the
i. aor. ind. act. of τίθημι ii. aor. ind. act. of φέρω iii. pres. ind. act. of αἰτέω iv. aor. ind. act. of αἰτέω v. aor. ind. act. of ἐσθίω

B. Translate into English
1. ἔδωκαν 2. ἀπώλεσας 3. ἐγράψαμεν 4. τίθημι 5. ἔδειξας 6. ἐθήκαμεν 7. ἀπέστειλεν 8. ἐλαλήσαμεν 9. ἔστησα 10. ἀπόλλυμι 11. ἄφηκεν 12. πείθεις 13. βλέπουσιν 14. ἦλθεν 15. ἐστήσαμεν 16. ἀφίημι 17. εἰσέρχεσθε 18. ἐπείσατε 19. ἀφῆκας 20. ἀπέστειλας 21. ἠγάγομεν 22. ἐγένετο 23. ἤνεγκα 24. ἵστημι 25. ἐστήσατε 26. ἐφάγετε 27. ἀπέστειλα 28. δίδωμι 29. ἔβλεψεν 30. ἀπωλέσαμεν 31. εἶπεν 32. δείκνυμι 33. ἐμαρτύρησαν 34. ἐπέσατε

35. ἐδείξατε 36. ἔσχες 37. ἠρώτησας 38. ἐδώκατε 39. ἀφήκατε 40. ἀπεκρίθη 41. ἄγετε 42. βάλλεις 43. ἔθηκα 44. ἐποίησαν 45. εἶδον 46. ἤνεγκαν 47. ἠγάπησα 48. πέμπετε 49. παρέδωκεν 50. ἀποθνήσκουσιν 51. ἀπωλέσατε 52. ἐρωτᾷς 53. ἐβάλετε 54. ἔλαβες 55. ἐδείξαμεν 56. ἦν 57. ἔθηκαν 58. ἐδόξασας 59. ὁρᾷ 60. ἐγέννησα 61. ᾐτήσατε 62. σῴζομεν 63. ποιοῦμεν 64. παρεδώκαμεν 65. δοξάζω 66. ἔπεσας 67. πίπτεις 68. ἐπέσαμεν 69. πίπτομεν

C. Translate into Greek
70. I give 71. I gave 72. They send 73. They sent 74. She destroyed 75. He answered 76. They placed 77. You (sing.) showed

D. Translate into idiomatic English
78. ἐγὼ ἀποστέλλω τὸν ἄγγελον. 79. ἐγὼ ἀπέστειλα τὸν ἄγγελον. 80. σὺ ἀποστέλλεις τὸν ἄγγελον. 81. σὺ ἀπέστειλας τὸν ἄγγελον. 82. ὁ κύριος ἀποστέλλει τὸν ἄγγελον. 83. ὁ κύριος ἀπέστειλεν τὸν ἄγγελον. 84. ὁ Ἰησοῦς φέρει τὰς ἁμαρτίας τοῦ λαοῦ. 85. ὁ Ἰησοῦς ἤνεγκεν τὰς ἁμαρτίας τοῦ κόσμου. 86. δώδεκα ἀπόστολοί εἰσιν;

87. ὁ Ἰησοῦς ἔστησεν τὸ παιδίον ἐν τῷ μέσῳ. 88. τότε ὁ Ἰησοῦς ἄφηκεν τὴν Γαλιλαίαν. 89. ἐπηρώτησαν αὐτόν, Εἶ σὺ ὁ Χριστός; καὶ ἀπεκρίθη, Οὐ. 90. ἐπηρώτησαν αὐτὸν εἰ ἦν ὁ Χριστός, καὶ ἀπεκρίθη, Οὐ. 91. ὁ γὰρ Ἰησοῦς

Part 2 119

ἔδειξεν αὐτοὺς τὴν ὁδὸν τῆς δικαιοσύνης, ἀλλὰ οὐκ ἐπίστευσαν αὐτῷ. **92.** ὁ κύριος ἦλθεν πάλιν εἰς τὴν Γαλιλαίαν.

93. τότε ὁ κύριος ἦλθεν εἰς τὴν Γαλιλαίαν. **94.** ὁ Ἰησοῦς ὁ Χριστὸς ἔδωκεν αἰώνιον ζωὴν πρὸς ἀνθρώπους. **95.** ὁ Ἰησοῦς ἀφῆκεν ἁμαρτίας. **96.** τότε ὁ Ἰησοῦς ἀπεκρίθη αὐτοὺς ἐν παραβολαῖς. **97.** χαρὰ ὁ καρπὸς τῆς ἀγαπῆς ἐστιν. **98.** τότε ὁ Ἰησοῦς εἶπεν αὐτοῖς ἐν παραβολαῖς … **99.** ὅτε ὁ δίκαιος ἄνθρωπος ἠρώτησεν, ὁ θεὸς ἀπέστειλε τὸν ἄγγελον αὐτοῦ ἀπὸ τῶν οὐρανῶν. **100.** τότε ὁ κύριος ἄφηκεν τὴν Ἱεροσόλυμαν. **101.** ὁ γὰρ Ἰησοῦς ἤνεγκε τὰς ἁμαρτίας τῶν ἀνθρώπων. **102.** ἄλλοι δὲ εἶπον ὅτι ὁ Χριστός ἐστιν. **103.** ἐγένετο δὲ ὅτε ὁ Ἰησοῦς εἰσῆλθεν εἰς τὴν Ἰερουσαλήμ … **104.** ὁ θεὸς ἔδωκε τοὺς νόμους αὐτοῦ πρὸς τούς ἀνθρώπους. **105.** οὕτως γὰρ ὁ κύριος ἀφῆκεν ὑμᾶς.

E. Sentences and Phrases from the Greek New Testament

106. Ἄλλην παραβολὴν παρέθηκεν ¹ αὐτοῖς … **107.** ἀλλὰ ἔχω κατὰ σοῦ² ὅτι τὴν ἀγάπην σοῦ τὴν πρώτην ἀφῆκας. **108.** Καὶ ἐγένετο ὅτε ἐτέλεσεν³ ὁ Ἰησοῦς τοὺς λόγους τούτους,⁴ μετῆρεν⁵ ἀπὸ τῆς Γαλιλαίας καὶ ἦλθεν εἰς τὰ ὅρια⁶ τῆς Ἰουδαίας⁷ πέραν⁸ τοῦ Ἰορδάνου⁹ **109.** καὶ ἔδωκαν κλήρους¹⁰ αὐτοῖς καὶ ἔπεσεν ἡ κλῆρος ἐπὶ Μαθθίαν.¹¹

110. Τότε παραλαμβάνει¹² αὐτὸν ὁ διάβολος¹³ εἰς τὴν ἁγίαν city καὶ ἔστησεν αὐτὸν ἐπὶ τὸ πτερύγιον¹⁴ τοῦ ἱεροῦ, καὶ λέγει αὐτῷ, Εἰ υἱὸς εἶ τοῦ θεοῦ, throw yourself down … **111.** καὶ when he called παιδίον ἔστησεν αὐτὸ ἐν μέσῳ αὐτῶν καὶ εἶπεν, Ἀμὴν λέγω ὑμῖν … **112.** ἀφῆκεν τὴν Ἰουδαίαν¹⁵ καὶ ἀπῆλθεν πάλιν εἰς τὴν Γαλιλαίαν.

113. ἐγένετο Ἰωάννης … ἐν τῇ ἐρήμῳ¹⁶ **114.** πάλιν ἀπέστειλεν ἄλλους δούλους … **115.** ἄλλους ἔσωσεν, himself he cannot save.

Vocabulary help for questions 102-111 (above)

[1.] (qu. 106) παρατίθημι (παρα + τιθημι; 19) "I put before; place along side of" (followed by dative) [2] (qu. 107) σοῦ is the genitive singular of σύ, you. [3.] (qu. 108) τελέω (28) "I bring to an end, finish, complete, perform, accomplish, pay" [4.] (qu. 108) τούτους is the acc. pl. of οὗτος, "this, these" [5.] (qu. 108) μεταίρω (2) "I go away." This is a compound word (μετα + αἰρω). The aorist of αἰρω is ἦρα. It takes the same endings as ἔλυσα, but without the σ. [6.] (qu. 108) ὅριον (12) "boundary"; pl. "region, district" [7.] (qu. 108) Ἰουδαία (44) "Judea" [8.] (qu. 108) πέραν (23) on the other side [9.] (qu. 108) Ἰορδάνης (15) "Jordan." This is a masculine first declension noun [10.] (qu. 109) κλῆρος (11) "lot, portion, share" [11.] (qu. 109) Μαθθαῖος (5) "Matthew, Matthaias" [12.] (qu. 110) παραλαμβάνω (49) "I take with, take over, receive" [13.] (qu. 110) διάβολος (37) "slanderer, Devil" [14.] (qu. 110) πτερύγιον (2) "pinnacle, summit" [15.] (qu. 110) Ἰουδαία (44) "Judea" [16.] (qu. 113) ἔρημος, ἡ (47) "wilderness, grassland, desert"; adj. "abandoned, empty, desolate." Like ὁδός, ἔρημος uses the pattern of λόγος, but is feminine.

Chapter 13: The Demonstrative Adjective οὗτος

The demonstrative pronoun οὗτος has already been met a number of times in translating sentences from the Greek New Testament. Nor is this surprising, as the word is used 1,388 times in the New Testament. It has the basic meaning of "this" (plural: "these"). Often οὗτος functions as a pronoun – meaning "this man," "this woman" or "this thing"– and in such instances may be translated with the word "he" or "she" or "it" in English.

Here is the way οὗτος declines:

οὗτος, αὕτη, τοῦτο			
	Masc	Fem	Neut
Nom	οὗτος	αὕτη	τοῦτο
Acc	τοῦτον	ταύτην	τοῦτο
Gen	τούτου	ταύτης	τούτου
Dat	τούτῳ	ταύτῃ	τούτῳ
Nom	οὗτοι	αὗται	ταῦτα
Acc	τούτους	ταύτας	ταῦτα
Gen	τούτων	τούτων	τούτων
Dat	τούτοις	ταύταις	τούτοις

Here is how οὗτος is translated:

Translation of οὗτος			
	Masc	Fem	Neut
Nom	this, he	this, she	this, it
Acc	this, him	this, her	this, it
Gen	of this, his	of this, hers	of this, its
Dat	this, him, it	this, her, it	this, it
Nom	these, they	these, they	these
Acc	these, them	these, them	these
Gen	their	their	of these
Dat	these, them	these, them	these

Notes:
1. There are some tricky parts to this declension. Notice particularly that the genitive plurals of both feminine and neuter are τούτων (not ταύτων as the rest of the pattern might lead you to expect). The nom. fem. sing. αὕτη

Part 2

(this) is also to be distinguished from the nom. fem. sing. αὐτή (she) [of αὐτός] by the difference in breathing mark. The endings of the nominative neuter are rather like the endings of the neuter article, not the neuter second declension noun. In fact, it might be a good idea to take another look at the paradigm of αὐτός in Chapter 10, to compare it with οὗτος, to note where it is the same and where it is different.
2. Translating οὗτος from Greek into English is not generally a problem. It takes the gender and number of the noun that it replaces (rather like αὐτός). When translating from English to Greek, however, it should be remembered that οὗτος goes outside of the article: thus "these men" would be translated as οὗτοι οἱ ἄνθρωποι or οἱ ἄνθρωποι οὗτοι. This is different from other adjectives which go between the article and the noun.

Vocabulary 13

οὗτος, αὕτη, τοῦτο (1388) this, these, he, she, it

Exercise 13

Translate into English

1. τοῦτο τὸ σάββατον 2. αὕτη ἡ θάλασσα 3. αὕτη ἡ βασιλεία 4. τοῦτο τὸ πλοῖον 5. ταῦτα τὰ πλοῖα 6. αὗται αἱ χαραί 7. αὕτη ἡ ἐξουσία 8. οὗτος ὁ δοῦλος 9. οὗτοι οἱ δοῦλοι 10. οὗτοι οἱ υἱοί

Translate into Greek

11. These days   12. This lord   13. This way   14. His boats   15. The work of these men

Sentences and Phrases from the Greek New Testament

16. Καὶ ἐγένετο ὅτε ἐτέλεσεν ὁ Ἰησοῦς τοὺς λόγους τούτους ... 17. Καὶ ἐγένετο ὅτε ἐτέλεσεν ὁ Ἰησοῦς τὰς παραβολὰς ταύτας ... 18. ἀλλὰ τοῦτο ἔχεις, ὅτι μίσεις τὰ ἔργα τῶν Νικολαϊτῶν ... 19. εἶπαν, Σκληρός ἐστιν ὁ λόγος οὗτος ... ὁ Ἰησοῦς ... εἶπεν αὐτοῖς, Τοῦτο ὑμᾶς σκανδαλίζει; 20. ὁ δὲ εἶπεν αὐτοῖς, Ἐχθρὸς ἄνθρωπος τοῦτο ἐποίησεν.

Vocabulary help for questions 16-20 (above)

1. (qu. 16 & 17) τελέω (28) I bring to an end, complete, perform, accomplish, pay 2. (qu. 18) μισέω (39) I hate 3. (qu. 18) Νικολαΐτης (2) Nicolaitan 4. (qu. 19) εἶπαν weak aorist endings are sometimes found on strong aorist verbs. The form εἶπαν is found no less than 95 times in the NT. 5. (qu. 19) σκληρός, -ά, -όν (5) hard, rough, harsh 6. (qu. 19) σκανδαλίζω (29) I give offence to, anger; I cause to sin 7. (qu. 20) ὁ δε and he [an idiom which will be met formally in Vocab. 18] 8. (qu. 20) The original verb has been changed to something you should recognize 9. (qu. 20) ἐχθρός (32) noun: enemy; adjective [ἐχθρός, -ά, -όν] hostile, hated.

Chapter 14: Third Declension Nouns

First-declension feminine nouns are already familiar from Chapter 6, and second-declension masculine and neuter nouns from Chapters 3 and 4. As there are only three declensions of Greek nouns, the third-declension nouns are the last type of noun yet to be met, and introducing them is the main purpose of this chapter.

There are two broad categories of third-declension nouns: masculine and feminine nouns form one category, while neuter nouns form another, and the first two parts of this chapter deal separately with these two categories. The third part of the chapter will introduce a commonly found third-declension adjective (πᾶς, πᾶσα, πᾶν), as well as the frequently used third-declension indefinite and interrogative pronouns, τις and τίς.

Within the basic categories of third-declension nouns are found many different sub-types, but most of them follow a reasonably similar pattern. It is this pattern that will be highlighted in the following explanations.

14.1.1 Masculine and Feminine Third Declension Nouns

14.1.1.1 The Basic Pattern Used by Masc. and Fem. 3rd Decl. Nouns

The sheer number of different types of third declension nouns look difficult at first, but most of the masculine and feminine third declension nouns follow the same basic pattern. The trick is to recognize this basic pattern. The mnemonic ςαοςι εςαςωνσιν (s-a-os-i es-as-ōn-sin) should help – it includes all the endings of the different cases used by most masculine and feminine third-declension nouns:

	Singular	Plural
Nom	[-ς]	-ες
Acc	-α	-ας
Gen	-ος	-ων
Dat	ι	-σι(ν)

Some third declension nouns lack a sigma [-ς] for their nom. masc. sing. These are nouns which end with consonants like ρ, λ, μ, ν which do not tolerate an immediately following sigma except under certain circumstances, and which make compensation for this. So what might at first sight appear

Part 2 123

to be exceptions to the nom. masc. sing. ending ς are not.

14.1.1.2 Third Decl. Nouns with Stems that End in a Guttural, Labial or Dental

The nominative singular and the dative plural both involve a σ. In the light of what was learnt about the weak aorists, it is probably no surprise to find that this σ causes changes to occur in these cases for words which end with gutturals, labials or dentals. As well as this, some words which end in a vowel also interact with the endings. At first sight, this leads to a rather daunting list of different-looking third declension nouns, but a bit of cool thinking soon reveals that the changes that take place are relatively regular. For example, when a σ is added to gutturals, labials and dentals, the following changes take place:

guttural (γ, κ, χ) + σ becomes ξ
labial   (β, π, φ) + σ becomes ψ
dental   (δ, τ, θ) + σ becomes σ

Therefore, the feminine third declension word σάρξ, σαρκός, ἡ (flesh), which has a noun stem σαρκ-, combines with the endings ςαοςι εςαςωνσι(ν) as follows:

σάρξ, σαρκός, ἡ (flesh)		
	Singular	Plural
Nom / Voc	σάρξ	σάρκες
Acc	σάρκα	σάρκας
Gen	σαρκός	σαρκῶν
Dat	σαρκί	σαρξί(ν)

The guttural κ, combines with the ς to make ξ for the nom. sing. and dat. pl.. Notice that σαρξ is listed in the vocabulary as σάρξ, σαρκός, ἡ. This indicates that the noun is feminine (ἡ is the feminine article; third declension nouns can be either masculine or feminine), and that its genitive is σαρκος. The genitive case is listed, because it is possible to derive the full noun from the genitive stem which is found by taking off the -ος from σαρκός to discover σαρκ-, and then add the appropriate endings. This is true of most nouns of the third declension, and the genitive of third declension nouns is listed in Vocabulary lists and dictionaries to show which noun pattern the noun uses (*see also* 14.1.2 on dictionaries).

Several of the third declension nouns occurring over 50 times in the Greek New Testament can be worked out in terms of these rules [ἡ ἐλπίς, -ιδος "hope"; ἡ νύξ, -κτος "night"; ἡ χάρις, -ιτος "grace"; ὁ πούς, -οδος "foot"—note: the articles are included to indicate if they are feminine or masculine nouns]:

	ἐλπίς	νύξ	χάρις	πούς
N/V	ἐλπίς	νύξ	χάρις	πούς
Acc	ἐλπίδα	νύκτα	χάριν	πόδα
Gen	ἐλπίδος	νυκτός	χάριτος	ποδός
Dat	ἐλπίδι	νυκτί	χάριτι	ποδί
N/V	ἐλπίδες	νύκτες	χάριτες	πόδες
Acc	ἐλπίδας	νύκτας	χάριτας	πόδας
Gen	ἐλπίδων	νυκτῶν	χαρίτων	ποδῶν
Dat	ἐλπίσι(ν)	νυξί(ν)	χάρισι(ν)	ποσί(ν)

Most of the changes can be explained in terms of the rules outlined above:
- ἐλπιδ + σ becomes ἐλπίς because the dental δ disappears.
- νυκτ + σ becomes νύξ because the dental τ disappears and the guttural κ combines with σ to make ξ.
- ποδ + σ becomes πούς because the dental δ disappears (the υ is added to make a fuller sound in the vowel—there is no particular reason for this apart from the fact that it sounds better when said).
- χαριτ + σ becomes χάρις because the dental τ disappears. χάριν is irregular. It is found 50 times in the NT. The more expected χάριτα is found only twice (Acts 24:27 and Jude 1:4).

14.1.1.3 Third Declension Nouns with Stems that End in a ρ

While the σ of the third-declension nominative singular and dative plural interacts with the gutturals, labials and dentals in a predictable manner, the same predictability is not found with third-declension nouns which have a stem that ends with a ρ. Observe, for example, how the words ὁ ἀνήρ,-δρος "man"; ἡ μήτηρ, -τρος "mother"; ὁ πατήρ, -τρος "father"; ἡ χείρ, -ρος "hand" decline:

	ἀνήρ	**μήτηρ**	**πατήρ**	**χείρ**
Nom	ἀνήρ	μήτηρ	πατήρ	χείρ
Voc	ἄνερ	μῆτερ	πάτερ	χείρ
Acc	ἄνδρα	μητέρα	πατέρα	χείρα
Gen	ἀνδρός	μητρός	πατρός	χειρός
Dat	ἀνδρί	μητρί	πατρί	χειρί
Nom	ἄνδρες	μητέρες	πατέρες	χείρες
Voc	ἄνδρες	μητέρες	πατέρες	χείρες
Acc	ἄνδρας	μητέρας	πατέρας	χείρας
Gen	ἀνδρῶν	μητερῶν	πατέρων	χειρῶν
Dat	ἀνδράσι(ν)	μητράσι(ν)	πατράσι(ν)	χερσί(ν)

Part 2 125

While there is more variation with these words than was found with third-declension masculine and feminine nouns that ended with gutturals, and it can be seen that some changes have been made for easier pronunciation [μητρός, μητρί, μητράσιν, πατρός, πατρί, πατράσιν, χερσίν], again the overall pattern holds good. It is still largely –αοςι εςαςωνσιν.

14.1.1.4 Other Third Declension Nouns

Two other third declension nouns have a stem which ends in a consonant and occur more than 50 times in the Greek NT: ὁ αἰών, -ῶνος (eon, age), and ἡ γυνή, -αικός (woman, wife). Their declensions are as follows:

	αἰών	γυνή
Nom	αἰών	γυνή
Voc	αἰών	γύναι
Acc	αἰῶνα	γυναῖκα
Gen	αἰῶνος	γυναικός
Dat	αἰῶνι	γυναικί
Nom	αἰῶνες	γυναῖκες
Voc	αἰῶνες	γυναῖκες
Acc	αἰῶνας	γυναῖκας
Gen	αἰώνων	γυναικῶν
Dat	αἰῶσι(ν)	γυναιξί(ν)

The noun ὁ αἰών has a stem which ends in the nasal ν. This causes changes to the word when a σ is involved: in one case the σ is absorbed (the nom. sing.), and in the other case the ν is absorbed (the dat. pl.).

The noun ἡ γυνή has something of an irregularity in the nominative singular. Care should be taken not to confuse this as a first declension feminine noun.

14.1.1.5 Summing Up

There are a great many different types of third declension noun, all with little quirks. So many, in fact, that everyone is forced to generalize an overall pattern from them for themselves. But if you use your wits, and know ςαοςι εςαςωνσιν, you are almost there. If you are studying under the guidance of a teacher, you will need to take direction from him/her as to which of these forms you should memorize. If you are working through this book on your own, you must know ςαοςι εςαςωνσιν, and how to use it to work out the different nouns. It is probably a good idea to practice writing them out until you can get them down on paper from memory. This should not take a great deal of memory work once you have seen the basic pattern, and realize that any changes from the basic pattern are to help in pronouncing the words. If you are taking examinations in Greek, you should be aware that asking students to write out some third declension nouns is almost always a standard question in any examination on Greek grammar.

You may find it heartening that third declension nouns are generally found with the article. The article is often of considerable assistance in translating from the Greek, because if you fail to recognize the case and/or gender of the third declension noun, the article gives a quick indication of case, gender, and number.

14.1.2 Dictionaries

This is perhaps the right moment to introduce some of the features of dictionaries, and how the Greek words are recorded in them. Nouns are recorded under their nominative singular forms, adjectives under their nominative masculine singular forms, and verbs in the first person singular present indicative active. Verbs are shown in their uncontracted form. In other words, -εω, -αω, and -οω verbs are listed with the vowel on the verb stem.

For **nouns** the dictionary indicates whether the noun is masculine or feminine, and shows which noun pattern it follows by listing its genitive singular. For example, the word λόγος would be listed as: "λόγος, ου m something said (e.g. word; saying ...)" With this information [that λόγος is a masculine noun, and its genitive singular is λόγου], and by knowing the basic patterns that are available for a noun to follow, it is possible to work out the rest of the forms the noun takes.

With **verbs** there is generally only one listing for each verb, under the present indicative active. This means that an irregular aorist like ἔφαγον would generally only be listed under ἐσθίω, although some dictionaries take pity on beginners and list some – but not many – of these irregular verbs under two entries: one for the aorist stem, and one for the present stem. Thus, it is doubly important to be able to recognize strong aorists, which is why they have been listed as separate vocabulary items in this book. In a dictionary, the verb would be followed by a listing of the different tenses where it shows an irregularity. After this, the various possible meanings of the verb are given. For example, ἐσθίω is listed in one dictionary as "ἐσθίω and ἔσθω (fut. φάγομαι; aor. ἔφαγον, inf. φαγεῖν) eat, consume." The irregular aorist of ἐσθίω was covered in Chapter 12.1. The verb also has an irregular future and infinitive. Futures and infinitives are covered in future chapters [Chaps. 15 & 25], but you might recognize the φαγ part of the strong (irregular) verb stem. Any part of the verb that is not listed is assumed to be formed in a regular way, either following the pattern of λύω, or derived from one of the parts listed by the dictionary.

Part 2

Adjectives are listed in dictionaries pretty much as they have been given in the vocabularies in this book, although with a wider range of possible meanings. The nominative endings are provided for masc. fem. neut. If only two nominative endings are given, the adjective uses the same endings for both masc. and fem. This is all the information needed to show which declension the adjective follows for its various genders. Third declension adjectives are also normally listed with their genitive singular forms.

Vocabulary 14.1

Third declension masc. & fem. nouns with consonant endings which occur more than 50 times in the NT

αἰών, αἰῶνος, ὁ (123) — age, aeon, forever
ἀνήρ, ἀνδρός, ὁ (216) — man
γυνή, γυναικός, ἡ (209) — woman, wife
ἐλπίς, ἐλπίδος, ἡ (53) — hope
μήτηρ, μητρός, ἡ (84) — mother
νύξ, νυκτός, ἡ (61) — night
πατήρ, πατρός, ὁ (415) — father
πούς, ποδός, ὁ (93) — foot
σάρξ, σαρκός, ἡ (147) — flesh
Σίμων, Σίμωνος,[2] ὁ (75) — Simon
χάρις, χάριτος, ἡ (155) — grace, favor
χείρ, χειρός, ἡ (176) — hand

Other words

εἰρήνη, ης, ἡ (91) — peace
ἤ [3] (342) — or, than
κεφαλή, ας, ἡ (75) — head
μένω (118) — [aor. ἔμεινα] I remain, abide
μή (1055) — not[4]
οἰκία (94) — house, household[5]
οὐδέ (139) — and not, but not; not even [= οὐ + δέ]
οὐδείς, οὐδεμία, οὐδέν (226) — no one, not one (= οὐδέ + εἷς, μία, ἕν)
οὖν[6] (493) — therefore, then, so
Παῦλος (158) — Paul
ὡς (505) — as, when, after, while, about

Notes on Vocabulary 14.1

1. In learning the third declension nouns from vocabulary cards, it is helpful to say aloud the nominative and genitive forms. For example, for ἐλπίς, -ιδός, ἡ say aloud "ἐλπίς, ἐλπίδος, ἡ." This will develop an aural memory of the genitive form, and its gender.
2. Σίμων, as may be gathered from -ωνος, uses the same pattern as αἰών.
3. Note the difference between ἤ meaning "or," and ἡ, the nom. fem. sing. article.
4. There are rules for when οὐ should be used, and when μή should be used. They will be explained as examples of their use arise [see 6.3 of *Intermediate New Testament Greek Made Easier* for a fuller explanation]. Translating from Greek to English generally is not dependent on knowing these rules – although it can help with interpretation.
5. Cf. οἰκία, ας, ἡ and οἶκος, ου, ὁ, "house, household" from Vocabulary 3.2.
6. Like δέ and γάρ, οὖν does not begin a sentence in Greek, it is always the second word of a sentence. In translating οὖν into English, it is often best to place it first in the sentence.

Exercise 14.1

A. Declensions: Write or type out in full the declension of
i. νύξ   ii. πούς   iii. ἀνήρ

B. Translate into English
1. πατήρ μου 2. ἡ χεὶρ τοῦ θεοῦ 3. νὺξ καὶ ἡμέρα 4. ἡ οἰκία τοῦ Σίμωνος Πέτρου 5. τὰ ἔργα τῆς σαρκός 6. τὰ ἔργα τούτου τοῦ αἰῶνος 7. ἡ κεφαλὴ τοῦ ἀνδρός 8. αἱ κεφαλαὶ τῶν ἀνδρῶν 9. ὁ καρπὸς τῆς ἐλπίδος 10. οἱ καρποὶ τῆς χάριτος 11. ἡ μήτηρ τοῦ Ἰησοῦ 12. ἡ χεὶρ ἢ ὁ πούς 13. ὁ θάνατος τῆς ἐλπίδος 14. ἡ τυφλὴ γυνή 15. ὁ κύριος ἔδωκεν εἰρήνην πρὸς τοὺς ἄνδρας.

16. ὁ Ἰησοῦς ὁ Χριστός ἐστιν ἡ κεφαλὴ τῆς ἐκκλησίας. 17. αὕτη ἐστὶν ἡ οἰκια τῆς μητρὸς τοῦ Σίμωνος Πέτρου. 18. ἡ χάρις τοῦ θεοῦ ἔσωσεν ὑμᾶς. 19. ὁ Ἰησοῦς οὖν ἀπεκρίθη καὶ εἶπεν, Μου[1] λόγοι μένουσιν εἰς τὸν αἰῶνα.[2] 20. οἱ ἄνδρες καὶ αἱ γυναῖκες αὐτῶν εἰσῆλθον εἰς τὴν οἰκίαν. 21. ἡ βασιλεία τοῦ θεοῦ μένει εἰς τὸν αἰῶνα. 22. ἡ χεὶρ τοῦ ἀνδρός ἐστιν κατὰ μου. 23. ἡ χεὶρ τοῦ ἀνδρός ἦν κατὰ μου. 24. ὑμεῖς δέχεσθε εἰρήνην καὶ χάριν ἀπὸ τοῦ θεοῦ. 25. οἱ νόμοι τοῦ θεοῦ μένουσιν εἰς τὸν αἰῶνα.

Notes on questions 1-25 (above)
[1] (qu. 19) New Testament Greek uses an upper case letter at the beginning of quoted speech. It also uses one at the beginning of a new paragraph, and for names of people and places. [2] (qu. 19 & 25) εἰς τὸν αἰῶνα is a common idiom, usually translated, "forever."

C. Sentences and Phrases from the Greek New Testament

26. ὁ δὲ δοῦλος οὐ μένει ἐν τῇ οἰκίᾳ εἰς τὸν αἰῶνα, ὁ υἱὸς μένει εἰς τὸν αἰῶνα. **27.** Σοφίαν δὲ λαλοῦμεν ἐν τοῖς τελείοις,[1] σοφίαν δὲ οὐ τοῦ αἰῶνος τούτου οὐδὲ τῶν ἀρχόντων[2] τοῦ αἰῶνος τούτου. **28.** Be subject to one another out of reverence for Christ, αἱ γυναῖκες τοῖς ἰδίοις ἀνδράσιν ὡς τῷ κυρίῳ, ὅτι ἀνήρ ἐστιν κεφαλὴ τῆς γυναικὸς ὡς καὶ ὁ Χριστὸς κεφαλὴ τῆς ἐκκλησίας.

29. Παῦλος δοῦλος θεοῦ, ἀπόστολος δὲ Ἰησοῦ Χριστοῦ ... ἐπ'[3] ἐλπίδι ζωῆς αἰωνίου ... **30.** ... κατ' ἐλπίδα ζωῆς αἰωνίου. **31.** λέγει ἡ μήτηρ τοῦ Ἰησοῦ πρὸς αὐτόν, Οἶνον[4] οὐκ ἔχουσιν. **32.** Ἦν δὲ ἄνθρωπος ἐκ τῶν Φαρισαίων, ... οὗτος ἦλθεν πρὸς αὐτὸν νυκτὸς[5] καὶ εἶπεν αὐτῷ ... **33.** ... παρέλαβεν[6] τὸ παιδίον καὶ τὴν μητέρα αὐτοῦ νυκτὸς[7] καὶ ἀνεχώρησεν[8] εἰς Αἴγυπτον,[9] ...

34. ὁ πατὴρ ἀγαπᾷ τὸν υἱόν **35.** ... ἐν τῇ δόξῃ τοῦ πατρὸς αὐτοῦ ... **36.** Εἰ δὲ ἡ χείρ σου ἢ ὁ πούς σου σκανδαλίζει[10] σε[11] ... **37.** ἔρχεται οὖν πρὸς Σίμωνα Πέτρον· λέγει αὐτῷ, Κύριε, σύ μου νίπτεις[12] τοὺς πόδας; ἀπεκρίθη Ἰησοῦς καὶ εἶπεν αὐτῷ ... **38.** λέγει αὐτῷ Σίμων Πέτρος, Κύριε, μὴ τοὺς πόδας μου μόνον ἀλλὰ καὶ[13] τὰς χεῖρας καὶ τὴν κεφαλήν. λέγει αὐτῷ ὁ Ἰησοῦς ...

39. Καὶ ὁ λόγος σὰρξ ἐγένετο ... **40.** Φανερὰ[14] δέ ἐστιν τὰ ἔργα τῆς σαρκός ... **41.** χάρις ὑμῖν καὶ εἰρήνη ἀπὸ θεοῦ πατρὸς ἡμῶν[15] καὶ κυρίου Ἰησοῦ Χριστοῦ. **42.** Καὶ ὅτε εἶδον αὐτόν, ἔπεσα[16] πρὸς τοὺς πόδας αὐτοῦ ὡς νεκρός.

Vocabulary help for questions 26-40 (above)

[1] (qu. 26) τέλειος -α -ον (19) perfect, mature [2] (qu. 27) ἄρχων, -οντος, ὁ (37) ruler [3] (qu. 29) Notice that ἐπί looses its ι when a vowel begins the next word. This is to make the two words easier to pronounce together. Several prepositions do this. The process of omitting the last vowel of the word because the next word begins with a vowel is called **elision**. [4] (qu. 30) οἶνος (34) wine [5] (qu. 32) Here the genitive indicates time (33.3.6). So translate this as "by night," or "at night." [6] (qu. 33) παραλαμβάνω (παρά + λαμβάνω) (49) take with, take over, receive [7] (qu. 33) The genitive case here is, as in qu. 32, a reference to time. Translate as "by night" or "at night." [8] (qu. 33) ἀναχωρέω (14) I go away, return, withdraw, retire, take refuge [9] (qu. 33) Αἴγυπτος, ου, ἡ (25) Egypt [10] (qu. 36) σκανδαλίζω (29) I cause to sin, fall, give offence; cause to stumble [11] (qu. 36) σέ is the accusative singular of σύ, you [12] (qu. 37) νίπτω (17) I wash [13] (qu. 38) Remember καί can mean "also." [14] (qu. 40) φανερός, -ά, -όν (18) clear, evident [15] (qu. 41) ἡμῶν is the genitive plural of ἐγώ, and is translated "our." [16] (qu. 42) ἔπεσα is an example of a strong aorist with a weak aorist ending, which is found from time to time in the NT (and other *Koine* documents).

14.2.1 Neuter Third Declension Nouns

Neuter nouns of the second declension vary only slightly from the second declension masculine nouns. Something similar is also true of most third declension neuter nouns. For example the third declension neuter nouns τὸ πνεῦμα (spirit), τὸ φῶς (light), and τὸ ἔθνος (nation), τὸ γένος ([20] family, race, descendent, kind) are declined it the following manner:

	πνεῦμα	φῶς	ἔθνος	γένος
N/V	πνεῦμα	φῶς	ἔθνος	γένος
Acc	πνεῦμα	φῶς	ἔθνος	γένος
Gen	πνεύματος	φωτός	ἔθνους	γένους
Dat	πνεύματι	φωτί	ἔθνει	γένει
N/V	πνεύματα	φῶτα	ἔθνη	γένη
Acc	πνεύματα	φῶτα	ἔθνη	γένη
Gen	πνευμάτων	φώτων	ἐθνῶν	γενῶν
Dat	πνεύμασι(ν)	φωσί(ν)	ἔθνεσι(ν)	- [not in NT]

The endings for the genitive and dative are the same as for the other third declension nouns that have been met so far. Thus there is only one other complication to be remembered—the endings on the nominative and accusative, both singular and plural.

Notes on neuter nouns:
1. The way other 3rd declension neuter nouns found in Vocabulary 14.2 decline can be worked out by analogy with the nouns listed above. For example, αἷμα, θέλημα, ὄνομα, ῥῆμα, στόμα, and σῶμα follow the pattern of πνεῦμα; while ὄρος follows the pattern of γένος.
2. As with the other neuter nouns, third declension neuter plural nouns take a singular verb when used as a subject.
3. There is one class of third declension neuter nouns which appears rather different. These are the ones that end in -ος (yes, these must be distinguished from masculine second declension nouns). There are two examples of this type that occur over 50 times in the Greek NT: ἔθνος (nation) and ὄρος (mountain); ὄρος is declined in the same pattern as ἔθνος (although note ὀρέων): ὄρος, ὄρος, ὄρους, ὄρει, ὄρη, ὄρη, ὀρέων, ὄρεσι(ν).

Part 2 131

Vocabulary 14.2

The neuter third declension nouns that occur more than 50 times in the Greek NT:

αἷμα, αἵματος, τό (97)	blood
ἔθνος, ἔθνους, τό (162)	nation; pl.: nations, Gentiles
θέλημα, -τος, τό (62)	will, wish, desire[1]
ὄνομα, -τος, τό (228)	name
ὄρος, ὄρους, τό (62)	mountain
πνεῦμα, -τος, τό (379)	spirit, wind
πῦρ, πυρός, τό (71)	fire[2]
ῥῆμα, ῥήματος, τό (68)	word; thing, object
στόμα, στόματος, τό (78)	mouth
σῶμα, σώματος, τό (142)	body
ὕδωρ, ὕδατος, τό[3] (76)	water
φῶς, φωτός, τό (73)	light

Other words:

ἀλήθεια, ἡ (109)	truth
βαπτίζω (77)	I baptize
ἡμῶν [4] (359)	our
θρόνος, ὁ (62)	throne
Ἰουδαῖος, -α, -ον (195)	a Jew; Jewish; Judean
καρδία, ἡ (156)	heart[5]
μακάριος, -α, -ον (50)	blessed, fortunate, happy
μέν … [δε] (181)	on the one hand … on the other hand; some … others
ὅπου (82)	where

Notes on Vocabulary 14.2

1. Cf. θέλημα and θέλω, "I will, wish," from Vocabulary 2.
2. The noun πῦρ does not occur in the plural in the NT. Its singular declines: πῦρ, πῦρ, πῦρ, πυρός, πυρί.
3. The dat. pl. of ὕδωρ, is ὕδασιν, found once in NT at Matt 8:32.
4. Note the difference between ἡμῶν, "our" and ὑμῶν, "your."
5. Cf. the English words "cardiology" or "cardiac surgery."

Exercise 14.2

A. Translate into English
1. σάρξ καὶ αἷμα 2. τὸ θέλημα τοῦ πνεύματος 3. τὸ θέλημα τῶν πνευμάτων 4. πῦρ καὶ ὕδωρ 5. τὰ ὄρη τῆς Γαλιλαίας 6. τὰ ῥήματα τοῦ θεοῦ 7. τὸ φῶς τοῦ σώματος 8. τὸ στόμα τοῦ κυρίου 9. ὁ θρόνος τῆς καρδίας 10. ἡ ζωὴ ἐν τῷ πνεύματι 11. τὰ ἐθνὴ τούτου τοῦ κόσμου 12. μακάριος εἶ 13. τὰ ὀνόματα ἡμῶν 14. ἡ οἰκία τῶν πνευμάτων 15. καὶ τὸ ὄνομα αὐτῷ ἦν Ἰωάννας 16. ὁ Ἰησοῦς εἶπεν, Ἐγώ εἰμι τὸ φῶς τοῦ κόσμου. 17. ἡμῶν πατήρ, ὁ ἐν τοῖς οὐρανοῖς 18. ἀγαπῶμεν τὴν ἀλήθειαν; 19. ὁ Ἰησοῦς ἀπέστειλεν αὐτοὺς πρὸς τὰ ὄρη. 20. καὶ τὸ ὄνομα αὐτῷ ἦν Παῦλος. 21. Ἰωάννης εἶδεν τὸν θρόνον τοῦ θεοῦ ἐν τοῖς οὐρανοῖς. 22. καὶ εἰσῆλθεν ὅπου ἦν τὸ παιδίον.

B. Sentences and Phrases from the Greek New Testament
23. Ἦν δὲ ἄνθρωπος ἐκ τῶν Φαρισαίων, Νικόδημος ὄνομα αὐτῷ, ἄρχων[1] τῶν Ἰουδαίων· οὗτος ἦλθεν πρὸς αὐτὸν νυκτὸς καὶ εἶπεν αὐτῷ, ... 24. Ὑμεῖς ἐστε τὸ φῶς τοῦ κόσμου. 25. ... τοῦτό ἐστιν τὸ σῶμά μου. 26. τὸ δὲ ῥῆμα κυρίου μένει εἰς τὸν αἰῶνα. 27. οἱ πατέρες ἡμῶν ἐν τῷ ὄρει τούτῳ προσεκύνησαν· καὶ ὑμεῖς λέγετε ὅτι ἐν Ἱεροσολύμοις ἐστὶν the place where men ought to worship.

28. ... Σίμων Πέτρος εἶπεν, Σὺ εἶ ὁ Χριστὸς ὁ υἱὸς τοῦ θεοῦ ... δὲ ὁ Ἰησοῦς εἶπεν αὐτῷ, Μακάριος εἶ, Σίμων Βαριωνᾶ,[2] ὅτι σὰρξ καὶ αἷμα οὐκ ἀπεκάλυψέν[3] σοι[4] ἀλλ' ὁ πατήρ μου ὁ ἐν τοῖς οὐρανοῖς. 29. οὕτως οὐκ ἔστιν θέλημα ἔμπροσθεν[5] τοῦ πατρὸς ὑμῶν τοῦ ἐν οὐρανοῖς that any of these little ones should perish. 30. ἐν αὐτῷ ζωὴ ἦν, καὶ ἡ ζωὴ ἦν τὸ φῶς τῶν ἀνθρώπων

31. Μακάριοι οἱ πτωχοὶ[6] τῷ πνεύματι, ὅτι αὐτῶν ἐστιν ἡ βασιλεία τῶν οὐρανῶν. 32. τὸ δὲ σῶμα οὐ τῇ πορνείᾳ[7] ἀλλὰ τῷ κυρίῳ, καὶ ὁ κύριος τῷ σώματι ... 33. ἀπεκρίθη αὐτῷ Σίμων Πέτρος, Κύριε, πρὸς whom will we go? ῥήματα ζωῆς αἰωνίου ἔχεις, and we have believed and know ὅτι σὺ εἶ ὁ ἅγιος τοῦ θεοῦ. ἀπεκρίθη αὐτοῖς ὁ Ἰησοῦς ... 34. ... κατὰ τὸ θέλημα τοῦ θεοῦ καὶ πατρὸς ἡμῶν ...

35. Ἐγώ εἰμι τὸ φῶς τοῦ κόσμου. 36. οὗτος ὁ θάνατος ὁ δεύτερός[8] ἐστιν, ἡ λίμνη[9] τοῦ πυρός. 37. καὶ λέγουσιν τοῖς ὄρεσιν καὶ ταῖς πέτραις,[10] "Fall on us ..." 38. This is he who came by water and blood, Ἰησοῦς Χριστός, οὐκ ἐν τῷ ὕδατι μόνον ἀλλ' ἐν τῷ ὕδατι καὶ ἐν τῷ αἵματι· καὶ τὸ πνεῦμα ἐστιν the witness, ὅτι τὸ πνεῦμά ἐστιν ἡ ἀλήθεια. 39. Ὑμῖν δὲ λέγω τοῖς ἔθνεσιν· ... εἰμι ἐγὼ ἐθνῶν ἀπόστολος ...

40. ... καὶ οἱ πόδες αὐτοῦ ὡς στῦλοι[11] πυρός. 41. ἐγὼ μὲν ὑμᾶς βαπτίζω ἐν ὕδατι εἰς μετάνοιαν,[12] but he who is coming after me is mightier than I, whose

Part 2

sandals I am not worthy to carry, this man will baptize you ἐν πνεύματι ἁγίᾳ καὶ πυρί. **42.** ... γὰρ ἠκούσαμεν ἀπὸ τοῦ στόματος αὐτοῦ. **43.** ... καὶ αὐτός ἐστιν ἡ κεφαλὴ τοῦ σώματος τῆς ἐκκλησίας· ...

44. τοῦτο γάρ ἐστιν τὸ θέλημα τοῦ πατρός μου ... **45.** ἡ γὰρ σὰρξ ἐπιθυμεῖ[13] κατὰ τοῦ πνεύματος, τὸ δὲ πνεῦμα κατὰ τῆς σαρκός, ... φανερὰ[14] δὲ ἐστιν τὰ ἔργα τῆς σαρκός, ... Ὁ δὲ καρπὸς τοῦ πνεύματός ἐστιν ἀγάπη, χαρὰ, εἰρήνη ... **46.** ... ὁ λαὸς εἶπεν, Τὸ αἷμα αὐτοῦ ἐφ᾽[15] ἡμᾶς καὶ ἐπὶ τὰ τέκνα ἡμῶν.

47. ὁ ἀγαθὸς ἄνθρωπος ἐκ τοῦ ἀγαθοῦ θησαυροῦ[16] τῆς καρδίας πρόφερει[17] τὸ ἀγαθόν, καὶ ὁ πονηρὸς ἐκ τοῦ πονηροῦ προφέρει τὸ πονηρόν· ἐκ γὰρ περισσεύματος[18] καρδίας λαλεῖ τὸ στόμα αὐτοῦ. **48.** Ἦλθεν οὖν πάλιν εἰς τὴν Κανὰ[19] τῆς Γαλιλαίας, ὅπου ἐποίησεν τὸ ὕδωρ οἶνον.[20]

Vocabulary help for questions 23-48 (above)

[1 (qu. 23)] ἄρχων, -οντος, ὁ (27) ruler [2 (qu. 28)] Βαριωνᾶ (1) Bar-Jona [son of Jona] [3 (qu. 28)] ἀποκαλύπτω (26) I reveal, disclose [In the Greek New Testament, the book of Revelation is called the Ἀποκάλυψις Ἰωάννου—the revelation of John] [4 (qu. 28)] σοί is the dative singular of σύ [5 (qu. 29)] ἔμπροσθεν (48) + gen. in front of, ahead, before. This word is used somewhat idiomatically in this sentence, although the basic meaning is easy enough to work out. Literally the sentence reads "Such [or: Thus] is not the will before [in the presence of] your father in the heavens." You can immediately see how this would be expressed in English. [6 (qu. 31)] πτωχός, -ή, -όν (34) poor [7 (qu. 32)] πορνεία, ἡ (25) sexual immorality [8 (qu. 35)] δεύτερος, -α, -ον (44) second [9 (qu. 35)] λίμνη, ἡ (11) lake [10 (qu. 37)] πέτρα, ἡ (15) rock [11 (qu. 40)] στῦλος, ὁ (4) pillar [12 (qu. 42)] μετάνοια, ἡ (22) repentance [13 (qu. 45)] ἐπιθυμέω (16) I desire [14 (qu. 45)] φανερός, -ά, -όν (18) clear, evident [15 (qu. 46)] Notice how ἐπί becomes ἐφ᾽ before a rough breathing. [16 (qu. 47)] θησαυρός, ὁ (17) treasure, storehouse [17 (qu. 47)] προφέρω (2) I bring out, produce [πρό + φέρω] [18 (qu. 47)] περίσσευμα, -ματος, τό (5) abundance [19 (qu. 48)] Κανά, ἡ (4) Cana [20 (qu. 48)] οἶνος, ὁ (34) wine

14.3.1 πᾶς, πᾶσα, πᾶν

The third declension adjective πᾶς (each, all, every) is used 1,243 times in the Greek New Testament. Its declension is as follows:

πᾶς, πᾶσα, πᾶν			
	Masc	Fem	Neut
N/V	πᾶς	πᾶσα	πᾶν
Acc	πάντα	πᾶσαν	πᾶν
Gen	παντός	πάσης	παντός
Dat	παντί	πάσῃ	παντί
N/V	πάντες	πᾶσαι	πάντα
Acc	πάντας	πάσας	πάντα
Gen	πάντων	πασῶν	πάντων
Dat	πᾶσι(ν)	πάσαις	πᾶσι(ν)

πᾶς uses third declension endings for both masculine and neuter, while the feminine uses first declension endings. πᾶς is an adjective, and normally presents little difficulty for the translator: "each," or "all" translates the word in most occurrences, as some examples will quickly show:

πᾶς ἄνθρωπος	each man
πάντες ἄνθρωποι	all men
πᾶσαι γυναῖκες	all women

14.3.2 τις, τι, and τίς, τί

The word τις, τι is used as an indefinite pronoun, so is translated by the words "anyone, anything, someone, something, a certain man/woman/thing, etc." It uses the same endings for both masculine and feminine, and has neuter forms. All of them are third declension type endings:

Part 2

τις, τι		
	Masc, Fem	Neut
N/v	τις	τι
Acc	τινα	τι
Gen	τινος	τινος
Dat	τινι	τινι
N/V	τινες	τινα
Acc	τινας	τινα
Gen	τινων	τινων
Dat	τισι(ν)	τισι(ν)

How the word is used is perhaps best demonstrated by means of examples:
    ἦν δέ τις ἄνθρωπος ...   and there was a <u>certain</u> man (John 5:5)
    τις ὀνόματι Λάζαρος   a <u>certain</u> man called Lazarus (Luke 16:20)
    εἰ ... τις ...   if <u>anyone</u> (Rom 8:9)

The word τίς, on the other hand, is the interrogative pronoun. In other words, it is used to ask questions, and is translated by the words "who...?, what...? which...?" One might almost say that the only difference between it and τις is that τίς has the accent.[1] It is declined in exactly the same way as τις:

τίς, τί		
	Masc, Fem	Neut
N/v	τίς	τί
Acc	τίνα	τί
Gen	τίνος	τίνος
Dat	τίνι	τίνι
N/V	τίνες	τίνα
Acc	τίνας	τίνα
Gen	τίνων	τίνων
Dat	τίσι(ν)	τίσι(ν)

Some examples will show how the word is used:
    τίς λέγει τοῦτο;   Who says this?
    τί ἐστιν τοῦτο;   What is this?

[¹Though a helpful generalization for beginners, it is not quite correct to say that τις never has an accent. It is true that an accent almost never appears on τις itself in the NT, but where possible, τις throws an (enclitic) accent on the previous word (see *Int*.7.3). In effect, then, the word τις *is* never found with an accent on it in the Greek New Testament, while the different forms of τίς are always found with accents.]

14.3.3 First and Second Person Pronouns: ἐγώ and σύ

Because the words are so commonly used, many of the different cases of ἐγώ and σύ have already been met. There are gathered together here for convenience. They are quite irregular, although in the singular they are somewhat similar to second declension nouns, and they have some of the characteristics of third declension nouns in their plurals.

Interestingly enough, English, which otherwise barely declines, does decline for many of the different cases of the pronouns:

	ἐγώ		σύ	
N/V	ἐγώ	I	σύ	you
Acc	[ἐ]μέ	me	σέ	you
Gen	[ἐ]μοῦ	my	σοῦ	your
Dat	[ἐ]μοί	to/for me	σοί	to/ you
N/V	ἡμεῖς	we	ὑμεῖς	you
Acc	ἡμᾶς	us	ὑμᾶς	you
Gen	ἡμῶν	our	ὑμῶν	your
Dat	ἡμῖν	to/for us	ὑμῖν	to/you

[Note: The oblique cases (μέ, μοῦ, μοί, σέ, σοῦ, σοί) of the 1st and 2nd personal pronouns singular are enclitic; in other words, where possible they throw their accent back onto the previous word (see *Int*.7.3 for further explanation).]

Vocabulary 14.3

πᾶς, πᾶσα, πᾶν (1226) each, all, every
τις, τι (518) someone, a certain [man/woman/thing] [indefinite pronoun]
τίς, τί (552) who ...? what ...? which ...? [interrogative pronoun]

Exercise 14.3

Sentences and Phrases from the Greek New Testament:
1. ὁ λογος ὁ σὸς[1] ἀλήθειά ἐστιν.   **2.** Ἀσπάζονται ὑμᾶς αἱ ἐκκλησίαι πᾶσαι τοῦ Χριστοῦ. **3.** εἰ δέ τις πνεῦμα Χριστοῦ οὐκ ἔχει, οὗτος οὐκ ἔστιν αὐτοῦ. **4.** ἐγὼ ἐν αὐτοῖς καί σὺ ἐν ἐμοί, ... **5.** καὶ τίς σοι ἔδωκεν τὴν ἐξουσίαν ταύτην; **6.** ἐγώ σε ἐδόξασα ἐπὶ τῆς γῆς   **7.** Ἐγὼ Ἰωάννης, ὁ ἀδελφὸς ὑμῶν ... **8.** ... ἐν πάσῃ σοφίᾳ ... ἐν παντὶ ἔργῳ ἀγαθῷ ...

9. ὁ δὲ εἶπεν αὐτοῖς, have you not read τί ἐποίησεν Δαυίδ... **10.** Τί σοι δοκεῖ, Σίμων; **11.** ... ἔδωκας αὐτῷ ἐξουσίαν πάσης σαρκός, ... **12.** So if you are offering your gift at the altar, and there remember ὅτι ὁ ἀδελφός σου ἔχει τι κατὰ σοῦ, ... **13.** Καὶ αὕτη ἐστὶν ἡ μαρτυρία[2] τοῦ Ἰωάννου, ὅτε ἀπέστειλαν πρὸς αὐτὸν οἱ Ἰουδαῖοι ἐξ[3] Ἱεροσολύμων priests and Levites in order to ask him, Σὺ τίς εἶ; And he confessed and did not deny, and confessed ὅτι Ἐγὼ οὐκ εἰμὶ ὁ Χριστός. καὶ ἠρώτησαν αὐτόν, Τί οὖν; Σὺ Ἠλίας[4] εἶ; καὶ λέγει, Οὐκ εἰμί.

Vocabulary help for questions 1-13 (above)
[1 (qu. 1)]σός, σή, σόν (27) your [possessive pronoun]   [2 (qu. 13)]μαρτυρία, ἡ (37) witness, testimony [cf. μαρτυρέω]   [3 (qu. 13)] ἐκ becomes ἐξ before a rough breathing   [4 (qu. 13)] Ἠλίας, ου, ὁ (29) Elijah

Chapter 15: The Infinitive Mood

Overview of Greek Moods

So far, all the verbs have been in the indicative mood. This chapter introduces the infinitive, another of the five moods the verb used in New Testament Greek. The following table summarizes the most common uses of the five moods:

Uses of Verb Moods	
Mood	Principal uses of the mood
Indicative mood	The mood used for making statements of fact and asking questions
Imperative mood	The mood used for giving orders / making [strong] requests
Subjunctive mood	The mood used to express contingencies or possibilities. Often found after certain conjunctions and in association with certain particles (e.g. ἵνα, ἄν, ἐάν, οὐ μή, etc)
Infinitive mood	The mood used after certain verbs (e.g. θέλω, δύναμαι, δεῖ, ἔξεστιν, μέλλω, ἄρχομαι, etc). Often most easily translated by the English infinitive: "to ..."
Participial mood	A mood difficult to equate to one thing in English grammar. Used with the article to mean "the one who ..."; otherwise, often best translated as a reference to time, "when ....," "while ..."; sometimes translated by the English participles, "... ing" (active), "... ed" (passive).

This chapter will describes the infinitive mood and its most common uses. The uses of the other moods will be introduced one by one in subsequent chapters.

15.1 The Infinitive Active

The majority of Greek infinitives are used much like English infinitives. Other uses of the infinitive will be dealt with as they arise in translation passages, and in a systematic way in Chapter 1 of *Intermediate New Testament Greek Made Easier* [see *Int*.1.3]. But for now, at least, the infinitives you meet should be straight-forward to translate.

The English infinitive is formed by placing the word "to" in front of the verb. For example, "to eat," "to cry," "to laugh," "to walk," "to play," etc. English-speakers find that they insert an infinitive after verbs that need one without thinking about it. The sentence "I want eat" sounds wrong to most English speakers because the English verb "to want" is usually followed by an infinitive, in this case "[I want] to eat." The same is true for "I want to cry," "I want to laugh," etc. In other words, the English verb "to want" is usually followed by an infinitive. This is also true of the verb "to be able": "I am able to walk," "I am able to swim," "I am able to play the piano," etc. The Greek verbs that are translated by "I want" and "I am able" are also usually followed by an infinitive.

Present infinitive active: λύειν
Aorist infinitive active: λῦσαι

Certain verbs are usually followed by the infinitive (e.g. δύναμαι "I am able [to ...]", δεῖ "it is necessary [to ...]", θέλω "I want [to ...]"). The infinitive is found in the two tenses that have been met so far: the present tense and the aorist tense. The infinitives of the regular verb follow the pattern of λύω:

The infinitive does not have different forms for the different personal subjects, and for each tense there is only the one form to learn. For example:

θέλω λύειν	I want to loose
θέλεις λύειν	you want to loose
θέλει λύειν	he wants to loose
θέλομεν λύειν	we want to loose
	etc.

15.1.1 The aorist infinitive of weak verbs with stems ending in a consonant

The aorist infinitive of weak verbs which have a stem ending in a consonant are formed much as might be expected: the σ combines with the letters according to the rules which were learnt for the weak aorists:

Verb	Pres Inf	Aor Inf	
γράφω	γράφειν	γράψαι	φ+σ=ψ
πέμπω	πέμπειν	πέμψαι	π+σ=ψ
δοξάζω	δοξάζειν	δοξάσαι	dz+σ=σ
σῴζω	σῴζειν	σῶσαι	dz+σ=σ

15.1.2 The infinitive of verbs which have a strong aorist indicative active

Examples are perhaps the best way to explain how verbs which have a strong aorist indicative active form their aorist infinitive active:

Verb	Pres Inf	Aor Ind	Aor inf
ἄγω	ἄγειν	ἤγαγον	ἀγαγεῖν
βάλλω	βάλλειν	ἔβαλον	βαλεῖν
ἔρχομαι	ἔρχεσθαι	ἦλθον	ἐλθεῖν
ἐσθίω	ἐσθίειν	ἔφαγον	φαγεῖν
λαμβάνω	λαμβάνειν	ἔλαβον	λαβεῖν
λέγω	λέγειν	εἶπον	εἰπεῖν
εὑρίσκω	εὑρίσκειν	εὗρον	εὑρεῖν
ὁράω	[not in NT]	εἶδον	ἰδεῖν

From the above examples it may be seen that the aorist stem is used to form the aorist infinitive active, using the ending normally associated with the present infinitive active.

15.1.3 Verbs that end in -εω or -αω

As they did in the weak (regular) aorists, verbs that end in -εω or -αω generally lengthen the ε or α into an η before the σ:

Verb	Pres Inf Act	Aor Inf Act
αἰτέω	αἰτεῖν	αἰτῆσαι
ἐρωτάω	ἐρωτᾶν	ἐρωτῆσαι
ποιέω	ποιεῖν	ποιῆσαι
προσκυνέω	προσκυνεῖν	προσκυνῆσαι

[Notice that there is no iota subscript in the present infinitive active of ἐρωτάω. This is likewise true of all -άω verbs. It is because the infinitive ending was originally -εεν. This original ending contracted following the rule ε + ε becomes ει to give -ειν. But there is no iota to become a subscript when εε contracted with α.]

15.1.4 Infinitives of middle and passive verbs

The present infinitive for middle and passive verbs is indicated by the ending -εσθαι, the aorist infinitive by either the ending -σασθαι (middle voice) or -θηναι (passive voice):

Verb	Pres Inf	Aor Inf
ἀποκρίνομαι	ἀποκρίνεσθαι	ἀποκριθῆναι
ἀσπάζομαι	ἀσπάζεσθαι	[not in NT]
γίνομαι	γίνεσθαι	γενέσθαι
δέχομαι	δέχεσθαι	δέξασθαι
ἔρχομαι	ἔρχεσθαι	ἐλθεῖν
πορεύομαι	πορεύεσθαι	πορευθῆναι
προσεύχομαι	προσεύχεσθαι	προσεύξασθαι

Notes:
1. The verb γίνομαι has a strong aorist infinitive, γενέσθαι, which is found 37 times in the NT
2. ἐλθεῖν: see 15.1.2 re. ἐλθεῖν.

15.1.5 The meaning of the tense in the infinitive mood

Thus far the aorist tense has been associated with past events. A little experimentation will convince the reader that there is nothing associated with past or present in the English infinitives. They take their tense from the verb with which they are found with – e.g. "I want to eat," "I wanted to eat." This is also true in Greek. The different tenses of the Greek infinitive, therefore, do not refer to time, but rather refer to the type of action involved. The present infinitive implies a continuous action, while the aorist tense implies either a single action, or carries no implication regarding the type of action involved. The present infinitive is only used when the continuous action of the verb is stressed, which means that the aorist infinitive is the most frequently encountered.

Perhaps the following example might illustrate the difference between the present and aorist infinitive. If one of my students said, θέλω εἰπεῖν [I want to speak] I would allow him to speak. But if a student said, θέλω λέγειν [I want to speak] I would not allow him to speak. Why? Because the student who said, θέλω λέγειν wanted to speak continuously, perhaps for the whole class period.

This distinction between the aorist and present infinitive is not particularly easy to show in translation, and generally no difference is made in translating θέλω εἰπεῖν and θέλω λέγειν. They both would be translated, "I want to speak." The translator, but not the reader of the English translation, would know the distinction.

15.1.6 Notes:
1. You will quickly learn to expect an infinitive after certain verbs, especially θέλω (I want [to …]), δύναμαι (I am able [to …]), and δεῖ (it is necessary [to …]).
2. Notice that because **the aorist infinitive** does not refer to the past tense, it **receives no augment**. Thus the aorist infinitive active of ἄγω is ἀγαγεῖν [*not* ἠγαγεῖν], and the aorist infinitive active of ἔρχομαι is ἐλθεῖν [*not* ἠλθεῖν].
3. Accents: a. The usual rules for verbs in the indicative apply to the **present** infinitive (e.g. λύειν, γράφειν, δοξάζειν). b. In a **weak aorist** infinitive the accent is on the second to last syllable (the penult – whether acute or circumflex must be determined by observation; e.g. λῦσαι, σῶσαι, γράψαι, φοξάσαι); while the **strong aorist** infinitive takes a circumflex accent on the last syllable (the ultima; e.g. ἀγαγεῖν, βαλεῖν).

15.1.7 Further examples
θέλομεν ἰδεῖν τὸν κύριον   We wish to see the Lord
θέλεις προσεύξασθαι τῷ θεῷ; Do you wish to pray to God?

15.2 δύναμαι

The verb δύναμαι (I am able) is followed by an infinitive. It follows a paradigm which has not yet been covered, but it occurs frequently enough in the New Testament to make it necessary to learn it now:

δύναμαι
δύνασαι
δύναται
δυνάμεθα
δύνασθε
δύνανται

Its infinitive is δύνασθαι, "to be able."

15.3 Parsing

Now that two different tenses (present and aorist), and two different moods of the verb (indicative and infinitive) have been met, it is sensible to formally introduce the correct method to parse a verb. Some examples will show the correct pattern to follow:

15.3.1 For Verbs
ἔλαβεν is the third person sing., strong aorist indicative active of λαμβάνω, I take

Part 2   143

λέγετε is the second person plural, present indicative active of λέγω, I say
γράψαι is the weak aorist infinitive active of γράφω, I write
ἐρχόμεθα is the first person plural present indicative middle of ἔρχομαι, I go

The options for parsing verbs met so far are:
[1st/2nd/3rd pers. sing./pl.] pres./aor. ind./inf. act./mid./pass, of ...

The basic pattern to follow in parsing a verb is:
[person] + [number] + tense + mood + voice + "of" + dictionary form + dictionary meaning

15.3.2 For Nouns

The following examples illustrate how to parse nouns:
ἡμέρας is the accusative feminine plural of ἡμέρα, -ας, day
δοῦλοι is the nominative masculine plural of δοῦλος, -ου, servant
φωτός is the genitive neuter singular of φῶς, -ωτος, light

The options that you have for parsing nouns are:
nom./voc./acc./gen./dat.   masc./fem./neut sing./pl. . of ...

The basic pattern to follow in parsing a noun is:
case + gender + number + dictionary form [+ genitive] + dictionary meaning

Parsing will become second nature to you as you master Greek. It is a good measure of how well the basic forms of the language are known, and consequently is almost always asked in Greek examinations.

Vocabulary 15

Verbs usually followed by an infinitive
δεῖ (102) [+ inf]   it is necessary [to ...]
δύναμαι (209) [+ inf]   I am able [to ...]
ἔξεστιν (31) [+ inf]   it is lawful [to ...]
θέλω (207) [+ inf]   I will, wish, want [from Vocab 2]

Infinitives of selected verbs
γενέσθαι (37)   to become [aor. inf. of γίνομαι]
δοῦναι (33+11)   to give [aor. inf. act. of δίδωμι]
εἶναι (123+7)   to be [present infinitive of εἰμί]
ζῆν (12)   to live [present infinitive of ζάω]
ἰδεῖν (37)   to see [aor. inf. act. of ὁράω]

Other words
γραφή (50)	writing, scripture
διά (483) + acc.	because of, on account of
διά + gen.:	through; [note: διὰ τί (27) = "why ...?"]
ἐγείρω (143)	I raise, wake [aor. ἤγειρα]
λίθος (58)	stone
οὐχί (53)	not, no [a variation of οὐ]
πῶς (104)	how ...? In what way ...?
σημεῖον (77)	sign
τόπος (95)	place
ὑπάγω (79)	I go away, withdraw
ψυχή (101)	soul, life

Exercise 15

A. Translate into English
1. ἐγὼ δύναμαι γράφειν 2. αὐτὸς θέλει δοξάζειν τὸν θεόν 3. ἡμεῖς θέλομεν ἐσθίειν; 4. σὺ δύνασαι γράψαι; 5. αὐτὸς δύναται ἀγάγειν; 6. αὐτὸς δύναται ποιῆσαι τοῦτον 7. οὐχὶ θέλω φαγεῖν λίθους 8. ὑμεῖς θέλετε βλέπειν τὸν θεόν; 9. ὑμεῖς θέλετε ἰδεῖν τὸν θεόν; 10. δεῖ τηρεῖν τὸν νόμον 11. Πέτρος ἦλθεν ἀσπάζεσθαι τὸν Ἰησοῦν. 12. αὐτοὶ εὗρον ἄρτον δοῦναι πρὸς τὸν Ἰησοῦν. 13. διὰ τί θέλεις ποιεῖν τοῦτον; 14. οὗτός ἐστιν ὁ τόπος ὅπου ἔπεσεν, καὶ οὗτος ὁ τόπος ὅπου ἔθηκαν αὐτόν. 15. πῶς θέλεις ὑπάγειν; 16. ὅτε αὐτοὶ ἦλθον πρὸς τὸν τόπον, εὗρον καρπὸν φαγεῖν. 17. θέλω εἶναι ὡς τὸν Ἰησοῦν. σὺ, θέλεις εἶναι ὡς τὸν Ἰησοῦν; 18. ὁ Ἰησοῦς ἤγειρεν Λάζαρον ἐκ τῶν νεκρῶν. 19. τηροῦμεν τὰς ἐντολὰς διὰ ἀγάπην. 20. τίς ψυχή ἐστιν; 21. ὁ Ἰησοῦς θέλει ἐλθεῖν διὰ Γαλιλαίας. 22. ὁ Ἰησοῦς οὐχὶ θέλει ἐλθεῖν διὰ Γαλιλαίας. 23. θέλει ἰδεῖν τὸν Ἰησοῦν ποιεῖ σημεῖον. 24. ἀγαπῶμεν τὸν Ἰησοῦν ὅτι αὐτός ἠγάπησεν πρῶτον ἡμᾶς.
[Note for qu. 18: Λάζαρος, -ου, ὁ (15) Lazarus]

B. Parsing
25—35. Parse the underlined words in the exercises numbered 1 to 24.

C. Translate into Greek
36. I am able to throw 37. Are you able to throw? 38. He found stones to throw. 39. They want to pray 40. He took bread to eat. 41. He found bread to eat.

Part 2 145

D. Sentences and Phrases from the Greek New Testament
42-52. *Parse the words underlined in the following passages*
53. ἐραυνᾶτε[1] τὰς γραφάς, ὅτι ὑμεῖς δοκεῖτε ἐν αὐταῖς ζωὴν αἰώνιον ἔχειν· and it is they that bear witness to me; καὶ οὐ θέλετε ἐλθεῖν πρός με so that you might have life. **54.** And do not presume to say to yourselves, Πατέρα ἔχομεν τὸν Ἀβραάμ. λέγω γὰρ ὑμῖν ὅτι δύναται ὁ θεὸς ἐκ τῶν λίθων τούτων ἐγεῖραι[2] τέκνα τῷ Ἀβραάμ. **55.** εὑρίσκει Φίλιππος[3] τὸν Ναθαναὴλ[4] καὶ λέγει αὐτῷ, "We have found him of whom Moses in the law and also the prophets wrote, Jesus, son of Joseph, from Nazareth. καὶ εἶπεν αὐτῷ Ναθαναήλ, Ἐκ Ναζαρὲτ[5] δύναταί τι ἀγαθὸν εἶναι;

56. καὶ εὗρον αὐτὸν καὶ λέγουσιν αὐτῷ ὅτι Πάντες ζητοῦσίν σε. **57.** εἰ δὲ θέλεις εἰς τὴν ζωὴν εἰσελθεῖν, keep the commandments. **58.** For he knew who would betray him; διὰ τοῦτο εἶπεν ὅτι Οὐχὶ πάντες καθαροί[6] ἐστε. **59.** καὶ εἰ θέλετε δέξασθαι, αὐτός ἐστιν Ἠλίας[7] ... **60.** καὶ ὅτε ἤκουσα καὶ ἔβλεψα, ἔπεσα προσκυνῆσαι ἔμπροσθεν[8] τῶν ποδῶν τοῦ ἀγγέλου ...

61. οἱ πατέρες ἡμῶν ἐν τῷ ὄρει τούτῳ προσεκύνησαν· καὶ ὑμεῖς λέγετε ὅτι ἐν Ἱεροσολύμοις ἐστὶν ὁ τόπος ὅπου προσκύνειν δεῖ. **62.** εἶπεν, Τί θέλετέ μοι δοῦναι, and I will betray him? **63.** θέλομεν ἀπὸ σοῦ σημεῖον ἰδεῖν. **64.** ἔλεγεν γὰρ ὁ Ἰωάννης τῷ Ἡρῴδῃ[9] ὅτι Οὐκ ἔξεστίν[10] σοι ἔχειν τὴν γυναῖκα τοῦ ἀδελφοῦ σου. **65.** ἐπείνασα[11] γὰρ καὶ ἐδώκατέ μοι φαγεῖν ...

66. Πῶς δύναται οὗτος ἡμῖν δοῦναι τὴν σάρκα [αὐτοῦ] φαγεῖν; εἶπεν οὖν αὐτοῖς ὁ Ἰησοῦς, Ἀμὴν ἀμὴν λέγω ὑμῖν ... **67.** Σκληρός[12] ἐστιν ὁ λόγος οὗτος· τίς δύναται αὐτοῦ ἀκούειν[13]; **68.** δεῖ δὲ καὶ μαρτυρίαν[14] καλὴν ἔχειν ἀπὸ those outside. **69.** τίς ἐξ ὑμῶν convicts me of sin? εἰ ἀλήθειαν λέγω, διὰ τί ὑμεῖς οὐ πιστεύετέ μοι; He who is ἐκ τοῦ θεοῦ τὰ ῥήματα τοῦ θεοῦ ἀκούει· διὰ τοῦτο ὑμεῖς οὐκ ἀκούετε, ὅτι ἐκ τοῦ θεοῦ οὐκ ἐστέ.

70. οὐ δύναται ὁ κόσμος μισεῖν[15] ὑμᾶς, ἐμὲ δὲ μισεῖ, ὅτι ἐγὼ μαρτυρῶ concerning it ὅτι τὰ ἔργα αὐτοῦ πονηρά ἐστιν. **71.** ὅπου ἐγὼ ὑπάγω ὑμεῖς οὐ δύνασθε ἐλθεῖν. **72.** Now among those who went up to worship at the feast were some Greeks; οὗτοι οὖν προσῆλθον Φιλίππῳ ... and asked him, saying, Κύριε, θέλομεν τὸν Ἰησοῦν ἰδεῖν. ἔρχεται ὁ Φίλιππος καὶ λέγει τῷ Ἀνδρέᾳ, ἔρχεται Ἀνδρέας καὶ Φίλιππος καὶ λέγουσιν τῷ Ἰησοῦ. ὁ δὲ Ἰησοῦς ...

73. Τότε προσῆλθεν αὐτῷ ἡ μήτηρ τῶν υἱῶν Ζεβεδαίου with her sons ... ὁ δὲ[16] εἶπεν αὐτῇ, Τί θέλεις; **74.** ἀπεκρίθη οὖν αὐτῷ ὁ ὄχλος, Ἡμεῖς ἠκούσαμεν ἐκ τοῦ νόμου ὅτι ὁ Χριστὸς μένει εἰς τὸν αἰῶνα, καὶ πῶς λέγεις σὺ ὅτι δεῖ ... τὸν υἱὸν τοῦ ἀνθρώπου to be lifted up? τίς ἐστιν οὗτος ὁ υἱὸς τοῦ ἀνθρώπου; **75.** διὰ τοῦτό με ὁ πατὴρ ἀγαπᾷ, ὅτι ἐγὼ τίθημι τὴν ψυχήν μου.

76. Ἐγένετο δὲ ἐν ταῖς ἡμέραις ταύταις he went out εἰς τὸ ὄρος προσεύξασθαι.
77. If a man says he has faith but not works, μὴ δύναται ἡ πίστις[17] σῶσαι αὐτόν;[18]   **78.** ... δεῖ ἡμᾶς εἰσελθεῖν εἰς τὴν βασιλείαν τοῦ θεοῦ.

Vocabulary help for questions 53-78 (above)

[1 (qu. 53)]ἐραυνάω (6) I search, examine   [2 (qu. 54)]Aorist infinitive of ἐγείρω   [3 (qu. 55)]Φίλιππος (36) Philip   [4 (qu. 55)]Ναθαναήλ (6) Nathanael   [5 (qu. 55)]Ναζαρέτ, Ναζαρέθ (10) Nazareth   [6 (qu. 58)]καθαρός, -ά, -όν (26) clean   [7 (qu. 58)]Ἡλίας, ὁ (29) Elijah   [8 (qu. 60)]ἔμπροσθεν + gen. (48) before   [9 (qu. 64)] Ἡρῴδης, ου, ὁ (43) Herod   [10 (qu. 64)]ἔξεστι(ν) (31) It is lawful, it is permitted, it is possible, proper [followed by infinitive]   [11 (qu. 65)]πεινάω (23) I hunger, am hungry   [12 (qu. 67)]σκληρός, -ά, -όν (5) hard, rough, harsh   [13 (qu. 67)]ἀκούω takes the accusative of the person heard, and the genitive of that which is heard   [14 (qu. 68)]μαρτυρία (37) witness, testimony. Cf. μαρτυρέω.   [15 (qu. 70)]μισέω (39) I hate   [16 (qu. 73)]Often ὁ δε is best translated as "And he ..."   [17 (qu. 77)]πίστις is a third declension noun of a type that will be met in Chapter 28. The word means "belief, faith."   [18 (qu. 77)]μή in a question, suggests that the answer to the question should be "no."

Part 2 147

Chapter 16: The Subjunctive Mood

Subjunctives and participles are not only used very frequently in the NT, they are used very differently in NT Greek than they are in English. That this should be the case should not be a surprise – after all, one of the reasons that students of the NT learn Greek is so that they might understand its original meaning, and one language expresses ideas differently than another. Indeed, sometimes something can be said in one language, but not another. Greek is not English just written using different words! Thus an essential step in a serious study of the NT is to read what is said in the original Greek.

Although this is self evident, it is also the reason that subjunctives can be disconcerting to students, at least at first. There is no English equivalent by which to make sense of many uses of the subjunctive. But the news is good – although initially confusing, in the end subjunctives are one of the easiest moods of the verb to translate. Many a weary student has welcomed the presence of an easy-to-understand subjunctive construction in one or other of the more difficult passages in the Greek NT. The same is not true, alas, of participles. But they can wait for a later chapter (see Chap. 20).

For the curious, the subjunctive mood of the English verb is used to express uncertainty, supposition, and polite requests and wishes. In some contexts the words "might" or "could" or the like are found associated with the verb in the subjunctive. These words will also turn up in many translations of the Greek subjunctive, and the concepts of uncertainty, supposition, polite requests and wishes will also be found to be important uses of the Greek subjunctive in Chapter 1 of *Intermediate New Testament Greek Made Easier*. But at this stage of your learning the language, it may be best to put this aside, and just to learn the various uses of the subjective outlined below as something different from that which happens in English. The chapter will first introduce how subjunctives are formed, and then describe some of their more common uses in the Greek NT.

16.1 Forms of the Subjunctive

Comparing the forms used for the subjunctive mood with those used for the indicative mood quickly reveals one of the nice things about the subjunctive—there is not a great deal of memory work involved in learning the different forms of the subjunctive:

16.1.1 Present Indicative Compared to Present Subjunctive

Person	Pres Ind Act	Pres Subj Act
1st p sing	λύω	λύω
2nd p sing	λύεις	λύῃς
3rd p sing	λύει	λύῃ
1st pers pl	λύομεν	λύωμεν
2nd pers pl	λύετε	λύητε
3rd pers pl	λύουσι(ν)	λύωσι(ν)

Person	Pres Ind Mid/Pass	Pres Subj Mid/Pas
1st p sing	δέχομαι	δέχωμαι
2nd p sing	δέχῃ	δέχῃ
3rd p sing	δέχεται	δέχηται
1st pers pl	δεχόμεθα	δεχώμεθα
2nd pers pl	δέχεσθε	δέχησθε
3rd pers pl	δέχονται	δέχωνται

16.1.2 Aorist Indicative Compared to Aorist Subjunctive

Person	Aor Ind Act	Aor Subj Act
1st p sing	ἔλυσα	λύσω
2nd p sing	ἔλυσας	λύσῃς
3rd p sing	ἔλυσε(ν)	λύσῃ
1st pers pl	ἐλύσαμεν	λύσωμεν
2nd pers pl	ἐλύσατε	λύσητε
3rd pers pl	ἔλυσαν	λύσωσι(ν)

Person	Str Aor Ind Act	Str Aor Subj Act
1st p sing	ἔλαβον	λάβω
2nd p sing	ἔλαβες	λάβῃς
3rd p sing	ἔλαβεν	λάβῃ
1st pers pl	ἐλάβομεν	λάβωμεν
2nd pers pl	ἐλάβετε	λάβητε
3rd pers pl	ἔλαβον	λάβωσι(ν)

Part 2   149

16.1.3 Aor. Subj. Middle [of δέχομαι]

Person	Aor Ind Act	Aor Subj Mid
1st p sing	[see 24.1.5, 28.3 & Appendix B]	δέξωμαι
2nd p sing		δέξῃ
3rd p sing		δέξηται
1st pers pl		δεξώμεθα
2nd pers pl		δέξησθε
3rd pers pl		δέξωνται

[Note: This is the form of the aorist subjunctive used by the verbs ἀσπάζομαι, δέχομαι, προσεύχομαι, and others like them. The verbs ἀποκρίνομαι, πορεύομαι, φοβέομαι, and others like them, use a passive form for their aorist. A fuller explanation will be given in 24.1.5, 28.3 and *Int*.4.3. δέξωμαι is actually δεχ-σ-ωμαι, and the usual rules apply for verb stems that end in a guttural, labial or dental.]

16.1.4 The Present Tense of the Subjunctive Mood

The foregoing examples illustrate that the subjunctive of the present tense is formed by the lengthening of the vowel at the beginning of the suffix (with the iota turning into a subscript). This is also true for middle and passive verbs.

16.1.5 Aorist Tenses of the Subjunctive Mood for the Active Voice

The aorist tenses are formed using the endings of the present subjunctive. The weak aorists add a σ, which can combine with the final consonant of the verb stem in the usual way, and then add the subjunctive endings. The strong aorists use the strong aorist verb stem and then add the subjunctive endings.

Examples of weak aorist subjunctives:

Pres ind act	Pres subj act	Aor ind act	Aor sub act
βλέπω βλέπεις etc	βλέπω βλέπῃς etc	ἔβλεψα ἔβλεψας etc	βλέψω βλέψῃς etc [π+σ = ψ]
δοξάζω δοξάζεις etc	δοξάζω δοξάζῃς etc	ἐδόξασα ἐδόξασας etc	δοξάσω δοξάσῃς etc [dz+σ = σ]
πείθω πείθεις etc	πείθω πείθῃς etc	ἔπεισα ἔπεισας etc	πείσω πείσῃς etc [θ+σ = σ]

Examples of strong aorist subjunctives

Pres ind act	Pres subj act	Aor ind act	Aor sub act
ἄγω ἄγεις etc	ἄγω ἄγῃς etc	ἤγαγον ἤγαγες etc	ἀγάγω ἀγάγῃς etc
βάλλω βάλλεις etc	βάλλω βάλλῃς etc	ἔβαλον ἔβαλες etc	βάλω βάλῃς etc
ἐσθίω ἐσθίεις etc	ἐσθίω ἐσθίῃς etc	ἔφαγον ἔφαγες etc	φάγω φάγῃς etc
λαμβάνω λαμβάνεις etc	λαμβάνω λαμβάνῃς etc	ἔλαβον ἔλαβες etc	λάβω λάβῃς etc
λέγω λέγεις etc	λέγω λέγῃς etc	εἶπον εἶπες etc	εἴπω εἴπῃς etc
ὁρῶ [ie ὁράω] ὁρᾷς etc	ὁρῶ ὁρᾷς etc	εἶδον εἶδες etc	ἴδω ἴδῃς etc

16.1.6 The Subjunctive of εἰμί

The present subjunctive active of εἰμί is as follows:

ὦ
ᾖς
ᾖ
ὦμεν
ἦτε
ὦσι(ν)

Notice that the forms listed are the subjunctive endings for the present subjunctive active verb, without the verb stem, and with a breathing mark. Thus there are no separate forms to be memorized, only recognized, although remember that you will be expected to be able to write these forms out in examinations and tests.

16.1.7 The Subjunctives of –μι Verbs

With the exception of δίδωμι, even the -μι verbs use the same endings for their subjunctives:

	Pres subj act	Aor subj act
ἵστημι I place	ἱστῶ ἱστῇς ἱστῇ ἱστῶμεν ἱστῆτε ἱστῶσι(ν)	στῶ στῇς στῇ στῶμεν στῆτε στῶσι(ν)
τίθημι I place	τιθῶ τιθῇς τιθῇ τιθῶμεν τιθῆτε τιθῶσι(ν)	θῶ θῇς θῇ θῶμεν θῆτε θῶσι(ν)
δίδωμι I give	διδῶ διδῷς διδῷ διδῶμεν διδῶτε διδῶσι(ν)	δῶ δῷς, or δοῖς δῷ, δοῖ, or δώη δῶμεν δῶτε δῶσι(ν)
ἀφίημι I forgive	ἀφιῶ ἀφιῇς ἀφιῇ ἀφιῶμεν ἀφιῆτε ἀφιῶσι(ν)	ἀφῶ ἀφῇς ἀφῇ ἀφῶμεν ἀφῆτε ἀφῶσι(ν)

The following table has been provided to alert students and teachers that they should concentrate on the aorist subjunctives of -μι verbs; and to bring to their attention the frequency (and importance) of participles (Chapter 20) and indicatives (Chapters 12 & 27) of -μι verbs:

\multicolumn{9}{c	}{Frequency in Greek NT}
Verb and compounds	Total NT	Indicative	Infinitive	Subjunctive	Subj Active	Present Subj Act	Aorist Subj Act	Participle
ἀφίημι	143	76	7	12	9	0	9	20
δείκνυμι	66	32	10	3	0	0	0	10
δίδωμι	616	377	65	42	38	2	36	82
ἵστημι	477	225	43	19	15	0	15	161
τίθημι	258	153	21	20	16	2	14	53

16.1.7 The Subjunctives of -εω and -αω Verbs

The subjunctives of -εω and -αω verbs can be worked out by applying the rules of vowel contractions met when the verbs were introduced (Chapters 5 & 8; cf. Appendix G). For the -εω verbs, for example, this means that the ε disappears for the present subjunctive, and generally lengthens to an η before the σ of the aorist. For example:

The 2nd pers. pl. pres. subj. act. of λαλέω is λαλῆτε
The 2nd pers. pl. aor. subj. act. of λαλέω is λαλησῆτε
The 3rd pers. pl. pres. subj. act. of ἀγαπάω is ἀγαπῶσι(ν)
The 3rd pers. pl. aor. subj. act. of ἀγαπάω is ἀγαπησῶσι(ν)

16.2 Common Uses of the Subjunctive

16.2.1 In Purpose (or Final) Clauses

The most common use of the subjunctive mood is with ἵνα, which is translated "in order that." ἵνα is used 673 times in the Greek New Testament, and is almost always followed by the subjunctive. Thus, ἵνα is usually an indication that there will be a subjunctive verb. Translating ἵνα clauses is easy: use "in order that ... might ..." [or "in order to"] for ἵνα, and translate the rest of the sentence using good English. Some examples will make this clear.

- John 5:40 reads: καὶ οὐ θέλετε ἐλθεῖν πρός με ἵνα ζωὴν ἐχῆτε. This translates as, "and you do not wish to come to me, in order that you might have life." The ἵνα is an indication that the verb (ἐχῆτε) will be in the subjunctive.
- John 3:17 reads: οὐ γὰρ ἀπέστειλεν ὁ θεὸς τὸν υἱὸν εἰς τὸν κόσμον ἵνα κρίνῃ τὸν κόσμον This translates as, "For God did not send his son into the world in order to condemn the world." [κρίνω (114) I judge (often in negative sense, hence, it can also be translated "condemn")]

16.2.2 In [More Probable Future] Conditional Clauses

The word ἐάν, "if," is normally followed by the subjunctive.

- John 8:51 reads: ἐάν τις τὸν ἐμὸν λόγον τηρήσῃ, θάνατον οὐ μὴ θεωρήσῃ εἰς τὸν αἰῶνα, which would be translated, "If anyone keeps my word, he will not see death for ever."
- John 6:53 reads: ἐὰν μὴ φάγητε τὴν σάρκα τοῦ υἱοῦ τοῦ ἀνθρώπου ... οὐκ ἔχετε ζωήν, which would be translated, "If you do not eat the flesh of the son of man ... you have not life." [or "Unless you eat the flesh of the son of man, ... you have not life."]

16.2.3 Other Uses

The vocabulary list includes a number of words which are regularly followed by the subjunctive mood: ἐὰν μή, ὃς ἄν or ὃς ἐὰν, ὅταν, and οὐ μή.

16.2.4 Notes on the Subjunctive

1. As has already been said at the beginning of the chapter, the difficult thing about subjunctives for beginners is that there is no clearly defined part of English that neatly translates them. The subjunctive mood implies possibilities. It does not state things that are, but things that might be (e.g., if so-and-so happens then ...). Therefore the words "might," or "may" sometimes appear in translations of subjunctives. With familiarity, though, subjunctives are some of the easiest forms to translate. This is especially true of subjunctives following ἵνα and ἐάν. Either of these words should arouse the expectation that the verb which follows will be in the subjunctive, and that the meaning of the sentence will be relatively straightforward.
2. Notice the aorist subjunctive does not receive the augment. As with infinitives, the difference between the aorist and present subjunctives is with regard to the kind of action described. The present subjunctive is used when the stress is placed upon the continuous nature of the action, otherwise the aorist subjunctive is used [This means the aorist subjunctive is the more common of the two]. It is often said that the aorist infinitive indicates punctilliar action. While this can be true, the aorist infinitive is also used of actions viewed as a whole [see *Int*.3.3]. The distinction between the two tenses, while it can be important in interpreting the meaning of a verse, usually cannot be adequately translated into English. In effect, then, present and aorist subjunctives of the same verb almost always yield the same English translation.
3. Accents: a. The usual rules for verbs in the indicative apply to the present and both strong and weak aorist subjunctive active of -ω verbs (e.g. λύω, λύῃς, ..., λύσω, λύσῃς, ..., λάβω, λάβῃς, ...). b. In the present and aorist subjunctive active of -μι verbs, the long syllable of the subjunctive ending receives a circumflex accent (e.g. τιθῶ, τιθῇς ...; θῶμαι, θῇ, ...).

Vocabulary 16

Items relating to subjunctives in some way

ἄν (166)   -ever[1]
ἐάν + subj. (343)   if
ἐάν μή + subj. (48)   unless, except [note: εἰ μή (103) + ind. also means, "unless, except"]
ἵνα + subj. (673)   in order that, so that
ὃς ἄν or ὃς ἐάν + subj. (92) whoever
ὅταν + subj. (123)   whenever, when
οὐ μή + subj. (83)   no, definitely not [strong denial]

Subjunctives of the -μι verbs[4]

Pres Ind Act	Meaning	Pres. Subj. Act.	Aor. Subj. Act.
ἀφίημι	I forgive	[ἀφιῶ (0)]	ἀφῶ (9)
δίδωμι	I give	[διδῶ (2)]	δῶ (36)
ἵστημι	I place	[ἱστῶ (0)]	στῶ (15)
τίθημι	I place	[τιθῶ (2)]	θῶ (14)

Other Words

ἀλλήλων [2] (100) — of one another
ἀνοίγω (78) — I open [aor. ἀνέῳξα, ἠνέῳξα, or ἤνοιξα]
ἐκεῖνος, -η, -ο (243) — that [pl.: those]; he/she/it
ἐμός, ἐμή, ἐμόν (76) — my [possessive pronoun]
ἔξω (62) — outside, outer
ἔπιον — I drank [aor. ind. act. of πίνω]
κηρύσσω (61) — I announce, proclaim, preach [aor. ἐκήρυξα]
κρίνω (114) — I judge
μετά (467) — + acc.: after, behind
μετά (467) — + gen.: with
ὀφθαλμός (100) — eye
περί (331) — + acc.: around, about, near
περί (331) — + gen.: about, concerning
πίνω (73) — I drink
τέ (201) — and[3] [τέ ... καί or τέ ... δέ can mean "both ... and"]
χρόνος (54) — time
ὧδε (61) — here
ὥρα, ἡ (106) — hour, time

Notes on Vocabulary 16

1. ἄν makes a noun or adverb indefinite, which generally means that it is followed by the subjunctive: for example, ὅπου means "where," ὅπου ἄν means "wherever"; ὅτε means "when," ὅτε + ἄν = ὅταν means "whenever"; etc. ἄν is also used in contrary to fact conditional sentences, which speak of possibilities which did not happen—in such sentences it is not translated (see *Int*.2.2.2).

2. ἀλλήλων is given in its genitive form because the nominative form is not found. The word is also found in accusative (ἀλλήλους, "one another"), and dative (ἀλλήλοις, "to/for one another"). These are the regular endings for second declension masculine nouns.

3. τέ is a very weak "and," and is often not translated into English. It is never found as the first word of a sentence, and throws its accent back onto the previous word if it can accept it.

Part 2

4. Those using vocabulary cards will find it helpful to make separate cards for the aorist subjunctive forms.

Exercise 16

A. Paradigms: Write in full the ...
i. Pres. subj. act. of γράφω   ii. Aor. subj. act. of πέμπω   iii. Aor. subj. act. of ἐσθίω   iv. Aor. subj. act. of τίθημι

B. Translate into English
1. ὁ Ἰησοῦς ἦλθεν ἵνα ἀνθρώπους σώσῃ. 2. ὁ Ἰησοῦς ἦλθεν ἀνθρώπους σῶσαι. 3. ὁ Ἰησοῦς ἦλθεν δοῦναι ζωὴν πρὸς πάντας ἀνθρώπους. 4. ὁ Ἰησοῦς ἦλθεν ἵνα δίδῳ ζωὴν πρὸς πάντας ἀνθρώπους. 5. οἱ τυφλοὶ ἄνδρες ἦλθον πρὸς τὸν Ἰησοῦν ἵνα ἀνοίξῃ τοὺς ὀφθαλμοὺς αὐτῶν. 6. ὁ Ἰησοῦς ἤνοιξεν τοὺς ὀφθαλμοὺς τῶν τυφλῶν ἀνθρώπων ἵνα ἴδωσιν. 7. ὃς ἂν θέλῃ δικαιοσύνην δύναται αἰτῆσαι τὸν θεὸν περὶ αὐτῆς. 8. ὁ Ἰησοῦς ἀγαπᾷ ἡμᾶς ἵνα ἀγαπήσωμεν ἀλλήλους. 9. μετὰ τὸν θάνατον τοῦ Ἰωάννου περιεπάτησεν ἐν Γαλιλαίᾳ. 10. ἐάν τις πιστεύῃ ἐν Ἰησοῦ, he will be saved. 11. ὃς ἂν πιστεύῃ ἐν Ἰησοῦ will be saved. 12. ἡ ὥρα ἦλθεν ὅτε ὁ Ἰησοῦς ἦν ἀποθανεῖν. 13. ὧδέ ἐστιν ὁ τόπος ὅπου ἔθηκαν αὐτόν. 14. Ἰωάννας κηρύσσει τὴν βασιλείαν τῶν οὐρανῶν. 15. Ἰωάννας ἐκήρυξε τὴν βασιλείαν τῶν οὐρανῶν. 16. ὁ Ἰησοῦς ἦν μετὰ αὐτῶν. 17. οὐχί, οὐ μὴ πίνω.

C. Parsing
18-25. Parse the words underlined in the following passages.

D. Sentences and Phrases from the Greek New Testament
26. The Jews then disputed among themselves, saying, Πῶς δύναται οὗτος ἡμῖν <u>δοῦναι</u> τὴν σάρκα [αὐτοῦ] <u>φαγεῖν</u>; εἶπεν οὖν αὐτοῖς ὁ Ἰησοῦς, Ἀμὴν ἀμὴν λέγω ὑμῖν, ἐὰν μὴ φάγητε τὴν σάρκα τοῦ υἱοῦ τοῦ ἀνθρώπου καὶ πίητε αὐτοῦ τὸ αἷμα, οὐκ ἔχετε ζωήν ... 27. καὶ ἐὰν ἀσπάσησθε τοὺς <u>ἀδελφοὺς</u> ὑμῶν μόνον, τί περισσὸν[1] ποιεῖτε; οὐχὶ καὶ οἱ ἐθνικοὶ τὸ αὐτὸ[2] <u>ποιοῦσιν</u>;

28. [a leper speaking to Jesus] <u>Κύριε</u>, ἐὰν θέλῃς δύνασαί με καθαρίσαι.[3]
29. ὅταν ἐν τῷ <u>κοσμῷ</u> ὦ, φῶς εἰμι τοῦ κόσμου. 30. εἶπεν οὖν ὁ Ἰησοῦς πρὸς αὐτόν, Ἐὰν μὴ σημεῖα καὶ τέρατα[4] ἴδητε, οὐ μὴ πιστεύσητε. 31. καὶ ἐὰν τίς μου ἀκούσῃ τῶν ῥημάτων καὶ μὴ φυλάξῃ,[5] ἐγὼ οὐ κρίνω αὐτόν· οὐ γὰρ ἦλθον ἵνα κρίνω τὸν κόσμον, ἀλλ' ἵνα σώσω τὸν κόσμον.

32. καὶ <u>ἐποίησεν</u> δώδεκα ... ἵνα ὦσιν μετ' αὐτοῦ καὶ ἵνα ἀποστέλλῃ αὐτοὺς κηρύσσειν καὶ ἔχειν ἐξουσίαν ἐκβάλλειν τὰ δαιμόνια ... 33. καὶ ὃς ἂν θέλῃ ἐν ὑμῖν εἶναι πρῶτος shall be ὑμῶν δοῦλος, ... 34. ἐγὼ ἦλθον ἵνα ζωὴν ἔχωσιν καὶ περισσὸν[6] ἔχωσιν. 35. καὶ ὅπου ἂν εἰσπορεύηται[7] εἰς κώμας[8] ...
36. Ὅταν δὲ τὸ ἀκάθαρτον[9] πνεῦμα ἐξέλθῃ ἀπὸ τοῦ ἀνθρώπου, ... 37. ... and

Jesus ... said, "What do you wish me to do for you? λέγουσιν αὐτῷ, Κύριε, ἵνα <u>ἀνοιγῶσιν</u> οἱ ὀφθαλμοὶ ἡμῶν.

38. οἱ Ἰουδαῖοι ... εἶπαν αὐτῷ, Οὐ καλῶς[10] λέγομεν ἡμεῖς ὅτι Σαμαρίτης εἶ σὺ καὶ δαιμόνιον ἔχεις; ἀπεκρίθη Ἰησους, Ἐγὼ δαιμόνιον οὐκ ἔχω, ἀλλὰ τιμῶ[11] τὸν πατέρα μου, καὶ ὑμεῖς ἀτιμάζετέ[12] με. ἐγὼ δὲ οὐ ζητῶ τὴν δόξαν μου· ... ἀμὴν ἀμὴν λέγω ὑμῖν, ἐάν τις τὸν ἐμὸν λόγον τηρήσῃ, θάνατον οὐ μὴ θεωρήσῃ εἰς τὸν αἰῶνα. εἶπον οὖν αὐτῷ οἱ Ἰουδαῖοι, now we know ὅτι δαιμόνιον ἔχεις. Ἀβραὰμ ἀπέθανεν καὶ οἱ προφῆται,[13] καὶ σὺ λέγεις, Ἐάν τις τὸν λόγον μου τηρήσῃ, οὐ μὴ γεύσηται[14] θανάτου εἰς τὸν αἰῶνα.

39. Ἤκουσεν Ἰησοῦς ὅτι ἐξέβαλον αὐτὸν ἔξω καὶ when he found him εἶπεν, Σὺ πιστεύεις εἰς τὸν υἱὸν τοῦ ἀνθρώπου; ἀπεκρίθη ἐκεῖνος καὶ εἶπεν, Καὶ τίς ἐστιν, κύριε, ἵνα πιστεύσω εἰς αὐτόν; εἶπεν αὐτῷ ὁ Ἰησοῦ ... **40.** ὃς δ'[24] ἂν βλασφημήσῃ[15] εἰς τὸ πνεῦμα τὸ ἅγιον, οὐκ ἔχει ἄφεσιν[16] εἰς τὸν αἰῶνα.
41. Ὅταν δὲ ἔλθῃ ὁ υἱὸς τοῦ ἀνθρώπου ἐν τῇ δόξῃ αὐτοῦ καὶ πάντες οἱ ἀγγελοὶ μετ' αὐτοῦ, τότε he will sit ἐπὶ θρονοῦ δόξης αὐτοῦ ...
42. ἐάν τις περιπατῇ ἐν τῇ ἡμέρᾳ, οὐ προσκόπτει,[17] ὅτι τὸ φῶς τοῦ κόσμου τούτου βλέπει· ἐὰν δέ τις περιπατῇ ἐν τῇ νυκτί, προσκόπτει, ὅτι τὸ φῶς οὐκ ἔστιν ἐν αὐτῷ. ταῦτα εἶπεν, καὶ μετὰ τοῦτο λέγει αὐτοῖς, Λάζαρος ... sleeps.
43. But I have spoken these things to you, ἵνα ὅταν ἔλθῃ ἡ ὥρα αὐτῶν μνημονεύητε[18] αὐτῶν ὅτι ἐγὼ εἶπον ὑμῖν.

44. καὶ ἔδωκα αὐτῇ χρόνον ἵνα μετανοήσῃ,[19] καὶ οὐ θέλει μετανοῆσαι ἐκ τῆς πορνείας[20] αὐτῆς. **45.** καὶ γὰρ χεὶρ κυρίου ἦν μετ' αὐτοῦ. **46.** [Ἰωάννης ...]· οὗτος ἦλθεν εἰς μαρτυρίαν[21] ἵνα μαρτυρήσῃ περὶ τοῦ φωτός, ἵνα πάντες πιστεύσωσιν δι' αὐτοῦ. οὐκ ἦν ἐκεῖνος τὸ φῶς, ἀλλ' ἵνα μαρτυρήσῃ περὶ τοῦ φωτός.

47. ἡ οὖν Μαριὰμ ὡς ἦλθεν ὅπου ἦν Ἰησοῦς, when she saw him ἔπεσεν αὐτοῦ πρὸς τοὺς πόδας saying to him, Κύριε, εἰ ἦς[22] ὧδε οὐκ ἄν μου ἀπέθανεν ὁ ἀδελφός. **48.** ἐάν τε γὰρ ζῶμεν, τῷ κυρίῳ ζῶμεν, ἐάν τε ἀποθνῄσκωμεν, τῷ κυρίῳ ἀποθνῄσκομεν.

49. You did not choose me, but I chose you and appointed you ἵνα ὑμεῖς ὑπάγητε καὶ καρπὸν φέρητε καὶ ὁ καρπὸς ὑμῶν μένῃ, ἵνα whatever αἰτήσητε τὸν πατέρα ἐν τῷ ὀνόματί μου δῷ ὑμῖν. ταῦτα ἐντέλλομαι[23] ὑμῖν, ἵνα ἀγαπᾶτε ἀλλήλους. **50.** ἐὰν εἴπῃ ὁ πούς, Ὅτι οὐκ εἰμὶ χείρ, οὐκ εἰμὶ ἐκ τοῦ σώματος, ...

51. ὃς δ'[24] ἂν πίῃ ἐκ τοῦ ὕδατος which I will give him, will not thirst forever.
52. οὗτος ἦν μετὰ Ἰησοῦ. **53.** Then they bought children to him, ἵνα τὰς

Part 2 157

χεῖρας ἐπιθῇ[25] αὐτοῖς καὶ προσεύξηται ... **54.** ἐν τούτῳ ἐστὶν ἡ ἀγάπη, οὐχ ὅτι ἡμεῖς have loved God, ἀλλ᾽ ὅτι αὐτὸς ἠγάπησεν ἡμᾶς καὶ ἀπέστειλεν τὸν υἱὸν αὐτοῦ ἱλασμὸν[26] περὶ τῶν ἁμαρτιῶν ἡμῶν.

Vocabulary help for questions 26-54 (above)
[1 (qu. 27)]περισσός, -η, -ον (6) extraordinary, remarkable [2 (qu. 27)]In this instance, αὐτός means "same." [3 (qu. 28)]καθαρίζω (31) I purify, cleanse [4 (qu. 30)]τέρας, -ατος, το (16) wonder, portent, omen [5 (qu. 31)]φυλάσσω (31) I keep, guard. The noun, φύλαξ, -ακος, ὁ (3) guard, sentry, shows that the root of this verb ends with a kappa. This combines in the σ of the aorist to give a ξ. [6 (qu. 34)]περισσός, ή, όν (6) abundant, over and above [7 (qu. 35)]εἰς + πορεύομαι; the tense of this verb has been changed from that which appears in the Greek New Testament. [8 (qu. 35)]κώμη, ἡ (27) village, small town [9 (qu. 36)]ἀκάθαρτος, -ον (31) unclean, impure [10 (qu. 38)]καλῶς (37) adv.: rightly, well [11 (qu. 38)]τιμάω (21) I honor [12 (qu. 38)]ἀτιμάζω (7) I dishonor [13 (qu. 38)]προφήτης, ου, ὁ, prophet [14 (qu. 38)]γεύομαι + gen (15) I taste [15 (qu. 40)]βλασφημέω (34) I blaspheme, slander [16 (qu. 40)]ἄφεσιν is the accusative singular of ἄφεσις, εως, ἡ (17) forgiveness; which is a third declension noun of a type which will be met in chapter 28. Cf. the verb ἀφίημι, I send away, forgive. [17 (qu. 42)]προσκόπτω (8) I stumble [18 (qu. 43)]μνημονεύω + gen. (21) I remember [cf. the English word mnemonic] [19 (qu. 44)]μετανοέω (34) I repent [20 (qu. 44)]πορνεία, ἡ (25) sexual immorality, unfaithfulness, fornication [21 (qu. 46)]μαρτυρία, ἡ (37) witness, testimony [22 (qu. 47)]ἦς is the 2nd. pers. sing. imperf. (past) tense of εἰμι. "You were." [23 (qu. 49)]ἐντέλλομαι (14) I command [24 (qu. 51)]δ᾽ = δέ before a vowel [25 (qu. 53)]ἐπιτίθημι (40) I lay or put upon, inflict [26 (qu. 54)]ἱλασμός, ὁ (2) expiation, propitiation

Chapter 17: Review of Parts 1 & 2

Progress thus far

Since the last review chapter, Chapter eleven, you have begun to make remarkable progress in your learning of New Testament Greek. You already know several of the most common tenses and moods of the Greek verb, and have mastered the majority of the different types of nouns and adjectives. Not only that, you have begun to translate from the New Testament itself. With all this new information comes the danger of information overload, so it is perhaps a good idea to pause for one chapter and to review all that has been covered to date.

Grammar covered to date includes:

The Verb
Paradigms for the following verbal forms have been met:
    For -ω, -εω, -αω and -ομαι verbs:
        Tenses: present and [for -ω, -εω and -αω verbs] aorist
        Moods: indicative, infinitive, subjunctive
    For -μι verbs:
        Tense: aorist for indicative; present and aorist for infinitive and
            subjunctive
        Moods: indicative, infinitive, subjunctive
Parsing: you have learnt to parse verbs in all the above tenses and moods

Uses of Tenses of the Indicative Verb Covered in Parts 1-2			
Tense	Form of λύω	Closest English Tense(s)	Normal Translation
Indicative Active:			
Present	λύω	Simple present act Pres continuous act Present emphatic act	I loose I am loosing I do loose
Aorist	ἔλυσα	Simple past active	I loosed

Uses of Verb Moods Covered in Parts 1-2	
Mood	Principal uses of the mood
Indicative mood	The mood used for making statements of fact and asking questions
Subjunctive mood	The mood used to express contingencies or possibilities. Often found after certain conjunctions and in association with certain particles (e.g. ἵνα, ἄν, ἐάν, οὐ μή, etc)
Infinitive mood	The mood used after certain verbs (e.g. θέλω, δύναμαι, δεῖ, ἔξεστιν, μέλλω, ἄρχομαι, etc). Often most easily translated by the English infinitive: "to ..."

Note: The difference between present and aorist tenses of verbs in the infinitive or subjunctive mood is a difference in type of action. The present tense of infinitives and subjunctives emphasize continuous action; while the aorist tense may indicate punctiliar action. The tense of the main verb indicates whether the action takes place in the present, past, or future, not the tense of the verb in the infinitive or subjunctive.

The Noun and Adjective

Most nouns of the first, second and third declensions have already been met in Parts 1 and 2 [Note: Appendix E lists the declensions of nouns and adjectives. There are some there which will be met later, but the majority have been covered.] The most common uses of cases have also been met (see Chapter 3; in fact, it may be a good idea to re-read what was said about case in Chapter 3).

Vocabulary

Your vocabulary is slowly building up. There is a cumulative vocabulary list for Part 1 & Part 2 in Appendix H, and it probably is a good idea to begin your revision by going through it.

Formation of the Aorist Tense

The two different types of aorist are formed in different ways. Perhaps it would be helpful to gather together some examples of the various ways they are formed.

Examples of weak aorists:

	Aor ind act	Aor inf act	Aor subj act
λύω λύεις etc	ἔλυσα ἔλυσας etc	λῦσαι	λύσω λύσῃς etc
γράφω γράφεις etc	ἔγραψα ἔγραψας etc	γράψαι	γράψω γράψῃς etc

	Aor ind act	Aor inf act	Aor subj act
δοξάζω δοξάζεις etc	ἐδόξασα ἐδόξασας etc	δοξάσαι	δοξάσω δοξάσῃς etc
πέμπω πέμπεις etc	ἔπεμψα ἔπεμψας etc	πέμψαι	πέμψω πέμψῃς etc

Examples of strong Aorists

	Aor ind act	Aor inf act	Aor subj act
ἄγω ἄγεις etc	ἤγαγον ἤγαγες etc	ἀγαγεῖν	ἀγάγω ἀγάγῃς etc
βάλλω βάλλεις etc	ἔβαλον ἔβαλες etc	βαλεῖν	βάλω βάλῃς etc
ἐσθίω ἐσθίεις etc	ἔφαγον ἔφαγες etc	φαγεῖν	φάγω φάγῃς etc
λαμβάνω λαμβάνεις etc	ἔλαβον ἔλαβες etc	λαβεῖν	λάβω λάβῃς etc
λέγω λέγεις etc	εἶπον εἶπες etc	εἰπεῖν	εἴπω εἴπῃς etc
ὁρῶ [ὁράω] ὁρᾷς etc	εἶδον εἶδες etc	ἰδεῖν	ἴδω ἴδῃς etc

Note: The formation of the aorist indicative/ infinitive/ subjunctive of -μι verbs has been learnt as part of the different vocabulary lists.

How can it be determined if a verb has a strong or weak aorist? If the aorist of the word has appeared in a vocabulary, and that aorist finished with -ov (the strong aorist ending), it has a strong aorist. Other verbs are weak. In other words: you will be told when a verb has a strong aorist. If you have not been told, it is most likely that the verb is weak. After their main entry for a verb, dictionaries also list the aorist or other tenses if they are strong, or show other irregularities.

Translation strategies:

There is no set of rules which will make translation easy, but if the following are tried in the order suggested, the meaning of the sentence will usually be clear:

1. First, note the **punctuation marks**, and discover where the sentence breaks into smaller parts. A short sentence is easier to translate than a longer one, and many Greek sentences break up into a number of small self-contained units, which are then easier to translate.

Part 2 161

2. Next, identify and parse the **main verb**(s). The main verb is usually the verb in the indicative mood. Each complete sentence will have a main verb, and the meaning of the sentence as a whole is built upon this verb.
3. Next, find the noun(s) which is(/are) in the **nominative case**. These are usually the subject of the main verb.
4. If a noun in the **accusative case** is present, it is usually the direct object of the verb.
5. Next, look for **special constructions** such as infinitives or ἵνα clauses. These are generally self-contained units of meaning that can be translated independently, and then combined into the larger sentence.
6. Next look at the **prepositional phrases**. These are phrases which begin with a preposition, and make up a unit of meaning.
7. Finally, combine all of this together to make the complete sentence.

It is unlikely that all seven of these ingredients will be met in any given Greek sentence, but for complicated sentences the procedure will almost always work well.

Indicators of Subjunctives and Infinitives

Parsing is probably the most important skill in translating any language. Thus far the indicative, infinitive and subjunctive moods have been covered. The **indicative** mood is the one generally used, as it is used to make statements of fact.

The **subjunctive** mood is usually easy to recognize. For example:
ἵνα   — is normally followed by a subjunctive
οὐ μή   — is always followed by a subjunctive
ἄν   — is normally followed by a subjunctive

Thus, one of these words indicates that it is likely that a subjunctive verb follows. They are welcome finds in a sentence because they are generally easy to translate. They should likewise be a welcome sight in a translation passage in an exam, because they should yield easy marks!

The **infinitive** is generally associated with another verb. Where Greek has two or more verbs in one phrase, then the main verb is normally in the indicative, and the other verb(s) is (/are) normally an infinitive or a participle. You would expect:
θέλω to be followed by an infinitive (although there are exceptions);
δύναμαι to be followed by an infinitive;
δεῖ to be followed by an infinitive.

Tricky bits

In the first review exercise there was only one set of words which were closely similar (εἰ, "if" and εἶ, "you are" [second person singular, εἰμι]), but as the cumulative vocabulary has grown, there are now more words that need to be distinguished from each other by small clues:

Words which differ only in accent and/or breathing:

αὐτῆ	she (nom. fem. sing. of αὐτός)
αὕτη	this (nom. fem. sing. of οὗτος)
αὐταί	they (nom. fem. pl. of αὐτός)
αὗται	these (nom. fem. pl. of οὗτος)
εἰ	if
εἶ	you are (second person singular, εἰμί)
ἤ	or, than
ἡ	the (nom. fem. sing. article)
ᾖ	(3rd. pers. sing. pres. subj. act. of εἰμί)
τις, τι	someone, a certain [man/woman/thing]
τίς, τί	who ...? what ...? which ...?

Words which are rather similar:

αὐτός, -ή, -όν	he/she/it, etc.
οὗτος αὕτη, τοῦτο	this
οὕτως	thus, so
ἡμεῖς	us [nom. pl. of ἐγώ]
ὑμεῖς	you [nom. pl. of σύ]
ἡμῶν	our [gen. pl. of ἐγώ]
ὑμῶν	your [gen. pl. of σύ]
ὅτε	when, while, as long as
ὅτι	because, that

Using Logos to Search for Examples of Grammatical Features

Using Logos to do grammatical searches is relatively straight forward, once you have worked out the power of searches using @.

Example 1: if you wished to see all the examples of an aorist subjunctive active in the NT, you would begin by choosing the Greek NT, and then typing @ in the search box. This brings up a list of grammatical forms, of which you would choose "verb." Logos then shows @V in the search box. Clicking the arrow to the side of the search box reveals that there are 28,113 verbs in the New Testament. If you click on the search box again, you can choose "aorist," and after another click, "active" and another click, "subjunctive." Then click on the arrow at the right of the search box, and you will be given a list of all the verses in the NT in which an aorist subjunctive active is found. It turns out that there are 943 examples (the number is listed in the right side of the search box).

Exaample 2: In another example, suppose you were trying to find all the aorist subjunctive active instances of δίδωμι and its compounds (e.g. παραδίδωμις [119], etc). After clearing any previous search (you can do this

Part 2 163

by deleting the previous search, and then pressing return), start typing δίδωμι into the search function. One of the options that come up is root:δίδωμι. This searches not just δίδωμι, but all of its compounds (the option, lemma, only searches for δίδωμι and not its compounds). Then type an immediate @ thus: root:δίδωμι@. What comes up is a series of choices, once of which is "verb" Choose it, and Logos will enter root:δίδωμι@V in the search box. You can search on that. But you also have other options, so if you were wanting all of the subjunctives of all the compounds of δίδωμι, you can click in the search box again to bring up the menu, and choose "subjunctive" and Logos will then generate root:δίδωμι@V??S.

Exapmle 3: If you wanted to add a combined search, say for occurrences of ἵνα with the subjunctives of δίδωμι, just type a space after the previous search (i.e. root:δίδωμι@V??S), and then put the new search item in. It produced, "root:δίδωμι@V??S lemma:ἵνα" for that search. Clicking the arrow at the right of the search box will generate a list of all examples in the NT where ἵνα is followed by the aorist subjunctive of δίδωμι – all 41 of them. Try it for yourself. You will find that it sounds more complex than it actually is, once you realize you just ad @ after the verb lemma or root.

Checklist for revision

◊ Revise the uses of the subjunctive and infinitive moods of the verb, and how they are formed.
◊ Carefully look at what happens to the verb in the aorist tenses, and practice writing out the paradigm of various aorists in the indicative, subjunctive and infinitive moods.
◊ Revise vocabulary [there is a cumulative vocabulary list for Part 2 in Appendix H].
◊ Revise parsing. Questions 47-80 of the review exercise are devoted to parsing practice, and you should be able to tell from that how well you have mastered the art by seeing how well you handle those questions.
◊ Do translation passage 17 and the review exercise 17; then check your answers against those in Appendix A.
◊ Repeat *all* of the translations from the New Testament (which start in Chapter 12).

Translation Passage 17: John 1:1-11

It is time to give yourself a reward for all the work that you have put into learning Greek so far. You now have enough grammar to begin translating larger passages from the Greek New Testament. We will begin with John 1:1-11.

[1] Ἐν ἀρχῇ ἦν ὁ λόγος, καὶ ὁ λόγος ἦν πρὸς τὸν θεὸν, καὶ θεὸς ἦν ὁ λόγος. [2] οὗτος ἦν ἐν ἀρχῇ πρός τὸν θεὸν, [3] πάντα δι' αὐτοῦ ἐγένετο, καὶ χωρὶς αὐτοῦ ἐγένετο οὐδὲ ἕν. What became [4] ἐν αὐτῷ ζωὴ ἦν, καὶ ἡ ζωὴ ἦν τὸ φῶς τῶν ἀνθρώπων· [5] καὶ τὸ φῶς ἐν τῇ σκοτίᾳ φαίνει, καὶ ἡ σκοτία αὐτὸ οὐ κατέλαβεν.

[6] Ἐγένετο ἄνθρωπος, sent from God, ὄνομα αὐτῷ Ἰωάννης. [7] οὗτος ἦλθεν εἰς μαρτυρίαν ἵνα μαρτυρήσῃ περὶ τοῦ φωτός, ἵνα πάντες πιστεύσωσιν δι' αὐτοῦ. [8] οὐκ ἦν ἐκεῖνος τὸ φῶς, ἀλλ' ἵνα μαρτυρήσῃ περὶ τοῦ φῶτος. [9] Ἦν τὸ φῶς τὸ ἀληθινόν, which φωτίζει πάντα ἄνθρωπον, which was coming εἰς τὸν κόσμον. [10] ἐν τῷ κόσμῳ ἦν, καὶ ὁ κόσμος δι' αὐτοῦ ἐγένετο, καὶ ὁ κόσμος αὐτὸν οὐκ ἔγνω. [11] εἰς τὰ ἴδια ἦλθεν, καὶ οἱ ἴδιοι αὐτὸν οὐ παρέλαβον.

Vocabulary help for Translation Passage 17: John 1:1-11
χωρίς + gen. (41) without, apart from   σκοτία (17) darkness   φαίνω (31) I give light, shine   καταλαμβάνω (13) I overtake, seize, apprehend, understand   φωτίζω (11) I shine, give light to, illuminate   This is the irregular 3rd pers. sing. aor. ind. act. of γινώσκω (29.2).   παραλαμβάνω (49) I receive, accept

Exercise 17 (Review)

The following exercise includes one example of all vocabulary items, and generally only one. Thus, even though it looks somewhat long, you will need to do it all if you wish to cover all the vocabulary and grammar of Parts 1 and 2. Take particular note of parts of verbs and other words with which you have difficulty.

A. Translate into English
1. ὁ Ἰησοῦς ἦλθεν ἵνα ἔχωμεν αἰώνιον ζωὴν. 2. ὁ θεὸς θέλει δοῦναι δικαιοσύνην πρὸς ὑμᾶς. 3. ἐγὼ ἤνοιξα τὸ στόμα μου καὶ εἶπον αὐτῷ, οὐκ Φοβοῦμαι ἄνθρωπον. 4. προσεύχονται πρὸς τὸν πατέρα νύκτα καὶ ἡμέραν. 5. τὸ πνεῦμα τοῦ θεοῦ ἦν ἐπὶ τοῦ προσώπου τῶν ὑδάτων. 6. Ἰωάννης τε καὶ Πέτρος κηρύσσουσι περὶ τῆς βασιλείας τοῦ οὐρανοῦ. 7. Ἀβραὰμ δὲ ἔκαλεσεν ἐπὶ τοῦ ὀνόματος τοῦ κύριου ἐν ἐκείνῳ τόπῳ. 8. ἡ μήτηρ τοῦ τέκνου ᾔτησεν τὸν Ἰησοῦν θεῖναι[1] τὴν χεῖρα αὐτοῦ ἐπὶ τῆς κεφαλῆς τοῦ παιδίου. [[1]θεῖναι is the aor. inf. act. of τίθημι. The pres. inf. act. of τίθημι is τιθέναι.] 9. ἀπεθάνομεν τῇ ἁμαρτίᾳ ἵνα ζῶμεν τῷ θεῷ. 10. ὁ Ἰησοῦς εἶπεν ὅτι οἱ Φαρισαῖοι περιπάτουσι κατὰ τὰς ἐντολὰς τῶν ἀνθρώπων, καὶ κατὰ τοὺς νόμους τοῦ τούτου κόσμου, ἀλλὰ οὐ κατὰ τοὺς νόμους τοῦ θεοῦ.

11. Σίμων Πέτρος περιεπάτησε διὰ τῶν ὄρων τοῦ Γαλιλαίας πρὸς τὴν θάλασσαν τοῦ Γαλιλαίας. 12. οἱ Ἰουδαῖοι ἔβαλον Παῦλον ἐκ αὐτῶν συναγωγῆς. 13. χαίρομεν ἐν τῇ σοφίᾳ τοῦ Χριστοῦ. 14. ὁ τυφλὸς ἔπεσεν πρὸς

Part 2 165

τοὺς πόδας τοῦ Ἰησοῦ, καὶ παρεκάλεσεν αὐτὸν ἵνα ἀνοίξῃ τοὺς ὀφθαλμοὺς αὐτοῦ. 15. τίς δύναται εἶναι ἅγιον ἐὰν μὴ πιστεύῃ ἐν τῇ ἐπαγγελίᾳ τοῦ θεοῦ; 16. Ἰωάννης ἐβάπτισεν ὕδατι, ἀλλὰ Πέτρος καὶ Παῦλος ἐβάπτισαν ὕδατι καὶ πνεύματι. 17. σὰρξ γὰρ καὶ αἷμα μόνη οὐ δύνανται εἰσέρχεσθαι εἰς τὴν βασιλείαν. 18. δοκῶ ὅτι δαιμόνια ζητεῖ ἀπολέσαι τούς ἁγίους τῶν ἐκκλησίων. 19. μακάριός ἐστιν ὁ ἀνὴρ ὅτι ἀγαπᾷ τὴν γυναῖκα αὐτοῦ. 20. ὁ ὄχλος ἀκολουθεῖ τὴν ὁδὸν τούτου αἰῶνος.

21. ἡ ὥρα κρίνειν τὸν κόσμον ἦλθεν. 22. τούς νεκρους ἐγείρουσιν ἐκ τῆς γῆς οἱ ἀδελφοί. 23. καὶ ἐγένετο ἐν ἐκείναις ἡμέραις ὅτι ὁ Ἰησοῦς εὗρον πονηροὺς ἀνθρώπους ἐν τῷ ἱερῷ. 24. δεῖ δοῦναι δόξαν πρὸς τὸν θεόν. 25. πονηρὸς λαὸς ἔλαβεν λίθους καὶ ἔδωκεν ὀνόματας αὐτοῖς καὶ καλεῖ αὐτοὺς θεοὺς καὶ προσεκύνησεν αὐτοῖς. 26. ἀπεκρίθη καὶ εἶπεν ὅτι Ἐγὼ ἦλθον ἵνα ὁ Χριστὸς λαλήσῃ ἀλήθειαν μοι. 27. ὁ Ἰησοῦς ἄφηκεν ἡμῶν ἁμαρτίαν ἵνα ἀφίωμεν τὰς ἁμαρτίας ἀλλήλων. 28. ὁ Ἰησοῦς ἦλθεν πρὸς τὰ ἴδια, ἀλλὰ οἱ ἴδιοι αὐτὸν οὐ δέχονται. 29. αὐτὸς οὖν εἶπεν, Ἀμὴν ἀμὴν λέγω ὑμῖν ὅτι ὅταν τὸ ἅγιον πνεῦμα ἔλθῃ, ... 30. ὁ θεὸς ἀπώλεσεν τὰ ἔθνη διὰ τὰ πονηρὰ ἔργα αὐτῶν.

31. πάντες ἀγαθαὶ καρδίαι φέρει τὸν καρπὸν τῆς ἀγάπης. 32. τὸ σάββατον ἦν σημεῖον πρὸς τοὺς υἱοὺς τοῦ Ἀβραάμ. 33. ὁ ὄχλος συνήγαγεν πάλιν ἀκούειν τὰς παραβολάς. 34. οἱ Φαρισαῖοι ἀπέστειλαν τινας ἐκ τῶν δούλων αὐτῶν ἐρωτᾶν τὸν Ἰωάννης εἰ ἦν ὁ Χριστὸς, καὶ ἀπεκρίθη, Οὐ. 35. οἱ ἀπόστολοι ἔφαγον τὸν ἄρτον ἐν χαρᾷ ὅτι ἔσχον εἰρήνην ἐν ταῖς καρδίαις αὐτῶν. 36. ἀγάπη τῆς γραφῆς γεννᾷ σοφίαν καὶ δίκαια ἔργα. 37. Σίμων Πέτρος πορεύεται σὺν τῷ δώδεκα ἐπερωτᾶν τὸν Ἰησοῦν περὶ τοῦ λόγου. 38. ἔστησα ἐμὸν ἐλπὶς ἐπὶ τῇ πιστῷ ἐπαγγελίᾳ. 39. οὐ γινώσκει τὴν ὥραν ὅτε ὁ κύριος αὐτοῦ ἔρχεται ἀλλὰ ὁ πιστὸς δοῦλος ἔτι ποιεῖ καλὰ ἔργα. 40. τὰ ἑπτὰ πλοῖα ἔμεινεν ἐν μέσῳ τῆς θαλάσσης. 41. οἱ δύο ἀδελφοὶ ἀπέλυσαν τοὺς δούλους μετὰ ἐλάλησαν αὐτοῖς. 42. ὁ Ἰησοῦς σῴζει τε σῶμα καὶ ψυχήν, ἢ δύναται μόνον σῶσαι τὸν ψυχήν; 43. οἱ νεκροὶ ἔχουσιν οὐχὶ ἐξουσίαν. 44. ἀπέστειλα μου ἀποστόλους πρὸς τὴν οἰκίαν τοῦ Δαυὶδ λέγειν μου ῥήματα 45. ὁρῶ καὶ καλὸν καὶ κακὸν ἐν τῇ ἐκκλησίᾳ. 46. ἡ ἀγαπήτη ἀρχὴ οὐ πίπτει.

B. Parse
47. ἀπέρχονται 48. γινῇ 49. βιβλίων 50. γράψαι 51. πιστεύομεν 52. ἀποθνήσκετε 53. ἀσπαζόμεθα 54. ἐδόξασαν 55. διδῷ 56. πέμψαι 57. ἐξήλθετε 58. ἀπέρχεσθε 59. λύειν 60. ἔδειξαν 61. ἐξέβαλες 62. ἀφῇ 63. ἀγαπᾷς 64. ἐμαρτύρησα 65. προσέρχεσθε 66. συνήγαγεν 67. χαίρομεν 68. δῷς 69. ἐτηρήσαμεν 70. εἴδετε 71. ἐστήσαμεν 72. ἠνέγκατε 73. ἔθηκας 74. ᾖ 75. ἤγαγον 76. ἐπίομεν 77. ἐπέμψατε 78. στῶμεν 79. ἱστῶ 80. τιθῇς

C. Tricky bits
Write down the meaning of the following, and parse if possible:
Words which differ only in accent: 81. ἢ 82. ἡ 83. ᾗ 84. αὐτή 85. αὕτη 86. αὐταί 87. αὗται 88. τις, τι 89. τίς, τί 90. εἰ 91. εἶ

Words which are rather similar: 92. ὅτε 93. ὅτι 94. ἡμεῖς 95. ὑμᾶς 96. ἡμῶν 97. ὑμῶν 98. αὐτός, -ή, -ό 99. οὗτος, αὕτη, τοῦτο 100. οὕτως

D. Prepositions (fill in the gaps):
101. σύν + _____ : _____
102. κατά   + accusative: _____
                + genitive: _____
103. πρός   + _____ : toward, with, against
                + gen. : to the advantage of
                + _____ : near, at, by
104. ἐπί   + acc.: _____
                + gen.: _____
                + dat.: _____
105. ἀπό   + _____ : from
106. ἐκ, ἐξ   + genitive: _____
107. ἐν   + _____ : _____
108. διά   + acc.: _____
                + gen.: _____

E. Miscellaneous Vocabulary Items:
Write down the meaning of: 109. μή 110. πῶς 111. ἔξω 112. ἄν 113. ὡς 114. οὐ μή + _____ = _____? 115. ὅπου 116. ἐάν + _____ = _____? 117. δείκνυμι 118. πείθω 119. μέν ... [δέ] 120. φῶς 121. πῦρ 122. ὑπάγω 123. οὕτως 124. διά τί 125. ὧδε 126. ἀπόλλυμι 127. χρόνος 128. πρῶτος 129. ὃς ἄν + _____ = _____?

F. Write out in full
The declension of 130. οἰκία 131. φωνή 132. θέλημα 133. ἄλλος

The paradigm for: 134. The present infinitive active of βάλλω 135. The aorist infinitive active of βάλλω 136. The aorist infinitive active of δοξάζω 137. The present indicative middle of γίνομαι 138. The aorist indicative active of παραδίδωμι 139. The present subjunctive active of βάλλω

G. Translate into Greek
140. Jesus sent Peter and John into the temple. 141. The house of the mother of David. 142. The angels see the face of God. If man saw the face of God he would die. 143. God forgave our sins by grace. 144. The crowd came from Jerusalem to see John.

H. Correct the Mistakes in the following
Underline the mistake, and write the correct Greek next to it: 145. τὰ τέκνα ἔλαβον ἄρτον. 146. ὁ Πέτρος ἔβαλεν ὁ λίθος. 147. ὁ Ἰησοῦς ἔρχεται ἵνα σῶσαι. 148. οἱ δοῦλοι πορεύομαι. 149. ὁ θεὸς οὐ ἐστὶν ἄνθρωπον.

Part 3

Participles, the perfect and imperfect tenses, and beginning to translate whole chapters from the Gospel of John

Chapter 18: The Relative Pronoun

The Greek relative pronoun is often used in a way that is similar to the English relative pronoun ("who, whom, which, that"). Interestingly enough, the relative pronoun is one of the parts of English that declines:

The English Relative Pronoun			
	Masc	Fem	Neut
Nom s	who	who	which/that
Acc s	whom	whom	which/that
Gen s	whose	whose	of which
Dat s	to whom	to whom	to which
Nom pl	who	who	which/that
Acc pl	whom	whom	which/that
Gen pl	whose	whose	of which
Dat pl	to whom	to whom	to which

Some of these forms have fallen into disuse in some varieties of regional English (e.g. "who" is often used for "whom"), so students will do well to take advice from their teacher whether to use all the forms or not. For most external exams, though, it is wise to continue to use all of them, including "whom."

Like other pronouns in Greek, the relative pronoun exists in singular and plural, masculine, feminine and neuter, and in nominative, accusative, genitive and dative (but not the vocative):

The Greek Relative Pronoun			
	Masc	Fem	Neut
Nom s	ὅς	ἥ	ὅ
Acc s	ὅν	ἥν	ὅ
Gen s	οὗ	ἧς	οὗ
Dat s	ᾧ	ᾗ	ᾧ
Nom pl	οἵ	αἵ	ἅ
Acc pl	οὕς	ἅς	ἅ
Gen pl	ὧν	ὧν	ὧν
Dat pl	οἷς	αἷς	οἷς

Note: The forms used are somewhat familiar as they are rather like the endings of the first and second declension nouns, with a hard breathing added. There is one learning difficulty, though, as aside from the accent, the relative pronoun looks exactly like the article in some of its forms. As a consequence, the accents for οἵ, ἥ, αἵ, and ὅ have to be specifically learned. Please notice the following differences between the relative pronoun, and other things that already have been met in earlier chapters:

ὅ   which, that (nom./acc. neut. sing. rel. pron.)
ὁ   the (nom. masc. sing. article)
ἥ   who, that (nom. fem. sing. rel. pron.)
ἡ   the (nom. fem. sing. article)
ἤ   or, than
ᾖ   he/she/it might be (3rd. pers. sing. pres. subjunctive act. of εἰμί, I am)
ᾗ   to whom (dat. fem. sing. rel. pron.)
οὗ   whose, of whom (gen. masc./neut. sing. rel. pron.)
οὐ   not
ᾧ   to whom, to which (dat. masc./neut. sing. rel. pron.)
ὦ   (1st. pers. sing. pres. subjunctive act. of εἰμί, I am)
οἵ   who, that (nom. masc. pl. rel. pron.)
οἱ   the (nom. masc. pl. article)
αἵ   who (nom. fem. pl. rel. pron.)
αἱ   the (nom. fem. pl. article)

Most relative pronouns are not difficult to translate, as they usually correspond reasonably closely to the English relative pronoun, aside, of course, from the added complications of gender and case. The relative pronoun takes its number and gender from the noun/pronoun to which it refers, but its case generally depends on its whereabouts in the sentence in which it is found [*Int*.2.7.1 deals with the attraction of relative pronouns, a significant exception to this general rule. Further, a list of the use of relative pronouns with various prepositions may be found in *Int*.2.7.3]. The noun/pronoun to which the relative pronoun refers is called the **antecedent** of the relative pronoun.

Some examples will illustrate the use of the relative pronoun:

- John 4:29 Come and see ἄνθρωπον ὃς εἶπέν μοι … Come and see a man who said to me … [ὅς is masculine singular, because of its antecedent (ἄνθρωπον). It is in the nominative case because it is the subject of the verb λέγω]
- Matt 12:32 ὃς ἂν εἴπῃ κατὰ τοῦ πνεύματος τοῦ ἁγίου … Whoever speaks against the holy spirit [ὅς is nominative, as it is the subject of the verb λέγω. The indefinite particle ἄν makes the "who" into "whoever".]
- John 11:2 ἦν δὲ Μαριὰμ … ἧς ὁ ἀδελφὸς … And it was Mary … whose brother … [This translates naturally into the English. The relative pronoun ἧς is singular feminine because it refers to Mary. It is genitive, because it expresses her relationship to her brother.]
- John 3:2 ταῦτα τὰ σημεῖα … ἃ σὺ ποιεῖς These signs which you do [The

Part 3   171

relative pronoun ἅ is neuter plural because "these signs" is neuter plural. It is nominative, because it is the subject of the verb ποιέω.]

18.2 Using the Dictionary Functions of *Logos*

Many electronic resources provide a very efficient method of obtaining access to dictionary meanings of words. This, in fact, is one of their greatest advantages. Much time can be spent just looking words up in dictionaries.

In the biblical languages pack of *Logos*, for example, the basic meaning of words can be obtained by loading the Greek New Testament (I suggest UBS4), and just pointing a curser at any word. The word will be parsed in a box at the foot of the screen. There are other dictionaries that can be accessed very efficiently. The steps to do so will now be explained, although if you have had *Logos* for a while, you will most likely have already attended to or experimented with some of the steps outlined below.

The following steps will give you access to the dictionary functions of *Logos*:

1. Start *Logos*. If it is the first time you have done so, you will find yourself at a home screen. At the top right of your *Logos* window you will see a heading "Layouts." You can choose which-ever layout that appeals to you. I use one that had two windows, and usually have the Greek text in one, and the English text in another (I use the English to access *TDNT* – see below).
2. Now that you have two windows, click on the + symbol on one of them. You wish to add the United Bible Society Greek New Testament – UBS4 is what you should search for. Add that. Also add a modern translation of the Bible to the other window – e.g. the RSV or the NRSV. Once you have done this, you have *very* fast access to any given text (just type the reference in the box just above the text of the Greek NT), and the basic meaning of every Greek word can be quickly ascertained by just pointing the curser at that word. The word will be parsed in a small panel at the bottom of the screen. The basic meaning of the word is provided there as a part of the parsing process.
3. Sometimes, you will be interested to find out more about the meaning and usage of a particular word. For example, to discover more about the usage of δόξα, "glory," click on the "Search" tab, and change your keyboard to Greek Polytonic. Then type δοξα, and search for it (you do not need to include the accent in searches). As you look at the search results, you will see that it has found all the places in the NT which has exactly that word, in exactly that form. You will no doubt want to find all the uses of δόξα, not just those in the nominative singular case. So, click on the box is the UBS4 column for the search item that has been found (e.g. John 8:54; although any of them will do). It should show you the Greek text of John 8:54, with the word δόξα highlighted.

4. Right click on δόξα, and you will be given a menu box, that includes "look up, look up in new tab, etc." Look down in the middle box, and you will find the option "morph. search δόξα" [don't choose "morph. search δόξαNNSF" as that will only search for the nominative singular examples]. It will give you a listing of all the places where δόξα is found in the New Testament. You could then look at each of these texts and write you own summary of what you find (that is actually a good exercise), but you may also wish to consult *TDNT*.
5. *TDNT* is the abbreviation of the *Theological Dictionary of the New Testament*. Once you use this, you will see why it has become the standard reference work for word studies in the New Testament. You can get to this resource several ways, although the way I like to do so is through the English text.
6. Go back to your search results for δόξα. This time click on a box for a modern translation such as the NSRV (I know this one works for what we are trying to do; not all of the English Bibles do). You can use any of the results, but why not chose John 8:54 again.
7. Now that you have the text in front of you, look up at the second row of instructions above the biblical text. There are a number of icons, including one called "Display." Click on the arrow next to "Display" and click on "Inline." This will bring up an interlinear display [you may have to adjust it as little to get the text you were looking at back again]. The first line is the English text. Under each English word you will find the corresponding Greek word. Underneath that you will find its dictionary form. Then a coded parsing. For example, "glory" in John 8:54, the word δόξα is listed as both the form found in the text, and the dictionary form. It is parsed NNSF (for Noun Nominative Singular Feminine – hover the curser over it, and the full explanation will appear towards the bottom of the window). Underneath are two numbers: 1391 and 33.357. You may hover the curser over each of them, and it will give you a little window for each. The first one, 1391, will bring you to *TDNT*, which is what you want. The other leads to a lexicon, which is fine for quick word meanings, but not for the type of in-depth research available through *TDNT*.
8. Click on the top number (i.e. 1391), and a new window will open, with the entry for δόξα that is found in *TDNT*. Glance down the entry, and you will discover that almost all of the background you would ever want is available to you (in fact, usually much more than you would ever want). It gives the background in classical Greek, the Hebrew Bible, the Septuagint (the LXX, or Greek version of the Bible translated and available to Jesus, Paul and the early Christians), in Palestinian Judaism, and the New Testament Usage. You can read as much or little as you want. By the way, you can quickly navigate around the article by clicking on the >> icon at the extreme left of the line just above the text. It will then

provide a table of contents which can be expanded to show more or less detail. You can also access all the articles for other words in the work, which are available under the alphabetical heading.

18.3 Using Burer & Miller's or Kubo's *Reader's Greek-English Lexicon*

There are several paper-based options for dictionaries. Prior to the widespread availability of electronic resources, a very efficient way to gain access to the basic meaning of words was to use Sakae Kubo's, *A Reader's Greek-English Lexicon of the New Testament* (Berrien Springs, MI: Andrews University Press, 1975), although there are many other choices available (including the very helpful if concise dictionary often included with the United Bible Societies' Greek New Testament). A more recently published Reader's Greek-English Lexicon is that of Michael H. Burer and Jeffrey E. Miller, *A New Reader's Lexicon of the Greek New Testament* (Grand Rapids, MI: Kregel, 2008), although a second-hand copy of Kubo is more than adequate if you can obtain one cheaply.

Burer & Miller's lexicon is arranged by New Testament verse. In their preface, Burer and Miller explain: "The NRL [New Readers Lexicon ...] lists and concisely defines in context every word that occurs fewer than fifty times in the New Testament (NT). There is no special vocabulary section for each NT book, and proper names and places are included. This format is designed to facilitate uninterrupted reading and translation of the NT. The contextual definitions were drawn from W. Bauer, F. W. Danker, W. F. Arndt, and F. W. Gingrich, *A Greek-English Lexicon of the New Testament and Other Early Christian Literature*, 3d ed. (Chicago: University of Chicago Press, 2000)" (p. 13). In other words, Burer & Miller list the meaning of all the words in each verse of the Bible that occur less than 50 times. Words that occur more than fifty times in the Greek New Testament will have already been included in the vocabularies in this textbook. So you should not need to refer to Burer & Miller's appendix of words that occur more than fifty times – though it is there for those times when you forget. Each word has a range of meanings, and Burer & Miller have listed the meaning from the standard Greek-English lexicon of the New Testament that they consider best fits the use of the word in the verse under consideration. As they themselves point out, it is often very helpful to know the other possible meanings a word might have. These can be found by consulting standard reference works such as Bauer, Danker, Arndt and Gingrich, or using the efficient search functions of a program like Logos, which gives quick access to a range of dictionaries, including TDNT. Burer and Miller also note, "Twenty percent (or one in five) of all NT words occurs fewer than fifty times. ... Only 525 verses do not contain a single word that occurs fewer than fifty times" (p. 17). By the way, keep an eye out for second-hand copies of Bauer, Danker, Arndt and Gingrich. It is a fabulously useful addition to your personal reference library if you can obtain one.

With Kubo's lexicon there is an extra step in looking up the meaning of a word. In Kubo, each book of the Bible has a section at the beginning which contains all the words that occur more than five times in that book called "Special Vocabulary." The rest of the words are listed under their verse, except for words that are repeated in the space of two verses. Thus, the first place to look for a word you do not know is under the heading for the specific verse you are reading or in the verse preceding it. Secondly, check in the "Special Vocabulary" listed at the beginning of that particular New Testament book. Lastly, check the list of words that occur more than fifty times (and blush as you do so!). If that does not locate the word, you need to start thinking about strong aorists, or perhaps you have made a mistake and need to start again.

18.4 Gentle exhortation and encouragement

You will have noticed that each new part of the book introduces a significant new level of difficulty. By the end of each part things have begun to make sense again, and you are then ready to move on to the next challenge. The significant new level of difficulty for Part 3 is that you are now lacking the vocabulary shelter that you have had to this point, and you have to go outside of the textbook to find words you don't know. Most students find it challenging to get used to using Logos or Burer & Miller, or Kubo as a source for vocabulary items. Everybody eventually learns how to use a dictionary as they have to in order to survive, but it takes some perseverance. The ever-present temptation is to use an interlinear. Because the eye automatically reads the English, not the Greek, *it can be a bad mistake to use an interlinear,* including that which is available in Logos. Likewise, it is likely to be a mistake to make an interlinear out of the exercises by writing the English meaning above the words. If you take a shortcut at this stage, then it will be that much harder to learn later. I have known a few students attempting to memorize whole chapters of their English Bible to try to pass their exam before they finally take the plunge to use Burer & Miller or another dictionary! Surely, the extra effort to learn how to use Burer & Miller or a dictionary has to be less than the effort to memorize this much English text. Thusss ... take the extra time to find those words from Kubo or another dictionary. Its worth it in the long run.

Vocabulary 18

ἰδού (200)   look, behold
νῦν (148)   now

Part 3   175

ὁ δε   and he, but the[1]
ὅς, ἥ, ὅ (1369)   who, which, what, that [relative pronoun]
ὅσος, ὅση, ὅσον (110)   as much as
ὅστις, ἥτις, ὅτι[2] (154)   whoever; such a one who; who
οὐαί (45)   woe, alas!
παρά (191)   + acc.: **by**, along, near, more than, against
παρά (191)   + gen.: from
παρά (191)   + dat.: **at**, by, beside, near
τοιοῦτος, τοιαύτη, τοιοῦτον (56)   such a kind, such as this

Notes on Vocabulary 18.

1. "And he" is often the best way to translate ὁ δέ, although it hardly needs pointing out that it should only be used when the article is not associated with a noun. In that case the best translation would be "But the ..."
2. Note that ὅστις = ὅς + τις, and that both parts of the word decline. Notice also that the word ὅτι, "because, that," has exactly the same form as the nominative neuter singular of this word

Exercise 18

Sentences and Phrases from the Greek New Testament:

Please note: In earlier chapters, words in the phrases, sentences and passages taken from the NT that you have not previously met in a vocabulary, have been provided in the notes. From now on you will be expected to be able to use a lexicon to discover the meaning of words that you have not yet met (or have forgotten) for the texts from the New Testament (see 18.2 & 18.3 above regarding dictionaries such Burer & Miller, and the dictionary function of Logos).

1. τὰ ἔργα ἃ ποιεῖς (John 7:3). **2.** καὶ ὃς οὐ λαμβάνει τὸν σταυρὸν αὐτοῦ καὶ ἀκολουθεῖ ὀπίσω μου, οὐκ ἔστιν μου ἄξιος (Matt 10:38). **3.** οὐαὶ τῷ κόσμῳ ἀπὸ τῶν σκανδάλων· ἀνάγκη γὰρ ἐλθεῖν τὰ σκάνδαλα, πλὴν οὐαὶ τῷ ἀνθρώπῳ δι' οὗ τὸ σκάνδαλον ἔρχεται (Matt 18:7). **4.** Καὶ ἐξῆλθεν πάλιν παρὰ τὴν θάλασσαν (Mark 2:13). **5.** καὶ ἰδοὺ φωνὴ ἐκ τῶν οὐρανῶν εἶπεν,[1] Οὗτός ἐστιν ὁ υἱός μου ὁ ἀγαπητός, ἐν ᾧ εὐδόκησα (Matt 3:17).

6. Πᾶς οὖν ὅστις ἀκούει μου τοὺς λόγους τούτους καὶ ποιεῖ αὐτούς ... (Matt 7:24). **7.** ἐγὼ δὲ οὐ παρὰ ἀνθρώπου τὴν μαρτυρίαν λαμβάνω (John 5:34). **8.** Ἀποκάλυψις Ἰησοῦ Χριστοῦ, ἣν ἔδωκεν αὐτῷ ὁ θεός, δεῖξαι[2] τοῖς δούλοις αὐτοῦ ἃ δεῖ γενέσθαι[3] ἐν τάχει, καὶ ἐσήμανεν by sending διὰ τοῦ ἀγγέλου αὐτοῦ τῷ δούλῳ αὐτοῦ Ἰωάννῃ, ὃς ἐμαρτύρησεν τὸν λόγον τοῦ θεοῦ καὶ τὴν μαρτυρίαν Ἰησοῦ Χριστοῦ, ὅσα εἶδεν (Rev 1:1-2). **9.** καὶ ἐπέστρεψα βλέπειν τὴν φωνὴν ἥτις ἐλάλησε[4] μετ' ἐμοῦ, καὶ when I turned εἶδον ἑπτὰ λυχνίας χρυσᾶς (Rev 1:12).

10. Ἄγουσιν αὐτὸν πρὸς τοὺς Φαρισαίους τόν ποτε τυφλόν. ἦν δὲ σάββατον ἐν ᾗ ἡμέρᾳ τὸν πηλὸν ἐποίησεν ὁ Ἰησοῦς καὶ ἀνέῳξεν αὐτοῦ τοὺς ὀφθαλμούς. πάλιν οὖν ἠρώτησαν αὐτὸν καὶ οἱ Φαρισαῖοι πῶς ἀνέβλεψεν. ὁ δὲ εἶπεν αὐτοῖς, Πηλὸν ἐπέθηκέν μου ἐπὶ τοὺς ὀφθαλμοὺς, καὶ I washed, καὶ βλέπω. ἔλεγον οὖν ἐκ τῶν Φαρισαίων τινές, Οὐκ ἔστιν οὗτος παρὰ θεοῦ ὁ ἄνθρωπος, ὅτι τὸ σάββατον οὐ τηρεῖ. ἄλλοι δὲ ἔλεγον, Πῶς δύναται ἄνθρωπος ἁμαρτωλὸς τοιαῦτα σημεῖα ποιεῖν; καὶ σχίσμα ἦν ἐν αὐτοῖς (John 9:13-16).

11. οὗτος ἦλθεν εἰς μαρτυρίαν ἵνα <u>μαρτυρήσῃ</u> περὶ τοῦ φωτός, ἵνα πάντες πιστεύσωσιν δι' αὐτοῦ. οὐκ ἦν ἐκεῖνος τὸ φῶς, ἀλλ' ἵνα μαρτυρήσῃ περὶ τοῦ φωτός. Ἦν τὸ φῶς τὸ ἀληθινόν, <u>ὃ</u> φωτίζει πάντα ἄνθρωπον, coming εἰς τὸν κόσμον (John 1:7-9). **12.** λέγει ἡ μήτηρ αὐτοῦ τοῖς <u>διακόνοις</u>, Ὅ τι ἂν λέγῃ ὑμῖν do (John 2:5).

13. ... καὶ οὐ θέλετε <u>ἐλθεῖν</u> πρός με ἵνα ζωὴν <u>ἔχητε</u>. Δόξαν παρὰ ἀνθρώπων οὐ λαμβάνω ... (John 5:40-41). **14.** Καὶ εἶδον θρόνον μέγαν λευκὸν, and he who sat upon it, οὗ ἀπὸ τοῦ προσώπου ἔφυγεν ἡ γῆ καὶ ὁ οὐρανός (Rev 20:11). **15.** εἶδεν ὁ Ἰησοῦς τὸν Ναθαναὴλ coming πρὸς αὐτὸν καὶ λέγει περὶ αὐτοῦ, Ἰδοὺ [5] ἀληθῶς Ἰσραηλίτης ἐν <u>ᾧ</u> δόλος οὐκ ἔστιν (John 1:47).

16. λέγω δὲ ὑμῖν ὅτι ὃς ἂν ἀπολύσῃ τὴν <u>γυναῖκα</u> αὐτοῦ μὴ ἐπὶ πορνείᾳ καὶ γαμήσῃ ἄλλην μοιχᾶται (Matt 19:9). **17.** νῦν δὲ καυχᾶσθε ἐν ταῖς ἀλαζονείαις ὑμῶν· πᾶσα καύχησις τοιαύτη πονηρά ἐστιν (Jam 4:16). **18.** ἐγὼ <u>ὅσους</u> ἐὰν φιλῶ ἐλέγχω καὶ παιδεύω ... (Rev 3:19). **19.** εἴ τις τὸν ναὸν τοῦ θεοῦ φθείρει, will destroy τοῦτον ὁ θεός· ὁ γὰρ ναὸς τοῦ θεοῦ ἅγιός ἐστιν, οἵτινές ἐστε <u>ὑμεῖς</u> (1 Cor 3:17).

20. Ἡ οὖν σπεῖρα καὶ ὁ χιλίαρχος καὶ οἱ ὑπέρεται [6] τῶν Ἰουδαίων <u>συνέλαβον</u> τὸν Ἰησοῦν καὶ ἔδησαν αὐτὸν καὶ ἤγαγον πρὸς Ἄνναν πρῶτον· ἦν γὰρ πενθερὸς τοῦ Καϊάφα, ὃς ἦν high priest that year (John 18:12-13).

Parsing:
21-30. Parse the words underlined in the previous sentences.

Notes on questions 1-20: Sentences from the Greek New Testament

[1] (qu. 5) The mood of εἶπεν has been changed from participial to indicative. Participles will be met in chapter 20. A similar change was made to ἠρώτησαν in question 10. [2] (qu. 8) δεῖξαι is the aor. inf. act. of δείκνυμι. [3] (qu. 8) γενέσθαι is the aor. inf. of the middle verb γίνομαι. [4] (qu. 9) The tense of ἐλάλησε has been changed from imperfect to aorist. Imperfects will be met in chapter 22; like the aorist, the imperfect normally refers to past time. [5] (qu. 15) The imperative Ἴδε has been changed to Ἰδού, a word in Vocabulary 18. [6] (qu. 20) ὑπηρέτης is listed in the section at the beginning of the Gospel of John as one of the words that is used more than five times in this gospel.

Chapter 19: Translation of 1 John 2:1-11

By now you are able to recognize an increasing percentage of the words and forms in the Greek New Testament. While there are still several important things that still need to be learned, you are now in a position to try your hand at translating a longer New Testament passage.

The most notable deficiency in your grammar at the moment is the lack of a knowledge of participles, which are very common in Greek. Indeed, most of the forms you will not recognize in 1 John 2:1-11 are either participles (see Chap. 20) or the perfect tense (see Chap. 21). As participles will be dealt with in the next chapter, take a close look at how they work as you meet them in 1 John 2:1-11. Where there is a new form it will be identified and translated in a note. Remember, you are expected to find the words that are not already part of your vocabulary by looking them up in Burer & Miller, or some other dictionary.

Vocabulary 19

ἁμαρτάνω (42)	I sin, do wrong
ἄρτι (36)	now
ἕως (145)	till, until
ἤδη (60)	already
ἥμαρτον (19)	I sinned [aor. ind. act. of ἁμαρτάνω. The weak aorist root ἁμαρτησ- is also found in moods other than the indicative]
καθώς (178)	just as
καινός, -η, -ον (42)	new
μισέω (39)	I hate
ὅλος, -η, -ον (108)	whole, entire; complete
ὀφείλω (35)	I owe, am obligated to, am bound, ought
ποῦ (47)	where

Translation Passage 19: 1 John 2:1-11

[1] Τεκνία μου, ταῦτα γράφω ὑμῖν ἵνα μὴ ἁμάρτητε. καὶ ἐάν τις ἁμάρτῃ, παράκλητον ἔχομεν πρὸς τὸν πατέρα Ἰησοῦν Χριστὸν δίκαιον· [2] καὶ αὐτὸς ἱλασμός ἐστιν περὶ τῶν ἁμαρτιῶν ἡμῶν, οὐ περὶ τῶν ἡμετέρων δὲ μόνον ἀλλὰ καὶ περὶ ὅλου τοῦ κόσμου. [3] Καὶ ἐν τούτῳ γινώσκομεν ὅτι ἐγνώκαμεν[1] αὐτόν, ἐὰν τὰς ἐντολὰς αὐτοῦ τηρῶμεν. [4] ὁ λέγων[2] ὅτι Ἔγνωκα[3] αὐτὸν καὶ τὰς ἐντολὰς αὐτοῦ μὴ τηρῶν,[4] ψεύστης ἐστὶν καὶ ἐν τούτῳ ἡ ἀλήθεια οὐκ ἔστιν· [5] ὃς δ' ἂν τηρῇ αὐτοῦ τὸν λόγον, ἀληθῶς ἐν τούτῳ ἡ ἀγάπη τοῦ θεοῦ τετελείωται,[5] ἐν τούτῳ γινώσκομεν ὅτι ἐν αὐτῷ ἐσμεν. [6] The one who says he abides in him, ὀφείλει καθὼς ἐκεῖνος περιεπάτησεν ... περιπατεῖν [7] Ἀγαπητοί, οὐκ ἐντολὴν καινὴν γράφω ὑμῖν ἀλλ' ἐντολὴν παλαιὰν ἣν εἴχετε[6] ἀπ' ἀρχῆς· ἡ ἐντολὴ ἡ παλαιά ἐστιν ὁ λόγος ὃν ἠκούσατε. [8] πάλιν ἐντολὴν καινὴν γράφω ὑμῖν, ὅ ἐστιν ἀληθὲς ἐν αὐτῷ καὶ ἐν ὑμῖν, ὅτι ἡ σκοτία παράγεται[7] καὶ τὸ φῶς τὸ ἀληθινὸν ἤδη φαίνει. [9] ὁ λέγων[8] ἐν τῷ φωτὶ εἶναι καὶ τὸν ἀδελφὸν αὐτοῦ μισῶν[9] ἐν τῇ σκοτίᾳ ἐστὶν ἕως ἄρτι. [10] ὁ ἀγαπῶν[10] τὸν ἀδελφὸν αὐτοῦ ἐν τῷ φωτὶ μένει καὶ σκάνδαλον ἐν αὐτῷ οὐκ ἔστιν· [11] ὁ δὲ μισῶν[11] τὸν ἀδελφὸν αὐτοῦ ἐν τῇ σκοτίᾳ ἐστὶν καὶ ἐν τῇ σκοτίᾳ περιπατεῖ καὶ οὐκ οἶδεν[12] ποῦ ὑπάγει, ὅτι ἡ σκοτία ἐτύφλωσεν τοὺς ὀφθαλμοὺς αὐτοῦ.

Notes on 1 John 2:1-11

[1] (v. 3) ἐγνώκαμεν is the irregular 1st. pers. pl. perfect ind. act. of γινώσκω. Translate as "we have known" [the word "have" is the indicator of the English perfect tense].   [2] (v. 4) λέγων is the nom. masc. sing. pres. participle act. of λέγω. ὁ λέγων may be translated as "the one who says," or "he who says," or "the [one] saying."   [3] (v. 4) Ἔγνωκα is the 1st. pers. sing. perfect ind. act. of γινώσκω. "I have known."   [4] (v. 4) τηρῶν is the nom. masc. sing. pres. part. act. of τηρέω. Used this way, the participle is a reference to time. Translate as, "... while [not] keeping"   [5] (v. 5) τετελείωται is the 3rd. pers. sing. perfect ind. passive of τελειόω. Translate as "has been made perfect."   [6] (v. 7) εἴχετε is the 2nd pers. pl. imperfect ind. act. of ἔχω. Here the imperfect is used as a continuous past tense. Translate as either "you were having," or "you had."   [7] (v. 8) παράγεται is the 3rd pers. sing. pres. ind. passive of παρ-άγω. The passive of this verb, when used intransitively means "pass away, depart."   [8] (v. 9) See note number 2.   [9] (v. 9) μισῶν is the nom. masc. sing. pres. participle act. of μισέω. The participle here is best translated as a reference to time (i.e. as a temporal clause), with some phrase such as "while he hates."   [10] (v. 10) ἀγαπῶν is the nom. masc. sing. pres. part. act. of ἀγαπάω. "The one who loves" or "the one loving," or "he who loves."   [11] (v. 11) μισῶν is the nom. masc. sing. pres. part. act. of μισέω. "The one who hates," or "he who hates."   [12] (v. 11) οἶδεν is the 3rd pers. sing. of the verb, οἶδα, "he/she/it knows."

Part 3

Chapter 20: Participles

The most significant mood of the verb yet to be met is the participle. Participles are found in 4,275 verses of the approximately 7,570 verses of the Greek New Testament, and therefore they must be mastered, or at least tamed, before it is possible to translate from Greek to English. They perhaps constitute the greatest challenge yet remaining in learning New Testament Greek.

At first, participles can seem a bit overwhelming. There appears to be a great number of forms to be learned, and they are used in ways that often have no real equivalent in English. A more careful examination, though, reveals that all the forms of the participle have been met already, and you will become comfortable with the different uses of the participle as they become more familiar. The gratifying part of learning participles is that understanding them will allow much more of the New Testament to be accessible than before. While you will still not recognize every verbal form on any given page of the Greek New Testament, with the addition of participles you should now be able to recognize most of them. It is worthwhile taking the trouble to become familiar with participles! As the chapter unfolds, both the forms of the participle, and the three most common uses of the mood will be met. It will turn out that only one of these uses will correspond to the English participle in any significant way. We begin with how participles are formed.

20.1.1 The Present Participle Active

The present participle active of λύω			
	Masc	Fem	Neut
N,V	λύων	λύουσα	λῦον
A	λύοντα	λύουσαν	λῦον
G	λύοντος	λυούσης	λύοντος
D	λύοντι	λυούσῃ	λύοντι
N,V	λύοντες	λύουσαι	λύοντα
A	λύοντας	λυούσας	λύοντα
G	λυόντων	λυουσῶν	λυόντων
D	λύουσι(ν)	λυούσαις	λύουσι(ν)

The participle not only has tense (present) mood (participle) and voice (active) like a verb, it also has case (nominative, vocative, accusative, genitive, dative), gender (masculine, feminine, neuter) and number (singular, plural) as well. It looks, in fact, rather like an adjective, and uses the forms of a third declension adjective. In *Intermediate New Testament Greek Made Easier* (*Int*.1.2), there will be opportunity to return to the observation that a participle is both verbal and adjectival. For now, though, it is nice to see that there is no real need to learn anything new about the way it is declined. The masculine follows the paradigm of a regular third declension masculine noun (notice the endings: [- or ς] -α -ος -ι -ες -ας -ων -σιν). The neuter likewise follows the paradigm of a third declension neuter noun. As is true of other third declension feminine adjectives, the feminine follows the paradigm of first declension feminine nouns. In this case the pattern of δόξα.

Consequently, the only learning needing to be done is to learn that the present participle active of λύω is λύων, λύουσα, λῦον, and has the masculine genitive λύοντος. Once this is known, the rest can easily be derived. Of course, it is still a good idea to practice writing out some of these participles in full.

The accents of participles tend to remain on the syllable on which they are found in the nominative case, as far as is consistent with the general rules of accents [see 2.8b].

20.1.2 The Weak Aorist Participle Active

	The weak aorist participle active of λύω		
	Masc	Fem	Neut
N,V	λύσας	λύσασα	λῦσαν
A	λύσαντα	λύσασαν	λῦσαν
G	λύσαντος	λυσάσης	λύσαντος
D	λύσαντι	λυσάσῃ	λύσαντι
N,V	λύσαντες	λύσασαι	λύσαντα
A	λύσαντας	λυσάσας	λύσαντα
G	λυσάντων	λυσασῶν	λυσάντων
D	λύσασι(ν)	λυσάσαις	λύσασι(ν)

Like both the aorist infinitive and aorist subjunctive, the aorist participle does not have an augment. Some examples are perhaps the best way to illustrate the formation of the weak aorist participle active:

Part 3

Verb	Aor Ind Act	Weak Aorist Participle		
		Masc	Fem	Neut
αἰτέω	ᾔτησα	αἰτήσας αἰτήσαντα	αἰτήσασα αἰτήσασαν	αἰτῆσαν etc
ἀγαπάω	ἠγάπησα	ἀγάπησας ἀγαπήσαντα	ἀγαπήσασα ἀγαπήσασαν	ἀγαπῆσαν etc
ἀποστέλλω	ἀπέστειλα	ἀπόστειλας ἀποστείλαντα	ἀποστείλασα ἀποστείλασαν	ἀποστεῖλαν etc
βλέπω	ἔβλεψα	βλέψας βλέψαντα	βλέψασα βλέψασαν	βλεψαν etc
γράφω	ἔγραψα	γράψας γράψαντα	γράψασα γράψασαν	γρᾶψαν etc
καλέω	ἐκάλεσα	κάλεσας καλέσαντα	καλέσασα καλέσασαν	καλεσαν etc
λαλέω	ἐλάλησα	λάλησας λαλήσαντα	λαλήσασα λαλήσασαν	λαλῆσαν etc
πείθω	ἔπεισα	πείσας πείσαντα	πείσασα πέσασαν	πεῖσαν etc
σῴζω	ἔσωσα	σώσας σώσαντα	σώσασα σώσασαν	σῶσαν etc

Notes

1. ἀποστέλλω is a liquid verb (the stem στελλ- ends with the liquid λ), which doesn't tolerate a σ immediately after the verb stem. The verb stem lengthens to compensate, and the σ is dropped. It forms its aorist participle (and indeed its aorist indicative) according to the paradigm of a weak aorist participle. [See *Int*.6.15.1 for other liquid verbs.]
2. Remember, καλέω is one of the few -εω verbs that does not lengthen the ε to η before the σ [see 12.2.3].
3. The aorist participle (both strong and weak aorist) may convey a reference to past time, but this past time is relative to the main verb of the sentence.

20.1.3 The Strong Aorist Participle Active

Those verbs which have a strong aorist indicative, also have a strong aorist participle. For example, the aorist participle active of λαμβάνω (which has the strong aorist indicative active, ἔλαβον) is:

The strong aorist participle active of λαμβάνω		
	Masc	Fem	Neut
N,V	λαβών	λαβοῦσα	λαβόν
A	λαβόντα	λαβοῦσαν	λαβόν
G	λαβόντος	λαβούσης	λαβόντος
D	λαβόντι	λαβούσῃ	λαβόντι
N,V	λαβόντες	λαβοῦσαι	λαβόντα
A	λαβόντας	λαβούσας	λαβόντα
G	λαβόντων	λαβουσῶν	λαβόντων
D	λαβοῦσι(ν)	λαβούσαις	λαβοῦσι(ν)

The strong aorist participle of λαμβάνω is formed from the verb stem of the strong aorist indicative (without the augment) together with the endings for the present participle active. Other strong participle actives are formed the same way. For example:

Verb	Aor Ind Act	Strong Aorist Participle		
		Masc	Fem	Neut
ἄγω	ἤγαγον	ἀγαγών ἀγαγόντα	ἀγαγοῦσα ἀγαγοῦσαν	ἀγαγόν etc
ἀποθνήσκω	ἀπέθανον	ἀποθανών ἀποθανόντα	ἀποθανοῦσα ἀποθανοῦσαν	ἀποθανόν etc
βάλλω	ἔβαλον	βαλών βαλόντα	βαλοῦσα βαλοῦσαν	βαλόν etc
ἔρχομαι	ἦλθον	ἐλθών ἐλθόντα	ἐλθοῦσα ἐλθοῦσαν	ἐλθόν etc
ἐσθίω	ἔφαγον	φαγών φαγόντα	φαγοῦσα φαγοῦσαν	φαγόν etc
εὑρίσκω	εὗρον	εὑρών εὑρόντα	εὑροῦσα εὑροῦσαν	εὑρόν etc
λέγω	εἶπον	εἰπών εἰπόντα	εἰποῦσα εἰποῦσαν	εἰπόν etc
ὁράω	εἶδον	ἰδών ἰδόντα	ἰδοῦσα ἰδοῦσαν	ἰδόν etc
πίπτω	ἔπεσα	πεσοῦσα πεσοῦσαν	πεσοῦσα πεσοῦσαν	πεσόν etc

20.1.4 The Present Participle Active of the Verb εἰμί

	The present participle active of εἰμί		
	Masc	Fem	Neut
N,V	ὤν	οὖσα	ὄν
A	ὄντα	οὖσαν	ὄν
G	ὄντος	οὔσης	ὄντος
D	ὄντι	οὔσῃ	ὄντι
N,V	ὄντες	οὖσαι	ὄντα
A	ὄντας	οὔσας	ὄντα
G	ὄντων	οὐσῶν	ὄντων
D	οὖσι(ν)	οὔσαις	οὖσι(ν)

The present participle active of εἰμί looks like the endings for the present participle active with accents and breathing marks added. Notice that ὤν (nom/voc masc. sing. pres. part. act. of εἰμί) is to be distinguished from ὧν (the gen. masc/fem/neut pl. of the relative pronoun), and ὄν (nom/acc/voc neut. sing. pres. part. act. of εἰμί) is to be distinguished from ὅν (the acc. masc. sing of the relative pronoun).

20.1.5 The English Participle

The English participle is generally formed by adding -ing (present participle) or -ed (past participle) to the verb, although the English past participle often has many irregularities. The English participle of a verb may be discovered by using the auxiliary verbs "is ..." for the present participle, and "has ..." for the past participle. For example, the present participle of love is "loving" and of say is "saying" ("is *loving*", "is *saying*"), while the past participle of love is "loved" and of say is "said" ("has *loved*", "has *said*"). Some examples of the English participle follow (note: eat, find, go, say are irregular in English, as they are in Greek):

Examples of English Participles		
pres ind	pres part [I am ...]	past part [I have ...]
Regular verbs		
love	loving	loved
save	saving	saved
place	placing	placed
judge	judging	judged
remain	remaining	remained
Irregular verbs		
eat	eating	eaten
find	finding	found
go	going	gone
say	saying	said

The Greek participle is indeed used where English would use a participle. But the Greek participle is much more often used in ways that find no equivalent in English grammar. These varied uses will be introduced through the rest of this textbook, starting with some of the most frequent uses. [For your reference, all the uses of the participle are gathered together in *Int.1.2*.]

20.1.6 Uses of the Participle 1: "The One Who ..."

Participles can often be translated as "The one who ..." The translation set in chapter 19 (1 John 2:1-11) included several participles, and most of them were translated "the one who ...," or "those who ...." These are examples of a very common use of the participle. For example:
- ὁ λέγων   "The one who says ..." [1 John 2:4, 6, 9]
         [in plural: οἱ λεγόντες "Those who say ..." Matt 23:16,]
- ὁ ἀγαπῶν   "The one who loves ..." [1 John 2:10]
- ὁ μισῶν   "The one who hates ..." [1 John 2:11]

Notes:
1. With this kind of use, the participle is usually preceded by the article (as it is in the examples above).
2. It is sometimes possible to translate this type of participle with a phrase which uses an English participle
   ὁ λέγων   "The [one] saying ..."
   ὁ ἀγαπῶν   "The [one] loving ..."
   ὁ μισῶν   "The [one] hating ..."
   This does not exhaust the ways in which it is possible to translate this type

Part 3 185

of participle. For example, ὁ ἀγαπῶν could be translated as "the one who loves," or "the one loving," or "he who loves," "the lover," etc.
3. Greek sometimes forms nouns from participles. For example, the verb σπείρω means "I sow." Matt 13:3b reads, Ἰδοὺ ἐξῆλθεν <u>ὁ σπείρων</u> τοῦ σπείρειν ["behold <u>the sower</u> went out to sow"]. The word σπείρων, "sower" is a noun made from the verb, σπείρω. English does something similar to this [e.g. sower, speaker, lover, etc], and even, on occasion, uses a participle to do so [e.g. the living, the missing, etc.]. A participle used as a noun is one kind of an English "gerund."
4. It scarcely needs to be pointed out that the Greek usage of the participle described here is much different to the use of the English participle.
5. Grammars often describe this kind of usage as the "adjectival use of participles."

Exercise 20.1

Write out in full
1. The present participle active of λέγω 2. The aorist participle active of ἀγαπάω 3. The aorist participle active of ἐσθίω 4. The present participle active of ποιέω 5. The aorist participle active of γράφω

Review of parsing: Parsing demonstrates the ability to correctly recognize the grammatical form of the verb. Parsing has already been introduced in Chapter 15, but perhaps it is a good idea to give a quick review of it together with some examples for the different moods of the verb that have been met so far. The options now available for verbs are:
- Tense: present and aorist
- Mood: indicative, infinitive, subjunctive, participle
- Voice: active, middle, passive
- Person: 1st, 2nd, 3rd [NB: person only found with indicative and subjunctive moods]
- Case: nominative, vocative, accusative, genitive, dative [NB: case only found with participial mood of verb; plus, of course, nouns, adjectives, articles and pronouns]

The verbs in the following exercise are drawn from each of these possibilities, although there are proportionately more participles, as is appropriate for a chapter introducing them. Some examples of parsing follow [NB: all verbs have tense, mood and voice; in addition, indicatives and subjunctives have person, while participles have case]:

Examples of verbs in the indicative and subjunctive moods [which have person]:

ἔβαλες is the 2nd pers. sing. aor. ind. act. of βάλλω, I throw
ἄφωμεν is the 1st. pers. pl. aor. subj. act. of ἀφίημι, I forgive
λέγουσιν is the 3rd. pers. pl. pres. ind. act. of λέγω, I say
Examples of verbs in the infinitive mood [which have neither person or case]:
πέμπειν is the pres. inf. act. of πέμπω, I send
ἀγαγεῖν is the aor. inf. act. of ἄγω, I lead
Examples of verbs in the participial mood [which have case]:
λαβούσῃ is the dat. fem. sing. [strong] aor. part. act. of λαμβάνω, I take
ὄντων is the gen. masc/neut. pl. pres. part. act. of εἰμί, I am

Parse the following:
6. λύοντα 7. λυούσαις 8. λῦον 9. λυόντων 10. λύσαντας 11. λῦσαν
12. λύσασαι 13. ὤν 14. βαλλούσης 15. ἦλθες 16. λεγών 17. δοξάζουσιν
18. φαγόντα 19. πιών 20. ὁρῶν 21. ἰδών 22. φέρουσιν 23. εἰπών 24. γράψας
25. βλέψασα 26. ἔπεσεν 27. βαλόντι 28. ᾔτησαν 29. ἔβλεψας 30. λύῃς
31. ἐσθίων 32. εὑρούσης 33. ὄντα 34. αἰτήσαν 35. διδῷς 36. ὄντος

37. πίπτουσαν 38. ἀγαπᾷς 39. δοξάζειν 40. πείσας 41. ἤγαγον 42. ἄγαγον
43. γράψαντες 44. φάγῃ 45. ἠγάπησεν 46. πορεύησθε 47. εἶπεν 48. ἀγάπων
49. ἀφῆκα 50. ἔπεισαν 51. βλέποντες 52. ὅν 53. ὄν 54. ἀγαπήσασαν
55. πεσοῦσαν 56. δοξάσαι 57. ἔστησας 58. ἀποστέλλει 59. δέξωμαι
60. ἐλθόντες 61. γραψάσης 62. ἀπέθανον 63. βλέψαν 64. ἔθηκα 65. εὕρομεν

66. ἐσώσαμεν 67. ἀπωλέσαμεν 68. βαλόντι 69. ἔφαγον 70. ἐλάλησαν
71. λεγόντων 72. αἰτησάσῃ 73. δῶτε 74. ἀπέστειλα 75. οὐσῶν 76. ὦμεν
77. ἔβαλετε 78. πεῖσαν 79. γράφοντα 80. ἀπόστειλας 81. βλεψάσῃ
82. ἀποθάνοντος 83. ἰδόντες 84. βαλοῦσα 85. ἀγαπήσαντι 86. σώσασαν
87. εὑρών 88. ἔδειξεν 89. λαλῆσαν 90. σῴζει

Translate into English
91. ὁ λέγων 92. ὁ σῴζων 93. ὁ καλῶν 94. ὁ βαλών 95. ὁ φαγών 96. ὁ ἰδών
97. ὁ πίπτων 98. ὁ ὤν 99. ὁ ἀγάπων 100. ὁ κρίνων 101. ὁ εὕρων 102. ὁ γεννῶν

Vocabulary 20.1 (John 5:19-32)

ἀληθής, -ές (26)   true[1]
ἀνάστασις, -εως, ἡ (42)   resurrection
ἑαυτοῦ, -ῆς, -οῦ (320)   [of] himself, herself, itself [3rd pers. reflexive pronoun[2]]
ἐμαυτοῦ, -ῆς (37)   [of] myself [1st pers. reflexive pronoun]
εἷς, μία, ἕν (337)   one
θαυμάζω (42)   I wonder, marvel
κρίσις, -εως, ἡ (47)   judgment, judging, condemnation

μαρτυρία (37)　　　　　witness, testimony [cf. μαρτυρέω Vocab. 5]
μέγας, μεγάλη, μέγα (194) great
μείζων, -ον gen. sing. μείζονος (48) greater [than] [3]
μηδέ (57)　　　　　　and not, but not; not even [= μη + δε, cf. οὐδέ
　　　　　　　　　　　(Vocab 14.1)]
μηδείς, μηδεμία, μηδέν (85) no one, nothing [= μηδέ + εἰς, μια, ἐν; cf. οὐδείς]
οὐδείς, οὐδεμία, οὐδέν [226] no one, nothing [= οὐδέ + εἰς, μια, ἐν]
σεαυτοῦ, -ῆς (43)　　　　[of] yourself [2nd pers. reflexive pronoun]
ὥσπερ (36)　　　　　　just as

Notes on Vocabulary 20.1

1. ἀληθής, -ές is an adjective which follows a third declension paradigm [and is listed in full in Appendix E]. The acc. masc./fem. sing. and nom./acc. neut. pl. is ἀληθῆ. This word has the same forms for masculine and feminine, and separate neuter forms. The noun ἀλήθεια, ας, "truth"; and the adverb ἀληθῶς, "truly, really," may be found in other vocabularies [see Vocabs. 14.2 & 29.1]. Cf. also ἀληθινός, -ή, -όν, (26) "true, genuine."
2. The reflexive pronouns, ἐμαυτοῦ, σεαυτοῦ and ἑαυτοῦ do not have a nominative or vocative case, but examples of accusative, genitive and dative occur in the New Testament. The 1st and 2nd pers. reflexive pronouns ἐμαυτοῦ and σευαυτοῦ have masculine and feminine forms, while the 3rd person reflexive pronoun has masculine, feminine and neuter. The reflexive pronouns function in Greek like the reflexive pronouns, "myself, yourself, himself/herself/itself" do in English.
3. μείζων is the comparative of the adjective μέγας, μεγάλη, μέγα, large, great. μείζων uses the forms of the third declension for masc. and neut. It has no separate feminine forms, but uses masc. forms for them. Comparatives are usually followed by the genitive case [see *Int*.6.7.5 & *Int*.5.3.5].

Translation Passage 20.1: John 5:19-32

[Note: Footnotes provide information on grammatical forms that have yet to be met as well as help with other features of the passage that might prove difficult.]

　　　[19] ... ὁ Ἰησοῦς ... ἔλεγεν αὐτοῖς, Ἀμὴν ἀμὴν λέγω ὑμῖν, οὐ δύναται ὁ υἱὸς ποιεῖν ἀφ'[1] ἑαυτοῦ οὐδὲν ἐὰν μή τι βλέπῃ τὸν πατέρα ποιοῦντα·[2] ἃ γὰρ ἂν ἐκεῖνος ποιῇ, ταῦτα καὶ ὁ υἱὸς ὁμοίως ποιεῖ. [20] ὁ γὰρ πατὴρ φιλεῖ τὸν υἱὸν καὶ πάντα δείκνυσιν[3] αὐτῷ ἃ αὐτὸς ποιεῖ, καὶ μείζονα τούτων[4] δείξει[5] αὐτῷ ἔργα, ἵνα ὑμεῖς θαυμάζητε. [21] ὥσπερ γὰρ ὁ πατὴρ ἐγείρει τοὺς νεκροὺς καὶ ζῳοποιεῖ, οὕτως καὶ ὁ υἱὸς οὓς θέλει ζῳοποιεῖ.

[22] οὐδὲ γὰρ ὁ πατὴρ κρίνει οὐδένα,⁶ ἀλλὰ τὴν κρίσιν⁷ πᾶσαν δέδωκεν⁸ τῷ υἱῷ, [23] ἵνα πάντες τιμῶσι τὸν υἱὸν καθὼς τιμῶσι τὸν πατέρα. ὁ μὴ τιμῶν τὸν υἱὸν οὐ τιμᾷ τὸν πατέρα τὸν πέμψαντα αὐτόν. [24] Ἀμὴν ἀμὴν λέγω ὑμῖν ὅτι ὁ τὸν λόγον μου ἀκούων⁹ καὶ πιστεύων τῷ πέμψαντί με ἔχει ζωὴν αἰώνιον καὶ εἰς κρίσιν οὐκ ἔρχεται, ἀλλὰ μεταβέβηκεν¹⁰ ἐκ τοῦ θανάτου εἰς τὴν ζωήν.

[25] ἀμὴν ἀμὴν λέγω ὑμῖν ὅτι ἔρχεται ὥρα καὶ νῦν ἐστιν ὅτε οἱ νεκροὶ ἀκούσουσιν¹¹ τῆς φωνῆς τοῦ υἱοῦ τοῦ θεοῦ καὶ οἱ ἀκούσαντες ζήσουσιν.¹² [26] ὥσπερ γὰρ ὁ πατὴρ ἔχει ζωὴν ἐν ἑαυτῷ, οὕτως καὶ τῷ υἱῷ¹³ ἔδωκεν ζωὴν ἔχειν ἐν ἑαυτῷ. [27] καὶ ἐξουσίαν ἔδωκεν αὐτῷ κρίσιν¹⁴ ποιεῖν, ὅτι υἱὸς ἀνθρώπου ἐστίν.

[28] μὴ θαυμάζετε¹⁵ τοῦτο, ὅτι ἔρχεται ὥρα ἐν ᾗ πάντες οἱ ἐν τοῖς μνημείοις ἀκούσουσιν¹⁶ τῆς φωνῆς αὐτοῦ [29] καὶ ἐκπορεύσονται οἱ τὰ ἀγαθὰ ποιήσαντες¹⁷ εἰς ἀνάστασιν¹⁸ ζωῆς, οἱ δὲ τὰ φαῦλα πράξαντες εἰς ἀνάστασιν κρίσεως.

[30] Οὐ δύναμαι ἐγὼ ποιεῖν ἀπ' ἐμαυτοῦ οὐδέν· καθὼς ἀκούω κρίνω, καὶ ἡ κρίσις ἡ ἐμὴ δικαία ἐστίν, ὅτι οὐ ζητῶ τὸ θέλημα τὸ ἐμὸν ἀλλὰ τὸ θέλημα τοῦ πέμψαντός με.

[31] Ἐὰν ἐγὼ μαρτυρῶ περὶ ἐμαυτοῦ, ἡ μαρτυρία μου οὐκ ἔστιν ἀληθής· [32] ἄλλος ἐστὶν ὁ μαρτυρῶν περὶ ἐμοῦ, καὶ οἶδα¹⁹ ὅτι ἀληθής ἐστιν ἡ μαρτυρία ἣν μαρτυρεῖ περὶ ἐμοῦ...

Notes on John 5:19-32

[1] (v. 19) ἀπό + rough breathing on next word = ἀφ' ... [2] (v. 19) The participle ποιοῦντα can be translated by the English participle "doing." [3] (v. 20) δείκνυσιν is the 3d. pers. *sing.* pres. ind. act. of δείκνυμι [see Appendix D]. [4] (v. 20) The genitive case is frequently used in comparisons [see *Int.*6.7 & *Int.*5.3.5], hence τούτων is in the genitive. [5] (v. 20) δείξει, "he will show," is the 3d pers. sing. future ind. act. of δείκνυμι. Future tenses will be met officially in Chapter 25. [6] (v. 22) οὐδένα is the acc. masc. sing. of οὐδείς, "no one" [7] (v. 22) κρίσιν is the acc. fem. sing. of κρίσις, "judgment" [8] (v. 22) δέδωκεν, "he has given," is the 3d. pers. sing. perfect ind. act. of δίδωμι [see Chapter 21]. [9] (v. 24) Notice that τὸν λόγον μου comes between the article and the participle [ὁ ... ἀκούων]. This kind of construction is relatively common in Greek. The only difficulty in translating this is to observe that the article belongs to the participle. [10] (v. 24) μεταβέβηκεν is the 3d. pers. perfect ind. act. of μεταβαίνω. "He has passed" [see Chapter 21]. [11] (v. 25) ἀκούσουσιν, "they will hear," is the 3d pers. pl. future ind. act. of ἀκούω [see Chapter 25]. [12] (v. 25) ζήσουσιν, "they will live," is the 3d pers. sing. future ind. act. of ζάω [see Chapter 25]. [13] (v. 26) The dative case τῷ υἱῷ is used in conjunction with the verb δίδωμι to indicate an indirect object, "to the son" [14] (v. 27) See note 7 on v. 22. [15] (v. 28) θαυμάζετε, "do not marvel ...," is the 2d.

Part 3 189

pers. pl. pres. imperative act. of θαυμάζω [see Chapter 26]. [16] [(v. 22)]ἀκούσουσιν see note 11 on v. 25. [17] [(v. 29)]See note 9 on v. 24. The construction is similar. [18] [(v. 29)]ἀνάστασιν is the acc. fem. sing. of ἀνάστασις [cf. κρίσιν]. [19] [(v. 32)]οἶδα, "I know." This verb uses a perfect form with present meaning. It has already occurred in the passages set from the Greek New Testament, and will be officially learnt in Vocabulary 21.2.

20.2.1 Present & Aorist Participles of -μι Verbs

-μι verbs are used frequently, and are often found in the participial mood. So it is important to be at ease with the participles of these verbs. It will probably come as no surprise to discover that the -μι verbs are somewhat irregular in their participles. Their active participles do follow recognizable third declension adjective patterns, though, and they are readily recognized as participles when they are met in the Greek text. The only challenge with these verbs is to recognize whether or not they are present participles or aorist participles. The following examples show these differences:

Indicative act	Participle active		
	Masc	Fem	Neut
Presesent δίδωμι	διδούς διδόντα διδόντος etc	διδοῦσα διδοῦσαν διδούσης	διδόν διδόν διδόντος
Aorist ἔδωκα	δούς δόντα δόντος etc	δοῦσα δοῦσαν δούσης	δόν δόν δόντος
Present ἵστημι	ἱστάς ἱστάντα ἱστάντος etc	ἱστᾶσα ἱστᾶσαν ἱστάσης	ἱστάν ἱστάν ἱστάντος
Aorist ἔστησα	στάς στάντα στάντος etc	στᾶσα στᾶσαν στάσης	στάν στάν στάντος
Present τίθημι	τιθείς τιθέντα τιθέντος etc	τιθεῖσα τιθεῖσαν τιθείσης	τιθέν τιθέν τιθέντος

Indicative act	Participle active		
	Masc	Fem	Neut
Aorist ἔθηκα	θείς θέντα θέντος etc	θεῖσα θεῖσαν θείσης	θέν θέν θέντος
Present δείκνυμι	δεικνύς δεικνύντα δεικνύντος etc	δεικνεῦσα δεικνεῦσαν δεικνεύσης	δεικνύν δεικνύν δεικνύντος
Aorist ἔδειξα	No examples of active voice in NT		

Notes:
1. The present participle of δίδωμι is found 14 times in the NT and 18 further times in compound verbs, but only in masculine and neuter forms. Its aorist participle is used 29 times, and a further 11 times in compound verbs. The nom. neut. sing. pres. part. act. form ἀποδιδοῦν is found in Rev 22:2, and the nom. neut. pl. pres. part. act. form διδόντα is found in 1 Cor 14:7. Eric G. Jay, *New Testament Greek* (London: SPCK, 1970), p. 312 gives the nom. neut. sing. form as διδόν, which has been followed in this text.
2. The present participle of ἵστημι is not found in the NT, but it is found 10 times in compound verbs. Its aorist participle active is found 6 times (plus a further 64 times in compounds), and its perfect 43 times (plus 23 in compounds). The perfect participle of ἵστημι [ἑστώς, -, ἑστός, ἑστωτ-], is found only in masculine and neuter. Important note: perfect participles of ἵστημι usually have a present meaning (an explanation is given in *Int*.6.14; perfect participles will be met in the next chapter).
3. The present participle of τίθημι is found twice in the NT (Mark 10:16; 15:19), and 8 times more in compound verbs. Its aorist participle is found 8 times, and a further 21 times in compound verbs.
4. The aorist participle of δείκνυμι occurs only once in the NT (acc. masc. sing. aor. part. pass, δειχθέντα in Heb 8:5). There is one present participle formed in a regular way from the verb δεικνύω in Rev 22:8, and two present participle actives (Acts 18:28 & 2 Thes 2:4) and four present participle middles of compounds of δείκνυμι.
5. No dative plural participle of δίδωμι and τίθημι occurs in the NT, and they are found only once in their compounds (παραδεδωκόσι, the dat. masc. pl. perf. part. act. of παραδίδωμι, "I hand or give over"; Acts 15:26).

20.2.2 The Present Participle Middle & Passive

	The present participle middle & passive of δέχομαι		
	Masc	Fem	Neut
N,V	δεχόμενος	δεχομένη	δεχόμενον
A	δεχόμενον	δεχομένην	δεχόμενον
G	δεχομένου	δεχομένης	δεχομένου
D	δεχομένῳ	δεχομένῃ	δεχομένῳ
N,V	δεχόμενοι	δεχόμεναι	δεχόμενα
A	δεχομένους	δεχομένας	δεχόμενα
G	δεχομένων	δεχομενῶν	δεχομένων
D	δεχομένοις	δεχομέναις	δεχομένοις

As with the present participle active, the form of the participle is that of an adjective, but this time, an adjective like ἀγαθός, -ή, -όν, which uses patterns from first and second declension.

20.2.3 Uses of the Participle 2: "When/while/as/After ..."

A very common use of the participle is translated by an English temporal clause. These are introduced by such words as "when ...," "while ...," "as ...," "before ...," "after ...," etc. For example:
- Καὶ <u>ἐλθὼν</u> ὁ Ἰησοῦς εἰς τὴν οἰκίαν Πέτρου εἶδεν ... And <u>after</u> Jesus <u>came into</u> the house of Peter, he saw ... (Matt 8:14)
- Ταῦτα <u>εἰπὼν</u> Ἰησοῦς ἐξῆλθεν σὺν τοῖς μαθηταῖς αὐτοῦ After he <u>said</u> these things, Jesus went out with his disciples (John 18:1)
- καὶ <u>ἐξελθὼν</u> εἶδεν πολὺν ὄχλον καὶ ... And <u>after he went out</u> he saw a great crowd and ... (Matt 14:14)
- καὶ εὑρὼν αὐτὸν εἶπεν, ... And <u>after he found</u> him he said ... (John 9:35)

This usage is quite different from English grammar, and it causes beginners to feel a certain amount of disorientation. But an examination of the above examples will reveal the pattern of such uses, and after a while this usage will become familiar. The aorist tense of the participles in the examples show the action of the participle took place before the action of the main verb [see *Int.* 1.2.5], thus the time sense of the participle is best represented by the English word "after."

This is the kind of translation which should be tried first for a participle without an article. Grammarians call this a temporal adverbial use of the participle [temporal = a reference to time].

20.2.4 Uses of the Participle 3: "-ing"

Another common use of the Greek participle is generally translated with a verb ending in "-ing." A very common example of this is λέγων, "saying":
Ἄγγελος δὲ κυρίου ἐλάλησεν πρὸς Φίλιππον λέγων, ... An angel of the Lord spoke to Phillip, saying, ... (Acts 8:26)
Πάλιν οὖν αὐτοῖς ἐλάλησεν ὁ Ἰησοῦς λέγων, . . Therefore Jesus spoke to them again, saying ... (John 8:12)
ἀπεκρίθη αὐτοῖς ὁ Ἰωάννης λέγων, ... John answered them, saying ... (John 1:26)

20.2.5 Translation Strategies for Participles

It takes some time to become comfortable with translating participles, but most of those found in the Gospels can be handled by the following three strategies (listed in the order they should be tried):
1. Does the participle have an article? If it does, its translation is straightforward. Translate as "the one who ..."
2. If the participle does not have an article, try translating it as a time reference: "while/when/as ..."
3. If the first two possibilities do not work, then try translating it with an English participle ("...ing" or "..ed"). This is often quite satisfactory, or can give clues as to what the function of the participle might be in the sentence.

Many participles can be handled in this fashion. Other uses of participles will be dealt with as examples crop up in the translation passages, and will be dealt with systematically in *Int*.1.2. For now, though, you should see enough of these three uses of participles to begin to develop your translation skills.

Vocabulary 20.2.1 (for Ex 20.2)

Participles of -μι verbs:
διδούς, διδοῦσα, διδόν, διδοντ- (14+18[1]) pres. part. act. of δίδωμι
δούς, δοῦσα, δόν, δοντ- (29+11) aor. part. act. of δίδωμι
θείς, θεῖσα, θέν, θεντ- (8+21) aor. part. act. of τίθημι
στάς, στᾶσα, στάν, σταντ- (6+64) aor. part. act. of ἵστημι
τιθείς, τιθεῖσα, τιθέν, τιθεντ- (2+8) pres. part. act. of τίθημι
ὤν, οὖσα, ὄν, ὀντ- (154+) pres. part. act. of εἰμί

[1]Note: (14+18) indicates that the present participle of δίδωμι is found 14 times in the NT, while at the same time being used in compounds of the verb a further 18 times.

Other words:
ἀναβαίνω (81)   I go up, ascend [ἀνά + βαίνω]
εὐθύς (54)   immediately, at once
καταβαίνω (81)   I go down, come down [κατά + βαίνω]
πεσών, πεσοῦσα, πεσόν (27)   aorist participle active of πίπτω [note: πίπτω uses weak aorist forms for the indicative mood, and strong aorist forms for infinitivesl, participles, and imperatives]

Exercise 20.2

Parse the following
1. πορευομένης 2. πορευόμενας 3. πορευομένοις 4. λύσαντα 5. λύσας 6. πορεύηται 7. λύοντας 8. στάν 9. φοβεῖται 10. ἀπερχομένῳ 11. προσευχομένοις 12. θῶμεν 13. ἔλαβεν 14. λῦον 15. οὖσα 16. ἱστάντας 17. ἀποκρινόμεναι 18. ἀσπαζομένοις 19. ἰδεῖν 20. λύσασας 21. φοβουμένους 22. ὄντι 23. προσευχομένην 24. φαγών 25. στάσαις 26. γινόμεθα 27. ἔστησαν 28. οὔσας 29. ἀποκρινομένων 30. ἐξέρχεσθε 31. ἀσπαζομένη 32. δεχόμενα 33. προσερχομένου 34. λάβωσιν 35. φοβουμένας 36. εἰσερχομένου 37. ἐξερχομένη 38. προσευχόμενοι 39. δῶτε 40. ἐσθίειν 41. τιθέντος 42. δοξάσας 43. οὔσαις 44. θέν 45. δούς 46. δεικνεύσαι

Write in full
47. The present participle passive of φοβέομαι 48. The present participle of εἰμί 49. The aorist participle active of δίδωμι

Translate into idiomatic English
50. Πάλιν οὖν αὐτοῖς ἐλάλησεν ὁ Ἰησοῦς λέγων, Ἐγώ εἰμι τὸ φῶς τοῦ κόσμου, ὁ ἀκολουθῶν ἐμοὶ οὐ μὴ περιπατήσῃ ἐν τῇ σκοτίᾳ (John 8:12). 51. Ταῦτα τὰ ῥήματα ἐλάλησεν ἐν τῷ γαζοφυλακίῳ διδάσκων ἐν τῷ ἱερῷ (John 8:20). 52. Καὶ παράγων εἶδεν ἄνθρωπον τυφλὸν ἐκ γενετῆς (John 9:1-2a). 53. ἀπεκρίθη αὐτοῖς ὁ Ἰωάννης λέγων, ... (John 1:26). 54. Καὶ ἐγένετο ἐν ἐκείναις ταῖς ἡμέραις ἦλθεν Ἰησοῦς ἀπὸ Ναζαρὲτ τῆς Γαλιλαίας and was baptized in the Jordan by John. καὶ εὐθὺς ἀναβαίνων ἐκ τοῦ ὕδατος εἶδεν σχιζομένους τοὺς οὐρανοὺς καὶ τὸ πνεῦμα ὡς περιστερὰν καταβαῖνον εἰς αὐτὸν καὶ φωνὴ ἐγένετο ἐκ τῶν οὐρανῶν, Σὺ εἶ ὁ υἱός μου ὁ ἀγαπητός, ἐν σοὶ εὐδόκησα (Mark 1:9-11). 55. Καὶ παράγων παρὰ τὴν θάλασσαν τῆς Γαλιλαίας εἶδεν Σίμωνα καὶ Ἀνδρέαν τὸν ἀδελφὸν Σίμωνος ἀμφιβάλλοντας ἐν τῇ θαλάσσῃ ... (Mark 1:16). 56. Καὶ ἐξελθὼν ὁ Ἰησοῦς ἀπὸ τοῦ ἱεροῦ ... προσῆλθον οἱ μαθηταὶ αὐτοῦ ἐπιδεῖξαι αὐτῷ τὰς οἰκοδομὰς τοῦ ἱεροῦ (Matt 24:1). 57. Καὶ ἐκπορευομένων αὐτῶν ἀπὸ Ἰεριχὼ ἠκολούθησεν αὐτῷ ὄχλος πολύς. καὶ ἰδοὺ δύο τυφλοὶ καθήμενοι παρὰ τὴν ὁδόν, ἀκούσαντες ὅτι

Ἰησοῦς παράγει, ἔκραξαν λέγοντες, ... υἱὸς Δαυίδ have mercy upon us (Matt 20:29-30). [Translate ἐκπορευομένων αὐτῶν as "while they were going." The phrase is built around a participle and a pronoun, both of which are in the genitive case. It is an example of a genitive absolute construction. You will learn about such constructions later (see *Int*.1.2.3). For now, just observe how this one works.]

Vocabulary 20.2.2 (John 9:1-41)

ἁμαρτωλός, -όν (47) sinful [as noun: sinner; cf. ἁμαρτάνω, I sin]
δεύτερος (44) second
ἐπιτίθημι (40) place upon [= ἐπί + τίθημι]
ἐργάζομαι (41) I work, labor [cf. ἔργον, work]
κάθημαι (91) I sit
μαθητής,[1] ὁ (262) disciple, pupil
οἶδα (321) I know[2]
ὅμοιος (45) like, resembling
ποτέ (29) once, formerly
προφήτης[1] (144) prophet
φωνέω (42) I call, invite

Notes on Vocabulary 20.2.2

1. Μαθητής and προφήτης are examples of first declension masculine nouns. They may be readily parsed by what is already known. The full declension of προφήτης is provided in Appendix E. Students who are aiming at a grade of distinction or better would probably wish to learn this declension.
2. οἶδα uses perfect tense forms with present tense meaning (perfect tenses will be met in the next chapter). It is used often in John.

Translation Passage 20.2: John 9:1-41

You are now in a position where you can begin to directly use the Greek New Testament, with *Logos* or Burer & Miller's *Reader's Lexicon* or some other Greek-English dictionary to help with the vocabulary. Furthermore, the addition of participles gives you much greater facility with the Greek of the New Testament. While there are still several things that are missing from your grammar, you should be able to recognize most of the grammatical forms in many New Testament passages.

From now on you will be expected to have access to a copy of the Greek New Testament for translation passages. If you have been using the biblical languages pack of *Logos*, you already have the Greek NT available (see instructions in Exercise 18). For printed versions, a good Greek New

Part 3 195

Testament to use is the United Bible Societies' *The Greek New Testament* with dictionary, although a Nestle edition is equally satisfactory. The advantage of the UBS Greek NT with dictionary is that you will have an alphabetic dictionary, as well as Burer & Miller's *New Reader's Lexicon*. If your Greek NT does not have a dictionary, you may want to think of also purchasing a New Testament Greek to English dictionary as there will be times when you need one.

Notes for the translation passages will be provided. These notes will deal with grammar that has not yet been met or items of difficulty. There are some further notes in the answers. For the next few exercises many of the participles will be listed in the answers with a suggested translation. Some other things are also noted there that should be known already, but which are to be a difficulty for some students. It is best to attempt the translation before reading the notes in the answers of course, but they are there if you get stuck.

John chapter nine:

v. 1. See notes in answers on παράγων. The answers also provide translation hints for other participles that are found in John 9.

v. 2. γεννηθῇ is from the verb γεννάω, and is a 3rd pers. sing. subjunctive (after all, it follows a ἵνα!). It is an aorist passive subjunctive; and the phrase should be translated, "so that he was born blind."

v. 3. Οὔτε ... οὔτε "neither ... nor" will officially be met in Vocab. 25. Like γεννηθῇ in v. 2, φανερωθῇ is 3rd. pers. sing. aor. subj. passive: "so that the works of God might become manifest by[/in/through] him."

v. 6. Kubo lists ἐπιτίθημι for this verse. In the United Bible societies' 3rd ed. of the Greek NT this is given as one of the possible textual variants to the word ἐπέχρισεν. The UBS editors considered it to be a B reading—an indication that they were fairly sure of the reading, although there is a little room for doubt [their top rating is an A reading, about which they are sure, while their bottom rating is a D reading, about which they are totally uncertain]. This variant is not listed in the 4th edition of the UBS Greek NT. Textual variants and how to choose between them will be considered in *Intermediate New Testament Greek Made Easier*, Chapter 8. ἐπιχρίω is a verb which occurs twice in the Greek New Testament (here and in v. 11). It means "I smear, spread on" and is formed from ἐπί + χρίω. χρίω means "I anoint" and is the word from which Χριστός (the anointed one) is derived. It is followed by a genitive.

v. 7. ὕπαγε is the 2nd pers. sing. pres. imperative act. of ὑπάγω. It is the command, "Go!" ἑρμηνεύεται "is translated" is the 3rd. pers. sing. pres. ind. passive of ἑρμενεύω, "I translate." ἀπεσταλμένος is the nom. masc. sing. perf. part. passive of ἀποστέλλω: "sent." The whole phrase, which has been put in brackets in the Greek New Testament because it is an explanatory note provided by the evangelist, may be translated: "(which is interpreted, 'sent')."

vv. 8, 9, 10, 16. ἔλεγον is the 1st/3rd pers. sing./pl. imperfect. ind. act. of λέγω. The imperfect tense will be met in Chapter 22. In practice there is little or no difference in meaning between the imperfect and aorist of λέγω.

v. 9 Here ὅτι is used rather like speech marks are in English: it introduces the exact words said [i.e. in this instance, it indicates direct speech; cf. *Int*.6.1].

v. 10. ἠνεῴχθησαν is yet another passive. It is the 3rd pers. pl. aor. ind. passive of ἀνοίγω. Here "[How] were [your eyes] opened?"

v. 11. See comments on ἐπέχρισεν in v. 6 [Kubo does list the word for this verse], and on ὕπαγε in v. 7. ὁ λεγόμενος is the nom. masc. sing. pres. part. passive of λέγω. Here "the one called ..." νιψάμενος is the nom. masc. sing. aor. part. middle of νίπτω, "I wash." The middle voice is used for such actions as dressing and undressing, and washing [see *Int*.4.2].

v. 12. Sometimes weak aorist endings are found on strong aorist verbs (e.g. εἶπαν).

v. 14. ἐν ᾗ ἡμέρᾳ: ἐν ᾗ means "while...," or "until..." [see *Int*.2.3.5], it is probably best translated by the word "when" in this context.

v. 15. ἠρώτων may look like a participle but is not (note the augment); it is, in fact, the 3rd pers. sing. imperfect ind. act. of ἐρωτάω [α + ον = ων; see Chap. 22 for imperfect tense]. Translate: "asked" or "began to ask." ἐνιψάμην is the 1st pers. sing. aor. ind. middle of νίπτω, "I wash." Here "I washed [myself]" [see *Int*.4.2 for middle voice].

v. 19. ἐγεννήθη "was born," is the 3rd pers. sing. aor. ind. passive of γεννάω.

v. 20. ἐγεννήθη: see comments on v. 19.

v. 21. ἐρωτήσατε "ask," is the 2nd pers. pl. aor. imperative act. of ἐρωτάω. A command (or in this context, a request; cf. *Int*.1.4.2); λαλήσει "he will speak," is the 3rd pers. sing. future ind. act. of λαλέω.

v. 22. ἐφοβοῦντο "they were afraid of," is the 3rd pers. pl. imperfect ind. of the passive verb φοβέομαι. συνετέθειντο is the 3d pers. pl. pluperfect ind. middle of συντίθημι which in the active voice means "put together"; but in the middle voice means "make an agreement, agree, decide." Translate as "they had agreed." Further information on imperfect tenses may be found in Chapter 22, while the pluperfect tense is discussed at *Int*.3.5.3.

v. 23. ἐπερωτήσατε = ἐπι + ἐρωτήσατε. On ἐρωτήσατε see comment on v. 21.

v. 24. δός "give," is the 2nd pers. sing. pres. imperative act. of δίδωμι, a command.

v. 25. ἕν "one [thing]," is the acc. neut. sing. of εἷς, μία, ἕν, "one"; ὤν "although I was blind," is a concessive adverbial participle [see *Int*.1.2.2.4].

v. 27. μή indicates that the questioner expects an answer of "no" [*Int*.6.3]. This information is nigh impossible to convey in English translation. In

Part 3 197

this verse, it is best not to try to fit a "no" in the translation.

- **v. 29**. Μωϋσεῖ is dative [see 4.4]. λελάληκεν "has spoken," is the 3rd pers. sing. perfect ind. act. of λαλέω.
- **v. 32**. ἠκούσθη "has been heard," is the 3rd pers. sing. aor. ind. passive of ἀκούω. γεγεννημένου "[of] one who has been born blind," is the gen. masc. sing. perfect part. passive of γεννάω.
- **v. 33**. ἠδύνατο "would not have been able [to do]," is the irregular imperfect indicative of δύναμαι.
- **v. 34**. ἐγεννήθης see comments on v. 19. This is the second pers. sing.
- **v. 37**. ἑώρακας "you have seen," is the [slightly irregular] 2nd pers. sing. perfect ind. act. of ὁράω. The sentence is constructed around καί ... καί. In English it is usually best to translate these as "both ... and ...," but in this instance it is probably best not to translate the first καί.
- **v. 38**. ἔφη "said," is the imperfect ind. act. of φήμι, "I say, affirm."
- **v. 39**. γένωνται "might become blind," is the 3rd pers. pl. aor. subjunctive mid. of γίνομαι.
- **v. 40**. This verse is not very easy to translate—once you have had a good try at translating it on your own, you may want to refer to the answers where some help is given. Also, see comments on v. 27 for the use of μή in questions.

Chapter 21: The Perfect Tense

This chapter deals with the perfect tense. It provides an explanation of what it is, and how it is formed in Greek. Practice in using it is found in both the exercise and the translation passage set from the Gospel of John.

21.1 The Perfect Tense in English

In English the perfect tense is formed with the help of the auxiliary verb "to have," plus the English past participle. Thus "I have read," "he has eaten," "they have fought," and "we have finished" are all perfect tenses. The time sense conveyed is that something happened in the past, and its effects are still felt in the present. For example, "He has eaten" may imply that "he is no longer hungry."

There is a large overlap in meaning between the English and Greek perfect tenses, and this makes them relatively easy to translate: simply add the English auxiliary word "have/has" and the rest of the translation falls into place. Some examples will make this clear, but they will have to wait until it is seen how the perfects are formed in Greek.

21.2 The Perfect Indicative Active

The perfect indicative active of λύω	
Form of λύω	Meaning
λέλυκα	I have loosed
λέλυκας	you have loosed
λέλυκεν	he/she/it has loosed
λελύκαμεν	we have loosed
λελύκατε	you have loosed
λελύκασιν	they have loosed

21.2.1 Reduplication

As well as the personal endings, the initial consonant of the word is repeated with the addition of an ε to form the perfect. This repetition of the initial consonant is called, reduplication.

Examples of Reduplication in the Perfect Tense

Meaning	Present Ind. Act.	Perfect Ind. Act	Meaning of perfect
I believe	πιστεύω	πεπίστευκα	I have believed
I beget	γεννάω	γεγέννηκα	I have begotten
I speak	λαλέω	λελάληκα	I have spoken
I do, make	ποιέω	πεποίηκα	I have done/made
I save	σῴζω	σέσωκα	I have saved
I keep	τηρέω	τετήρηκα	I have kept

As might be expected, -εω verbs, and -αω verbs usually lengthen the ε and the α before the personal ending which is added to the verb stem. Several examples of this may be observed in the examples given above (e.g. γεγέννηκα, λελάληκα).

Verbs which begin with a vowel sometimes lengthen their initial vowel:

Meaning	Present Ind. Act.	Perfect Ind. Act	Meaning of perfect
I love	ἀγαπάω	ἠγάπηκα	I have loved
I ask	αἰτέω	ᾔτηκα	I have asked
I sin	ἁμαρτάνω	ἡμάρτηκα	I have sinned
I hope	ἐλπίζω	ἤλπικα	I have hoped

Verbs that begin with an aspirate show a distinctive pattern. It is very hard to say two aspirates together (try to say φεφ-, or θεθ-!), so what these verbs do to reduplicate their initial consonant makes sense. For example,

Meaning	Present Ind. Act.	Perfect Ind. Act	Meaning of perfect
I love	φιλέω	πεφίληκα	I have loved

21.2.2 Irregular Perfects

Many verbs have irregular perfects, which is not surprising in the light of the problem of reduplicating the beginning sound of verb stems that begins with a vowel, and because the personal endings begin in a guttural. Some of the irregular perfects of verbs which have already been met are listed below, together with the perfects of some -μι verbs.

Meaning	Pres. Ind. Act.	Perf. Ind. Act.	Meaning of perfect
I hear	ἀκούω	ἀκήκοα	I have heard
I go	-βαίνω[1]	-βέβηκα	I have gone
I throw	βάλλω	βέβληκα	I have thrown
I know	γινώσκω	ἔγνωκα	I have known
I write	γράφω	γέγραφα	I have written
I give	δίδωμι	δέδωκα	I have given
I come	ἔρχομαι	ἐλήλυθα	I have come
I stand	ἵστημι	ἕστηκα or ἕστακα	I stand[2]
I take	λαμβάνω	εἴληφα	I have taken

I say	λέγω	εἴρηκα	I have said
I see	ὁράω	ἑώρακα	I have seen
I persuade	πείθω	πέποιθα	I have persuaded
I fall	πίπτω	πέπτωκα	I have fallen
I place	τίθημι	τέθεικα	I have placed
I bear	φέρω	ἐνήνοχα	I have borne

Notes:
1. The verb -βαίνω only occurs in compounds in the Greek New Testament. Two of these have already been vocabulary items: ἀναβαίνω and καταβαίνω [see Vocab. 20.2].
2. The verb ἵστημι takes a direct object [i.e. is transitive] in the present tense. It uses the perfect tense as an intransitive present tense [i.e. where there is no direct object]. Consequently, ἕστηκα should be translated "I stand ...," not by an English perfect [see *Int*.6.14].
3. Irregular perfects use the same personal endings as the regular perfects, although they continue to leave off the κ if they lack it in the first person singular:

Paradigm of the Irregular Perfect Indicative Active

1st pers sing	γέγραφα	I have written
2nd pers sing	γέγραφας	you have written
3rd pers sing	γέγραφεν	he/she/it has written
1st pers pl	γεγράφαμεν	we have written
2nd pers pl	γεγράφατε	you have written
3rd pers pl	γεγράφασιν	they have written

21.3 The Perfect Participle Active

	The perfect participle active of λύω		
	Masc	Fem	Neut
N	λελυκώς	λελυκυῖα	λελυκός
A	λελυκότα	λελυκυῖαν	λελυκός
G	λελυκότος	λελυκυίας	λελυκότος
D	λελυκότι	λελυκυίᾳ	λελυκότι
N	λελυκότες	λελυκυῖαι	λελυκότα
A	λελυκότας	λελυκυίας	λελυκότα
G	λελυκότων	λελυκυιῶν	λελυκότων
D	λελυκόσι(ν)	λελυκυίαις	λελυκόσι(ν)

21.4 The Perfect Indicative of Middle and Passive Verbs

The perfect indicative of the middle-passive verb πορεύομαι	
Form of πορεύομαι	Meaning
πεπόρευμαι	I have gone
πεπόρευσαι	you have gone
πεπόρευται	he/she/it has gone
πεπορεύμεθα	we have gone
πεπόρευσθε	you have gone
πεπόρευνται	they have gone

21.5 The Perfect Participle Middle and Passive

The perfect participle of the middle-passive verb πορεύομαι			
	Masc	Fem	Neut
N	πεπορευμένος	πεπορευμένη	πεπορευμένον
A	πεπορευμένον	πεπορευμένην	πεπορευμένον
G	πεπορευμένου	πεπορευμένης	πεπορευμένου
D	πεπορευμένῳ	πεπορευμένῃ	πεπορευμένῳ
N	πεπορευμένοι	πεπορευμέναι	πεπορευμένα
A	πεπορευμένους	πεπορευμένας	πεπορευμένα
G	πεπορευμένων	πεπορευμένων	πεπορευμένων
D	πεπορευμένοις	πεπορευμέναις	πεπορευμένοις

21.6 The Perfect Infinitive

The perfect infinitive is found 38 times in the active voice, and 9 times in the middle and passive voices.

The perfect infinitive active of λύω is λελυκέναι "to have loosed"
The perfect infinitive of the middle-passive verb πορεύομαι is πεπορεύσθαι "to have gone"

21.7 Examples of Translating the Perfect Tense

Usually the English perfect tense is a good translation of the Greek perfect tense, as might be illustrated by several examples of the perfect tense which have already been met in the translation passages:
- 1 John 2:3: Καὶ ἐν τούτῳ γινώσκομεν ὅτι ἐγνώκαμεν αὐτόν, ἐὰν τὰς ἐντολὰς αὐτοῦ τηρῶμεν. And by this we know that we have known him, if we keep his commandments.
- 1 John 2:4: ὁ λέγων ὅτι Ἔγνωκα αὐτὸν καὶ τὰς ἐντολὰς αὐτοῦ μὴ τηρῶν, ψεύστης ἐστίν. The one who says, "I have known him," while not keeping his commandments, is a liar.
- John 9:29: ἡμεῖς οἴδαμεν ὅτι Μωϋσεῖ λελάληκεν ὁ θεός ... We know that God has spoken to Moses ...

Vocabulary 21.1 (for Ex 21)

More Frequently Occurring Irregular Perfects:
δέδωκα [27+]   I have given [perf. ind. act. of δίδωμι]
ἔγνωκα [19]   I have known [perf. ind. act. of γινώσκω]
ἐλήλυθα [31+]   I have come/gone [perf. ind. act. of ἔρχομαι]
ἕστηκα or ἕστακα [20+] I stand [perf. ind. act. of ἵστημι; used as a intransitive present tense (i.e. in cannot take a direct object); the present tense of ἵστημι is transitive (i.e. it can take a direct object)]
ἑστώς or ἑστηκώς, -, ἑστός [43+] perf. part. act. of ἵστημι
ἑώρακα [31+]   I have seen [perf. ind. act. of ὁράω]
πέποιθα [16]   I have persuaded [perf. ind. act. of πείθω]

Other Irregular Perfects:
ἀκήκοα[1] [10]   I have heard [perf. ind. act. of ἀκούω]
-βέβηκα [5]   I have gone [perf. ind. act. of -βαίνω]
βέβληκα [1+]   I have thrown [perf. ind. act. of βάλλω]
γέγραφα [1+]   I have written [perf. ind. act. of γράφω]
εἴληφα [7]   I have taken [perf. ind. act. of λαμβάνω]
εἴρηκα [8+]   I have said [perf. ind. act. of λέγω]
-ενήνοχα [1+]   I have borne [perf. ind. act. of φέρω]
πέπτωκα [3]   I have fallen [perf. ind. act. of πίπτω]
τέθεικα [4+]   I have placed [perf. ind. act. of τίθημι]

Other words:
ἐλπίζω (30)   I hope [perf. ἤλπικα]
σήμερον (41)   (adv.) today
φιλέω (25)   I love, kiss

φίλος, η, ον (29)   adj: loving; as noun: friend

[1]Note on ἀκήκοα: The o on the end of the perfect verb stem ἀκηκο- does not coalesce with the vowels of the endings. Thus the perf. ind. act. of ἀκούω is: ἀκήκοα, ἀκήκοας, ἀκήκοε(ν), ἀκηκόαμεν, ἀκηκόατε, ἀκηκόασι(ν).

Exercise 21

Translate into English
1. λύεις 2. λελύκατε 3. ἔλυσας 4. λέλυκας 5. βέβληκεν 6. βεβλήκασιν 7. βάλλουσιν 8. ἔβαλον 9. σεσώκαμεν 10. ἐσώσαμεν 11. σεσώκατε 12. σῴζομεν 13. βέβηκας 14. γέγραφα 15. ἀκήκοα 16. ἐλήλυθεν 17. πεφίληκας 18. γεγέννηκας 19. ἔγνωκεν 20. δεδώκατε 21. πεπόρευσαι 22. ἠκούσατε 23. ἐλήλυθας 24. ἑστήκασιν 25. πεπιστεύκασιν 26. πεποιήκασιν 27. λαλοῦμεν

28. δεδώκαμεν 29. βέβληκεν 30. ἀκηκόασιν 31. ἐξεληλύθαμεν 32. ἔδωκαν 33. εἴληφα 34. ἐγράψαμεν 35. ἕστακεν 36. πεπροσκύνηκας 37. εἰσεληλύθατε 38. καταβεβήκαμεν 39. ἐγνώκασιν 40. δέδωκεν 41. εἰρήκασιν 42. εἶπες 43. πέπτωκα 44. γέγραφας 45. ἐδώκατε 46. τέθεικα 47. πεφίληκεν 48. ἐνήνοχεν 49. εἴρηκας 50. ἀναβεβήκατε 51. εἰλήφαμεν 52. λελάληκεν 53. ἐπέσαμεν

54. ᾔτηκας 55. τεθείκατε 56. ἐνηνόχασιν 57. ἤνεγκα 58. ἤλπικας 59. ἀγαπᾷ 60. ἔγραψαν 61. ᾐτήκαμεν 62. ἠγάπηκα 63. τετήρηκεν

Parse the following:
64. πεπορευμένας   65. λελυκότες   66. γεγεννηκυῖαι   67. δέδωκας 68. πεποίθαμεν 69. πεποίηκεν 70. ἑωρακυῖα 71. τεθεικώς 72. πεφιληκυιῶν

Translate the following into idiomatic English:
73. Ἀμὴν ἀμὴν λέγω ὑμῖν ὅτι ὁ τὸν λόγον μου ἀκούων καὶ πιστεύων τῷ πέμψαντί με ἔχει ζωὴν αἰώνιον καὶ εἰς κρίσιν οὐκ ἔρχεται, ἀλλὰ μεταβέβηκεν ἐκ τοῦ θανάτου εἰς τὴν ζωήν (John 5:24). 74. Ἰησοῦς ... εἶπεν, Σὺ πιστεύεις εἰς τὸν υἱὸν τοῦ ἀνθρώπου; ἀπεκρίθη ἐκεῖνος καὶ εἶπεν, Καὶ τίς ἐστιν, κύριε, ἵνα πιστεύσω εἰς αὐτόν; εἶπεν αὐτῷ ὁ Ἰησοῦς, Καὶ ἑώρακας αὐτὸν καὶ ὁ λαλῶν μετὰ σοῦ ἐκεῖνός ἐστιν (John 9:35-37). 75. Τίνι γὰρ εἶπέν ποτε τῶν ἀγγέλων, Υἱός μου εἶ σύ, ἐγὼ σήμερον γεγέννηκά σε; (Heb 1:5) 76. ἤδη ὑμεῖς καθαροί ἐστε διὰ τὸν λόγον ὃν λελάληκα ὑμῖν (John 15:3). 77. ἀλλὰ ταῦτα λελάληκα ὑμῖν ἵνα ὅταν ἔλθῃ ἡ ὥρα αὐτῶν μνημονεύητε αὐτῶν ὅτι ἐγὼ εἶπον ὑμῖν (John 16:4). [μνημονεύω is followed by a genitive of the thing remembered] 78. Ταῦτα ἐλάλησεν Ἰησοῦς καὶ ἐπάρας τοὺς ὀφθαλμοὺς αὐτοῦ εἰς τὸν οὐρανὸν εἶπεν, Πάτερ, ἐλήλυθεν ἡ ὥρα (John 17:1). 79. κἀγὼ ἑώρακα καὶ μεμαρτύρηκα ὅτι οὗτός ἐστιν ὁ υἱὸς τοῦ θεοῦ (John 1:34; note κἀγώ = καί + ἐγώ). 80. θεὸν οὐδεὶς ἑώρακεν πώποτε (John 1:18). 81. καὶ ἡμεῖς πεπιστεύκαμεν καὶ ἐγνώκαμεν ὅτι σὺ εἶ ὁ ἅγιος τοῦ θεοῦ (John 6:69).

Vocabulary 21.2 (for John 8:12-59)

ἀποκτείνω¹ (74)   I kill [ao. ἀπέκτεινα]
γνώσομαι (10)   I shall know [mid. fut. of γινώσκω]
διδάσκαλος (59)   teacher
διδάσκω (95)   I teach
εἰδῶ (10)   I might know [subj. of οἶδα²]
εἰδώς, εἰδυῖα, εἶδος, εἰδοτ- (51) perf. part. act. (with present meaning) of οἶδα
κἀγώ (84)   and I, I also [= καί + ἐγώ]
καλῶς (37)   adv.: rightly, well
οἶδα (321)   I know³
πολύς, πολλή, πολύ (353) many, much
χαίρω (74)   I rejoice

Notes on Vocabulary 21.2

1. ἀποκτείνω = ἀπό + κτείνω; this verb is sometimes spelt as ἀποκτέννω, or ἀποκτεννύω.
2. The subj. act. of οἶδα, εἰδῶ follows the pattern that might be expected: εἰδῶ, εἰδῇς, εἰδῇ, etc.]
3. οἶδα uses perfect tense forms with present tense meaning.

Translation Passage 21: John 8:12-59

The following notes are intended to help with some of the grammatical forms which have not yet been met. There are some further comments on these verses in Appendix A.

John chapter eight:

v. 12. ἕξει "will have," is the (slightly irregular) 3rd pers. sing. future ind. act. of ἔχω.

v. 14. κἄν = καὶ ἐάν; "even if," or "and if." The contraction is found 16 times in the NT.

v. 17. γέγραπται is found in 67 verses in the NT. The reduplication of the γ of γράφω shows that it is a perfect. It is, in fact, the 3rd pers. sing. perf. ind. passive. Translate as "it has been written."

v. 19. οὔτε ... οὔτε "neither ... nor." ᾔδειτε "you knew," is the 2nd pers. pl. pluperfect ind. act. of οἶδα. οἶδα uses perfect forms for present meaning, and pluperfect forms for past meaning. The second occurrence of ᾔδειτε follows ἄν, but in this case, ἄν indicates a contrary to fact conditional sentence [see *Int*.2.2.2]. In contrary to fact conditional sentences, the

Part 3

imperfect tense is used for present meaning, and the aorist or pluperfect for past meaning.

v. 20. ἐλήλυθει "had ... come," is the 3d pers. sing. pluperfect ind. act. of the middle verb ἔρχομαι. ἐπίασεν is aorist of πιάζω.

vv. 21-22. ζητήσετε "you will seek," is the 2d pers. pl. future ind. act. of ζητέω; ἀποθανεῖσθε "you will die" is the 2nd pers. sing. future ind. mid. of ἀποθνήσκω; ἀποκτενεῖ "he will kill himself," is the 3d pers. sing. future ind. act. of ἀποκτείνω.

v. 27. ἔγνωσαν is the 3rd pers. pl. aor. ind. act. of γινώσκω [see 28.2].

v. 30. The phrase, Ταῦτα αὐτοῦ λαλοῦντος "after/when he said these things", forms a genitive absolute construction (genitive absolute constructions form around a participle in the genitive case; everything else in the phrase that can take case becomes genitive). Here the genitive absolute has temporal meaning.

v. 33. γενήσεσθε "you will become," is the 2nd pers. pl. fut. ind. mid. of γίνομαι.

v. 36. ἔσεσθε "you will be," is the 2nd pers. pl. fut. ind. act. of εἰμί [see Vocab. 25].

v. 39. This verse involves an interesting textual variant, as well as grammar that has yet to be met. The UBS text reads ἐποιεῖτε, the the imperfect ind. act. of ποιέω. Imperfects are used in the second half of contrary to fact conditions with present reference. Thus this verse might be translated "If you are children of Abraham [which you aren't], you would do the deeds of Abraham." A textual variant has ποιεῖτε in place of ἐποιεῖτε, an imperative instead of an imperfect. If this reading were adopted, the text would be translated, "If you are children of Abraham, do the deeds of Abraham [a command]." Contrary to fact conditions, and a brief introduction to textual variants are covered in *Intermediate New Testament Greek Made Easier* Chapters 2 [*Int*.2.2.2] and 8.

v. 41. γεγεννήμεθα "we have been begotten," is a perfect (note the reduplicated γ). It is the 1st pers. pl. perf. ind. passive of γεννάω.

v. 42. The verb ἥκω "I have come" is in a present tense form, but is translated as a perfect. Εἰ ... ἄν ἐμέ is a contrary to fact condition [note ἄν in the "then" clause; see also *Int*.2.2.2]; Jesus implies that because his hearers do not love him, they do not, in fact, have God as their father.

v. 43. διὰ τί = "why"?

v. 50. The verb ἐστίν can sometimes be used in an impersonal sense. Here it might be translated "There is [one who seeks and judges]."

v. 53. μή in questions has already been met while translating John 9:27. They are not translated into English, and indicate that the question expects a "no" answer [see *Int*.6.3].

v. 55. ἔσομαι "I will be" is the 1st pers. sing. fut. ind. act. of εἰμί [see Vocab. 25].
v. 56. No doubt you recognized ἴδῃ as the aor. subj. act. of ὁράω [see 16.1]. ἠγαλλιάσατο is the 1st pers. sing. aor. ind. middle of ἀγαλλιάω, translate "rejoiced." ἐμήν is from the possessive adjective ἐμός, ή, όν "my, mine."
v. 58. πρίν is followed by an infinitive, and means "before" [see *Int.*1.3.3].
v. 59. ἐκρύβη is the 3d pers. sing. aor. ind. passive of κρύπτω. Translate as "was hidden ...," or with Kubo, "hid himself ..."

Chapter 22:
The Imperfect Indicative Active

New Testament Greek has four main tenses in the indicative mood which deal with past events in some way: the imperfect, the aorist, the perfect, and the pluperfect. The aorist and perfect tenses have been met in Chapters 12 and 21. The aorist tense is the default past tense, and is usually translated by the simple past tense in English; while the Greek perfect tense deals with events from the past that still have effect in the present, and is most often best translated with the English perfect tense. This chapter will introduce the imperfect tense, looking first at how it is formed, and then at how it is usually translated. Amongst other things, it will be discovered that the imperfect tense can refer to either continuous action in the past, or the start of an action in the past.

22.1 The Paradigm of the Imperfect Indicative Active

The imperfect indicative active of λύω	
Form of λύω	English meaning
ἔλυον	I was loosing/began to loose
ἔλυες	you were loosing/began ..
ἔλυεν	he/.. was loosing/began ..
ἐλύομεν	we were loosing/began ..
ἐλύετε	you were loosing/began ..
ἔλυον	they were loosing/began ..

[Note: Many grammers of New Testament Greek specify that the third person singular imperfect indicative active has a moveable ν. This is not true for most imperfect indicatives in the New Testament. The -εω verbs form the largest group of exceptions. The end of the third person singular imperfect indicative active of -εω verbs is always ε-ε, which, after contraction, produces an -ει ending. As this is invariably the case, -εω verbs do not use a moveable ν for their third person singular imperfect indicative actives either.]

Like the aorist tense, the imperfect tense involves both adding an augment to the beginning of the word, and an ending to the end of the word. Familiarity with the aorist tense will make the different kinds of augment on

the imperfect tense look natural. The augment is one of the indications of past time. Examples
- ἐγίνωσκον is the imperfect [ind. act.] of γίνωσκω.
- ἔλεγον is the imperfect of λέγω.
- ἤθελον is the imperfect of θέλω [one of the rare irregular forms found in the imperfect tense].
- ἠρώτων [-αον] is the imperfect of ἐρωτάω.
- ἐπηρώτων [-αον] is the imperfect of ἐπερωτάω.
- ἠκουλουθουν [-εον] is the imperfect of ἀκολουθέω.
- ἐλάλουν [-εον] is the imperfect of λαλέω.
- περιεπάτουν [-εον] is the imperfect of περιπατέω.
- ἐποίουν [-εον] is the imperfect of ποιέω.

The imperfect tense only exists in the indicative. In other words, there are no imperfect participles, subjunctives, infinitives, imperatives or optatives [see Appendix B].

22.2 The Imperfect Indicative of -εω and -αω Verbs

The rules for the contraction of vowels that have already been met are applied in the same manner to the imperfect tense, and the imperfect tenses of the -εω and -αω verbs can be easily derived [the rules of contraction are listed in Appendix G if a reminder is needed; note the moveable ν is missing from the 3d per. sing. for both -εω and -αω verbs]:

The Imperfect Indicative Active of λαλέω:
ἐλάλουν
ἐλάλεις
ἐλάλει
ἐλαλοῦμεν
ἐλαλεῖτε
ἐλάλουν

The Imperfect Indicative Active of ἀγαπάω:
ἠγάπων
ἠγάπας
ἠγάπα
ἠγαπῶμεν
ἠγαπᾶτε
ἠγάπων

22.3 The Translation of the Imperfect Tense

There are two common ways to translated the imperfect tense:

1. "was/were ...-ing" (the **continuous imperfect**): The imperfect tense often implies continuous action. Thus ἔβαλλον could be translated as "I was throwing" (the English verb "was/were" is added to show the continuous nature of the action). For example:
   - ἤσθιον, ἔπινον, ἐγάμουν they were eating, they were drinking, they were marrying (Luke 17:27)
   - καὶ πολλοί πλούσιου ἔβαλλον πολλά And many rich people were casting [in] much (Mark 12:41)

2. "... began ..." (the **inceptive or ingressive imperfect**): Many imperfects may be translated by adding the English word "began." In English "began" is either followed by an infinitive (I began to study) or by a present participle (I began studying). Either of these is acceptable as a translation of the inceptive imperfect. For example:
   - When he saw the crowd he went up into the mountain, and when he sat down his disciples came to him, and opening his mouth he began to teach them ... (ἐδίδασκεν αὐτούς ...) (Matt 5:1-2)
   - When the bridegroom was delayed, they all grew tired and began to sleep (ἐκάθευδον) (Matt 25:5)

Exercise 22.1

[Note: This exercise is provided to allow those teachers who wish to cover the imperfect tense before the aorist tense to do so. In other words, it may be done after Chapter 11, and uses vocabulary known by the end of that chapter. It may be regarded as an optional exercise for those who have completed up to Chapter 21.]

Provide two English translations for each of the following corresponding to the continuous and inceptive imperfects:
1. ἔλεγον 2. ἔγραφεν 3. ἦγον 4. ἐκεβάλλετε 5. σύνηγες 6. ἤκουες
7. ἀπέθνησκον 8. ἐκαλοῦμεν 9. ἐβάλλομεν 10. ἀπελύετε 11. ἤτουν
12. ἐγέννων 13. ἐδοκεῖτε 14. ἠρώτων 15. ἐγίνωσκεν

22.4 The Imperfect Indicative of Middle and Passive Verbs

The imperfect indicative middle of δέχομαι is:
ἐδεχόμην
ἐδέχου
ἐδέχετο
ἐδεχόμεθα
ἐδέχεσθε
ἐδέχοντο

22.5 The Imperfect Indicative of εἰμί

Several of the imperfect forms of εἰμί in the following table should be familiar as they have already appeared in set passages from the Greek New Testament, and the 3rd pers. sing. was listed as early as Vocabulary 12.1. Here, then, is the complete paradigm of the imperfect of εἰμί:

ἤμην
ἦς or ἦσθα
ἦν
ἦμεν or ἤμεθα
ἦτε
ἦσαν

The imperfect of εἰμί is translated, "I was," "you were," "he/she/it was," "we were" etc. An alternate form ἦσθα instead of ἦς is used twice in the New Testament (Matt 26:69, Mark 14:67); ἦς itself is used 6 times. In the first person plural, the form ἦμεν is used 8 times, and ἤμεθα is used 4 times. The first person singular ἤμην is used 15 times, while the third person forms ἦν and ἦσαν are used 289 and 93 times, respectively.

There are no aorist or perfect tenses of εἰμί.

22.6 The Difference Between the Imperfect and the Aorist Tenses

Although the endings of the imperfect are the same as the endings for the strong aorist tense, there is no real confusion, because the imperfect is formed from the verb stem used in the present tense (the present verb stem), and strong verbs use an aorist verb stem that is different from the present

Part 3 211

verb stem. Some examples will make this clear:

Examples to illustrate formation of imperfect vs aorist tenses		
Pres ind act	Imp ind act	Aor ind act
ἄγω	ἦγον	ἤγαγον
βάλλω	ἔβαλλον	ἔβαλον
ἐσθίω	ἤσθιον	ἔφαγον
ἔχω	εἶχον	ἔσχον
λαμβάνω	ἐλάμβανον	ἔλαβον
λέγω	ἔλεγον	εἶπον
πίνω	ἔπινον	ἔπιον
πίπτω	ἔπιπτον	ἔπεσα

The imperfect tense is not listed in principal parts because in almost every instance it is formed regularly [although notice that ἔχω and μέλλω, which have 1st pers. imp. ind. actives of εἶχον and ἤμελλον resp. (see Vocab. 22), form their augment for the imperfect in an irregular manner – they are some of the very few verbs to do so. See also ἤθελον at 22.1].

It is natural to compare the imperfect and the aorist tenses. For example, they are both past tenses. The difference is that the imperfect may be used to stress either the **inceptive** or **continuous** nature of the action, while the aorist describes the action as a whole and can usually be translated by a simple past tense in English. At times the aorist tense makes no reference to the kind of action involved. It it is more often used where the action takes place only once [**punctiliar use**], or intermittently [**iterative use**]. [See *Int*.3.2.2 & *Int*.3.5.1 for further uses of the aorist and imperfect tenses]

Examples:

ἔβαλεν	He threw
ἔβαλλεν	He was throwing [continuous action] / He began to throw [inceptive action]
ἔφαγον	I ate
ἤσθιον	I was eating / I began eating
ἔπεσας	You fell
ἔπιπτες	You were falling / You began to fall

Note: the imperfect of λέγω (ἔλεγον) is found often in the Gospels. Frequent use appears to have worn away the differences between the imperfect ἔλεγον and the aorist εἶπον [cf. *Int*.3.5.1.7], and it is often very hard to distinguish any difference of meaning between them. There is no need to distinguish between them in translation.

Vocabulary 22

ἄρα (49) then, therefore
εἶχον (51) I was having, I began to have [irregular imp. ind. act. of ἔχω]
ἐκεῖ (95) there
ἐνώπιον (93) + gen. before, in the presence of
εὐαγγελίζω (54) I proclaim, preach, bring good news [note: εὐαγγελίζω = εὐ + ἀγγελίζω; thus its 1st pers. imp. ind. act. is εὐηγγέλιζον]
εὐαγγέλιον (76) good news, gospel
Ἠλίας, -ου (29) Elijah
θεραπεύω (43) I heal
καθίζω (46) I seat, sit [cf. κάθημαι, I sit]
κράζω (55) I cry out, scream
μέλλω (110) [usually + inf.] I am about to, on the point of [imp. ind. act. ἤμελλον (14) or ἔμελλον (4); fut. μελλήσω (2); not found in aor.]
πλείων, πλεῖον (55) more, greater (comparative of πολύς, great)
ὑπάρχω (60) I am [= εἰμί], exist, have at my disposal [Note also that τὰ ὑπάρχοντα = property, possessions]
φόβος (47) fear [cf. φοβέομαι, I fear; cf. also the English word "phobia"]
ὥστε (84) therefore, so that [note: ὥστε + infinitive is used to express result, "with the result that."]

Exercise 22.2

[Note: numbers 1-14, 16-27 may be done after exercise 12.2 if your teacher so wishes.]

Translate into English
Provide two translations for imperfect tenses—one translated as an inceptive imperfect, one as a continuous imperfect:

1. ἔλεγες 2. εἶπες 3. ἐπέσαμεν 4. ἐπίπτομεν 5. ἔβλεπεν 6. ἔβλεψεν 7. ἄγετε 8. ἠγάγετε 9. ἤγετε 10. ἔπεισα 11. ἔπειθον 12. βάλλετε 13. ἐβάλλετε 14. ἐβάλετε 15. βεβλήκατε 16. ἦσθα 17. ᾔτησαν 18. ᾔτουν 19. ᾖς 20. ἠγάπα 21. ἠγάπησεν 22. ἠγαπᾶτε 23. εἶχε 24. ἔσχεν 25. ἤρωτα 26. ἠρώτησας 27. ἠρώτησε 28. ἦν 29. ἔπεμψαν 30. ἔπεμπον 31. ἦσαν 32. εἴληφας 33. ἔλαβες 34. ἐλάμβανες

35. ἀπήλθομεν 36. ἀπηρχόμεθα 37. ἐπίετε 38. ἔπιες 39. ἔπινες 40. ἤμην 41. ἦτε 42. ἐπροσευχόμην 43. ἐμαρτυρήσατε 44. ἐμαρτυρεῖτε 45. ἐδεχόμην 46. ἤμεθα 47. ἠσθίομεν 48. ἐφάγομεν 49. ἐφοβοῦντο 50. ἐγίνοντο 51. προσήρχεσθε 52. ἔγεννα 53. ἐποιοῦμεν 54. προσήρχου

From the Greek New Testament

55. And they were filled with great fear καὶ ἔλεγον πρὸς ἀλλήλους, Τίς ἄρα οὗτός ἐστιν ὅτι καὶ ὁ ἄνεμος καὶ ἡ θάλασσα ὑπακούει αὐτῷ; (Mark 4:41).

56. ἔλεγον οὖν αὐτῷ, Ποῦ ἐστιν ὁ πατήρ σου; ... ἔλεγον οὖν οἱ Ἰουδαῖοι, Μήτι ἀποκτενεῖ ἑαυτόν, ὅτι λέγει, Ὅπου ἐγὼ ὑπάγω ὑμεῖς οὐ δύνασθε ἐλθεῖν; καὶ ἔλεγεν αὐτοῖς, Ὑμεῖς ἐκ τῶν κάτω ἐστέ ...ἔλεγον οὖν αὐτῷ, Σὺ τίς εἶ; ... Ἔλεγεν οὖν ὁ Ἰησοῦς πρὸς τοὺς πεπιστευκότας αὐτῷ Ἰουδαίους, Ἐὰν ὑμεῖς μείνητε ἐν τῷ λόγῳ τῷ ἐμῷ, ἀληθῶς μαθηταί μού ἐστε ... (John 8:19, 22, 23, 25, 31).

57. Καὶ καθίσας κατέναντι τοῦ γαζοφυλακίου ἐθεώρει πῶς ὁ ὄχλος βάλλει χαλκὸν εἰς τὸ γαζοφυλάκιον. καὶ πολλοὶ πλούσιοι ἔβαλλον πολλά. καὶ ἐλθοῦσα μία χήρα πτωχὴ ἔβαλεν λεπτὰ δύο, ... καὶ προσκαλεσάμενος τοὺς μαθητὰς αὐτοῦ εἶπεν αὐτοῖς, Ἀμὴν λέγω ὑμῖν ὅτι ἡ χήρα αὕτη ἡ πτωχὴ πλεῖον πάντων ἔβαλεν τῶν βαλλόντων εἰς τὸ γαζοφυλάκιον. πάντες γὰρ ἐκ τοῦ περισσεύοντος αὐτοῖς ἔβαλον, αὕτη δὲ ἐκ τῆς ὑστερήσεως αὐτῆς πάντα ὅσα εἶχεν ἔβαλεν ὅλον τὸν βίον αὐτῆς (Mark 12:41-44).

58. Μετὰ ταῦτα ἦλθεν ὁ Ἰησοῦς καὶ οἱ μαθηταὶ αὐτοῦ εἰς τὴν Ἰουδαίαν γῆν καὶ ἐκεῖ διέτριβεν μετ᾽ αὐτῶν καὶ ἐβάπτιζεν (John 3:22). **59.** οὐδεὶς ... παρρησίᾳ ἐλάλει περὶ αὐτοῦ διὰ τὸν φόβον τῶν Ἰουδαίων (John 7:13). **60.** καὶ ἦν τις βασιλικὸς οὗ ὁ υἱὸς ἠσθένει ἐν Καφαρναούμ. οὗτος ἀκούσας ὅτι Ἰησοῦς ἥκει ἐκ τῆς Ἰουδαίας εἰς τὴν Γαλιλαίαν ἀπῆλθεν πρὸς αὐτὸν καὶ ἠρώτα ἵνα καταβῇ καὶ ἰάσηται αὐτοῦ τὸν υἱόν, ἤμελλεν γὰρ ἀποθνήσκειν (John 4:46b-47).

61. Καὶ περιῆγεν ἐν ὅλῃ τῇ Γαλιλαίᾳ διδάσκων ἐν ταῖς συναγωγαῖς αὐτῶν καὶ κηρύσσων τὸ εὐαγγέλιον τῆς βασιλείας καὶ θεραπεύων πᾶσαν νόσον καὶ πᾶσαν μαλακίαν ἐν τῷ λαῷ ... Καὶ περιῆγεν ὁ Ἰησοῦς all the cities and villages διδάσκων ἐν ταῖς συναγωγαῖς αὐτῶν καὶ κηρύσσων τὸ εὐαγγέλλιον τῆς βασιλείας καὶ θεραπεύων πᾶσαν νόσον καὶ πᾶσαν μαλακίαν (Matt 4:23; 9:35).

62. καὶ ἐγένετο θάμβος ἐπὶ πάντας καὶ συνελάλουν πρὸς ἀλλήλους λέγοντες, Τίς ὁ λόγος οὗτος ὅτι ἐν ἐξουσίᾳ καὶ δυνάμει ἐπιτάσσει τοῖς ἀκαθάρτοις πνεύμασιν καὶ ἐξέρχονται; (Luke 4:36) **63.** καὶ ἰδοὺ γυνὴ χαναναία ἀπὸ τῶν ὁρίων ἐκείνων ἐξελθοῦσα ἔκραζεν λέγουσα, "Have mercy on me, κύριε υἱὸς Δαυίδ ... (Matt 15:22). **64.** καὶ ἠκολούθησαν αὐτῷ ὄχλοι πολλοί, καὶ ἐθεράπευσεν αὐτοὺς ἐκεῖ (Matt 19:2).

65. ὅπου γάρ ἐστιν ὁ θησαυρός σου, ἐκεῖ ἔσται καὶ ἡ καρδία σου (Matt 6:21).
66. καὶ διελογίζοντο πρὸς ἀλλήλους ὅτι ἄρτους οὐκ ἔχουσιν (Mark 8:16).
67. καὶ ἰδοὺ ἦλθεν ἀνὴρ ᾧ ὄνομα Ἰάϊρος καὶ οὗτος ἄρχων τῆς συναγωγῆς ὑπῆρχεν, καὶ πεσὼν παρὰ τοὺς πόδας τοῦ Ἰησοῦ παρεκάλει αὐτὸν εἰσελθεῖν εἰς τὸν οἶκον αὐτοῦ, ὅτι θυγάτηρ μονογενὴς ἦν αὐτῷ ὡς ἐτῶν δώδεκα καὶ αὐτὴ ἀπέθνησκεν (Luke 8:41-42).

68. καὶ τὰ πνεύματα τὰ ἀκάθαρτα, ὅταν αὐτὸν ἐθεώρουν, προσέπιπτον αὐτῷ καὶ ἔκραζον λέγοντες ὅτι Σὺ εἶ ὁ υἱὸς τοῦ θεοῦ (Mark 3:11). **69.** καὶ ἐξελθόντος αὐτοῦ ἐκ τοῦ πλοίου εὐθὺς ὑπήντησεν αὐτῷ ἐκ τῶν μνημείων

ἄνθρωπος ἐν πνεύματι ἀκαθάρτῳ, ὃς τὴν κατοίκησιν εἶχεν ἐν τοῖς μνήμασιν, καὶ οὐδὲ ἁλύσει οὐκέτι οὐδεὶς ἐδύνατο αὐτὸν δῆσαι ... καὶ διὰ παντὸς νυκτὸς καὶ ἡμέρας ἐν τοῖς μνήμασιν καὶ ἐν τοῖς ὄρεσιν ἦν κράζων καὶ κατακόπτων ἑαυτὸν λίθοις (Mark 5:2-4, 5).

70. ἄλλοι ἔλεγον ὅτι Οὗτός ἐστιν, ἄλλοι ἔλεγον, Οὐχί, ἀλλὰ ὅμοιος αὐτῷ ἐστιν. ἐκεῖνος ἔλεγεν ὅτι, Ἐγώ εἰμι (John 9:9). **71.** ἐν ἡμέρᾳ ὅτε κρίνει ὁ θεὸς τὰ κρυπτὰ τῶν ἀνθρώπων κατὰ τὸ εὐαγγέλιόν μου διὰ Χριστοῦ Ἰησοῦ (Rom 2:16). **72.** καὶ καθὼς ἐγένετο ἐν ταῖς ἡμέραις Νῶε, οὕτως ἔσται καὶ ἐν ταῖς ἡμέραις τοῦ υἱοῦ τοῦ ἀνθρώπου· ἤσθιον, ἔπινον, ἐγάμουν, ... καὶ ἦλθεν ὁ κατακλυσμὸς καὶ ἀπώλεσεν πάντας (Luke 17:26-27).

73. ἀλλ' ἐν ταῖς ἡμέραις τῆς φωνῆς τοῦ ἑβδόμου ἀγγέλου, ὅταν μέλλῃ σαλπίζειν, and the mystery of God is finished, ὡς εὐηγγέλισεν τοὺς ἑαυτοῦ δούλους τοὺς προφήτας (Rev 10:7). **74.** καὶ οἱ προάγοντες καὶ οἱ ἀκολουθοῦντες ἔκραζον, Ὡσαννά ... (Mark 11:9). **75.** λέγει πρὸς Φίλιππον, Πόθεν ἀγοράσωμεν ἄρτους ἵνα φάγωσιν αὐτοί; τοῦτο δὲ ἔλεγεν πειράζων αὐτόν· αὐτὸς γὰρ ᾔδει τί ἔμελλεν ποιεῖν (John 6:5c-6)

76. Πολλὰ μὲν οὖν καὶ ἄλλα σημεῖα ἐποίησεν ὁ Ἰησοῦς ἐνώπιον τῶν μαθητῶν αὐτοῦ which have not been written in this book (John 20:30). **77.** ἔκραξεν οὖν ἐν τῷ ἱερῷ διδάσκων ὁ Ἰησοῦς καὶ λέγων, Κἀμὲ οἴδατε καὶ οἴδατε πόθεν εἰμί· καὶ ἀπ' ἐμαυτοῦ οὐκ ἐλήλυθα, ἀλλ' ἔστιν ἀληθινὸς ὁ πέμψας με, ὃν ὑμεῖς οὐκ οἴδατε ... (John 7:28). **78.** ... Ζακχαῖος εἶπεν πρὸς τὸν κύριον, Ἰδοὺ τὰ ἡμίσιά μου τῶν ὑπαρχόντων, κύριε, τοῖς πτωχοῖς δίδωμι, ... (Luke 19:8).

79. καὶ αὐτὸς προελεύσεται ἐνώπιον αὐτοῦ ἐν πνεύματι καὶ δυνάμει Ἠλίου, ἐπιστρέψαι καρδίας πατέρων ἐπὶ τέκνα καὶ ἀπειθεῖς ἐν φρονήσει δικαίων, ἑτοιμάσαι κυρίῳ λαὸν prepared. Καὶ εἶπεν Ζαχαρίας πρὸς τὸν ἄγγελον, Κατὰ τί γνώσομαι τοῦτο; ἐγὼ γάρ εἰμι πρεσβύτης καὶ ἡ γυνή μου προβεβηκυῖα ἐν ταῖς ἡμέραις αὐτῆς. καὶ ἀποκριθεὶς ὁ ἄγγελος εἶπεν αὐτῷ, Ἐγώ εἰμι Γαβριὴλ ὁ παρεστηκὼς ἐνώπιον τοῦ θεοῦ καὶ ἀπεστάλην λαλῆσαι πρὸς σὲ καὶ εὐαγγελίσασθαί σοι ταῦτα ... (Luke 1:17-19) [ἀπεστάλην is the strong aorist indicative passive of ἀποστέλλω. It will be met officially after the review chapter, and may be translated "I was sent."]

Part 3

Chapter 23: Review of Parts 1-3

For most students the two greatest challenges to mastering New Testament Greek are participles and the way the verb changes between tenses. Substantial progress has now been made in mastering both these difficulties. As you have seen from translating John 8 & 9, you now stand on the verge of being able to translate freely from the easier parts of the Greek New Testament – significant progress indeed!

The next section of the textbook will introduce several new grammatical forms, the most important being the forms of the passive voice, the future tense and the imperative mood. It is probably sensible, though, to take some time to be comfortable with the material already covered *before* moving on to new work.

The Major Things Learnt Thus Far

A list of topics found in Chapters 1 to 22:

Verb tenses (active voice): Present [except -μι verbs], aorist, imperfect [except -μι verbs], perfect
Verb Tenses (middle and passive voice): Present, imperfect, perfect
Moods of the verb: Indicative, subjunctive, infinitive, participle
Nouns: First declension feminine; second declension masculine and neuter; third declension masculine, feminine and neuter

Meanings of the tenses

Uses of Verb Tenses Covered in Parts 1-3			
Indicative Active:			
Tense	Form of λύω	Closest English Tense(s)	Normal Translation (indicative mood)
Present	λύω	Simple present active Present continuous active Present emphatic active	I loose I am loosing I do loose
Aorist	ἔλυσα	Simple past active	I loosed
Imperfect	ἔλυον	Past continuous Past inceptive	I was loosing I began to loose
Perfect	λέλυκα	Perfect active	I have loosed

Uses of the mood

So far, the indicative, subjunctive, infinitive and participial moods have been covered. In summary, these moods are used in the following way:

Uses of Verb Moods Covered in Parts 1-3	
Mood	Principal uses of the mood
Indicative mood	The mood used for making statements and asking questions about real events
Subjunctive mood	The mood used to express contingencies. Often found after certain conjunctions (e.g. ἵνα, ἄν, ἐάν, οὐ μή, etc)
Infinitive mood	The mood used after certain verbs (e.g. θέλω, δύναμαι, ἔξεστιν, etc). Often most easily translated by the English infinitive: "to ..."
Participial mood	A mood difficult to equate to one thing in English grammar. Used with the article to mean "the one who ..."; often best translated as a reference to time, "when ...," "while ...," etc.; and sometimes translated by the English participles, "-ing" (active), "-ed" (passive).

A Checklist for revision:

◊ Revise the uses of the subjunctive, participial and infinitive moods of the verb.
◊ Carefully look at what happens to the verb in the different tenses, especially the irregular verbs. Learn the tables of principal parts in this chapter
◊ Revise vocabulary.
◊ Practice writing out the different paradigms and declensions. They are most easily found in Appendices B, D and E. The present tense of the –μι verbs in appendix D may be ignored at this time, as well as those paradigms and declensions in the other two appendices that have not yet been met.
◊ Ensure that you have mastered the art of parsing. A significant part of the review exercise is devoted to parsing practice, and you should be able to tell from that how well you have mastered the art. If more practice at parsing is needed, most of the exercises in Part 3 have a section devoted to parsing. If the odd numbered exercises are chosen, it will be possible to check your answer against those in Appendix A.
◊ Do Review Exercise 23.
◊ Repeat *all* of the translations from the New Testament [sentences from the NT start in Chapter 11], giving particular attention to John 1:1-11 [Chapter

Part 3 217

21]; 1 John 2:1-11 [Chapter 19], John 5:19-32 & 9:1-41 [Chapter 21]; John 8:12-59 [Chapter 22].

Tricky bits:

The last review chapter gave a list of words which were only slightly different from each other. With the addition of the relative pronouns and the present participle of εἰμί this list has grown considerably [there is a fuller list given in appendix F]:

Words which differ only in accent or breathing mark:
αἱ the (nom. fem. pl. of the article, ὁ, ἡ, τό)
αἵ who (nom. fem. pl. of the relative pronoun, ὅς, ἥ, ὅ)
αὐτή she (nom. fem. sing. of αὐτός)
αὐτῇ to this (dat. fem. sing. of αὐτός)
αὕτη this (nom. fem. sing. of οὗτος)
αὐταί they (nom. fem. pl. of αὐτός)
αὗται these (nom. fem. pl. of οὗτος)
εἰ if
εἶ you are (second person singular, εἰμί)
ἐν in
ἕν one (nom./acc. neut. sing. of εἷς, μία, ἕν)
ἤ or, than
ἡ the (nom. fem. sing. article)
ἥ who, that (nom. fem. sing. rel. pron.)
ᾖ (3rd. pers. sing. pres. subj. act. of εἰμί)
ᾗ to whom (dat. fem. sing. rel. pron.)
ἦν I was (1st pres. sing. imperfect. ind. act. of εἰμί, I am)
ἥν who (acc. fem. sing. of the relative pron. ὅς, who)
ἦς you were (2nd pers. sing. imperfect ind. act. of εἰμί)
ᾖς you might be (2nd pers. sing. pres. subj. act. of εἰμί)
ὅ which, that (nom./acc. neut. sing. rel. pron.)
ὁ the (nom. masc. sing. article)
οἵ who, that (nom. masc. pl. rel. pron.)
οἱ the (nom. masc. pl. article)
ὄν being (nom/acc neut. sing. pres. part. act. of εἰμί)
ὅν who, that (the acc. masc. sing of the relative pronoun).
οὐ not
οὗ whose, of whom (gen. masc./neut. sing. rel. pron.)
τις, τι someone, a certain [man/woman/thing]
τίς, τί who ...? what ...? which ...?
ᾧ to whom (dat. masc./neut. sing. rel. pron.)
ὦ I might be (1st. pers. sing. pres. subjunctive act. of εἰμί, I am)

ὤν (nom. masc. sing. pres. part. act. of εἰμί, I am)
ὧν of whom (gen. masc./fem./neut. pl. of the relative pronoun)

Words which differ only in one letter:
αὐτός, -ή, -ό he/she/it, etc.
οὗτος, αὕτη, τοῦτο this, he/she/it
ἡμεῖς we [nom. pl. of ἐγώ]
ὑμεῖς you [nom. pl. of σύ]
ὑμᾶς you [acc. pl. of σύ]
ἡμῶν our [gen. pl. of ἐγώ]
ὑμῶν your [gen. pl. of σύ]
ἔτι still, yet
ἐπί + acc.: across, to, against
   + gen.: upon, near, before, over, on the basis
   + dat.: at, by, on
ὅτε when, while, as long as
ὅτι because, that
οὗτος, αὕτη, τοῦτο this, he/she/it
οὕτως thus, so (adverb)
ποτέ once, formerly
τότε then, at that time; next

Words which differ in meaning, but not in form:
ὅτι because, that
ὅτι whoever, whatever (nom. neut. sing. of ὅστις)

Principal Parts of Regular and Irregular Verbs

One of the standard ways of learning irregular verbs is to learn their principal parts. It is also a standard examination question to ask a student to write out the principal parts of a verb. The principal parts of a verb are all from the indicative mood. They are the present, future, aorist and perfects of the active voice, and the aorist and perfect of the passive voice. The passive voice will not be met until Chapter 24 and the future tense will be met in Chapter 25, but perhaps it would be helpful to write out the principal parts of the tenses that have been met so far for the active voice of some of the irregular verbs. They have been classified into ones that *must* be known, and ones that *should* be known. Further lists of principal parts may be found at 24.1.7, 30.5 and in Appendix C. Many of the verbs which at this moment appear in the classification of verbs that should be known will later be reclassified at 30.5 as verbs that must be known. A gap in the listing means that there is no occurrence of that tense of the verb in the New Testament. Just about all of these principal parts should be familiar from previous vocabularies.

| Partial Table of Selected Principal Parts that *Must* be Known ||||
| Active Voice ||||
Verb	Meaning	Aorist	Perfect
βάλλω	throw	ἔβαλον	βέβληκα
δίδωμι	give	ἔδωκα	δέδωκα
ἔρχομαι	come	ἦλθον	ἐλήλυθα
λαμβάνω	take	ἔλαβον	εἴληφα
λέγω	say	εἶπον	εἴρηκα
λύω	loose	ἔλυσα	λέλυκα
ὁράω	see	εἶδον	ἑώρακα

Notes on principal parts

1. It is well worth while to thoroughly learn these principal parts, because dictionaries only list the present indicative form of the verb, and the present form of an irregular verb either has to be known or a guess made of what its present form might be. This can be nigh impossible for some verbs. For example, not too many would be able to guess that the present indicative of εἴληφα is λαμβάνω.
2. The verb θνῄσκω, listed in the table of principal parts that should be known, is most commonly found in the compound ἀποθνῄσκω [= ἀπό + θνῄσκω].
3. There are several compounds of ὄλλυμι in the New Testament. The only one met thus far is ἀπόλλυμι [= ἀπό + ὄλλυμι].
4. στέλλω almost entirely occurs in compounds in the New Testament; e.g. ἀποστέλλω [= ἀπό + στέλλω].

| Partial Table of Selected Principal Parts that *Should* be Known ||||
| Active Voice ||||
Verb	Meaning	Aorist	Perfect
ἀγαπάω	love	ἠγάπησα	ἠγάπηκα
ἄγω	lead	ἤγαγον	
αἰτέω	ask for	ᾔτησα	ᾔτηκα
ἀκούω	hear	ἤκουσα	ἀκήκοα
ἀνοίγω	open	ἀνέῳξα	ἀνέῳγα
		ἤνοιξα	
		ἠνέῳξα	

Partial Table of Selected Principal Parts that *Should* be Known			
Active Voice			
Verb	Meaning	Aorist	Perfect
ἀποκτείνω	kill	ἀπέκτεινα	
ἀφίημι	forgive	ἀφῆκα	ἀφεῖκα
-βαίνω	go	-ἔβην	-βέβηκα
γεννάω	beget	ἐγέννησα	γεγέννηκα
γίνομαι	become	ἐγενόμην	γέγονα
γινώσκω	know	ἔγνων	ἔγνωκα
γράφω	write	ἔγραψα	γέγραφα
δείκνυμι	show	ἔδειξα	δέδειχα
ἐλπίζω	hope	ἤλπισα	ἤλπικα
ἐσθίω	eat	ἔφαγον	
εὑρίσκω	find	εὗρον	εὕρηκα
ἔχω	have	ἔσχον	ἔσχηκα
-θνῄσκω[2]	die	-ἔθανον	τέθνηκα
ἵστημι	place	ἔστην	ἕστηκα
		ἔστησα	ἕστακα
καλέω	call	ἐκάλεσα	κέκληκα
κρίνω	judge	ἔκρινα	κέκρικα
λαλέω	speak	ἐλάλησα	λελάληκα
μένω	remain	ἔμεινα	μεμένηκα
-όλλυμι[3]	destroy	-ώλεσα	-όλωλα
πείθω	persuade	ἔπεισα	πέποιθα
πίνω	drink	ἔπιον	πέπωκα
πίπτω	fall	ἔπεσα	πέπτωκα
στέλλω	send	-έστειλα	-έσταλκα
τίθημι	place	ἔθηκα	τέθεικα
φέρω	bear	ἤνεγκα	-ενήνοχα

Note: ἕστακα (perfect of ἵστημι) is used transitively (i.e. is used where the verb takes a direct object), while ἕστηκα is used intransitively (i.e. where the verb cannot take an object). The perfect tenses ἕστακα and ἕστηκα are often translated with an English present tense.

Part 3 221

Exercise 23 (Review)

[Note: the following exercise uses almost every word that has appeared in vocabularies to this point at least once, and also endeavors to use the different tenses and moods of the verbs. It may look a long exercise, but most parts of the verb or vocabulary items are only used once. Clearly, it is of advantage to work through the entire exercise. If you are hesitant or make a mistake with a particular question make a note of it, as it is a learning difficulty.]

Verbs
Translate into English
1. ἔρχῃ 2. λέγουσιν 3. οἴδασιν 4. λέλυκας 5. ἐργάζονται 6. ἐπείθομεν 7. ἐβάλετε 8. ἐλάμβανεν 9. ᾐτήσατε 10. ἠκούσαμεν 11. ἀφίημι 12. ἀπέλυσας 13. δέδωκας 14. λύειν 15. ἔγραφες 16. εἴπετε 17. ἀποκρίνεται 18. ἐφάγετε 19. ἐγίνωσκεν 20. καλῶ 21. ἐλήλυθα 22. ἀκήκοεν 23. ἐσῴζετε 24. ἐξεβάλομεν 25. ἄφηκας 26. ἤλπισας 27. ἤλπιζες 28. ἔλαβες 29. ἔγραψαν 30. δύναμαι βλέψαι

31. καλοῦμεν 32. ἤσθιον 33. φωνοῦμεν 34. δεῖ ἐσθίειν 35. ἤνοιξας 36. πίνεις 37. ἤκουεν 38. δίδωμι 39. ἀφῆκαν 40. ἦσαν 41. ᾐτήκαμεν 42. τίθημι 43. βεβλήκασιν 44. ἔλυσα 45. εἰρήκαμεν 46. ἀνέβαινον 47. ἤλπικεν 48. ἐγνώκαμεν 49. ἔλυον 50. ἠγαπήκασιν 51. ἐκάλουν 52. ἵστημι 53. κεκλήκατε 54. εὑρίσκομεν 55. ὁρῶ 56. καταβαίνετε 57. ἀγαπᾶτε 58. γίνεσθε

59. ἐστήσατε 60. εὑρήκαμεν 61. γεγράφατε 62. ἐκάλεσεν 63. δείκνυμι 64. βάλλουσιν 65. εἶδον 66. λαλεῖτε 67. ἄγομεν 68. ἀφείκατε 69. εὗρεν 70. ἤλθετε 71. ἐδώκατε 72. λαβεῖν 73. ἐγένετο 74. πέμπεις 75. ἦν 76. ἀνέβην 77. γέγονα 78. ἔστησεν 79. ἀπώλεσας 80. ἐπίετε 81. ἤνεγκεν 82. ἑώρακας 83. βέβηκας 84. εἶχες 85. ἔκρινον 86. κρίνεις 87. μισεῖτε 88. πεπτώκασιν

89. βεβλήκαμεν 90. ἔδειξεν 91. τεθείκασιν 92. ἀνέῳξαν 93. ἀπέστελλον 94. ἐστάλκατε 95. ἀπεστείλαμεν 96. ἀποστέλλω 97. θέλω λέγειν 98. γινόμεθα 99. ἔγνων 100. καταβέβηκεν 101. ἀπώλεσας 102. ἔσχεν 103. ἐγέννησεν 104. εἰσήλθετε 105. ἐγείρομεν 106. ἀναβαίνομεν 107. ἠγάγετε 108. βάλλομεν 109. ἀσπάζονται 110. ἐσμέν 111. ἐξέρχῃ 112. ἐπίνομεν 113. ἀπεκρίθη

114. ἐνήνοχα 115. μαρτυρῶ 116. προσεύχονται 117. φοβούμεθα 118. ὁ πιστεύων 119. ὁ ἑωρακώς 120. πιστεύεις 121. ἐδώκαμεν 122. ἰδεῖν 123. ἦγον 124. ἔθηκας 125. ἐφέρομεν 126. πέποιθα 127. ὀφείλεις 128. ἐτηρεῖ 129. θαυμάζουσιν 130. ἀπέθνησκεν 131. ἀπώλεσα 132. ἀπέστειλας 133. ἀπέκτεινεν 134. ἐπερωτᾶτε 135. παρέδωκεν 136. ἠγάπας 137. ἠγάπησα 138. ἔσχηκα

139. ἀνεῴγατε 140. ἐδείξαμεν 141. πέπωκεν 142. ἀπολώλασιν 143. ἀπωλέσατε 144. τεθνήκασιν 145. ἔπιπτον 146. πεποίθασιν 147. ἐθήκατε 148. ἀπέκτεινες 149. κάθημαι 150. συνηγάγομεν 151. ἔπεισεν 152. ἔπεσεν 153. ἦτε 154. προσκυνεῖτε 155. χαίρεις 156. ζητοῦμεν 157. ἔλεγεν 158. εἴληφα 159. ἀπεθάνετε 160. ἐλάλησεν 161. φέρετε 162. πίπτεις

Parse the following
163. λῦσαι 164. λύητε 165. ζῶμεν 166. ἔρχωνται 167. εἰπόντες 168. λύσωμεν 169. λαβόντι 170. βαλεῖν 171. ἠγάπηκος 172. δῷ 173. λύσαντας 174. οὔσης 175. λυσασῶν 176. φαγεῖν 177. εἶναι 178. ἀγάγειν 179. ἀφεικυίας 180. ἀφηκόντι 181. ἐλαλοῦν 182. ἀγαπήσῃ 183. τιθέντας 184. βάλῃ 185. λελυκυίαις 186. ἀγόντα 187. ἀφιῇς 188. ἀφῶ 189. ὤν 190. δούς 191. ἐλθόντος 192. διδόντες 193. ἰδεῖν 194. ἱστῆτε 195. στῶσιν 196. δεικνύοντος 197. ἴδῃς 198. τιθῶμεν 199. εἰδυῖα 200. στάντος 201. θελήματα 202. ἔδειξεν 203. ὦ 204. διδούς 205. θῶ 206. ἔθνει 207. ἥμαρτες

Paradigms and Declensions
Write out in full: **208.** The declension of the adjective κακός. **209.** The aorist participle active of γράφω. **210.** The present indicative active of ζάω. **211.** The present indicative passive of φοβέομαι. **212.** The aorist indicative active of αἰτέω. **213.** The aorist indicative active of εὑρίσκω. **214.** The imperfect indicative active of πίνω. **215.** The perfect indicative active of λαλέω. **216.** The present participle middle of προσεύχομαι. **217.** The declension of the noun νύξ. **218.** The aorist participle active of δίδωμι.

Principal Parts:
From memory, write out the principal parts that have been learnt so far of the following verbs: 219. ἔρχομαι 220. λέγω 221. ἀποστέλλω 222. ἔχω

Prepositions
Fill in the spaces:

Preposition		Case	Meaning
223.	περί	_____	around, about, near
224.	παρά	+ dat.	_____
225.	ἐπί	+ dat.	_____
226.	σύν	_____	with
227.	παρά	+ acc.	_____
228.	ἐκ, ἐξ	_____	from, out of, away from
229.	παρά	+ gen.	_____
230.	ἀπό	+ gen.	_____
231.	ἐπί	_____	upon, near, before, over, on the basis
232.	μετά	+ acc.	_____

Part 3   223

233. διά   + acc.   _____
234. πρός   + gen.   to the advantage of [see notes to Vocab. 9]
235. κατά   _____   according to
236. εἰς   _____   into, towards
237. πρός   + acc.   _____
238. μετά   _____   with
239. διά   + gen.   _____
240. ἐπί   + acc.   _____
241. _____   + dat.   in, by (instrument)
242. κατά   _____   down, against
243. περί   + gen.   _____
244. πρός   + dat.   near, at, by [see notes to Vocab. 9]

Tricky bits
Write down the meaning of the following, and parse where appropriate:
245. εἰ 246. εἶ 247. ἡμῶν 248. ὑμῶν 249. αὐτή 250. αὕτη 251. οἵ 252. οἱ 253. ἦν 254. ἥν 255. ἐν 256. ἕν 257. ὅτε 258. ὅτι 259. ὅ 260. ὁ 261. ἡμεῖς 262. ὑμᾶς 263. ὅν 264. ὄν 265. ποτέ 266. τότε 267. οὐ 268. οὗ 269. αὐταί 270. αὗται 271. αὐτός, -ή, -όν 272. οὗτος, αὕτη, τοῦτο 273. τις, τι 274. τίς, τί 275. ᾧ 276. ὦ 277. οὗτος 278. οὕτως 279. ἤ 280. ἡ 281. ἥ 282. ᾗ 283. Write down the two possible meanings of the word ὅτι

Translate into English
284. αἱ ἑπτὰ ἐκκλησίαι. 285. οὐδέ. 286. καλῶς. 287. ὁ πονηρὸς ὀφθαλμός. 288. οἱ ἅγιοι προφῆται. 289. σὰρξ καὶ αἷμα. 290. τὸν ἁμαρτωλὸν ἔργον. 291. πῶς. 292. ἐν ἐκείνῃ τῇ ὥρᾳ. 293. οὔτε ἄνθρωπος οὔτε γυνή. 294. ὁ οὐρανὸς καὶ ἡ γῆ. 295. ἡ ἐλπὶς τῆς ζωῆς αἰωνίου. 296. ἄλλα πλοῖα. 297. ἡ Γαλιλαία τῶν ἐθνῶν. 298. ὁ δέ. 299. τὸ πρόσωπον τῆς θαλάσσης.

300. οἱ δώδεκα μαθηταὶ αὐτοῦ. 301. ὅσοι δὲ ἔλαβον αὐτόν, ἔδωκεν αὐτοῖς ἐξουσίαν τέκνα θεοῦ γενέσθαι. 302. εἶπέν τις ἐξ αὐτῶν ἴδιος αὐτῶν προφήτη ... 303. διὰ τί. 304. ὥσπερ. 305. ἔτι. 306. ἄρτι. 307. οὐαί. 308. ὁ πιστὸς δοῦλος. 309. οὐ δύναται ὁ υἱὸς ποιεῖν ἀφ' ἑαυτοῦ οὐδὲν ἐὰν μή τι βλέπῃ τὸν πατέρα ποιοῦντα. 310. τὸ ὕδωρ τῆς ζωῆς. 311. ὁ κακὸς τόπος. 312. νὺξ καὶ ἡμέρα. 313. ὁ Πατὴρ τῶν πάντων. 314. ποῦ. 315. πάλιν. 316. χεὶρ καὶ πούς. 317. ὡς. 318. ὁ ἀληθὴς ἀπόστολος. 319. ὁ ὅλος κόσμος. 320. τοιοῦτος.

321. διδάσκαλος τῆς δικαιοσύνης. 322. νῦν. 323. ἐπιτίθημι. 324. πολὺ ἁμαρτία. 325. ὁ ἄγγελος τοῦ θανάτου. 326. ἕως. 327. ἡ κρίσις τῆς Ἰερουσαλήμ. 328. ὅστις. 329. καθώς. 330. οὕτως. 331. ὁ ἀγαπητὸς ἀδελφὸς τοῦ Ἀβραάμ. 332. ὁ ἐρωτῶν. 333. ὃς ἂν πιστεύῃ σῴζει. 334. ἡ ἐπαγγελία τῆς δόξης. 335. ὁ προσελθών. 336. οἱ χαίροντες ἐν τῷ κυρίῳ. 337. ἤδη.

338. κἀγώ. 339. ὁ μέγας οἶκος. 340. τὰ δύο δαιμόνια. 341. ἀνὴρ τῆς ἐξουσίας.

342. ὁ θρόνος τῆς βασιλείας. 343. ἡ σοφία τῶν τυφλῶν. 344. θέλω εἶναι ὅμοιον Ἰησοῦ. 345. ὁ Χριστός διδάσκει τὸν καινὸν νόμον; 346. ἡ ἀνάστασις τῶν νεκρῶν. 347. ὁ γὰρ μένων ἐν ὀνόματί μου εἰσὶν μακάριος. 348. οἱ μηθηταὶ τῶν Φαρισαίων. 349. ἡ φωνὴ τοῦ δεχομένου ἐμοῦ.

350. οἱ Ἰουδαῖοι οὖν προσκυνοῦσιν ἐν ταῖς συναγωγαῖς, ἀλλὰ οἱ ἀκολουθοῦντες τοῦ Χριστοῦ Ἰησοῦ προσκυνοῦσιν ἐν ἐκκλησίαις. 351. δοκεῖς ὅτι Δαυὶδ ἦν δίκαιος; 352. ὁ ἀληθὴς προσκυνῶν τοῦ μονου θεοῦ. 353. τὸ τέκνόν ἐστιν ἀγαθὸς ἀλλὰ ὁ ἀδελφὸς αὐτοῦ οὐκ ἐστίν. 354. τὰ ῥήματα τοῦ στόματός μου. 355. ὁ δε υἱός τοῦ θεοῦ μένει εἰς τούς αἰῶνας.

356. τὸ δεύτερον βιβλίον τοῦ Σίμωνος Πέτρου. 357. ψυχαὶ ὑμῶν ἀλλὰ οὐχὶ σώματα ὑμῶν. 358. Ἰησοῦς εἶπεν, Ἐγώ εἰμι ἡ ὁδός, ἡ ἀλήθεια καὶ ἡ ζωή. 359. αὐτὸς παρεκάλεσεν ἄρτον ἀπὸ τοῦ Ἰωάννας. 360. οἱ καρποὶ τοῦ πνεύματός εἰσιν ἀγάπη χαρὰ εἰρήνη. 361. ἡ πρῶτον τῶν σαββάτων. 362. ἡ μαρτυρία τοῦ Παύλου. 363. ὧδε. 364. ἡ μήτηρ σου. 365. τέ. 366. ἰδού.

367. ὁ δοξάζων ἐν ἐλπίδι. 368. ὁ χρόνος τῆς χάριτι. 369. ἵνα ἀπέλθῃ. 370. μείζων. 371. ἡ ἀρχὴ τοῦ ἱεροῦ. 372. τὸ πῦρ ὅ ἔδωκεν φῶτα. 373. καρδία τοῦ λίθου. 374. ὁ καλὸς λαὸς τοῦ ὄρους. 375. ἡ κεφαλὴ τῆς οἰκίας. 376. ὅπου. 377. ὅταν. 378. οἱ ἁμαρτάνοντες. 379. ἐν μέσῳ τοῦ ὄχλου. 380. αἱ ἐντολαὶ τῶν παιδίων. 381. ἀλλήλων. 382. ἀμήν. 383. αἱ γραφαί.

384. παραβολὴ τοῦ ὑπάγοντος αὐτοῦ. 385. πρῶτον. 386. οἱ λόγοι τοῦ σῴζοντος. 387. τὸ σημεῖον τοῦ προφήτου

Passages from the Greek New Testament:

It would be an excellent idea to take time now and go back over the passages that have been set from the Greek New Testament, beginning with those set for Part 3, and giving special attention to the longer passages (John 1:1-11 [Chapter 21]; 1 John 2:1-11 [Chapter 19], John 5:19-32 & 9:1-41 [Chapter 21]; John 8:12-59 [Chapter 22]).

Part 4

The passive voice, the future tense, the imperative mood, and the translation of John 1-11

Chapter 24: The Passive Voice

Thus far, all of the forms of the verb have been either active voice, or – in the case of verbs in the middle and passive voices that have been found in the exercises – translated by an English active voice. This chapter introduces the passive and middle voices. Each of the tenses and moods of the active voice has a corresponding passive and middle voice form. So does this mean the equivalent of what has taken the best part of 23 chapters to learn previously must now be learned in the space of one chapter? It might seem so at first glance as there appears to be a lot of paradigms to learn all at once. Closer inspection, though, reveals that almost all of them have already been met using δέχομαι as the pattern. This chapter will finally reveal the secret of middle and passive verbs that are translated with an English active voice [see 24.1.5]. Indeed, when a middle or passive form of the verb endings are met in the New Testament, it is just as likely to require a translation with the English active voice. But alongside of these uses of passive forms exist uses that require translation by an English passive voice.

This chapter is broken into two sections. In the first of these, an explanation will be provided of what is meant by passive voice, how they are formed in NT Greek, and how the passive and middle voice of the indicative mood should be translated from Greek into English. The second half of the chapter deals with the passive voice in the subjunctive, infinitive and participial moods. Along the way you will learn about principal parts, and have an opportunity to translate the third chapter of the Gospel of John.

24.1.1 The English Passive Voice

As there are many similarities between the English passive voice and that of Greek, a consideration of the English passive is a very suitable place to begin an introduction to the Greek passive. Some examples will demonstrate the difference between the active and passive voice in English:

Active voice;	*Passive voice*
The boy kicks the ball.	The ball is kicked by the boy.
John punches Bill.	Bill is punched by John.
John throws the stone.	The stone is thrown by John.

These examples illustrate that in the active voice the subject of the verb does the action, while in the passive voice the subject of the verb is the recipient of the action (the subject is "passive"). This is also true in Greek, and the English passive is normally a good guide to the meaning of the Greek passive, at least as far as voice is concerned.

24.1.2 The Indicative Passive of λύω

While there appears to be a considerable number of forms to remember all at once, examination reveals that, except for the aorist, all of the following forms have been covered previously in the various tenses of middle and passive verbs that are translated by an English active voice using δέχομαι as the pattern. The passive forms of λύω are as follows:

The Present Indicative Passive of λύω:
λύομαι
λύῃ
λύεται
λυόμεθα
λύεσθε
λύονται

[English translation: I am loosed, you are loosed, etc.]

The Imperfect Indicative Passive of λύω:
ἐλυόμην
ἐλύου
ἐλύετο
ἐλυόμεθα
ἐλύεσθε
ἐλύοντο

[English translation: I was being loosed, you were being loosed, etc.; I began to be loosed, you ..., etc.]

The Aorist Indicative Passive of λύω:
ἐλύθην
ἐλύθης
ἐλύθη
ἐλύθημεν
ἐλύθητε
ἐλύθησαν

[English translation: I was loosed, you were loosed, etc.]

The Perfect Indicative Passive of λύω:
λέλυμαι
λέλυσαι
λέλυται
λελύμεθα
λέλυσθε
λέλυνται

[English translation: I have been loosed, you have been loosed, etc.]

24.1.3 Translating the Tenses of the Indicative Passive

The following table shows the different tenses of the verb "kill" and how they would be translated in the active and the passive voice:

Examples of How the Various Greek Tenses for Active and Passive Voice Might Be Translated		
Tense	Active	Passive
Present	I kill	I am killed
Imperfect	I began to kill / I was killing	I began to be killed / I was being killed
Aorist	I killed	I was killed
Perfect	I have killed	I have been killed

It can be seen that the features of the tense system from the active voice are preserved in the passive voice. The English passive adds the auxiliary verb "to be" [am, be, was, been, being], but this is the only difference. You may like to try the same thing for the verb "to throw," and should also be able to write out the Greek forms for that verb, both active and passive. Other examples from Greek to English will further illustrate how the passive voice is translated:

Examples of Translating Tenses for Active and Passive Voice from Greek

Tenses of Active Indicative

Present	ὁ Ἰησοῦς βάπτιζει	Jesus baptises
Imperf.	ὁ Ἰάκωβος ἐβάπτιζεν	James was baptising, or: James began to baptise
[Future	ὁ Ἰωάννης κάλεσει	John will call — see chapter 25]
Aorist	ὁ Ἰωάννης ἐβάπτισα	John baptised
Perfect	ὁ Ἰωάννης λέλυκεν	John has loosed

Tenses of the Passive Indicative

Present	ὁ Ἰησοῦς βαπτίζεται	Jesus is baptised
Imperf.	ὁ Ἰάκωβος ἐβαπτίζετο	James was being baptised, or: James began to be baptised
[Future	Ἰωάννης καλεθήσεται	John will be called]
Aorist	ὁ Ἰωάννης ἐβαπτίσθη	John was baptised
Perfect	ὁ Ἰωάννης λέλυται	John has been loosed

24.1.4 Agent and Instrument

In the passive voice, the subject of the verb is the recipient of the action. The person that performs the action is called the agent. If an inanimate object performs the action, it is called an instrument. Examples will make this clear:
- In the sentence, "The ball is kicked by the boy," the verb is passive. The subject of the verb is "the ball" (which is the passive recipient of the action), while "the boy" is the agent (the one who performs the action).
- In the sentence, "The stone is thrown by John," John is the agent. He is the one who performs the action (the subject of the verb, "the stone," is the passive recipient of the action).
- In the sentence, "The soldier was killed by a sword," the sword performs the action. It is inanimate, thus it is the instrument.

The difference between an agent and an instrument, is that an agent is living (e.g. "the boy," "John"), while an instrument is inanimate (e.g. "the sword").

The normal way to express **agent** is by ὑπό + **genitive**, although διά + **genitive** can also be used [usually of an intermediate agent; see *Int*.4.1]:
- Ἰησοῦς ... ἐβαπτίσθη εἰς τὸν Ἰορδάνην <u>ὑπὸ Ἰωάννου</u> [Mark 1:9] Jesus was baptised <u>by John</u> in the Jordan
- οὕτως γὰρ γέγραπται <u>διὰ τοῦ προφήτου</u> [Matt 2:5] For thus it has been written <u>by the prophet</u>

Instrument is expressed by either the **dative** case alone or by ἐν + **dative**:
- τῇ γὰρ <u>χάριτί</u> ἐστε σεσῳσμένοι [Eph 2:8] For you are saved <u>by grace</u>

Instrument can also be found with the active voice:
- ἐξέβαλεν τὰ πνεύματα <u>λόγῳ</u> [Matt 8:16] He cast out the spirits <u>by a word</u>
- Ἐγὼ βαπτίζω <u>ἐν ὕδατι</u> [John 1:26] I baptise <u>with water</u>

24.1.5 Middle and Passive Voices and their Translation

The Greek of the New Testament has distinctive grammatical forms for three voices, which are identified in Grammars as active, middle (or MP1) and passive (or MP2). To further complicate things, a quick consultation of Appendix B reveals that the grammatical forms of the middle and passive are the same for the present, imperfect and perfect tenses. Furthermore, because English lacks a middle voice, it is usually challenging for students to grasp the possible meanings of the Greek middle voice. As English does have a passive voice, the passive voice is usually something that is comprehensible, which is why, even though historically the middle voice developed first in Greek, this chapter began with a consideration of the passive voice. Another complication is that often the best translation of the middle voice is some form of an

English active voice. What follows is a brief explanation of the three voices, with further discussion on the translation of the so-called deponent verbs.

The three voices may be distinguished by the relationship of the grammatical subject of the verb with the action of the verb. In the active voice, the action of the verb is initiated by the grammatical subject of the verb. In the middle voice, the action of the verb is both initiated by the grammatical subject and experienced by the grammatical subject. Other uses of the middle voice include reflexive and reciprocal. One might summarize by stating that in the middle voice the subject of the verb participates in the action. In the passive voice, the action of the verb is experienced by the subject (i.e. happens to the subject). Helpful diagrams may be found at: http://jonathanpennington.com/wp-content/themes/jtp2011/AfterDeponencyPaperHandoutPenningtonSBL2012.pdf

Most of the usages in the middle voice in the NT are best translated by the English active voice. For example, while ἔρχομαι ("I go, come") is indeed a middle voice in Greek (i.e. this is something that the subject of the verb initiates, but happens to the subject), in English this is best translated by the English active voice. Verbs of washing [oneself] and clothing [oneself or others] are expressed in the middle voice in Greek, but in the first person are often best translated by the English reflexive in the active voice ("I wash myself," "I clothe myself") [by the way, none of the verbs of washing or clothing occur more than 50 times in the NT, so will not appear in your vocabulary lists].

The shorthand term, "deponent," is used to describe verbs that do not have active forms that are usually translated by the English active voice. Most of them use middle forms, although a smaller group only has passive forms, and a still smaller group sometimes uses one or the other. For example, of the verbs you have met so far, ἀσπάζομαι, δέχομαι, ἐργάζομαι and προσεύχομαι have both middle and passive forms, and their middle form is usually translated with an English active voice, and their passive with an English passive voice. The verbs ἀποκρίνομαι, γίνομαι, δύναμαι, φοβέομαι are only found with passive forms. Only the context will determined whether they should be translated with the active or passive voice. The verb πορεύομαι has a middle form in the future, and but a passive form in the aorist. [Note: a more complete list of middle and passive deponents is given in *Int.* 4.3.]

In summary, it is not true to describe verbs with middle or passive forms that are translated by the English active voice as using the middle and passive voice to express active meaning. It is better to describe such verbs as being best translated by the English active voice, especially given that English does not have a middle voice. Such verbs are also occasionally used in a manner which requires them to be translated as passive. If they have middle and passive forms, when they are met in their passive form (which can be distinguished in the future and aorist tenses), then they usually should be translated by the English passive voice.

24.1.6 Irregular Passives

The endings of the aorist and perfect passive begin with a consonant. This means that verbs which have a verb stem that ends in a consonant often undergo certain changes in these tenses. As a result, there are many irregularities in the perfect and aorist passive tenses. Some of these irregularities are predictable, especially for verbs with stems that end in gutturals, labials or dentals. The aorist passive endings all begin with θ. They consistently follow the following changes:

Before θ:
    guttural (γ, κ, χ)   + θ becomes χθ
    labial   (β, π, φ)   + θ becomes φθ
    dental (δ, τ, θ)   + θ becomes ?*
    *The result varies—the first dental often becomes a σ.

Thus the aorist indicative passive of:
ἄγω	is	ἤχθην	(γ + θ = χθ)
ἀνοίγω	is	ἠνοίχθην	(γ + θ = χθ)
διώκω	is	ἐδιώχθην	(κ + θ = χθ)
δοξάζω	is	ἐδοξάσθην	(ζ + θ = σθ)
ἑτοιμάζω	is	ἡτοιμάσθην	(ζ + θ = σθ)
-λέγω	is	-ελέχθην	(γ + θ = χθ)

Note: the usual aor. ind. pass. of λέγω is ἐρρέθην. The form ἐλέχθην is found but once in the NT: διελέχθησαν, the 3rd pers. pl. aor. ind. pass. of διαλέγομαι, "I discuss, debate" (Mark 9:34)

| πείθω | is | ἐπείσθην | (θ + θ = σθ) | etc. |

Some of the changes in the perfect indicative passives can be understood by the following rules:

Before μ:
    guttural (γ, κ, χ)   + μ becomes γμ
    labial   (β, π, φ)   + μ becomes μμ
    dental (δ, τ, θ)   + μ becomes σμ

Before σ:
    guttural (γ, κ, χ)   + σ becomes ξ
    labial (β, π, φ)   + σ becomes ψ
    dental (δ, τ, θ)   + σ becomes σ

Part 4   233

Before τ:
> guttural (γ, κ, χ)   + τ becomes κτ
> labial   (β, π, φ)   + τ becomes πτ
> dental   (δ, τ, θ)   + τ becomes ?*
> *The result varies—the first dental often becomes a σ.

Thus the 1st pers. perf. ind. pass. of:
γράφω	is	γέγραμμαι	(φ + μ = μμ)
δείκνυμι	is	δέδειγμαι	(κ + μ = γμ)
διώκω	is	δεδίωγμαι	(κ + μ = γμ)
πείθω	is	πέπεισμαι	(θ + μ = σμ) etc.

The rules also explain how the 2nd and 3rd persons of the verb are formed. E.g. The perf. ind. pass. of γράφω is as follows:
> γέγραμμαι   (φ + μ = μμ)
> γέγραψαι   (φ + σ = ψ)
> γέγραπται   (φ + τ = πτ), etc.

[Note: while there are 225 middle and passive in the NT, only 8 of them are in the 3rd person plural. Six of these 8 are ἀφέωνται, the 3rd pers. pl. perf. ind. pass. of ἀφίημι. In other words, you need not know how to form the 3rd pers. pl. of any perfect indicative passive verbs; just as well, because ν can react unpredictably when combined with other consonants (see *Int.* 6.15)].

Some of the changes to the verb stem that take place in the perfect passive are similar to those found with the irregular perfect active verbs:

Pres. ind. act.	Perf. ind. act.	Perf. ind. pass.
βάλλω ...	βέβληκα ...	βέβλημαι ...
καλέω ...	κέκληκα ...	κέκλημαι ...
λαμβάνω ...	εἴληφα ...	εἴλημμαι ...
λέγω ...	εἴρηκα ...	εἴρημαι ... etc.

24.1.7 Principal Parts

Principal Parts of the active voice of the verb were introduced in Chapter 23. Now that the passive voice has been introduced, the two parts of the passive verb that are usually included in principal parts (the perfect and aorist passive forms) may be added. It is usually possible to know how the other moods of the verb are formed by knowing only the principal parts of a verb. An examination of the table of principal parts in Appendix C will give you a bit of a feel for how the passive aorists and perfects are formed. Eventually you will want to know a reasonable number of these principal parts because the principal parts of a verb need to be known before its meaning may be accessed in a dictionary.

At this stage the following principal parts should be known [Notes on Table of Principal Parts: (i) a gap in the table indicates that there are no occurrences of that tense of the verb in the Greek New Testament; (ii) although you will not meet the future tense until the next chapter, they are included here for the sake of completeness; (iii) eBook readers will likely need to change screen orientation to "Landscape" to see entire table]:

Principal Parts of Some Common Verbs					
\multicolumn{4}{c|}{Active Voice}	\multicolumn{2}{c}{Passive Voice}	
Verb		Future	Aorist	Perfect	Perfect	Aorist
βάλλω	throw	βαλέω	ἔβαλον	βέβληκα	βέβλημαι	ἐβλήθην
δίδωμι	give	δώσω	ἔδωκα	δέδωκα	δέδομαι	ἐδόθην
ἔρχομαι	come	ἐλεύσομαι	ἦλθον	ἐλήλυθα		
ἵστημι	place	στήσω	ἔστην...	ἕστηκα..	..[intrans.]	ἐστάθην
			ἔστησα.	ἕστακα..	..[trans.]	
λαμβάνω	take	λήμψομαι	ἔλαβον	εἴληφα	-εἴλημμαι	-ἐλήμφθην
λέγω	say	ἐρέω	εἶπον	εἴρηκα	εἴρημαι	ἐρρέθην
λύω	loose	λύσω	ἔλυσα	λέλυκα	λέλυμαι	ἐλύθην
ὁράω	see	ὄψομαι	εἶδον	ἑώρακα		ὤφθην
τίθημι	place	θήσω	ἔθηκα	τέθεικα	τέθειμαι	ἐτέθην
φέρω	bear	οἴσω	ἤνεγκα	ἐνήνοχα		ἠνέχθην

Vocabulary 24.1

ὑπό (217) + acc.: under, below; + gen.: by [agent]

Irregular aorist passives
ἐβλήθην (11+)   I was thrown [aor. ind. pass. of βάλλω]
ἐγήγερμαι (9+)   I have been raised [perf. ind. pass. of ἐγείρω]
ἐδόθην (36+)   I was given [aor. ind. pass. of δίδωμι]
ἐκλήθην (16+)   I was called [aor. ind. pass. of καλέω]
ἐρρέθη (11+)   it was said [aor. ind. pass. of λέγω]
ἐτέθην (9+)   I was placed [aor. ind. pass. of τίθημι]
εὑρέθην (17+)   I was found [aor. ind. pass. of εὑρίσκω]
ἠγέρθην (20+)   I was raised [aor. ind. pass. of ἐγείρω]
ὤφθην (20+)   I was seen [aor. ind. pass. of ὁράω]

Less frequently occurring irregular aorist and perfect passives
ἀπεστάλην (6+) I was sent [aor. ind. pass. of ἀποστέλλω]
ἀφέθην (4+)   I was forgiven [aor. ind. pass. of ἀφίημι]
ἀφέωμαι (6+)   I have been forgiven [perf. ind. pass. of ἀφίημι]; only occurs in the 3rd pers. pl. in the NT: ἀφέωνται]
βέβλημαι (2+)   I have been thrown [perf. ind. pass. of βάλλω]

δέδομαι (5+)   I have been given [perf. ind. pass. of δίδωμι]
-είλημμαι (1+)   I have been taken [perf. ind. pass. of λαμβάνω]
εἴρημαι (4+)   I have been said [perf. ind. pass. of λέγω]
-ελήμφθην (5+)   I was taken [aor. ind. pass. of λαμβάνω]
ἐστάθην (6+)   I was stood [aor. ind. pass. of ἵστημι]
ἠνέχθην (6+)   I was carried, borne [aor. ind. pass. of φέρω]

Note: The + in the frequencies above–e.g. (6+)–means that this form occurs at least 6 times in the NT in the indicative passive in the verb noted and that it is also found in compounds of that verb. A dash in front of an entry means that the particular form is found only in compounds of the verb.

Exercise 24.1

Translate into English

1. λαμβάνομαι 2. ἐλαμβανόμην 3. ἐλήμφθημεν 4. ἐλήμφθην 5. εἴλημμαι
6. λαμβάνω 7. ἐλάμβανον 8. ἔλαβον 9. εἴληφα 10. ἐλύθημεν 11. ἐλυόμεθα
12. λυόμεθα 13. λελύμεθα 14. ἐλύομεν 15. ἐλύσαμεν 16. λελύκαμεν
17. δεδώκασιν 18. δέδομαι 19. ἐδώκατε 20. ἐδόθησαν 21. ἔδωκαν
22. βάλλεσθε 23. λέγεται 24. ἐτέθην 25. ἠνέχθη 26. ἐβλήθητε

27. ἐλέγετο 28. ἐλέχθη 29. ἔθηκα 30. βεβλήκατε 31. τέθειμαι 32. ἤχθη
33. ὤφθησαν 34. εἴρηκας 35. εἴρηται 36. ἀπεστάλην 37. βέβλησθε
38. ἑωράκασιν 39. ὤφθημεν 40. ἤνεγκεν 41. φέρει 42. εἶπες 43. ἔλεγες
44. γέγραπται 45. ἐβάλλετε 46. ἐβάλετε 47. τέθεικα 48. ἐνήνοχεν 49. ἠνοίχ-
θημεν 50. πέπεισμαι 51. ἐθήκατε 52. ἐλέγετο 53. ἐρρέθη

54. ἐβάλετε 55. ἀφέθην 56. ἐκλήθημεν 57. ἠγέρθην 58. τίθημι 59. ἐπείσθη
60. ἀφέωνται 61. ἐγήγερται 62. ἐδοξάσθην 63. ἀπεστάλητε 64. εὑρέθησαν
65. εἴχετε

From the Greek New Testament:
66. οὕτως γὰρ γέγραπται διὰ τοῦ προφήτου ... (Matt 2:5b)   67. Ἰακὼβ δὲ ἐγέννησεν τὸν Ἰωσὴφ τὸν ἄνδρα Μαρίας, ἐξ ἧς ἐγεννήθη [73] Ἰησοῦς ὁ λεγόμενος Χριστός. (Matt 1:16). 68. Πάντα μοι παρεδόθη [74] ὑπὸ τοῦ πατρός [75] μου, καὶ οὐδεὶς ἐπιγινώσκει τὸν υἱὸν εἰ μὴ ὁ πατήρ, οὐδὲ τὸν πατέρα τις ἐπιγινώσκει εἰ μὴ ὁ υἱὸς καὶ ᾧ ἐὰν βούληται ὁ υἱὸς ἀποκαλύψαι (Matt 11:27). 69. λέγει αὐτῷ Ναθαναήλ, Πόθεν με γινώσκεις; ἀπεκρίθη [76] Ἰησοῦς καὶ εἶπεν αὐτῷ, Πρὸ τοῦ σε Φίλιππον φωνῆσαι ὄντα ὑπὸ τὴν συκῆν εἶδόν [77] σε (John 1:48; note πρὸ τοῦ + inf. = before [see *Int*.1.3.3]). 70. καὶ ἐγένετο [78] ἐν ἐκείναις ταῖς ἡμέραις ἦλθεν Ἰησοῦς ἀπὸ Ναζαρὲτ τῆς Γαλιλαίας καὶ ἐβαπτίσθη [79] εἰς τὸν Ἰορδάνην ὑπὸ Ἰωάννου (Mark 1:9). 71. Let no one who is tempted say ὅτι Ἀπὸ θεοῦ πειράζομαι· ὁ γὰρ θεὸς ἀπείραστός ἐστιν κακῶν, πειράζει δὲ αὐτὸς οὐδένα. ἕκαστος δὲ πειράζεται ὑπὸ τῆς ἰδίας ἐπιθυμίας ...

(James 1:13-14). **72.** οὗτός ἐστιν περὶ οὗ <u>γέγραπται</u> [80]· ἰδοὺ ἐγὼ ἀποστέλλω τὸν ἄγγελόν μου πρὸ προσώπου σου (Matt 11:10).

Parsing
73-80. Parse the words underlined in the translation passages above.

24.2.1 The Subjunctive Passive of λυω

The Present Subjunctive Passive of λυω is:

λύωμαι
λύῃ
λύηται
λυώμεθα
λύησθε
λύωνται

As with the pres. subj. act., the subjunctive passive looks somewhat like the indicative, except the initial vowels in the endings have been lengthened.

The Aorist Subjunctive Passive of λυω is:

λυθῶ
λυθῇς
λυθῇ
λυθῶμεν
λυθῆτε
λυθῶσι(ν)

This is like the present indicative subjunctive, except that a θ has been added before the ending. [Some verbs form a strong aorist subjunctive passive by a change in the verbal stem, and omit the θ. E.g. χαρῆτε (1 Pet 4:13) is the 2nd pers. pl. aor. subj. pass. of χαίρω; while φανῶσιν (Matt 6:5) is the 3rd pers. pl. aor. subj. pass. of φαίνω. In practice these strong aorist passive subjunctives are readily recognized.]

Examples of the Use of Passive Subjunctives:
Subjunctive passives are used in ways analogous to subjunctive actives. E.g.
- οὐ γὰρ ἀπέστειλεν ὁ θεὸς τὸν υἱὸν εἰς τὸν κόσμον ἵνα κρίνῃ τὸν κόσμον, ἀλλ' ἵνα <u>σωθῇ</u> ὁ κόσμος δι' αὐτοῦ. God did not send his son into the world to condemn the world, but in order that the world <u>might be saved</u> through him. [ἵνα + subjunctive in purpose clause; John 3:17]
- ... ἐὰν μὴ <u>στραφῆτε</u> καὶ γένησθε ὡς τὰ παιδία, οὐ μὴ εἰσέλθητε εἰς τὴν βασιλείαν τῶν οὐρανῶν. "... unless you <u>are inwardly changed</u> and become as children, you will certainly not enter the kingdom of heaven." [ἐὰν μή + subjunctive = unless; Matt 18:3]
- ... οὐ μὴ <u>ἀφεθῇ</u> ὧδε λίθος ἐπὶ λίθον. "... there will not <u>be left</u> here stone

upon stone." [οὐ μὴ + subjunctive = strong denial; Mark 13:2], etc.

24.2.2 The Infinitive Passive of λύω

The forms of the infinitive for the passive voice are:
Present infinitive passive: λύεσθαι to be loosed
[Future infinitive passive: λυθήσεσθαι *does not occur in NT*]
Aorist infinitive passive: λυθῆναι to be loosed
Perfect infinitive passive: λελύσθαι to have been loosed

The difference between aorist and present infinitives is not that of time (which is given by the main verb of the sentence) but the nature of the action: present infinitives are used when the continuous nature of the action is stressed, otherwise an aorist is used. [Note: amongst the 159 aor. inf. passives found in the NT, 154 are formed regularly. The strong aorist exceptions are κρυβῆναι in Matt 5:14, 2 Thes 2:10, τεθῆναι in Rev 11:9, and χαρῆναι in Luke 16:32, 1 Cor 15:32]

Examples of the Use of Passive Infinitives:

Passive infinitives are used in ways analogous to active infinitives. E.g.
- ἐκέλευσεν ἄγεσθαι αὐτὸν εἰς τὴν παρεμβολήν "he ordered him to be [led/] brought into the barracks" (Acts 21:34).
- ἐκέλευσεν τὸν Παῦλον ἀχθῆναι "he ordered Paul to be brought" (Acts 25:6).
- Δεῖ ὑμᾶς γεννηθῆναι ἄνωθεν "It is necessary for you to be born again/from above" (John 3:7).

24.2.3 The Passive Participles of λύω

The present and perfect participle passive endings are the same as those already learnt for middle verbs. The only really new forms to learn are those of the aorist participle passive.

The **present participle passive of** λυω is:

Masculine	Feminine	Neuter
λυόμενος	λυομένη	λυόμενον
λυόμενον	λυομένην	λυόμενον
λυομένου	λυομένης	λυομένου
λυομένῳ	λυομένῃ	λυομένῳ
λυόμενοι	λυόμεναι	λυόμενα
λυομένους	λυομένας	λυόμενα
λυομένων	λυομένων	λυομένων
λυομένοις	λυομέναις	λυομένοις

The **aorist participle passive of** λυω is:

Masculine	Feminine	Neuter
λυθείς	λυθεῖσα	λυθέν
λυθέντα	λυθεῖσαν	λυθέν
λυθέντος	λυθείσης	λυθέντος
λυθέντι	λυθείσῃ	λυθέντι
λυθέντες	λυθεῖσαι	λυθέντα
λυθέντας	λυθείσας	λυθέντα
λυθέντων	λυθεισῶν	λυθέντων
λυθεῖσι(ν)	λυθείσαις	λυθεῖσι(ν)

The **perfect participle passive of** λυω is:

Masculine	Feminine	Neuter
λελυμένος	λελυμένη	λελυμένον
λελυμένον	λελυμένην	λελυμένον
λελυμένου	λελυμένης	λελυμένου
λελυμένῳ	λελυμένῃ	λελυμένῳ
λελυμένοι	λελυμέναι	λελυμένα
λελυμένους	λελυμένας	λελυμένα
λελυμένων	λελυμένων	λελυμένων
λελυμένοις	λελυμέναις	λελυμένοις

[Note: some verbs form a strong aorist passive participle by changing the verb stem, and omitting the θ. E.g. στραφέντες (Matt 7:6) is the nom. masc. pl. aor. part. pass. of στρέφω; while σπαρεις (Matt 13:19) is the nom. masc. sing. aor. part. pass. of σπείρω. In practice these strong aorist passive participles are as readily recognized as other passive participles.]

What has already been learned about the participle is directly applicable to passive participles as well. In translating a passive participle, first check to see if it has an article (in which case the translation is "the one who is..."), then try a reference to time ("while ..."). Finally try the English passive participle ("...ed") and see if the sentence can be made to make sense.

Examples of the Use of Passive Participles:

- Matt 10:2 Σίμων ὁ λεγόμενος Πέτρος "Simon, <u>the one who is called</u> Peter" [article + participle = "the one who ..." — adjectival use]
- John 9:32 ἐκ τοῦ αἰῶνος οὐκ ἠκούσθη ὅτι ἠνέῳξέν τις ὀφθαλμοὺς τυφλοῦ <u>γεγεννημένου</u> "Never was it heard that anyone opened the eyes of <u>one who had been born</u> blind." [adjectival use, but without an article in this instance]
- Matt 3:16 <u>βαπτισθεὶς</u> δὲ ὁ Ἰησοῦς ... "<u>After</u> Jesus <u>was baptised</u> ..." [a reference to time "when/while/as, etc." or in this case "after ..." — temporal adverbial participle]

Vocabulary 24.2

αἴρω (101) I lift up, take up, remove
ἄρχω (85) I rule; [in middle:] I begin
ἔμπροσθεν (48) as a preposition with gen.: in front of, before; as an adverb: ahead, forward, in front
ἦρα (56) I lifted up [aor. ind. act. of αἴρω; aor. pass. ἤρθην (8)]
ἱμάτιον (60) garment
ὅπως (53) conj.: [+ subj.] in order that [similar to ἵνα]
πράσσω (39) I do, practice [aor. act ἔπραξα (5); perf. act. πέπραχα (2); perf. pass. πέπραγμαι (2)]
σπείρω (52) I sow [aor. ἔσπειρα; perf. pass. ἔσπαρμαι; aor. pass. ἐσπάρην]
φυλακή (46) prison, guard, watch

Exercise 24.2

Parse

[Please note: numbers 1-27 are all from λύω, and include examples from each of the different tenses/voices/moods that have been learned to date. Most tense/mood/voice combinations are used only once. Note any mistake made on any of nos. 1-27, because this may indicate a need to go back and revise that particular tense/mood/voice. Answers are provided for all of 1-27, and for the odd numbers for 28-45. Occasional notes are provided for 42-49.]

1. λυθῆτε 2. λυθείς 3. ἐλυόμεθα 4. λυθῆναι 5. λυόμενα 6. λύεται 7. λύητε 8. λῦσαι 9. λελύμενοι 10. λύεσθαι 11. λύων 12. λύσητε 13. λυομένοις 14. λυθῇς 15. λελύκασιν 16. λυθείσῃ 17. λελυμένην 18. ἐλύσατε 19. λυόντων 20. λύησθε 21. λελύσθαι 22. λύθεντας 23. λελυκυίᾳ 24. λυθῶμεν 25. λύειν 26. λυθέν 27. λύσασα 28. βάλληται 29. βέβλημαι 30. ἐβάλλετε 31. βλήθω 32. ἐβλήθην

33. βεβλήμενοι 34. εἰλημμένους 35. λήμφθω 36. ἐλέγου 37. ῥέθεις 38. ἤρθη 39. ἄρθεντι 40. σπείροντες 41. λαμβανόμεναι

From the Greek New Testament:

[Note: extra help is provided in the answers for nos. 42, 43 and 46]

42. παντὸς ἀκούοντος τὸν λόγον τῆς βασιλείας καὶ μὴ συνιέντος ἔρχεται ὁ πονηρὸς καὶ ἁρπάζει τὸ ἐσπαρμένον ἐν τῇ καρδίᾳ αὐτοῦ, οὗτός ἐστιν ὁ παρὰ τὴν ὁδὸν σπαρείς. ὁ δὲ ἐπὶ τὰ πετρώδη σπαρείς, οὗτός ἐστιν ὁ τὸν λόγον ἀκούων καὶ εὐθὺς μετὰ χαρᾶς λαμβάνων αὐτόν, οὐκ ἔχει δὲ ῥίζαν ἐν ἑαυτῷ ἀλλὰ πρόσκαιρός ἐστιν, γενομένης δὲ θλίψεως ἢ διωγμοῦ διὰ τὸν λόγον εὐθὺς σκανδαλίζεται. ὁ δὲ εἰς τὰς ἀκάνθας σπαρείς, οὗτός ἐστιν ὁ τὸν λόγον ἀκούων, καὶ ἡ μέριμνα τοῦ αἰῶνος καὶ ἡ ἀπάτη τοῦ πλούτου συμπνίγει τὸν λόγον καὶ ἄκαρπος γίνεται. ὁ δὲ ἐπὶ τὴν καλὴν γῆν σπαρείς, οὗτός ἐστιν ὁ τὸν λόγον ἀκούων καὶ συνιείς, ὃς δὴ καρποφορεῖ καὶ ποιεῖ ὃ μὲν ἑκατόν, ὃ δὲ ἑξήκοντα, ὃ δὲ τριάκοντα (Matt 13:19-23).

43. διὰ τοῦτο λέγω ὑμῖν ὅτι ἀρθήσεται ἀφ᾽ ὑμῶν ἡ βασιλεία τοῦ θεοῦ καὶ δοθήσεται ἔθνει ποιοῦντι τοὺς καρποὺς αὐτῆς (Matt 21:43). **44.** γέγραπται γὰρ ὅτι Τοῖς ἀγγέλοις αὐτοῦ ἐντελεῖται περὶ σοῦ καὶ ἐπὶ χειρῶν ἀροῦσίν σε, μήποτε προσκόψῃς πρὸς λίθον τὸν πόδα σου (Matt 4:6). [Note: ἐντελεῖται is the 3rd pers. sing. fut. ind. middle of the verb ἐντέλλομαι.] **45.** Ὅταν οὖν ποιῇς ἐλεημοσύνην, μὴ σαλπίσῃς ἔμπροσθέν σου, ὥσπερ οἱ ὑποκριταὶ ποιοῦσιν ἐν ταῖς συναγωγαῖς καὶ ἐν ταῖς ῥύμαις, ὅπως δοξασθῶσιν ὑπὸ τῶν ἀνθρώπων· ἀμὴν λέγω ὑμῖν, ἀπέχουσιν τὸν μισθὸν αὐτῶν (Matt 6:2). [Note on μὴ σαλπίσῃς: μή with an aorist subjunctive is used to convey a prohibition (negative command)—"do not ..." (see *Int*.1.1.5)]

46. ... φιλοῦσιν ἐν ταῖς συναγωγαῖς καὶ ἐν ταῖς γωνίαις τῶν πλατειῶν ἑστῶτες προσεύχεσθαι, ὅπως φανῶσιν τοῖς ἀνθρώποις (Matt 6:5b). **47.** καὶ ἐγένετο ἐν ἐκείναις ταῖς ἡμέραις ἦλθεν Ἰησοῦς ἀπὸ Ναζαρὲτ τῆς Γαλιλαίας καὶ ἐβαπτίσθη εἰς τὸν Ἰορδάνην ὑπὸ Ἰωάννου. καὶ εὐθὺς ἀναβαίνων ἐκ τοῦ ὕδατος εἶδεν σχιζομένους τοὺς οὐρανοὺς καὶ τὸ πνεῦμα ὡς περιστερὰν καταβαῖνον εἰς αὐτόν· καὶ φωνὴ ἐγένετο ἐκ τῶν οὐρανῶν, Σὺ εἶ ὁ υἱός μου ὁ ἀγαπητός, ἐν σοὶ εὐδόκησα (Mark 1:9-11).

48. Ἔλεγεν οὖν τοις ἐκπορευομενοις ὀχλοις βαπτισθηναι ὑπ᾽ αὐτου, Γεννηματα ἐχιδνων, τίς ὑπεδειξεν ὑμιν φυγειν ἀπο της μελλουσης ὀργης; (Luke 3:7). **49.** καὶ ἔσεσθε μισούμενοι ὑπὸ πάντων διὰ τὸ ὄνομά μου. ὁ δὲ ὑπομείνας εἰς τέλος οὗτος σωθήσεται (Mark 13:13). **50.** ἴδετε ποταπὴν ἀγάπην δέδωκεν ἡμῖν ὁ πατήρ, ἵνα τέκνα θεοῦ κληθῶμεν, καὶ ἐσμέν (1 John 3:1). [Note on ἴδετε, "behold." This is the 2nd pers. imperative ind. act. of ὁράω (aor. ind. act. εἶδον; aor. inf. act. ἰδεῖν). Imperatives are covered in Chapter 26.]

Translation Passage 24.2: John 3:1-36

v. 1 Ἦν, "There was," is used impersonally.

v. 2 νυκτός: the genitive is used to convey the concept of time [see *Int*.5.3.6]. Translate as "by night." Help is provided in the answers if you do not recognize ἐλήλυθας or ᾖ.

v. 3 ἄνωθεν has two possible meanings, "from above" and "again." Jesus clearly means "from above," while Nicodemus misunderstands him to say "again." This subtlety is clear to those able to read the Greek text, but very difficult to translate into English.

v. 4 Help is provided in the answers if you do not recognize ὤν or how to translate it.

v. 6 Help is provided in the answers if you do not recognize τὸ γεγεννημένον.

v. 7 μὴ θαυμάσῃς: μή + aor. subj. is used to express aorist prohibitions

Part 4 241

[*Int*.1.1.5]. Translate as "do not marvel"
v. 8 πνεῦμα means both spirit and wind, and the meaning of this verse depends on this double meaning. Because English uses different words and the connection is lost, it is not possible to translate this ambiguity into English.
v. 9 γενέσθαι is the aor. infinitive middle of γίνομαι [cf. Vocab 15].
v. 12 πιστεύσετε is the 2d pers. pl. future ind. act. of πιστεύω "... you will believe ..."
v. 13 Help is provided in the answers if you do not recognize καταβάς.
v. 16 ἀπόληται is the aor. subj. middle of ἀπόλλυμι. The middle voice is used here to indicate something of benefit (or detriment) to the subject of the verb – those believing.
v. 21 ἐστιν εἰργασμένα, "have been worked." Like Greek, English has periphrastic tenses, which is the term used to describe tenses formed from the verb "to be" + participle [see *Int*.3.7].
v. 24 Like ἐστιν εἰργασμένα, "are worked," in v. 21, ἦν βεβλημένος, "had [not yet] been thrown" is a periphrastic construction made up of a form of the verb "to be" plus a participle; βεβλημένος is a nom. masc. sing. perf. part. pass. of Βάλλω [see principal parts in 24.1.7 & Appendix C] and such a participle when used used with the imperfect tense of εἰμί forms periphrastic pluperfect tense, "had ..." [see *Int*.3.7.6 & 3.5.3].
v. 27 ᾖ δεδομένον. If the column dealing with the subjunctive mood in the full paradigm of the verb given as Appendix B is consulted, it may be noted that the perfect tense of the subjunctive mood is formed from the subjunctive of the verb εἰμί plus a perfect participle. This is the construction here: i.e. it is a perfect subjunctive (formed periphrastically – see comment on v. 21).
v. 28 Ἀπεσταλμένος is the perfect passive participle of ἀποστέλλω [check out the principal parts of στέλλω in Appendix C].
v. 31 See answers on v. 4 if you do not recognize ὤν.
v. 34 δίδωσιν is the 3rd pers. sing. pres. ind. act. of δίδωμί, which will not be met officially until Chapter 27.
v. 36 ὄψεται is the 3rd pers. sing. future ind. middle of ὁράω [see principal parts in 24.1.7 & Appendix C].

Chapter 25: The Future Tense

As might be expected, the future tense is used of events that will or might happen in the future. This is true for both the English future tense, and the Greek future tense.

25.1 The Future Indicative

25.1.1 The Paradigm of the Future Indicative Active of λύω:

As can be seen in the following table, the future indicative active is the same as the present indicative active with the addition of a -σ- before the ending.

Future Indicative Active of λύω		
1st pers s	λύσω	I shall loose
2nd pers s	λύσεις	you will loose
3rd pers s	λύσει	he/.. will loose
1st pers pl	λύσομεν	we shall loose
2nd pers pl	λύσετε	you will loose
3rd pers pl	λύσουσι(ν)	they will loose

25.1.2 The Future of Passive Verbs

The future indicative passive of λύω is formed by the addition of -θησ- before the ending:

λυθήσομαι
λυθήσῃ
λυθήσεται
λυθησόμεθα
λυθήσεσθε
λυθήσονται

[English translation: I shall be loosed, you will be loosed, etc.]

25.1.3 The Future of Middle Verbs

The middle verbs πορεύομαι and προσεύχομαι form their futures by using a -σ- before the endings -ομαι, -ῃ, -εται, -ομεθα, -εσθε, -ονται, and the irregular futures γενήσομαι, ἐλεύσομαι, ἔσομαι, λήμψομαι, ὄψομαι, listed in Vocabulary 25, follow this same pattern. The future indicative middle of

Part 4

πορεύομαι is as follows:

πορεύσομαι
πορεύσῃ
πορεύσεται
πορευσόμεθα
πορεύσεσθε
πορεύσονται

English translation: I shall go, you will go, ...

25.1.4 Notes on the Future Tense

1. As the English future corresponds rather well with the Greek future, translating Greek futures to English is relatively straight forward, as the following examples will show:

ἐγώ βλέψω τὸν κύριον	I shall see the Lord	[future]
ἐγώ βλέπω τὸν κύριον	I see the Lord	[present]
ζήσομεν ἐν τῷ οὐρανῷ	We shall live in Heaven.	[future]
ζῶμεν ἐπὶ τῆς γῆς	We live on the earth.	[present]

etc.

2. The σ causes modifications with certain verbs, although most of these changes will be familiar by now:

   (i) The σ contracts with the last letter of verb stems that end with dentals, labials and gutturals according to the following rules:

   guttural (γ, κ, χ) + σ becomes ξ
   labial   (β, π, φ) + σ becomes ψ
   dental (δ, τ, θ) + σ becomes σ

   Some examples of the future tense of verbs with stems that end in gutturals, labials and dentals are:

Meaning	Present	Future (English)	Future (Greek)	
I lead	ἄγω	I shall lead	ἄξω	(γ+σ=ξ)
I baptise	βαπτίζω	I shall baptize	βαπτίσω	(dz+σ=σ)
I see	βλέπω	I shall see	βλέψω	(π+σ=ψ)
I write	γράφω	I shall write	γράψω	(φ+σ=ψ)
I send	πέμπω	I shall send	πέμψω	(π+σ=ψ)
I glorify	δοξάζω	I shall glorify	δοξάσω	(dz+σ=σ)
I persuade	πείθω	I shall persuade	πείσω	(θ+σ=σ)
I pray	προσεύχομαι	I shall pray	προσεύξομαι	(χ+σ=ξ)
I save	σῴζω	I shall save	σώσω	(dz+σ=σ)

   (ii) The ε of -εω verbs, and the α of -αω verbs generally become η in front of the σ.

   Some examples of the future tense of -εω and -αω verbs are:

Meaning	Present	Future (English)	Future (Greek)
I ask	αἰτέω	I shall ask	αἰτήσω
I love	ἀγαπάω	I shall love	ἀγαπήσω

I beget	γεννάω	I shall beget	γεννήσω
I ask	ἐρωτάω	I shall ask	ἐρωτήσω
I live	ζάω	I shall live	ζήσω or ζήσομαι
I seek	ζητέω	I shall seek	ζητήσω
I call	καλέω	I shall call	καλέσω
I speak	λαλέω	I shall speak	λαλήσω
I bear witness	μαρτυρέω	I shall bear witness	μαρτυρήσω
I walk	περιπατέω	I shall walk	περιπατήσω
I do	ποιέω	I shall do	ποιήσω
I fear	φοβέομαι	I shall fear	φοβηθήσομαι

καλέω is the only verb in this list which does not lengthen the ε or α before the σ. καλέω was also an odd-one-out in the way it formed its aorist: ἐκάλεσα (not ἐκάλησα [see 12.2.3]).

3. Some verbs have irregular futures, which have to be learnt. The futures of the following irregular verbs appear in the vocabulary: ἀποθνήσκω, ἀπόλλυμι, ἀποστέλλω, ἀφίημι, βάλλω, γίνομαι, γινώσκω, δίδωμι, δείκνυμι, ἐγείρω, εἰμί, ἔρχομαι, ἐσθίω, εὑρίσκω, ἔχω, ἵστημι, κρίνω, λαμβάνω, λέγω, μένω, ὁράω, πίνω, πίπτω, τίθημι, φέρω. Many of these irregular futures use the same root as they do for their strong aorist, so they may look familiar.

4. The future tense of εἰμί is almost regular. It looks as though it is a deponent verb with the root ἐσ-. It is found in 173 verses in the NT, and declines as follows:

ἔσομαι
ἔσῃ
ἔσται
ἐσόμεθα
ἔσεσθε
ἔσονται

Translation: I shall be, you will be, ...

5. The uncontracted 1st pers. sing. future ind. of ἀποθνήσκω is ἀποθανέομαι, of ἀποστέλλω is ἀποστελέω, of βάλλω is βαλέω, of κρίνω is κρινέω, of λέγω is ἐρέω, of μένω is μενέω, and of πίπτω is πεσέω. The normal rules of contraction will give the other forms of the future of these verbs. For example, the future of πίπτω is πεσῶ, πεσεῖς, πεσεῖ, πεσοῦμεν, πεσεῖτε, πεσοῦσιν.

6. Some verbs which are not deponent in their present tense, have an irregular future deponent, but one that is built on their present stem, as, for example, the futures of γινώσκω, λαμβάνω and ὁράω, which are γνώσομαι, λήμψομαι, and ὄψομαι, resp. On the other hand, the deponent future of ἔρχομαι (ἐλεύσομαι) is formed from a stem quite different from that used to form the present stem.

25.2 The Future Participle

The future participle is rarely used in the New Testament (Gramcord reports only 13 verses in which it finds a future participle, compared to more than 1800 occurrences of aorist participles). Students tend to confuse it with the weak aorist participle, and so it is tempting to omit it altogether. But as it is formed in a completely regular way, it is easily learned, and with a little care they should be recognized in those few places where they are met. Do remember, though, not to confuse the much more frequently found weak aorist participles with future participles.

In the indicative mood, the future of regular verbs is formed by inserting a σ after the verb stem. Consulting the paradigm of the verb found in Appendix B will reveal that future participles are formed in a similar way: in their active and middle voices, future participles add a σ after the verb stem, but otherwise use the endings of the present participle. Passive verbs add a -θησ- instead of -σ- in their future indicative tense, and do the same in future participles [see Appendix B]. If a verb has an irregular future with a deponent form, then the future participle is also deponent. The following [irregular deponent] future participles occur in two places the Greek New Testament (ἐσόμενον in Luke 22:49; and γενησόμενον in 1 Cor 15:37):

The Future Participle of γίνομαι and εἰμί

Verb	Fut Ind	Future Participle
γίνομαι	γενήσομαι	γενησόμενος, η, ον
εἰμί	ἔσομαι	ἐσόμενος, η, ον

Vocabulary 25

Irregular futures:

βαλέω (βαλῶ) (11+) I shall throw [fut. ind. act. of βάλλω]
γενήσομαι (12) I shall become [fut. ind. dep. of γίνομαι]
γνώσομαι (18) I shall know [fut. ind. dep. of γινώσκω]
δώσω (47+) I shall give [fut. ind. act. of δίδωμι]
ἐλεύσομαι (22+) I shall come/go [fut. ind. dep. of ἔρχομαι]
ἕξω ² (14+) I shall have [fut. ind. act. of ἔχω]
ἐρέω (ἐρῶ) (46+) I shall say, speak [fut. ind. act. of λέγω]
ἔσομαι (173) I shall be [fut. ind. dep. of εἰμί]
εὑρήσω (22) I shall find [fut. ind. act. of εὑρίσκω]
θήσω (9+) I shall place [fut. ind. act. of τίθημι]
κρινέω (κρινῶ) ³ (17+) I shall judge [fut. ind. act. of κρίνω]
λήμψομαι (17+) I shall take [fut. ind. dep. of λαμβάνω]
ὄψομαι (34) I shall see [fut. ind. dep. of ὁράω]
στήσω (6+) I shall stand [fut. ind. act. of ἵστημι]

Less Frequently Occurring Irregular futures:

ἀπολέσω (9)	I shall destroy [fut. ind. act. of ἀπόλλυμι]
ἀφήσω (7)	I shall forgive [fut. ind. act. of ἀφίημι]
ἀποθανέομαι (3)	I shall die [fut. ind. dep. of ἀποθνήσκω]
ἀποστελέω (5)	I shall send [fut. ind. act. of ἀποστέλλω]
δείξω (8)	I shall show [fut. ind. act. of δείκνυμι]
ἐγερέω (ἐγερῶ) (5)	I shall rise [fut. ind. act. of ἐγείρω]
μενέω (μενῶ) [3] (6+)	I shall remain [fut. ind. act. of μένω]
οἴσω (2+)	I shall bear [fut. ind. act. of φέρω]
πεσέομαι (6)	I shall fall [fut. ind. dep. of πίπτω]
πίομαι (4)	I shall drink [fut. ind. dep. of πίνω]
φάγομαι (4)	I shall eat [fut. ind. dep. of ἐσθίω]

Other words:
οὔτε ... οὔτε (91) neither ... nor

Notes on Vocabulary 25

1. The plus in the frequency counts means that at least that many occurrences of the form occur in the NT; still further examples may be found in compounds of the verb.
2. Notice that the future of ἔχω is almost regular—the only unexpected part is a change from the smooth to the rough breathing (ἕξω *not* ἔξω).
3. In the New Testament, the future and present for both κρίνω and μένω are differentiated by only a difference in accent – their futures have the circumflex accent, while the present tenses have the acute accent. This is because the future tenses of κρίνω and μένω are actually κρινέω and μενέω resp. and they are accented in the manner of -εω verbs. The end result is that in the futures of these two verbs, the accent falls on the endings, rather than on the verb stem. Here, then, is the presend and future indicative active of these two verbs:

κρίνω		μένω	
Present	Future	Present	Future
κρίνω	κρινῶ	μένω	μενῶ
κρίνεις	κρινεῖς	μένεις	μενεῖς
κρίνει	κρινεῖ	μένει	μενεῖ
κρίνομεν	κρινοῦμεν	μένομεν	μενοῦμεν
κρίνετε	κρινεῖτε	μένετε	μενεῖτε
κρίνουσι(ν)	κρινοῦσι(ν)	μένουσι(ν)	μενοῦσι(ν)

Part 4   247

[This difference is potentially important in the Gospel of John, where μένω and κρίνω are both key words in its theology, and are used frequently in some important passages (e.g. John 3:17-18; 8:15-50; 12:24-48; 15:4-16), although largely in the present tense (but see the future tense in John 12:48).]

Exercise 25

Translate into English:
1. ἀκούσω 2. ἀφίημι 3. βάλλεις 4. λαλήσετε 5. βλέψουσιν 6. ἀποστελῶ 7. αἰτήσουσιν 8. πείσομεν 9. ἐρωτήσει 10. οἴσω 11. ἄξω 12. δίδωμι 13. δοῦναι 14. φέρουσιν 15. ἔβλεψαν 16. στήσω 17. πείθετε 18. ἤκουσα 19. ἀφήσει 20. πίῃ 21. ἀπόλλυμι 22. βλέψαι 23. οἴσεις 24. ἐρωτήσουσιν 25. ἔφαγες 26. βλέπει 27. μενῶ 28. μένω 29. δώσεις 30. ἀποθάνῃ 31. ἀπολύσετε 32. εἰσελεύσονται 33. βαλοῦμεν 34. ἐπερωτήσεις 35. φοβηθήσεσθε 36. ἔστησεν 37. ἔσῃ 38. φαγεῖν 39. πίομαι 40. καλοῦμεν 41. ἄξετε 42. ἠνέγκαμεν 43. ἔβαλες 44. ἀφήσουσιν 45. φάγονται 46. λαλοῦμεν 47. ἀποστελοῦμεν 48. προσελευσόμεθα 49. μενοῦμεν

50. φοβηθησόμεθα 51. δώσετε 52. ἐρῶ 53. ἀποθανοῦμαι 54. ἐρωτήσομεν 55. λαλήσεις 56. γενήσεται 57. αἰτήσομεν 58. μενεῖτε 59. βαλεῖν 60. στήσεις 61. καλέσει 62. ἀπέστειλα 63. ἐσθίουσιν 64. πίνω 65. ἀπολέσει 66. ἠνέγκατε 67. ἐρωτᾷ 68. παρακαλέσουσιν 69. εἶπον 70. ἀφῆκεν 71. τίθημι 72. ἠγάπησα 73. ἐλάλησαν 74. θήσετε 75. γενήσῃ 76. κρίνω 77. ἐδώκαμεν 78. ἐρεῖς 79. οἴσει 80. ἵστημι 81. ἰδεῖν 82. ἀπωλέσαμεν 83. ἐθήκατε 84. ᾔτησεν 85. κρινοῦμεν 86. ἔσχες 87. ἀποστέλλεις 88. ἐλευσόμεθα 89. ἐξελεύσῃ 90. ἐστέ 91. εὕρετε 92. προσεύξονται 93. γίνῃ 94. ἔχεις 95. ἀπολέσετε 96. ζήσεις 97. πείσεις 98. ᾐτήσαμεν 99. ἀπελεύσομαι 100. ἐρεῖτε 101. γράψεις 102. ὄψεται

103. ἐξήλθετε 104. γενήσονται 105. ζητεῖτε 106. εὑρήσεις 107. σώσεις 108. προσεύξεσθε 109. ἀγαπᾷς 110. ζήσομεν 111. λήμψῃ 112. πεσοῦμαι 113. δοξάσει 114. ζῶ 115. σῶσαι 116. ἐκάλεσας 117. ζητήσομεν 118. γράψετε

119. γενήσεται 120. ἀγαπήσομεν 121. σώσετε 122. ἔσονται 123. θήσομεν 124. κρινεῖτε 125. ποιήσετε 126. λημψόμεθα 127. ἕξομεν 128. οἴσομεν 129. εὑρήσει 130. ἐλεύσονται

Translate into Greek
131. I shall ask 132. You (pl) persuaded 133. He saw 134. We shall forgive 135. She will say 136. I shall call 137. He will destroy 138. I shall give 139. They will drink 140. He sent 141. We shall be 142. She will find 143. They will become 144. They will judge 145. They judge 146. They will have 147. They had 148. They have 149. We shall write 150. He threw

151. I sought 152. You (sing) asked
153. They will bear 154. They will hear 155. You (pl.) will send 156. I shall save 157. You (pl.) will go 158. They will lead 159. You (pl) throw 160. We shall remain 161. I saved 162. He loves 163. He will love 164. He loved 165. I shall send 166. I sent 167. She will glorify 168. They will take 169. They will walk 170. We shall do 171. I shall eat 172. He will bear witness 173. They saw 174. They see 175. They will see

Parsing
176-185. Parse the words underlined in the following exercises.

Sentences and Phrases from the Greek New Testament
186. And I heard a great voice from the throne, saying, Ἰδοὺ ἡ σκηνὴ τοῦ θεοῦ μετὰ τῶν ἀνθρώπων, καὶ σκηνώσει μετ' αὐτῶν, καὶ αὐτοὶ λαοὶ αὐτοῦ ἔσονται, καὶ αὐτὸς ὁ θεὸς μετ' αὐτῶν ἔσται, αὐτῶν θεός, καὶ <u>ἐξαλείψει</u> [176] πᾶν δάκρυον ἐκ τῶν <u>ὀφθαλμῶν</u> [177] αὐτῶν, καὶ ὁ θάνατος οὐκ ἔσται ἔτι οὔτε πένθος οὔτε κραυγὴ οὔτε πόνος οὐκ ἔσται ἔτι, ὅτι τὰ πρῶτα ἀπῆλθαν (Rev 21:3-4).

187. πολλοὶ[1] <u>ἐροῦσίν</u> [178] μοι ἐν ἐκείνῃ τῇ ἡμέρᾳ, Κύριε κύριε, οὐ τῷ σῷ ὀνόματι ἐπροφητεύσαμεν, καὶ τῷ σῷ ὀνόματι δαιμόνια ἐξεβάλομεν, καὶ τῷ σῷ ὀνόματι δυνάμεις[2] πολλὰς ἐποιήσαμεν; (Matt 7:22). **188.** Ἰδοὺ <u>ἔρχεται</u> [179] μετὰ τῶν νεφελῶν, καὶ ὄψεται αὐτὸν πᾶς ὀφθαλμός ...(Rev 1:7). **189.** ὃς γὰρ ἂν ποιήσῃ τὸ <u>θέλημα</u> [180] τοῦ θεοῦ, οὗτος ἀδελφός μου καὶ ἀδελφὴ καὶ μήτηρ ἐστίν (Mark 3:35).

190. καὶ ὅ τι ἂν <u>αἰτήσητε</u> [181] ἐν τῷ ὀνόματί μου τοῦτο ποιήσω, ἵνα δοξασθῇ ὁ πατὴρ ἐν τῷ υἱῷ· ἐάν τι αἰτήσητέ με ἐν τῷ ὀνόματί μου ἐγὼ ποιήσω (John 14:13-14). **191.** ἐγώ εἰμι ὁ ἄρτος τῆς <u>ζωῆς</u> [182] οἱ πατέρες ὑμῶν <u>ἔφαγον</u> [183] ἐν τῇ ἐρήμῳ τὸ μάννα καὶ ἀπέθανον. οὗτός ἐστιν ὁ ἄρτος which comes down from heaven, ἵνα τις ἐξ αὐτοῦ φάγῃ καὶ μὴ ἀποθάνῃ. I am the living bread which came down from heaven, ἐάν τις φάγῃ ἐκ τούτου τοῦ ἄρτου <u>ζήσει</u> [184] εἰς τὸν αἰῶνα, καὶ ὁ ἄρτος δὲ ὃν ἐγὼ δώσω ἡ σάρξ μού ἐστιν ... (John 6:48-51).

192. εἶπεν οὖν ὁ Ἰησοῦς πρὸς αὐτόν, Ἐὰν μὴ σημεῖα καὶ τέρατα <u>ἴδητε</u> [185], οὐ μὴ πιστεύσητε (John 4:48). **193.** καὶ ἐξουσίαν ἔδωκεν αὐτῷ κρίσιν[3] ποιεῖν, ὅτι υἱὸς ἀνθρώπου ἐστίν. Do not wonder at this, ὅτι ἔρχεται ὥρα ἐν ᾗ πάντες οἱ ἐν τοῖς μνημείοις ἀκούσουσιν τῆς φωνῆς αὐτοῦ καὶ ἐκπορεύσονται ... (John 5: 27-29a). **194.** ὃς δ' ἂν πίῃ[4] ἐκ τοῦ ὕδατος οὗ ἐγὼ δώσω αὐτῷ, οὐ μὴ διψήσει εἰς τὸν αἰῶνα, ἀλλὰ τὸ ὕδωρ ὃ δώσω αὐτῷ γενήσεται ἐν αὐτῷ πηγὴ ὕδατος ... (John 4:14).

Notes on questions 186-194: Sentences from the Greek New Testament

[1(qu.187)]Nom. masc. pl. of πολύς, "much, many" [2(qu.187)]ἡ δύναμις (118) "power, ability, miracle." This is a type of third declension noun that will not be met officially until Chapter 28, although it may not be difficult to work out even now. [3(qu.193)]κρίσις, εως, ἡ occurs more than five times in the Gospel of John and is listed in the special vocabulary at the beginning of the Gospel's listing in Kubo. κρίσιν is the acc. sing. of κρίσις, a third declension noun of a type that will be met in Chapter 28. [4(qu.194)]πίῃ is the aorist subjunctive of πίνω.

Chapter 26: The Imperative Mood

26.1 Imperative Mood

The imperative mood is mainly used to give commands. The forms of the imperative are:

Active Voice:
Present Imperative Active
2nd person	λῦε	loose!	λύετε	loose!
3rd person	λυέτω	let him loose	λυέτωσαν	let them loose

[Weak] Aorist Imperative Active
2nd person	λῦσον	loose!	λύσατε	loose!
3rd person	λυσάτω	let him loose	λυσάτωσαν	let them loose

Passive Voice:
Present Imperative Passive
2nd person	λύου	be loosed	λύεσθε	be loosed
3rd person	λυέσθω	let him be loosed	λυέσθωσαν	let them be loosed

Aorist Imperative Passive
2nd person	λύθητι	be loosed	λύθητε	be loosed
3rd person	λυθήτω	let him be loosed	λυθήτωσαν	let them be loosed

Notes:
1. There is no difference in form between the 2nd pers. pl. pres. *indicative* act. found in 356 verses of the Greek NT, and and the 2nd pers. pl. pres. *imperative* act. which is found in 269 verses (modelled on λύετε in both cases). This is also true of the 2nd pers. sing. aor. *imperative* act. used approximately 140 times in the NT, and the nom./acc. neut sing. fut. *participle* act. which is found in 12 verses (both are modelled on λῦσον). The only way to tell these apart is by the context.
2. There are no first person imperatives. Where these are needed, New Testament Greek uses a subjunctive mood, and grammarians call this the hortatory use of the subjunctive [see *Int*.1.1.4 for further explanation and examples].
3. Verbs which have strong aorists form their aorist imperatives by using their aorist stem with the endings of the present imperative. For example:
   - the pres. imp. act. of βάλλω is βάλλε, βαλλέτω, βάλλετε, βαλλέτωσαν
   - the aor. imp. act. of βάλλω is βάλε, βαλέτω, βάλετε, βαλέτωσαν

It is perhaps helpful to give a table showing how both the strong and weak verbs form their imperatives [Note: because the imperatives lack first person, the examples of the imperative will be in the second person singular].

Examples of Imperative Mood: **Active Voice**			
Pres ind [1st pers]	Pres imp [2nd pers]	Aor ind [1st pers]	Aor imp [2nd pers]
ἀγαπάω	ἀγᾶπα [α+ε]	ἠγάπησα	ἀγάπησον
ἄγω	ἄγε	ἤγαγον	ἄγαγε
αἰτέω	αἰτει [ε+ε]	ᾔτησα	αἴτησον
ἀκούω	ἄκουε	ἤκουσα	ἄκουσον
ἀποκτείνω	ἀπόκτεινε	ἀπέκτεινα	ἀπόκτεινον
βάλλω	βάλλε	ἔβαλον	βάλε
γράφω	γράφε	ἔγραψα	γράψον
εὑρίσκω	εὕρισκε	εὗρον	εὗρε
ἐλπίζω	ἔλπιζε	ἤλπισα	ἔλπισον
ἔρχομαι	ἔρχου	ἦλθον	ἐλθέ
κρίνω	κρίνε	-	-
λαμβάνω	λάμβανε	ἔλαβον	λάβε
λέγω	λέγε	εἶπον	εἰπέ
λύω	λῦε	ἔλυσα	λῦσον
ὁράω	ὅρα [α+ε]	εἶδον	ἴδε

Examples of Imperative Mood: **Passive Voice**				
Pres ind act [1st pers]	Pres ind pass [1st pers]	Pres imp pass [2nd pers]	Aor ind pass [1st pers]	Aor Imp pass [2nd pers]
ἀγαπάω	ἀγάπωμαι	ἀγαπῶ [α+ου]	ἠγαπήθην	ἀγαπήθητι
ἄγω	ἄγομαι	ἄγου	ἤχθην	ἄχθητι
αἰτέω	αἰτοῦμαι	αἰτοῦ	ᾐτήθην	αἰτήθητι
ἀκούω	ἀκούομαι	ἀκούου	ἠκούσθην	ἀκούσθητι
ἀποκτείνω [mid.-deponent] βάλλω	ἀποκτείνομαι ἀσπάζομαι βάλλομαι	ἀποκτείνου ἀσπάζου βάλλου	ἀπεκτάνθην [ἠσπασάμην] ἐβλήθην	ἀποκτάνθητι ἄσπασαι] βλήθητι
εὑρίσκω λέγω [pass.-deponent]	εὑρίσκομαι λέγομαι φοβέομαι	εὑρίσκου λέγου φοβοῦ	εὑρέθην ἐρρέθην ἐφοβήθη	εὑρέθητι ῥέθητι φοβήθητι

An examination of the above table should give confidence in determining how the imperatives are formed for the different kinds of verbs. Once the principal parts for a verb are known, it should be possible to derive its imperatives. Notice that there is no augment in the aorist imperative. The augment is an indication of past time, and the aorist imperative is distinguished from the present imperative not by a time referent, but rather by kind of action (see next note).
4. The difference between the aorist and present imperative is not related to time, but to the type of action referred to. The present imperative is used where the continuous nature of the action is stressed. By their nature, all imperatives refer to events that can only take place at some future time.
5. Examples of imperatives:
Μὴ κρίνετε, ἵνα μὴ κριθῆτε Do not judge, so that you are not judged (Matt 7:1)
ἤκουσα τοῦ δευτέρου ζῴου λέγοντες, Ἔρχου I heard the second living [being] say, "Come" (Rev 6:3)
Κατὰ τὴν πίστιν ὑμῶν γενηθήτω ὑμῖν According to your faith let it happen to you (Matt 9:29)
6. There are four, and only four, perfect imperatives in the NT: ἔρρωσθε [Acts 15:29], ἴστε [Eph 5:5; Jam 1:19], and πεφίμωσο [Mark 4:39].

26.2 The Present Imperative Mood of εἰμί

2nd p	ἴσθι	be!	ἔστε	be!
3rd p	ἔστω	let him be	ἔστωσαν	let them be

26.3 The Aorist Imperative of βαίνω & γινώσκω

2nd p	-βηθι or -βα	-βατε	γνῶθι	γνῶτε
3rd p	-βάτω	-βάτωσαν	γνώτω	γνώτωσαν

26.4 The Imperative Active of -μι Verbs

ἀφίημι

	Pres sing	Pres pl	Aor Sing	Aor pl
2nd p	-	ἀφίετε	ἄφες	ἄφετε
3rd p	ἀφιέτω	-	-	-

[note: only the parts indicated occur in the New Testament, either in ἀφίημι, or other compounds of -ιημι]

δίδωμι

	Pres sing	Pres pl	Aor Sing	Aor pl
2nd p	δίδου	δίδοτε	δός	δότε
3rd p	διδότω	διδότωσαν	δότω	δότωσαν

ἵστημι

	Pres sing	Pres pl	Aor Sing	Aor pl
2nd p	ἵστη	ἵστατε	στῆθι or -στα	στῆτε
3rd p	ἱστάτω	ἱστάτωσαν	στήτω	στήτωσαν

τίθημι

	Pres sing	Pres pl	Aor Sing	Aor pl
2nd p	τίθει	τίθετε	θές	θέτε
3rd p	τιθέτω	τιθέτωσαν	θέτω	θέτωσαν

Vocabulary 26

ἄφες (15)   allow! permit, forgive [2nd pers. sing. aor. imp. act. of ἀφίημι]
γλῶσσα (50)   tongue, language
δεξιός, -ά, -όν (54)   right [opposite of left]
δεῦρο, [pl. δεῦτε] (21)   adv.: come! come on! [δεῦρο is an adverb that acts like an imperative]
διό (53)   therefore
διώκω (44)   I persecute, pursue, strive for
δός (16)   give [2nd pers. sing. aor. imp. act. of δίδωμι]
ἐλεέω (32)   I have mercy, am merciful
ἐπεί (26)   conj.: because, since, when
ἕτερος, -α, -ον (98)   other
εὐλογέω (42)   I bless
μᾶλλον (80)   more, rather
ὀργή (36)   anger, wrath
ὑπέρ (149)   + acc.: over and above, beyond
ὑπέρ (149)   + gen.: for, in behalf of, because of
φημί (66)   I say, affirm [pres. ind.: 3rd pers. sing. φησίν, 3rd pres. pl. φασίν; imperf. ind.: 3rd sing. ἔφη]

Exercise 26

Translate into English:

1. κρῖνε 2. κρίνει 3. μὴ κρῖνε 4. αἶτε 5. δός 6. ἐβάλετε 7. βάλετε 8. εὗρε 9. δεῦτε 10. φάγε 11. ἔφαγον 12. στῆτε 13. ἔστησαν 14. στήτωσαν

15. ἀναβαίνουσιν 16. ἀναβάτω 17. θές 18. λυέσθωσαν 19. ἔστω 20. ἀχθήτω 21. εἶπε 22. λέγε 23. αἰτηθήτωσαν 24. βάτωσαν 25. ἀκουσθήτωσαν 26. γνῶτε 27. ὄφθητι

Parse

28-34. Parse the verbs underlined in the following sentences:

From the Greek New Testament:

35. Δεῦτε πρός με πάντες οἱ κοπιῶντες καὶ πεφορτισμένοι, κἀγὼ ἀναπαύσω ὑμᾶς. ἄρατε [28] τὸν ζυγόν μου ἐφ᾽ ὑμᾶς καὶ μάθετε [29] ἀπ᾽ ἐμοῦ, ὅτι πραΰς εἰμι καὶ ταπεινὸς τῇ καρδίᾳ, καὶ εὑρήσετε [30] ἀνάπαυσιν ταῖς ψυχαῖς ὑμῶν· ὁ γὰρ ζυγός μου χρηστὸς καὶ τὸ φορτίον μου ἐλαφρόν ἐστιν (Matt 11:28-30). 36. κἀγὼ ὑμῖν λέγω, αἰτεῖτε [31] καὶ δοθήσεται [32] ὑμῖν, ζητεῖτε καὶ εὑρήσετε, κρούετε καὶ ἀνοιγήσεται ὑμῖν· πᾶς γὰρ ὁ αἰτῶν λαμβάνει [33] καὶ ὁ ζητῶν εὑρίσκει καὶ τῷ κρούοντι ἀνοιγήσεται (Luke 11:9-10). 37. ἔστω [34] δὲ ὁ λόγος ὑμῶν ναὶ ναί, οὒ οὔ· τὸ δὲ περισσὸν τούτων ἐκ τοῦ πονηροῦ ἐστιν (Matt 5:37).

38. Ἠκούσατε ὅτι ἐρρέθη, Ὀφθαλμὸν ἀντὶ ὀφθαλμοῦ καὶ ὀδόντα ἀντὶ ὀδόντος. [39] ἐγὼ δὲ λέγω ὑμῖν μὴ ἀντιστῆναι τῷ πονηρῷ· ἀλλ᾽ ὅστις σε ῥαπίζει εἰς τὴν δεξιὰν σιαγόνα σου, στρέψον αὐτῷ καὶ τὴν ἄλλην· [note on ἀντιστῆναι: Greek, like English, can use the infinitive to express commands. This translates naturally into an English command] [40] καὶ τῷ θέλοντί σοι κριθῆναι καὶ τὸν χιτῶνά σου λαβεῖν, ἄφες αὐτῷ καὶ τὸ ἱμάτιον· [41] καὶ ὅστις σε ἀγγαρεύσει μίλιον ἕν, ὕπαγε μετ᾽ αὐτοῦ δύο. [42] τῷ αἰτοῦντί σε δός, καὶ τὸν θέλοντα ἀπὸ σοῦ δανίσασθαι μὴ ἀποστραφῇς. [note on ἀποστραφῇς: here the aor. subj. is used instead of the aor. imperative. This happens with prohibitions (negative commands) where the aorist tense is used (*Int*.1.1.5)] [43] Ἠκούσατε ὅτι ἐρρέθη, Ἀγαπήσεις τὸν πλησίον σου καὶ μισήσεις τὸν ἐχθρόν σου. [44] ἐγὼ δὲ λέγω ὑμῖν, ἀγαπᾶτε τοὺς ἐχθροὺς ὑμῶν καὶ προσεύχεσθε ὑπὲρ τῶν διωκόντων ὑμᾶς [45] ὅπως γένησθε υἱοὶ τοῦ πατρὸς ὑμῶν τοῦ ἐν οὐρανοῖς, ὅτι τὸν ἥλιον αὐτοῦ ἀνατέλλει ἐπὶ πονηροὺς καὶ ἀγαθοὺς καὶ βρέχει ἐπὶ δικαίους καὶ ἀδίκους. [46] ἐὰν γὰρ ἀγαπήσητε τοὺς ἀγαπῶντας ὑμᾶς, τίνα μισθὸν ἔχετε; οὐχὶ καὶ οἱ τελῶναι τὸ αὐτὸ ποιοῦσιν; [47] καὶ ἐὰν ἀσπάσησθε τοὺς ἀδελφοὺς ὑμῶν μόνον, τί περισσὸν ποιεῖτε; οὐχὶ καὶ οἱ ἐθνικοὶ τὸ αὐτὸ ποιοῦσιν; [48] Ἔσεσθε οὖν ὑμεῖς τέλειοι ὡς ὁ πατὴρ ὑμῶν ὁ οὐράνιος τελειός ἐστιν. (Matt 5:38-48)

39. οὕτως καὶ ὑμεῖς, ἐπεὶ ζηλωταί ἐστε πνευμάτων, πρὸς τὴν οἰκοδομὴν τῆς ἐκκλησίας ζητεῖτε ἵνα περισσεύητε. [13] διὸ ὁ λαλῶν γλώσσῃ προσευχέσθω ἵνα διερμηνεύῃ. [14] ἐὰν γὰρ προσεύχωμαι γλώσσῃ, τὸ πνεῦμά μου προσεύχεται, ὁ δὲ νοῦς μου ἄκαρπός ἐστιν. [15] τί οὖν ἐστιν; προσεύξομαι τῷ πνεύματι, προσεύξομαι δὲ καὶ τῷ νοΐ· ψαλῶ τῷ πνεύματι, ψαλῶ δὲ καὶ τῷ νοΐ. [16] ἐπεὶ ἐὰν εὐλογῇς ἐν πνεύματι, ὁ ἀναπληρῶν τὸν τόπον τοῦ ἰδιώτου πῶς ἐρεῖ τὸ Ἀμήν ἐπὶ τῇ σῇ εὐχαριστίᾳ; ἐπειδὴ τί λέγεις οὐκ οἶδεν· [17] σὺ

μὲν γὰρ καλῶς εὐχαριστεῖς ἀλλ᾽ ὁ ἕτερος οὐκ οἰκοδομεῖται. [18] εὐχαριστῶ τῷ θεῷ, παντῶν ὑμῶν μᾶλλον γλώσσαις λαλῶ· [19] ἀλλὰ ἐν ἐκκλησίᾳ θέλω πέντε λόγους τῷ νοΐ μου λαλῆσαι, ἵνα καὶ ἄλλους κατηχήσω, ἢ μυρίους λόγους ἐν γλώσσῃ. (1 Cor 14:12-19)

40. οὐκ ἔστιν μαθητὴς ὑπὲρ τὸν διδάσκαλον· κατηρτισμένος δὲ πᾶς ἔσται ὡς ὁ διδάσκαλος αὐτοῦ. (Luke 6:40) **41.** Βαρτιμαῖος, τυφλὸς προσαίτης, ἐκάθητο παρὰ τὴν ὁδόν. καὶ ἀκούσας ὅτι Ἰησοῦς ὁ Ναζαρηνός ἐστιν ἤρξατο κράζειν καὶ λέγειν, Υἱὲ Δαυὶδ Ἰησοῦ, ἐλέησόν με. καὶ ἐπετίμων αὐτῷ πολλοὶ ἵνα σιωπήσῃ· ὁ δὲ πολλῷ μᾶλλον ἔκραζεν, Υἱὲ Δαυίδ, ἐλέησόν με. καὶ στὰς ὁ Ἰησοῦς εἶπεν, Φωνήσατε αὐτόν. καὶ φωνοῦσιν τὸν τυφλὸν λέγοντες αὐτῷ, Θάρσει, ἔγειρε, φωνεῖ σε. (Mark 10:46b-49)

42. ὅς γὰρ οὐκ ἔστιν καθ᾽ ὑμῶν, ὑπὲρ ἡμῶν ἐστιν. (Mark 9:40) **43.** ἔφη αὐτῷ ὁ Ἰησοῦς, Εἰ θέλεις τέλειος εἶναι, ὕπαγε πώλησόν σου τὰ ὑπάρχοντα καὶ δὸς τοῖς πτωχοῖς, καὶ ἕξεις θησαυρὸν ἐν οὐρανοῖς, καὶ δεῦρο ἀκολούθει μοι. (Matt 19:21) **44.** πολλῷ οὖν μᾶλλον δικαιωθέντες νῦν ἐν τῷ αἵματι αὐτοῦ σωθησόμεθα δι᾽αὐτοῦ ἀπὸ τῆς ὀργῆς. (Rom 5:9) **45.** Ἔρχεται γυνὴ ἐκ τῆς Σαμαρείας ἀντλῆσαι ὕδωρ. λέγει αὐτῇ ὁ Ἰησοῦς, Δός μοι πεῖν. ... λέγει πρὸς αὐτὸν ἡ γυνή, Κύριε, δός μοι τοῦτο τὸ ὕδωρ, ἵνα μὴ διψῶ μηδὲ διέρχωμαι ἐνθάδε ἀντλεῖν. (John 4:7, 15)

Chapter 27: Present & Imperfect Indicative Active of -μι Verbs

The aorist indicative active (12.3.1), the subjunctive active (16.1), active participles (20.2.3), perfect actives (21.2), and the imperative active (26.4) of -μι verbs have already been met. Not only this, from the principal parts already learnt, the future active, and also the aorist and perfect passive forms of these verbs are known. So only their present and imperfect forms in the active and passive voices need to be introduced. These have been delayed to this point because they exhibit irregularities, and they form these tenses in a way that is quite different from other verbs.

While there are irregularities, an examination of the different verbs shows that there are general patterns that they all follow, and with some practice it becomes relatively straightforward to recognize and translate them. These verbs are used very frequently. For example, δίδωμι and compound verbs involving δίδωμι are found in 556 verses of the NT, over 50 of them in the present and imperfect indicative; while ἵστημι and its compounds are found in 265 verses, 20 of which are in the present and imperfect indicative. So the effort required to become familiar with them quickly pays dividends, though, in fact, much of the effort required for the mastery of these verbs has already taken place earlier in the book. They are listed below, in order of frequency (most frequent to less frequent).

The Active Voice:

Δίδωμι present	Δίδωμι imperfect	Ἵστημι present	Ἀφίημι present
δίδωμι	ἐδίδουν	ἵστημι	ἀφίημι
δίδως	ἐδίδους	ἵστης	ἀφεῖς
δίδωσι(ν)	ἐδίδου	ἵστησι(ν)	ἀφίησιν
δίδομεν	ἐδίδομεν	ἵσταμεν	ἀφίομεν
δίδοτε	ἐδίδοτε	ἵστατε	ἀφίετε
διδόασι(ν)	ἐδίδοσαν	ἵστασι(ν)	ἀφίασι(ν)

Τίθημι present	Τίθημι imperfect	Δείκνυμι present	Δείκνυμι imperfect
τίθημι	ἐτίθην	δείκνυμι	ἐδείκνυν
τίθης	ἐτίθεις	δείκνυς	ἐδείκνυς
τίθησι(ν)	ἐτίθεται	δείκνυσι(ν)	ἐδείκνυ
τίθεμεν	ἐτίθεμεν	δείκνυμεν	ἐδείκνυμεν
τίθετε	ἐτίθετε	δείκνυτε	ἐδείκνυτε
τιθέασι(ν)	ἐτίθεσαν	δεικνύασι(ν)	ἐδείκνυσαν

Note: the imperfect active of ἵστημι and ἀφίημι do not occur in the Greek NT.

The Middle and Passive Voice:

Δίδωμι present	Δίδωμι imperfect	Ἵστημι present	Ἵστημι imperfect
δίδομαι	ἐδιδόμην	ἱστάμην	ἱστάμην
δίδοσαι	ἐδίδοσο	ἵστασο	ἵστασο
δίδοται	ἐδίδοτο	ἵστατο	ἵστατο
διδόμεθα	ἐδιδόμεθα	ἱστάμεθα	ἱστάμεθα
δίδοσθε	ἐδίδοσθε	ἵστασθε	ἵστασθε
δίδονται	ἐδίδοντο	ἵσταντο	ἵσταντο

Τίθημι present	Τίθημι imperfect	Δείκνυμι present	Δείκνυμι imperfect
τίθεμαι	ἐτιθέμην	δείκνυμαι	ἐδεικνύμην
τίθεσαι	ἐτίθεσο	δείκνυσαι	ἐδείκνυσο
τίθεται	ἐτίθετο	δείκνυται	ἐδείκνυτο
τιθέμεθα	ἐτιθέμεθα	δεικνύμεθα	ἐδεικνύμεθα
τίθεσθε	ἐτίθεσθε	δείκνυσθε	ἐδείκνυσθε
τίθενται	ἐτίθεντο	δείκνυνται	ἐδείκνυντο

Notes:
1. The verb ἀπόλλυμι is declined like δείκνυμι
2. See Vocabulary 26 for the verb φημί, "I say"
3. The [pres. and impf.] passive voice of τίθημι is supplied by κεῖμαι, which is conjugated rather like a perfect mid. or pass.: pres: κεῖμαι, κεῖσαι, κεῖται, καίμεθα, κεῖσθε, κεῖνται; imp: ἐκείμην, ἔκεισο, ἔκειτο, ἐκείμεθα, ἔκεισθε, ἔκειντο.
4. Appendix D is devoted to -μι verbs. Perhaps it would be a good idea to take the time to look at it now, and become familiar with all the parts of those verbs, and ensure that the different moods and tenses are known.

Vocabulary 27

ἀμπελών, -ῶνος, ὁ (23)	vineyard
ἀνίστημι (107)	I rise, appear, rebel, etc.
ἀποδίδωμι (47)	I give away, give up, give out, pay, grant, give back, render
εἴτε ... εἴτε (65)	if ... if, whether ... or
ἕκαστος, -η, -ον (81)	each, every
ἔξεστιν (31)	it is lawful, permitted, possible, proper
ἔσχατος, -η, -ον (52)	last
καιρός (85)	time
λοιπός, -ή, -όν (55)	rest, remaining, other [note: [τὸ] λοιπόν can be used as an adverb, when it means "finally; from now on, still, in addition"]
μυστήριον (27)	mystery
παραλαμβάνω (49)	I take with, take over, rejoin
προσφέρω (47)	I offer
Σατανᾶς, ὁ (36)	Satan
συνίημι (26)	I understand, perceive [συνίημι = σύν + -ίημι; ἀφίημι = ἀπό + -ίημι. Thus συνίημι follows the paradigm of ἀφίημι]

Exercise 27

Parse the following

[Most of the different tenses and moods are only represented once. So, if you do not recognize the answer immediately, note that there is a need to do some revision of that tense/mood/voice]:

1. ἵστασι 2. τίθησιν 3. δίδως 4. δός 5. ἄφηκεν 6. ἐδίδου 7. ἵστωμεν 8. διδόασι 9. οὖσαν 10. δείκνυτε 11. τίθησιν 12. τιθέασιν 13. ἵστανται 14. ἵσταται 15. δίδωσιν 16. θῇ 17. ἀφίασιν 18. ἀφίησιν 19. στῶ 20. δίδοσαι 21. ἐθήκαμεν 22. στάν 23. δόν 24. τέθεικα 25. θείς 26. ἐδείκνυ 27. ἔδειξα 28. ἐτίθεσαν 29. ἐδίδοσαν 30. δείξω 31. ἵσταντα 32. δούς 33. διδότω 34. ἐδείκνυσο

35. δῶ 36. ἀφῇ 37. δεικνύοντος 38. ἐδίδουν 39. θές 40. δοῦναι 41. -έστακα 42. ἵστατε 43. φησίν 44. φασίν 45. ἐτέθην 46. δεδώκαμεν 47. στῆθι 48. τίθει 49. στήσω 50. ἐστάθη 51. δείκνυσθε 52. ἐδώκατε 53. θήσει 54. ἐδόθης 55. δίδοτε 56. τιθῶ 57. ἵσταντο 58. ἔστησας 59. ἐδίδοσθε 60. τέθεισαι

From the Greek New Testament

61. Πάλιν παραλαμβάνει αὐτὸν ὁ διάβολος εἰς ὄρος ὑψηλὸν λίαν καὶ δείκνυσιν αὐτῷ πάσας τὰς βασιλείας τοῦ κόσμου καὶ τὴν δόξαν αὐτῶν καὶ εἶπεν αὐτῷ, Ταῦτά σοι πάντα δώσω, ἐὰν πεσὼν προσκυνήσῃς μοι. τότε λέγει αὐτῷ ὁ Ἰησοῦς, Ὕπαγε, Σατανᾶ· γέγραπται γάρ, Κύριον τὸν θεόν σου προσκυνήσεις καὶ αὐτῷ μόνῳ λατρεύσεις. Τότε ἀφίησιν αὐτὸν ὁ διάβολος, καὶ ἰδοὺ ἄγγελοι προσῆλθον καὶ διηκόνουν αὐτῷ. (Matt 4:8-11)
62. καὶ πέμψας ἀπεκεφάλισεν τὸν Ἰωάννην ἐν τῇ φυλακῇ. καὶ ἠνέχθη ἡ κεφαλὴ αὐτοῦ ἐπὶ πίνακι καὶ ἐδόθη τῷ κορασίῳ, καὶ ἤνεγκεν τῇ μητρὶ αὐτῆς (Matt 14:10-11). **63.** μέλλει γὰρ ὁ υἱὸς τοῦ ἀνθρώπου ἔρχεσθαι ἐν τῇ δόξῃ τοῦ πατρὸς αὐτοῦ μετὰ τῶν ἀγγέλων αὐτοῦ, καὶ τότε ἀποδώσει ἑκάστῳ κατὰ τὴν πρᾶξιν αὐτοῦ (Matt 16:27).

64. ὅταν οὖν ἔλθῃ ὁ κύριος τοῦ ἀμπελῶνος, τί ποιήσει τοῖς γεωργοῖς ἐκείνοις; λέγουσιν αὐτῷ, Κακοὺς κακῶς ἀπολέσει αὐτοὺς καὶ τὸν ἀμπελῶνα ἐκδώσεται ἄλλοις γεωργοῖς, οἵτινες ἀποδώσουσιν αὐτῷ τοὺς καρποὺς ἐν τοῖς καιροῖς αὐτῶν (Matt 21:40-41). **65.** ἄλλα δὲ ἔπεσεν ἐπὶ τὴν γῆν τὴν καλὴν καὶ ἐδίδου καρπόν, ὁ μὲν ἑκατόν, ὁ δὲ ἑξήκοντα, ὁ δὲ τριάκοντα (Matt 13:8).
[Note on ἄλλα: This is not the conjunction ἀλλά, but is the neut. pl. of the adjective ἄλλος, -η, -ο "another, other"]

66. Ἐπηρώτων δὲ αὐτὸν οἱ μαθηταὶ αὐτοῦ τίς αὕτη εἴη ἡ παραβολή. ὁ δὲ εἶπεν, Ὑμῖν δέδοται γνῶναι τὰ μυστήρια τῆς βασιλείας τοῦ θεοῦ, τοῖς δὲ λοιποῖς ἐν παραβολαῖς, ἵνα, βλέποντες μὴ βλέπωσιν καὶ ἀκούοντες μὴ συνιῶσιν (Luke 8:9-10). [Note on τίς ... εἴη: εἴη is the optative of εἰμί. The sense is "what (this parable) might mean." Grammatically, it could either be a potential optative (with ἄν omitted), or as an indirect question [see later comments on optatives in *Int*.1.5).]

67. θέλω δὲ τούτῳ τῷ ἐσχάτῳ δοῦναι ὡς καὶ σοί· ἢ οὐκ ἔξεστίν μοι ὃ θέλω ποιῆσαι ἐν τοῖς ἐμοῖς; ἢ ὁ ὀφθαλμός σου πονηρός ἐστιν ὅτι ἐγὼ ἀγαθός εἰμι; Οὕτως ἔσονται οἱ ἔσχατοι πρῶτοι καὶ οἱ πρῶτοι ἔσχατοι (Matt 20:14b-16). **68.** ὥστε μηδεὶς καυχάσθω ἐν ἀνθρώποις· πάντα γὰρ ὑμῶν ἐστιν, εἴτε Παῦλος εἴτε Ἀπολλῶς εἴτε Κηφᾶς εἴτε κόσμος εἴτε ζωὴ εἴτε θάνατος, εἴτε ἐνεστῶτα εἴτε μέλλοντα· πάντα ὑμῶν, ὑμεῖς δὲ Χριστοῦ, Χριστὸς δὲ θεοῦ (1 Cor 3:21-22).

69. Δύνοντος δὲ τοῦ ἡλίου ἅπαντες ὅσοι εἶχον ἀσθενοῦντας νόσοις ποικίλαις ἤγαγον αὐτοὺς πρὸς αὐτόν· ὁ δὲ ἑνὶ ἑκάστῳ αὐτῶν τὰς χεῖρας ἐπιτιθεὶς ἐθεράπευεν αὐτούς (Luke 4:40). **70.** ἴσθι εὐνοῶν τῷ ἀντιδίκῳ σου ταχύ, ἕως ὅτου εἶ μετ' αὐτοῦ ἐν τῇ ὁδῷ, μήποτέ σε παραδῷ ὁ ἀντίδικος τῷ κριτῇ καὶ ὁ κριτὴς τῷ ὑπηρέτῃ καὶ εἰς φυλακὴν βληθήσῃ· ἀμὴν λέγω σοι, οὐ μὴ ἐξέλθῃς ἐκεῖθεν, ἕως ἂν ἀποδῷς τὸν ἔσχατον κοδράντην (Matt 5:25-26).

71. λέγει οὖν αὐτοῖς ὁ Ἰησοῦς, Ὁ καιρὸς ὁ ἐμὸς οὔπω πάρεστιν, ὁ δὲ καιρὸς ὁ ὑμέτερος πάντοτέ ἐστιν ἕτοιμος (John 7:6). **72.** ἔλαβεν τοὺς ἑπτὰ ἄρτους καὶ τοὺς ἰχθύας καὶ εὐχαριστήσας ἔκλασεν καὶ ἐδίδου τοῖς μαθηταῖς, οἱ δὲ μαθηταὶ τοῖς ὄχλοις (Matt 15:36). **73.** Τότε προσηνέχθησαν αὐτῷ παιδία ἵνα τὰς χεῖρας ἐπιθῇ αὐτοῖς καὶ προσεύξηται· οἱ δὲ μαθηταὶ ἐπετίμησαν αὐτοῖς. ὁ δὲ Ἰησοῦς εἶπεν, Ἄφετε τὰ παιδία καὶ μὴ κωλύετε αὐτὰ ἐλθεῖν πρός με, τῶν γὰρ τοιούτων ἐστὶν ἡ βασιλεία τῶν οὐρανῶν. καὶ ἐπιθεὶς τὰς χεῖρας αὐτοῖς ἐπορεύθη ἐκεῖθεν (Matt 19:13-15).

74. ἡ δὲ Μαρία ἡ Μαγδαληνὴ καὶ Μαρία ἡ Ἰωσῆτος ἐθεώρουν ποῦ τέθειται (Mark 15:47). **75.** οὐδὲ καίουσιν λύχνον καὶ τιθέασιν αὐτὸν ὑπὸ τὸν μόδιον ἀλλ' ἐπὶ τὴν λυχνίαν, καὶ λάμπει πᾶσιν τοῖς ἐν τῇ οἰκίᾳ (Matt 5:15). **76.** καὶ ἰδοὺ προσέφερον αὐτῷ παραλυτικὸν ἐπὶ κλίνης βεβλημένον. καὶ ἰδὼν ὁ Ἰησοῦς τὴν πίστιν αὐτῶν εἶπεν τῷ παραλυτικῷ, Θάρσει, τέκνον, ἀφίενταί σου αἱ ἁμαρτίαι (Matt 9:2).

77. ἰδὼν δὲ ὁ Σίμων ὅτι διὰ τῆς ἐπιθέσεως τῶν χειρῶν τῶν ἀποστόλων δίδοται τὸ πνεῦμα, προσήνεγκεν αὐτοῖς χρήματα λέγων, Δότε κἀμοὶ τὴν ἐξουσίαν ταύτην ἵνα ᾧ ἐὰν ἐπιθῶ τὰς χεῖρας λαμβάνῃ πνεῦμα ἅγιον (Acts 8:18). **78.** Οὕτως καὶ ὁ πατήρ μου ὁ οὐράνιος ποιήσει ὑμῖν, ἐὰν μὴ ἀφῆτε ἕκαστος τῷ ἀδελφῷ αὐτοῦ ἀπὸ τῶν καρδιῶν ὑμῶν (Matt 18:35).

Chapter 28: Potpourri

This chapter gathers together several somewhat unrelated topics which should be covered in an introduction to New Testament Greek, but which have yet to receive attention. These topics include -οω verbs, the unthematic aorists of βαίνω, γινώσκω and δύνω, the aorist tense of deponent verbs, third declension nouns whose stem ends in a vowel, other translations of the present tense, and μέγας and πυλύς.

28.1 -οω Verbs

Verbs which end in -εω and -αω were met very early in this textbook. There is one other class of verbs which has stems ending in a vowel that have yet to be explained. These are the -οω verbs. There is only one example which occurs more than 50 times in the Greek New Testament, and that is πληροω (I fulfil, fill), although several other important verbs also show the same kinds of endings (e.g. δικαιοω, I justify, vindicate, show justice). The contractions undergone by ο are:

ο + ε   becomes ου
ο + η   becomes ω
ο + ο   becomes ου
ο + ου   becomes ου
ο + ω   becomes ω
ο + ?ι (any combination containing ι, even if it is an iota subscript) becomes οι

The contractions of omicron may be simplified to the following three rules:

ο + short vowel or ου becomes ου
ο + long vowel becomes ω
ο + any iota becomes οι

Verbs which end in -οω show these contractions in the present and imperfect tenses (both active and passive). Like the -εω and -αω verbs, the -οω verbs are nearly always regular.

Thus the present and imperfect tenses of the indicative mood of πληρόω are:

πληρόω			
Present act	Imperfect act	Present pass	Impefect Pass
πληρῶ	ἐπλήρουν	πληροῦμαι	ἐπληρούμην
πληροῖς	ἐπλήρους	πληροῖ	ἐπληροῦ
πληροῖ	ἐπλήρου	πληροῦται	ἐπληροῦτο
πληροῦμεν	ἐπληροῦμεν	πληρούμεθα	ἐπληρούμεθα
πληροῦτε	ἐπληροῦτε	πληροῦσθε	ἐπληροῦσθε
πληροῦσι(ν)	ἐπλήρουν	πληροῦνται	ἐπληροῦντο

As might be expected, the o lengthens to ω in the future and aorist tenses. The principal parts of πληρόω are: πληρόω, πληρώσω, ἐπλήρωσα, πεπλήρωκα, πεπλήρωμαι, ἐπληρώθην. -οω verbs are accented on the same principles as -εω and -αω verbs (see 5.2, 8.2 & *Int.*7.2.2).

28.2 The Unthematic Aorists of βαίνω, γινώσκω and δύνω

The term unthematic is used because the aorists of βαίνω "I go", δύνω "I set [of the sun]" and γινώσκω "I know" do not use vowels in forming their personal endings. Their aorists are as follows:

Aorist of βαίνω "I go"	Aorist of δύνω "I set"	Aorist of γινώσκω "I know"
-έβην	ἔδυν	ἔγνων
-έβης	ἔδυς	ἔγνως
-έβη	ἔδυ	ἔγνω
-έβημεν	ἔδυμεν	ἔγνωμεν
-έβητε	ἔδυτε	ἔγνωτε
-έβησαν	ἔδυσαν	ἔγνωσαν

Notes:
1. The aor. inf. act. of γινώσκω is γνῶναι, its aor. part. act. is γνούς, γνοῦσα, γνόν, γνοντ-.
2. The aor. inf. act. of -βαίνω is -βῆναι, its aor. part. act. is -βάς, -βάσα, -βάν.
3. The aorist imperative of both γινώσκω and -βαίνω have already been met in 26.3.
4. Both -βαίνω and -δύνω exist only as compounds in the Greek New Testament.

28.3 The Aorist Indicative Middle

The aorist indicative middle of λύω is:
ἐλυσάμην
ἐλύσω
ἐλύσατο
ἐλυσάμεθα
ἐλύσασθε
ἐλύσαντο

All the regular rules of combining consonants with σ apply:
guttural (γ, κ, χ) + σ becomes ξ
labial (β, π, φ) + σ becomes ψ
dental (δ, τ, θ) + σ becomes σ

Thus the aorist indicative middle of δέχομαι "receive" is:
ἐδεξάμην
ἐδέξω
ἐδέξατο
ἐδεξάμεθα
ἐδέξασθε
ἐδέξαντο

The middle endings are -σαμην, -σω, -σατο, -σαμεθα, -σασθε, -σαντο. The χ of δέχομαι combines with the σ of the endings to make ξ.

English & Greek Present; English and Greek Aorist
I greet   ἀσπάζομαι   I greeted   ἠσπασάμην   dz + σ = σ
I receive δέχομαι   I received ἐδεξάμην   χ + σ = ξ
I pray   προσεύχομαι   I prayed   προσευξάμην   χ + σ = ξ

[προσεύχομαι is actually a compound verb (πρός + εὔχομαι). The diphthong ευ is unchanged by the augment in this case.]

28.4 The Other Moods of the Middle Voice

28.4.1 The Aorist Subjunctive Middle
The aorist subjunctive middle of λύω is:
λύσωμαι
λύσῃ
λύσηται
λυσώμεθα
λύσησθε
λύσωνται

28.4.2 The Aorist Imperative Middle
The aorist imperative middle of λύω is
λῦσαι
λυσάσθω
λῦσαι
λυσάσθω

28.4.3 The Aorist Participle Middle
The aorist participle middle of λυω is:

Case	Masc	Fem	Neut
N	λυσάμενος	λυσαμένη	λυσάμενον
A	λυσάμενον	λυσαμένην	λυσάμενον
G	λυσαμένου	λυσαμένης	λυσαμένου
D	λυσαμένῳ	λυσαμένῃ	λυσαμένῳ
N	λυσάμενοι	λυσάμεναι	λυσάμενα
A	λυσαμένους	λυσαμένας	λυσάμενα
G	λυσαμένων	λυσαμένων	λυσαμένων
D	λυσαμένοις	λυσαμέναις	λυσαμένοις

28.5 Third Declension Nouns that Have a Stem which Ends in a Vowel

There is one major class of third declension nouns that has not yet been covered. These are third declension nouns which have a stem that ends with a vowel. There are several types of these, but the two most common follow either the declension of ἡ πόλις or the declension of ὁ βασιλεύς:

	βασιλεύς	πόλις
Nom	βασιλεύς	πόλις
Voc	βασιλεῦ	πόλι
Acc	βασιλέα	πόλιν
Gen	βασιλέως	πόλεως
Dat	βασιλεῖ	πόλεσι(ν)
Nom	βασιλεῖς	πόλεις
Voc	βασιλεῖς	πόλεις
Acc	βασιλεῖς	πόλεις
Gen	βασιλέων	πόλεων
Dat	βασιλεῦσι(ν)	πόλεσι(ν)

As the vocabulary shows, there are several quite common nouns that follow the declension of these two nouns.

28.6 Other Translations of the Present Tense

The present indicative may be used of either repeated action, punctiliar action, or iterative action. Thus the possible translations of λύω range from "I loose" (punctiliar), "I am loosing" (continuous), "I repeatedly loose" (iterative), as well as "I do loose" (emphatic).

28.7 μέγας and πολύς

The full declension of the irregular adjectives μέγας "large, great" and πολύς "much, many" are listed in Appendix E. Students seeking a grade of credit or above should take time to familiarize themselves with these two adjectives at this juncture.

Vocabulary 28

-οω verbs
δικαιόω (39)   I justify, vindicate, show justice
πληρόω (86)   I fulfil, fill
σταυρόω (46)   I crucify
φανερόω (49)   I make known, reveal, show; pass.: I am revealed, it is evident

masc. & fem. third decl. nouns with vowel endings:
ἀρχιερεύς, -έως, ὁ (122)   high priest
βασιλεύς, -έως, ὁ (115)   king
γραμματεύς, -έως, ὁ (62)   scribe

δύναμις, -εως, ἡ (118)   power, ability, miracle
ἱερεύς, -έως, ὁ (31)   priest
πίστις, -εως, ἡ (243)   belief, faith
πόλις-, -εως, ἡ (161)   city

Other words
γνούς, γνοῦσα, γνόν, γνοντ- (18) [aor. part. act. of γινώσκω]
γνῶναι (15) to know   [aor. inf. act. of γινώσκω]
ἐγγίζω [+ dat.] (42) I approach, draw near
ἔγνων (42) I knew [aor. ind. act. of γινώσκω]
μετανοέω (34) I repent
πρεσβύτερος (65) older, elder
τρεῖς, τρία (67) three
χωρίς (41)   prep. + gen.: without, apart from
   adv.: separately, by itself

Exercise 28

Sentences and Phrases from the Greek New Testament:
1. ἀποκριθεὶς δὲ ὁ Ἰησοῦς εἶπεν πρὸς αὐτόν, Ἄφες ἄρτι, οὕτως γὰρ πρέπον ἐστὶν ἡμῖν πληρῶσαι πᾶσαν δικαιοσύνην. τότε ἀφίησιν αὐτόν (Matt 3:15).
2. ἐν τῷ κόσμῳ ἦν, καὶ ὁ κόσμος δι' αὐτοῦ ἐγένετο, καὶ ὁ κόσμος αὐτὸν οὐκ ἔγνω. εἰς τὰ ἴδια ἦλθεν, καὶ οἱ ἴδιοι αὐτὸν οὐ παρέλαβον (John 1:10-11).

3. λέγει αὐτοῖς ὁ Πιλᾶτος, Τί οὖν ποιήσω Ἰησοῦν τὸν λεγόμενον Χριστόν; λέγουσιν πάντες, Σταυρωθήτω. ὁ δὲ ἔφη, Τί γὰρ κακὸν ἐποίησεν; οἱ δὲ περισσῶς ἔκραζον λέγοντες, Σταυρωθήτω. ... σταυρώσαντες δὲ αὐτὸν διεμερίσαντο τὰ ἱμάτια αὐτοῦ βάλλοντες κλῆρον ...Τότε σταυροῦνται σὺν αὐτῷ δύο λῃσταί, εἷς ἐκ δεξιῶν καὶ εἷς ἐξ εὐωνύμων. (Matt 27:22-23, 35, 38)

4. καὶ εἰσῆλθεν εἰς τὸν οἶκον Ζαχαρίου καὶ ἠσπάσατο τὴν Ἐλισάβετ. καὶ ἐγένετο ὡς ἤκουσεν τὸν ἀσπασμὸν τῆς Μαρίας ἡ Ἐλισάβετ, ἐσκίρτησεν τὸ βρέφος ἐν τῇ κοιλίᾳ αὐτῆς, καὶ ἐπλήσθη πνεύματος ἁγίου ἡ Ἐλισάβετ (Luke 1:40-41a). **5.** Ταύτην ἐποίησεν ἀρχὴν τῶν σημείων ὁ Ἰησοῦς ἐν Κανὰ τῆς Γαλιλαίας καὶ ἐφανέρωσεν τὴν δόξαν αὐτοῦ, καὶ ἐπίστευσαν εἰς αὐτὸν οἱ μαθηταὶ αὐτοῦ (John 2:11).

6. καὶ τότε ὁμολογήσω αὐτοῖς ὅτι Οὐδέποτε ἔγνων ὑμᾶς· ἀποχωρεῖτε ἀπ' ἐμοῦ οἱ ἐργαζόμενοι τὴν ἀνομίαν (Matt 7:23). **7.** Ἀπὸ τότε ἤρξατο ὁ Ἰησοῦς κηρύσσειν καὶ λέγειν, Μετανοεῖτε· ἤγγικεν γὰρ ἡ βασιλεία τῶν οὐρανῶν (Matt 4:17). **8.** ὅτε οὖν ἦλθεν εἰς τὴν Γαλιλαίαν, ἐδέξαντο αὐτὸν οἱ Γαλιλαῖοι πάντα ἑωρακότες ὅσα ἐποίησεν ἐν Ἱεροσολύμοις ἐν τῇ ἑορτῇ, καὶ αὐτοὶ γὰρ ἦλθον εἰς τὴν ἑορτήν (John 4:45).

Part 4   267

9. μεμέρισται ὁ Χριστός; μὴ Παῦλος ἐσταυρώθη ὑπὲρ ὑμῶν, ἢ εἰς τὸ ὄνομα Παύλου ἐβαπτίσθητε; (1 Cor 1:13) [μή is used to introduce a question which expects the answer "no." It is not generally translated into English, although sometimes it is possible to convey something of the expected "no" answer *(Int.*7.3)]. **10.** ἵνα πληρωθῇ τὸ ῥηθὲν διὰ Ἡσαΐου τοῦ προφήτου λέγοντος ... (Matt 12:17) [ῥηθέν is the aor. pass. part. of λέγω (ἐρρέθην, the aor. ind. passive, has already been met in an Vocab. 24.1)].

11. Μετὰ ταῦτα ἦν ἑορτὴ τῶν Ἰουδαίων καὶ ἀνέβη Ἰησοῦς εἰς Ἱεροσόλυμα (John 5:1). **12.** ὥσπερ γὰρ ἦν Ἰωνᾶς ἐν τῇ κοιλίᾳ τοῦ κήτους τρεῖς ἡμέρας καὶ τρεῖς νύκτας, οὕτως ἔσται ὁ υἱὸς τοῦ ἀνθρώπου ἐν τῇ καρδίᾳ τῆς γῆς τρεῖς ἡμέρας καὶ τρεῖς νύκτας (Matt 12:40). **13.** Καὶ ἤρξατο διδάσκειν αὐτοὺς ὅτι δεῖ τὸν υἱὸν τοῦ ἀνθρώπου πολλὰ παθεῖν καὶ ἀποδοκιμασθῆναι ὑπὸ τῶν πρεσβυτέρων καὶ τῶν ἀρχιερέων καὶ τῶν γραμματέων καὶ ἀποκτανθῆναι καὶ μετὰ τρεῖς ἡμέρας ἀναστῆναι (Mark 8:31).

14. οὐ γὰρ Δαυὶδ ἀνέβη εἰς τοὺς οὐρανούς (Acts 2:34a). **15.** καὶ ἀρξάμενος ἀπὸ Μωϋσέως καὶ ἀπὸ πάντων τῶν προφητῶν διερμήνευσεν αὐτοῖς ἐν πάσαις ταῖς γραφαῖς τὰ περὶ ἑαυτοῦ (Luke 24:27). **16.** καὶ ἀνέβησαν ἐπὶ τὸ πλάτος τῆς γῆς καὶ ἐκύκλευσαν τὴν παρεμβολὴν τῶν ἁγίων καὶ τὴν πόλιν τὴν ἠγαπημένην, καὶ κατέβη πῦρ ἐκ τοῦ οὐρανοῦ καὶ κατέφαγεν αὐτούς (Rev 20:9).

17. Μηδενὶ μηδὲν ὀφείλετε εἰ μὴ τὸ ἀλλήλους ἀγαπᾶν· ὁ γὰρ ἀγαπῶν τὸν ἕτερον νόμον πεπλήρωκεν (Rom 13:8) [ἀγαπᾶν is an infinitive. The last α of ἀγαπάω contracts with the -εεν of the infinitive ending. See 15.1.3] **18.** δικαιοσύνη γὰρ θεοῦ ἐν αὐτῷ ἀποκαλύπτεται ἐκ πίστεως εἰς πίστιν (Rom 1:17). **19.** Καὶ ἦλθεν εἷς ἐκ τῶν ἑπτὰ ἀγγέλων τῶν ἐχόντων τὰς ἑπτὰ φιάλας τῶν γεμόντων τῶν ἑπτὰ πληγῶν τῶν ἐσχάτων καὶ ἐλάλησεν μετ' ἐμοῦ λέγων, Δεῦρο, δείξω σοι τὴν νύμφην τὴν γυναῖκα τοῦ ἀρνίου. καὶ ἀπήνεγκέν με ἐν πνεύματι ἐπὶ ὄρος μέγα καὶ ὑψηλόν, καὶ ἔδειξέν μοι τὴν πόλιν τὴν ἁγίαν Ἰερουσαλὴμ καταβαίνουσαν ἐκ τοῦ οὐρανοῦ ἀπὸ τοῦ θεοῦ (Rev 21:9-10).

20. πολλοὶ ἐροῦσίν μοι ἐν ἐκείνῃ τῇ ἡμέρᾳ, Κύριε κύριε, οὐ τῷ σῷ ὀνόματι ἐπροφητεύσαμεν, καὶ τῷ σῷ ὀνόματι δαιμόνια ἐξεβάλομεν, καὶ τῷ σῷ ὀνόματι δυνάμεις πολλὰς ἐποιήσαμεν; (Matt 7:22). **21.** οὐαὶ δὲ ὑμῖν, γραμματεῖς καὶ Φαρισαῖοι ὑποκριταί, ὅτι κλείετε τὴν βασιλείαν τῶν οὐρανῶν ἔμπροσθεν τῶν ἀνθρώπων, ὑμεῖς γὰρ οὐκ εἰσέρχεσθε οὐδὲ τοὺς εἰσερχομένους ἀφίετε εἰσελθεῖν (Matt 23:13).

22. Καὶ ἀναβαίνων ὁ Ἰησοῦς εἰς Ἱεροσόλυμα παρέλαβεν τοὺς δώδεκα μαθητὰς κατ' ἰδίαν καὶ ἐν τῇ ὁδῷ εἶπεν αὐτοῖς, Ἰδοὺ ἀναβαίνομεν εἰς Ἱεροσόλυμα, καὶ ὁ υἱὸς τοῦ ἀνθρώπου παραδοθήσεται τοῖς ἀρχιερεῦσιν καὶ γραμματεῦσιν, καὶ κατακρινοῦσιν αὐτὸν θανάτῳ καὶ παραδώσουσιν αὐτὸν τοῖς ἔθνεσιν εἰς τὸ ἐμπαῖξαι καὶ μαστιγῶσαι καὶ σταυρῶσαι, καὶ τῇ τρίτῃ ἡμέρᾳ ἐγερθήσεται. [Note the use of the dative case to indicate (location in) time in the phrase τῇ τρίτῃ ἡμέρᾳ (*Int*.5.4.4)] (Matt 20:17-19) **23.** Καὶ ἀπήγαγον τὸν Ἰησοῦν πρὸς τὸν ἀρχιερέα, καὶ συνέρχονται πάντες οἱ ἀρχιερεῖς καὶ οἱ πρεσβύτεροι καὶ οἱ γραμματεῖς (Mark 14:53).

24. Νυνὶ δὲ χωρὶς νόμου δικαιοσύνη θεοῦ πεφανέρωται μαρτυρουμένη ὑπὸ τοῦ νόμου καὶ τῶν προφητῶν, δικαιοσύνη δὲ θεοῦ διὰ πίστεως Ἰησοῦ Χριστοῦ εἰς πάντας τοὺς πιστεύοντας (Rom 3:21-22a). [Note on μαρτυρουμένη: This participle is a concessive adverbial participle (see *Int*.1.2.2.4). It is generally translated as: "although ... bear witness," or "although being witnessed to ..."] **25.** καὶ οἱ ἀστέρες ἔσονται ἐκ τοῦ οὐρανοῦ πίπτοντες, καὶ αἱ δυνάμεις αἱ ἐν τοῖς οὐρανοῖς σαλευθήσονται. καὶ τότε ὄψονται τὸν υἱὸν τοῦ ἀνθρώπου ἐρχόμενον ἐν νεφέλαις μετὰ δυνάμεως πολλῆς καὶ δόξης (Mark 13:25-26).

Chapter 29: Translation of John 1-11

It is now time to spoil ourselves. Most people learn Koine Greek so that they can read the Greek New Testament, and after a good deal of effort your grammar is now to a level where you can handle many of the texts that might be put before you. Now is the time to reap the benefit of all that hard work, and to translate your first extended passage – chapters one through eleven of the Gospel of John. Many of these passages will be old friends from previous exercises, but now they can all be linked together. John 1-11 has been divided into 3 sections (John 1-2, 3-6 and 7-11), each of which has an associated vocabulary. Notes have also been provided to explain points of grammar that have not yet been met [the references in square brackets give the place where the appropriate grammar or syntax is covered in *Intermediate New Testament Greek Made Easier*], as well as point to some other features of the set passage that is of interest or provides difficulty for beginners.

Vocabulary 29.1 (For John 1-2)

ἀδελφή (26)   sister
ἀληθινός (28)   true, genuine
ἀληθῶς (18)   adv.: truly, really
ἄξιος, -α, -ον (41) worthy, befitting
ἀρνέομαι (32)   I deny
ἀσθενέω (33)   I am sick, weak
ἐγγύς (31)   adv.: near
ἔρημος, ἡ (47)   desert, wilderness [declined like λογος, but feminine]
θύρα (39)   door
κλάω (14)   I break
κλαίω (38)   I weep
κλείω (16)   I shut, lock
μνημεῖον (37)   tomb, grave
ναός (45) temple, inner part of temple
ὀπίσω (35) prep. + gen.: after, behind, away from; adv.: back, behind
οὐκέτι (48) adv.: no longer, no more
πάντοτε (41)   always
παρρησία (31) openness; ἐν παρρησία be known publicly
πρό + gen (47) before

πρόβατον (37) sheep
φαίνω (31) I give light; mid.: appear
χρεία (49) need, necessity

Notes on Translation Passage 29.1: John 1-2

Chapter 1
1:1 καὶ θεὸς ἦν ὁ λόγος. This is a much-discussed phrase. Jehovah's Witnesses, for example, would like to translate this as "... and the word was a god." This is less likely than the translation "the word was divine," or "the word was God." Elsewhere in John, the article can be included where a specific reference is intended, and omitted where a generalized reference is meant (cf. John 9:5 ὅταν ἐν τῷ κόσμῳ ὦ, φῶς εἰμι τοῦ κόσμου – where φῶς is used without the article, in a generic sense, although it would be translated "the light" in English). Further, that John can use two articles with the verb εἰμί is evident (e.g. καὶ ἡ ζωὴ ἦν τὸ φῶς τῶν ἀνθρώπων in 1:4). There are occasions, though, where one article is omitted with the verb εἰμι to indicate which is the subject of the verb: e.g. 3:29 ὁ ἔχων τὴν νύμφην νυμφίος ἐστίν or 3:6 τὸ γεγεννημένον ἐκ τοῦ σαρκὸς σάρξ ἐστιν, καὶ τὸ γεγεννημένον ἐκ τοῦ πνεύματος πρεῦμά ἐστιν. By Colwell's law [see *Int*.6.8.2] the phrase καὶ θεὸς ἦν ὁ λόγος could have any one of the three translations mentioned above, only context will determine which is correct. On the other hand, it is hard to imagine that a Gospel which includes Thomas's confession, Ὁ κύριός μου καὶ ὁ θεός μου (20:28), would hesitate to attribute full divinity to Jesus.

1:3 The small letters [c] [d] etc. in the UBS text indicates that there is some variation between translators in the way they punctuate vv. 3-4. Either is possible, and only your sense of how the text should read will tell you what you prefer. Punctuation marks were added hundreds of years after the Gospel of John was written.

1:6 ἀπεσταλμένος is the nom. masc. sing. perf. part. pass. of ἀποστέλλω.

1:13 Notice the connection between οἳ ... ἐγεννήθησαν, "those who were born."

1:15 Ὁ ὀπίσω μου ἐρχόμενος ἔμπροσθέν μου γέγονεν, ὅτι πρῶτός μου ἦν: With difficult texts it is sometimes a good idea to go back to first principles (i.e. first look for the main verb, then the subject, then the direct object, etc....). The main verb is γέγονεν, the perfect of γίνομαι, a verb which has a range of meanings, but which has the root meaning of "become." The subject of the sentence is Ὁ ... ἐρχόμενος, "the one who comes." Thus the basic sentence might read: "The one who comes has become ..." The direct object of the sentence is ἔμπροσθέν [μου]. Adding the last phrase:

"The one who comes after me has become before me, because he was my πρῶτος. This last word, πρῶτος, may hold the clue to the meaning of the sentence: it could either be a reference to time (cf. John 8:58 "Before Abraham was, I am"), or a reference to status – Jesus was more important than John the Baptist. As with many other sentences and phrases in John, the phrase might be deliberately constructed so as to carry both meanings. Alas, one cannot adequately translate this kind of ambiguity (which is, after all, why you are learning Greek, so that you can recover some of the dimensions of the original language that are lost in translation). You will have to choose which of these possibilities attracts you most, and translate in a manner which carries that idea, and which is still good English.

1:18 μονογενὴς θεός vs μονογενὴς υἱὸς θεοῦ vs ὁ μονογενής There is a small footnote number next to the word θεὸς in this verse in the UBS text. The footnote indicates that the editors thought that this reading had a probability rating of "B" ("A" being a near certain reading, "B" a most probable reading, "C" a likely reading, "D" a reading about which it is impossible to be sure). Several of the ancient manuscripts have different readings for this verse. The editors preferred μονογενὴς θεός, probably on the grounds of its wider attestation, the fact that other variants can be explained as being derived from this reading, and because it is the more difficult reading (it is unlikely that the difficulty would have been introduced, it is more likely it would have been removed). There is ongoing academic dabate about this particular variant. On the other hand, that the Fourth Gospel is comfortable with attributing the epithet θεός to Jesus is clear from John 20:28.

1:24 ἀπεσταλμένοι This is the perfect passive participle of ἀποστέλλω [check out στέλλω in the verb chart in Appendix C].

1:28 ἦν ... βαπτίζων, "was baptising." The participle is used with the verb εἰμί. This kind of construction is called a periphrastic tense, and is used as it is in English—to stress the continuous nature of the action [see *Int*.3.7].

1:29 The dative case of Τῇ ἐπαύριον is a locative dative with respect to time [see *Int*.5.4.4]. Translate "On the next day."

1:30 ὑπέρ + acc. means "over and above, beyond," + gen. "for, in behalf of, because of." Here it is perhaps best translated "concerning" or "about." See also the comments on v. 15.

1:31, 33, 34 κἀγώ = καὶ ἐγώ, "and I"

1:31, 33 ᾔδειν is the [1st pers. sing.] pluperfect [ind. act.] of the verb οἶδα. This verb uses the perfect tense for present meaning. The pluperfect is the past tense which corresponds with the perfect tense. Thus, this should be translated as a past tense. With the οὐ, this might be translated as: "did not know" (v. 33).

1:35 As in 1:29, the dative case of Τῇ ἐπαύριον is a locative dative with respect to time [see *Int*.5.4.4]. Translate "On the next day." εἱστήκει is the [3rd pers. sing.] pluperfect [ind. act.] of ἵστημι. The perfect active of ἵστημι (i.e. ἕστηκα, ...) is intransitive (I stood), and used with present tense meaning. The pluperfect is the past tense that corresponds to the perfect tense, thus this should be translated as a past tense: "was standing."

1:43 As in 1:29 & 1:35, the dative case of Τῇ ἐπαύριον is a locative dative with respect to time [see *Int*.5.4.4]. Translate "On the next day." The verb θέλω is irregular in both its imperfect (ἤθελον) and, as in this verse, its aorist (ἠθέλησα).

1:48 Πρὸ τοῦ + inf. (φωνῆσαι) is used of antecedent time "before" [see *Int*.1.3.3]

1:50 μείζω is followed by a genitive of comparison (τούτων) [see *Int*.5.3.5]

1:51 ἀνεῳγότα is the perf. part. of ἀνοίγω.

Chapter 2

2:1 τῇ ἡμέρᾳ τῇ τρίτῃ is a locative dative, giving location in time [see *Int*.5.4.4]

2:3 ὑστερήσαντος οἴνου is a genitive absolute (a participle and other nouns etc. in the genitive [see *Int*.1.2.3]). In this case, translate as for a temporal adverbial participle – "After they ran short of wine ..."

2:4 Τί ἐμοὶ καὶ σοί, γύναι; This is an idiomatic phrase found elsewhere in the Greek New Testament, and also in the LXX. Cf. Mark 5:7, 2 Sam 16:10. In the society in which Jesus lived he was under strong obligation to render obedience to his mother. Perhaps he was pointing out to her that she had no right to make this request of him on the basis of her family relationship.

2:9 γεγενημένον is the perfect participle of γίνομαι; the participle is used in an adjectival sense here [see *Int*.1.2.1]: οἶνον γεγενημένον means "which had become wine" [the tense of a participle is with respect to the action of the main verb, which is aorist, thus "have" becomes "had" (see *Int*.1.2.5)]. The verbs ᾔδει, ᾔδεισαν are both pluperfect forms of the verb οἶδα which has perfect form and present meaning. Pluperfects are used as the past tense for this verb [see *Int*.3.5.3].

2:15 τε ... καί "both ... and"

2:17 γεγραμμένον ἐστίν is a perfect periphrastic construction, literally "has been written" [see *Int*.3.7]

2:22 καί ... καί "both ... and"

2:24 διὰ τὸ αὐτὸν γινώσκειν πάντας This is an articular infinitive construction (which just means that the article is used with an infinitive). The rule is that the infinitive is considered to be neuter, and the subject is expressed in the accusative (!) case. διὰ τὸ + infinitive = because [see *Int*.1.3.3]. Thus, the phrase might be best translated, "because he knew all [men/things]."

2:25 οὐ χρείαν εἶχεν ἵνα τις μαρτυρήσῃ περὶ τοῦ ἀνθρώπου: the subordinate conjunction ἵνα is usually used to form a final or purpose clause ("in order that"), but sometimes the ἵνα-clause acts as the complement of a verb [see comments on ἵνα in *Int*.6.12]. In such cases ἵνα is often best translated by the word "that," although "for" works best with the English expression "to have need": "He did not have need of anybody to bear witness to him about humans."

Vocabulary 29.2 (For John 3-6)

ἀγοράζω [+ gen.] (30) I buy
ἅπας, ἅπασα, ἅπαν (32) all, whole; pl.: everyone, everything [alternative form of πᾶς]
διάβολος (37) devil
διέρχομαι (42) I go through [διά + ἔρχομαι]
ἐκπορεύομαι (33) I come/go forth
ἔτος, -ους, το (49) year
εὐθέως (33)   adv.: immediately, at once
εὐχαριστέω (38) I give thanks
μικρός, -ά, -όν (46) little, small
οἶνος (34)   wine
ὁμοίως (31)   adv.: in the same way, likewise, similarly [cf. ὅμοιος]
παραγίνομαι (36) I come, arrive
πειράζω (38) I test, tempt
πέντε (38)   five
σωτηρία (45) salvation
χείρων (11)   worse [irregular comparative of κακος]

Notes on Translation Passage 29.2: John 3-6

Chapter 3

3:1 Ἦν is used impersonally: "There was." αὐτῷ is a dative of possession [see *Int*.5.4.5].

3:2 νυκτός: the genitive is used to convey the concept of time [see *Int*.5.3.6]. Translate as "by night."

3:3 γεννηθῇ 3rd pers. sing. aor. subj. pass. of γεννάω. The word ἄνωθεν means both "from above" (cf. ἄνω in 2:7, and other words which have a -θεν ending which indicate direction [e.g. ἐκεῖθεν from ἐκεῖ]), and "again." It is clear from the context that Jesus intends Nicodemus to understand that he must be born "from above" (cf. John 3:31; 19:11), but Nicodemus gets it all wrong. He (as a Jewish leader) is at this time thinking in terms of "below." He can only ask how is it possible to be born "again."

3:8 πνεῦμα means both spirit and wind, and the meaning of this verse depends on this double meaning. Because English uses different words and the connection is lost, it is not possible to translate this ambiguity into English.

3:16 ἀπόληται is the aor. subj. middle of ἀπόλλυμι. The middle voice is used here to indicate something of benefit (or detriment) to the subject of the verb – those believing. Chrys Caragounis points out that this verse is one of only two places in the NT where ὥστε is followed by an indicative (rather than an infinitive; the other is Gal 2:13). In classical usage ὥστε + indicative "expressed an actual occurrence" while ὥστε + subj. "expressed only a resulting possibility," although he goes on to say that in the NT ὥστε + inf. "are used mostly to express actual result" [Chrys C. Caragounis, *The Development of Greek and the New Testament* (Tübingen: Mohr Siebeck, 2006), 182-83; see also *Int*.1.3.6]. It is likely that in this verse the indicative is chosen over the infinitive to emphasise the reality of the result.

3:28 Ἀπεσταλμένος see comments on John 1:24

Chapter 4

4:3 ἔδει is the imperf. ind. active of the impersonal verb δεῖ, "it is necessary," although as ἔδει is in the imperfect tense, it should be translated "it was necessary."

4:6 κεκοπιακώς is the nom. masc. sing. perf. part. active of κοπιάω, "I work hard; grow weary." This is a causal adverbial participle [see *Int*.1.2.2.2], translate as: "... because he had grown weary ..."

4:8 ἀπεληλύθεισαν is the 3rd pers. pl. strong pluperfect indicative active of ἀπέρχομαι, "I leave" [see *Int*.4.8 on pluperfects]. Translate: "... had gone ..."

4:9 Both ὤν and οὔσης are concessive participles [see *Int*.1.2.2.4]. Just translate the the first participle thus: "... although you are a Jew ..."

4:10 The ἄν indicates that this is a contrary to fact conditional sentence [see *Int*.2.2.2]. On the second person form ᾔδεις see on ᾔδειν, the equivalent first person form in 1:31, 33 above.

4:12 μή is used in questions that expect an answer of "no" [see *Int*.6.2].

4:31, 40 ἠρώτων is not a participle! Do you recognize it? [It is the imperfect. The verb ἐρωτάω contracts.]

4:42 αὐτοὶ γὰρ ἀκηκόαμεν For we ourselves [αὐτος used in the sense of "self"] have heard ...

4:44 αὐτὸς ... Ἰησοῦς "Jesus himself"

4:46 ἠσθενεῖ is from ἀσθενέω

4:47 ἠρώτα is the 3rd pers. sing. imperf. ind. act. of ἐρωτάω. As the next word begins with a vowel, ἠρώτα-ε-(ν) drops the ν. The α + ε contract to α.

4:49 πρίν + inf. = before [see *Int*.1.3.3].

4:51 ἤδη δὲ αὐτοῦ καταβαίνοντος — the participle and pronoun in this phrase are in the genitive case. It is an example of a special construction called a genitive absolute [see *Int*.1.2.3]. Translate "While he was going down ..."

Chapter 5
5:2 ἔστιν is used impersonally: "There is ..."
5:4 The best manuscripts omit this verse (see discussion of text criticism in *Intermediate New Testament Greek Made Easier* Chapter 38).
5:7 ἄνθρωπον οὐκ ἔχω ἵνα ὅταν ταραχθῇ τὸ ὕδωρ βάλῃ με εἰς τὴν κολυμβήθραν: the subordinate conjunction ἵνα is usually used to form a final or purpose clause ("in order that"), but sometimes the ἵνα-clause is used where otherwise one might expect an infinitive [see comments on ἵνα in *Int*.6.12]. Here ἵνα ... βάλῃ could be translated "to put."
5:10 ἆραι is the aor. inf. act. of αἴρω (see principal parts in Appendix C).
5:13 ᾔδει is the 3rd pers. sing. pluperfect. ind. act. of οἶδα, which while perfect in form is present in meaning. The pluperfect is the past tense of οἶδα, translated as "knew" [see *Int*.4.8] Translate ὄχλου ὄντος ἐν τῷ τόπῳ as, "Because there was a crowd in that place" (this is a genitive absolute construction, used as a causal adverbial clause — [see *Int*.1.2.2.3; *Int*.1.2.3; *Int*.2.6]).
5:17 κἀγώ = καὶ ἐγώ, "and I," or, in this instance, "I also."
5:29 The tense of a participle is with respect to the action of the main verb [see *Int*.3.3]. The the two aorist participles ποιήσαντες, πράξαντες are prior to the action of the main verb, ἐκπορεύσονται, which has a future tense. Thus the deeds which determine whether one partakes of the resurrection of life or the resurrection of judgment could be future actions. They include all actions prior to the future resurrection.
5:35 The verb θέλω has an irregular augment for both the imperfect (ἤθελον) and the aorist (ἠθέλησα).
5:36 μείζω: "greater than," irregular comparative of μέγας [see *Int*.6.7.2]; the genitive case of τοῦ Ἰωαννου is a genitive of comparison [see *Int*.5.3.5].
5:44 λαμβάνοντος should be translated "since you receive" (it is a causal adverbial participle [see *Int*.1.2.2.2])
5:46 The ἄν indicates a contrary to fact conditional sentence (cf. John 4:10 [see *Int*.2.2.2])

Chapter 6
6:6 ᾔδει: see on John 1:31, 33 [see also *Int*.3.5.3.2]
6:11 The verb θέλω has an irregular augment for both the imperfect (ἤθελον) and the aorist (ἠθέλησα).
6:15 γνούς: is a causal adverbial participle [see *Int*.1.2.2.2]; translate, "Because [Jesus] knew"

6:17 ἐγεγόνει is the 3rd pers. sing. pluperfect ind. act. of γίνομαι, and ἐληλύθει is the 3rd pers. sing. pluperfect ind. act. of ἔρχομαι The pluperfect is the past tense associated with the perfect tense, translated as "had ..." [see *Int*.3.5.3]. Here, "had already become dark," and "had come" respectively.

6:18 ἀνέμου μεγάλου πνέοντος is a genitive absolute construction [see *Int*.1.2.3]. Here in a causal adverbial sense: "because a great wind was blowing"

6:19 ἐληλακότες is the perf. part. act. of ἐλαύνω.

6:21 The verb θέλω has an irregular augment for both the imperfect (ἤθελον) and the aorist (ἠθέλησα).

6:22 Τῇ ἐπαύριον — the dative case is sometimes used with reference to location in time [see on 1:35, 43, etc. and *Int*.5.4.4]. ἐπαυριον does not decline.

6:29 τοῦτό ἐστιν τὸ ἔργον τοῦ θεοῦ, ἵνα πιστεύητε εἰς ὃν ἀπέστειλεν ἐκεῖνος: the subordinate conjunction ἵνα is usually used to form a final or purpose clause ("in order that"), but sometimes the ἵνα-clause acts as the complement of a verb [see comments on ἵνα in *Int*.6.12]. In such cases ἵνα is often best translated by the word "that." Thus this phrase might be translated, "This is the work of God, that you believe in the one who he sent."

6:37 ἥξει: "will have come." It is the future of the verb ἥκω. This verb has a perfect meaning in the present tense, and preserves it in the future. The form here is not to be confused with ἕξω (the fut. of ἔχω, I have) or ἄξω (the future of ἄγω, I lead).

6:39 τοῦτο δέ ἐστιν τὸ θέλημα τοῦ πέμψαντός με, ἵνα πᾶν ὃ δέδωκέν μοι μὴ ἀπολέσω ἐξ αὐτοῦ: the subordinate conjunction ἵνα is usually used to form a final or purpose clause ("in order that"), but sometimes the ἵνα-clause acts as the complement of a verb [see comments on ἵνα in *Int*.6.12]. In such cases ἵνα is often best translated by the word "that." Thus this phrase might be translated, "This is the will of the one who sent me, that I should loose nothing of all that he has given me" [cf. v. 29].

6:40 This is another example where ἵνα should be translated as "that" [cf. 6:29, 39].

6:44 κἀγώ = καὶ ἐγώ, "and I"

6:46 οὐχ ὅτι ... τις "not that anyone"

6:54, 56, 57 κἀγώ = καὶ ἐγώ, "and I"

6:57 κἀκεῖνος = καὶ ἐκεῖνος, "and that one / he"

6:64 ᾔδει: see on John 1:31, 33 [see also *Int*.3.5.3.2]

6:65 ᾖ δεδομένον: is a perfect passive subjunctive, which is formed periphrastically (i.e. with a perfect participle and a subjunctive of the verb εἰμί [for periphrastic tenses see *Int*.3.7; for the perfect passive form of the subjunctive see Appendix B]).

Part 4   277

6:67 μή is used in questions to either indicate an answer "no," or to indicate uncertainty [see *Int*.6.3].

Vocabulary 29.3 (For John 7-11)

ἀπαγγέλλω (45)   I announce, report
βλασφημέω (34)   I blaspheme, slander, insult
δέω (41)   I bind
διδαχή (30)   teaching
ἐπιθυμία (38)   desire
κρατέω [+ gen.] (47) I grasp, hold
λογίζομαι (40)   I consider, reckon
περιτέμνω (17)   I circumcise [περί + τέμνω (τέμνω = I cut)]
περιτομή (35)   circumcision
πλανάω (39)   I lead astray, deceive
σπέρμα, ατος, το (44) seed, offspring
τρίτος, -η, -ον (56) third

[note: vocabulary entries to this point cover all words listed in Kubo as occurring over 50 times, and all listed in Metzger as occurring over 46 times (the number of occurrences listed for each word at times differs slightly between Metzger and Kubo). The vocabularies for Parts 1-4 accounts for 90,590 words of the approximately 137,500 words in the Greek New Testament, or about 66% of the total.]

Notes on Translation Passage 29.3: John 7-11

Chapter 7
7:1 The verb θέλω has an irregular augment for both the imperfect (ἤθελον) and the aorist (ἠθέλησα).
7:3 If you have problems parsing Μετάβηθι, you may wish to check the imperative of βαίνω as it is listed in 26.3.
7:15 οἶδεν μὴ μεμαθηκώς "<u>Since</u> we know he has not learned": the perfect participle μεμαθηκώς carries a <u>concessive</u> meaning in this verse [see *Int*.1.2.2.4].
7:30 ἐληλύθει, which has already been met at John 6:17, is the 3rd pers. sing. pluperfect ind. act. of ἔρχομαι. The pluperfect is the past tense associated with the perfect tense, translated as "had ..." [see *Int*.3.5.3.1]. Here, "had already become dark," and "had come" respectively.
7:31 μή in questions: see comments on John 7:52. ὧν is a genitive of comparison [see *Int*.5.3.5]: "than those which ..."
7:35 μή in questions: see comments on John 7:52

7:37 εἱστήκει: see comments on John 1:35
7:41 μή in questions: see comments in John 7:52
7:44 The verb θέλω has an irregular augment for both the imperfect (ἤθελον) and the aorist (ἠθέλησα).
7:45 Διά τί = "why?"
7:46 οὕτως is an adverb. Thus the phrase Οὐδέποτε ἐλάλησεν οὕτως conveys a meaning something like: "No man spoke in this way at any [previous] time."
7:48, 51 μή in questions expects an answer "no" (cf. 7:52).
7:52 Μὴ καὶ σὺ ἐκ τῆς Γαλιλαίας εἶ; "Are you also a Galilean?" Μή is used in questions which expect an answer "no," or which are purely suppositional ("perhaps" [see *Int*.6.3]). Frequently the μή in these kinds of questions should not be translated. Here is a further example where the one who reads the Greek has extra information unavailable to the English-only reader. One can hear the incredulity or sarcasm in the question with its negative answer.

Chapter 8

[Note: if you are using Kubo you will notice that the vocabulary listing for 7:53–8:11 is relegated to a list at the end of the Gospel of John. The UBS Greek New Testament places brackets around this section, although it is considered an "A" (i.e. virtually certain) reading. Some early manuscripts omit this section, while others have it at different places in John, or Luke's Gospel. Major commentaries carry comments on whether or not this passage should be included, and most conclude that the omission of the passage is an early example of censorship. Indeed, it is hard to imagine anybody in the early church making up such a story about Jesus.]

8:2 Ὄρθρος means "dawn, early morning." Note the use of the genitive for time [see *Int*.5.3.6]: "When it was dawn ..."
8:5 λιθάζειν This infinitive is used to give the content of the command of Moses [see *Int*.1.3.8 and cf. the usage of κελεύω in *Int*.1.3.1].
8:6 τῷ δακτύλῳ This is an example of the instrumental dative [see *Int*.5.4.3]: "with his finger."
8:9 εἷς καθ' εἷς. The καθ' is actually κατά: the "'" indicating that the vowel is omitted, while the τ becomes θ in front of a hard breathing. This is the distributive use of κατά [see *Int*.6.11.2], and the phrase should be translated "one by one."
8:12 οὐ μὴ περιπατήσῃ. Οὐ μή is used with the subjunctive to express strong denial. It can be seen that the subjunctive indicates potential, because in English it feels most natural to translate this as a future. This is often the case with subjunctives.
8:14 κἄν = καὶ ἐάν, "even if ..."

8:16, 18 ὁ πέμψας με πατήρ: "he who sent me, the father." πατήρ is used in apposition here – it adds further information as to the "he."

8:19 ἤδειτε is the pluperfect of οἶδα. See on 1:31, 33

8:20 ἐληλύθει is the 3rd pers. sing. pluperfect ind. act. of ἔρχομαι, "had come" [see *Int*.3.5.3.1]

8:22 Μήτι is used rather like μή in questions (see comments on 7:52): it is used to indicate that the answer to the question is "no," or to indicate uncertainty, in which case it is translated "perhaps." In this instance, "perhaps" is probably the best translation.

8:25 Τὴν ἀρχὴν ὅ τι καὶ λαλῶ ὑμῖν; As indicated in the textual apparatus of the UBS Greek New Testament, there are two possible ways to translate this passage, one using the text as written, another, reading ὅ τι as ὅτι (which is perfectly possible because the original manuscripts were all majuscules; in other words, they were written all in capital letters with no spaces between the words). Neither option appeals immediately to the beginning student. Possible translations range from "Why should I speak to you at all?" (NEB) to "What I told you from the beginning" (RSV; which takes the accusative as a reference to the extent of time, [see *Int*.5.2.7]).

8:26 κἀγώ = καὶ ἐγώ, "and I"

8:31 τοὺς πεπιστευκότας: the action of a participle is with respect to the action of the main verb [see *Int*.1.2.5; *Int*.3.4], which in this case is Ἔλεγεν, and in a past tense. Thus the perfect participle is perfect with respect to a past event, and τοὺς πεπιστευκότας should be translated as "those who had believed in him" (*not* "those who have believed in him").

8:39 has an interesting textual variant, for which the UBS gives a C rating. The reading accepted takes the sentence as a simple condition, the variant adds ἄν, which makes the sentence a contrary to fact condition [see *Int*.2.2.1 and *Int*.2.2.2]. If it was decided that the variant was correct, and that the sentence was a contrary to fact condition, then Jesus would be making the telling point that his listeners were *not*, in fact, children of Abraham.

8:42 Εἰ ... ἄν ἐμε is a contrary to fact condition [see *Int*.2.2.2]; Jesus implies that because his hearers do not love him, they do not, in fact, have God as their father.

8:42 καλῶς is an adverb, meaning "well, correctly," and modifies the verb λέγομεν. Thus καλῶς λέγομεν might be translated, "did we not correctly say," or in more natural English, "were we not right in saying."

8:50 ἔστιν is best translated impersonally here: "There is ..."

8:51 οὐ μὴ θεωρήσῃ See comments on 8:12.

8:53 μὴ in a question expects the answer, "no" [see *Int*.6.2]

8:55 κἄν = καὶ ἐάν, "even if ..." πρίν + inf. = "before"

8:56 Ἀβραὰμ ... ἠγαλλιάσατο <u>ἵνα ἴδῃ</u> τὴν ἡμέραν τὴν ἐμή: the subordinate conjunction ἵνα is usually used to form a final or purpose clause ("in order that"), but sometimes the ἵνα-clause acts as the complement of a verb as a substitute for an infinitive [see comments on ἵνα in *Int*.6.12]. This sentence could be translated "Abraham ... rejoiced <u>to see</u> my day." ἐχάρη is the 3rd pers. sing. strong aorist passive-deponent of χαίρω.

Chapter 9

9:2 <u>ἵνα</u> τυφλὸς <u>γεννηθῇ</u>; A ἵνα-clause is usually a purpose clause [see *Int*.2.4.1]; here, though, it is a result clause [see *Int*.2.5]. This is adequately expressed in English as "... <u>so that</u> <u>he was born</u> blind."

9:3 By way of contrast to v. 2, the ἵνα-clause in this verse is clearly a purpose clause [see *Int*.2.4.1], as are the vast majority of ἵνα-clauses.

9:6 ἐπέχρισεν αὐτοῦ: αὐτοῦ is in the genitive case, because ἐπιχρίω, like other verbs of touching and laying hold of, takes the genitive [see *Int*.5.3.3].

9:7 νίψαι: is an infinitive of purpose [see *Int*.1.3.5]

9:8 Οὐχ is used in questions that expect an answer "yes" [see *Int*.6.3].

9:11 ἀπελθὼν ... καὶ νιψάμενος are both in the aorist tense. The tense of participles is usually with respect to the action of the main verb [see *Int*.3.4], which in this case is the aorist ἀνέβλεψα, the action taking place in the past. Thus ἀπελθὼν ... καὶ νιψάμενος might be translated, "When I <u>had</u> gone ... and <u>had</u> washed."

9:18 ἕως ὅτου: "until" [see *Int*.2.2.1.iii]

9:22 συνετέθειντο is the pluperfect middle of συντίθημι, which in the middle voice means to make an agreement, agree, decide: "they had decided" [see *Int*.3.5.3.2 for pluperfect tenses]; <u>ἵνα</u> ἐάν τις αὐτὸν ὁμολογήσῃ χριστόν, ἀποσυνάγωγος γένηται: the subordinate conjunction ἵνα is usually used to form a final or purpose clause ("in order that"), but sometimes the ἵνα-clause acts as the complement of a verb [see comments on ἵνα in *Int*.6.12]. In such cases ἵνα is often best translated by the word "that." Thus this phrase might be translated, "For the Jews had already decided <u>that</u> if anyone ..." [cf. v. 6:29, 39].

9:28-29 Both the genitive (Μωϋσέως) and the dative (Μωϋσεῖ) of Μωϋσῆς is found in the space of two verses [see 4.4].

9:31 The verb ἀκούω should take the genitive of the person heard, and the accusative of what was heard [see Chap. 11 & *Int*.5.3.3].

9:41 Εἰ τυφλοὶ ἦτε, οὐκ ἂν εἴχετε ἁμαρτίαν is a contrary to fact condition–the Pharisees were not physically blind. That the construction is contrary to fact is indicated by the ἄν in the apodosis (the "then clause") [see *Int*.2.2.2].

Chapter 10

10:3 The verb ἀκουω here takes the genitive of the person heard, and the accusative of what was heard [see *Int*.5.3.3].

10:4 αὐτῷ: The verb ἀκολουθέω takes a dative [see *Int*.5.4.10].
10:15 κἀγώ = καὶ ἐγώ, "and I"
10:16 κἀκεῖνα = καὶ ἐκεῖνα.
10:20 αὐτοῦ: the verb ἀκούω here takes the genitive of the person heard [see on 9:31 & *Int*.5.3.3].
10:21 μή in a question expects the answer "no" [see *Int*.7.3].
10:24 παρρησίᾳ is a dative of manner [see *Int*.5.4.9].
10:27, 28 κἀγώ = καὶ ἐγώ, "and I"
10:33 ὤν is a concessive participle: "although you are [a man]" [see *Int*.1.2.2.4].
10:35 Notice that both ἐκείνους and θεούς are in the accusative. Some verbs take two accusatives [see *Int*.5.2.3], and λέγω is one of these. Thus this section of the verse might be translated: "If he calls them gods ..."
10:38 κἄν = καὶ ἐάν, "even if ..." You already know that the rather irregular aorist of γινώσκω is ἔγνων [see 28.2]. Thus you should recognize γνῶτε as the 2nd pers. pl. aor. subj. act. of γινώσκω. κἀγώ = καὶ ἐγώ, "and I"

Chapter 11

11:7 Ἄγωμεν is the 1st pers. sing. pres. subj. act. It illustrates a use of the subjunctive that is yet to be met, the so-called "hortatory" subjunctive [see *Int*.1.1.4]. It is best translated, "Let us go ..." The subjunctive is here used to express an exhortation (hence, it is called, hortatory).
11:13 εἰρήκει is the pluperfect ind. act. of λεγω, "he had spoken" [see *Int*.3.7].
11:16 See 11:7 on hortatory subjunctives.
11:18 Note the use of the genitive, τῶν Ἱεροσολύμων to indicate spatial separation (i.e. distance; [see *Int*.5.3.4]).
11:19 ἐληλύθεισαν is the 3rd pers. pl. pluperfect ind. act. of ἔρχομαι. The pluperfect in the past tense associated with the perfect tense, and thus this might be translated, "they had come."
11:21 The ἄν indicates a contrary to fact conditional sentence (cf. John 4:10; 5:46 [see *Int*.2.2.2]).
11:25 κἄν = καὶ ἐάν, "even if ..."
11:28 εἰποῦσα: εἰπών, the nom. masc. sing. aor. part. of λέγω, has become very familiar. Here, though, is found the feminine form of the participle; it is feminine because Martha is speaking.
11:29 ἠγέρθη is a passive form of ἐγείρω. The passive of this verb can sometimes be used intransitively – "she got up."
11:30 ἐληλύθει is the 3rd pers. sing. pluperfect ind. act. of ἔρχομαι. See on 11:19.
11:35 Ἴδε is the aor. imperative act. of ὁράω.
11:38 ἐπέκειτο. κεῖμαι is used for the passive voice of τιθημι.
11:42 ᾔδειν is the pluperfect of οἶδα. See on 1:31, 33.

11:44 περιεδέδετο is the 3rd pers. sing. pluperfect ind. pass. of περιδίδομι, "had been wrapped" [see *Int*.3.5.3.1].

11:50, 53 Just as in John 6:29, 39; 9:22, the two uses of ἵνα in these verses are probably best translated by the word "that." The ἵνα in v. 52, on the other hand, is expresses purpose, "in order that."

11:54 κἀκεῖ = καὶ ἐκεῖ, "and there."

11:57 δεδώκεισαν is the 3rd pers. pl. pluperfect ind. act. of δίδωμι, "had given" [see *Int*.3.5.3.1]. Just as in John 6:29, 39; 9:22, the ἵνα in this verses is probably best translated by the word "that."

Part 4   283

Chapter 30: Comprehensive Review of Parts 1-4

It is time to congratulate yourself. You now know enough grammar to successfully translate long passages from John and the other Gospels. Looking back over the early chapters of the book will show you just how far you have come from the time you began learning the Greek alphabet. Well done! Of course, there is more to do before you will be comfortable with Paul's letters and Acts, and *Intermediate New Testament Greek Made Easier* will provide a natural next step in that process. It will give you a more sophisticated and methodical grasp of Greek grammar which should allow you to translate just about anything in the Greek New Testament. But that is for the future. For now it is desirable to gather up all the things that have been learnt so far and ensure that they are well established in both memory and understanding.

30.1 Verbs

A verb may be used to express an action, an intention, a state of being, or a state of mind. In NT Greek, verbs decline to differentiate tense, mood and voice.

30.1.1 Tense

Tenses are used in NT Greek to indicate *type of action*, and in the indicative and participial moods, whether the *time of the action* is past, present or future. In the indicative mood, the aorist, imperfect, perfect [and pluperfect] tenses represent different types of action in past time, the present tense represents action in the present time, and the future tense represents action in the future. In the infinitive, subjunctive and imperative moods, the distinction between present and aorist tenses is often represents a difference in the kind of action envisioned. The present tense almost always denotes a continuous (or repeated) action, while the aorist tense often denotes punctiliar action. With participles the present, aorist or future tenses are often used to indicate the time of the action of the verb in the participle relative to the action of the main verb (see *Int*.3.5).

The following table lists the English tense which usually best translates each Greek tense:

Uses of Tenses in the Indicative Verb Covered in Parts 1-4			
Tense	Form of λύω	Closest English Tense(s)	Normal Translation
Indicative Active:			
Present	λύω	Simple present active Present continuous active Present emphatic active	I loose I am loosing I do loose
Imperfect	ἔλυον	Past continuous active Past inceptive	I was loosing I began loosing
Future	λύσω	Future active	I shall loose
Aorist	ἔλυσα	Simple past active	I loosed
Perfect	λέλυκα	Perfect active	I have loosed
Indicative Passive			
Present	λύομαι	Simple present passive Continuous present passive	I am loosed I am being loosed
Imperfect	ἐλυόμην	Past continuous passive Past inceptive passive	I was being loosed I began to be loosed
Future	λυθήσομαι	Future passive	I shall be loosed
Aorist	ἐλύθην	Simple past passive	I was loosed
Perfect	λέλυμαι	Perfect passive	I have been loosed

30.1.2 Mood

The following table lists the uses of the various moods of the verb in NT Greek to which you have been introduced:

Uses of Verb Moods Covered in Parts 1-4	
Mood	Principal uses of the mood
Indicative mood	The mood used for making statements of fact and asking questions
Imperative mood	The mood used for giving orders / making [strong] requests
Subjunctive mood	The mood used to express contingencies or possibilities. Often found after certain conjunctions and in association with certain particles (e.g. ἵνα, ἄν, ἐάν, οὐ μή, etc)

Infinitive mood	The mood used after certain verbs (e.g. θέλω, δύναμαι, δεῖ, ἔξεστιν, μέλλω, ἄρχομαι, etc). Often most easily translated by the English infinitive: "to ..."
Participial mood	A mood difficult to equate to one thing in English grammar. Used with the article to mean "the one who ..."; often best translated as a reference to time, "when ...," "while ..."; sometimes translated by the English participles, "... ing" (active), "... ed" (passive).

30.1.3 Principal Parts

Note: users of eBook will likely need to switch to landscape screen mode to see the entire table of principal parts.

Active Voice					Passive Voice	
Verb		Future	Aorist	Perfect	Perfect	Aorist
ἀγαπάω	love	ἀγαπήσω	ἠγάπησα	ἠγάπηκα	ἠγάπημαι	ἠγαπήθην
ἄγω	lead	ἄξω	ἤγαγον		ἦγμαι	ἤχθην
ἀκούω	hear	ἀκούσω	ἤκουσα	ἀκήκοα		ἠκούσθην
ἀφίημι	forgive	ἀφήσω	ἀφῆκα	ἀφεῖκα	ἀφέωμαι	ἀφέθην
-βαίνω	go	-βήσομαι	-ἔβην	-βέβηκα		
βάλλω	throw	βαλέω	ἔβαλον	βέβληκα	βέβλημαι	ἐβλήθην
γεννάω	beget	γεννήσω	ἐγέννησα	γεγέννηκα	γεγέννημαι	ἐγεννήθην
γίνομαι	become	γενήσομαι	ἐγενόμην	γέγονα	γεγένημαι	ἐγενήθην
γινώσκω	know	γνώσομαι	ἔγνων	ἔγνωκα	ἔγνωσμαι	ἐγνώσθην
δείκνυμι	show	δείξω	ἔδειξα		δέδειγμαι	ἐδείχθην
δίδωμι	give	δώσω	ἔδωκα	δέδωκα	δέδομαι	ἐδόθην
δύναμαι	am able	δυνήσομαι	ἐδυνήθην ἠδυνήθην			
ἐγείρω		ἐγερέω	ἤγειρα		ἐγήγερμαι	ἠγέρθην
ἔρχομαι	raise come	ἐλεύσομαι	ἦλθον	ἐλήλυθα		
ἐσθίω	eat	φάγομαι	ἔφαγον			
εὑρίσκω	find	εὑρήσω	εὗρον	εὕρηκα		εὑρέθην
ἔχω	have	ἕξω	ἔσχον	ἔσχηκα		
-θνῄσκω	die	-θανέομαι	-ἔθανον	τέθνηκα		
ἵστημι	place	στήσω	ἔστην.... ἔστησα..	ἕστηκα... -ἕστακα..	..(intrans.) ....(trans.)	ἐστάθην
καλέω	call	καλέσω	ἐκάλεσα	κέκληκα	κέκλημαι	ἐκλήθην

	Active Voice				Passive Voice	
Verb		Future	Aorist	Perfect	Perfect	Aorist
κρίνω	judge	κρινέω	ἔκρινα	κέκρικα	κέκριμαι	ἐκρίθην
λαλέω	speak	λαλήσω	ἐλάλησα	λελάληκα	λελάλημαι	ἐλαλήθην
λαμβάνω	take	λήμψομαι	ἔλαβον	εἴληφα	-εἴλημμαι	-ελήμφθην
λέγω	say	ἐρέω	εἶπον	εἴρηκα	εἴρημαι	ἐρρέθην
λύω	loose	λύσω	ἔλυσα	λέλυκα	λέλυμαι	ἐλύθην
μένω	remain	μενέω	ἔμεινα	μεμένηκα		
ὄλλυμι	destroy	ὀλέσω, ὀλέω	ὤλεσα	ὄλωλα		
ὁράω	see	ὄψομαι	εἶδον	ἑώρακα		ὤφθην
πίπτω	fall	πεσέομαι	ἔπεσα	πέπτωκα	πεπλήρωμαι	
πληρόω	fill, fulfil	πληρώσω	ἐπλήρωσα	πεπλήρωκα		ἐπληρώθην
στέλλω	send	-στελέω	-έστειλα	-έσταλκα	-έσταλμαι	-ἐστάλην
τίθημι	place	θήσω	ἔθηκα	τέθεικα	τέθειμαι	ἐτέθην
φέρω	bear	οἴσω	ἤνεγκα	-ενήνοχα		ἠνέχθην

Learning these principal parts thoroughly is an important step to mastering the language. Indeed students seeking a distinction or high distinction grade may well wish to learn the slightly fuller list of principal parts in Appendix C at this time. [Note: Appendix C in *Intermediate New Testament Greek Made Easier* gives further lists of principal parts, including two listings for irregular verbs that occur infrequently in the NT. Everybody will need to consult this appendix from time to time as they translate from the Greek NT.]

30.1.4 Voice

The Greek verb has three voices: active, middle, and passive. In the active voice the subject initiates the action inherent in the verb; in the middle voice the subject participates in the action, while in the passive voice the subject is the recipient of the action [see 24.1.1, 24.1.3 & 24.1.4]. On many, if not most, occasions, because English does not have a middle voice, the Greek middle voice is translated by the English active voice. This is also true of some passive verbs: they are translated by the English active voice. The word "deponent" is often used to describe such verbs. Note that the verb ἄρχω, which means "rule" in the active voice, means "begin" in the middle voice [see Vocab. 28], while the verb φαίνω "give light" means "appear" in the middle voice [see Vocab 29.1].

30.1.5 The Paradigm of the Verb

Much has been learned in early chapters about regular verbs, contracted verbs (i.e. those with verb stems ending in α, ε, ο [see 12.2.3, 15.1.3, 16.1.7,

25.2, 28.1 & Chaps. 5, 8]), verbs with stems that end in a guttural, labial or dental [see 12.2.2, 15.1.1, 15.1.5, 25.2], strong verbs [see 12.1, 15.1.2, 16.1.5] and -μι verbs [see 12.3.1, 16.1.7, 20.2.1 and Chap. 27]. The complete paradigm of the regular verb my be found in Appendix B, while the regular contractions used in the present and imperfect tenses (both active and passive) of the contracting verbs are given in Appendix G, the principal parts of the regular and irregular verbs are listed in Appendix C, and the paradigms of -μι verbs are given in Appendix D.

30.2 Nouns

A noun might be the name of an object or creature (in which case it is a common noun), the name of a collection of things or creatures (a collective noun), the name of a quality (an abstract noun), or the name of a place or a person (a proper noun). In NT Greek, nouns decline to differentiate five cases: nominative, vocative accusative, genitive and dative. Nouns formulate their cases in several ways. In ancient times, grammarians classified nouns as first, second and third declension nouns on the basis of similarities between various nouns in the way that they formed their cases. The three declensions of the noun are gathered in Appendix E. While there are some rare types of third declension nouns have not been met, essentially all the different types of nouns and adjectives have received treatment, and may be found gathered in that appendix.

30.2.1 Uses of Case

The following uses of these cases have been introduced [see 3.1.5, 3.2]:

Nominative:	Subject of verb
Vocative:	Used in direct speech directed to an individual
Accusative:	Direct object of verb, certain prepositions
Genitive:	Possessive, certain prepositions and verbs
Dative:	Indirect object, instrument, certain prepositions and verbs

30.3 Adjectives

An adjective is used to describe a noun more exactly. It has the effect of limiting the number of instances to which a noun might refer. For example, while the noun "man" might refer a very significant proportion of the population, far fewer would fit the description "good man," or "elderly man." The declension of adjectives of the second and first declension, and adjectives of the third and first declension may be found in Appendix E.

30.4 Conjunctions

Conjunctions are words that are used to join various grammatical units such as nouns, phrases and clauses. The conjunctions that have appeared in vocabularies are as follows:

ἀλλά [414] but, indeed
ἄρα, ἆρα [52] therefore, then
γάρ [990] for, since, indeed, certainly
δέ [2271] but, rather, and, moreover, then, now
διό [52] therefore, for this reason
ἐάν + subj. [306] if, even if
ἐὰν μή + subj. (47) unless
εἰ [535] if
ἕως [137] until, while
ἤ or, but
ἵνα + subj. [673] in order that, so that
καί [8947] and, also, even, and yet, however
μέν: μέν ... δέ [104] on the one hand ... on the other

μηδέ [57] and not, but not; not even [cf. οὐδέ]
ὅπου [82] where, whereas
ὅταν + subj. [123] whenever
ὅπως [52] in order that
ὅτε [102] when, while, whenever
ὅτι [1187] that, because
οὐδέ [139] and not, but not; not even [cf. μηδέ]
οὖν [490] therefore, then, thus, so
οὔτε ... οὔτε [91; 39 verses] neither ... nor
τότε [158] then, next, after that
ὡς [442] as, like; as long as, while, when; so that
ὥστε [673] with a result that, so

Note: the (postpositive) conjunctions δέ, γάρ, μέν, οὖν, τε are usually the second word in a sentence. They almost always should be appear first in the English translation.

30.5 Pronouns

A pronoun takes the place of a noun. The following pronouns have appeared in vocabularies:

First person pronoun: ἐγώ, ἐμέ or με, ἐμοῦ or μου, ἐμοί or μοι, ἡμεῖς, ἡμᾶς, ἡμῶν, ἡμῖν (I, me, my, to me, us, us, our, to us, resp.).

Second person pronoun: σύ, σέ or σε, σοῦ or σου, σοί or σοι, ὑμεῖς, ὑμᾶς, ὑμῶν, ὑμῖν (you, you, your, to you, you, you, your, to you, resp.).

Third person pronoun: αὐτός, ή, ό (he, she, it, etc.) [see Chap. 10]

The demonstrative adjectives οὗτος, η, ο (this, these) and ἐκεῖνος, η, ο (that, those) [often used as pronouns; see Chap. 13 and Vocab. 16]

Relative pronoun: ὅς, ἥ, ὅ (who, whom, whose, which, that) [see Chap. 18]

Interrogative pronoun: τίς, τί (who, what, which) [see 14.3.2]

Indefinite pronoun: τις, τι (a certain ...) [14.3.2]

Note: με, μου, μοι, σέ, σοῦ, σοῖ, τις, τι all throw their accents on the previous word if it is able to receive it (i.e., they are enclitic).

30.6 Prepositions

A preposition is used to show the relation between a noun and something else. Propositions may be used to express relationships in space or time. They are found before their nouns. The following prepositions have appeared in vocabularies:

ἀπό (645) + gen:	from, away from
διά (666) + acc:	because of, on account of
διά + gen:	through
εἰς (1753) + acc:	into, towards
ἐκ, ἐξ (915) + gen:	from, out of, away from
ἔμπροσθεν (48) prep:	+ gen: in front of, before
ἔμπροσθεν	adv: ahead, forward, in front
ἐν (2713) + dat:	in, by (instrument)
ἐνώπιον (93) + gen:	before, in the presence of
ἐπί (878) + acc:	**across**, to, against
ἐπί + gen:	**upon**, near, before, over, on the basis of, in the time of
ἐπί + dat:	**at**, by, **on**
κατά (471) + acc:	according to
κατά + gen:	down, against
μετά (467) + acc:	**after**, behind
μετά + gen:	**with**
ὀπίσω (35)	prep + gen: after, behind, away from
ὀπίσω:	adv: back, behind
παρά (191) + acc:	**by**, along, near, more than, against
παρά + gen:	from
παρά + dat:	**at**, by, beside, near
περί (331) + acc:	**around**, about, near
περί + gen:	**about**, concerning
πρό (47) + gen:	before
πρός (696) + acc:	toward, to, with, against
πρός + dat:	near, at, by
σύν (127) + dat:	with
ὑπέρ (149) + acc:	over and above, beyond
ὑπέρ + gen:	for, on behalf of, because of
ὑπό (217) + acc:	under, below
ὑπό + gen:	by [agent]
χωρίς (41):	prep + gen: without, apart from
χωρίς:	adv: separately, by itself

30.7 Adverbs

Adverbs, as their name suggests, modify the meaning of verbs. They are to be distinguished from adjectives which modify nouns. It can be important to keep in mind the relationship between an adverb and its verb when translating. The following adverbs have appeared in the vocabularies:

ἐκεί [104] there
ἔτι [82] still, yet
εὐθέως, εὐθύς [86] immediately
ἤδη [56] now, already
οὕτως [203] so, thus

πάλιν [136] again
πρῶτον [65] firstly
τότε [158] then
ὧδε [59] hither, here

30.8 Vocabulary

Appendix H gives a cumulative listing of all the vocabularies. It may be a good idea to cast your eye down this and ensure that you remember all the words and make an effort to re-capture the ones which will have slipped your memory. These cumulative vocabularies include all the words that occur over 46 times in the Greek New Testament, as well as many more of those that occur over 30 times. Together they represent approximately 66% of all the words in the Greek New Testament.

A Checklist for revision:

◊ Revise the paradigm of the regular verb [see Appendix B – by now you should know all of this paradigm except for the optative mood; some students find it very helpful to spend the first ten minutes of their final exam writing out the verb paradigm from memory].

◊ Revise how to form the different tenses of the indicative mood, especially the irregular verbs [see Chaps 12, 21, 22, 25]. Learn the tables of principal parts in this chapter [see 30.1.3].

◊ Revise the appropriate translation of the present, imperfect, future, aorist, and perfect tenses of the verb [see 30.1.1 & Chaps. 12, 21, 22, 25].

◊ Revise the uses of the subjunctive, participial and infinitive moods of the verb, and how these various moods are formed [see 30.1.2 & Chaps 15, 16, 20].

◊ Revise the uses of the active and passive voices of the verb [see 30.4 & Chap. 24].

◊ Revise vocabulary [see Appendix H].

◊ Revise the three declensions of nouns and adjectives [see Appendix E].

◊ Ensure that you have mastered the art of parsing. A significant part of

Part 4   291

the review exercise is devoted to parsing practice, and you should be able
to tell from that how well you have mastered the art. If more practice
at parsing is needed, most of the exercises in Parts 3 & 4 have a section
devoted to parsing. If the odd numbered exercises are chosen, it will be
possible to check your answer against those in Appendix A.
◊   Complete Review Exercise 30.
◊   Repeat all of the translations from the New Testament (which start in
    Chapter 11), concentrating especially on John 1-11 [see Chap. 29].

Exercise 30: Review of Parts 1-4

Note: this exercise covers each form of the verb, and each principal part of
irregular verbs at least once, and usually only once. If you do not recognize
something in the exercise, that reveals a learning error which needs to be
noted and addressed.

The Verb

Translate into English
1. λύσω 2. λέλυκα 3. λύομαι 4. ἐλύθην 5. ἔλυον 6. λύω 7. λέλυμαι 8. ἔλυσα
9. λυθήσομαι 10. σπείρετε 11. παραλαμβάνει 12. ἀγαπᾷς 13. ἐπλανήθη
14. λογιζόμεθα 15. στήσω 16. ἦν 17. ὤφθης 18. ὑπάρχω 19. περιτέμνουσιν
20. ἐσθίομεν 21. ἐπληρώθη 22. εὐλογοῦμεν 23. πίῃ 24. προσέρχεσθε
25. εὑρέθη 26. εὐηγγελίζετε 27. αἰτοῦμεν 28. εἶπες 29. δείξομεν 30. ἦτε
31. ἐστί 32. ἐγένετο 33. πειράζετε 34. ἐλογίσθη 35. ἔσπειρας 36. ἔστησα
37. παρέλαβε 38. ἐτέθησαν 39. φάγονται 40. κηρύξουσιν 41. πεπλήρωται
42. εὐχαριστεῖς 43. εἶδεν 44. ἐτηροῦν 45. ἐκράτησαν 46. ἐφώνησεν
47. πεσοῦμαι 48. ἐβάλετε 49. δεδώκατε 50. εἰμί 51. εὑρίσκουσιν
52. παρεδόθης 53. ἠνέχθην 54. ἐστάλην 55. ἀγοράζομεν 56. ἠγοράσατε

57. πέπτωκας 58. ἐδίδασκεν 59. γνώσονται 60. ἐπίομεν 61. κρατοῦμεν
62. ἤρθησαν 63. ἐστάθης 64. φαίνω 65. αἴρεις 66. πεποίθαμεν 67. δώσουσι
68. ἤγειρα 69. ἑωράκαμεν 70. ἀπέδωκα 71. γενήσομαι 72. εἰσί 73. λήμψῃ
74. ἠγέρθητε 75. ὄψεσθε 76. φέρετε 77. ἀροῦμεν 78. ἔσπαρμαι
79. ἀρνοῦνται 80. ἐλήμφθη 81. ἐγνώκαμεν 82. γέγραφας 83. ἦσθα
84. δείκνυσιν

85. ἐθεράπευσεν 86. ἐλεοῦμεν 87. ἄρχουσιν 88. ἤρξατο 89. ὀφείλουσι
90. εἰρήκατε 91. ἔχεις 92. προσεύχομαι 93. βέβληκεν 94. βέβηκε
95. ἀκολουθοῦμεν 96. δοῦναι 97. ἀσθενεῖτε 98. οἴσεις 99. φανεροῦμεν
100. ἐξεπορεύσασθε 101. εἰλήμμεθα 102. ἐλεύσῃ 103. εἶ 104. φοβοῦμαι
105. ἐκλήθησαν 106. προσφέρομεν 107. οἶδεν 108. ἐδείξατε 109. καθίζετε

110. πέπραχεν 111. εἶχες 112. τέθειται 113. ἀφέθημεν 114. ἤλπιζεν 115. δοξάζειν 116. ἐβλέψατε 117. ἐδόθην 118. ἀφίεται 119. ὄψεσθε 120. ἐκηρύξατε 121. ἐγήγερται 122. κλαίω 123. κλάω 124. κλείω 125. ἔκλαυσα 126. ἔκλεισα 127. ἔκλασα 128. κλαύσω 129. ποσηνέγκατε 130. βλασφημῶ 131. μισήσεις 132. ἐπορευσάμην 133. ἐνηνόχασιν 134. βαλοῦμεν

135. βάλλομεν 136. ἔδωκα 137. μενεῖ 138. μένει 139. ἕξετε 140. ἥξω 141. εἰλήφατε 142. ὁρᾷ 143. ἐγγίζειν 144. ἤγγικεν 145. παραγίνῃ 146. διεληλύθατε 147. δέδοσαι 148. ζά 149. ἐπεθήκατε 150. ἀφήσω 151. ἀκούετε 152. ἐδίωξαν 153. συνίημι 154. ἐργαζόμεθα 155. ἀποστέλλουσι 156. ἀποστέλουσι 157. μετανοῦμεν 158. δικαιωθήσονται 159. ἔρεις

160. ἐπίστευσαν 161. κρινῶ 162. κρίνω 163. ἔσομαι 164. ἐβαπτίζοντο 165. ἀποκτένω 166. ἀποκτείνω 167. ἀκηκόαμεν 168. ἐδείκνυτε 169. ἐσπάρης 170. ἦρκας 171. ἐδικαιώθη 172. πίπτουσιν 173. ἠμέλλετε 174. κατέβη 175. ἑστήκασιν 176. ἀπεστάλμεθα 177. ἁμαρτάνεις 178. ἀπήλθετε 179. ἔσται 180. ζητεῖτε 181. διώκεις 182. ἐσταυρώθησαν 183. θήσομεν 184. εὗρεν

185. εὑρήσετε 186. ἀπολέσεις 187. ἀναβεβήκατε 188. ἐρρέθη 189. κράζειν 190. τέθεικα 191. θαυμασθῆναι 192. δύνασαι 193. μέλλουσι 194. σπέρει 195. ἐδιώξαμεν 196. περιπάτει 197. ἡμάρτομεν 198. ἀποθανοῦμαι 199. ἄφηκεν

Parse the following

200. λῦσαι 201. λυέτω 202. λύσαντος 203. λυσῇς 204. λύειν 205. λυσάτωσαν 206. λύεσθαι 207. λύωμαι 208. λυθῆτι 209. λυθεῖσα 210. λύου 211. λυομένη 212. λυθῆτε 213. φασίν 214. ἀποθνήσκουσι 215. ἦρα 216. στάς 217. ᾧ 218. καθίσαντος 219. δεδιωγμένοι 220. θέλων 221. τίθεισα 222. εἰδότος 223. ἀφῆτε 224. γνῶναι 225. εἰδῇς 226. προσκυνῆσαι 227. καθημένου

228. κράξαντες 229. ἐλέησον 230. δόν 231. εἶναι 232. χαῖρε 233. γνόν 234. ἱστάντας 235. ἤνοιξα 236. ἔφη 237. θείς 238. ἀφιῶμεν 239. διδόντα 240. στῇς 241. δίδητε 242. τίθωμεν 243. ὤν 244. ἐρρέθην 245. ἀπεκρίθη 246. ἱστῇ 247. δῶ 248. ἔσῃ 249. καλέσασα 250. τεθείκασαν 251. ἵστησιν 252. ἵστασιν 253. ἐγενήθην

Translate

254. ἐδεξάμην 255. εἰσερχόμεθα 256. λαλεῖ 257. ἀπεστείλατε 258. ἀποκρίνομαι 259. παρακάλουμεν 260. ἀνέῳξας 261. ἔφαγον 262. ἀπελύθητε 263. ἔγραψας 264. ἐξεβλήθητε 265. τιθέασιν 266. ἀσπάζῃ 267. γίνῃ 268. ἐξήλθετε 269. θήσουσιν 270. λαμβάνω 271. ὁρᾷς 272. ἀπωλέσαμεν 273. πεπλήρωκε 274. γέννα 275. ἐπέρωτα 276. ἔλεγεν 277. ἀπέθανον 278. ἐδίδους

279. ἐδίδοσαν 280. εἶδεν 281. ἠγαπήθην 282. γινώσκουσι 283. ἠρωτήσαμεν 284. μαρτυρήσω 285. βέβλησαι 286. δίδωσι 287. διδόασι 288. ἠγάπημαι 289. ἄφεικας 290. εὑρήκατε 291. καλέσομεν 292. πεπτώκατε 293. ἐπλήρωσαν 294. ἠνέγκαμεν 295. ἤγαγον 296. πείθουσιν 297. ἠγάπηκας 298. ἄφηκεν 299. ἐδυνήθημεν 300. ἔξουσιν 301. κεκρίκαμεν 302. ἠγάπησε 303. ἠκούσθην

304. ἀφήσομεν 305. δυνήσεται 306. ἔσθει 307. ἐκάλεσεν 308. ἔμεινεν 309. ἐπέσαμεν 310. κεκρίμεθα 311. ἤκουσον 312. ἀναβήσομαι 313. ἐδείχθης 314. ἔσχηχας 315. κέκληκας 316. ἀκούσετε 317. ἐλάλησε 318. ἐκρίνατε 319. ἀγαπήσομεν 320. ἀποτέθνηκε 321. γεννήσουσιν 322. ἐλαλήθη 323. ἀκούσομαι 324. δέδειγμαι 325. λελάληται 326. λαλήσεις 327. ἐγέννησα

328. ἀπολέσεις 329. γέγονα 330. ἐγεννήθην 331. ἐδείχθην 332. ἔγνωσμαι 333. ἀποθανούμεθα 334. κέκλημαι 335. ἐγνώσθητε 336. ἐκρίθησαν 337. λελαλήκατε 338. εἰρήκασιν 339. γεγένησαι 340. γεγέννησαι 341. ἔγνων 342. εἴρηται 343. ἐστάθητε 344. γεγενήμεθα 345. μεμένηκας 346. ἀπολῶ 347. γεγέννηκεν

Principal Parts

Write out from memory the principal parts of the following verbs: 348. ἀγαπάω 349. ἀφίημι 350. βαίνω 351. γίνομαι 352. δίδωμι 353. εὑρίσκω 354. ἔχω 355. λαμβάνω 356. μένω 357. ὄλλυμι 358. ὁράω 359. φέρω

Declensions and Paradigms

Write out in full the declension of: 360. βιβλίον 361. ἐπαγγελία 362. πούς 363. φῶς 364. τυφλός, ή, όν 365. μέγας

Write in full the paradigm of: 366. The aor. part. act. of λύω 367. The aor. ind. pass. of ἀγαπάω 368. The aor. ind. act. of γινώσκω 369. The perf. part. act. of κρίνω 370. The aor. subj. act. of τίθημι 371. The perf. ind. pass. of ἐγείρω 372. The perf. ind. act. of ἀκούω 373. The aor. ind. act. of κρίνω 374. The aor. ind. pass. of στέλλω 375. The perf. ind. act. of ἔρχομαι 376. The fut. ind. act. of βαίνω 377. The fut. ind. act. of βάλλω 378. The perf. ind. pass. of δίδωμι 379. The pres. ind. act. of τίθημι 380. The aor. ind. act. of πληρόω 381. The imperf. ind. act. of λαλέω 382. The aor. ind. mid. of προσεύχομαι 383. The imperf. ind. pass. of λαμβάνω

[etc.: There are much such questions you could be asked. You may wish to go over the paradigms again, including those of the -μι verbs, and contracted verbs, and to practice writing out some of them. These are very common exam questions, and should be gift marks.]

Prepositions
What should be placed in the spaces?:
384. πρός + acc: _____
    + dat (infreq): near, at, by
    + gen (rare): to the advantage of
385. διά + _____ : through
    + _____ : because of
386. σύν + _____ : _____
387. ἀπό + gen: _____
388. ὀπίσω prep + gen: _____
    adv: _____
389. εἰς + _____ : into, towards
390. χωρίς prep + gen: _____
    adv: _____
391. ἐπί + _____ : at, by, on
    + _____ : upon, near, over
    + _____ : across, to, against
392. περί + acc: _____
    + gen: _____
393. κατά + gen: _____
    + acc: _____
394. _____ + dat: in, by (instr.)
395. μετά + acc: _____
    + gen: _____
396. παρά + dat: _____
    + gen: _____
    + acc: _____
397. ἔμπροσθεν
    prep + gen: _____
    adv: _____
398. ἐκ, ἐξ + _____ : from, out of
399. ὑπέρ + acc: _____
    + gen: _____
400. πρό + _____ : _____
401. ἐνώπιον + gen: _____
402. ὑπό + acc: _____
    + gen: _____

Sentences
The following sentences contain many of the different grammatical constructions that have been met thus far.
Translate into idiomatic English:

403. λέγω γὰρ ὑμῖν ὅτι δύναται ὁ θεὸς ἐκ τῶν λίθων τούτων ἐγεῖραι τέκνα τῷ Ἀβραάμ. **404.** εἰ δὲ θέλεις εἰς τὴν ζωὴν εἰσελθεῖν, τήρησον τὰς ἐντολάς. **405.** ἀμὴν ἀμὴν λέγω ὑμῖν, ἄν τι αἰτήσητε τὸν πατέρα ἐν τῷ ὀνόματί μου δώσει ὑμῖν. **406.** καὶ τὴν πόλιν τὴν ἁγίαν Ἰερουσαλὴμ καινὴν εἶδον καταβαίνουσαν ἐκ τοῦ οὐρανοῦ ἀπὸ τοῦ θεοῦ. **407.** καὶ πᾶς ὁ ζῶν καὶ πιστεύων εἰς ἐμὲ οὐ μὴ ἀποθάνῃ εἰς τὸν αἰῶνα. **408.** κἀγὼ ὑμῖν λέγω, αἰτεῖτε καὶ δοθήσεται ὑμῖν, ζητεῖτε καὶ εὑρήσετε, κρούετε καὶ ἀνοιγήσεται ὑμῖν· πᾶς γὰρ ὁ αἰτῶν λαμβάνει καὶ ὁ ζητῶν εὑρίσκει καὶ τῷ κρούοντι ἀνοιγήσεται. **409.** ἐγὼ δὲ οὐ πάρα ἀνθρώπου τὴν μαρτυρίαν λαμβάνω, ἀλλὰ ταῦτα λέγω ἵνα ὑμεῖς σωθῆτε etc.

You may wish to go back over the different chapters and to re-do some of the translation passages from the Greek New Testament, especially John 1-11. Passages from the New Testament start in exercises after chapter eleven.

Chapter 31: Where to Go From Here

If you have carefully worked through this book, you will have achieved a fair degree of proficiency in translating from the Gospel of John. The question naturally arises: what is the next logical step?

First, you will want to make sure that you keep the Greek that you have learned. Once they have passed their Greek exams, some students let the language lapse, and this can only be described as a sad waste of hard work. There is good news and bad news when it comes to learning languages. Studies have shown that if unused, language proficiency tends to diminish very rapidly, but that whatever is retained of a language for a period of 5 years, is likely to remain in memory for the next 25 to 30 years [Harry P. Bahrick, "Semantic Memory Content in Permastore: Fifty Years of Memory for Spanish Learned in School," *Journal of Experimental Psychology: General* 113 (1984) 1-29; see also *idem*, "Long Term Maintenance of Knowledge," in Endel Tulving and Furgus I. M. Craik, *The Oxford Handbook of Memory* (Oxford: University Press, 2000), 247-362]. A short period of time devoted to reading from the Greek New Testament each day is a convenient way to keep up an acceptable proficiency in the language.

Second, you may be interested in taking the next step, and expanding your knowledge of grammar and syntax to the place where you will be able to translate from anywhere in the Greek New Testament, even the more challenging passages. This second level of Greek is usually called intermediate Greek, and there is a good selection of intermediate and advanced grammars available. But if you were wishing to use an intermediate grammar that:

(1) starts with those topics that will most dramatically increase your mastery of NT Greek (i.e. moods, sentences and clauses), while at the same time allowing topics to be studied in any order;

(2) Provides multiple examples of every type of construction;

(3) Includes exercises and answers;

(4) Allows you to apply your new knowledge to passages from the New Testament selected to illustrate the grammar and syntax that you have just learned [there are questions, answers and notes that cover 41 whole chapters of the New Testament from which to choose];

(5) includes a comprehensive coverage of grammar and syntax sufficient be able to act as a reference grammar;

... then *Intermediate New Testament Greek Made Easier* may well be the book for you. This companion volume to *Beginning New Testament Greek Made Easier* makes the study of Greek easier by providing ample opportunity for practice and application, and gives immediate feedback on your mastery of the concepts in each chapter. Working systematically through this book will provide you with the knowledge and skills that will allow you to translate anything in the Greek New Testament.

Appendices

Appendix A: Answers to Exercises

Part 1

Answers to Exercise 1.1

1. [Luke 3:23-38]:
[23] Kai autos ēn Iēsous archomenos hōsei etōn triakonta, ōn huios, hōs enomizeto Iōsēph tou Ēli [24] tou Maththat tou Leui tou Melchi tou Iannai tou Iōsēph [25] tou Mattathiou tou Amōs tou Naoum tou Hesli tou Naggai [26] tou Maath tou Mattathiou tou Semeïn tou Iōsēch tou Iōda [27] tou Iōanan tou Hrēsa tou Zorobabel tou Salathiēl tou Nēri [28] tou Melchi tou Addi tou Kōsam tou Elmadam tou Ēr [29] tou Iēsou tou Eliezer tou Iōrim tou Maththat tou Leui [30] tou Sumeōn tou Iouda tou Iōsēph tou Iōnam tou Eliakim [31] tou Melea tou Menna tou Mattatha tou Natham tou Dauid [32] tou Iessai tou Iōbēd tou Boos tou Sala tou Naassōn [33] tou Aminadab tou Admin tou Arni tou Hesrōm tou Phares tou Iouda [34] tou Iakōb tou Isaak tou Abraam tou Thara tou Nachōr [35] tou Serouch tou Hragau tou Phalek tou Eber tou Sala [36] tou Kaïnam tou Arphaxad tou Sēm tou Nōe tou Lamech [37] tou Mathousala tou Henōch tou Iaret tou Maleleēl tou Kaïnam [38] tou Enōs tou Sēth tou Adam tou Theou.

2. [Matthew 1:6-11]:
[6] Ἰεσσαι δε ἐγεννησεν τον Δαυιδ τον βασιλεα. Δαυιδ δε ἐγεννησεν τον Σολομωνα ἐκ της του Οὐριου, [7] Σολομων δε ἐγεννησεν τον Ῥοβοαμ, Ῥοβοαμ δε ἐγεννησεν τον Ἀβια, Ἀβια δε ἐγεννησεν τον Ἀσαφ, [8] Ἀσαφ δε ἐγεννησεν τον Ἰωσαφατ, Ἰωσαφατ δε ἐγεννησεν τον Ἰωραμ, Ἰωραμ δε ἐγεννησεν τον Ὀζιαν, [9] Ὀζιας δε ἐγεννησεν τον Ἰωαθαμ, Ἰωαθαμ δε ἐγεννησεν τον Ἀχαζ, Ἀχαζ δε ἐγεννησεν τον Ἑζεκιαν, [10] Ἑζεκιας δε ἐγεννησεν τον Μανασση, Μανασσης δε ἐγεννησεν τον Ἀμως, Ἀμως δε ἐγεννησεν τον Ἰωσιαν, [11] Ἰωσιας δε ἐγεννησεν τον Ἰεχονιαν και τους ἀδελφους αὐτου ἐπι της μετοικεσιας Βαβυλωνος.

Answers to Exercise 1.2

Compare your typed answer to the original from the textbook.

Answers to Exercise 2.1

A. i. ἀκούω ἀκούεις ἀκούει ἀκούομεν ἀκούετε ἀκούουσι(ν)
ii. θέλω θέλεις θέλει θέλομεν θέλετε θέλουσι(ν)
iii. γράφω γράφεις γράφει γράφομεν γράφετε γράφουσι(ν)
iv. ἔχω ἔχεις ἔχει ἔχομεν ἔχετε ἔχουσι(ν)

B. 1. He/she/it says 3. They write 5. I have 7. They eat 9. He/she/it has 11. I eat 13. We write 15. I say 17. You take 19. We hear 21. We say 23. They find

C. 25. θέλω 27. λέγουσι(ν) 29. ἀκούω 31. λέγετε 33. γράφω 35. ἔχεις 37. λαμβάνουσι(ν) 39. ἔχομεν 41. θέλουσι(ν) 43. ἐσθίετε 45. ἔχετε 47. ἐσθίει

Answers to Exercise 2.2

1. λέγει 3. γράφουσιν 5. ἔχω 7. ἐσθίουσιν 9. ἔχει

Answers to Exercise 3.1

1. The men find the slaves. 3. The men find slaves. 5. The man finds the slave. 7. The Christ finds a slave. 9. The son receives (or takes) the people. 11. Abraham wants sons and slaves. 12. The people have gods [note: in English, when used as the subject of a sentence, the collective noun "people" takes a plural verb. In Greek, on the other hand, the subject λαός takes a singular verb if the noun is singular in form–λαοί would take a plural verb. Languages have different conventions, and the only time you will need to think about this one is when translating from English into Greek. Your English will usually provide the correct translation of the word λαός without you needing to think about it.] 13. God has a people. 15. John has a brother. 17. Abraham has a son and David has a son. 19. Jesus says words. 21. ὁ δοῦλος ἔχει ἀδελφόν. 23. οἱ ἀδελφοὶ ἔχουσι δούλους. 25. ὁ δοῦλος ἔχει ἀδελφούς. 27. ὁ λαὸς ἐσθίει ἄρτον. 29. ὁ Χριστὸς ἔχει λαόν. 31. ὁ Ἰησοῦς εὑρίσκει τοὺς δούλους καὶ λέγει λόγους.

Answers to Exercise 3.2

i. δοῦλος δοῦλε δοῦλον δούλου δούλῳ δοῦλοι δούλους δούλων δούλοις
ii. νόμος νόμε νόμον νόμου νόμῳ νόμοι νόμους νόμων νόμοις
iii. λαός λαέ λαόν λαοῦ λαῷ λαοί λαούς λαῶν λαοῖς
iv. ὄχλος ὄχλε ὄχλον ὄχλου ὄχλῳ ὄχλοι ὄχλους ὄχλων ὄχλοις

1. The house of the slave. 3. The house of the angel. 5. A man takes the house of the slave. 7. The man takes the houses of the slave. 9. John says a word to the crowd. 11. Do you know the law of God? 13. The son eats bread in the house. 15. I believe [in] God. 17. Does Jesus speak [say] the words of God? 19. Does the crowd believe? 21. The sons take the slave from the house. 23. πιστεύω ἐν ἀγγέλοις. 25. ὁ Χριστὸς ἔχει τὸν λαὸν τοῦ θεοῦ. 27. ὁ Ἀβραὰμ ἐσθίει ἄρτον ἐκ τοῦ οἴκου. 29. ὁ Ἰησοῦς λέγει τῷ κόσμῳ.

Answers to Exercise 3.3

1. γινώσκεις τὸν νόμον τοῦ θεοῦ; 3. ἐσθίει ἄρτον ἐν τῷ οἴκῳ ὁ υἱός. 5. πιστεύω ἐν τῷ θεῷ. 7. λέγει τοὺς λόγους τοῦ θεοῦ ὁ Ἰησοῦς; 9. ὁ ὄχλος πιστεύει;

Appendix A: Answers to Exercises

Answers to Exercise 4

i. τέκνον τέκνον τέκνου τέκνῳ τέκνα τέκνα τέκνων τέκνοις
ii. βιβλίον βιβλίον βιβλίου βιβλίῳ βιβλία βιβλία βιβλίων βιβλίοις
iii. κόσμος, κόσμε κόσμον κόσμου κόσμῳ κόσμοι κόσμους κόσμων κόσμοις
iv. παιδίον παιδίον παιδίου παιδίῳ παιδία παιδία παιδίων παιδίοις
[note on iii.: the nominative of the word, κόσμος, ends with -ος, it is therefore a second declension masculine word, not neuter like the other three words, which have nominatives which end in -ον.]

1. Abraham is a man of God. 3. Are you the Christ? 5. You are the messenger [or angel] from God. 7. I am David from Jerusalem [literally: I am David, the one from Jerusalem]. 9. Demons are in the world. 11. If you are Jesus, you are the Christ of God. 13. The brothers take the books of the child. 15. Does Jesus want works of the law? 17. We are the servants [or slaves] of the people. 19. Jesus and the brother of David find the children in the temple. 21. The slave knows the faces of the children. 23. Demons know the son of God. 25. We are the people of the law. 27. Jesus is from God. 29. The law is from God. 31. δαιμόνιά ἐστιν ἐν τῷ κόσμῳ. [Remember: neuter plural subjects take a singular verb] 33. ὁ Ἰησοῦς ἐστιν ὁ υἱὸς τοῦ θεοῦ. 35. ἐσμὲν ὁ λαὸς τοῦ Χριστοῦ. 37. ὁ Ἀβραὰμ γινώσκει τὸν θεόν. 39. πιστεύεις [or πιστεύετε] ἐν δαιμονίοις;

Answers to Exercise 5.1

i. τηρῶ τηρεῖς τηρεῖ τηροῦμεν τηρεῖτε τηροῦσι(ν)
ii. ποιῶ, ποιεῖς ποιεῖ ποιοῦμεν ποιεῖτε ποιοῦσι(ν)
iii. λαμβάνω λαμβάνεις λαμβάνει λαμβάνομεν λαμβάνετε λαμβάνουσι(ν)
iv. καλῶ καλεῖς καλεῖ καλοῦμεν καλεῖτε καλοῦσι(ν)
[note on iii.: λαμβάνω is not an -εω verb, so follows the regular pattern of λύω]

1. The brother walks according to the law of [the] God. 3. The children walk according to the laws of [the] God. 5. The son walks according to the law of [the] God. 7. We seek Jesus. 9. We worship Jesus and keep the law of God. 11. I bear witness against Jerusalem. 13. The crowd does not walk according to the law of the world. 15. We do not worship man. 17. You do not keep the law of God. 19. I believe [or think] that demons are in the world. 21. Jesus calls men out of the world. 23. The crowd seeks Jesus. 25. I think/believe that you are the Christ of God. 27. Jesus bears witness against Jerusalem. 29. Jesus speaks according to the law of God. 31. Jesus does the deeds of God. 33. We follow Jesus. [Remember that the idiom is different in Greek—it uses the dative case after the verb ἀκολουθέω. Notice also how helpful the article with the name Jesus can be—it helps us distinguish here between dative and genitive forms of his name.] 35. οἱ υἱοὶ οὐ περιπατοῦσι κατὰ τοὺς νόμους ἀνθρώπου. 37. λαλεῖτε λόγους τῷ ὄχλῳ.

Answers to Exercise 5.2

1. μαρτυρῶ κατὰ τοῦ Ἰερουσαλήμ. 3. ὁ ὄχλος οὐ περιπατεῖ κατὰ τὸν νόμον τοῦ κόσμου. 5. προσκυνοῦμεν οὐκ ἀνθρώπῳ. 7. τηρεῖτε οὐ τὸν νόμον τοῦ θεοῦ. 9. δοκῶ ὅτι δαιμόνια ἐστιν ἐν τῷ κόσμῳ.

Answers to Exercise 6

i. φωνή φωνήν φωνῆς φωνῇ φωναί φωνάς φωνῶν φωναῖς
ii. σοφία σοφίαν σοφίας σοφίᾳ σοφίαι σοφίας σοφιῶν σοφίαις
iii. χαρά χαράν χαρᾶς χαρᾷ χαραί χαράς χαρῶν χαραῖς
iv. ἄρτος, ἄρτε ἄρτον ἄρτου ἄρτῳ, ἄρτοι ἄρτους ἀρτῶν ἄρτοις
v. πρόσωπον, πρόσωπον, προσώπου, προσώπῳ, πρόσωπα, πρόσωπα, προσώπων, προσώποις
vi. ζωή, ζωήν, ζωῆς, ζωῇ, ζωαί, ζωάς, ζωῶν, ζωαῖς

1. The church of God keeps the law of God. 3. The love of God is the beginning of wisdom. 5. The commandment of Jesus has authority. 7. The glory of the church is in [the] love of the brethren [or brothers]. 9. I rejoice in the law of God. 11. I do not rejoice in the commandments of men. 13. The commandments of men have no authority. 15. I seek the wisdom of God. 17. John speaks against the sin of men. 19. Jesus bears witness that God is love. 21. The sons of God walk according to the commandment of God. 23. I hear the sound of joy in Jerusalem. 25. Sin does not have the promise of life. 27. The sons of God do the commandments of God. 29. The beginning of sin. 31. Do you rejoice in Jesus? 33. Do you keep the commandments of Jesus? 35. Jesus calls men from sin. 37. ἡ γῆ τοῦ Δαυίδ. 39. ἔχει τὴν ἐξουσίαν ἐπαγγελίας. 41. οἱ υἱοὶ τοῦ θεοῦ περιπατοῦσι κατὰ τὴν ἐντολὴν τοῦ θεοῦ. 43. ἀκούω τὴν φωνὴν τῆς χαρᾶς ἐν Ἰερουσαλήμ. 45. ἔχει οὐχ ἡ ἁμαρτία τὴν ἐπαγγελίαν τῆς ζωῆς. 47. οἱ υἱοὶ τοῦ θεοῦ ποιοῦσι τὰς ἐντολὰς τοῦ θεοῦ. 49. ἡ ἀρχὴ τῆς ἁμαρτίας. 51. χαίρετε ἐν τῷ Ἰησοῦ; 53. τηρεῖτε τὰς ἐντολὰς τοῦ Ἰησοῦ; 55. ὁ Ἰησοῦς καλεῖ ἀνθρώπους ἀπὸ ἁμαρτίας.

Answers to Exercise 7

i. masc.: κακός, κακέ, κακόν, κακοῦ, κακῷ, κακοί, κακούς, κακῶν, κακοῖς
fem.: κακή, κακή, κακήν, κακῆς, κακῇ, κακαί, κακάς, κακῶν, κακαῖς
neut.: κακόν, κακόν, κακόν, κακοῦ κακῷ, κακά, κακά, κακῶν, κακοῖς
ii. masc.: νεκρός, νεκρέ, νεκρόν, νεκροῦ, νεκρῷ, νεκροί, νεκρούς, νεκρῶν, νεκροῖς
fem.: νεκρά, νεκρά, νεκράν, νεκρᾶς, νεκρᾷ, νεκραί, νεκράς, νεκρῶν, νεκραῖς
neut.: νεκρόν, νεκρόν, νεκρόν, νεκροῦ, νεκρῷ, νεκρά, νεκρά, νεκρῶν, νεκροῖς

1. The good man 3. The good man 5. The good day 7. The good day 9. The good deed [work] 11. The good deed [work] 13. The dead man 15. The dead man 17. The dead church 19. The dead church 21. The dead work [deed] 23. The dead work 25. The holy book 27. The beloved slave 29. The blind child 31. We worship the only God. 33. The child has a pretty [beautiful, etc] face. 35. If you have Christ, you have eternal life. 37. My God is righteous 39. The faithful people have eternal life. 41. You are a good child. 43. Abraham is a righteous man. 45. The dead do not know God. 47. I think/consider that God is righteous. 49. The commandment of Jesus is good. 51. ὁ πονηρὸς δοῦλος 53. ὁ ἅγιος ἄνθρωπος 55. αἱ ἅγιαι ἡμέραι 57. τὰ νεκρὰ ἔργα 59. τὰ ἔργα τὰ νεκρά 61. οἱ ἅγιοι ἄγγελοι 63. τὰ πονηρὰ δαιμόνια 65. ἡ ἐκκλησία ἡ πιστή 67. κακοὶ ἄνθρωποι ποιοῦσι πονηρὰ ἔργα. 69. ἡ ἐκκλησία ἔχει οὐ δικαιοσύνην, Χριστὸς μόνος ἔχει δικαιοσύνην.

Appendix A: Answers to Exercises 303

Answers to Exercise 8.1

i. γεννῶ, γεννᾷς, γεννᾷ, γεννῶμεν, γεννᾶτε, γεννῶσι(ν)
ii. ἐρωτῶ, ἐρωτᾷς, ἐρωτᾷ, ἐρωτῶμεν, ἐρωτᾶτε, ἐρωτῶσι(ν)
iii. ζητῶ, ζητεῖς, ζητεῖ, ζητοῦμεν, ζητεῖτε, ζητοῦσι(ν)
iv. συνάγω, συνάγεις, συνάγει, συνάγομεν, συνάγετε, συνάγουσι(ν)

1. We see 3. He/she/it loves 5. You send away 7. You ask 9. He/she/it begets 11. γεννῶσι(ν) 13. ζῇς 15. ἐρωτῶμεν or ἐπερωτῶμεν 17. Righteousness begets love. 19. Do you see sin in the church? 21. God loves the world, but the world does not love God. 23. The wisdom of God does not beget sin. 25. We see the love of God in the face of Jesus. 27. You write the law of man, but I speak commandments of authority. 29. I love my brother. 31. The man sends [or dismisses] the slaves away from the house. 33. I see Jesus with Peter. 35. Jesus bears witness against the commandments of the synagogue. 37. Jesus does not love the sins of the world. 39. Evil men speak against the law of God. 41. You speak evil words, but I speak the words of life. 43. Jesus sends the crowd from the house. 45. οἱ ἄγγελοι ἀπολυουσι τους ἀποστολους. 47. ὁ λαος οὐχ ὁρᾳ τον θεον.

Answers to Exercise 8.2

1. ὁ ἀπόστολος ἐρωτᾷ τὸν Ἰησοῦν. 3. ὁ Ἰησοῦς ζῇ σὺν τῷ Πέτρῳ. 5. ἀπολύει τὸν ὄχλον ὁ Ἰησοῦς. 7. οἱ ἀδελφοὶ καὶ οἱ δοῦλοι ἐπερωτῶσι τὸν Ἰησοῦν. 9. ὁ θεὸς ἀποστέλλει τὸν ἀπόστολον ἐκ τοῦ ἁγίου ἱεροῦ.

Answers to Exercise 9

i. προσεύχομαι, προσεύχῃ, προσεύχεται, προσευχόμεθα, προσεύχεσθε, προσεύχονται
ii. παρακαλῶ, παρακαλεῖς, παρακαλεῖ, παρακαλοῦμεν, παρακαλεῖτε, παρακαλοῦσι(ν)
iii. φοβοῦμαι, φοβῇ, φοβεῖται, φοβούμεθα, φοβεῖσθε, φοβοῦνται

1. They receive or They take 3. We receive 5. You answer 7. I go away 9. You pray 11. You become 13. προσευχόμεθα 15. φοβοῦνται 17. φοβεῖται 19. John greets Jesus. 21. The son of man comes/goes into the world. 23. The son of man comes/goes out of the world. 25. Jesus goes to Nazareth [note: no doubt you recognized Ναζαρὲθ as Nazareth; the name of the town of Nazareth is found 12 times in the Greek New Testament, and spelled three different ways: Ναζαρά, Ναζαρέθ, Ναζαρέτ]. 27. John comes/goes out of Jerusalem. 29. I go to eternal life [or I am approaching eternal life]. 31. The slave receives/takes the holy book from the righteous man. 33. My words do not become law, but the words of Jesus [do] become law. 35. The children go into the house. 37. David receives the bread from the good/beautiful slave. 39. The world does not receive the Christ. 41. Bad men become righteous if they believe in Jesus. 43. δεχόμεθα τὴν ζωὴν ἀπὸ τοῦ θεοῦ. 45. ὁ λαὸς ἀσπάζεται τὸν Ἰησοῦν. 47. φοβῇ τὸν θεόν; or φοβεῖσθε τὸν θεόν; 49. ὁ υἱὸς τοῦ ἀνθρώπου ἔρχεται ἐκ τοῦ κόσμου. 51. ὁ Ἰησοῦς πορεύεται πρὸς τὴν Ἰερουσαλήμ. 53. ὁ Ἰωάννης ἔρχεται ἀπὸ τῆς Ἰερουσαλήμ. 55. φοβούμεθα οὐκ ἄνθρωπον.

Answers to Exercise 10

1. Jesus comes to his people, but his people do not receive him. 3. Jesus bears the sins of the world, but the world does not know him. 5. David puts his book in his house. 7. Peter approaches his boat. 9. They find Peter at [or: by / on] the boat. 11. Peter himself finds them on [or near] the boat. 13. Jesus dies. 15. We worship God and keep his laws. 17. The Lord comes to his people. 19. The Lord comes into his holy temple. 21. John speaks across the crowd to Peter. 23. Jesus Christ is the Lord. 25. They do not die in their houses. 27. Jesus casts demons out of the child. 29. The Lord finds the blind man near [or: before / upon] the house. 31. The slave carries his child. 33. Angels lead the church of God. 35. The slaves fall upon their faces. 37. God does not die. 39. ὁ ἀδελφὸς ἄγει τὸ τέκνον / παιδίον αὐτοῦ. 41. προσκυνοῦμεν τῷ κυρίῳ. 43. ὁ Ἰησοῦς λέγει λόγους αὐτοῖς [or πρὸς αὐτούς].

Answers to Exercise 11 (Review)

Notes:
1. All the answers are provided for this exercise. This is so that you can more readily test yourself to discover how well you are doing. There is no need to remind you to use these answers responsibly (i.e., as a check of work you have already done).
2. For most of the answers, only one of the different options is given. Any of the other meanings listed in the vocabularies is also correct in almost all cases.

1. We eat 2. You ask 3. You seek 4. I pray 5. You bear 6. They see 7. He/she/it sends 8. You glorify 9. He/she/it receives 10. You think 11. They become 12. I live 13. We fear 14. He/she/it takes 15. You know 16. We walk 17. You beget 18. I will, wish 19. They rejoice 20. You die 21. I come 22. He/she/it gathers 23. We bear witness 24. You find 25. I believe 26. We call 27. He/she/it loves 28. They depart 29. I fall 30. You hear 31. I do 32. They ask 33. You answer 34. He/she/it throws 35. You say 36. He/she/it asks 37. You release 38. I go, come 39. You write 40. They greet 41. You enter/go in 42. I have 43. You cast out 44. We go out 45. You lead 46. You approach 47. You worship 48. You keep 49. We are 50. You speak 51. θέλομεν 52. φοβῇ 53. φοβεῖσθε (ε+ε=ει) 54. συνάγουσι(ν) 55. δοκοῦμεν 56. γεννᾷ 57. προσεύχονται 58. δοξάζω 59. ἀσπάζῃ

60. The holy day 61. The promise of eternal life 62. Beloved church 63. The beginning of wisdom 64. His death 65. Dead works 66. The commandments of the Lord 67. The only child 68. The son of man 69. The good earth 70. If you are the Christ 71. The righteous apostles 72. The temple of God 73. My book 74. The evil slaves 75. The voice of authority 76. The brothers from Jerusalem 77. The world of demons 78. The faithful angel 79. The blind children 80. The bad law 81. The joys of righteousness 82. The good words 83. The people of Abraham 84. Peter and John 85. In the synagogue 86. The love of sin 87. The glories of the church 88. Their bread 89. The crowds from the house 90. The face of Jesus 91. ὁ ἅγιος ἄνθρωπος 92. οἱ ἅγιοι ἄνθρωποι 93. ἡ ἁγία ἡμέρα 94. αἱ ἅγιαι ἡμέραι 95. ὁ μόνος θεός 96. τὸ νεκρὸν παιδίον [or τέκνον] 97. οἱ λόγοι αὐτοῦ 98. οἱ λόγοι αὐτῶν 99. τὸ τέκνον τῆς συναγωγῆς 100. τὸ ἔργον [τῶν] δαιμονίων

Appendix A: Answers to Exercises

101. α 102. ῳ 103. ει 104. ᾳ 105. ῳ 106. ῳ 107. ῳ 108. ει 109. α 110. Genitive 111. ἐκ, ἐξ 112. With 113. To the advantage of 114. Accusative 115. Dative 116. Genitive 117. Accusative 118. Accusative 119. Genitive 120. Dative 121. Dative 122. Accusative 123-136. See relevant sections of book.

137. ἡ ἀγαθὴ ἡμέρα. [The adjective must agree with the noun it qualifies] The good day 138. οἱ ἀπόστολοι ἔρχονται πρὸς τὸν Ἰησοῦν. [The plural subject requires a plural verb] The apostles come to Jesus 139. ὁ Πέτρος εὑρίσκει αὐτοὺς ἐν τῷ οἴκῳ. [ἐν is followed by the dative case] Peter finds them in the house. 140. ἐγὼ ἀκούω τοῦ Πέτρου. [ἀκουω is followed by the genitive of the person heard] I hear Peter. 141. ὁ θεός ἐστιν ἀγάπη. [εἰμὶ has the nominative case for both subject and complement] God is love. 142. ὁ Δαυὶδ λαμβανει ἄρτον ἐκ τοῦ ἱεροῦ. [The subject of the sentence (David) required the verb to be in the third person singular; ἐκ is followed by the genitive] David takes bread from the temple. 143. δαιμόνια οὐκ ἐσθίει τὸν ἄρτον. [Neuter plural subjects are followed by third person singular verbs] Demons do not eat bread. 144. ἐγὼ προσκυνῶ θεῷ. ["I" is first person, and takes a first person verb; the verb προσκυνέω is followed by a dative] I worship God. 145. φοβούμεθα οὐκ ἄνθρωπον. [The stem of the verb is φοβε-. The ε + ο = ου] We do not fear man. 146. We call upon the Lord. 147. I know that God is good but man is evil. 148. Evil men throw [cast] Peter and John out of the synagogue because they believe that Jesus is the Christ. 149. Jesus says, I am the son of man. If you believe in the son of man you have eternal life [or: life for ever]. 150. Sin begets death, but righteousness begets life. 151. ἄγγελοι ἄγουσι δικαίους ἀνθρώπους. 152. ὁ Ἰησοῦς καλεῖ τοὺς νεκροὺς πρὸς ζωήν. 153. ἀγαθοὶ ἄνθρωποι μόνοι τηροῦσι τὸν νόμον τοῦ θεοῦ;

Part 2

Answers to Exercise 12.1

i. εἶπον, εἶπες, εἶπεν, εἴπομεν, εἴπετε, εἶπον ii. εἶδον, εἶδες, εἶδεν, εἴδομεν, εἴδετε, εἶδον iii. ἦλθον, ἦλθες, ἦλθεν, ἤλθομεν, ἤλθετε, ἦλθον 1. He/she/it throws 3. We threw 5. You threw 7. You throw 9. I/they saw 11. You saw 13. He/she/it came 15. I come 17. You ate 19. We ate 21. I take 23. You took 25. He/she/it died 27. I/they died 29. He/she/it led 31. You led 33. You had 35. We had 37. He/she/it said 39. You said 41. You cast out 43. You saw 45. He/she/it approached 47. He/she/it approaches 49. The Pharisees had their laws. 51. Abraham saw God. 53. I saw the Lord. 55. The two children take bread. 57. The seven children ate bread. 59. ἐσθίομεν 61. εἴδομεν 63. ἀπέθανον 65. λέγει

[Note: The teacher's manual has the Bible references for the even numbered questions for the "Sentences and Phrases from the Greek New Testament" sections of this and subsequent exercises. So, if needed, your teacher will be able to tell you where they are taken from.] **67.** Jesus said to them, "I am the bread of life" (from John 6:35). **69.** In [the] beginning was the word, and the word was with God, and the word was God. He was in [the] beginning with God … in him was life, and the life was the light of humankind [lit.: men] (from John 1:1-5). **71.** John, to the seven churches that are in Asia (from Rev 1:4). [lit.: "John, to the seven churches, the [ones] in Asia." You will notice that Greek sometimes uses the definite article in places that it would not be used in English. In this text it is used with the name of a region, Asia.] **73.** These things he said in a synagogue ... in Capernaum (from John 6:59).

Answers to Exercise 12.2

i. ἔβλεψα, ἔβλεψας, ἔβλεψεν, ἐβλέψαμεν, ἐβλέψατε, ἔβλεψαν
ii. ἐλάλησα, ἐλάλησας, ἐλάλησεν, ἐλαλήσαμεν, ἐλαλήσατε, ἐλάλησαν
iii. ἔπεισα, ἔπεισας, ἔπεισεν, ἐπείσαμεν, ἐπείσατε, ἔπεισαν
iv. ἐγέννησα, ἐγέννησας, ἐγέννησεν, ἐγεννήσαμεν, ἐγεννήσατε, ἐγέννησαν

1. He/she/it sends **3.** We sent **5.** You dismissed **7.** You begat **9.** You wrote **11.** You write **13.** They said **15.** I saved **17.** They saved **19.** We made/We did **21.** He/she/it glorified **23.** He/she/it led **25.** You asked **27.** We saw **29.** You persuaded **31.** He/she/it asked **33.** We threw **35.** You say **37.** We asked **39.** We said **41.** You saved **43.** He/she/it called **45.** You glorified **47.** They saw **49.** You had **51.** You bore witness **53.** You led **55.** We said **57.** ἀγαπῶμεν **59.** γράφω **61.** ἐβάλομεν **63.** ἔγραψαν **65.** Jesus saved you. **67.** Jesus saved them. **69.** The heavens still tell [of] the glory of God. **71.** Did the kingdom come in Jesus? **73.** Jesus came to his own. **75.** I saw the boat on the sea. **77.** She saw the boat on the sea. **79.** You saw the boat on the sea. **81.** Truly, truly [or Verily, verily] I say to you that I am the Christ. **83.** Abraham walked upon the path of righteousness. **85.** David wrote laws and commandments. **87.** Did you save? **89.** The Pharisees asked Jesus. **91.** Was Peter the first of the apostles? **93.** εἶδες τὸν Ἰησοῦν; or ἔβλεψας τὸν Ἰησοῦν; **95.** ὁ Χριστὸς ἦλθεν ἐκ τῶν οὐρανῶν. **97.** John 1:11: He came to his own, and [his] own did not accept him. **99.** John 9:14: But the day Jesus made clay was a Sabbath. [The English idiom used to express time is different from that used by Greek, although a word-for-word translation clearly indicates what is meant: "But it was the Sabbath in the day Jesus made the clay."]

Answers to Exercise 12.3

i. ἔθηκα, ἔθηκας, ἔθηκεν, ἐθήκαμεν, ἐθήκατε, ἔθηκαν
ii. ἤνεγκα, ἤνεγκας, ἤνεγκεν, ἠνέγκαμεν, ἠνέγκατε, ἤνεγκαν
iii. αἰτῶ, αἰτεῖς, αἰτεῖ, αἰτοῦμεν, αἰτεῖτε, αἰτοῦσι(ν)
iv. ᾔτησα, ᾔτησας, ᾔτησεν, ᾐτήσαμεν, ᾐτήσατε, ᾔτησαν
v. ἔφαγον, ἔφαγες, ἔφαγεν, ἐφάγομεν, ἐφάγετε, ἔφαγον

1. They gave **3.** We wrote **5.** You showed **7.** He/she/it sent **9.** I placed **11.** He/she/it forgave **13.** They see **15.** We placed **17.** You enter **19.** You forgave **21.** We led **23.** I carried / bore **25.** You placed **27.** I sent away **29.** He/she/it saw **31.** He/she/it said **33.** They bore witness **35.** You showed **37.** You asked **39.** You forgave **41.** You lead **43.** I placed **45.** I/they saw **47.** I loved **49.** He/she/it delivered **51.** You ruined **53.** You threw **55.** We showed **57.** They placed **59.** He/she/it sees **61.** You asked **63.** We do **65.** I glorify **67.** You fall **69.** We fall **71.** ἔδωκα **73.** ἀπέστειλαν **75.** ἀπεκρίθη **77.** ἔδειξας **79.** I sent the messenger. **81.** You sent the messenger. **83.** The lord sent the messenger. **85.** Jesus bore the sins of the world. **87.** Jesus

Appendix A: Answers to Exercises 307

stood the child in the middle. **89.** They asked him, "Are you the Christ?" And he answered, "No." **91.** For Jesus showed them the way of righteousness, but they did not believe him. **93.** Then the Lord went into Galilee. **95.** Jesus forgave sins. **97.** Joy is the fruit of love. **99.** When the righteous man asked, God sent his angel from heaven. **101.** For Jesus bore the sins of men [note: γάρ is the second word in the Greek sentence, but is placed first in the English sentence]. **103.** And it came to pass when Jesus entered Jerusalem ... **105.** For thus the Lord forgave you. **107.** Rev 2:4 But I have against you that you left your first love. **109.** Acts 1:26a And they cast lots for them, and the lot fell upon Matthew. [Here again is an idiom which is slightly different from English. Literally the sentence reads: "And they gave lots to them, and the lot fell upon Matthew." In Greek you "give lots," in English you "cast lots."] **111.** Matt 18:2b And when he called a child, he placed it/him/her in their midst, and said, "truly I say to you ... **113.** Mark 1:4a John appeared in the desert. [note: Beginners often find ἐγένετο difficult to translate. It has the basic meaning of "become, happen." Literally, "John happened/became in the desert," or in English idiom, "John appeared ..." ἐγένετο also can be used where English would translate it as: "it came to pass."] **115.** Matt 27:42a He saved others, himself he cannot save.

Answers to Exercise 13

1. This Sabbath 3. This kingdom 5. These boats 7. Her authority 9. These slaves 11. αὗται αἱ ἡμέραι 13. αὕτη ἡ ὁδός [Remember, though ὁδός declines like λόγος, it is feminine.] 15. τὸ ἔργον τούτων τῶν ἀνθρώπων 17. Matt 13:53 And it came to pass when Jesus finished these parables. [*see* comment on answer no. 113 of exercise 12.3.] 19. From John 6:60-61: They said, "This word is harsh/difficult." ... Jesus said to them, "Are you offended at this?" [or: "Does this offend you?"]

Answers to Exercise 14.1

i. νύξ, νύκτα, νυκτός, νυκτί, νύκτες, νύκτας, νυκτῶν, νυξί(ν)
ii. πούς, πόδα, ποδός, ποδί, πόδες, πόδας, ποδῶν, ποσί(ν)
iii. ἀνήρ, ἄνερ, ἄνδρα, ἀνδρός, ἀνδρί, ἄνδρες, ἄνδρας, ἀνδρῶν, ἀνδράσι(ν)

1. My father 3. Night and day 5. The works of the flesh 7. The head of man 9. The fruit of hope 11. The mother of Jesus 13. The death of hope 15. The Lord gave peace to [the] men 17. This is the house of the mother of Simon Peter 19. Therefore Jesus answered and said, "My words remain forever." [Note: It is important to follow the conventions of English punctuation in translating into English. In other words, please always include speech marks where English would include them in direct speech.] 21. The kingdom of God remains forever. 23. The hand of man was against me. 25. The laws of God remain forever. 27. 1 Cor 2:6 And we speak a wisdom among [in] the perfect, but a wisdom not of this age, neither of the rulers of this age. 29. Tit 1:1-2 Paul, a servant of God, and an apostle of Jesus Christ ... upon [the] hope of eternal life. 31. John 2:3 The mother of Jesus says to him, "They have no wine." 33. Matt 2:14 He took [with him] the child and his mother by night and took refuge in Egypt. 35. Mark 8:38b ... in the glory of his father ... 37. John 13:6 Therefore he comes to Simon Peter; he says to him, "Lord, do you wash my feet?" Jesus answered and said to him ... 39. John 1:14 And the word became flesh.

[Like εἰμί, ἐγένετο takes nominative for both subject and complement; see further comments on ἐγένετο in no. 113. of exercise 12.3] **41.** Rom 1:7, 1 Cor 1:3 & 2 Cor 1:2 Grace to you and peace from God our father and [from] the Lord Jesus Christ.

Answers to Exercise 14.2

1. Flesh and blood 3. The will of the spirits 5. The mountains of Galilee 7. The light of the body 9. The throne of the heart 11. The nations of this world 13. Our names 15. And his name was John [lit.: and the name to him was John] 17. Our father, the [one] in heaven. [or: Our heavenly father] 19. Jesus sent them to the mountains. 21. John saw the throne of God in heaven. **23.** John 3:1-2: There was a man of the Pharisees, named Nicodemus, a ruler of the Jews; he came to him by night and said to him … **25.** Mark 14:22b: This is my body. **27.** John 4:20: Our fathers worshipped in this mountain, and you say that [in] Jerusalem is the place where men ought to worship. **29.** Matt 18:14: Thus is not the will of your heavenly father, that any of these little ones should perish. [lit. Thus is not the will before your heavenly father …] **31.** Matt 5:3: Blessed [are] the poor in spirit, because of them is the kingdom of heaven. **33.** John 6:68: Simon Peter answered him, "Lord, to whom will we go? You have words of eternal life, and we have believed and know that you are the holy [one] of God." Jesus answered them … **35.** John 8:12: I am the light of the world. **37.** Rev 6:16: And they say to the mountains and to the rocks, "Fall on us …" **39.** Rom 11:13: But I say to you Gentiles; … I am [the] apostle of the Gentiles. **41.** Matt 3:11: I [on the one hand] baptize by water for repentance … in/with [the] Holy Spirit and fire. **43.** Col 1:18: … and he is the head of the body of the church; … **45.** Gal 5:17, 19, 22: For the flesh lusts/desires against the spirit and the spirit against the flesh … the works of the flesh are clear … But the fruit of the spirit is love, joy, peace, … **47.** Luke 6:45 The good man out of the good treasure of the heart produces good, but the evil man out of evil produces evil; for his mouth speaks from the abundance of the heart.

Answers to Exercise 14.3

1. John 17:17b: Your word is truth. **3.** Rom 8:9: And if any[one] does not have the spirit of Christ, he is not his. **5.** Matt 21:23: And who gave you this authority? **7.** Rev 1:9a: I am John, your brother … **9.** Matt 12:3a: And he said to them, have you not read what David did … **11.** John 17:2a: … you gave him authority over all flesh … **13.** John 1:19-21: And this is the witness of John, when the Jews from Jerusalem sent priests and Levites to him in order to ask him, "Who are you?" And he confessed and did not deny, and confessed, "I am not the Christ." And they asked him, "Then who [are you]? Are you Elijah?" And he said, "I am not."

Answers to Exercise 15

1. I am able to write. 3. Do we wish to eat? 5. Is he able to lead? 7. I do not wish to eat stones 9. Do you wish to see God? 11. Peter came to greet Jesus. 13. Why do you wish to do this? 15. How do you wish to leave? 17. I wish to be like Jesus. You, do you wish to be like Jesus? 19. We keep the commandments because of love.

Appendix A: Answers to Exercises 309

21. Jesus wishes to go through Galilee. 23. He wishes to see Jesus make a sign. 25. δοξάζειν is the pres. inf. act. of δοξάζω, I glorify 27. ἀσπάζεσθαι is the pres. inf. mid. of ἀσπάζομαι, I greet 29. ἔπεσεν is the 3rd pers. sing. [str.] aor. ind. act. of πίπτω, I fall 31. ἦλθον is the 3rd pers. pl. [str.] aor. ind. act. of ἔρχομαι, I come [The subject of the verb is plural, which means that ἦλθον cannot be in the first person in this sentence] 33. εἶναι is the pres. inf. act. of εἰμί, I am 35. ἀγαπῶμεν is the 1st pers pl. pres. ind. act. of ἀγαπάω, I love 37. δύνασαι βαλεῖν; 39. θέλουσι προσεύξασθαι 41. αὐτὸς εὗρεν ἄρτον φαγεῖν 43. εὑρίσκει is the 3rd pers. sing. pres. ind. act. of εὑρίσκω, I find 45. εἰσελθεῖν is the [str.] aor. inf. act. of εἰσέρχομαι, I enter 47. ὄρει is the dat. neut. sing. of ὄρος, mountain [Note the dat. sing. article τῷ in τῷ ὄρει —thus even had you forgotten the declension of ὄρος, it still should be possible to parse ὄρει.] 49. πιστεύετε is the 2nd pers. pl. pres. ind. act. of πιστεύω, I believe 51. προσεύξασθαι is the aor. inf. mid. of προσεύχομαι, I pray **53.** John 5:39-40 You search the writings because in them you think to have eternal life; and it is they that bear witness to me; and you do not wish to come to me so that you might have life. [or, more idiomatically: You search the scriptures because you think you have eternal life in them ...] **55.** John 1:45-46 Philip finds Nathanael and says to him ... And Nathanael said to him, "Can any good thing come from Nazareth [lit.: Is there able to be anything good from Nazareth]?" **57.** Matt 19:17 If you wish to enter into life ... **59.** Matt 11:14 And if you wish to receive [him], he is Elijah ... **61.** John 4:20 Our fathers worshipped on this mountain; and you say that Jerusalem is the place where it is necessary to worship. **63.** Matt 12:38 We wish to see a sign from you. **65.** Matt 25:35 For I was hungry and you gave me [something] to eat ... **67.** John 6:60 This saying is harsh; who is able to hear [it]? **69.** John 8:46-47 Who of you convicts me of sin? If I speak truly, why do you not believe in me? He who is of God hears the words of God; because of this you do not hear, because you are not of God. **71.** John 8:21 Where I go you are not able to come. **73.** Matt 20:20-21a Then the mother of the sons of Zebedee approached him with her sons ... and he said to her, "What do you wish/want?" **75.** John 10:17 Because of this the father loves me, because I place/lay down my soul/life. **77.** Jam 2:14 If a man says he has faith but not works, is his faith able to save him? [μη in a question expects an answer of "no." [cf. 38.10]

Answers to Exercise 16

i. γράφω, γράφῃς, γράφῃ, γράφωμεν, γράφητε, γράφωσι(ν)
ii. πέμψω, πέμψῃς, πέμψῃ, πέμψωμεν, πέμψητε, πέμψωσι(ν)
iii. φάγω, φάγῃς, φάγῃ, φάγωμεν, φάγητε, φάγωσι(ν)
iv. θῶ, θῇς, θῇ, θῶμεν, θῆτε, θῶσι(ν)

1. Jesus came in order that he might save men [or: Jesus came in order to save men]. **3.** Jesus came to give life to all men. **5.** The blind men came to Jesus in order that he might open their eyes. **7.** Whoever wants righteousness is able to ask God concerning it. **9.** After the death of John he walked in Galilee. **11.** Whoever believes in Jesus will be saved. **13.** Here is the place where they put him. **15.** John preached the kingdom of heaven. **17.** No, I [definitely] do not drink. **19.** φαγεῖν is the [str.] aor. inf. act. of ἐσθίω, I eat **21.** ποιοῦσιν is the 3rd pers. pl. pres. ind. act. of ποιέω, I do

23. κόσμῳ is the dat. masc. sing. of κόσμος, world **25.** ἀνοιγῶσιν is the 3rd pers. pl. pres. subj. act. of ἀνοίγω, I open **27.** Matt 5:47 And if you greet your brothers only, what do you do [that is] extraordinary[1]? Do not even/also the Gentiles do the same? [[1]This word is hard to translate adequately into English. The concept is "above and beyond what is normally expected." Those wishing to establish righteousness by doing good deeds, need to do something more (something extra-ordinary) than the heathen Gentiles.] **29.** John 9:5 While I am in the world, I am the light of the world. [Remember, ὦ is the 1st pers. sing. pres. subj. act. of εἰμί] **31.** John 12:47 And if anyone hear of my words and does not keep [them], I do not judge him; for I did not come in order to judge the world, but in order that I might save the world. **33.** Matt 20:27 And whoever wishes to be first among (ἐν) you, shall be your slave. **35.** Mark 6:56a And whenever he enter(s/ed) into a village ... [the tense of the verb has been changed to one you know] **37.** Matt 20:33 ... They said to him, "Lord, in order that our eyes might open ..." [or better: "Lord, that our eyes might open." The subjunctive here is used to make a very polite request] **39.** John 9:35-36 Jesus heard that they cast him out, and when he found him he said, "Do you believe in the son of man?" He answered and said, "And who is [he], Lord, so that I might believe in him? Jesus said to him ... **41.** Matt 25:31a But when the son of man comes in his glory and all the angels with him, then he will sit upon the throne of his glory. **43.** John 16:4 "But I have spoken these things to you, so that when their hour comes you might remember them, that I spoke [them] to you." **45.** Luke 1:66c For the hand of the Lord was with him. [English does not tolerate, "And for ..."] **47.** John 11:32 Therefore, as Mary came where Jesus was, when she saw him she fell at his feet, saying to him, "Lord, if you were here, my brother would not [have] died." **49.** John 15:16-17 You did not choose me, but I chose you and appointed you in order that you might go and bear fruit, and [that] your fruit remain, so that whatever you ask the father in my name, he will/might give [it] to you. These things I command you, so that you might love one another. **51.** John 4:14 Whoever drinks from the water ... **53.** Matt 19:13 Then they brought children to him, so that he might place [his] hands on them and pray ...

Translation Passage 17: John 1:1-11

[1] In [the] beginning was the word, and the word was with [in the presence of] God, and the word was God. [2] He was in [the] beginning with God. [3] All things came to be [lit.: became] through him, and apart from him not one thing came to be. What came to be [became] [4] in him was life, and the life was the light of men. [5] And the light shines in the darkness, and the darkness did not understand it.

[6] There was a man, sent from God, named John. [7] He came as a witness, in order that he might witness concerning the light, in order that all might believe through him. [8] He [lit.: that man] was not the light, but [came] in order that he might witness concerning the light. [9] The true light, which lightens every man, was coming into the world. [10] He was in the world, and the world came to be [lit.: became] through him, and the world did not know him. [11] He came to his own, and his own did not accept him. [Note on vs. 9: το φῶς τὸ ἀληθινόν is either the neuter

Appendix A: Answers to Exercises 311

nominative (in which case the sentence would be translated: "He was the true light, which lightens all men, coming into the world") or neuter accusative (which is the way it has been translated here). The neuter accusative was chosen because it better fits the context. The transition between "He [John] was not the light …" and "He [Jesus] was the true light …" is somewhat abrupt.]

Answers to Exercise 17 (Review)

Translate into English

1. Jesus came in order that we might have eternal life. 2. God wishes to give righteousness to you. 3. I opened my mouth and said to him, "I fear no man." [Remember to follow the conventions of English and put direct speech in speech marks.] 4. Day and night they pray to the father. 5. The Spirit of God was upon the face of the waters. 6. Both John and Peter preach about[/concerning] the kingdom of heaven. 7. And Abraham called upon the name of the Lord in that place. 8. The child's mother asked Jesus to place his hand upon the head of the child. 9. We died to sin in order that we might live to God. 10. Jesus said that the Pharisees walk according to the commandments of men, and according to the laws of this world, but not according to the laws of God. 11. Simon Peter walked through the mountains of Galilee to[wards] the sea of Galilee. 12. The Jews cast Paul out of their synagogue. 13. We rejoice in the wisdom of Christ. 14. The blind [man] fell towards the feet of Jesus, and entreated him [in order] that he might open his eyes. 15. Who is able to be holy unless [except] he believes in the promise of God? 16. John baptized by water, but Peter and Paul by water and the spirit. 17. For flesh and blood alone are [or: is] not able to enter into the kingdom. 18. I think that demons seek to destroy the saints of the churches. 19. Happy [blessed] is the man who loves his wife. 20. The crowd follows the way of this age. 21. The hour to judge the world came. 22. The brothers raise the dead from the earth. 23. And it came to pass in those days that Jesus found evil men in the temple. 24. It is necessary to give glory to God. 25. An evil people took stones and gave them names and called them gods and worshipped them. 26. He answered and said, "I came in order that the Christ might speak truth to me." 27. Jesus forgave our sin in order that we might forgive the sins of one another. 28. Jesus came to his own, but his own do not receive him. 29. Therefore he said, "Truly truly I say to you that when the holy spirit comes …" 30. God destroyed the nations because of their evil works. 31. All good hearts bear the fruit of love. 32. The Sabbath was a sign to the sons of Abraham. 33. The crowd gathered again to hear the parables. 34. The Pharisees sent some of their servants to ask John if he was the Christ, and he answered, "No." 35. The apostles ate the bread with joy because they had peace in their hearts. 36. Love of the scripture begets wisdom and righteous deeds. 37. Simon Peter goes with the twelve to ask Jesus concerning the matter. 38. I placed my hope upon the faithful promise. 39. He does not know the hour when his lord comes, but the faithful servant still does good works. 40. The seven boats remained in the midst of the sea. 41. The two brothers dismissed the slaves after they spoke to them. 42. Does Jesus save both the body and soul, or is he able to save only the soul? 43. The dead have no authority. 44. I sent my mes-

sengers to the house of David to speak my words. 45. I see both good and evil in the church. 46. The beloved ruler does not fall.

Parse

47. 3rd pers. pl. pres. ind. mid. of ἀπέρχομαι, I go away 48. 2nd pers. sing. pres. ind. mid. of γίνομαι, I become 49. gen. neut. pl. of βιβλίον, book 50. aor. inf. act. of γράφω, I write 51. 1st pers. pl. pres. ind. act. of πιστεύω, I believe 52. 2nd pers. pl. pres. ind. act. of ἀποθνῄσκω, I die 53. 1st pers. pl. pres. ind. mid. of ἀσπάζομαι, I greet 54. 3rd pers. pl. aor. ind. act. of δοξάζω, I glorify 55. 1st pers. sing. pres. subj. act. of δίδωμι, I give 56. aor. inf. act. of πέμπω, I send 57. 2nd pers. pl. aor. ind. act. of ἐξέρχομαι, I go out 58. 2nd pers. pl. pres. ind. mid. of ἀπέρχομαι, I go away, depart 59. pres. inf. act. of λύω, I loose 60. 3rd pers. pl. aor. ind. act. of δείκνυμι, I show 61. 2nd pers. sing. [str.] aor. ind. act. of ἐκβάλλω, I throw out 62. 3rd pers. sing. aor. subj. act. of ἀφίημι, I forgive, let go 63. 2nd pers. sing. pres. ind. act. of ἀγαπάω, I love 64. 1st pers sing. aor. ind. act. of μαρτυρέω, I bear witness 65. 2nd pers. pl. pres. ind. mid. of προσέρχομαι, I come to 66. 3rd pers. sing. aor. ind. act. of συνάγω, I gather 67. 1st pers. pl. pres. ind. act. of χαίρω, I rejoice 68. 2nd pers. sing. aor. subj. act. of δίδωμι, I give 69. 1st pers. pl. [wk.] aor. ind. act. of τηρέω, I keep 70. 2nd pers. pl. [str.] aor. ind. act. of ὁράω, I see 71. 1st pers. pl. aor. ind. act. of ἵστημι, I place 72. 2nd pers. pl. [str.] aor. ind. act. of φέρω, I bear 73. 2nd pers. sing. aor. ind. act. of τίθημι, I place 74. 3rd pers. sing. pres. subj. act. of εἰμί, I am 75. 1st[/3rd] pers. sing.[/pl.] [str.] aor. ind. act. of ἄγω, I lead 76. 1st pers. pl. [str.] aor. ind. act. of πίνω, I drink 77. 2nd pers. pl. [wk.] aor. ind. act. of πέμπω, I send 78. 1st pers. pl. aor. subj. act. of ἵστημι, I place 79. 1st pers. sing. pres. subj. act. of ἵστημι, I place 80. 2nd pers. sing. pres. subj. act. of τίθημι, I place

Tricky bits

Words which differ only in accent: 81. ἤ or, than 82. ἡ the (nom. fem. sing. article) 83. ᾖ (3rd. pers. sing. pres. subj. act. of εἰμί) 84. αὐτή she (nom. fem. sing. of αὐτός) 85. αὕτη this (nom. fem. sing. of οὗτος) 86. αὐταί they (nom. fem. pl. of αὐτός) 87. αὗται these (nom. fem. pl. of οὗτος) 88. τις, τι someone, a certain [man/woman/thing] 89. τίς, τί who ...? what ...? which ...? 90. εἰ if 91. εἶ you are (second person singular, εἰμί)

Words which are rather similar: 92. ὅτε when, while, as long as 93. ὅτι because, that 94. ἡμεῖς we [nom. pl. of ἐγώ] 95. ὑμᾶς you [acc. pl. of σύ] 96. ἡμῶν our [gen. pl. of ἐγώ] 97. ὑμῶν your [gen. pl. of σύ] 98. αὐτός, -ή, -όν he/she/it, etc. 99. οὗτος -η, -ο this 100. οὕτως thus, so

Prepositions

101. σύν   + dat.: with
102. κατά   + acc.: according to
                 + gen.: down, against
103. πρός   + acc.: toward, with, against
                 + gen.: to the advantage of
                 + dat.: near, at, by

Appendix A: Answers to Exercises 313

104. ἐπὶ   + acc.: across, to, against
      + gen.: upon, near, before, over, on the basis of, at the time of
      + dat.: at, by, on
105. ἀπὸ   + gen.: from, away from
106. ἐκ, ἐξ   + gen.: from, out of, away from
107. ἐν   + dat.: in, by (instrument)
108. διὰ   + acc.: because of, on account of
      + gen.: through

Miscellaneous vocabulary items:

109. Not 110. How ...? 111. Outside 112. -ever 113. As, when, after 114. Subj.; no [strong denial] 115. Where 116. Subj.; if, -ever 117. I show 118. I persuade 119. On the one hand ... on the other 120. Light 121. Fire 122. I go away 123. Thus, so 124. Why 125. Here 126. I destroy 127. Time 128. First 129. Subj.; whoever

Write out in full

The declension of: 130. οἰκία οἰκία οἰκίαν οἰκίας οἰκίᾳ οἰκίαι οἰκίας οἰκιῶν οἰκίαις 131. φωνή φωνή φωνήν φωνῆς φωνῇ φωναί φωνάς φωνῶν φωναῖς 132. θέλημα, θέλημα θελήματος θελήματι θελήματα θελήματα θελημάτων θελήμασιν 133. ἄλλος ἄλλη ἄλλο, ἄλλον ἄλλην ἄλλο, ἄλλου etc.

The paradigm for: 134. βάλλειν 135. βαλεῖν 136. δοξάσαι 137. γίνομαι, γίνῃ, γίνεται, γινόμεθα, γίνεσθε, γίνονται 138. παρέδωκα παρέδωκας παρέδωκε(ν) παρεδώκαμεν παρεδώκατε παρέδωκαν 139. βάλλω, βάλλῃς, βάλλῃ, βάλλωμεν, βάλλητε, βάλλωσι(ν)

Translate into Greek

140. ὁ Ἰησοῦς ἀπέστειλε τὸν Πέτρον καὶ τόν Ἰωάννης εἰς τὸ ἱερόν. 141. ὁ οἶκος τῆς μητρὸς τοῦ Δαυίδ. 142. οἱ ἀγγελοί βλέπουσι τὸν πρόσωπον τοῦ θεοῦ. ἐὰν ἄνθρωπος ἴδῃ τὸν πρόσωπον τοῦ θεοῦ ἀποθάνῃ. 143. θεὸς ἄφηκε τὰς ἁμαρτίας ἡμῶν ἐν χάριτι. 144. ὁ ὄχλος ἐξῆλθεν ἐκ Ἱεροσόλυμα ἰδεῖν/βλεψαι τὸν Ἰωάννης.

Correct the mistakes in the following

145. τὰ τέκνα <u>ἔλαβον</u> ἄρτον. A neuter plural subject is followed by a 3rd person <u>singular</u> verb: τὰ τέκνα <u>ἔλαβεν</u> ἄρτον. 146. ὁ Πέτρος ἔβαλεν <u>ὁ λίθος</u>. The direct object should be in the accusative case: ὁ Πέτρος ἔβαλεν <u>τὸν λίθον</u>. 147. ὁ Ἰησοῦς ἔρχεται <u>ἵνα σῶσαι</u> ἁμαρτωλούς. You can say this *either* by ἵνα and a subjunctive, or by an infinitive alone, but you cannot mix the two kinds of construction. Thus the correct answer would be either: ὁ Ἰησοῦς ἔρχεται <u>σῶσαι</u> or: ὁ Ἰησοῦς ἔρχεται <u>ἵνα σώσῃ</u>. 148. οἱ δοῦλοι <u>πορεύομαι</u>. An explicit subject demands a third person verb: οἱ δοῦλοι <u>πορεύονται</u>. 149. ὁ θεὸς <u>οὐ</u> ἐστίν <u>ἄνθρωπον</u>. The verb εἰμί is copulative (i.e. uses the nominative case for both the subject and the complement. It equates the two parts of the sentence): ὁ θεὸς <u>οὐκ</u> ἐστὶν <u>ἄνθρωπος</u>.

Part 3

Answers to Exercise 18

1. The works which you do. **3.** Woe to the world because of enticement; for it is necessary that enticement come [lit. it is necessary to come enticement—but this needs to be translated into idiomatic English], but woe to the man through whom the enticement comes. **5.** And behold, a voice from heaven said, "This is my beloved son, in whom I am well pleased." **7.** But I do not receive testimony from man. **9.** And I turned to see the voice which spoke with me, and when I turned I saw seven golden lampstands. **11.** He [this man] came to witness, so that he might bear witness concerning the light, so that all might believe through him. He was not the light, but in order to witness concerning the light. It was the true light, which lightens all humans, which came into the world. **13.** And you do not wish to come to me in order that you might have life. I do not receive glory from men. **15.** Jesus saw Nathanael coming to him and said concerning him, "Behold a true Israelite in whom is no deceit." **17.** As it is, you boast in your arrogance. All such boasting is evil. **19.** If any[body] destroy the temple of God, God will destroy him [lit. this one]; for the temple of God is holy, which you are. **21.** 3rd. pers. sing. aor. subj. act. of μαρτυρέω, I bear witness **23.** dat. masc. pl. of διάκονος, slave **25.** 2nd. pers. pl. pres. subj. act. of ἔχω, I have **27.** acc. fem. sing. of γυνή, γυναικός, woman wife **29.** nom. masc. pl. of the second personal pronoun, σύ, you

Answers to Exercise 20.1

1. masc. λέγων, λέγοντα, λέγοντος, λέγοντι, λέγοντες, λέγοντας, λεγόντων, λέγουσι(ν)
fem. λέγουσα, λέγουσαν, λεγούσης, λεγούσῃ, λέγουσαι, λεγούσας, λεγουσῶν, λεγούσαις
neut. λέγον, λέγον, λέγοντος, λέγοντι, λέγοντα, λέγοντα, λεγόντων, λέγουσι(ν)

2. masc. ἀγαπήσας, ἀγαπήσαντα, ἀγαπήσαντος, ἀγαπήσαντι, ἀγαπήσαντες, ἀγαπήσαντας, ἀγαπησάντων, ἀγαπήσασι(ν)
fem. ἀγαπήσασα, ἀγαπήσασαν, ἀγαπησάσης, ἀγαπησάσῃ, ἀγαπήσασαι, ἀγαπησάσας, ἀγαπησασῶν, ἀγαπησάσαις
neut. ἀγαπῆσαν, ἀγαπῆσαν, ἀγαπήσαντος, ἀγαπήσαντι, ἀγαπήσαντα, ἀγαπήσαντα, ἀγαπησάντων, ἀγαπήσασι(ν)

3. masc. φαγών, φαγόντα, φαγόντος, φαγόντι, φαγόντες, φαγόντας, φαγόντων, φαγοῦσι(ν)
fem. φαγοῦσα, φαγοῦσαν, φαγούσης, φαγούσῃ, φαγοῦσαι, φαγούσας, φαγουσῶν, φαγούσαις
neut. φαγον, φαγον, φαγοντος, φαγοντι, φαγοντα, φαγοντα, φαγοντων, φαγοῦσι(ν)

4. masc. ποιῶν, ποιοῦντα, ποιοῦντος, ποιοῦντι, ποιοῦντες, ποιοῦντας, ποιούντων, ποιοῦσι(ν)
fem. ποιοῦσα, ποιοῦσαν, ποιούσης, ποιούσῃ, ποιοῦσαι, ποιούσας, ποιουσῶν, ποιούσαις
neut. ποιοῦν, ποιοῦν, ποιοῦντος, ποιοῦντι, ποιοῦντα, ποιοῦντα, ποιούντων, ποιοῦσι(ν)

Appendix A: Answers to Exercises 315

5. masc. γράψας, γράψαντα, γράψαντος, γράψαντι, γράψαντες, γράψαντας, γραψάντων, γράψασι(ν)
fem. γράψασα, γράψασαν, γραψάσης, γραψάσῃ, γράψασαι, γραψάσας, γραψασῶν, γραψάσαις
neut. γρᾶψαν, γρᾶψαν, γράψαντος, γράψαντι, γράψαντα, γράψαντα, γραψάντων, γράψασι(ν)

7. dat. fem. pl. pres. part. act. of λύω, I loose 9. gen. masc/neut. pl. pres. part. act. of λύω, I loose 11. nom./voc./acc. neut. sing. aor. part. act. of λύω, I loose 13. nom./voc. masc. sing. pres. part. act. of εἰμί, I am 15. 2nd. pers. sing. aor. ind. act. of ἔρχομαι, I go 17. 3rd. pers. pl. pres. ind. act. [or: dat. masc./neut. pl. pres. part. act.] of δοξάζω, I glorify 19. nom./voc. masc. sing. aor. part. act. of πίνω, I drink 21. nom./voc. masc. sing. aor. part. act. of ὁράω, I see 23. nom./voc. masc. sing. aor. part. act. λέγω, I say 25. nom./voc. fem. sing. aor. part. act. of βλέπω, I see 27. dat. masc./neut. sing. aor. part. act. of βάλλω, I throw 29. 2nd. pers. sing. aor. ind. act. of βλέπω, I see 31. nom./voc. masc. sing. pres. part. act. of ἐσθίω, I eat 33. nom./voc./acc. neut. sing. [also: acc. masc.] pres. part. act. of εἰμί, I am 35. 2nd. pers. sing. pres. subj. act. of δίδωμι, I give 37. acc. fem. sing. pres. part. act. of πίπτω, I fall 39. pres. inf. act. of δοξάζω, I glorify 41. 1st (3rd) pers. sing. (pl.) aor. ind. act. of ἄγω, I lead 43. nom./voc. masc. pl. aor. part. act. of γράφω, I write 45. 3rd. pers. sing. aor. ind. act. of ἀγαπάω, I love 47. 3rd. pers. sing. aor. ind. act. of λέγω, I say 49. 1st. pers. sing. aor. ind. act. of ἀφίημι, I forgive 51. nom./voc. masc. pl. pres. part. act. of βλέπω, I see 53. nom./voc./acc. neut. sing. pres. part. act. of εἰμί, I am 55. acc. fem. sing. aor. part. act. of πίπτω, I fall 57. 2nd. pers. sing. aor. ind. act. of ἵστημι, I place 59. 1st. pers. sing. aor. subj. mid. of δέχομαι, I receive 61. gen. fem. sing. aor. part. act. of γράφω, I write 63. nom./voc./acc. neut. sing. aor. part. act. of βλέπω, I see 65. 1st. pers. pl. [str.] aor. ind. act. of εὑρίσκω, I find 67. 1st. pers. pl. aor. ind. act. of ἀπόλλυμι, I destroy 69. 1st.[/3rd.] pers. sing. [/pl.] aor. ind. act. of ἐσθίω, I eat 71. gen. masc./neut. pl. pres. part. act. of λέγω, I say 73. 2nd pers. pl. aor. subj. act. of δίδωμι, I give 75. gen. fem. pl. pres. part. act. of εἰμί, I am 77. 2nd. pers. pl. aor. ind. act. of βάλλω, I throw 79. acc. (nom./voc./acc.) masc. (neut.) sing. (pl.) pres. part. act. of γράφω, I write 81. dat. fem. sing. aor. part. act. of βλέπω, I see 83. nom./voc. masc. pl. aor. part. act. of ὁράω, I see 85. dat. masc./neut. sing. aor. part. act. of ἀγαπάω, I love 87. nom./voc. masc. sing. str. aor. part. act. of εὑρίσκω, I find 89. nom./voc./acc. neut. sing. aor. part. act. of λαλέω, I say 91. The one who says 93. The one who calls 95. The one who eats 97. The one who falls 98. The one who is [note: this is one of the terms for the ultimate God; cf. the LXX of Exod 3:14] 99. The lover [or: the one who loves] 101. The one who finds

Answers to Exercise 20.2

1. gen. fem. sing. pres. part. mid. of πορεύομαι, I go 3. dat. masc./neut. pl. pres. part. mid. of πορεύομαι, I go 5. nom./voc. masc. sing. aor. part. act. of λύω, I loose 7. acc. masc. pl. pres. part. act. of λύω, I loose 9. 3rd pers. sing. pres. ind. pass. of φοβέομαι, I fear 11. dat. masc./neut. pl. pres. part. mid. of προσεύχομαι, I pray 13. 3rd pers. sing. aor. ind. act. of λαμβάνω, I take 15. nom./voc. fem. sing. pres.

part. act. of εἰμί, I am **17.** nom. fem. pl. pres. part. pass. of ἀποκρίνομαι, I answer **19.** aor. inf. act. of ὁράω, I see **21.** acc. masc. pl. pres. part. pass. of φοβέομαι, I fear **23.** acc. fem. sing. pres. part. mid. of προσεύχομαι, I pray **25.** dat. fem. pl. aor. part. act. of ἵστημι, I stand **27.** 3rd pers. pl. aor. ind. act. of ἵστημι, I stand **29.** gen. masc./fem./neut. pl. pres. part. pass. of ἀποκρίνομαι, I answer **31.** dat. fem. sing. pres. part. mid. of ἀσπάζομαι, I greet **33.** gen. masc./neut. sing. pres. part. mid. of προσέρχομαι, I approach **35.** acc. fem. pl. pres. part. pass. of φοβέομαι, I fear **37.** dat. fem. sing. pres. part. mid. of ἐξέρχομαι, I go out **39.** 2nd pers. pl. aor. subj. act. of δίδωμι, I give **41.** gen. masc./neut. sing. pres. part. act. of τίθημι, I place **43.** dat. fem. pl. pres. part. act. of εἰμί, I am **45.** nom. masc. sing. aor. part. act. of δίδωμι, I give

47.   φοβούμενος   φοβουμένη   φοβούμενον
         φοβούμενον   φοβουμένην   φοβούμενον
         φοβούμενου   φοβουμένης   etc.

48.   see 20.1.4

49.   δούς   δοῦσα   δόν
         δόντα   δοῦσαν   δόν
         δόντος   δούσης   etc.

50. The two participles in this verse should not create difficulty: λέγων .. saying; ὁ ἀκολουθῶν .. the one who follows **51.** διδάσκων .. while [he was] teaching, or when teaching **52.** παράγων .. while/as he was going along, as he was passing by **53.** λέγων .. saying **54.** ἐγένετο, met first in Vocabulary 12.3, is often best tranlated as "it came to pass." It is from the verb γίνομαι. ἀναβαίνων .. as he went up; σχιζομένους .. opened; καταβαῖνον .. coming down. Notice the contrast between ἀναβαίνων and καταβαῖνον; ἀνα-βαίνων and κατα-βαῖνον: κατά means "down"; ἀνά means "up." **55.** παράγων .. as he was going; while going; ἀμφιβάλλοντας .. casting **56.** ἐξελθών .. while leaving **57.** [they] ἐκπορευομένων .. while they were leaving; καθήμενοι .. sitting; λέγοντες .. saying

Further Notes on Translation Passage 20.2: John 9:1-41

Verse: **1.** παράγων "as he was passing by" **2.** λέγοντες "saying" **4.** τοῦ πέμψαντος "(of) the one who sent" **6.** εἰπών "when he had said" [or: "having said"] **7.** Ἀπεσταλμένος "sent" [the English past participle of "to send"]; βλέπων "seeing" **8.** οἱ θεωροῦντες "those who saw"; ὁ καθήμενος "the one who sat"; προσαιτῶν "begged." Note that the article of ὁ καθήμενος could stand with both participles, in which case the phrase would read, "the one who sat and the one who begged." In English this would be rather cumbersome, so it is probably best translated as "the one who sat and begged." **11.** ἀπελθών ... καὶ νιψάμενος "when I went and washed" **18.** τοῦ ἀναβλέψαντος "[of] the one who recovered his sight" **19.** λέγοντες "saying" **22.** γένηται is the 3rd pers. sing. aor. subj. of γίνομαι (ἵνα is followed by a subjunctive; γένηται is a strong aorist subjunctive middle). **35.** εὑρών "when he found him" **39.** οἱ βλέποντες "those who see" **40.** ὄντες is a participial form of εἰμί (as you remembered?). οἱ ... ὄντες "those who were." This phrase is actually quite difficult, but with a little care you should be able to translate it. The main verb is Ἤκουσαν, which is a 3rd pers. pl. aorist, "they heard." The subject of the sentence is οἱ μετ' αὐτοῦ ὄντες,

Appendix A: Answers to Exercises

"those who are/were with him." The ταῦτα is the direct object of the verb, "these things." The ἐκ τῶν Φαρισαίων is a prepositional phrase which can be added last to the translation. The whole verse might be translated: "Those who were with him of the Pharisees heard these things ..." Less literally: "Those Pharisees who were with him heard these things ..."

Answers to Exercise 21

1. You loose 3. You loosed 5. He/she/it has thrown 7. They throw 9. We have saved 11. You have saved 13. You have gone 15. I have heard 17. You have loved 19. He/she/it has known 21. You have gone 23. You have gone 25. They have believed 27. We speak [pres. ind. act.] 29. He/she/it has thrown 31. We have gone out 33. I have taken 35. He/she/it stands [remember, the perfect tense of ἵστημι is translated with an English transitive present tense] 37. You have gone into 39. They have known 41. They have said 43. I have fallen 45. You gave 47. He/she/it has loved 49. You have said 51. We have taken 53. We fell 55. You have placed 57. I carried / bore 59. He/she/it loves 61. We have asked 63. He/she/it has kept **65.** nom./voc. masc. pl. perf. part. act. of λύω, I loose **67.** 2nd pers. sing. perf. ind. act. of δίδωμι, I give **69.** 3rd pers. sing. perf. ind. act. of ποιέω, I do **71.** nom./voc. masc. sing. perf. part. act. of τίθημι, I place **73.** ὁ μισῶν ... he who hates. **74.** ὁ ... ἀκούων καὶ πιστεύων ... the one who hears and believes [or he who hears and believes]; τῷ πεμφαντί ... [in] the one who sent **75.** Καί ... καί, often means "both ... and," although whether it should be translated in this way in this instance is debatable; ὁ λαλῶν .. he who speaks.

Notes on Translation Passage 21: John 8:12-59

John chapter eight, verse:
12. ὁ ἀκολουθῶν "the one who follows"; οὐ μή + subj. expresses strong negation.
16. ὁ πέμψας "the one who sent"; ὁ πέμψας με πατήρ "the father who sent me"
20. διδάσκων "while teaching"
21. The future of [ἀπο]θνήσκω is [ἀπο]θανοῦμαι [see Chap. 25], which appears to follow a verb stem [ἀπο]θανέ-, whence the 2nd pers. pl. future of [ἀπο]θνήσκω is ἀποθανεῖσθε.
30. λαλοῦντος "when he said"

Answers to Exercise 22.1

1. I was/they were speaking; I/they began speaking 3. I was/they were leading; I/they began to lead 5. You were gathering; You began gathering 7. I was/they were dying; I/they began to die 9. We were throwing; We began to throw 11. I was/they were asking; I/they began to ask 13. You were thinking; You began thinking 15. He/she/it was knowing; He/she/it began to know

Answers to Exercise 22.2

1. You were saying; You began to say 2. You said 3. We fell 4. We were falling; We began to fall 5. He/she/it was seeing; He/she/it began to see 6. He/she/it saw 7. You

lead 8. You led 9. You were leading; You began to lead 11. I[/they] was[/were] persuading; I/they began persuading 13. You were throwing; You began to throw 15. You have thrown 17. They asked 19. You were 21. He/she/it loved 23. He/she/it was having; He/she/it began to have 25. He/she/it was asking; He/she/it began to ask 27. He/she/it asked 29. They sent 31. They were 33. You took 35. We departed 37. You drank 39. You were drinking; You began drinking 41. You were [This might also be parsed as a subjunctive, whereupon it could be translated as "you might be."] 43. You bore witness 45. I was receiving; I began to receive 47. We were eating; We began to eat 49. They were afraid; They began to fear 51. You were approaching; You began approaching 53. We were doing; We began to do **57.** προσκαλεσάμενος "when he had called/summoned." You will recognize that this is an aorist middle middle form of the verb προσκαλέομαι, which Kubo lists as προσκαλέω in the special vocabulary for Mark. Other dictionaries list it as a deponent verb, προσκαλέομαι. **60.** ἠσθένει the 3rd pers. sing. aor. ind. act. of ἀσθενέω. Note that the ending ε + ε(ν) has contracted to ει. ἀκούσας when he heard; ἠρώτα is the 3rd pers. imp. ind. act. of ἐρωτάω. ἤμελλεν is the irregular imperfect of μέλλω. **67.** Like εἰμί, the verb ὑπάρχω has a nominative case for both the subject and direct object of the verb. **69.** The phrase, καὶ οὐδὲ ἁλύσει οὐκέτι οὐδεὶς ἐδύνατο αὐτὸν δῆσαι, takes a little thinking before it can be translated, although you have all the necessary vocabulary and grammar, and if you apply the translation rules that you have long known about [first find the verb, then the subject and the direct object, and then add all the other bits in], they will work. The verb is ἐδύνατο ... δῆσαι. Δῆσαι is the infinitive of δέω, I bind, and so the heart of the sentence is "was able to bind [him]." The subject is οὐδείς, no one—thus the last part of the sentence is [using the Greek word order] no longer [was] anybody able to bind him. The last fragment is οὐδὲ ἁλύσει, which means, "not even [with] chains." Thus the whole phrase is: "And nobody was any longer able to bind him, not even with chains," or: "And it was no longer possible to bind him, even with chains." **77.** διδάσκων "while he was teaching"

Answers to Revision Exercise 23

1. You go/come 2. They say 3. They know 4. You have loosed 5. They work 6. We were pursuading/began to persuade 7. You threw 8. He/she/it was taking / began to take 9. You asked 10. We heard 11. I forgive 12. You released 13. You have given 14. To loose 15. You were writing / began to write 16. You said 17. He/she/it answers 18. You ate 19. He/she/it was knowing / began to know 20. I call 21. I have gone/come 22. He/she/it has heard 23. You were saving / began to save 24. We threw out 25. You forgave 26. You hoped 27. You were hoping / began to hope 28. You took 29. They wrote 30. I am able to see

31. We call 32. I/they were eating / began to eat 33. We call 34. It is necessary to eat 35. You opened 36. You drink 37. He/she/it were hearing / began to hear 38. I give 39. They forgave 40. They were 41. We have asked 42. I place 43. They have thrown 44. I loosed 45. We have said 46. I /They were ascending / began to ascend 47. He/she/it has hoped 48. We have known 49. I / They were loosing / began to loose 50. They have loved 51. I / They were calling / began to call 52. I stand 53. You have called 54. We find 55. I see 56. You were descending / began to descend 57. You love 58. You become

Appendix A: Answers to Exercises 319

59. You stood 60. We have found 61. You have written 62. He/she/it called 63. I show 64. They throw 65. I/they saw 66. You speak 67. We lead 68. You have forgiven 69. He/she/it found 70. You came 71. You gave 72. To take 73. He/she/it became, happened 74. You send 75. He/she/it was 76. I went up/ascended 77. I have become 78. He/she/it stood 79. You destroyed 80. You drank 81. He/she/it bore 82. You have seen 83. You have gone 84. You were having / began to have 85. I / They were judging / began to judge 86. You judge 87. You hate 88. They have fallen

89. We have thrown 90. He / she / it showed 91. They have placed 92. They opened 93. I / They were sending / began to send 94. You have sent 95. We sent 96. I send 97. I wish to say 98. We become 99. I knew [aor. of γινώσκω] 100. He/she/it has descended 101. You destroyed 102. He/she/it had 103. He/she/it begat 104. You entered 105. We raise/wake 106. We go up/ascend 107. You led 108. We throw 109. They greet 110. We are 111. You go out 112. We were drinking / began to drink 113. He/she/it answered

114. I have borne 115. I testify 116. They pray 117. We fear 118. The one who believes 119. The one who has seen 120. You believe 121. We gave 122. To see 123. I/They were leading / began to lead 124. You placed 125. We were bearing / began to bear 126. I have persuaded 127. You owe 128. He/she/it was keeping / began to keep 129. They wonder 130. He/she/it was dying / began to die 131. I destroyed 132. You sent [away] 133. He/she/it was killing / began to kill 134. You ask 135. He/she/it delivered, entrusted 136. You were loving / began to love 137. I loved 138. I have had

139. You have opened. 140. We showed 141. He/she/it has drunk 142. They have destroyed 143. You destroyed 144. They have died 145. I / they were falling / began to fall 146. They have persuaded 147. You placed 148. You were killing / began to kill 149. I sit 150. We gathered 151. He/she/it persuaded 152. He/she/it fell 153. You were [see 22.5] 154. You worship 155. You rejoice 156. We seek 157. He/she/it said / was saying / began to say 158. I have taken 159. You died 160. He/she/it spoke 161. You bear 162. You fall

163. aor. inf. act. of λύω, I loose **164**. 2nd pers. pl. pres. subj. act. of λύω, I loose **165**. 1st. pers. pl. pres. ind./subj. act. of ζάω, I live **166**. 3rd. pers. pl. pres. subj. mid./mid. of ἔρχομαι, I come **167**. nom. masc. pl. aor. part. act. of λέγω, I say **168**. 1st pers. pl. aor. subj. act. of λύω, I loose **169**. dat. masc./neut. sing. aor. part. act. of λαμβάνω, I take **170**. aor. inf. act. of βάλλω, I throw **171**. nom./acc. neut. sing. perf. part. act. of ἀγαπάω, I love **172**. 3rd. pers. sing. aor. subj. act. of δίδωμι, I give

173. acc. masc. pl. aor. part. act. of λύω, I loose **174**. gen. fem. sing. pres. part. act. of εἰμί, I am **175**. gen. fem. pl. aor. part. act. of λύω, I loose **176**. aor. inf. act. of ἐσθίω, I eat **177**. pres. inf. act of εἰμί, I am **178**. aor. inf. act. of ἄγω, I lead **179**. gen. fem. sing. [or acc. fem. pl.] perf. part. act. of ἀφίημι, I forgive **180**. dat. masc./neut. sing. aor. part. act. of ἀφίημι, I forgive **181**. 1st pers sing. / 3rd pers. pl. imperf. ind. act. of λαλέω, I speak **182**. 3rd. pers. sing. aor. subj. act. of ἀγαπάω, I love

183. acc. masc. pl. pres. part. act. of τίθημι, I place **184**. 3rd. pers. sing. aor. subj. act. of βάλλω, I throw **185**. dat. fem. pl. perf. part. act. of λύω, I loose **186**. acc. [nom./acc.] masc.[neut.] sing [pl.] pres. part. act. of ἄγω, I lead **187**. 2nd pers. sing.

pres. subj. act. of ἀφίημι, I forgive **188**. 1st pers. sing. aor. subj. act. of ἀφίημι, I forgive **189**. nom. masc. sing. pres. part. act. of εἰμί, I am **190**. nom. masc. sing. aor. part. act. of δίδωμι, I give **191**. gen. masc./neut. sing. aor. part. act. of the verb ἔρχομαι, I go/come **192**. nom. masc. pl. pres. part. act. of δίδωμι, I give

193. aor. inf. act. of ὁράω, I see **194**. 2nd pers. pl. pres. subj. act. of ἵστημι, I place **195**. 3rd pers. pl. aor. subj. act. of ἵστημι, I place **196**. gen. masc./neut. sing. pres. part. act. of δείκνυμι, I show **197**. 2nd pers. sing. aor. subjunctive act. of ὁράω, I see **198**. 1st pers. pl. pres. subj. act. of τίθημι, I place **199**. nom. fem. sing. perf. part. act. of οἶδα, I know **200**. gen. masc./neut. sing. aor. part. act. of ἵστημι, I place **201**. nom./acc. neut. pl. of θέλημα, -ατος, τό, will **202**. 3rd pers. sing. aor. ind. act. of δείκνυμι, I show **203**. 1st pers. sing. pres. subj. act. of εἰμί, I am **204**. nom. masc. sing. pres. part. act. of δίδωμι, I give **205**. 1st pers. sing. aor. subj. act. of τίθημι, I place **206**. dat. neut. sing. of ἔθνος, τό nation **207**. 2nd pers. sing. aor. ind. act. of ἁμαρτάνω, I sin

208. N   κακός   κακή   κακόν
        A   κακόν   κακήν   κακόν, etc
209. N   γράψας   γράψασα   γρᾶψαν
        A   γράψαντα   γραψάσαν   γρᾶψαν
        G   γράψαντος   γραψάσης   γράψαντος, etc

210. ζῶ, ζῇς, ζῇ, ζῶμεν, ζῆτε, ζῶσι(ν) **211**. φοβοῦμαι, φοβῇ, φοβεῖται, φοβούμεθα, φοβεῖσθε, φοβοῦνται **212**. ᾔτησα, ᾔτησας, ᾔτησεν, ᾐτήσαμεν, ᾐτήσατε, ᾔτησαν **213**. εὗρον, εὗρες, εὗρεν, εὕρομεν, εὕρετε, εὗρον **214**. ἔπινον, ἔπινες, ἔπινεν, ἐπίνομεν, ἐπίνετε, ἔπινον **215**. λελάληκα, λελάληκας, λελάληκεν, λελαλήκαμεν, λελαλήκατε, λελαλήκασιν

216. N   προσευχόμενος   προσευχομένη   προσευχόμενον
         A   προσευχόμενον   προσευχομένην   προσευχόμενον, etc.
217. νύξ, νύκτα, νυκτός, νυκτί, νύκτες, νύκτας, νυκτῶν, νυξί(ν)
218. N   δούς   δοῦσα   δόν
         A   δόντα   δοῦσαν   δόν
         G   δόντος   δούσης   δόντος, etc.

219. ἔρχομαι, ἦλθον, ἐλήλυθα **220**. λέγω, εἶπον, εἴρηκα **221**. ἀποστέλλω, ἀπέστειλα, ἀπέσταλκα **222**. ἔχω, ἔσχον, ἔσχηχα **223**. περί + acc. **around**, about, near **224**. παρά + dat. **at, by, beside, near** **225**. ἐπί + dat. **at, by, on** **226**. σύν + dat. with **227**. παρά + acc. **by, along, near, more than, against** **228**. ἐκ, ἐξ + gen. from, out of, away from **229**. παρά + gen. from **230**. ἀπό + gen. from **231**. ἐπί + gen. **upon**, near, before, over, on the basis **232**. μετά + acc. **after**, behind **233**. διά + acc. because of, on account of **234**. πρός + gen. to the advantage of **235**. κατά + acc. according to **236**. εἰς + acc. into, towards **237**. πρός + acc. toward, with, against **238**. μετά + gen. **with** **239**. διά + gen. through **240**. ἐπί + acc. across, to, against **241**. ἐν + dat. in, by (instrument) **242**. κατά + gen. down, against **243**. περί + gen. **about, concerning** **244**. πρός + dat. near, at, by

245. εἰ if **246**. εἶ you are (second person singular, εἰμι, I am) **247**. ἡμῶν our [gen. pl. of ἐγώ] **248**. ὑμῶν your [gen. pl. of σύ] **249**. αὐτή she (nom. fem. sing. of αὐτός) **250**. αὕτη this (nom. fem. sing. of οὗτος) **251**. οἵ who, that (nom. masc. pl. rel. pron.) **252**. οἱ the (nom. masc. pl. article) **253**. ἦν I was (1st pres. sing. im-

Appendix A: Answers to Exercises 321

perfect. ind. act. of εἰμί, I am) **254.** ἥν who (acc. fem. sing. of the relative pron. ὅς, who) **255.** ἐν in **256.** ἕν one (nom./acc. neut. sing. of εἷς, μία, ἕν) **257.** ὅτε when, while, as long as **258.** ὅτι because, that **259.** ὅ which, that (nom./acc. neut. sing. rel. pron.) **260.** ὁ the (nom. masc. sing. article) **261.** ἡμεῖς we [nom. pl. of ἐγώ] **262.** ὑμᾶς you [acc. pl. of σύ] **263.** ὄν being (nom/acc neut. sing. pres. part. act. of εἰμί) **264.** ὅν who, that (acc. masc. sing of the relative pronoun). **265.** ποτέ once, formerly **266.** τότε then, at that time; next **267.** οὐ not **268.** οὗ whose, of whom (gen. sing. masc./neut. rel. pron) **269.** αὐταί they (nom. fem. pl. of αὐτός) **270.** αὗται these (nom. fem. pl. of οὗτος) **271.** αὐτός, -ή, -όν he/she/it, etc. **272.** οὗτος, αὕτη, τοῦτο this **273.** τις, τι someone, a certain [man/woman/thing] **274.** τίς, τί who ...? what ...? which ...? **275.** ᾧ to whom (dat. masc./neut. sing. rel. pron.) **276.** ὦ I might be (1st. pers. sing. pres. subjunctive act. of εἰμί, I am) **277.** οὗτος this (nom. masc. sing. of οὗτος, αὕτη, τοῦτον **278.** οὕτως thus, so **279.** ἤ or, than **280.** ἡ the (nom. fem. sing. article) **281.** ἥ who, that (nom. fem. sing. rel. pron.) **282.** ᾖ [he might be] (3rd. pers. sing. pres. subj. act. of εἰμι) **283.** Write down the two possible meanings of the word ὅτι: ὅτι because, that ὅτι whoever, whatever (nom. neut. sing. of ὅστις)

284. The seven churches **285.** And/but not **286.** Rightly, well **287.** The evil eye **288.** The holy prophets **289.** Flesh and blood **290.** The sinful deed **291.** How ...? **292.** In that hour **293.** Neither man nor woman **294.** Heaven and earth **295.** The hope of eternal life **296.** Other boats **297.** Galilee of the Gentiles/nations **298.** And he **299.** The face of the sea

300. His twelve disciples **301.** As many as received him, he gave authority to become children of God **302.** One of their own prophets said ... [Tit 1:12] **303.** Why ...? **304.** Just as **305.** Still, yet **306.** Now **307.** Woe **308.** The faithful slave **309.** The Son is able to do nothing of himself, except what he sees the Father doing [John 5:19] **310.** The water of life **311.** The evil place **312.** Night and day **313.** The father of all **314.** Where ...? **315.** Again **316.** Hand and foot **317.** As **318.** The true apostle **319.** The whole world/cosmos **320.** Such a kind

321. A teacher of righteousness **322.** Now **323.** I place upon **324.** Much sin **325.** The angel of death **326.** Till, until **327.** The judgment of Jerusalem **328.** Whoever **329.** Just as **330.** Thus, so **331.** The beloved brother of Abraham **332.** The one who asks **333.** Whoever believes saves **334.** The promise of glory **335.** The one who approaches **336.** Those who rejoice in the Lord **337.** Already

338. And I, I also **339.** The great house **340.** The two demons **341.** A man of authority **342.** The throne of the kingdom **343.** The wisdom of the blind **344.** I wish to be like Jesus **345.** Does the Christ teach the new law? **346.** The resurrection of the dead **347.** For he who remains in my name will be blessed/happy **348.** The disciples of the Pharisees **349.** The voice of he who meets/receives me

350. Therefore, the Jews worship in synagogues, but those who follow Christ Jesus worship in churches. **351.** Do you think that David was righteous? **352.** The true worshipper of the only God **353.** The child is good, but his brother is not **354.** The words of my mouth **355.** The Son of God remains/abides forever

356. The second book of Simon Peter 357. Your souls but not your bodies 358. Jesus said, I am the way, the truth and the life 359. He asked bread from John 360. The fruits of the spirit are love, joy, peace ... 361. The first of the Sabbaths [i.e. the first day of the week] 362. The witness/testimony of Paul 363. Here 364. Your mother 365. And 366. Behold

367. The one who glorifies in hope 368. The time of grace 369. So that he might depart 370. Greater 371. The ruler of the temple 372. The fire which gave light 373. A heart of stone 374. The good people of the mountain 375. The head of the house 376. Where 377. Whenever 378. Those who sin 379. In the midst of the crowd 380. The commandments of children 381. [Of] one another 382. Amen [truly] 383. The writings/scriptures 384. A parable of his departure 385. First 386. The words of the one who saves 387. The sign of the prophet

Part 4

Answers to Exercise 24.1

1. I am taken 2. I was being taken / began to be taken 3. We were taken 4. I was taken 5. I have been taken 6. I take 7. I was taking / began to take 8. I took 9. I have taken 10. We were loosed 11. We were being loosed 12. We are loosed 13. We have been loosed 14. We were loosing 15. We loosed 16. We have loosed 17. They have given 19. You gave 21. They gave 23. It is said 25. He/she/it was borne 27. It was being said 29. I placed 31. I have been placed 33. They were seen 35. It has been said 37. You have been thrown 39. We were seen 41. He/she/it bears 43. You were saying 45. You were throwing 47. I have placed 49. We were opened 51. You placed 53. It was said 55. I was forgiven 57. I was raised 59. He/she/it was persuaded 61. He/she/it has been raised 63. You were sent 65. You were having 73. 3rd pers. sing. aor. ind. pass. of γεννάω, I beget 75. gen. masc. sing. of πατήρ, πατρός, ὁ, father 76. 3rd pers. sing. aor. ind. pass. [used in an active sense] of ἀποκρίνομαι, I answer 77. 1st pers. sing. aor. ind. act. of ὁράω, I see 79. 3rd pers. sing. aor. ind. pass. of βαπτίζω, I baptize

Answers to Exercise 24.2

1. 2nd pers. pl. aor. sub. pass. of λύω, I loose **2.** nom. masc. sing. aor. part. pass. of λύω, I loose **3.** 1st. pers. pl. imp. ind. pass. of λύω, I loose **4.** aor. inf. pass. of λύω, I loose **5.** nom./acc. neut. pl. pres. part. pass. of λύω, I loose **6.** 3rd pers. sing. pres. ind. pass. of λύω, I loose **7.** 2nd pers. pl. pres. sub. act. of λύω, I loose **8.** aor. inf. act. of λύω, I loose **9.** nom. masc. pl. perf. part. pass. of λύω, I loose **10.** pres. inf. pass. of λύω, I loose **11.** nom. masc. sing. pres. part. act. of λύω, I loose **12.** 2nd pers. pl. aor. sub. act. of λύω, I loose **13.** dat. masc./neut. pl. pres. part. pass. of λύω, I loose **14.** 2nd. pers. sing. aor. subj. pass. of λύω, I loose **15.** 3rd. pers. pl. perf. ind. act. of λύω, I loose **16.** dat. fem. sing. aor. part. pass. of λύω, I loose **17.** acc. fem. sing. perf. part. pass. of λύω, I loose **18.** 2nd. pers. pl. aor. ind. act. of λύω, I loose **19.** gen. masc./neut. pl. pres. part. act. of λύω, I loose

Appendix A: Answers to Exercises 323

20. 2nd pers. pl. pres. sub. pass. of λύω, I loose 21. perf. inf. pass. of λύω, I loose 22. acc. masc. pl. aor. part. pass. of λύω, I loose 23. dat. fem. sing. perf. part. act. of λύω, I loose 24. 1st pers. pl. aor. subj. pass. of λύω, I loose 25. pres. inf. act. of λύω, I loose 26. nom./acc. neut. sing. aor. part. pass. of λύω, I loose 27. nom. fem. sing. aor. part. act. of λύω, I loose 29. 1st. pers. sing. perf. ind. pass. of βάλλω, I throw 31. 1st pers. sing. aor. subj. pass. of βάλλω, I throw 33. nom. masc. pl. perf. part. pass. of βάλλω, I throw 35. 1st pers. sing. aor. subj. pass. of λαμβάνω, I take 37. nom. masc. sing. aor. part. pass. of λέγω, I say

39. dat. masc./neut. sing. aor. part. pass. of αἴρω, I lift up 41. nom. fem. pl. pres. part. pass. of λαμβάνω, I take 42. ἀκούοντος — those hearing; συνιέντος — gen. masc. sing. pres. part. act. of συνίημι. This matches ἀκούοντος, and the basic idea is "all those who hear and do not understand ..."; ὁ παρὰ τὴν ὁδὸν σπαρείς is easier if you realize that the basic idea is ὁ ... σπαρείς. σπαρείς is the aor. part. pass. of σπείρω. γενομένης ... "when ... becomes [arises]." συνιείς is the nom. masc. sing. pres. part. act. of συνίημι. 43. ἀρθήσεται is the fut. ind. pass. of αἴρω, while δοθήσεται is the fut. ind. pass. of δίδωμι. 46. ἑστῶτες perf. ind. part. of ἵστημι, used intransitively, with present meaning ["standing / while standing"; see *Int*.6.14].

Notes on Translation Passage 24.2: John 3:1-36

v. 2 ἐλήλυθας is perfect ind. act. of ἔρχομαι, while ᾖ is the subj of εἰμί
v. 4 ὤν is the nom. masc. sing. pres. part. act. of εἰμί; either "being," or "when ..."
v. 6 τὸ γεγεννημένον is the nom. neut. sing. perf. part. pass. of γεννάω (note article): "that which has been born ..."
v. 13 καταβάς is the nom. masc. sing. aor. part. act. of καταβαίνω

Answers to Exercise 25

1. I shall hear 3. You throw 5. They will see 7. They will ask 9. He/she/it will ask 11. I shall lead 13. To give 15. They saw 17. You persuade 19. He/she/it will forgive 21. I destroy 23. You will bear 25. You ate 27. I shall remain [notice accent!] 29. You will give 31. You will release 33. We shall throw 35. You will fear 37. You will be 39. I shall drink 41. You will lead 43. You threw 45. They will eat 47. We shall send 49. We shall remain 51. You will give

53. I shall die 55. You will speak 57. We shall ask 59. To throw 61. He/she/it will call 63. They eat 65. He/she/it will destroy 67. He/she/it asks 69. I/they said 71. I place 73. They said 75. You will become 77. We gave 79. He/she/it will bear 81. To see 83. You placed 85. We shall judge 87. You send 89. You will go out 91. You found 93. You become 95. You will destroy 97. You will persuade 99. I shall depart 101. You will write 103. You went out 105. You seek

107. You will save 109. You love 111. You will take 113. He/she/it will glorify 115. To save 117. We shall seek 119. He/she/it will become 121. You will save 123. We shall place 125. You will do 127. We shall have 129. He/she/it will find 131. αἰτήσω 133. εἶδεν 135. ἐρεῖ 137. ἀπολέσει 139. πίονται 141. ἐσόμεθα 143. γενήσονται 145. κρίνουσι(ν) 147. ἔσχον 149. γράψωμεν 151. ἐζήτησα 153. οἴσουσι(ν) 155. ἀποστέλετε 157. ἐλεύσεσθε 159. βάλλετε

161. ἔσωσα 163. ἀγαπήσει 165. ἀπόστελω 167. δοξάσει 169. περιπατήσουσι(ν) 171. φάγομαι 173. εἶδον 175. ὄψονται **177.** Gen. masc. pl. of ὀφθαλμός, eye **179.** 3rd. pers. sing. pres. ind. mid. of ἔρχομαι, I go/come **181.** 2nd. pers. pl. fut. ind. act. of αἰτέω, I ask **183.** 3rd. pers. pl. aor. ind. act. of ἐσθίω, I eat **185.** 2nd. pers. pl. aor. subj. act. of ὁράω, I see **187.** Many will say to me on that day, "Lord lord, did we not prophecy in your name, and cast out demons in your name, and perform many miracles in your name?"

189. For whoever does the will of God, he is my brother and sister and mother. **191.** I am the bread of life. Your fathers ate the manna in the desert and died. This is the bread which comes down from heaven, so that anybody might eat from it and not die. I am the living bread which came down from heaven; if anybody eat from this bread he will live for ever, and the bread which I give is my flesh.

193. And he gave authority to him to make/do judgment, because he is the son of man. Do not wonder at this, because an hour comes in which all those in the tombs will hear his voice and will come forth ...

Notes on Translation Passage 25

v. 6: This verse is quite difficult to translate, so the words that cause most of the difficulty have been omitted from the translation passage. The full sentence reads, 6 ὁ λέγων ἐν αὐτῷ μένειν ὀφείλει καθὼς ἐκεῖνος περιεπάτησεν καὶ αὐτὸς [οὕτως] περιπατεῖν. Translated word for word, the sentence reads thus: "The one who says to remain in him ought, as that man walked, he thus to walk." The biggest difficulty in the sentence is that the infinitives are not used in the way an English infinitive is used. In the chapter on infinitives, it was said that most English infinitives are used in a way similar to English infinitives, and these are easy to translate. Those that are not used like English infinitives are not always easy to translate, and in this sentence illustrates that. The meaning of the first phrase should be clear though. "The one who says to remain in him" is best expressed in English by using a second main verb in the indicative (Greek sometimes uses the infinitive in reported speech [see 36.1]: "The one who says he remains in him." This part is clear. The rest of the sentence is hard. The basic bones of it are: ὀφείλει ... περιπατεῖν: "He aught to walk," or (using a slightly different English idiom, meaning the same thing:) "He should walk." The phrase, καθὼς ἐκεῖνος περιεπάτησεν, is a subordinate clause (easily translated as "as that man [i.e. Jesus] walked," or "as he walked"), and the καὶ αὐτὸς οὕτως is "also he [repeating the subject of the sentence] thus [his manner of walking]" Therefore, while there is no really good translation, the sentence might be translated, "He who says he remains in him should, as that man walked, also likewise walk." By the way, the square brackets around the [οὕτως] indicate that the word [οὕτως] was added by the editors to try and make sense out of the sentence. There was no manuscript evidence for its addition, but even the editors found it hard enough to need to add something to make it make sense.

v. 9 also has a an infinitive used for indirect speech [see 36.1]. Literally, the sentence begins, "The one who says in the light to be ..." English would not use an infinitive for indirect speech here, but would use a second indicative verb: "The one who says he is in the light ..."

Appendix A: Answers to Exercises 325

Answers to Exercise 26

1. Judge 3. Do not judge 5. Give 7. Throw 9. Come 11. I/they ate 13. They stood 15. They go up 17. Place 19. Let him/her/it be 21. Speak 23. Let them be asked 25. Let them be heard 27. Be seen 28. 2nd pers. pl. aor. imperative act. of αἴρω I take 29. 2nd pers. pl. aor. imperative act. of μανθάνω I learn 30. 2nd pers. pl. fut. ind. act. of εὑρίσκω, I find 31. 2nd pers. pl. pres. imperative act. of αἰτέω, I ask 32. 3rd pers. sing. fut. ind. pass. of δίδωμι, I give 33. 3rd pers. sing. pres. ind. act. of λαμβάνω, I receive 34. 3rd pers. sing. pres. imperative act. of εἰμί, I am 40. "A disciple is not beyond/above the teacher but when prepared he will be in all [ways/things] like his teacher." [Note: it is also possible to take the πᾶς as the subject of the verb, in which case the sentence might be translated: "A disciple is not beyond/above the teacher, but every [disciple], when he is fully prepared/instructed, will be like his teacher."]

Answers to Exercise 27

1. 3rd pers. pl. pres. ind. act. of ἵστημι, I place 3. 2nd pers. sing. pres. ind. act. of δίδωμι, I give 5. 3rd pers. sing. aor. ind. act. of ἀφίημι, I let go, forgive 7. 1st pers. pl. pres. subj. act. of ἵστημι, I place 9. acc. fem. sing. pres. part. act. of εἰμί, I am 11. 3rd pers. sing. pres. ind. act. of τίθημι, I place 13. 3rd pers. pl. pres. ind. pass. of ἵστημι, I place 15. 3rd pers. sing. pres. ind. act. of δίδωμι, I give [also 3rd pers. pl. pres. subj. act.] 17. 3rd pers. pl. pres. ind. act. of ἀφίημι, I let go, forgive 19. 1st pers. sing. aor. subj. act. of ἵστημι, I place 21. 1st pers. pl. aor. ind. act. of τίθημι, I place 23. nom./acc. neut. sing. aor. part. act. of δίδωμι, I give 25. nom. masc. sing. aor. part. act. of τίθημι, I place 27. 1st pers. sing. aor. ind. act. of δείκνυμι 29. 3rd pers. pl. imperf. ind. act. of δίδωμι, I give 31. acc. masc. sing. pres. part. act. of ἵστημι, I place [also nom./voc./acc. neut. pl.] 33. 3rd pers. sing. pres. imperative act. of δίδωμι, I give 35. 1st pers. sing. aor. subj. act. of δίδωμι, I give 37. gen. masc. sing. pres. part. act. of δείκνυμι, I show 39. 2nd pers. sing. aor. imperative act. of τίθημι, I place 41. 1st pers. sing. perf. ind. act. of ἵστημι, I place 43. 3rd pers. sing. pres. ind. act. of φημί, I say [see Vocab. 26] 45. 1st pers. sing. aor. ind. pass. of τίθημι, I place 47. 2nd pers. sing. aor. imperative active of ἵστημι, I place 49. 1st pers. sing. fut. ind. act. of ἵστημι, I place 51. 2nd pers. pl. pres. ind. pass. of δείκνυμι, I show 53. 3rd pers. sing. fut. ind. act. of τίθημι, I place 55. 2nd pers. pl. pres. subj. act. of δίδωμι, I give 57. 3rd pers. pl. imperf. ind. pass. of ἵστημι, I place 59. 2nd pers. pl. imperf. ind. pass. of δίδωμι, I give

Answers to Exercise 28 & 29

Use a relatively literal tranlation of the Bible.

Answers to Exercise 30 (Review)

The Verb

Translate into English: **1.** I shall loose (fut. ind. act.) **2.** I have loosed (perf. ind. act.) **3.** I am loosed (pres. ind. pass.) **4.** I was loosed (aor. ind. pass.) **5.** I was loosing (imperfect ind. act.) **6.** I loose (pres. ind. act.) **7.** I have been loosed (perf. ind. pass.) **8.** I loosed (aor. ind. act.) **9.** I shall be loosed (fut. ind. pass.) **10.** You sow (pres. ind. act.) **11.** He/she/it takes with (pres. ind. act.) **12.** You love (pres. ind. act.) **13.** He/she/it was led astray (aor. ind. pass.) **14.** We consider, reckon (pres. ind. act.) **15.** I shall stand (fut. ind. act. of ἵστημι) **16.** He/she/it was (imperfect. ind. act. of εἰμί) **17.** You were seen (aor. ind. pass. of ὁράω) **18.** I am, exist (pres. ind. act.) **19.** They circumcise (pres. ind. act.) **20.** We eat (pres. ind. act.) 21. It was fulfilled (aor. ind. pass.) **22.** We bless (pres. ind. act.) **23.** You will drink (fut. ind. act. of πίνω) **24.** You come to (pres. ind. mid. verb) **25.** He/she/it was found (aor. ind. pass. of εὑρίσκω) **26.** You were preaching (imperfect ind. act.) **27.** We ask (pres. ind. act.) **28.** You said (aor. ind. act. of λέγω) **29.** We shall show **30.** You were (imperfect ind. act. of εἰμί) **31.** He/she/it is (3rd pers. sing. pres. ind. act. of εἰμί) **32.** He/she/it became (aor. ind. act.) **33.** You tempt (pres. ind. act.) **34.** It/he/she was reckoned (aor. ind. pass. of λογίζομαι) **35.** You sowed (aor. ind. act.) **36.** I placed (aor. ind. act. of ἵστημι) **37.** He/she/it took over (aor. ind. act. of παραλαμβάνω) **38.** They were placed (aor. ind. pass. of τίθημι) **39.** They will eat (fut. ind. act. of ἐσθίω) **40.** They will announce (fut. ind. act. of κηρύσσω) **41.** It has been fulfilled (perf. ind. pass. of πληρόω) **42.** You give thanks (pres. ind. act.) **43.** He/she/it saw (aor. ind. act. of ὁράω) **44.** I was/they were keeping (imperfect ind. act. of τηρεω) **45.** They grasped (aor. ind. act.) **46.** He/she/it called (aor. ind. act.) **47.** I shall fall (fut. ind. act. of πίπτω) **48.** You threw (aor. ind. act. of βάλλω) **49.** You have given (perf. ind. act. of δίδωμι) **50.** I am (pres. ind. act.)

51. They find (pres. ind. act.) **52.** You were delivered up (aor. ind. pass. of παραδίδωμι) **53.** I was borne/carried (aor. ind. pass. of φέρω) **54.** I was sent (aor. ind. pass. of στέλλω) **55.** We buy (pres. ind. act.) **56.** You bought (aor. ind. act. of ἀγοράζω) **57.** You have fallen (perf. ind. act. of πίπτω) **58.** He/she/it was teaching (imperfect ind. act. of διδάσκω) **59.** They will know (fut. ind. act. of γινώσκω) **60.** We drank (aor. ind. act. of πίνω) **61.** We grasp (pres. ind. act.) **62.** They were raised (aor. ind. pass. of αἴρω) **63.** You were stood (aor. ind. pass. of ἵστημι) **64.** I give light (pres. ind. act.) **65.** You lift up (pres. ind. act.) **66.** We have persuaded (perf. ind. act. of πείθω) **67.** They will give (fut. ind. act. of δίδωμι) **68.** I raised (aor. ind. act. of ἐγείρω) **69.** We have seen (perf. ind. act. of ὁράω) **70.** I gave away (aor. ind. act. of ἀποδίδομι) **71.** I shall become (fut. ind. act. of γίνομαι) **72.** They are (pres. ind. act. of εἰμί) **73.** You will take (fut. ind. act. of λαμβάνω) **74.** You were raised (aor. ind. pass. of ἐγείρω) **75.** You will see (fut. ind. act. of αἴρω) **76.** You carry (pres. ind. act. of φέρω) **77.** We shall lift up (ἀρέω is the fut. ind. act. of αἴρω) **78** . I have been sown (perf. ind. pass. of σπείρω) **79.** They deny (pres. ind. mid.) **80.** He/she/it was taken (aor. ind. pass. of λαμβάνω) **81.** We have known (perf. ind. act. of γινώσκω) **82.** You have written (perf. ind. act. of γράφω) **83.** You were (imperfect ind. act. of εἰμί) **84.** He/she/it shows (NB: 3rd pers. <u>sing</u> pres. ind. act. of δείκνυμι) **85.** He/she/it healed (aor./imperfect ind. act.) **86.** We are merciful **87.** They rule (pres. ind. act. — ἄρχω means "I rule" in active voice) **88.** He/she/it began (aor. ind. mid.— ἄρχω means "I begin" in middle voice) **89.** They owe/ought (pres. ind. act.) **90.** You have said (perf. ind. act. of λέγω) **91.** You have (pres. ind. act.) **92.** I pray (pres. ind. mid.) **93.** He/she/it has thrown (perf. ind. act. of βάλλω) **94.** He/she/it

Appendix A: Answers to Exercises 327

has gone (perf. ind. act. of βαίνω) 95. We follow (pres. ind. act.) 96. to give (aor. inf. act. of δίδωμι) 97. You are sick (pres. ind. act.) 98. You will bear (fut. ind. act. of φέρω) 99. We make known (pres. ind. act. of φανερόω)

100. You went out (aor. ind. mid. of the middle verb ἐκπορεύομαι) 101. We have been taken (perf. ind. pass. of λαμβάνω) 102. You will come (fut. ind. act. of ἔρχομαι) 103. You are (2nd pers. sing. of εἰμί) 104. I fear (pres. ind. mid. verb) 105. They were called (aor. ind. pass. of καλέω) 106. We offer (pres. ind. act.) 107. He/she/it knows 108. You showed (aor. ind. act. of δείκνυμι) 109. You seat (pres. ind. act.) 110. He/she/it has practiced (perf. of πράσσω) 111. You were having (imperfect. ind. act. of ἔχω) 112. He/she/it has been placed (perf. ind. pass. of τίθημι) 113. We were forgiven (aor. ind. pass. of ἀφίημι) 114. He/she/it was hoping (imperfect. ind. act. of ἐλπίζω) 115. To glorify (pres. inf. act.) 116. You saw (aor. ind. act. of βλέπω) 117. I was given (aor. ind. pass. of δίδωμι) 118. He/she/it is forgiven (pres. ind. pass. of ἀφιημι) 119. You will see (fut. ind. mid. of ὁραω) 120. You announced (aor. ind. act. of κηρύσσω) 121. He/she/it has been raised (perf. ind. pass. of ἐγείρω) 122. I weep (pres. ind. act.) 123. I break (pres.) 124. I shut (pres.) 125. I wept (aor.) 126. I shut (aor.) 127. I broke (aor.) 128. I shall weep (fut.) 129. You offered (aor. ind. act. of προσφέρω) 130. I blaspheme (pres. ind. act.) 131. You will hate (fut. ind. act.) 132. I went/came (aor. ind. mid. of the verb, πορεύομαι) 133. They have borne (perf. ind. act. of φέρω) 134. We shall throw (fut. ind. act. of βάλλω) 135. We throw (pres. ind. act.) 136. I gave (aor. ind. act. of δίμωμι) 137. He/she/it will remain (fut. ind. act.) 138. He/she/it remains (pres. ind. act.) 139. You will have (fut. ind. act. of ἔχω) 140. I have come (fut. ind. act. of ἥκω) 141. You have taken (perf. ind. act. of λαμβάνω) 142. He/she/it sees (pres. ind. act. of ὁράω) 143. To draw near (pres. inf. act.) 144. He/she/it has drawn near (perf. ind. act. of ἐγγίκεν) 145. You come (pres. ind. act.) 146. You have gone through (perf. ind. act. of διέρχομαι) 147. You have been given (perf. ind. pass. of δίδωμι) 148. He/she/it lives (pres ind. act. of ζάω) 149. You placed upon (aor. ind. act. of ἐπιτίθημι)

150. I shall forgive (fut. ind. act. of ἀφίημι) 151. You hear (pres. ind. act.) 152. They persecuted (aor. ind. act. of διώκω) 153. I understand (pres. ind. act.) 154. We work (pres. ind. mid. verb) 155. They send (pres. ind. act.) 156. They will send (fut. ind. act.) 157. We repent (pres. ind. act.) 158. They will be justified (fut. ind. pass. of δικαιόω) 159. You will speak (fut. ind. act. of λέγω) 160. They believed (aor. ind. act.) 161. I shall judge (fut. ind. act.) 162. I judge (pres. ind. act.) 163. I shall be (fut. ind. act. of εἰμί) 164. They were being baptised (imperfect ind. pass.) 165. I shall kill (fut. ind. act. of ἀποκτείνω) 166. I kill (pres. ind. act.) 167. We have heard (perf. ind. act. of ἀκούω) 168. You were showing (imperfect ind. act. of δείκνυμι) 169. You were sown (aor. ind. pass. of σπείρω) 170. You have lifted up (perf. ind. act. of αἴρω) 171. He/she/it was justified (aor. ind. pass. of δικαιόω) 172. They fall (pres. ind. act.) 173. You were about to (imp. ind. act. of μέλλω) 174. He/she/it came down (aor. ind. act. of καταβαίνω) 175. They have stood (perf. ind. act. of ἵστημι) 176. We have been sent (perf. ind. pass. of ἀποστέλλω) 177. You sin (pres. ind. act.) 178. You went away (aor. ind. act. of ἀπέρχομαι) 179. He/she/it will be (fut. ind. act. of εἰμί) 180. You seek (pres. ind. act. of ζητέω) 181. You persecute 182. They were crucified (aor. ind. pass.) 183. We shall place (fut. ind. act. of τίθημι) 184. He/

she/it found (aor. ind. act. of εὑρίσκω) 185. You will find (fut. ind. act. of εὑρίσκω) 186. You will destroy (fut. ind. act. of ἀπόλλυμι) 187. You have gone up (perf. ind. act. of ἀναβαίνω) 188. It was said (aor. ind. pass. of λέγω) 189. To cry out (pres. inf. act.) 190. I have placed (perf. ind. act. of τίθημι) 191. To be amazed (aor. inf. pass. of θαυμάζω) 192. You are able (pres. ind. act.) 193. They are about to (pres. ind. act.) 194. He/she/it will sow (fut. ind. act. of σπείρω) 195. We persecuted (aor. ind. act. of διώκω) 196. He/she/it walks (pres. ind. act.) 197. We sinned (aor. ind. act. of ἁμαρτάνω) 198. I shall die (fut. ind. act. of ἀποθνήσκω) 199. He forgave (aor. ind. act. of ἀφίημι)

Parse

200. aor. inf. act. of λύω, I loose 201. 3rd pers. sing. pres. imperative act. of λύω, I loose 202. gen. masc./neut. sing. aor. part. act. of λύω, I loose 203. 2nd pers. sing. aor. subj. act. of λύω, I loose 204. pres. inf. act. of λύω, I loose 205. 3rd pers. pl. aor. imperative act. of λύω, I loose 206. pres. inf. pass. of λύω, I loose 207. 1st pers. sing. pres. subj. pass. of λύω, I loose 208. 2nd pers. sing. aor. imperative pass. of λύω, I loose 209. nom. fem. sing. aor. part. pass. of λύω, I loose 210. 2nd pers. sing. pres. imperative pass. of λύω, I loose 211. nom. fem. sing. pres. part. pass. of λύω, I loose 212. 2nd pers. pl. aor. subj. pass. of λύω, I loose 213. 3rd pers. pl. pres. ind. act. of φημί, I say 214. 3rd pers. pl. pres. ind. act. of ἀποθνήσκω, I die 215. 1st pers. sing. aor. ind. act. of αἴρω, I lift up 216. nom. masc. sing. aor. part. act. of ἵστημι, I place 217. 1st pers. sing. pres. subj. act. of εἰμί, I am 218. gen. masc./neut. sing. aor. part. act. of καθίζω, I seat, sit 219. nom. masc. pl. perf. part. pass. of διώκω, I persecute

220. nom. masc. sing. pres. part. act. of θέλω, I will 221. nom. fem. sing. pres. part. act. of τίθημι, I place 222. gen. masc./neut. sing. perf. part. act. of οἶδα, I know 223. 2nd pers. pl. aor. subj. act. of ἀφίημι, I forgive 224. aor. inf. act. of γινώσκω, I know 225. 2nd pers. sing. pres. subj. act. of οἶδα, I know 226. aor. inf. act. of προσκυνέω, I prostrate myself before 227. gen. masc./neut. sing. pres. part. mid. of the verb κάθημαι, I sit 228. nom. masc. pl. aor. part. act. of κράζω, I cry out 229. 2nd pers. sing. aor. imperative act. of ἐλεέω, I have mercy 230. nom./acc. neut. sing. aor. part. act. of δίδωμι, I give 231. pres. inf. act. of εἰμί, I am 232. 2nd pers. sing. pres. imperative act. of χαίρω, I rejoice 233. nom./acc. neut. sing. aor. part. act. of γινώσκω, I know 234. acc. masc. pl. pres. part. act. of ἵστημι, I stand 235. 1st pers. sing. aor. ind. act. of ἀνοίγω, I open 236. 3rd pers. sing. aor. ind. act. of φημί, I say 237. nom. masc. sing. aor. part. act. of τίθημι, I place 238. 1st pers. pl. pres. subj. act. of ἀφίημι, I forgive 239. acc. masc. sing. [nom./acc. neut. pl.] pres. part. act. of δίδωμι, I give

240. 2nd pers. sing. aor. subj. act. of ἵστημι, I place 241. 2nd pers. pl. pres. subj. act. of δίδωμι, I give 242. 1st pers. pl. pres. subj. act. of τίθημι, I place 243. nom. masc. sing. pres. part. act. of εἰμί, I am 244. 1st pers. sing. aor. ind. pass. of λέγω, I say 245. 3rd pers. sing. aor. ind. pass. [used in active sense], of ἀποκρίνομαι, I answer 246. 3rd pers. sing. pres. subj. act. of ἵστημι, I place 247. 1st pers. sing. aor. subj. act. of δίδωμι, I give 248. 2nd pers. sing. fut. ind. act. of εἰμί, I am 249. nom. fem. sing. aor. part. act. of καλέω, I call 250. 3rd pers. pl. perf. ind. act. of τίθημι,

Appendix A: Answers to Exercises

I place 251. 3rd pers. sing. pres. ind. act. of ἵστημι, I stand 252. 3rd pers. pl. pres. ind. act. of ἵστημι, I stand 253. 1st pers. sing. aor. ind. pass. of γίνομαι, I become

Translate

254. I received (aor. ind. mid. of δέχομαι) 255. We enter (pres. ind. mid.) 256. He/she/it speaks (pres. ind. act.) 257. You sent (aor. ind. act. of ἀποστέλλω) 258. I answer (pres. ind. mid.) 259. We summon (pres. ind. act. of παρακαλέω) 260. You opened (aor. ind. act. of ἀνοίγω—there are three different ways in which this verb forms its aorist. Do you remember them?) 261. I/they ate (aor. ind. act. of ἐσθίω) 262. You were released (aor. ind. pass. of ἀπολύω) 263. You wrote (aor. ind. act.) 264. You were thrown out (aor. ind. pass. of ἐκβάλλω) 265. They place (pres. ind. act.) 266. You greet (pres. ind. mid.) 267. You become (pres. ind. mid.) 268. You went out (aor. ind. act.) 269. They will place (fut. ind. act. of τίθημι) 270. I take (pres. ind. act.) 271. You see (pres. ind. act. of ὁράω) 272. We destroyed (aor. ind. act. of ἀπόλλυμι) 273. He/she/it has fulfilled (perf. ind. act. of πληρόω) 274. He/she/it begets (pres. ind. act.) 275. He/she/it asks (pres. ind. act.) 276. He/she/it was saying (imperfect ind. act.) 277. I/they died (aor. ind. act. of ἀποθνήσκω) 278. You were giving (imperfect ind. act. of δίδωμι) 279. They were giving (imperfect ind. act. of δίδωμι)

280. He/she/it saw (aor. ind. act. of ὁράω) 281. I was loved (aor. ind. pass. of ἀγαπάω) 282. They know (pres. ind. act.) 283. We asked (aor. ind. act. of ἐρωτάω) 284. I shall bear witness (fut. ind. act.) 285. You have been thrown (perf. ind. pass. of βάλλω) 286. He/she/it gives (pres. ind. act. of δίδωμι) 287. They give (pres. ind. act.) 288. I have been loved (perf. ind. pass. of ἀγαπάω) 289. You have forgiven (perf. ind. act. of ἀφίημι) 290. You have found (perf. ind. act. of εὑρίσκω) 291. We shall call (fut. ind. act.) 292. You have fallen (perf. ind. act. of πίπτω) 293. They fulfilled (aor. ind. act. of πληρόω) 294. We bore (aor. ind. act. of φέρω) 295. I/they led (aor. ind. act. of ἄγω) 296. They persuade (pres. ind. act.) 297. You have loved (perf. ind. act. of ἀγαπάω) 298. He/she/it forgave (aor. ind. act. of ἀφίημι) 299. We were able (aor. ind. [pass.?—note, the verb carries within it a passive meaning. The form is passive, although listed in the table of principle parts as active! If you are in a classroom situation, your teacher will no doubt indicate a preference as to whether to call this active or passive] of δύναμαι)

300. They will have (fut. ind. act. of ἔχω) 301. We have judged (perf. ind. act. of κρίνω) 302. He/she/it loved (aor. ind. act. of ἀγαπάω) 303. I was heard (aor. ind. pass. of ἀκούω) 304. We shall forgive (fut. ind. act. of ἀφίημι) 305. He/she/it will be able (fut. ind. act. of δύναμαι) 306. He/she/it eats (pres. ind. act.; alternate form of ἐσθίω) 307. He/she/it called (aor. ind. act. of καλέω) 308. He/she/it remained (aor. ind. act. of μένω) 309. We fell (aor. ind. act. of πίπτω) 310. We have been judged (perf. ind. pass. of κρίνω) 311. I/they heard (imperf. ind. act. of ἀκούω) 312. I shall go up (fut. ind. act. of ἀνα-βαίνω) 313. You were shown (aor. ind. pass. δείκνυμι) 314. You have had (perf. ind. act. of ἔχω) 315. You have called (perf. ind. act. of καλέω) 316. You will hear (fut. ind. act.) 317. He/she/it spoke (aor. ind. act.) 318. You judged (aor. ind. act.) 319. We shall love (fut. ind. act.)

320. He/she/it died (perf. ind. act. ἀποθνήσκω) 321. They will beget (fut. ind. act.

of γεννάω) 322. It[/he/she] was said (aor. ind. pass. of λαλέω) 323. I shall hear (fut. ind. mid. of ἀκούω) 324. I have been shown (perf. ind. pass. of δείκνυμι) 325. It has been said (perf. ind. pass. of λαλέω) 326. You will speak (fut. ind. act.) 327. I begat (aor. ind. act. of γεννάω) 328. You will destroy (fut. ind. act. of ἀπ'-όλλυμι) 329. I have become (perf. ind. act. of γίνομαι) 330. I was begotten (aor. ind. pass. of γεννάω) 331. I was shown (aor. ind. pass. of δείκνυμι) 332. I have been known (perf. ind. pass. of γινώσκω) 333. We shall die (fut. ind. act. of ἀπο-θνήσκω) 334. I have been called (perf. ind. pass. of καλέω) 335. You were known (aor. ind. pass. of γινώσκω) 336. They were judged (aor. ind. pass. of κρίνω) 337. You have said (perf. ind. act.) 338. They have said (perf. ind. act. of λέγω) 339. You have become (perf. ind. act./or pass. of γίνομαι)

340. You have been begotten (perf. ind. pass. of γεννάω) 341. I knew ([non-thematic] aor. ind. act. of γινώσκω) 342. It has been said (perf. ind. pass. of λέγω) 343. You were stood (aor. ind. pass. of ἵστημι) 344. We have become (perf. ind. act. of γίνομαι) 345. You have remained (perf. ind. act. of μένω) 346. I shall destroy (fut. ind. act. of ἀπ'-όλλυμι) 347. He/she/it has begotten (perf. ind. act. of γεννάω)

Principle Parts
348-360 See table of principle parts in chapter 22, or in Appendix C.

Declensions and Paradigms
360. βιβλίον βιβλίον βιβλίου βιβλίῳ βιβλία βιβλία βιβλίων βιβλίοις 361. ἐπαγγελία ἐπαγγελίαν ἐπαγγελίας ἐπαγγελίᾳ ἐπαγγελίαι ἐπαγγελίας ἐπαγγελίων ἐπαγγελίαις 362. πούς πόδα ποδός ποδί πόδες πόδας ποδῶν ποσί(ν) 363. φῶς φῶς φωτός φωτί φῶτα φῶτα φωτῶν φωσί(ν) 364. masc.: τυφλός τυφλόν τυφλοῦ τυφλῷ τυφλοί τυφλούς τυφλῶν τυφλοῖς fem.: τυφλή τυφλήν τυφλῆς τυφλῇ τυφλαί τυφλάς τυφλῶν τυφλαῖς neut.: τυφλόν τυφλόν τυφλοῦ τυφλῷ τυφλά τυφλά τυφλῶν τυφλοῖς 365. See appendix E 366. See appendix B 367. ἠγαπήθην ἠγαπήθης ἠγαπήθη ἠγαπήθημεν ἠγαπήθητε ἠγαπήθησαν 368. ἔγνων ἔγνως ἔγνω ἔγνωμεν ἔγνωτε ἔγνωσαν 369. masc.: κεκρικώς κεκρικότα κεκρικότος κεκρικότι κεκρικότες κεκρίκας κεκρίκων κεκρίξιν fem.: κεκρικυῖα κεκρικυῖαν κεκρικυίας κεκρικυίᾳ κεκρικυῖαι κεκρικυίας κεκρικυιῶν κεκρικυίαις neut.: κεκρικός κεκρικός κεκρικότος κεκρικότι κεκρικότα κεκρικότα κεκρικότων κεκρίξιν 370. θῶ θῇς θῇ θῶμεν θῆτε θῶσιν 371. ἠγέρθην ἠγέρθης ἠγέρθη ἠγέρθημεν ἠγέρθητε ἠγέρθησαν 372. ἀκήκοα ἀκήκοας ἀκήκοεν ἀκηκόαμεν ἀκηκόατε ἀκηκόασιν 373. ἔκρινα ἔκρινας ἔκρινεν ἐκρίναμεν ἐκρίνατε ἔκριναν 374. ἐστάλην ἐστάλης ἐστάλη ἐστάλημεν ἐστάλητε ἐστάλησαν 375. ἐλήλυθα ἐλήλυθας ἐλήλυθεν ἐληλύθαμεν ἐληλύθατε ἐλήλυθαν 376. βήσομαι βήσῃ βήσεται βησόμεθα βήσεσθε βήσονται 377. βαλῶ βαλεῖς βαλεῖ βαλοῦμεν βαλεῖτε βαλοῦσι(ν) 378. δέδομαι δέδοσαι δέδοται δεδόμεθα δέδοσθε δέδονται 379. See Appendix D 380. ἐπλήρωσα ἐπλήρωσας ἐπλήρωσεν ἐπληρώσαμεν ἐπληρώσατε ἐπλήρωσαν 381. ἐλαλοῦν ἐλαλεῖς ἐλαλεῖν ἐλαλοῦμεν ἐλαλεῖτε ἐλαλοῦν 382. ἐπροσευξάμην ἐπροσεύξω ἐπροσεύξατο ἐπροσευξόμεθα ἐπροσεύξασθε ἐπροσεύξαντο 383. ἐλαμβανόμην ἐλαμβάνου ἐλαμβάνετο ἐλαμβανόμεθα ἐλαμβάνεσθε ἐλαμβάνοντο

Appendix A: Answers to Exercises 331

Prepositions
384. πρός + acc.: toward, with, against + dat.: near, at, by + gen.: to the advantage of 385. διά + gen.: through + acc.: because of, on account of 386. σύν + dat.: with 387. ἀπό + gen.: from 388. ὀπίσω prep. + gen.: after, behind, away from adv.: back, behind 389. εἰς + acc.: into, towards 390. χωρίς prep. + gen.: without, apart from adv.: separately, by itself 391. ἐπί + dat.: **at**, by, **on** + gen.: **upon**, near, before, over, on the basis of, in the time of + acc.: **across**, to, against 392. περί + acc.: **around**, about, near + gen.: **about**, concerning 393. κατα v + gen.: down, against + acc.: according to 394. ἐν + dat.: in, by (instrument) 395. μετά + acc.: **after**, behind + gen.: **with** 396. παρά + dat.: **at**, by, beside, near + gen.: from + acc.: **by**, along, near, more than, against 397. ἔμπροσθεν prep. + gen.: in front of, before adv.: ahead, forward, in front 398. ἐκ, ἐξ + gen.: from, out of, away from 399. ὑπέρ + acc.: over and above, beyond + gen.: for, on behalf of, because of 400. πρό + gen.: before 401. ἐνώπιον + gen.: before, in the presence of 402. ὑπό + acc.: under, below + gen.: by [agent]

Sentences
403. For I tell you that God is able to raise children to Abraham from these stones. [This sentence illustrates indirect speech and infinitives.] **404.** And if you wish to enter into life, keep the commandments. [This sentence illustrates a conditional sentence, and an imperative.] **405.** Truly, truly I say to you, whatever you ask the Father in my name he will give to you. [This sentence illustrates the use of ἄν + subjunctive, and contains a future tense.] **406.** And I saw the holy city, New Jerusalem, coming down out of heaven from God. [This sentence illustrates the strong aorist tense, adjectives, and one of the uses of the participle.] **407.** And everyone who lives and believes in me will not perish for ever. [This sentence illustrates one of the uses of the participle, οὐ μή + subjunctive as strong negation, and the idiomatic phrase εἰς τὸν αἰῶνα.] **408.** And I tell you, ask, and it will be given to you, seek and you will find, knock and it will be opened to you; for every one who asks receives, and the one who seeks finds, and to the one who knocks it will be opened. [This sentence illustrates imperatives, futures, passives, several cases of the participle, as well as variations in tense.] **409.** But I do not receive witness from men, but I say these things in order that you might be saved. [This sentence illustrates a ἵνα clause, and a passive subjunctive.]

There is a lot more that you have learned, but these few sentences should give you some indication of the kind of Greek that you should now handle with ease. You have made great progress since you began to learn the Greek alphabet!

APPENDIX B: Paradigm of the Regular Verb

Active Voice

Tense	No & Person	Indicative Mood	Imperative Mood	Subjunctive Mood	Optative Mood	Infinitive Mood	Participial Mood
Present [& Imperfect]	1 sing	λύω [3057] ἔλυον [1104]	[519]	λύω [345]	λύοιμι [19]	λύειν [657]	λύων, λύουσα, λῦον λυοντ- [2143]
	2	λύεις ἔλυες	λῦε	λύῃς	λύοις		
	3	λύει ἔλυε(ν)	λυέτω	λύῃ	λύοι		
	1 pl	λύομεν ἐλύομεν		λύωμεν	λύοιμεν		
	2	λύετε ἐλύετε	λύετε	λύητε	λύοιτε		
	3	λύουσι(ν) ἔλυον	λυέτωσαν	λύωσι(ν)	λύοιεν		
Future	1 sing	λύσω [633]				λύσειν [0]	λύσων, λύσουσα, λῦσον λυσοντ- [10]
	2	λύσεις					
	3	λύσει					
	1 pl	λύσομεν					
	2	λύσετε					
	3	λύσουσι(ν)					
Aorist	1 sing	ἔλυσα [3098]	[55]	λύσω [782]	λύσαιμι [18]	λῦσαι [836]	λύσας, λύσασα, λῦσαν λυσαντ- [1331]
	2	ἔλυσας	λῦσον	λύσῃς	λύσαις		
	3	ἔλυσε(ν)	λυσάτω	λύσῃ	λύσαι		
	1 pl	ἐλύσαμεν		λύσωμεν	λύσαιμεν		
	2	ἐλύσατε	λύσατε	λύσητε	λύσαιτε		
	3	ἔλυσαν	λυσάτωσαν	λύσωσι(ν)	λύσαιεν		
Perfect [& pluperfect]	1 sing	λέλυκα [522] [ἐ]λελύκειν [75]	[2]	λελυκὼς ὦ λελυκὼς ᾖς etc. (i.e. formed periphrastically) [1]		λελυκέναι [38]	λελυκώς, λελυκυῖα, λελυκός λελυκοτ- [220]
	2	λέλυκας [ἐ]λελύκεις	Both ἴστε				
	3	λέλυκεν [ἐ]λελύκει					
	1 pl	λελύκαμεν [ἐ]λελύκειμεν					
	2	λελύκατε [ἐ]λελύκειτε					
	3	λελύκασιν [ἐ]λελύκεισαν					

Numbers in brackets indicate the number of verses that this tense-mood-voice is found in the NT – as reported by Gramcord

Appendix B: Paradigm of Regular Verb

Middle Voice

Tense	No & Person	Indicative Mood	Imperative Mood	Subjunctive Mood	Optative Mood	Infinitive Mood	Participial Mood
Present [& Imperfect]	1 sing 2 3 1 pl 2 3	λύομαι [474] λύῃ λύεται λυόμεθα λύεσθε λύονται	ἐλυόμην [202] ἐλύου ἐλύετο ἐλυόμεθα ἐλύεσθε ἐλύοντο	[159] λύου λυέσθω λύεσθε λυέσθωσαν	λύωμαι [40] λύῃ λύηται λυώμεθα λύησθε λύωνται	λυοίμην [1] λύοιο λύοιτο λυοίμεθα λύοισθε λύοιντο	λύεσθαι [123]	λυόμενος, λυομένη, λυόμενον [546]
Future	1 sing 2 3 1 pl 2 3	λύσομαι [436] λύσῃ λύσεται λυσόμεθα λύσεσθε λύσονται					λύσεσθαι [5]	λυσόμενος, λυσομένη, λυσόμενον [2]
Aorist	1 sing 2 3 1 pl 2 3	ἐλυσάμην [602] ἐλύσω ἐλύσατο ἐλυσάμεθα ἐλύσασθε ἐλύσαντο	[69] λῦσαι λυσάσθω λύσασθε λυσάσθωσαν	λύσωμαι [167] λύσῃ λύσηται λυσώμεθα λύσησθε λύσωνται	λυσαίμην [19] λύσαιο λύσαιτο λυσαίμεθα λύσαισθε λύσαιντο	λύσασθαι [108]	λυσάμενος, λυσαμένη, λυσάμενον [294]
Perfect [& pluperfect]	1 sing 2 3 1 pl 2 3	λέλυμαι [26] λέλυσαι λέλυται λελύμεθα λέλυσθε λέλυνται	[ἐ]λελύμην [2] [ἐ]λέλυσο [ἐ]λέλυτο [ἐ]λελύμεθα [ἐ]λέλυσθε [ἐ]λέλυντο	[0] λέλυσο λελύσθω λέλυσθε λελύσθωσαν	λελυμένος ὦ λελυμένος ᾖς etc. (i.e. formed periphrastically) [1]	λελυμένος εἴην λελυμένος εἴης etc. (i.e. formed periphrastically) [0]	λελύσθαι [1]	λελυμένος, λελυμένη, λελυμένον [32]

Numbers in brackets indicate the number of verses that this tense-mood-voice is found in the NT – as reported by Gramcord

Passive Voice

Tense	No & Person	Indicative Mood		Imperative Mood	Subjunctive Mood	Optative Mood	Infinitive Mood	Participial Mood
Present [& Imperfect]	1 sing 2 3 1 pl 2 3	λύομαι [407] λύῃ λύεται λυόμεθα λύεσθε λύονται	ἐλυόμην [110] ἐλύου ἐλύετο ἐλυόμεθα ἐλύεσθε ἐλύοντο	[74] λύου λυέσθω λύεσθε λυέσθωσαν	λύωμαι [19] λύῃ λύηται λυώμεθα λύησθε λύωνται	λυοίμην [3] λύοιο λύοιτο λυοίμεθα λύοισθε λύοιντο	λύεσθαι [107]	λυόμενος, λυομένη, λυόμενον [388]
Future	1 sing 2 3 1 pl 2 3	λυθήσομαι [250] λυθήσῃ λυθήσεται λυθησόμεθα λυθήσεσθε λυθήσονται					λυθήσεσθαι [0]	λυθησόμενος, λυθησομένη, λυθησόμενον [1]
Aorist	1 sing 2 3 1 pl 2 3	ἐλύθην [774] ἐλύθης ἐλύθη ἐλύθημεν ἐλύθητε ἐλύθησαν		[71] λύθητι λυθήτω λύθητε λυθήτωσαν	λυθῶ [247] λυθῇς λυθῇ λυθῶμεν λυθῆτε λυθῶσι(ν)	λυθείην [5] λυθείης λυθείη λυθείημεν λυθείητε λυθείησαν	λυθῆναι [159]	λυθείς, λυθεῖσα, λυθέν λυθεντ- [380]
Perfect [& pluperfect]	1 sing 2 3 1 pl 2 3	λέλυμαι [199] λέλυσαι λέλυται λελύμεθα λέλυσθε λέλυνται	[ἐ]λελύμην [75] [ἐ]λέλυσο [ἐ]λέλυτο [ἐ]λελύμεθα [ἐ]λέλυσθε [ἐ]λέλυντο	[2] λέλυσο λελύσθω λέλυσθε λελύσθωσαν	λελυμένος ὦ λελυμένος ᾖς etc. (i.e. formed periphrastically) [1]	λελυμένος εἴην λελυμένος εἴης etc. (i.e. formed periphrastically) [0]	λελύσθαι [8]	λελυμένος, λελυμένη, λελυμένον [392]

Numbers in brackets indicate the number of verses that this tense-mood-voice is found in the NT – as reported by Gramcord

APPENDIX C: Selected Principal Parts of Regular & Irregular Verbs

Verb	Meaning	Future	Aorist	Perfect (Active)	Perfect (Passive)	Aorist (Passive)
ἀγαπάω	love	ἀγαπήσω	ἠγάπησα	ἠγάπηκα	ἠγάπημαι	ἠγαπήθην
-ἀγγέλλω[1]	announce	-αγγελέω	-ήγγειλα	-	-ήγγελμαι	-ηγγέλην
ἄγω	lead	ἄξω	ἤγαγον	-	ἦγμαι	ἤχθην
ἁγιάζω[2]	sanctify	ἁγιάσω	ἡγίασα	ἡγίακα	ἡγίασμαι	ἡγιάσθην
αἴρω	raise	ἀρέω	ἦρα	ἦρκα	ἦρμαι	ἤρθην
αἰτέω	ask for	αἰτήσω	ᾔτησα	ᾔτηκα	ᾔτημαι	ᾐτήθην
ἀκούω	hear	ἀκούσω[3]	ἤκουσα	ἀκήκοα	-	ἠκούσθην
ἀνοίγω	open	ἀνοίξω	ἤνοιξα	ἀνέῳγα	ἀνέῳγμαι	ἀνῴχθην
ἀνοίγω	open	ἀνοίξω	ἀνέῳξα	-	ἠνέῳγμαι	ἠνοίχθην
ἀνοίγω	open	ἀνοίξω	ἠνέῳξα	-	ἤνοιγμαι	ἠνεῴχθην
ἀποκτείνω[4]	kill	ἀποκτενέω	ἀπέκτεινα	-	-	ἀπεκτάνθην
ἀπόλλυμι	destroy	ἀπολέσω	ἀπώλεσα	ἀπόλωλα	-	-
ἀπόλλυμι	destroy	ἀπολέω				
ἀφίημι	forgive	ἀφήσω	ἀφῆκα	ἀφεῖκα	ἀφέωμαι	ἀφέθην
-βαίνω[5]	go	-βήσομαι	-έβην	-βέβηκα	-	-
βάλλω	throw	βαλέω	ἔβαλον[6]	βέβληκα	βέβλημαι	ἐβλήθην
γεννάω	beget	γεννήσω	ἐγέννησα	γεγέννηκα	γεγέννημαι	ἐγεννήθην
γίνομαι	become	γενήσομαι	ἐγενόμην	γέγονα	γεγένημαι	ἐγενήθην
γινώσκω	know	γνώσομαι	ἔγνων	ἔγνωκα	ἔγνωσμαι	ἐγνώσθην
δείκνυμι	show	δείξω	ἔδειξα	δεδείχα	δέδειγμαι	ἐδείχθην
δέχομαι	receive	-	ἐδεξάμην	-	δέδεγμαι	ἐδέχθην
δέω	bind	δήσω	ἔδησα	δέδεκα	δέδεμαι	ἐδέθην
δίδωμι	give	δώσω	ἔδωκα	δέδωκα	δέδομαι	ἐδόθην
δοκέω	think	δόξω	ἔδοξα[7]	-	-	-
δύναμαι	am able	δυνήσομαι	-	-	-	ἠδυνήθην
ἐγείρω	raise	ἐγερέω	ἤγειρα	-	ἐγήγερμαι	ἠγέρθην
ἐλπίζω	hope	ἐλπιέω	ἤλπισα	ἤλπικα	-	-
ἔρχομαι	come	ἐλεύσομαι	ἦλθον	ἐλήλυθα	-	-
ἐσθίω[8]	eat	φάγομαι	ἔφαγον	-	-	-
εὑρίσκω	find	εὑρήσω	εὗρον	εὕρηκα	-	εὑρέθην
ἔχω[9]	have	ἕξω	ἔσχον	ἔσχηκα	-	-
θέλω[10]	will	-	ἠθέλησα	-	-	-
-θνήσκω	die	-θανέομαι	-έθανον	τέθνηκα	-	-
ἵστημι	place	στήσω	ἔστην	ἕστηκα (intransitive)	-	ἐστάθην
ἵστημι	place	στήσω	ἔστησα	-έστακα (transitive)		
καλέω	call	καλέσω	ἐκάλεσα	κέκληκα	κέκλημαι	ἐκλήθην

κηρύσσω	proclaim	-	ἐκήρυξα	-	-	ἐκηρύχθην
κλαίω	weep	κλαύσω	ἔκλαυσα	-	-	-
κλάω	break	-	ἔκλασα	-	-	-εκλάσθην
κλείω	shut	κλείσω	ἔκλεισα	-	κέκλεισμαι	ἐκλείσθην
κράζω	cry out	κράξω	ἔκραξα	κέκραγα	-	-
κρίνω	judge	κρινέω	ἔκρινα	κέκρικα	κέκριμαι	ἐκρίθην
λαλέω	speak	λαλήσω	ἐλάλησα	λελάληκα	λελάλημαι	ἐλαλήθην
λαμβάνω	take	λήμψομαι	ἔλαβον	εἴληφα	-είλημμαι	-ελήμφθην
λέγω	say	ἐρέω	εἶπον	εἴρηκα	εἴρημαι	ἐρρέθην
λέγω	say	ἐρέω	εἶπα			
λύω	loose	λύσω	ἔλυσα	λέλυκα	λέλυμαι	ἐλύθην
μένω	remain	μενέω	ἔμεινα	μεμένηκα	-	-
ὁράω	see	ὄψομαι	εἶδον	ἑώρακα	-	ὤφθην
ὁράω	see	ὄψομαι	εἶδα	ἑόρακα		
πάσχω	suffer	-	ἔπαθον	πέπονθα	-	-
πείθω	persuade	πείσω	ἔπεισα	πέποιθα	πέπεισμαι	ἐπείσθην
πίνω	drink	πίομαι	ἔπιον	πέπωκα	-	-επόθην
πίπτω	fall	πεσέομαι	ἔπεσα	πέπτωκα	-	-
πίπτω	fall	πεσέομαι	ἔπεσα			
πληρόω	fill, fulfill	πληρώσω	ἐπλήρωσα	πεπλήρωκα	πεπλήρωμαι	ἐπληρώθην
πορεύομαι	go	πορεύσομαι	-	-	πεπόρευμαι	ἐπορεύθην
στέλλω	send	-στελέω	-έστειλα	-έσταλκα	-έσταλμαι	-εστάλην
σῴζω	save, heal	σώσω	ἔσωσα	σέσωκα	σέσωσμαι	ἐσώθην
σῴζω	save, heal	σώσω	ἔσωσα	σέσωκα	σέσωμαι	
τίθημι	place	θήσω	ἔθηκα	τέθεικα	τέθειμαι	ἐτέθην
φέρω	bear	οἴσω	ἤνεγκα	-ενήνοχα	-	ἠνέχθην
χαίρω	rejoice	χαρήσομαι	-εχάρησα	-	-	ἐχάρην

Notes on principal parts

[1] Aside from its appearance as a present participle active in John 20:18, the verb ἀγγέλλω only occurs in compounds in the New Testament. E.g. ἀναγγέλλω (13) I announce, report; ἀπαγγέλλω (45) I announce, report; ἐπαγγέλλω (15) I promise; καταγγέλλω (18) I proclaim; παραγγέλλω + dat. (30) I command. A dash in front of an entry means that verb or form of the verb only occurs in a compound. Thus future, aorist and passive forms of ἀγγέλλω only occur as compounds in the NT.

[2] There are a large number of verbs which end in -αζω or -ιζω, which follow the pattern of ἁγιάζω. The exceptions, γνωρίζω, ἐλπίζω, καθαρίζω, μακαρίζω, are all found in the appendix of principal parts in *Intermediate New Testament Year Greek Made Easier*, as are the verbs, ἀσπάζω, κράζω, παίζω, στενάζω which, in fact, all have guttural stems lengthened in the present by ι (which becomes ζ).

[3] The deponent 3rd pers. pl. form ἀκούσονται is found once in the NT (Acts 28:28)

[4] Verbal forms derived from the alternate spelling ἀποκτέννω (of ἀποκτείνω) are found at Matt 10:28; Mark 12:5 and Rev 6:11.

[5] The verb -βαίνω only occurs in compounds in the NT. E.g. ἀναβαίνω (81) I go up; ἐμβαίνω (18) I embark; καταβαίνω (81) I go down; μεταβαίνω (11) I depart.

[6] The 3rd pers. pl. form ἔβαλαν is found once in the NT (Acts 16:37).

Appendix C: Irregular Verbs

[7]The aor. ind. act. of δοκέω is found 7 times in the NT, and all follow the pattern of ἔδοξα – as though the verb was δόκω rather than δοκέω, and despite the fact that the verb shows the normal contractions of an -εω verb in the pres. ind. act. On the other hand, the compound verb εὐδοκέω (I am well pleased, take delight), found 21 times in the NT, 16 of which are aor. ind. act., follows the pattern εὐδόκησα in the aor. ind. act., as might be expected of an -εω verb.

[8]A verbal form derived from the alternate spelling ἔσθω (of ἐσθίω) is found at Luke 22:30.

[9]ἔχω has the irregular imperfect indicative active εἶχον.

[10]θέλω has the irregular imperfect indicative active ἠθέλησα.

[11]Sometimes a verb may have alternate forms (e.g. ἀνοίγω has three forms of the aorist). For the convenience of those using the eBook version of this text, ἀνοίγω is repeated three times in the table,to enable alternate forms to be listed; other verbs are repeated twice.

Note: A more comprehensive table of principal parts may be found in Appendix C of *Intermediate New Testament Greek Made Easier*

Appendix D: -μι Verbs

Δίδωμι

Principal parts
δίδωμι, δώσω, ἔδωκα, δέδωκα, δέδομαι, ἐδόθην

Indicative active:

present	imperfect
δίδωμι	ἐδίδουν
δίδως	ἐδίδους
δίδωσι(ν)	ἐδίδου
δίδομεν	ἐδίδομεν
δίδοτε	ἐδίδοτε
διδόασι(ν)	ἐδίδοσαν

Indicative passive:

Present	Imperfect
δίδομαι	ἐδιδόμην
δίδοσαι	ἐδίδοσο
δίδοται	ἐδίδοτο
διδόμεθα	ἐδιδόμεθα
δίδοσθε	ἐδίδοσθε
δίδονται	ἐδίδοντο

Participles:
pres act: διδούς, διδοῦσα, διδόν, διδόντα ... aor act: δούς, δοῦσα, δόν, δόντα, ... pres pass: διδόμενος, διδομένη, διδόμενον

Infinitives:
Active: pres διδόναι; aor. δοῦναι; Passive: pres δίδοσθαι

Subjunctives:
Active: pres. διδῶ, διδῷς, ...; aor. δῶ, δῷς, ...
Passive: pres. διδῶμαι, διδῷ, ...

Imperatives:
pres δίδου, διδότω, δίδοτε, διδότωσαν aor. δός, δότω, δότε, δότωσαν

Εἰμί

Principal parts
εἰμί, ἔσομαι

Indicative active:

present	imperfect
εἰμί	ἤμην
εἶ	ἦς, ἦσθα
ἐστίν	ἦν
ἐσμέν	ἦμεν, ἦμεθα
ἐστέ	ἦτε, ἦσθε
εἰσί(ν)	ἦσαν

fut.
ἔσομαι, ἔσῃ, ...

Participles
pres ὤν, οὖσα, ὄν, ὄντα, ...
fut ἐσόμενος, ἐσομένη, ἐσόμενον

Infinitives
pres εἶναι   fut ἔσεσθαι

Subjunctive
pres. ὦ, ᾖς, ᾖ, ὦμεν, ἦτε, ὦσι(ν)

Imperative
pres. ἴσθι, ἔστω (or ἤτω), ἔστε, ἔστωσαν (or ἤτωσαν)

Appendix D: -μι Verbs

-ἵημι

-ἵημι: ἀφιημι (143), συνιημι (26)
Principal parts
ἀφίημι, ἀφήσω, ἀφῆκα, ἀφεῖκα, ἀφέωμαι, ἀφέθην

Present indicative active:
ἀφίημι
ἀφεῖς
ἀφίησιν
ἀφίομεν
ἀφίετε
ἀφίασι(ν)

Present indicative middle / passive:
ἀφίεμαι
ἀφίεσαι
ἀφίεται
ἀφιέμεθα
ἀφίεσθε
ἀφίενται

Participles:
pres act: ἀφιείς, ἀφιεῖσα, ἀφιέν, ἀφιέντα ... aor act: ἀφεις, ἀφεισα, ἀφεν ...

Infinitives:
Active: pres. ἀφιέναι; aor. ἀφεῖναι

Subjunctives:
Active: pres ἀφιῶ, ἀφιῇς, ...; aor. ἀφῶ, ἀφῇς, ...

Imperatives:
pres. ἀφιει, ἀφιετω, ἀφιετε, ἀφιετωσαν
aor. ἄφες, ἄφετω, ἄφετε, ἀφέτωσαν

Ἵστημι

Principal parts: ἵστημι, στήσω, ἔστην or ἔστησα, ἔστηκα or -έστακα, —, ἐστάθην

Indicative active:
present: imperfect:
ἵστημι not in NT
ἵστης
ἵστησι(ν)
ἵσταμεν
ἵστατε
ἵστασι(ν)

strong aorist (intransitive)
[note: ἵστημι also has a transitive weak aorist, ἔστησα]
ἔστην ἔστημεν
ἔστης ἔστητε
ἔστη ἔστησαν

str. pluperf. act. (past meaning):
εἱστήκειν, ...

Indicative passive:
Present Imperfect
ἵσταμαι ἵσταμην
ἵστασαι ἵστασο
ἵσταται ἵστατο
ἱστάμεθα ἱστάμεθα
ἵστασθε ἵστασθε
ἵστανται ἵσταντο

Participles
pres. act: ἱστάς, ἱστᾶσα, ἱστάν, ἱστάντα ...; aor. act.: στάς, στᾶσα, στάν, στάντα, ...; strong perf. act. (pres. meaning) ἑστώς, ἑστῶσα, ἑστός, ἑστῶτα, ...; weak perf. act. (pres. meaning) ἑστηκώς, ἑστηκυῖα, ἑστηκός, ἑστηκότα, ...; pres. pass. ἱστάμενος, ἱσταμένη, ἱστάμενον

Infinitives
Active: pres. ἱστάναι aor. στῆναι Passive: pres. ἵστασθαι

Subjunctives
Active: pres. ἱστῶ, ἱστῇς, ... aor. στῶ, στῇς, ... Passive: pres. ἱστῶμαι, ἱστῇ, ...

Imperatives
pres. ἵστη, ἱστάτω, ἵστατε, ἱστάτωσαν
aor. στῆθι, στήτω, στῆτε, στήτωσαν

Τίθημι

Principal parts
τίθημι, θήσω, ἔθηκα, τέθεικα, τέθειμαι, ἐτέθην

Indicative active
present:	imperfect:
τίθημι	ἐτίθην
τίθης	ἐτίθεις
τίθησι(ν)	ἐτίθει
τίθεμεν	ἐτίθεμεν
τίθετε	ἐτίθετε
τιθέασι(ν)	ἐτίθεσαν

Indicative middle
[pass. pres. and impf. supplied by κεῖμαι]:
Present	Imperfect
τίθεμαι	ἐτιθέμην
τίθεσαι	ἐτίθεσο
τίθεται	ἐτίθετο
τιθέμεθα	ἐτιθέμεθα
τίθεσθε	ἐτίθεσθε
τίθενται	ἐτίθεντο

Participles
pres. act.: τιθείς, τιθεῖσα, τιθέν, τιθέντα ...; aor. act. θείς, θεῖσα, θέν, θέντα, ... ; pres. mid. τιθέμενος, τιθεμένη, τιθέμονον; aor. mid. θέμενος, θεμένη, θέμενον

Infinitives
Active: pres. τιθέναι, aor. θεῖναι;
Passive: pres. τίθεσθαι, aor. τεθῆναι

Subjunctives
Active: pres. τιθῶ, τιθῇς, ... aor. θῶ, θῇς, ... Passive: pres. τιθῶμαι, τιθῇς, ...

Imperatives
Active: pres. τίθει, τιθέτω, τίθετε, τιθέτωσαν aor. θές, θέτω, θέτε, θέτωσαν

Δείκνυμι

Principal parts
δείκνυμι, δείξω, ἔδειξα, δέδειχα, δέδειγμαι, ἐδείχθην

Indicative active
present	imperfect
δείκνυμι	ἐδείκνυν
δείκνυς	ἐδείκνυς
δείκνυσι(ν)	ἐδείκνυ
δείκνυμεν	ἐδείκνυμεν
δείκνυτε	ἐδείκνυτε
δεικνύασι(ν)	ἐδείκνυσαν

Indicative passive
present	imperfect
δείκνυμαι	ἐδεικνύμην
δείκνυσαι	ἐδείκνυσο
δείκνυται	ἐδείκνυτο
δεικνύμεθα	ἐδεικνύμεθα
δείκνυσθε	ἐδείκνυσθε
δείκνυνται	ἐδείκνυντο

Infinitives
Active: pres. δεικνύναι
Passive: pres. δείκνυσθαι

Subjunctives
Active: pres. δεικνύω, δεικνύῃς, ...

Appendix E: The Declension of Nouns & Adjectives

Nouns

First Declension

	γῆ	ἡμέρα	δόξα	προφήτης
Nom	γῆ	ἡμέρα	δόξα	προφήτης
Voc	γῆ	ἡμέρα	δόξα	προφῆτα
Acc	γῆν	ἡμέραν	δόξαν	προφήτην
Gen	γῆς	ἡμέρας	δόξης	προφήτου
Dat	γῇ	ἡμέρᾳ	δόξῃ	προφήτῃ
N/V	γαῖ	ἡμέραι	δόξαι	προφῆται
Acc	γᾶς	ἡμέρας	δόξας	προφήτας
Gen	γῶν	ἡμερῶν	δοξῶν	προφητῶν
Dat	γαῖς	ἡμέραις	δόξαις	προφήταις

Second Declension

	λόγος	ἔργον
Nom	λόγος	ἔργον
Voc	λόγε	ἔργον
Acc	λόγον	ἔργον
Gen	λόγου	ἔργου
Dat	λόγῳ	ἔργῳ
N/V	λόγοι	ἔργα
Acc	λόγους	ἔργα
Gen	λόγων	ἔργων
Dat	λόγοις	ἔργοις

Third Declension

		σάρξ	ἐλπίς	νύξ
N/V	[-ς]	σάρξ	ἐλπίς	νύξ
Acc	-α	σάρκα	ἐλπίδα	νύκτα
Gen	-ος	σαρκός	ἐλπίδος	νυκτός
Dat	ι	σαρκί	ἐλπίδι	νυκτί
N/V	-ες	σάρκες	ἐλπίδες	νύκτες
Acc	-ας	σάρκας	ἐλπίδας	νύκτας
Gen	-ων	σαρκῶν	ἐλπίδων	νυκτῶν
Dat	-σι(ν)	σαρξί(ν)	ἐλπίσι(ν)	νυξί(ν)

	χάρις	πούς	αἰών	γυνή
Nom	χάρις	πούς	αἰών	γυνή
Voc	χάρις	πούς	αἰών	γύναι
Acc	χάριν	πόδα	αἰῶνα	γυναῖκα
Gen	χάριτος	ποδός	αἰῶνος	γυναικός
Dat	χάριτι	ποδί	αἰῶνι	γυναικί
N/V	χάριτες	πόδες	αἰῶνες	γυναῖκες
Acc	χάριτας	πόδας	αἰῶνας	γυναῖκας
Gen	χαρίτων	ποδῶν	αἰώνων	γυναικῶν
Dat	χάρισι(ν)	ποσί(ν)	αἰῶσι(ν)	γυναιξί(ν)

The accusative singular of χάρις usually shows an irregularity: χάριν is used (50x in NT; instead of χάριτα which is found 2x) for the accusative singular.

	ἀνήρ	μήτηρ	πατήρ	χείρ
Nom	ἀνήρ	μήτηρ	πατήρ	χείρ
Voc	ἄνερ	μῆτερ	πάτερ	χείρ
Acc	ἄνδρα	μητέρα	πατέρα	χεῖρα
Gen	ἀνδρός	μητρός	πατρός	χειρός
Dat	ἀνδρί	μητρί	πατρί	χειρί
Nom	ἄνδρες	μητέρες	πατέρες	χεῖρες
Voc	ἄνδρες	μητέρες	πατέρες	χεῖρες
Acc	ἄνδρας	μητέρας	πατέρας	χεῖρας
Gen	ἀνδρῶν	μητερῶν	πατέρων	χειρῶν
Dat	ἀνδράσι(ν)	μητράσι(ν)	πατράσι(ν)	χερσί(ν)

Appendix E: Declensions

	πνεῦμα	φῶς	ἔθνος	γένος
N/V	πνεῦμα	φῶς	ἔθνος	γένος
Acc	πνεῦμα	φῶς	ἔθνος	γένος
Gen	πνεύματος	φωτός	ἔθνους	γένους
Dat	πνεύματι	φωτί	ἔθνει	γένει
N/V	πνεύματα	φῶτα	ἔθνη	γένη
Acc	πνεύματα	φῶτα	ἔθνη	γένη
Gen	πνευμάτων	φώτων	ἐθνῶν	γενῶν
Dat	πνεύμασι(ν)	φωσί(ν)	ἔθνεσι(ν)	- [not in NT]

	βασιλεύς	πόλις	βοῦς	ἰχθύς
Nom	βασιλεύς	πόλις	βοῦς	ἰχθύς
Voc	βασιλεῦ	πόλι	βοῦ	ἰχθύ
Acc	βασιλέα	πόλιν	βοῦν	ἰχθύν
Gen	βασιλέως	πόλεως	βοός	ἰχθύος
Dat	βασιλεῖ	πόλεσι(ν)	βοΐ	ἰχθύι
N,V	βασιλεῖς	πόλεις	βόες	ἰχθύες
Acc	βασιλεῖς	πόλεις	βόας	ἰχθύας
Gen	βασιλέων	πόλεων	βοῶν	ἰχθύων
Dat	βασιλεῦσι(ν)	πόλεσι(ν)	βουσί(ν)	ἰχθύσι(ν)

Adjectives

Adjectives of the Second and First Declension

Adjectives of the 1st & 2nd Declension			
	Masc	Fem	Neut
Nom	ἀγαθός	ἀγαθή	ἀγαθόν
Voc	ἀγαθέ	ἀγαθή	ἀγαθόν
Acc	ἀγαθόν	ἀγαθήν	ἀγαθόν
Gen	ἀγαθοῦ	ἀγαθῆς	ἀγαθοῦ
Dat	ἀγαθῷ	ἀγαθῇ	ἀγαθῷ
N,V	ἀγαθοί	ἀγαθαί	ἀγαθά
Acc	ἀγαθούς	ἀγαθάς	ἀγαθά
Gen	ἀγαθῶν	ἀγαθῶν	ἀγαθῶν
Dat	ἀγαθοῖς	ἀγαθαῖς	ἀγαθοῖς

Alpha-pure Adjectives of the 1st & 2nd Declension		
	Masc	Fem	Neut
Nom	ἅγιος	ἁγία	ἅγιον
Voc	ἅγιε	ἁγία	ἅγιον
Acc	ἅγιον	ἁγίαν	ἅγιον
Gen	ἁγίου	ἁγίας	ἁγίου
Dat	ἁγίῳ	ἁγίᾳ	ἁγίῳ
N,V	ἅγιοι	ἅγιαι	ἅγια
Acc	ἁγίους	ἁγίας	ἅγια
Gen	ἁγίων	ἁγίων	ἁγίων
Dat	ἁγίοις	ἁγίαις	ἁγίοις

εὐθύς, εὐθεῖα, εὐθύ		
	Masc	Fem	Neut
N,V	εὐθύς	εὐθεῖα	εὐθύ
Acc	εὐθύν	εὐθεῖαν	εὐθύ
Gen	εὐθέως	εὐθείας	εὐθέως
Dat	εὐθεῖ	εὐθείᾳ	εὐθεῖ
N,V	εὐθείς	εὐθεῖαι	εὐθέα
Acc	εὐθείς	εὐθείας	εὐθέα
Gen	εὐθέων	εὐθειῶν	εὐθέων
Dat	εὐθέσι(ν)	εὐθείαις	εὐθέσι(ν)

Adjectives of the Third and First Declension

πᾶς, πᾶσα, πᾶν		
	Masc	Fem	Neut
N/V	πᾶς	πᾶσα	πᾶν
Acc	πάντα	πᾶσαν	πᾶν
Gen	παντός	πάσης	παντός
Dat	παντί	πάσῃ	παντί
N/V	πάντες	πᾶσαι	πάντα
Acc	πάντας	πάσας	πάντα
Gen	πάντων	πασῶν	πάντων
Dat	πᾶσι(ν)	πάσαις	πᾶσι(ν)

Appendix E: Declensions

	μέλας, μέλαινα, μέλαν		
	Masc	Fem	Neut
N/V	μέλας	μέλαινα	μέλαν
Acc	μέλανα	μέλαιναν	μέλαν
Gen	μέλανος	μελαίνης	μέλανος
Dat	μέλανι	μελαίνῃ	μέλανι
N/V	μέλανες	μέλαιναι	μέλανα
Acc	μέλανας	μελαίνας	μέλανα
Gen	μελάνων	μελαινῶν	μελάνων
Dat	μέλασι(ν)	μελαίναις	μέλασι(ν)

Adjectives of the Third Declension

	ἄφρων, ἄφρον		ἀληθής, ἀληθές	
	Masc/Fem	Neut	Masc/Fem	Neut
N/V	ἄφρων	ἄφρον	ἀληθής	ἀληθές
Acc	ἄφρονα	ἄφρον	ἀληθῆ	ἀληθές
Gen	ἄφρονος	ἄφρονος	ἀληθοῦς	ἀληθοῦς
Dat	ἄφρονι	ἄφρονι	ἀληθεῖ	ἀληθεῖ
N/V	ἄφρονες	ἄφρονα	ἀληθεῖς	ἀληθῆ
Acc	ἄφρονας	ἄφρονα	ἀληθεῖς	ἀληθῆ
Gen	ἀφρόνων	ἀφρόνων	ἀληθῶν	ἀληθῶν
Dat	ἄφροσι(ν)	ἄφροσι(ν)	ἀληθέσι(ν)	ἀληθέσι(ν)

Irregular Adjectives

	μέγας, μεγάλη, μέγα		
	Masc	Fem	Neut
N/V	μέγας	μεγάλη	μέγα
Acc	μέγαν	μεγάλην	μέγα
Gen	μεγάλου	μεγάλης	μεγάλου
Dat	μεγάλῳ	μεγάλῃ	μεγάλῳ
N/V	μεγάλοι	μεγάλαι	μεγάλα
Acc	μεγάλους	μεγάλας	μεγάλα
Gen	μεγάλων	μεγάλων	μεγάλων
Dat	μεγάλοις	μεγάλαις	μεγάλοις

	πολύς, πολλή, πολύ		
	Masc	Fem	Neut
N/V	πολύς	πολλή	πολύ
Acc	πολύν	πολλήν	πολύ
Gen	πολλοῦ	πολλῆς	πολλοῦ
Dat	πολλῷ	πολλῇ	πολλῷ
N/V	πολλοί	πολλαί	πολλά
Acc	πολλούς	πολλάς	πολλά
Gen	πολλῶν	πολλῶν	πολλῶν
Dat	πολλοῖς	πολλαῖς	πολλοῖς

Pronouns

Personal Pronouns

	1st Pers Pronoun (ἐγώ)		2nd Pers Pronoun (σύ)	
N/V	ἐγώ	I	σύ	you
Acc	[ἐ]μέ	me	σέ	you
Gen	[ἐ]μοῦ	my	σοῦ	your
Dat	[ἐ]μοί	to/for me	σοί	to/ you
N/V	ἡμεῖς	we	ὑμεῖς	you
Acc	ἡμᾶς	us	ὑμᾶς	you
Gen	ἡμῶν	our	ὑμῶν	your
Dat	ἡμῖν	to/for us	ὑμῖν	to/you

Appendix E: Declensions

3rd Pers Pronoun (αὐτός, αὐτή, αὐτό)			
	Masc	Fem	Neut
N,V	αὐτός	αὐτή	αὐτό
Acc	αὐτόν	αὐτήν	αὐτό
Gen	αὐτοῦ	αὐτῆς	αὐτοῦ
Dat	αὐτῷ	αὐτῇ	αὐτῷ
N,V	αὐτοί	αὐταί	αὐτά
Acc	αὐτούς	αὐτάς	αὐτά
Gen	αὐτῶν	αὐτῶν	αὐτῶν
Dat	αὐτοῖς	αὐταῖς	αὐτοῖς

Demonstrative Adjectives [often used as Pronouns]

οὗτος, αὕτη, τοῦτο			
	Masc	Fem	Neut
Nom	οὗτος	αὕτη	τοῦτο
Acc	τοῦτον	ταύτην	τοῦτο
Gen	τούτου	ταύτης	τούτου
Dat	τούτῳ	ταύτῃ	τούτῳ
Nom	οὗτοι	αὗται	ταῦτα
Acc	τούτους	ταύτας	ταῦτα
Gen	τούτων	τούτων	τούτων
Dat	τούτοις	ταύταις	τούτοις

ἐκεῖνος, ἐκείνη, ἐκεῖνο			
	Masc	Fem	Neut
Nom	ἐκεῖνος	ἐκείνη	ἐκεῖνο
Acc	ἐκεῖνον	ἐκείνην	ἐκεῖνο
Gen	ἐκείνου	ἐκείνης	ἐκείνου
Dat	ἐκείνῳ	ἐκείνῃ	ἐκείνῳ
Nom	ἐκεῖνοι	ἐκεῖναι	ἐκεῖνα
Acc	ἐκείνους	ἐκείνας	ἐκεῖνα
Gen	ἐκείνων	ἐκείνων	ἐκείνων
Dat	ἐκείνοις	ἐκείναις	ἐκείνοις

Relative Pronoun & Indefinite Relative Pronoun*

	Relative Pronoun (ὅς, ἥ, ὅ)			Indefinite Relative Pronoun (ὅστις, ἥτις, ὅτι)		
	Masc	Fem	Neut	Masc	Fem	Neut
N	ὅς	ἥ	ὅ	ὅστις	ἥτις	ὅτι
A	ὅν	ἥν	ὅ	-	-	-
G	οὗ	ἧς	οὗ	ὅτου	-	ὅτου
D	ᾧ	ᾗ	ᾧ	-	-	-
N	οἵ	αἵ	ἅ	οἵτινες	αἵτινες	ἅτινα
A	οὕς	ἅς	ἅ	-	-	-
G	ὧν	ὧν	ὧν	-	-	-
D	οἷς	αἷς	οἷς	-	-	-

*only forms of ὅστις that are found in the NT are listed in this table

Correlative Pronoun & Indefinite Pronoun

	Correlative Pronoun (ὅσος, ὅση, ὅσον)			Indefinite Pronoun (τις, τι)	
	Masc	Fem	Neut	Masc, Fem	Neut
N	ὅσος	ὅση	ὅσον	τις	τι
A	ὅσον	ὅσην	ὅσον	τινα	τι
G	ὅσου	ὅσης	ὅσου	τινος	τινος
D	ὅσῳ	ὅσῃ	ὅσῳ	τινι	τινι
N	ὅσοι	ὅσαι	ὅσα	τινες	τινα
A	ὅσους	ὅσας	ὅσα	τινας	τινα
G	ὅσων	ὅσων	ὅσων	τινων	τινων
D	ὅσοις	ὅσαις	ὅσοις	τισι(ν)	τισι(ν)

The Definite Article

	Masc	Fem	Neut	Meaning
Nom s	ὁ	ἡ	τό	the
Acc s	τόν	τήν	τό	the
Gen s	τοῦ	τῆς	τοῦ	of the
Dat s	τῷ	τῇ	τῷ	to/for the
Nom pl	οἱ	αἱ	τά	the
Acc pl	τούς	τάς	τά	the
Gen pl	τῶν	τῶν	τῶν	of the
Dat pl	τοῖς	ταῖς	τοῖς	to/for the

APPENDIX F: Words Which Differ Only in Accent, Breathing Mark, or in Only One Letter

Words Which Differ Only in Accent or Breathing Mark

ἁγία holy (nom. sing. fem. of the adj. ἅγιος, holy)

ἅγια holy (nom./voc./acc. pl. neut. of the adj. ἅγιος)

ἄγων (nom. masc. sing. pres. part. act. of ἄγω, I lead)

ἀγών contest (3rd declension noun, ὁ ἀγών, ἀγῶνος, contest)

αἱ the (nom. fem. pl. of the article, ὁ, ἡ, τον)

αἵ who (nom. fem. pl. of the relative pronoun, ὅς, ἥ, ὅ)

ἀλλά but (a conjunction)

ἄλλα others (nom./acc. neut. pl. of the adjective ἄλλος, another, other)

ἄλλος, η, ο another, other; more, additional

ἄλλως adv.: otherwise

ἄρα then (a particle)

ἆρα ...? (interrogative particle)

αὐτή she (nom. fem. sing. of αὐτός)

αὐτῇ she (dat. fem. sing. of αὐτός)

αὕτη this (nom. fem. sing. of οὗτος)

αὐταί they (nom. fem. pl. of αὐτός)

αὗται these (nom. fem. pl. of οὗτος)

δώῃ (3rd pers. sing. aor. subj. act. of δίδωμι, I give)

δῴη (3rd pers. sing. aor. opt. act. of δίδωμι, I give)

εἰ if

εἶ you are (second person singular, εἰμί)

εἶπε he/she/it said (3rd pers. sing. aor. ind. act. of λέγω, I say)

εἰπέ say! (2nd pers. sing. aor. imperative act. of λέγω, I say)

εἰς into (preposition)

εἷς one (nom. masc. sing. of εἷς, μία, ἕν, one)

ἔξω outside

ἕξω I will have (1st pers. sing. fut. ind. act. of ἔχω)

ἐν in

ἕν one (nom./acc. neut. sing. of εἷς, μια, ἕν)

ἤ or, than

ἡ the (nom. fem. sing. article)

ἥ who, that (nom. fem. sing. rel. pron.)

ᾖ (3rd. pers. sing. pres. subj. act. of εἰμί)

ᾗ to whom (dat. fem. sing. rel. pron.)

ἦν I was (1st pres. sing. imperfect. ind. act. of εἰμί, I am)

ἤν if (another form of ἐάν, if)

ἥν who (acc. fem. sing. of the relative pron. ὅς, who)
ἦς you were (2nd pers. sing. imperfect ind. act. of εἰμί)
ᾖς you might be (2nd pers. sing. pres. subj. act. of εἰμί)
κρίνω I judge (pres.)
κρινῶ I will judge (fut.)
μένω I remain (pres.)
μενῶ I will remain (fut.)
ὅ which, that (nom. neut. sing. rel. pron.)
ὁ the (nom. masc. sing. article)
οἵ who, that (nom. masc. pl. rel. pron.)
οἱ the (nom. masc. pl. article)
ὄν (1) being (nom/acc neut. sing. pres. part. act. of εἰμί) [only Mark 4:31]
ὅν (157) who, that (the acc. masc. sing of the relative pronoun).
οὐ not
οὗ whose, of whom (gen. sing. masc./neut. rel. pron)
οὗ (24) adv.: where
πόσιν drinking (acc. sing. of the fem. 3rd decl. noun ἡ πόσις, drinking)
ποσίν to/for [the] feet (dat. pl. of the masc. 3rd decl. noun ὁ πούς, ποδός, foot)
πότε (17) when ...? (interrogative adverb)
ποτέ (28) once, at some time (enclitic indefinite particle)
πούς (3) where ...? (interrogative adverb)
ποῦ (43) where? (interrogative adverb)
πού (4) somewhere, anywhere (enclitic indefinite particle)
πῶς (99) how ...? (interrogative adverb)

πώς (14) anyhow (enclitic indefinite adverb)
ταῦτα these (nom./acc. neut. pl. of the pronoun οὗτος, η, ο, this)
ταὐτά the same things (contracted form of τα αὐτά, the neut. pl. of αὐτός, ή, ό, self, oneself, same)
τις, τι someone, a certain [man/woman/thing] (enclitic)
τίς, τί who ...? what ...? which ...?
φίλων (gen. masc./fem./neut. pl. of the adjective, φίλος, η, ον, friendly)
φιλῶν (nom. masc. sing. pres. part. act. of φιλέω, I love)
χειρῶν of hands (gen. pl. of the fem. 3rd decl. noun ἡ χείρ, χειρός, hand)
χείρων worse (irregular comparative of the adjective κακός, ή, όν, bad)
ᾧ to whom (dat. masc./neut. sing. rel. pron.)
ὦ I might be (1st. pers. sing. pres. subjunctive act. of εἰμι, I am)
ὦ Oh ... (with vocative)
ὤν (nom. masc. sing. pres. part. act. of εἰμί, I am)
ὧν of whom (gen. masc./fem./neut. pl. of the relative pronoun)

Verbal Forms Which Are the Same or Which Differ Only in Accent

βάλω I might throw (pres. subj. act. of βάλλω, I throw, put)
βαλῶ I will throw (fut. ind. act. of βάλλω, I throw, put)
λύετε You loose (2nd pers. pl. pres. ind. act. of λύω, loose)
λύετε loose ! (2nd pers. pl. pres. imperative act. of λύω, I loose)

Appendix F: Small Differences

λῦσον loose ! (2nd pers. sing. aor. imperative act. of λύω, I loose)
λῦσον (nom./acc. nuet. sing. fut. part. act. of λύω, I loose)
λύσω I shall loose (fut. ind. act.)
λύσω aor. subj. act.

Verb & Noun Forms which Are Similar

αἴρω I raise
αἱρέω I take
-βέβηκα I gave gone/come (perf. ind. act. of -βαίνω, I go/come)
βέβληκα I have thrown (perf. ind. act. of βάλλω, I throw)
ἐλείφην I was left (aor. ind. pass. of λείπω, I leave)
ἐλήμφθην I was taken (aor. ind. pass. of λαμβάνω, I take)
ἕξω I will have (fut. ind. act. of ἔχω, I have)
ἥξω I will have come (fut. ind. act. of the verb ἥκω, I have come—note: this verb has a perfect meaning in the present tense, and preserves this in the future tense)
ἄξω I will lead (fut. ind. act. of ἄγω, I lead)
ἔπεσα I fell
ἔπαισα I struck (aor. ind. act. of παίω, I strike)
ἔπεισα I persuaded (aor. ind. act. of πείθω, I persuade)
ἕστακα I stand (transitive use: perf. ind. act. of ἵστημι I stand)
ἔσταλκα I have sent (perf. ind. act. of στέλλω, I send)
ζήσω I will live (fut. ind. act. of ζάω, I live)
ζώσω I will gird (fut. ind. act. of ζώννυμι, I gird)
ζῶν nom. masc. sing. pres. part. act of ζάω, I live
ζῴων of living things, of animals (gen. masc. pl. of ζῷον, living creature, animal)

Words Which Differ Only in One Letter

ἀμήν verily, truly, amen
ἤμην I was (1st pers. sing. imp. ind. act. of εἰμι)
ἀλήθεια truth; reality
ἀληθής, ές true, honest; real, genuine
ἀληθῶς truly, actually [adverb]
ἔτι still, yet
ἐπί + acc.: **across**, to, against
  + gen.: **upon**, near, before, over, on the basis
  + dat.: **at**, by, **on**
αὐτός, -ή, -ό he/she/it, etc.
οὗτος, αὕτη, τοῦτο this
ἡμεῖς us (nom. pl. of ἐγώ)
ὑμεῖς you (nom. pl. of σύ)
ἡμᾶς us (acc. pl. of ἐγώ)
ὑμᾶς you (acc. pl. of σύ)
ἡμῶν our (gen. pl. of ἐγώ)
ὑμῶν your (gen. pl. of σύ)
καλός, -ή, -όν good (adj.)
καλῶς rightly, well (adv.)
ὅτε when, while, as long as
ὅτι because, that
οὗτος this (nom. masc. sing. of οὗτος, αὕτη, τοῦτο)
οὕτως thus, so (adv.)
ποτέ (28) once, formerly
πότε (17) when?
τότε () then, at that time; next
χήρα (26) widow
χώρα, ας, ἡ (28) district, country, land
χωρίς + gen. (41) without, apart from

Similar Sounding Words
καθαρίζω I cleanse
καθίζω I sit
σημεῖον sign
σήμερον today

Words Which Differ in Meaning, but not in Form
εἰμί I am
-εἶμι I go [this verb is only found in compound form in the New Testament: ἄπειμι (1) I go, come; εἴσειμι (4) I go in, come in; ἔξειμι (4) I go out or away, go on a journey; ἔπειμι (5) I come after, next, next day; σύνειμι (1) I come together. It has the same forms as the verb which means "I am" but means "I go"]
ἦτε you were (2nd pers. pl. imp. ind. act. of εἰμί)
ἦτε you might be (2nd pers. sing. pres. subj. act. of εἰμί)
ὅτι because, that
ὅτι whoever, whatever (nom. neut. sing. of ὅστις)
ὦ I might be (1st. pers. sing. pres. subjunctive act. of εἰμί, I am)
ὦ Oh ... (with vocative)

APPENDIX G: Modifications of Vowels and Consonants in Inflection

Vowels

ε + ε becomes ει
ε + ο becomes ου
ε + long vowel or diphthong becomes long vowel or diphthong

α + ε becomes α
α + η becomes α
α + ο becomes ω
α + ω becomes ω
α + ?ι: the iota in the second syllable becomes an iota subscript (e.g. αει becomes ᾳ).
α + ?υ : the υ in the second syllable disappears, and does not affect the way the other vowels contract (e.g. αου becomes what αο would become ω)

ο + ε becomes ου
ο + η becomes ω
ο + ο becomes ου
ο + ου becomes ου
ο + ω becomes ω
ο + ?ι (any combination containing ι, even if it is an iota subscript) becomes οι

Consonants

Before σ:
guttural (γ, κ, χ) + σ becomes ξ
labial (β, π, φ) + σ becomes ψ
dental (δ, τ, θ) + σ becomes σ

Before θ:
guttural (γ, κ, χ) + θ becomes χθ
labial (β, π, φ) + θ becomes φθ
dental (δ, τ, θ) + θ becomes ?*

Before μ
guttural (γ, κ, χ) + μ becomes γμ
labial (β, π, φ) + μ becomes μμ
dental (δ, τ, θ) + μ becomes σμ

Before τ
guttural (γ, κ, χ) + τ becomes κτ
labial (β, π, φ) + τ becomes πτ
dental (δ, τ, θ) + τ becomes ?*

Before δ
guttural (γ, κ, χ) + δ becomes γδ
labial (β, π, φ) + δ becomes βδ
dental (δ, τ, θ) + τ becomes ?*

*The result varies—the first dental often becomes a σ.

Appendix H: Cumulative Vocabularies

The number in square brackets after each entry refers to the number of the vocabulary the item is found in. The number in round brackets indicates frequency of occurrence in the Greek New Testament.

Cumulative Vocabulary for Part 1 (chaps. 1-11)

Ἀβραάμ (73) Abraham [1]
ἀγαθός, -η, -ον (104) good [7]
ἀγαπάω (141) I love [8]
ἀγάπη (116) love [6]
ἀγαπητός, -η, -ον (61) beloved [7]
ἄγγελος (175) angel, messenger [3.2]
ἅγιος, -α, -ον (233) holy, sacred, dedicated [7]
ἄγω (66) I lead, bring, take along, arrest [10]
ἀδελφός (343) brother [3.1]
αἱ the [nom. fem. pl. definite article] [6]
αἰτέω (70) I ask, demand [5]
αἰώνιος, -ον (70) eternal [7]
ἀκολουθέω (90) + dat. I follow [5]
ἀκούω (427) I hear, listen [2]
ἀλλά (635) but, yet, nevertheless [8]
ἁμαρτία (173) sin [6]
ἄνθρωπος (548) human being, man [3.4]
ἀπέρχομαι (116) I go away, depart (ἀπο + ἔρχομαι) [9]
ἀπό + gen. (645) from, away from [3.2]
ἀποθνῄσκω (113) I die [10]
ἀποκρίνομαι (231) I answer [9]
ἀπολύω (65) I release; dismiss, send away [8]
ἀποστέλλω (131) I send away, send [8]
ἀπόστολος (79) apostle, messenger [8]
ἄρτος (97) bread [3.1]
ἀρχή (55) beginning, ruler, authority [6]
ἀσπάζομαι (59) I greet [9]
αὐτός, ή, ό (5534) he/she/it [third person personal pronoun]; [him/her/-it]self; same [10]

αὐτοῦ his [10]
βάλλω (122) I throw; put, place, bring [10]
βιβλίον (34) book [4]
γεννάω (97) I beget; bear, produce [8]
γῆ (248) earth, ground, land [6]
γίνομαι (667) I become, come to be, happen [9]
γινώσκω (221) I know, learn [3.2]
γράφω (190) I write [2]
δαιμόνιον (63) demon [4]
Δαυίδ (59) David [1]
δέχομαι (56) I receive, take [9]
δίκαιος, -α, -ον (79) just, righteous [7]
δικαιοσύνη (91) righteousness, justice [7]
δοκέω (62) I think, believe; I seem [5]
δόξα (165) glory, splendor, fame [6]
δοξάζω (61) I glorify, praise [6]
δοῦλος (124) slave, servant [3.1]
ἐγώ (1713) I [8]
εἶ you are [4]
εἰ (513) if [4]
εἰμί (2450) I am [4]
εἰς (1753) + acc. into, towards [9]
εἰσέρχομαι (192) I come in, go in (εἰς + ἔρχομαι) [9]
εἰσίν they are [4]
ἐκ, ἐξ + gen. (915) out of, away from, from [3.2]
ἐκβάλλω (81) I cast out, send out, remove [10]
ἐκκλησία (114) church [6]
ἐν + dat. (2713) in, by (instrument) [3.2]

Appendix H: Cumulative Vocabularies

ἐντολή (68) commandment [6]
ἐξέρχομαι (216) I go out, come out (ἐκ + ἔρχομαι) [9]
ἐξουσία (102) authority, ability, right [6]
ἐπαγγελία (52) promise, pledge [6]
ἐπερωτάω (56) I ask [8]
ἐπί (878) + acc.: across, to, against [10]
  + gen.: upon, near, before, over, on the basis of, in the time of
  + dat.: at, by, on
ἔργον (169) deed, work [4]
ἔρχομαι (631) I go, come [9]
ἐρωτάω (62) I ask [8]
ἐσθίω (165) I eat [2]
ἐστίν is, he/she/it is, there is [4]
εὑρίσκω (176) I find [2]
ἔχω (705) I have [2]
ζάω (140) I live [8]
ζητέω (117) I seek [5]
ζωή (135) life [6]
ἡ the (nom. fem. sing. definite article) [6]
ἡμέρα (388) day [6]
θάνατος (120) death [10]
θέλω (207) I will, wish, want [2]
θεός (1314) God [1]
θεωρέω (58) I behold, see [5]
ἱερόν (70) temple [4]
Ἱεροσόλυμα (62) Ἰερουσαλήμ (77) Jerusalem [1]
Ἰησοῦς (919) Jesus [1]
Ἰωάννης, Ἰωαννᾶς (135) John [1]
καί (8947) and, also, even [3.1]
κακός, -ή, -όν (50) bad [7]
καλέω (148) I call [5]
καλός, -ή, -όν (99) good [7]
κατά (471) + acc.: according to [5]
  + gen.: down, against
κόσμος (185) world, adornment [3.2]
κύριος (718) lord, master [10]
λαλέω (298) I speak, utter [5]
λαμβάνω (258) I take, receive [2]
λαός (141) people (cf. "laity") [3.1]
λέγω (1318) I say, speak [2]
λόγος (331) word, matter, reason [3.1]
λύω (42) I loose [2]
μαρτυρέω (76) I testify, bear witness [5]

μόνος, -η, -ον (66) only, alone [7]
μού, or ἐμοῦ my (a genitive) [7]
Μωϋσῆς (80) Moses [4]
νεκρός, -ά, -όν (128) dead [7]
νόμος (191) law [3.2]
ὁ the [nom. masc. sing. definite article] [3.1]
οἱ the [nom. masc. pl. definite article] [3.1]
οἶκος (112) house, household [3.2]
ὁράω (114) I see [8]
ὅτι (1285) because, that, "" [5]
οὐ, οὐκ, οὐχ (1619) not [5]
ὄχλος (174) crowd [3.2]
παιδίον (52) child, infant [4]
παρακαλέω (109) I summon, request, entreat [5]
περιπατέω (95) I walk [5]
Πέτρος (156) Peter [1]
πίπτω (90) I fall [10]
πιστεύω (241) + dat. [or ἐν + dat.] I believe (in), I entrust [3.2]
πιστός, -ή, -όν (67) faithful, believing [7]
πλοῖον (66) boat [10]
ποιέω (565) I do, make [5]
πονηρός, -ά, -όν (78) evil, wicked [7]
πορεύομαι (150) I go [9]
πρός (696) + acc.: toward, to, with, against [9]
  + dat.: near, at, by
προσέρχομαι (87) + dat. I come or go to, approach [9]
προσεύχομαι (86) I pray [9]
προσκυνέω (59) + dat. I worship, prostrate myself before [5]
πρόσωπον (74) face [4]
σοφία (51) wisdom [6]
σύν + dat. (127) with [8]
συνάγω (59) I gather [8]
συναγωγή (56) synagogue, place of assembly [8]
τά the [nom./acc. neut. pl. definite article] [4]
ταῖς to/for the [dat. fem. pl. definite article] [6]
τάς the [acc. fem. pl. definite article] [6]

τέκνον (99) child [4]
τῇ to/for the [dat. fem. sing. definite article] [6]
τήν the [acc. fem. sing. definite article] [6]
τῆς of the [gen. fem. sing. definite article] [6]
τηρέω (70) I keep, watch [5]
τό the [nom./acc. neut. sing. definite article] [4]
τοῖς to the [dat. masc./neut. pl. definite article] [3.2]
τόν the [acc. masc. sing. definite article] [3.1]
τοῦ of the [gen. masc./neut. sing. definite article] [3.2]
τούς the [acc. masc. pl. definite article] [3.1]
τυφλός, -ή, -όν (50) blind [7]
τῷ to the [dat. masc./neut. sing. definite article] [3.2]
τῶν of the [gen. masc./neut./fem. pl. definite article] [3.2]
υἱός (375) son [3.1]
φέρω (68) I bear, bring, carry [10]
φοβέομαι (95) I fear [9]
φωνή (137) voice, sound [6]
χαίρω (74) I rejoice [6]
χαρά (59) joy [6]
Χριστός (531) Christ, christ [1]
The vocabulary for Part 1 accounts for 51,568 of the approximately 137,500 words in the Greek New Testament, or about 37% of the total.

Cumulative Vocabulary for Part 2 (chaps. 12-17)

αἷμα, -τος, το (97) blood [14.2]
αἰών, -ῶνος, ὁ (123) age, aeon [14.1]
ἀλήθεια, ἡ (109) truth [14.2]
ἀλλήλων (100) [of] one another [16]
ἄλλος, -η, -ο (155) other, another [12.3]
ἀμήν (126) so let it be, truly, amen [12.2]
ἄν (166) -ever [16]
ἀνήρ, ἀνδρός, ὁ (216) man [14.1]
ἀνοίγω (78) I open [aor. ἀνέῳξα, ἠνέῳξα, or ἤνοιξα] [16]
ἀπέθανον I died [aor. ind. act. of ἀποθνησκω] [12.1]
ἀπεκρίθη He/she/it answered [3rd pers. sing. aor. ind. pass. dep. of ἀποκρίνομαι, I answer] [12.3]
ἀπέστειλα I sent [aor. ind. act. of ἀποστέλλω] [12.3]
ἀπόλλυμι (90) I ruin, destroy, loose. In middle voice: perish, die [12.3]
ἀπώλεσα I destroyed [aor. ind. act. of ἀπόλλυμι I ruin] [12.3]
ἀφῆκα I forgave, let go, sent away, pardoned [aor. ind. act. of ἀφίημι I forgive] [12.3]
ἀφίημι (142) I forgive, cancel, remit (of sin or debts), leave, allow, divorce [12.3]
ἀφῶ 1st. p. s. aor. subj. act. of ἀφίημι, I forgive [16]
βαπτίζω (77) I baptize [14.2]
βασιλεία (162) kingdom [14.2]
βλέπω (132) I see [12.2]
Γαλιλαία (61) Galilee [12.3]
γάρ (1036) for; certainly, so, then [12.2]
γραφή (50) writing, scripture [15]
γυνή, -αικός, ἡ (209) woman, wife [14.1]
δέ (2271) but, and [12.2]
δεῖ (102) it is necessary [15]
δείκνυμι (33) I show, point out [12.3]
διά (483) + acc.: because of, on account of
 + gen.: through [note: διὰ τί = "why ...?"] [15]
δίδωμι (416) I give [12.3]
δοῦναι to give [aor. inf. act. of δίδωμι] [15]
δύναμαι (209) I am able [15]
δύο (136) two [12.1]
δῶ 1st. p. s. aor. subj. act. of δίδωμι, I give [16]
δώδεκα (75) twelve [12.3]
ἐάν + subj. (343) if [16]

Appendix H: Cumulative Vocabularies

ἐὰν μή + subj. (56) except, unless [16]

ἔβαλον I threw, put (aor. ind. act. of βάλλω) [12.1]

ἐγείρω (143) I raise, wake (aor. ἤγειρα) [15]

ἐγένετο He/she/it became, appeared, happened (3rd pers. sing. str. aor. ind. mid. dep. of γίνομαι, I become) [12.3]

ἔδειξα I showed (aor. ind. act. of δείκνυμι (32) I show, point out) [12.3]

ἔδωκα I gave (aor. ind. act. of δίδωμι, I give) [12.3]

ἔθηκα I placed (aor. ind. act. of τίθημι (101) I place) [12.3]

ἔθνος, -ους, το (162) nation; pl.: nations, Gentiles [14.3]

εἶδον I saw (aor. ind. act. of ὁράω) [12.1]

εἶναι to be (infinitive of εἰμί) [15]

εἶπον I said (aor. ind. act. of λέγω) [12.1]

εἰρήνη (91) peace [14.1]

ἐκεῖνος, -η, -ο (243) that, (pl.: those); he/she/it [16]

ἔλαβον I took (aor. ind. act. of λαμβάνω) [12.1]

ἔλεγε(ν) He/she/it said [3rd pers. sing. impf. ind. act. of λέγω, I say]

ἐλπίς, -ίδος, ἡ (53) hope [14.1]

ἐμός, ἐμή, ἐμόν (76) my (possessive pronoun) [16]

ἔξω (62) outside, outer [16]

ἔπεσα I fell (aor. ind. act. of πίπτω) [12.3]

ἔπιον I drank (aor. ind. act. of πίνω) [16]

ἑπτά (87) seven [12.1]

ἔσχον I had (aor. ind. act. of ἔχω) [12.1]

ἔστησα I placed (aor. ind. act. of ἵστημι I place) [12.3]

ἔτι (92) still, yet [12.2]

εὗρον I found (aor. ind. act. of εὑρίσκω) [12.2]

ἔφαγον I ate (aor. ind. act. of ἐσθιω) [12.1]

ἤ (342) or, than [14.1]

ἤγαγον I led (aor. ind. act. of ἄγω) [12.1]

ἠθέλησα I wished, wanted (aor. ind. act. of θέλω; note irregular augment) [12.2]

ἦλθον I came, went (aor. ind. act. of ἔρχομαι) [12.1]

ἡμῶν our (note the difference from ὑμῶν, your) [14.2]

ἦν He/she/it was, there was [12.1]

ἤνεγκα I bore (aor. ind. act. of φέρω) [12.3]

θάλασσα (91) sea [12.2]

θέλημα, -τος, το (62) will [14.2]

θρόνος, ὁ (62) throne [14.2]

θῶ 1st. p. s. aor. subj. act. of τίθημι, I place [16]

ἰδεῖν to see (aor. inf. act. of ὁράω) [15]

ἴδιος (113) one's own, private [12.2]

ἵνα + subj. (673) in order that, so that [16]

Ἰουδαῖος, -α, -ον (195) a Jew; Jewish; Judean [14.2]

ἵστημι (154) I place, set, put; stand; stop [12.3]

ἵστω 1st. p. s. pr. subj. act. ἵστημι, I place [16]

καρδία, ἡ (156) heart [14.2]

καρπός (66) fruit [14.3]

κεφαλή (75) head [14.1]

κηρύσσω (61) I announce, proclaim, preach (fut. κηρύξω; aor. ἐκήρυξα) [16]

κρίνω (114) I judge [16]

λίθος (58) stone [15]

μακάριος, -α, -ον (50) blessed, fortunate, happy [14.2]

μέν ... [δε] (181) on the one hand ... on the other hand; some ... others [14.2]

μένω (118) I remain, abide [14.1]

μέσος (56) middle, in the middle [12.3]

μετά (467) + acc.: after, behind [16]
+ gen.: with

μή (1055) not [14.1]

μήτηρ, -τρος, ἡ (84) mother [14.1]

νύξ, νυκτός, ἡ (61) night [14.1]

ὁδός, ἡ (101) way, path, road [12.2]
οἰκία (94) house, household [14.1]
ὄνομα, -τος, τό (228) name [14.2]
ὅπου (82) where [14.2]
ὄρος, -ους, τό (62) mountain [14.2]
ὅς ἄν + subj. whoever [16]
ὅταν + subj. (123) whenever, when [16]
ὅτε (102) when, while, as long as (note: the difference between this word and ὅτι, because, that) [12.3]
οὐδέ (139) and not, but not; not even (= οὐ + δε, cf. μηδε) [14.1]
οὐδείς, οὐδεμία, οὐδέν (226) no one, not one (= οὐδέ + εἷς, μία, ἕν) [14.1]
οὐ μή + subj. no (strong denial) [16]
οὖν (493) therefore, then, so [14.1]
οὐρανός (272) heaven [12.2]
οὗτος, αὕτη, τοῦτο this, pl.: these [13]
οὕτως (208) thus, so, in this way [12.3]
οὐχί (53) not, no (a variation of οὐ) [15]
ὀφθαλμός (100) eye [16]
πᾶς, πᾶσα, πᾶν (1226) each, all, every [14.3]
πατήρ, πατρός, ὁ (415) father [14.1]
Παῦλος (158) Paul [14.1]
πάλιν (139) again, once more [12.3]
παραβολή (50) parable [12.3]
παραδίδωμι (120) I deliver, entrust, commit, pass on [12.3]
πείθω (52) I convince, persuade; depend on, trust in [12.2]
πέμπω (79) I send [12.2]
πέραν (73) on the other side [12.3]
περί (331) + acc.: around, about, near [16]
  + gen.: about, concerning
πίνω (73) I drink [16]
πνεῦμα, -τος, τό (379) spirit, wind [14.2]
πούς, ποδός, ὁ (93) foot [14.1]
πρῶτον (60) adv.: first [12.2]
πρῶτος, -η -ον (92) adj.: first [12.2]
πῦρ, πυρός, τό (71) fire [14.2]
πῶς (104) how ...? in what way ...? [15]
ῥῆμα, -τος, τό (68) word; thing, object [14.2]
σάββατον (68) Sabbath [12.2]

σάρξ, σαρκός, ἡ (147) flesh [14.1]
σημεῖον (77) sign [15]
Σίμων, -ωνος, ὁ (75) Simon [14.1]
στόμα, -τος, τό (78) mouth [14.2]
στῶ 1st. p. s. aor. subj. act. ἵστημι, I place, set; stand, stop [16]
σύ (1057) you (sing. nom) [12.2]
σώζω (106) I save, heal [12.2]
σῶμα, -τος, τό (142) body [14.5]
τέ (201) and (note: this is a very weak "and," and is often not translated into English; τε ... και can mean "both ... and") [16]
τίθημι I place, put; I make [12.3]
τιθῶ 1st. p. s. pr. subj. act. of τίθημι, I place [16]
τις, τι (518) someone, a certain [man/woman/thing] (indefinite pronoun) [14.3]
τίς, τί (552) who ...? what ...? which ...? (interrogative pronoun) [14.3]
τόπος (95) place [15]
τότε (159) then [12.3]
ὕδωρ, ὕδατος, τό (76) water [14.2]
ὑμεῖς (1830) you (nom. pl. of σύ) [12.2]
ὑμῶν your (gen. pl. of σύ) [12.2]
ὑπάγω (79) I go away, withdraw [15]
Φαρισαῖος (99) Pharisee [12.1]
φῶς, φωτός, τό (73) light [14.2]
χάρις, -ιτος, ἡ (155) grace, favor [14.1]
χείρ, χειρός, ἡ (176) hand [14.1]
χρόνος (54) time [16]
ψυχή (101) soul, life [15]
ὧδε (61) here [16]
ὥρα, ἡ (106) hour, time [16]
ὡς (505) as, when, after, while, about [14.1]

The vocabulary for Part 2 accounts for 25,000 of the approximately 137,500 words in the Greek New Testament. Together with the vocabulary for Part 1, this is a total of 76,568 words, or about 55% of the total.

Cumulative Vocabulary for Part 3 (chaps 18-23)

ἀκήκοα I have heard (perf. ind. act. of ἀκούω) [21.1]

ἀληθής, -ές (26) true [20.1]

ἁμαρτάνω (42) I sin, do wrong [19]

ἁμαρτωλός, -όν (47) sinful (as noun: sinner; cf. ἁμαρτάνω, I sin) [20.2.2]

ἀναβαίνω (81) I go up, ascend (ἀνα + βαίνω) [20.2.1]

ἀνάστασις, -εως, ἡ (42) resurrection [20.1]

ἀποκτείνω (74) I kill (= ἀπο + κτείνω; aor. ind. act. ἀπέκτεινα; this verb is sometimes spelled as ἀποκτέννω, or ἀποκτεννύω) [21.2]

ἄρα (49) then, therefore [22]

ἄρτι (36) now [19]

-βέβηκα I have gone (perf. ind. act. of βαίνω) [21.1]

βέβληκα I have thrown (perf. ind. act. of βάλλω) [21.1]

γέγραφα I have written (perf. ind. act. of γράφω) [21.1]

δέδωκα I have given (perf. ind. act. of δίδωμι) [21.1]

δεύτερος, -α, -ον (44) second [20.2.2]

διδάσκαλος (59) teacher [21.2]

διδάσκω (95) I teach [21.2]

διδούς, διδούσα, διδόν, διδοντ- pres. part. act. of δίδωμι [20.2.1]

δούς, δούσα, δόν, δοντ- aor. part. act. of δίδωμι [20.2.1]

ἑαυτοῦ (320) [of] himself, herself, itself [20.1]

ἔγνωκα I have known (perf. ind. act. of γινώσκω) [21.1]

εἰδῶ (subj. act. of οἶδα, I know) [21.2]

εἰδώς, εἰδυια, εἰδος, εἰδοτ- perf. part. act. (with present meaning) of οἶδα [21.2]

εἴληφα I have taken (perf. ind. act. of λαμβάνω) [21.1]

εἴρηκα I have said (perf. ind. act. of λέγω) [21.1]

εἷς, μία, ἕν (337) one [21.1]

εἶχον I began to have / was having (irregular imp. ind. act. of ἔχω) [22]

ἕκαστος (81) each [22]

ἐλήλυθα I have come/gone (perf. ind. act. of ἔρχομαι) [21.1]

ἐλπίζω (31) I hope (cf. ἐλπίς) [21.1]

ἐμαυτοῦ (37) [of] myself [20.1]

-ενήνοχα I have borne (perf. ind. act. of φέρω) [21.1]

ἐνώπιον + gen. (93) before, in the presence of [22]

ἐπιτίθημι (40) I place upon (= ἐπί + τίθημι) [20.2.2]

ἐργάζομαι (41) I work, labor (cf. ἔργον, work) [20.2.2]

ἕστηκα or ἕστακα perf. ind. act. of ἵστημι [21.1]

ἑστώς or ἑστηκώς, -, ἑστός perf. part. act. of ἵστημι [21.1]

εὐαγγελίζω (54) I proclaim, preach, bring good news (note: εὐαγγελίζω = εὐ + ἀγγελίζω; thus its 1st pers. imp. ind. act. is εὐηγγέλιζον) [22]

εὐαγγέλλιον (76) good news, gospel [22]

εὐθύς (54) immediately, at once [20.2.1]

ἑώρακα I have seen (perf. ind. act. of ὁράω) [21.1]

ἕως (145) till, until, while [19]

ἤδη (60) already [19]

Ἡλίας, -ου (29) Elijah [22]

ἥμαρτον I sinned (aor. ind. act. of ἁμαρτάνω. The aorist root ἁμαρτησ- is also found in moods other than the indicative) [19]

θαυμάζω (42) I wonder, marvel [20.1]

θείς, θεῖσα, θέν, θεντ- aor. part. act. of τίθημι [20.2.1]

θεραπεύω (43) I heal [22]

ἰδού (200) look, behold [18]

κἀγώ (84) and I, I also (= και + ἐγω) [21.2]

κάθημαι (91) I sit [20.2.2]

καθίζω (46) I seat, sit (cf. κάθημαι, I sit) [22]

καθώς (178) just as [19]
καινός, -η, -ν (42) new [19]
καλῶς (37) rightly, well [21.2]
καταβαίνω (81) I go down, come down (κατα + βαίνω) [20.2.1]
κράζω (55) I cry out, scream [22]
κρίσις, -εως, ἡ (47) judgment, judging, condemnation [20.1]
μαθητής (262) disciple, pupil [20.2.2]
μαρτυρία (37) witness, testimony (cf. μαρτυρεω) [20.1]
μέγας, μέγαλη, μέγα (194) great [20.1]
μείζων, -ον gen. sing. μείζονος (48) greater (comparative of μέγας) [20.1]
μέλλω (110) I am about to, on the point of (imp. ind. act. ἤμελλον) [22]
μηδέ (57) and not, but not; not even (= μή + δέ, cf. οὐδέ) [20.1]
μηδείς, μηδεμία, μηδέν (85) no one, nothing (= μηδέ + εἷς, μία, ἕν; cf. οὐδείς) [20.1]
μισέω (39) I hate [19]
νῦν (148) now [18]
ὁ δέ and he, but the [18]
οἶδα (321) I know (uses perfect tense forms with present tense meaning) [20.2.2]
ὅλος (108) whole, entire; complete [19]
ὅμοιος, α, ον (45) adj.: like, resembling [20.2.2]
ὅς, ἥ, ὅ (1369) who, which, what, that (relative pronoun) [18]
ὅς ἄν or ὅς ἐάν + subj. whoever [18]
ὅσος, ὅση, ὅσον (110) as much as [18]
ὅστις, ἥτις, ὅτι (154) whoever; such a one who; who [18]
οὐαί (45) woe, alas! [18]
ὀφείλω (35) I owe, am obligated to, bound, ought [19]
παρά (191) + acc.: **by**, along, near, more than, against [18]
 + gen.: from
 + dat.: **at**, by, beside, near
πέποιθα I have persuaded (perf. ind. act. of πείθω) [21.1]
πέπτωκα I have fallen (perf. ind. act. of πίπτω) [21.1]
πλείων, πλεῖον (55) more [22]
πολύς, πολλή, πολύ (353) many, much [21.2]
ποτέ (29) once, formerly [20.2.2]
ποῦ (47) where [19]
προφήτης (144) prophet [20.2.2]
σεαυτοῦ (43) [of] yourself [20.1]
σήμερον (41) today [21.1]
στάς, στᾶσα, στάν, σταντ- aor. part. act. of ἵστημι [21.2.1]
τέθεικα I have placed (perf. ind. act. of τίθημι) [21.1]
τιθείς, τιθεῖσα, τιθέν, τινθεντ- pres. part. act. of τίθημι [20.2.1]
τοιοῦτος, -η, -ον (56) such a kind, such as this [18]
ὑπάρχω (60) I am (= εἰμί), exist, be at one's disposal (Note also that τα ὑπαρχοντα = property, possessions) [22]
φόβος (47) fear [cf. φοβεομαι, I fear; cf. also the English word "phobia"] [22]
φιλέω (25) I love [21.1]
φίλος, η, ον (29) loving; as noun: friend [21.1]
φωνέω (42) I call, invite [20.2.2]
χαίρω (74) I rejoice
ὤν, οὖσα, ὄν, ὀντ- aor. part. act. of εἰμί [20.2.1]
ὥστε (84) therefore, so that (note: ὥστε + infinitive is used to express result, "with a result that") [22]
ὥσπερ (36) just as [20.1]

The vocabulary for Part 3 accounts for 6,650 of the approximately 137,500 words in the Greek New Testament. Together with the vocabulary for Parts 1 & 2, this is a total of 83218 words, or about 60% of the total.

Cumulative Vocabulary for Part 4 (chaps 24-30)

ἀγοράζω + gen. (30) I buy [29.2]
ἀδελφή (26) sister [29.1]
αἴρω (101) I lift up, take up, remove [24.2]
ἀληθινός (28) true, genuine [29.1]
ἀληθῶς (18) adv.: truly, really [29.1]
ἀμπελών, ῶνος, ὁ (23) vineyard [27]
ἀνίστημι (107) rise, appear, rebel, etc. [27]
ἄξιος, α, ον (41) worthy, befitting [29.1]
ἀπαγγέλλω (45) I announce, report [29.3]
ἅπας, ἅπασα, ἅπαν (32) all, whole; pl.: everyone, everything (alternative form of πᾶς) [29.2]
ἀποδίδωμι (47) I give away, give up, give out, pay, grant, give back, render [27]
ἀποθανέομαι I shall die (fut. ind. of ἀποθνήσκω) [25]
ἀπολέσω I shall destroy (fut. ind. act. of ἀπόλλυμι) [25]
ἀποστελέω I shall send (fut. ind. act. of ἀποστέλλω) [25]
ἀρνέομαι (32) I deny [29.1]
ἀρχιερεύς, -έως ὁ (122) high priest [28]
ἄρχω (85) I rule, in middle: begin [28]
ἀσθενέω (33) I am sick, weak [29.1]
ἀφέθην I was forgiven (aor. ind. pass. of ἀφίημι) [24.1]
ἀφέωμαι I have been forgiven (perf. ind. pass. of ἀφίημι) [24.1]
ἀφήσω I shall forgive (fut. ind. act. of ἀφίημι) [25]
βαλέω I shall throw (fut. ind. act. of βάλλω) [25]
βασιλεύς, -έως, ὁ (115) king [28]
βέβλημαι I have been thrown [perf. ind. pass. of βάλλω] [24.1]
βλασφημέω (34) I blaspheme, slander, insult [29.3]
γενήσομαι I shall become (fut. ind. of γίνομαι) [25]
γλῶσσα (50) tongue, language [26]
γνούς, γνοῦσα, γνόν (aor. part. act. of γινώσκω) [28]
γνῶναι to know (aor. inf. act. of γινώσκω) [28]
γνώσομαι I shall know (fut. ind. of γινώσκω) [25]
γραμματεύς, -έως, ὁ (62) scribe [28]
δέδομαι I have been given (perf. ind. pass. of δίδωμι) [24.1]
δεξιός, -ά, -όν (954) right [26]
δεῦτε (41) come! come on! [26]
δέω (41) I bind [29.3]
διάβολος (37) devil [29.2]
διδαχή (30) teaching [29.3]
διέρχομαι (42) I go through (διά + ἔρχομαι) [29.2]
δικαιόω (39) I justify, vindicate, show justice [28]
διό (53) therefore [26]
διώκω (44) I persecute, pursue, strive for [26]
δός give (2nd pers. sing. aor. imp. act. of δίδωμι) [26]
δύναμις, -εως, ὁ (118) power, ability, miracle [28]
δώσω I shall give (fut. ind. act. of διδωμι) [25]
ἐβλήθην I was thrown [ao. ind. pass. of βάλλω] [24.1]
ἐγγίζω + dat. (42) I approach, draw near [28]
ἐγγύς (31) adv.: near [29.1]
ἐγήγερμαι I have been raised (perf. ind. pass. of ἐγείρω) [25.1]
ἔγνων (42) I knew [aor. ind. act. of γινώσκω] [28]
ἐδόθην I was given (aor. ind. pass. of δίδωμι) [25.1]
εἴτε ... εἴτε (65) if ... if, whether ... or [27]
-είλημμαι I have been taken [perf. ind. pass. of λαμβάνω] [24.1]
ἕκαστος, -η, -ον (81) each, every [27]

ἐκεῖ (95) there [24.1]
ἐκλήθην I was called (aor. ind. pass. of καλέω) [24.1]
ἐκπορεύομαι (33) I come/go forth [29.2]
ἐλεέω (32) I have mercy, am merciful [26]
ἐλεύσομαι I shall come/go (fut. ind. of ἔρχομαι) [25]
ἐλημφθην I was taken (aor. ind. pass. of λαμβάνω) [24.1]
ἐλέχθην I was said [aor. ind. pass. of λέγω] [24.1]
ἔμπροσθεν (48) as a preposition with gen.: in front of, before; as an adverb: ahead, forward, in front [24.2]
ἔξεστιν (31) it is lawful, permitted, possible, proper [27]
ἕξω I shall have (fut. ind. act. of ἔχω) [25]
ἐπεί (26) since, when [26]
ἐπιθυμία (38) desire [29.3]
ἐρέω (96) I shall say, speak (fut. ind. act. of λέγω) [25]
ἔρημος, ἡ (47) desert, wilderness [29.1]
ἐρρέθην I was said [aor. ind. pass. of λέγω] [24.1]
ἔσομαι I shall be (fut. ind. of εἰμί) [25]
ἐστάθην I was stood (aor. ind. pass. of ἵστημι) [24.1]
-εστάλην I was sent (aor. ind. pass. of -στέλλω) [24.1]
ἔσχατος, -η, -ον (52) last [27]
ἐτέθην I was placed (aor. ind. pass. of τίθημι) [24.1]
ἕτερος (98) other [26]
ἔτος, -ους, τό (49) year [29.2]
εὐθέως (33) adv.: immediately, at once [29.2]
εὐλογέω (42) I bless [26]
εὑρέθην I was found (aor. ind. pass. of εὑρίσκω) [24.1]
εὑρήσω I shall find (fut. ind. act. of εὑρίσκω) [25]
εὐχαριστέω (38) I give thanks [29.2]
ἠνέχθην I was borne (aor. ind. pass. of φέρω) [24.1]

ἦρα (56) I lifted up (aor. ind. act. of αἴρω) [24.2]
ἤρθην I was lifted up (aor. ind. pass. of αἴρω) [24.2]
ἠγέρθην I was raised (aor. ind. pass. of ἐγείρω) [24.1]
θήσω I shall place (fut. ind. act. of τίθημι) [25]
θύρα (39) door [29.1]
ἱμάτιον (60) garment [24.2]
ἱρεύς, έως, τό (31) priest [28]
καιρός (85) time [27]
κλαίω (38) I weep [29.1]
κλάω (14) I break [29.1]
κλείω (16) I shut, lock [29.1]
κρατέω + gen. (47) I grasp, hold [29.3]
κρινέω I shall judge (fut. ind. act. of κρίνω) [25]
λήμψομαι I shall take (fut. ind. of λαμβάνω) [25]
λογίζομαι (40) I consider, reckon [29.3]
λοιπός, -ή, -όν (55) rest, remaining, other (note: [τὸ] λοιπόν can be used as an adverb, when it means "finally; from now on, still, in addition") [27]
μᾶλλον (80) more, rather [26]
μενέω I shall remain (fut. ind. act. of μένω) [25]
μετανοέω (34) I repent [28]
μικρός, ά, όν (46) little, small [29.2]
μνημεῖον (37) tomb, grave [29.1]
μυστήριον (27) mystery [27]
ναός (45) temple, inner part of temple [29.1]
οἶνος (34) wine [29.2]
οἴσω I shall bear (fut. ind. act. of φέρω) [25]
ὁμοίως (31) adv.: in the same way, likewise, similarly (cf. ὅμοιος) [29.2]
ὀπίσω (35) prep. + gen.: after, behind, away from [29.1]
  adv.: back, behind
ὅπως (53) conj.: (+ subj.) in order that [24.2]
ὀργή (36) anger, wrath [26]
οὐκέτι (48) adv.: no longer, no more

Appendix H: Cumulative Vocabularies

οὔτε ... οὔτε (91) neither ... nor [25]
ὄψομαι I shall see (fut. ind. of ὁράω) [25]
πάντοτε (41) always [29.1]
παραγίνομαι (36) I come, arrive [29.2]
παραλαμβάνω (49) I take with, take over, rejoin [27]
παρρησία (31) openness; ἐν παρρησίᾳ be known publicly [29.1]
πειράζω (38) I test, tempt [29.2]
πέντε (38) five [29.2]
περιτέμνω (17) I circumcise [περί + τέμνω (τέμνω = I cut)] [29.3]
περιτομή (35) circumcision [29.3]
πεσέομαι I shall fall (fut. ind. of πίπτω) [25]
πίομαι I shall drink (fut. ind. of πίνω) [25]
πίστις, -εως, ἡ (243) belief, faith [28]
πλανάω (39) I lead astray, deceive [29.3]
πλείων greater (comparative of πολύς, great) [29.2]
πληρόω (86) I fulfil, fill [28]
πόλις, -εως, ἡ (161) city [28]
πράσσω (39) I do, practice (perf. act. πεπραχα; perf. pass. πεπραγμαι) [24.2]
πρεσβύτερος (65) older, elder [28]
πρό (47) + gen before [29.1]
πρόβατον (37) sheep [29.1]
προσφέρω (47) I offer [27]
Σατανᾶς, ὁ (36) Satan [27]
σπείρω (52) I sow (aor. ἔσπειρα; perf. pass. ἔσπαρμαι; aor. pass. ἐσπάρην) [24.2]
σπέρμα, ατος, το (44) seed, offspring [29.3]
σταυρόω (46) I crucify [28]
στήσω I shall stand (fut. ind. act. of ἴστημι) [25]
συνίημι (26) I understand, perceive [27]
σωτηρία (45) salvation [29.2]
τρεῖς, τρία (67) three [28]
τρίτος, η, ον (56) third [29.3]
ὑπέρ (149) + acc.: over and above, beyond [26]
+ gen.: for, in behalf of
ὑπό (217) + acc.: under, below
+ gen.: by [agent] [24.1]
φάγομαι I shall eat (fut. ind. of ἐσθίω) [25]
φαίνω (31) I give light [29.1]
φανερόω (49) I make known, reveal, show; pass.: I am revealed, it is evident [28]
φημί (66) I say, affirm (pres. ind.: 3rd pers. sing. φησιν, 3rd pres. pl. φασιν; imperf. ind.: 3rd sing. ἔφη) [26]
φυλακή (46) prison, guard, watch [24.2]
χείρων (11) worse (irregular comparative of κακος) [29.2]
χρεία (49) need, necessity [29.1]
χωρίς (41) prep. + gen.: without, apart from [28]
adv.: separately, by itself
ὤφθην I was seen (aor. ind. pass. of ὁράω) [24.1]

The vocabulary for Part 4 accounts for 7,372 of the approximately 137,500 words in the Greek New Testament. Together with the vocabulary for Parts 1-3, this is a total of 90,590 words, or about 66% of the total.

APPENDIX I: Pronunciation of Modern Greek

This appendix enables the comparison of the Erasmian or "classical" system of pronunciation with the way the language is pronounced in modern Greece. The guide to modern Greek pronunciation is taken from Caragounis, p. 352. The words in square brackets illustrate the appropriate sound in the letter which is underlined.

\multicolumn{4}{c}{Pronunciation Guide to Modern Greek}
lower case	UPPER CASE	"Classical" Sound	Modern Sound
α	Α	a	a [f<u>a</u>ther]
β	Β	b	v [<u>v</u>an]
γ	Γ	g [g<u>e</u>t]	y [<u>y</u>et, <u>w</u>oe]
δ	Δ	d	th [<u>th</u>en]
ε	Ε	e [m<u>e</u>t]	e [p<u>e</u>n]
ζ	Ζ	z or dz	z [<u>z</u>ero]
η	Η	ē [f<u>ê</u>te]	i [btwn: d<u>i</u>d–s<u>ee</u>]
θ	Θ	th [<u>th</u>en]	th [<u>th</u>in]
ι	Ι	i	i [btwn: d<u>i</u>d-s<u>ee</u>]
κ	Κ	k	k [<u>k</u>een, <u>k</u>oda<u>k</u>]
λ	Λ	l	l [<u>l</u>ad]
μ	Μ	m	m [<u>m</u>ada<u>m</u>]
ν	Ν	n	n [<u>n</u>ame]
ξ	Ξ	x	x [e<u>x</u>tra]
ο	Ο	o	o [d<u>o</u>t]
π	Π	p	p [<u>p</u>age]
ρ	Ρ	r	r [<u>r</u>ock]
σ, ς	Σ	s	s [<u>s</u>alt]
τ	Τ	t	t [<u>t</u>op]
υ	Υ	u	i [d<u>i</u>d]
φ	Φ	f	f [<u>f</u>act]
χ	Χ	ch [lo<u>ch</u>]	ch [German i<u>ch</u>; ba<u>ch</u>]
ψ	Ψ	ps [li<u>ps</u>]	ps [to<u>ps</u>y-turvy]
ω	Ω	ō [t<u>o</u>ne]	o [d<u>o</u>t]

Appendix I: Modern Greek   365

Diphthongs in Modern Greek
αι is pronounced as e in p<u>e</u>n
ει, οι, υι are pronounced as η (i.e. between d<u>i</u>d and s<u>ee</u>)
ου is pronounced as oo in l<u>oo</u>k
αυ, ευ, ηυ are pronounced <u>av</u>, <u>ev</u>, <u>iv</u> before vowels and γ, δ, λ, μ, ν, ρ; and as <u>af</u>, <u>ef</u>, <u>if</u> before all other consonants

There is much communality between classical and modern pronunciation: both agree on the pronunciation of α, ε, ι, κ, λ, μ, ν, ξ, ο, π, ρ, σ, τ, φ, ψ, ου. The biggest differences are with the pronunciation of consonants β, γ, δ (pronounced: v, y, th), and the vowels and dipthongs η, υ, ω, αι, ει, οι, υι, αυ, ευ, ηυ.

APPENDIX J: Abbreviations

The following abbreviations have been used:

acc.	accusative	mid.	middle
act.	active	ms. mss.	manuscript(s)
adj.	adjective	neut.	neuter
adv.	adverb	no.	*[numero]* number
ao.	aorist	nom.	nominative
aor.	aorist	NT	New Testament
C.	century	opt.	optative
cf.	*[confer]* compare	p. pp.	page, pages
chap(s).	chapter(s)	part.	participle
conj.	conjunction	pass.	passive
dat.	dative	perf.	perfect
dep.	deponent	pers.	person
E	easy [part 5]	pl.	plural
e.g.	*[exampli gratia]* for example	plperf.	pluperfect
		prep.	preposition
ed.	edition	pres.	present
etc.	*[et cetera]* and the others, and so forth	pron.	pronoun
		rel.	relative
fem.	feminine	resp.	respectively
fut.	future	rev.	revision, revised
gen.	genitive	sing.	singular
i.e.	*[id est]* that is	str.	strong
imp.	if mood: imperative; if tense: imperfect	subj.	subjunctive
		s.v.	*[sub verbo, sub voce]* under the word/entry
imperf.	imperfect		
impf.	imperfect	UBS	United Bible Societies' *The Greek New Testament*
imprv.	imperative		
impv.	imperative	v. (vv.)	verse(s)
ind.	indicative	VF	a very frequently occurring construction [Part 5]
inf.	infinitive		
Int.	Robert K. McIver, *Intermediate New Testament Greek Made Easier*	voc.	vocative
		vocab.	vocabulary
		wk.	weak
lit.	literally	1st	first
LXX	Septuagint	2nd	second
masc.	masculine	3rd	third